Colossians and Philemon

BAKER EXEGETICAL COMMENTARY
ON THE NEW TESTAMENT

ROBERT W. YARBROUGH
and JOSHUA W. JIPP, EDITORS

Volumes now available:

Matthew *David L. Turner*
Mark *Robert H. Stein*
Luke *Darrell L. Bock*
Acts *Darrell L. Bock*
Romans, 2nd ed. *Thomas R. Schreiner*
1 Corinthians *David E. Garland*
2 Corinthians *George H. Guthrie*
Galatians *Douglas J. Moo*
Ephesians *Frank Thielman*
Philippians, 2nd ed. *Moisés Silva*
Colossians and Philemon *G. K. Beale*
1–2 Thessalonians *Jeffrey A. D. Weima*
James *Dan G. McCartney*
1 Peter, 2nd ed. *Karen H. Jobes*
1–3 John *Robert W. Yarbrough*
Jude and 2 Peter *Gene L. Green*
Revelation *Thomas R. Schreiner*

G. K. Beale (PhD, University of Cambridge) is professor of New Testament and biblical theology at Westminster Theological Seminary in Philadelphia, Pennsylvania. He is the coeditor of the *Commentary on the New Testament Use of the Old Testament* and the author of numerous books, including *A New Testament Biblical Theology: The Unfolding of the Old Testament in the New* and commentaries on Revelation and 1 and 2 Thessalonians.

Colossians and Philemon

G. K. Beale

BAKER EXEGETICAL COMMENTARY
ON THE NEW TESTAMENT

Baker Academic
a division of Baker Publishing Group
Grand Rapids, Michigan

Published by Baker Academic
a division of Baker Publishing Group
Grand Rapids, Michigan
BakerAcademic.com

Printed in the United States of America

Library of Congress Cataloging-in-Publication Data
Names: Beale, G. K. (Gregory K.), 1949– author.
Title: Colossians and Philemon / G. K. Beale.
Description: Grand Rapids, MI : Baker Academic, [2019] | Series: Baker exegetical commentary on the New Testament | Includes bibliographical references and index.
Identifiers: LCCN 2018028040 | ISBN 9780801026676 (cloth : alk. paper)
Subjects: LCSH: Bible. Colossians—Commentaries. | Bible. Philemon—Commentaries.
Classification: LCC BS2715.53 .B43 2019 | DDC 227/.7077—dc23
LC record available at https://lccn.loc.gov/2018028040

 Square brackets indicate departures from its wording, underlining rather than italic is used for emphasis, and italic is not used to identify words supplied for English sense that are not found in the original Hebrew and Greek.

Baker Publishing Group publications use paper produced from sustainable forestry practices and postconsumer waste whenever possible.

24 25 26 27 28 29 30 10 9 8 7 6 5 4

To Wanda and Brian Cates and Charlene and Jeremy Cates,
who have welcomed us into their Maine Downeast community
and with whom my wife and I have had much good fellowship in the Lord

Contents

Philemon

Excursuses

Series Preface

The chief concern of the Baker Exegetical Commentary on the New Testament (BECNT) is to provide, within the framework of informed evangelical thought, commentaries that blend scholarly depth with readability, exegetical detail with sensitivity to the whole, and attention to critical problems with theological awareness. We hope thereby to attract the interest of a fairly wide audience, from the scholar who is looking for a thoughtful and balanced examination of the text to the motivated lay Christian who craves a solid but accessible exposition.

Nevertheless, a major purpose is to address the needs of pastors and others involved in the preaching and exposition of the Scriptures as the uniquely inspired Word of God. This consideration directly affects the parameters of the series. For example, serious biblical expositors cannot afford to depend on a superficial treatment that avoids the difficult questions, but neither are they interested in encyclopedic commentaries that seek to cover every conceivable issue that could be raised. Our aim, therefore, is to focus on those problems that have the most direct bearing on the meaning of the text (although selected technical details are treated in the additional notes) or that pose unavoidable challenges for interpretation.

Similarly, a special effort is made to avoid treating exegetical questions for their own sake, that is, in relative isolation from the thrust of the argument as a whole. This effort may involve (at the discretion of the individual contributors) abandoning the verse-by-verse approach in favor of an exposition that focuses on the paragraph as the main unit of thought. In all cases, however, the commentaries will stress the development of the argument and explicitly relate each passage to what precedes and follows it so as to identify its function in the flow of discourse as clearly as possible.

We believe, moreover, that a responsible exegetical commentary must take into account the latest scholarly research, regardless of its source. The contributors to this series, accordingly, attempt to avoid two pitfalls. On the one hand, they do not consider traditional opinions to be sacrosanct, and they are committed to doing justice to the biblical text in the light of compelling evidence regardless of whether it supports such opinions. On the other hand, they will not quickly abandon a long-standing view, if there is persuasive evidence in its favor, for the sake of theories perhaps currently more in vogue. Contributing to this balance is contributors' affirmation of the trustworthiness and essential unity of Scripture. They also consider that the historic formulations of

Christian doctrine, such as the ecumenical creeds and many of the documents originating in the sixteenth-century Reformation and its aftermath, arose from a legitimate reading of Scripture, thus providing a valuable framework for its subsequent interpretation. While respect for formulations of classic consensual Christianity (Thomas Oden) may risk an imposition of tradition on the text, we deny that it must necessarily do so or that rejection of any hermeneutic that comports with Christian tradition automatically results in more valid exegetical insights and exposition.

In other words, we do not consider exegetically justifiable theological convictions to be a hindrance to biblical interpretation. On the contrary, an exegete who hopes to understand the apostle Paul in a theological vacuum might just as easily try to interpret Aristotle without regard for the philosophical framework of his whole work or without having recourse to those subsequent philosophical categories that make possible a meaningful contextualization of his thought. At the same time, it bears mention that the contributors to the present series come from a variety of theological traditions and that they represent a considerable span of hermeneutical outlooks and ecclesial orientations. In the end, what matters is representing the original text, in light of all of the relevant data and considerations that can and ought to be brought to bear, accurately, clearly, and meaningfully to the contemporary reader.

Shading has been used to assist the reader in locating salient sections of the treatment of each passage. This occurs particularly in introductory comments and concluding summaries. Textual variants in the Greek text are signaled in the author's translation by means of half-brackets around the relevant word or phrase (e.g., ⌜Gerasenes⌝), thereby alerting the reader to turn to the additional notes at the end of each exegetical unit for a discussion of the textual problem. The documentation uses the author-date method, in which the basic reference consists of author's surname + year + page number(s): Fitzmyer 1992: 58. The only exceptions to this system are well-known reference works (e.g., BDAG, LSJ, *TDNT*). Full publication data and a complete set of indexes can be found at the end of the volume.

Robert W. Yarbrough
Joshua W. Jipp

Author's Preface

I began writing this commentary toward the latter part of 2012. When embarking on the task of commentary writing, one often asks oneself whether it is really necessary to write another commentary. This is especially the case with Colossians and Philemon. There is a multitudinous amount of commentaries and secondary literature on these two epistles. In the case of Colossians, I believed there was still a need for a commentary which did the following things: (1) study the OT allusions in a more trenchant manner than previously in order to determine how they might affect the interpretation of Colossians; (2) study how Jewish exegetical tradition interpreted these same OT allusions and how such interpretation related to the use in Colossians. I have found that OT allusions occur at what commentators consider to be key junctures of the epistle and have a significant impact on the exegesis and theology of Colossians. Others will have to judge whether or to what degree I have successfully achieved these goals and how well I have argued for the presence of OT allusions throughout Colossians. Philemon probably has no clear OT allusions, so my contribution to this epistle is not to be made in this area as in Colossians. Nevertheless, I have tried to interpret Philemon first on the basis of my own interaction with the Greek text before reading secondary literature. I followed the same pattern in Colossians. My intention in writing the commentary was to provide an exegesis of Colossians and Philemon that would be especially helpful to teachers, pastors, students, and others seriously interested in interpreting Colossians and Philemon for the benefit of the church. While the commentary discussion is detailed at various points, I have provided statements of exegetical ideas at the beginning of each section of the commentary, so the reader can perceive how I summarize the material that follows. These statements may serve as the core of homiletical ideas by those using the commentary for preaching and teaching Bible studies. I have also put much discussion into the additional notes, which appear at the end of the commentary unit. These appended sections go into more detail about, and provide further support for, various points argued in the comments. I have provided an English translation of most Greek words and phrases for the benefit of those not proficient in Greek.

I have interacted with what I believe to be the most relevant sources among the vast material on Colossians and Philemon, but I have not tried to interact with *all* the available secondary literature on Colossians and Philemon. The commentary is indebted to prior commentators, especially Douglas J. Moo,

J. D. G. Dunn, David E. Garland, Eduard Lohse, Peter T. O'Brien, David W. Pao, and N. T. Wright.

I am grateful to the administration and trustees of Westminster Theological Seminary for granting me the resources and the time (especially a sabbatical) to be able to complete this project. I am also indebted to my following graduate teaching assistants for help in proofing and various kinds of research efforts related to the writing of the commentary: Matt Dudreck, Brandon Szerlip, Todd Scacewater, Will Ross, Calvin Peronto, Danillo Santos, William Wood, and Laura Leon.

As with my former projects, I owe a debt of gratitude especially to my wife, Dorinda, who has helped me to understand Colossians and Philemon better as we discussed it. Above all, I am grateful to God, who gave me the desire to write this project and the energy to complete it. My prayer is that this book will give glory to him alone.

A few comments about some stylistic aspects and other features of the commentary are in order.

Instead of offering an original translation, I have relied on the New American Standard Bible (NASB) as the basis for this commentary, a departure from the normal practice for the BECNT series. I am grateful to the Lockman Foundation for permission to use their translation so extensively. Especially in the Scripture blocks that precede the comment sections, square brackets mark wherever I have departed from the NASB and have rendered the Greek text differently. Within the comment sections, I have more freely incorporated my own translation of key terms and phrases and have used underlining to draw attention to particular words in both the NASB and my own translations.

References to the Greek New Testament follow the text of NA^{28}. When discussing variant readings in the Greek text of Colossians and Philemon, I focus on textual variants that significantly affect the meaning of the text (these are usually treated in footnotes or in the additional notes).

With respect to translations of other ancient works, when the translation differs from the standard editions usually referred to, then it is my translation or someone else's (in the latter case, I indicate whose). Some of my discussions about the relation of the OT and Judaism to Colossians are the result of an integration and revision of my earlier work on the use of the OT in Colossians (Beale 2007: 841–70).

For the Greek OT, I used R. Hanhart's revision of *Septuaginta*, edited by A. Rahlfs (Stuttgart: Deutche Bibelgesellschaft, 2006). My default English translation of the Septuagint is L. C. L. Brenton, *The Septuagint Version of the Old Testament and Apocrypha with an English Translation* (London: Samuel Bagster & Sons, 1896; repr., Grand Rapids: Zondervan, 1972). This text is dependent on only Codex B. I have also consulted *A New English Translation of the Septuagint*, edited by A. Pietersma and B. G. Wright (New York: Oxford University Press, 2007).

My default for the Hebrew text of the Dead Sea Scrolls is the edition of M. G. Abegg Jr. accessed through Accordance Bible software. I sometimes refer to the Hebrew text edited by F. García Martínez and E. J. C. Tigchelaar, *The Dead Sea Scrolls: Study Edition*, 2 vols. (Leiden: Brill, 1997–98). My default English translation of the scrolls is that of M. O. Wise, M. G. Abegg Jr., and E. M. Cook, *The Dead Sea Scrolls: A New Translation*, rev. ed. (New York: Harper Collins, 2005). Other translations of these texts are cited by name (e.g., Dupont-Sommer, Vermès, García Martínez). When English renderings differ from all other translations, they are my own.

The Greek text and the English translation of Philo follow the Loeb Classical Library editions, though I sometimes cite the translation of Yonge 1993. Other variations from the English of the Loeb edition are my own translation.

The following English editions of various Jewish works were consulted, referred to, and sometimes quoted:

The Babylonian Talmud, ed. I. Epstein, 18 vols. (London: Soncino, 1948)

Mekilta de-Rabbi Ishmael, trans. and ed. J. Z. Lauterbach, 3 vols. (Philadelphia: Jewish Publication Society of America, 1976)

The Midrash on Proverbs, trans. B. L. Visotzky (New Haven: Yale University Press, 1992)

The Midrash on Psalms, trans. and ed. W. G. Braude, Yale Judaica Series 13.1–2 (New Haven: Yale University Press, 1976)

Midrash Rabbah, ed. H. Freedman and M. Simon, 10 vols. (London: Soncino, 1961)

Midrash Sifre on Numbers, trans. and ed. P. P. Levertoff, Translations of Early Documents, Series III: Rabbinic Texts (London: Golub, 1926)

Midrash Tanhuma, trans. and ed. J. T. Townsend, 2 vols. (Hoboken, NJ: Ktav, 1989)

Midrash Tanhuma-Yelammedenu: An English Translation of Genesis and Exodus from the Printed Version of Tanhuma-Yelammedenu with Introduction, Notes, and Indexes, trans. S. A. Berman (Hoboken, NJ: Ktav, 1996)

The Minor Tractates of the Talmud, ed. A. Cohen, 2 vols. (London: Soncino, 1965)

The Mishnah, trans. and ed. H. Danby (Oxford: Oxford University Press, 1980)

The Old Testament Pseudepigrapha, ed. J. H. Charlesworth, 2 vols. (Garden City, NY: Doubleday, 1983); sometimes reference was made to *The Apocrypha and Pseudepigrapha of the Old Testament*, vol. 2, *Pseudepigrapha*, ed. R. H. Charles (Oxford: Clarendon, 1977)

The Pesikta de-Rab Kahana, trans. and ed. W. G. Braude and I. J. Kapstein (Philadelphia: Jewish Publication Society of America, 1975)

Pesikta Rabbati, trans. and ed. W. G. Braude, Yale Judaica Series 18.1–2 (New Haven: Yale University Press, 1968)

Pirke de Rabbi Eliezer, trans. and ed. G. Friedlander (New York: Hermon, 1916)

Sifre: A Tannaitic Commentary on the Book of Deuteronomy, trans. and ed. R. Hammer, Yale Judaica Series 24 (New Haven: Yale University Press, 1986)

Tanna debe Eliyyahu, trans. and ed. W. G. Braude and I. J. Kapstein (Philadelphia: Jewish Publication Society of America, 1981)

The Targums of Onkelos and Jonathan Ben Uzziel on the Pentateuch, with the Fragments of the Jerusalem Targum, on Genesis and Exodus, trans. and ed. J. W. Etheridge (New York: Ktav, 1968); and the volumes published in *The Aramaic Bible: The Targums*, ed. M. McNamara (Collegeville, MN: Liturgical Press, 1987)

References and English translations of portions of the Apostolic Fathers are from *The Apostolic Fathers: Greek Texts and English Translations*, translated and edited by M. W. Holmes, 3rd ed. (Grand Rapids: Baker Academic, 2007).

G. K. Beale
Summer 2017

Abbreviations

Bibliographic and General

*	author's translation
§(§)	section(s), paragraph(s)
//	parallel to
×	times
ABD	*The Anchor Bible Dictionary*, ed. D. N. Freedman et al., 6 vols. (New York: Doubleday, 1992)
adj.	adjective
ANF	*The Ante-Nicene Fathers: Translations of the Writings of the Fathers down to A.D. 325*, ed. A. Roberts and J. Donaldson; rev. A. C. Coxe, 10 vols. (New York: Christian Literature, 1885–87; repr., Peabody, MA: Hendrickson, 1994)
ASV	American Standard Version
b.	*ben*, son of (with personal names); Babylonian Talmud (with tractate names)
BAA	*Griechisch-Deutsches Wörterbuch zu den Schriften des Neuen Testaments und der frühchristlichen Literatur*, by W. Bauer, K. Aland, and B. Aland, 6th ed. (Berlin: de Gruyter, 1988)
BCP	Book of Common Prayer
BDAG	*A Greek-English Lexicon of the New Testament and Other Early Christian Literature*, by W. Bauer, F. W. Danker, W. F. Arndt, and F. W. Gingrich, 3rd ed. (Chicago: University of Chicago Press, 2000)
BDF	*A Greek Grammar of the New Testament and Other Early Christian Literature*, by F. Blass, A. Debrunner, and R. W. Funk (Chicago: University of Chicago Press, 1961)
CEB	Common English Bible
cent.	century
cf.	*confer*, compare
chap(s).	chapter(s)
CSB	Christian Standard Bible
DJD	Discoveries in the Judaean Desert
DOTP	*Dictionary of the Old Testament: Pentateuch*, ed. T. D. Alexander and D. W. Baker (Downers Grove, IL: InterVarsity, 2003)
Douay	The Douay-Rheims Bible, 1899 American Edition
DPL	*Dictionary of Paul and His Letters*, ed. G. F. Hawthorne and R. P. Martin (Downers Grove, IL: InterVarsity, 1993)
DSS	Dead Sea Scrolls
ed(s).	edition, editor(s)

EDEJ	*The Eerdmans Dictionary of Early Judaism*, ed. J. J. Collins and D. C. Harlow (Grand Rapids: Eerdmans, 2010)
EDNT	*Exegetical Dictionary of the New Testament*, ed. H. Balz and G. Schneider, 3 vols. (Grand Rapids: Eerdmans, 1990–93)
e.g.	*exempli gratia*, for example
Eng.	English Bible versification differing from that of the LXX or MT
esp.	especially
ESV	English Standard Version
etc.	*et cetera*, and so forth, and the rest
forthc.	forthcoming
frag.	fragment
Geneva	Geneva Bible, 1599 ed.
HCSB	Holman Christian Standard Bible
i.e.	*id est*, that is
ISV	International Standard Version
JB	Jerusalem Bible
KJV	King James Version
κτλ	καὶ τὰ λοιπά (= and the rest; etc.)
L&N	*Greek-English Lexicon of the New Testament: Based on Semantic Domains*, ed. J. P. Louw and E. A. Nida, 2nd ed., 2 vols. (New York: United Bible Societies, 1988–89)
LCL	Loeb Classical Library
LEH	*Greek-English Lexicon of the Septuagint*, ed. J. Lust, E. Eynikel, and K. Hauspie, rev. ed. (Stuttgart: Deutsche Bibelgesellschaft, 2003)
lit.	literally
LSJ	*A Greek-English Lexicon*, compiled by H. G. Liddell and R. Scott; rev. and enlarged by H. S. Jones with R. McKenzie, 9th ed., with rev. supplement ed. P. G. W. Glare with A. A. Thompson (Oxford: Clarendon, 1996)
LXX	Septuagint: the Greek OT = Old Greek, translated in NETS
𝔐	Majority Text, including Byzantine Koine MSS
marg.	marginal reading (i.e., alternate translation in the margin of a Bible version)
MHT	*A Grammar of New Testament Greek*, vol. 1: *Prolegomena*, by J. H. Moulton, 3rd ed.; vol. 2: *Accidence and Word Formation*, by W. F. Howard; vol. 3: *Syntax*, by N. Turner; vol. 4: *Style*, by N. Turner (Edinburgh: T&T Clark, 1908–76)
MM	*The Vocabulary of the Greek Testament: Illustrated from the Papyri and Other Non-literary Sources*, by J. H. Moulton and G. Milligan (repr., Grand Rapids: Eerdmans, 1976)
MS(S)	manuscript(s)
MT	Masoretic Text of the Hebrew Bible
n(n).	note(s), footnote(s)
NA^{27}	*Novum Testamentum Graece*, 27th rev. ed., ed. [E. and E. Nestle], B. and K. Aland, J. Karavidopoulos, C. M. Martini, and B. M. Metzger (Stuttgart: Deutsche Bibelgesellschaft, 1993)

NA^{28} *Novum Testamentum Graece*, 28th rev. ed., ed. [E. and E. Nestle], B. and K. Aland, J. Karavidopoulos, C. M. Martini, and B. M. Metzger (Stuttgart: Deutsche Bibelgesellschaft, 2012)

NABRE New American Bible, revised edition (2010)

NASB New American Standard Bible (1995)

NEB New English Bible

NET The NET Bible (New English Translation)

NETS *A New English Translation of the Septuagint*, ed. A. Pietersma and B. G. Wright (New York: Oxford University Press, 2007), http://ccat.sas.upenn.edu/nets/edition/

NIDNTT *The New International Dictionary of New Testament Theology*, ed. L. Coenen, E. Beyreuther, and H. Bietenhard; English translation ed. C. Brown, 4 vols. (Grand Rapids: Zondervan, 1975–86)

NIV New International Version (2011)

NIV 1984 New International Version (1984)

NJB New Jerusalem Bible

NJPS *The Tanakh: The Holy Scriptures: The New JPS Translation according to the Traditional Hebrew Text* (1985)

NKJV New King James Version

NLT New Living Translation (2007)

NRSV New Revised Standard Version

n.s. new series

NT New Testament

OED *The Oxford English Dictionary*, 2nd ed. (Oxford: Clarendon, 2004)

OG Old Greek. *See* LXX

olim formerly, as for 1QH column numbers in Dupont-Sommer 1962

OT Old Testament

OTP *The Old Testament Pseudepigrapha*, ed. J. H. Charlesworth, 2 vols. (Garden City, NY: Doubleday, 1983–85)

$\mathfrak{P}$ papyrus, as in $\mathfrak{P}^{46}$

p(p). page(s)

par(r). parallel(s)

pl. plural

P.Oxy. Oxyrhynchus papyrus (+ number)

Ps.- Pseudo-

ptcp. participle

P.Tor. Choach. papyrus from Thebes, archived at Turin

R. Rabbi (before a rabbi's name)

REB Revised English Bible

rec. recension

repr. reprinted

rev.	revised
RSV	Revised Standard Version
sect.	section
Str-B	*Kommentar zum Neuen Testament aus Talmud und Midrasch*, by H. L. Strack and P. Billerbeck, 6 vols. (Munich: Beck, 1922–61)
s.v.	*sub verbo*, under the word
Sym.	Symmachus the Ebionite's Greek OT (late 2nd cent.)
TDNT	*Theological Dictionary of the New Testament*, ed. G. Kittel and G. Friedrich; trans. and ed. G. W. Bromiley, 10 vols. (Grand Rapids: Eerdmans, 1964–76)
Theod.	Theodotion's Greek OT (mid-2nd cent.), paralleled in NETS
TLG	*Thesaurus Linguae Graecae*, digital corpus (University of California, Irvine, 1972–; online, 2001–)
TLNT	*Theological Lexicon of the New Testament*, by C. Spicq; trans. and ed. J. D. Ernest, 3 vols. (Peabody, MA: Hendrickson, 1994)
TNIV	Today's New International Version
trans.	translated by, translator
UBS[5]	*The Greek New Testament*, 5th rev. ed., ed. B. Aland, K. Aland, J. Karavidopoulos, C. M. Martini, and B. M. Metzger (Stuttgart: Deutsche Bibelgesellschaft, 2014)
v(v).	verse(s)
vol(s).	volume(s)
Webster	Noah Webster's 1833 limited revision of the KJV

Hebrew Bible

Gen.	Genesis	Neh.	Nehemiah	Hosea	Hosea
Exod.	Exodus	Esther	Esther	Joel	Joel
Lev.	Leviticus	Job	Job	Amos	Amos
Num.	Numbers	Ps(s).	Psalm(s)	Obad.	Obadiah
Deut.	Deuteronomy	Prov.	Proverbs	Jon.	Jonah
Josh.	Joshua	Eccles.	Ecclesiastes	Mic.	Micah
Judg.	Judges	Song	Song of Songs	Nah.	Nahum
Ruth	Ruth	Isa.	Isaiah	Hab.	Habakkuk
1–2 Sam.	1–2 Samuel	Jer.	Jeremiah	Zeph.	Zephaniah
1–2 Kings	1–2 Kings	Lam.	Lamentations	Hag.	Haggai
1–2 Chron.	1–2 Chronicles	Ezek.	Ezekiel	Zech.	Zechariah
Ezra	Ezra	Dan.	Daniel	Mal.	Malachi

Greek Testament

Matt.	Matthew	John	John	1–2 Cor.	1–2 Corinthians
Mark	Mark	Acts	Acts	Gal.	Galatians
Luke	Luke	Rom.	Romans	Eph.	Ephesians

Phil.	Philippians	Titus	Titus	1–2 Pet.	1–2 Peter
Col.	Colossians	Philem.	Philemon	1–3 John	1–3 John
1–2 Thess.	1–2 Thessalonians	Heb.	Hebrews	Jude	Jude
1–2 Tim.	1–2 Timothy	James	James	Rev.	Revelation

Other Jewish and Christian Writings

Apoc.	Apocalypse (as part of LAE)
Apoc. Ab.	Apocalypse of Abraham
Apoc. Adam	Apocalypse of Adam
Apoc. El. (C)	Coptic Apocalypse of Elijah
Apoc. Mos.	Apocalypse of Moses
Apoc. Paul	Apocalypse of Paul
Apoc. Zeph.	Apocalypse of Zephaniah
1 Apol.	Justin Martyr, *First Apology*
Artap.	Artapanus
Bar.	Baruch
2 Bar.	2 (Syriac Apocalypse of) Baruch
3 Bar.	3 (Greek Apocalypse of) Baruch
4 Bar.	4 Baruch
Barn.	Barnabas
Cels.	Origen, *Against Celsus*
1–2 Clem.	1–2 Clement
Clem. Hom.	(Pseudo-)Clementine Homilies
Conf.	Augustine, *Confessions*
Eccl. Hist.	Eusebius, *Ecclesiastical History*
1 En.	1 (Ethiopic) Enoch
2 En.	2 (Slavonic) Enoch
3 En.	3 (Hebrew) Enoch
Ep. Virg.	Pseudo-Clement, *Epistle on Virginity*
1 Esd.	1 Esdras
2 Esd.	2 Esdras
Eup.	Eupolemos, earliest known Hellenistic-Jewish historian (ca. 158/157 BC)
Gk. Apoc. Ezra	Greek Apocalypse of Ezra
Gos. Eb.	Gospel of the Ebionites
Gos. Nic.	Gospel of Nicodemus
Hel. Syn. Pr.	Hellenistic Synagogal Prayers
Her.	Irenaeus, *Against Heresies*
Herm. *Sim.*	Shepherd of Hermas, *Similitude(s)*
Herm. *Vis.*	Shepherd of Hermas, *Vision(s)*
Hist. Rech.	History of the Rechabites
Ign. *Phld.*	Ignatius, *To the Philadelphians*
Jdt.	Judith
Jos. Asen.	Joseph and Aseneth
Jub.	Jubilees
LAB	Liber antiquitatum biblicarum (Pseudo-Philo)
LAE	Life of Adam and Eve
Let. Aris.	Letter of Aristeas
Liv. Pro.	Lives of the Prophets
1–4 Macc.	1–4 Maccabees
Mart. Ascen. Isa.	Martyrdom and Ascension of Isaiah
Mart. Pol.	Martyrdom of Polycarp
Misc.	Clement of Alexandria, *Miscellanies*
Odes Sol.	Odes of Solomon
Pol. *Phil.*	Polycarp, *To the Philippians*
Pre. Pet.	Preaching of Peter
Ps.-Phoc.	Pseudo-Phocylides
Pss. Sol.	Psalms of Solomon
Serm.	Augustine, *Sermons*
Sib. Or.	Sibylline Oracles
Sir.	Sirach (Ecclesiasticus)
T. Ab.	Testament of Abraham
T. Adam	Testament of Adam

T. Benj.	Testament of Benjamin	T. Levi	Testament of Levi
T. Dan	Testament of Dan	T. Reu.	Testament of Reuben
T. Gad	Testament of Gad	T. Sim.	Testament of Simeon
T. Isaac	Testament of Isaac	T. Sol.	Testament of Solomon
T. Iss.	Testament of Issachar	T. Zeb.	Testament of Zebulun
T. Job	Testament of Job	Tob.	Tobit
T. Jud.	Testament of Judah	Wis.	Wisdom of Solomon

Josephus

Ag. Ap.	*Against Apion*	*J.W.*	*The Jewish War*
Ant.	*Jewish Antiquities*		

Philo

Agr.	*On Agriculture*	*Migr.*	*On the Migration of Abraham*
Alleg.	*Allegorical Interpretation*	*Mos.*	*On the Life of Moses*
Cher.	*On the Cherubim*	*Names*	*On the Change of Names*
Conf.	*On the Confusion of Tongues*	*Plant.*	*On Planting*
Contempl.	*On the Contemplative Life*	*Post.*	*On the Posterity of Cain*
Creat.	*On the Creation of the World*	*Prelim.*	*On the Preliminary Studies*
Decal.	*On the Decalogue*	*QE*	*Questions and Answers on Exodus*
Dreams	*On Dreams*		
Drunk.	*On Drunkenness*	*QG*	*Questions and Answers on Genesis*
Emb.	*On the Embassy to Gaius*		
Etern.	*On the Eternity of the World*	*Rewards*	*On Rewards and Punishments*
Flacc.	*Against Flaccus*	*Sacr.*	*On the Sacrifices of Cain and Abel*
Flight	*On Flight and Finding*		
Giants	*On Giants*	*Sobr.*	*On Sobriety*
Good Pers.	*That Every Good Person Is Free*	*Spec.*	*On the Special Laws*
		Unchang.	*That God Is Unchangeable*
Heir	*Who Is the Heir?*	*Virt.*	*On the Virtues*
Hypoth.	*Hypothetica: Apology for the Jews*	*Worse*	*That the Worse Attacks the Better*

Rabbinic Tractates

The abbreviations below are used for the names of the tractates in the Mishnah (indicated by a prefixed m.), Tosefta (t.), Babylonian Talmud (b.), and Palestinian/Jerusalem Talmud (y.).

Avot	Avot	Hul.	Hullin	Qidd.	Qiddushin
B. Bat.	Bava Batra	Kelim	Kelim	Sanh.	Sanhedrin
Ber.	Berakhot	Ker.	Kerithot	Shevu.	Shevu'ot
Eruv.	Eruvin	Mak.	Makkot	Yevam.	Yevamot
Gerim	Gerim	Menah.	Menahot	Yoma	Yoma
Git.	Gittin	Parah	Parah		
Hag.	Hagigah	Pesah.	Pesahim		

Other Rabbinic Works

Exod. Rab.	Exodus Rabbah	Pesiq. Rab.	Pesiqta Rabbati
Gen. Rab.	Genesis Rabbah	Pirqe R. El.	Pirqe Rabbi Eliezer
Midr. Pss.	Midrash Psalms	Ruth Rab.	Ruth Rabbah
Midr. Tanh.	Midrash Tanhuma	Sifre Deut.	Sifre Deuteronomy
Num. Rab.	Numbers Rabbah	Tanh.	Tanhuma

Targumim

Targumim on the Writings and Prophets are indicated by the abbreviation Tg. appended in front of the usual abbreviation for the biblical book (see the above list). In the place of Tg., targumim on the Pentateuch use one of the following abbreviations:

Tg. Neof. 1	Targum Neofiti 1	Tg. Ps.-J.	Targum Pseudo-Jonathan
Tg. Onq.	Targum Onqelos		

Qumran/Dead Sea Scrolls

CD-A(B)	Damascus Document, copy A (or B)	4Q161	Isaiah Pesher[a]
1QapGen ar	Genesis Apocryphon, in Aramaic	4Q171	Psalms Pesher[a]
1QH	Thanksgiving Hymns (Hodayot)	4Q174	Florilegium
1QM	War Scroll (Milḥamah)	4Q213a	Aramaic Levi[b]
1QpHab	Pesher Habakkuk	4Q365	Reworked Pentateuch[c]
1QS	Rule of the Community	4Q400	Songs of the Sabbath Sacrifice[a]
1QSa	Rule of the Congregation (appendix a to 1QS)	4Q405	Songs of the Sabbath Sacrifice[f]
1QSb	Rule of the Blessings (appendix b to 1QS)	4Q418	Instruction[d]
1Q20	Genesis Apocryphon	4Q423	Instruction[g]
4Q158	Reworked Pentateuch[a]	4Q433a	Hodayot-like text B
		4Q434	Bless, Oh My Soul
		4Q504	Words of the Luminaries[a]
		4Q511	Songs of the Sage[b]
		11QT[a]	Temple Scroll[a] (11Q19)

Nag Hammadi Codices

Gos. Truth	Gospel of Truth (I 3; XII 2)
Three Forms	Three Forms of First Thought (XIII 1)

Greco-Roman Classics

Abst.	Porphyry, *On Abstinence*	*Art*	Galen, *The Art of Medicine* (Μεθόδου)
Acute	Hippocrates, *Regimen in Acute Diseases*	*Astyph.*	Isaeus, *On the Estate of Astyphilus*
Advice	Plutarch, *Advice to Bride and Groom* (in *Moralia*)	*Att.*	Cicero, *Letters to Atticus*
Anc. Med.	Hippocrates, *Ancient Medicine*	*Aug.*	Suetonius, *Divine Augustus*
Anger	Plutarch, *On the Control of Anger* (in *Moralia*)	*Bacch.*	Euripides, *Bacchae*
		Banq.	Athenaeus, *The Learned Banquet*

Beasts	Plutarch, *Beasts Are Rational* (in *Moralia*)
Borrow	Plutarch, *That We Ought Not to Borrow* (in *Moralia*)
Bus.	Plutarch, *On Being a Busybody* (in *Moralia*)
Chaer.	Chariton, *Chaereas and Callirhoe*
Claud.	Suetonius, *Divine Claudius*
Cyr.	Xenophon, *Cyropaedia*
Def. Orac.	Plutarch, *On the Defect of Oracles*
Dis.	Hippocrates, *Diseases*
Diss.	Epictetus, *Dissertations*
Dreams	Artemidorus Daldianus, *The Interpretation of Dreams*
Ed. Child.	Pseudo-Plutarch, *The Education of Children* (in *Moralia*)
El.	Euripides, *Electra*
Ench.	Epictetus, *Enchiridion* (*Handbook*)
Envy	Dio Chrysostom, *On Envy*
Ep.	Pliny the Younger, *Epistles*; Seneca (the Younger), *Moral Epistles*
Flac.	Cicero, *For Flaccus*
Herc.	Euripides, *Children of Hercules*
Hist.	Dio Cassius, *Roman History*; Herodian, *History of the Empire*; Polybius, *Histories*
Hist. Lib.	Diodorus of Sicily, *Historical Library*
Hunt.	Dio Chrysostom, *The Hunter*
Il.	Homer, *Iliad*
Inst.	Quintilian, *Institutes of Oratory*
Is. Os.	Plutarch, *Isis and Osiris*
Leoch.	Demosthenes, *Against Leochares*
Lit. Comp.	Dionysius of Halicarnassus, *On Literary Composition*
Lives	Diogenes Laertius, *Lives and Opinions of Eminent Philosophers*
Lives Soph.	Philostratus, *Lives of the Sophists*
Med.	Euripides, *Medea*; Marcus Aurelius, *Meditations*
Mem.	Xenophon, *Memorabilia*
Mor.	Plutarch, *Moralia*
Nic. Eth.	Aristotle, *Nicomachean Ethics*
Notes	Diogenes Laertius, *Pythagorean Notes* (*Hypomnemata*)
Od.	Homer, *Odyssey*
Oed. Col.	Sophocles, *Oedipus at Colonus*
Oed. King	Sophocles, *Oedipus the King*
Old Man	Plutarch, *Whether an Old Man Should Engage in Public Affairs* (in *Moralia*)
One	Pseudo-Menander, *One-Liners*
Or.	Dio Chrysostom, *Orations* (*Discourses*)
Orat.	Cicero, *On the Orator*
Peace	Plutarch, *Peace of Mind* (in *Moralia*)
Pers.	Aeschylus, *The Persians*
Pol.	Aristotle, *Politics*
Pyr.	Sextus Empiricus, *Outlines of Pyrrhonism*
Reg.	Hippocrates, *Regimen*
Rep.	Plato, *The Republic*
Rom.	Plutarch, *Romulus*
Rom. Ant.	Dionysius of Halicarnassus, *Roman Antiquities*
Rom. Hist.	Appian, *Roman History*
Shield	Hesiod, *Sheild of Heracles*
Spart.	Plutarch, *Sayings of Spartans* (in *Moralia*)
Talk.	Plutarch, *Concerning Talkativeness* (in *Moralia*)
Test. Frag. P.	Cratinus, *Testimonies and Fragments: The Poets of the Old Comedy*
Tib.	Suetonius, *Tiberius*
Tim.	Plato, *Timaeus*
T. Talk	Plutarch, *Table Talk in Nine Books* (in *Moralia*)
Unbeliev.	Palaephatus, *On Unbelievable Tales*
Univ.	Pseudo-Aristotle, *On the Universe*
Well	Plutarch, *Advice about Keeping Well* (in *Moralia*)

Transliteration

Hebrew

א	*ʾ*	בָ	*ā*	*qāmeṣ*
ב	*b*	בַ	*a*	*pataḥ*
ג	*g*	הַ	*a*	furtive *pataḥ*
ד	*d*	בֶ	*e*	*sĕgōl*
ה	*h*	בֵ	*ē*	*ṣērē*
ו	*w*	בִ	*i*	short *ḥîreq*
ז	*z*	בִ	*ī*	long *ḥîreq* written defectively
ח	*ḥ*	בָ	*o*	*qāmeṣ ḥāṭûp*
ט	*ṭ*	בוֹ	*ô*	*ḥōlem* written fully
י	*y*	בֹ	*ō*	*ḥōlem* written defectively
ך/כ	*k*	בוּ	*û*	*šûreq*
ל	*l*	בֻ	*u*	short *qibbûṣ*
ם/מ	*m*	בֻ	*ū*	long *qibbûṣ* written defectively
ן/נ	*n*	בָה	*â*	final *qāmeṣ hēʾ* (בָהּ = *āh*)
ס	*s*	בֶי	*ē*	*sĕgōl yōd* (בֶי = *ēy*)
ע	*ʿ*	בֵי	*ē*	*ṣērē yōd* (בֵי = *ēy*)
ף/פ	*p*	בִי	*î*	*ḥîreq yōd* (בִי = *îy*)
ץ/צ	*ṣ*	בֲ	*ă*	*ḥāṭēp pataḥ*
ק	*q*	בֱ	*ĕ*	*ḥāṭēp sĕgōl*
ר	*r*	בֳ	*ŏ*	*ḥāṭēp qāmeṣ*
שׂ	*ś*	בְ	*ə*	vocal *šəwāʾ*
שׁ	*š*			
ת	*t*			

Notes on the Transliteration of Hebrew

1. Accents are not shown in transliteration.
2. Silent *šəwāʾ* is not indicated in transliteration.
3. The spirant forms ב ג ד כ פ ת are usually not specially indicated in transliteration.
4. *Dāgēš forte* is indicated by doubling the consonant. Euphonic *dāgēš* and *dāgēš lene* are not indicated in transliteration.
5. *Maqqēp* is represented by a hyphen.

Greek

α	*a*	θ	*th*	ο	*o*	χ	*ch*
β	*b*	ι	*i*	π	*p*	ψ	*ps*
γ	*g/n*	κ	*k*	ρ	*r*	ω	*ō*
δ	*d*	λ	*l*	σ/ς	*s*	῾	*h*
ε	*e*	μ	*m*	τ	*t*		
ζ	*z*	ν	*n*	υ	*y/u*		
η	*ē*	ξ	*x*	φ	*ph*		

Notes on the Transliteration of Greek

1. Accents, lenis (smooth breathing), and *iota* subscript are not shown in transliteration.
2. The transliteration of asper (rough breathing) precedes a vowel or diphthong (e.g., ἁ = *ha*; αἱ = *hai*) and follows ρ (i.e., ῥ = *rh*).
3. *Gamma* is transliterated *n* only when it precedes γ, κ, ξ, or χ.
4. *Upsilon* is transliterated *u* only when it is part of a diphthong (i.e., αυ, ευ, ου, υι).

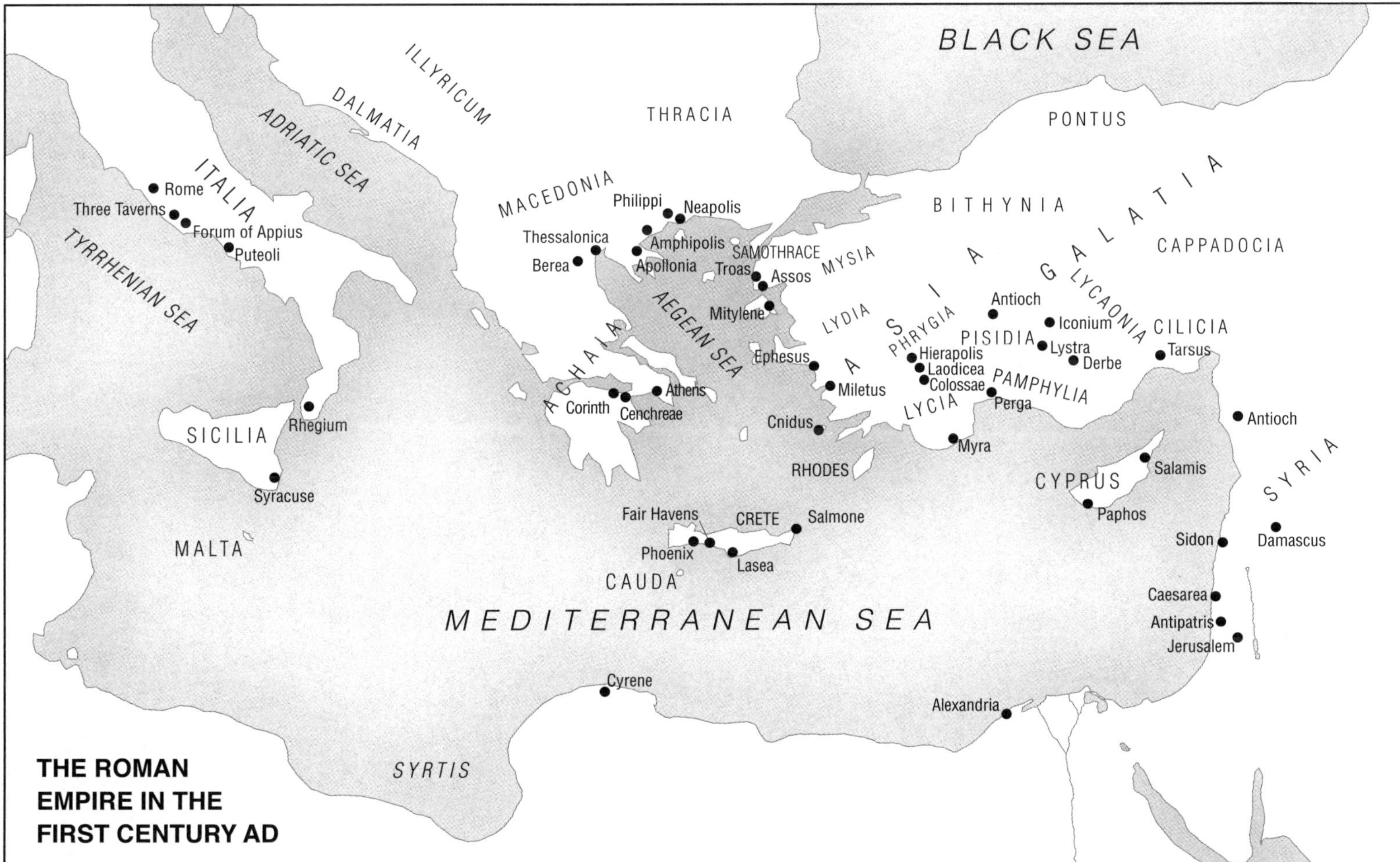

THE ROMAN EMPIRE IN THE FIRST CENTURY AD

Introduction to Colossians

Authorship

Arguments for a Pseudonymous Author

Vocabulary and Stylistic Considerations

Though anticipated in the nineteenth century, in the early twentieth century scholars set forth arguments that Paul did not write Colossians.[1]

One argument was that the vocabulary of Colossians was so different from Paul's other accepted genuine epistles that Colossians must be considered to have been written by someone else. The number of once-occurring words (thirty-four hapax legomena; see Pascuzzi 2013: 229) was seen to be so numerous that this pointed away from Paul being the author. If the epistle were authentic, would not more words be used that were in common with Paul's usual vocabulary?

However, a comparison of word statistics between one epistle and another to determine authorship is a precarious criterion to use. For example, there are among Paul's accepted authentic letters just as many once-occurring words as in purported pseudepigraphical letters.[2] In addition, there is insufficient data to determine Paul's standard style (Paul's seven purportedly authentic letters do not provide a big enough sample to determine this). Furthermore, it is plausible that the kinds of words used in writing to a particular church would be significantly shaped by the unique circumstances of the church and the particular occasion that prompted the writing of the letter. Finally, a person's writing style in choice of vocabulary can change significantly over time. Consider even today how a scholar's writing style usually changes significantly from student days to the time of retirement. Some have adduced the unique syntactical style of Colossians as evidence of non-Pauline authorship.[3] But, again, the very same argument adduced above against the vocabulary criterion

1. One estimate is that 60 percent of contemporary scholars believe that Colossians was not written by Paul; see D. Moo 2008: 29, who gives a sampling of scholars not holding to Pauline authorship and others holding to it. See J. White 2017: 90–91, listing recent German and English-speaking scholars holding to ultimate Pauline authorship of Colossians.

2. E.g., Colossians uses 87 words not found in the accepted seven authentic epistles, but Philippians (accepted as Pauline) contains 79 unique words; see D. Moo 2008: 30.

3. See, e.g., Schweizer 1982: 18, listing several kinds of syntactical constructions that occur in Colossians and do not occur in Paul's undisputed letters (such as combinations of synonymous constructions, how genitives are strung together, difficult and long sentences or relative clauses strung loosely together).

can equally be brought forward in response to syntactical arguments against Paul's authorship.[4] In fact, every unusual stylistic feature in Colossians, with the exception of ὅ (ἅ) ἐστιν (*ho* [*ha*] *estin*, which is, 2:17, 22), can be found in the so-called authentic letters, though with less frequency (see Pascuzzi 2013: 230).

In this connection, Paul may have coauthored the epistle with Timothy (cf. Col. 1:1), but this is unlikely due to the repeated use of "I" throughout the letter, capped by the conclusion of "I, Paul, write this letter in my own hand." However, one must also take into consideration the fact that Paul used secretaries and that there were a variety of ways in which authors dictated in the ancient world. For example, Cicero (*Att.* 333, 13.25) speaks of two kinds of dictation to secretaries: "Tiro, who is by way of taking down whole sections together," but "Spintharus" wrote down "syllable by syllable."[5] If Paul dictated this letter using the looser approach, then the letter could well reflect the secretary's choice of vocabulary with respect to synonyms and interpretative paraphrases. One argument along these lines of a looser dictation method is that of Dunn. Dunn actually believes technically that Paul did not even dictate the letter but that one of his disciples or coworkers (probably Timothy) composed it on his behalf; next Paul read it or had it read to him, and then he approved (and possibly revised?) it before it was sent to the Colossians. Accordingly, Paul's secretary would have been "familiar with the broad pattern of Paul's letter-writing" and possibly Paul was "content to leave it to the secretary to formulate the letter with a fair degree of license, perhaps under the conditions of his imprisonment, at that point able only to add the briefest of personal conclusions (see on 4:18)" (Dunn 1996: 38). Dunn concludes that what may appear to be different theological concepts or different theological emphases of the secretary are not contradictory to Paul's thought, since they would represent the secretary's interpretation of Paul's theology, which Paul would have condoned authoritatively as organic and consistent developments of his own thought. This is a speculative and convoluted view. Nevertheless, even this extreme view of secretarial use would still theoretically fall within the bounds of the epistle being considered ultimately to be by Paul (Dunn 1996: 38) and thus to bear his apostolic authority. Such a phenomenon occurs today in the United States, for example, with presidential speech writers. The speech writer writes a speech; the President looks it over, perhaps does some revision, and then delivers the speech.

Thus Paul either wrote the epistle himself or authorized it to be dictated to a secretary or coauthored it with Timothy. The first two options are the most probable. One could say that "Paul 'owned' the content even though its crafting and articulation may be the work of others" (Pascuzzi 2013: 227).

4. See O'Donnell (1999) for an elaboration of the fallacy of trying to discern authorship via the above criteria of vocabulary, syntax, and other facets of writing style, which I have subsequently found to be helpful (see excursus 1).

5. I am grateful to Gordon Fee for bringing this text from Cicero to my attention.

Theological Considerations

Commentators commonly acknowledge that one of the criteria for discerning non-Pauline authorship of Colossians is that some of its theological concepts do not appear to be consistent with Paul's theology in his seven supposedly authentic letters.[6] But such an idea is based on the assumption that Paul's thought developed along a linear chronological trajectory, beginning with less developed to more developed ideas, and that even more developed notions can be identified as too advanced for Paul. But how can one be sure that the purportedly more advanced ideas by Paul could not have arisen before the supposedly less developed. And how can one be certain that what is said to be too advanced for Paul is really so?[7] Accordingly, it is overly optimistic to think that one can define the degree of latitude a writer has before he comes to the point of self-contradiction[8] or a point beyond which he could not conceivably think. Among concepts usually adduced are Christology, eschatology, ecclesiology, and the Christian life.[9]

Christology, especially in 1:15–17, is usually seen to be more advanced than in Paul's undisputed letters. Here Christ is portrayed as existing eternally before the beginning of the first creation as a fully divine being. But certainly 1 Cor. 8:4–6 and Phil. 2:6–11 are virtually as explicit about Christ's deity (e.g., mentioned by Dunn 1995: 36), the latter also focusing on Christ's preexistence. But some see that the Christology of Col. 1:19–20 and 2:9 is even an explicit step beyond anything else in the accepted epistles of Paul (so Dunn 1995: 36). However, when these passages are placed within an OT temple context (see my comments on 1:19; 2:9), then they can be seen as a development of Paul's own temple theology, which is also elsewhere in Paul based on the OT (e.g., see 1 Cor. 3:9–17; cf. 2 Cor. 6:15–16).

The ecclesiological statement that Christ is "the head of the body" in 1:18a is seen as more in line with the ecclesiology of Eph. 1:21–23 (which is typically also viewed as pseudonymous) than anything one finds in Paul's seven accepted epistles (so Dunn 1995: 36). But why could this not be a development by Paul himself, especially since he has already discussed believers being the "body of Christ" (NIV: 1 Cor. 10:16; 12:27, the latter reading, "Now you are the body of Christ")?[10] Pascuzzi (2013: 238) argues that though Paul does not refer to Christ as "head" of the body in 1 Cor. 12, it does not mean that he could not

6. The seven NT letters accepted by all scholars to have been originally written by Paul are Romans, 1 Corinthians, 2 Corinthians, Galatians, Philippians, 1 Thessalonians, and Philemon.

7. See Pascuzzi (2013: 237) on raising questions about the assumptions concerning the way Paul's ideas developed.

8. See Carson and Moo 2005: 518, in dependence on L. T. Johnson 1972: 394–95.

9. E.g., see Dunn 1995: 36, listing these topics as typical theological issues that have raised questions about the authorship of Colossians. D. Moo (2008: 32–33) also mentions the view held by some that a pseudonymous author sought to attach Paul's apostolic authority to a generation of teachers who arose after Paul's death, which some think points to a time later than Paul, to which D. Moo well responds.

10. D. Moo (2008: 34) has pointed out the 1 Corinthians evidence.

have conceived the notion prior to the writing of Colossians, especially since 1 Cor. 11:3 says, "Christ is the head of every man," which comes close to Christ being the head of the whole church. Some contend that Paul apparently did not think of the church as a supralocal (i.e., universal) reality prior to Colossians, so that such an idea in the letter indicates that it cannot be genuinely Pauline. But, again, Pascuzzi argues, why could not Paul have genuinely developed this notion?[11] Indeed, it is evident that Paul conceived of the church as universal in his earlier so-called genuine epistles (Gal. 1:13; 1 Cor. 12:28; 15:9) and Col. 4:15–16 expresses a local use of church (so Brown 1997: 612).[12]

One of the most common theological objections to Pauline authorship is that Colossians has a "realized" view of eschatology, whereas in the undisputed letters the futuristic eschatology is purported to be typical. Many have responded to this by acknowledging the "inaugurated" emphasis in Colossians (1:13; 1:18; 1:26; 2:12–13; 3:1–3; 3:10) but also noting the presence of a definite future perspective (1:5; 1:27b; 3:4; 3:6; 3:24; 3:25). And in the undisputed epistles, in fact, Paul has a robust "already" and "not yet" view of eschatology.[13] The inaugurated eschatology in Colossians is due to the occasion of the false teachers questioning the believers' status in Christ and the sufficiency of their faith. Paul wants to assure them that they significantly participate already in end-time blessings in Christ (see Pascuzzi 2013: 240–41).

Some also see the household code in Col. 3:18–4:1 to be so different from the authentic Paul's portrayal of Christian living that it cannot be from Paul's hand (again, it is uniquely parallel in the Pauline corpus to the household code in Eph. 5:21–6:9, which is likewise viewed as non-Pauline). But why could not Paul himself have developed his own thought on this subject? Even if there were not responses to the objections about Christology, ecclesiology, and eschatology above, why could these not also be Paul's own legitimate developments of his thinking?[14]

Indeed, almost anything that appears in Colossians that does not appear in the undisputed Pauline writings is seen as evidence of inauthenticity, whether it be Paul's suffering for the church (1:24) or the explicit reference to the Spirit (1:8) or to the law as a shadow of future fulfillment (2:17; see Schweizer 1982: 16–18), in addition to the above-mentioned notions. This is an inaccurate

11. And Pascuzzi (2013) adds that if Col. 1:18a is a pre-Pauline hymn, which is almost universally held by scholars, then neither Paul nor even a pseudepigrapher was responsible originally for the idea of Christ being the head of the church body, since it was pre-Pauline tradition, though Paul (or the pseudonymous author) would have agreed with the view by incorporating it into his letter.

12. Pascuzzi (2013: 38) adds Phil. 3:6 and 1 Cor. 10:32 to passages in Paul's "accepted" letters that refer to the universal church, and she thinks that 1 Cor. 1:12 and 2 Cor. 1:1 can be included with these passages.

13. See Beale 2011: passim; e.g., see Rom. 6:1–13 for the inaugurated end-time resurrection and future resurrection; see also Rom. 8:1–25 for the present and future eschatological work of the Spirit.

14. See D. Moo (2008: 32–37) for good responses to most of these theological objections to Pauline authorship.

criterion, since one can find things in even an accepted epistle that cannot be found in the other accepted letters. But even if this were not the case, why cannot an author develop new thoughts in his own writings?

Conclusion on the Issue of Pseudonymity

I remember attending the New Testament Seminar at Cambridge University, where Harold Hoehner delivered a paper titled "Did Paul Write Galatians?" The paper facetiously concluded that Paul should not be considered to be the author of Galatians when that epistle is judged according to the typical pseudepigraphical criteria used to determine the non-Pauline authorship of Ephesians and the Pastoral Epistles. The point of the paper (later published as Hoehner 2006) was to show in detail that Pauline scholars are very inconsistent in judging Ephesians and the Pastoral Epistles to be inauthentic, while accepting that Paul wrote Galatians. Galatians has an impersonal style compared to the other six accepted epistles (Hoehner 2006: 153–55). In comparison to the other six supposedly authentic Pauline letters, Galatians also has thirty hapax legomena and quite a few vocabulary words that are uncommon, as well as historical and theological peculiarities (Hoehner 2006: 155–67). As Gupta (2013b: 213) says, "The whole scope and depth of research Hoehner offers against viewing Galatians as authentic is impressive." Hoehner shows convincingly that if these scholars applied the same criteria to Galatians as they have to the supposedly inauthentic letters, they should conclude that Galatians also is not genuine. As I recall, there was not much response to Hoehner's paper. This illustrates the subjective nature of the criteria commonly employed to determine non-Pauline authorship.

After all, as in each of the seven Pauline letters most frequently accepted by scholars as Pauline, Colossians is also said to be written by "Paul" (Col. 1:1). In Col. 4:18 Paul "writes this greeting with" his "own hand," which is a way of expressing the epistle's Pauline authenticity. It also assumes that most of the epistle has been dictated to a secretary (O'Brien 1982: 259). Use of secretaries was common in the Greco-Roman world, and often secretaries were not referred to or named.[15] Such a signature protected against false teachers writing in Paul's name (as warned against in 2 Thess. 2:2). This authoritative apostolic signature reminds the hearers of Paul's authority in all he says in the epistle, especially his warnings about and objections to the false teachers. His signature along with a note in his own hand (as in 1 Cor. 16:21; Gal. 6:11; Philem. 19) probably has the same significance. It is commonly known that such added signatures at the ends of letters were a feature in Greco-Roman letters as well (see references in Dunn 1996: 289; and Bruce 1984: 186, who also notes that such signatures were appended when a secretary wrote the letter).

15. So Pao (2012: 322, and sources cited there), who also notes that at the end of Romans (16:22), Paul does not supply an autograph, though he makes explicit that "Tertius" was his secretary.

In this light, if Paul did not write Colossians, then the pseudonymous author was deceiving by saying "I, Paul, write this greeting with my own hand." It does not ameliorate the deceptive motive by saying that this signature by an anonymous author was an attempt to give his letter an aura of Pauline authority, since deception would still be involved.

Many who hold to a non-Pauline author usually do not think the author was trying to deceive. But such commentators have difficulty in overcoming the evidence that the pseudonymous author was trying to deceive. In fact, they have failed to argue persuasively that no deception took place. It is hard to explain away an attempt to deceive, since the letter is said to be written by "Paul." Paul twice warns the readers against "delusion" (Col. 2:4) or "deception" (2:8). Would a pseudonymous author "who speaks of deceit like this put the name of Paul to a letter he himself had composed?" (Carson and Moo 2005: 349).

Further complications for proposals for a pseudonymous author are the personal comments and instructions that are given in Col. 4:7–18. If Paul himself did not write these, then they are a fiction, unless one speculates that Paul wrote these before his death and they were inserted here. But even if so, it would make it appear that Paul had written the entirety of the letter up to 4:7, which would still result in the majority of the letter being a fiction. And if this were a literary technique giving the fictitious author an air of Pauline authority, would the addressees not have known this, which would invalidate such an intent?[16] Alternatively, if the addressees were not aware that the letter was not authentic, then it is difficult to resist the idea that the anonymous author intended to deceive, even if the deception was aimed to bring about a good pastoral and theological goal (cf. similarly D. Moo 2008: 332–34). It has been argued that Col. 4:7–18 is meant to strengthen the Pauline authority of some anonymous writer (MacDonald 2000: 184). However, in what way could a pseudonymous letter enhance the authority of an author unknown to the readers?[17] "The hard evidence demands that we conclude either that some New Testament documents are pseudonymous and that the . . . authors intended to deceive their readers, or that the real authors intended to speak the truth and that pseudonymity is not attested in the New Testament."[18] The latter is more probable.

Some believe there was a pseudepigraphical genre that did not necessitate the notion of deception. This issue, in part, concerns whether there are other Greek and Jewish pseudepigraphical writings that are comparable to the genre of Colossians. Some contend that such pseudepigraphical letters can be found, but even these (like the Epistle of Jeremiah and the Letter of Aristeas) are substantially different from the epistolary genre of Colossians (so D. Moo 2008:

16. The personal and urgent request of Paul that is to be addressed by the Colossians to Archippus in 4:17 is an illustration of such details; following Witherington 2007: 201.

17. So Witherington 2007: 201–2; see also the introduction to 4:7–18 below.

18. Carson and Moo 2005: 350; and 346–50, discussing pseudonymity in relation to deception.

38). There are also no examples of recognized ancient pseudepigraphical writings composed within ten to twenty years after the purported author's death, which is a frame of time most of those supporting pseudonymity propose. Such writings were usually produced hundreds of years after the purported writer's death, and for the most part, the identity of the pseudonymous author was, and continues to remain, undiscoverable (Pascuzzi 2013: 232). And though many modern scholars accept pseudonymity among OT books, the early Christians apparently did not, so that there is no evidence they were consciously producing pseudonymous works that stood in line with some acceptable Jewish tradition (Pascuzzi 2013: 232–33). But even if Colossians were part of such an accepted pseudepigraphical genre that did not attempt to deceive, was it accepted widely enough in the church for recipients of the letter to appreciate that it was not an attempt to deceive? There is no such evidence. In fact, what evidence there is on the subject is to the contrary. In AD 200 Serapion, bishop of Antioch, said: "We receive both Peter and the other apostles as Christ, but the writings which falsely bear their names we reject, . . . knowing that such were not handed down to us."[19] Thus it is unlikely that such a pseudepigraphical genre that did not attempt to deceive ever existed within the church. So if Colossians was written by someone other than Paul, we must conclude that the author was trying to deceive.[20]

The unanimous patristic testimony to the authenticity of Colossians should be taken more seriously, since they were quite aware of some church writings that were pseudonymous and that they accordingly condemned. Indeed, the early church made distinctions on the basis of established criteria (style, content, and character) between accepted, genuine writings, disputed writings, and spurious writings.[21] This is especially the case at a time when reception history is becoming increasingly significant for interpretation of biblical texts (following here Gupta 2013b: 211–12).

Conclusion on Authorship

In the light of the preceding discussion, we judge that the following criteria are not sufficient to rule out Paul as the ultimate author of Colossians: vocabulary, literary style, theological development, and comparisons with other pseudepigraphical genre or writings. Paul's own development in his writing style and theology or his use of various kinds of secretaries or variations in circumstances sufficiently explain any significant differences from the seven accepted Pauline letters. The church fathers also testify to Colossians as authentically Pauline. Our conclusions are in line with that of Pascuzzi (2013: 245):

> Two key assumptions supporting the case for authenticity, namely that Paul's letters were occasional and that they were collaborative creations, are premises that are almost universally agreed on in Pauline scholarship today. They are

19. See D. Moo 2008: 38, citing Eusebius, *Eccl. Hist.* 6.12.1–6, where the citation is found.
20. See D. Moo (2008: 37–40) for secondary sources pro and con with respect to pseudepigraphy.
21. Pascuzzi 2013: 232, citing Eusebius, *Eccl. Hist.* 3.25.1–7.

> not determinative for establishing Colossians' authenticity. However, they have the advantage of being widely accepted, and they favor the letter's authenticity because they can best account for indisputable variations in style and developments, or changed emphases in theology. The circumstances in the Colossian community can explain the theological development and emphases in this letter. The collaborative aspect of composition can explain the stylistic variations. If we add to this the stylostatistical results of Neumann's study which puts Colossians within, or sufficiently close to, the range of authentic letters, the near certainty that the situation that occasioned the letter occurred during Paul's lifetime, and the threefold claim within the letter that Paul is its author, there is an accumulation of evidence that reinforces the probability that Colossians is authentic.

In light of this, the assumptions of pseudonymous practices in the early church and of a Pauline school (from which subsequent pseudonymous authors arose) are not compelling (Pascuzzi 2013: 245).

Place and Date of Writing

The close similarities of Colossians, Ephesians, and Philemon show Paul writing from a situation of imprisonment (see Col. 4:3, "the mystery of Christ, for which I have been also imprisoned"; 4:18 NIV, "remember my chains"; Eph. 4:1; 6:20, "I am an ambassador in chains"; Philem. 1, 9, 13 NIV, "I am in chains for the gospel").[22] This is likely the same imprisonment referred to in all three letters. So where is this imprisonment? Though there were other periods of imprisonment (cf. 2 Cor. 6:5; 11:23), the most likely options of the place of imprisonment proposed by different commentators are Ephesus (implied from 2 Cor. 1:8; 1 Cor. 15:32[?]), Caesarea (Acts 24:27), or Rome (Acts 28:16–31).

Among other reasons that he offers, the suggestion of N. Wright (1986) appears to point in the right direction. He says that it is more probable that Onesimus would have traveled to Ephesus to see Paul rather than to Rome. And it would have been easier for Paul to send Onesimus back to Colossae and possibly to request that the slave be returned to him again to assist him (cf. Philem. 13–14). Would it not be asking a lot for Onesimus to travel from Rome to Colossae and then return to Rome again, especially when he had already come to Rome initially from Colossae as a part of his escape from slavery? On top of this, Wright concludes, since Paul saw Rome as a staging post on his journey to Spain (Rom. 15:22–29), it is unlikely that Paul would be desiring to visit Philemon so soon after his hoped-for imminent release from prison in Rome (see N. Wright 1986: 35).

If this is correct, then the Letter to Colossae would have been written in the early 50s, during the time of Paul's extended ministry in Ephesus, which lasted for over two years (see Acts 19:8–10). Nevertheless, while Wright's speculation is plausible, it is hard to be confident about whether Paul wrote from Ephesus or Rome.

22. This section is a summary of N. Wright 1986: 34–39, though much of what Wright says is generally acknowledged.

Where Was Colossae, and Who Were the Colossians?

Colossae was situated in the region of Phrygia, which was in the Roman province of Asia Minor.[23] It was 15 miles south-southeast of Hierapolis, 11 miles southeast of Laodicea, and 120 miles east of Ephesus. Colossae was an important economic city at the time of the Roman imperial period. By that time Laodicea had become the most important city in the region. There was a significant Jewish population in the cities of the Lycus valley (among which was Colossae), perhaps as many as 7,500. This estimate is based on the amount of money confiscated for the temple tax by a Lucius Peducaeus in Laodicea in 62 BC (see Cicero, *Flac.* 28.68). Furthermore, according to Josephus (*Ant.* 12.145–53) the Seleucid king Antiochus III in 213 BC settled 2,000 Jewish families in the general region around Colossae (cited by D. Moo 2008: 27). Of course, the majority of the inhabitants of Colossae were Gentiles. The evidence from ancient coins found in the area reveals the worship of such deities as the Artemis of Ephesus, Zeus, Men of Phrygia, Hygeia, Athena, Boule, Demeter, and Selene, in addition to the Egyptian gods Isis and Serapis. After severe earthquakes in the region of Colossae, the populace moved to the nearby town of Chonae (Honaz), so that afterward Colossae was eventually abandoned.

Importance of the Old Testament in Colossians

Until recently there had been no book, monograph, or even article dedicated explicitly to a study of the OT in Colossians.[24] One reason for such little scholarly attention to this subject is that there are no formal quotations or citations from the OT in Colossians. Numerous commentators find difficulty detecting even any allusions in the letter, although there are a number of them. What Goppelt (1982: 198)[25] said in general about the NT is applicable to Colossians:

> In previous studies of the NT use of Scripture, far too much emphasis has been placed on actual quotations. . . . The NT use of Scripture is not restricted to the direct quotation of OT passages. Continual allusions to Scripture are found in the exposition of the writers. . . . This fact has been overlooked or has been evaluated negatively. . . . Much of the NT abounds with allusions to the OT. . . . These allusions make up the larger portion of the NT use of Scripture and form the heart of its view of Scripture.

23. This section is based on C. E. Arnold, *ABD* 1:1089–90.

24. Beetham wrote his doctoral dissertation on the subject (2005; published in 2008), Fee (2006) completed an essay on the subject, and I wrote the chapter on Colossians in Beale and Carson 2007: 841–70. The final form of both Fee's and Beetham's studies appeared too late for sufficient interaction with them in my 2007 work, although prepublication exposure to their studies revealed that their approach was similar to mine, and the OT allusions that they identified overlapped with a number of those that I discerned (esp. Beetham's work). In this commentary, I have in some cases abbreviated what I discussed in the earlier essay; in other cases, I have expanded on it, finding new allusions that I had not seen earlier.

25. I was attracted to this quotation in Beetham 2008: vii.

Some of the allusions are discussed in the various commentaries, which sometimes agree about the particular OT texts to which the author is alluding.[26] But even when commentators have observed allusions, there has been little attempt to demonstrate their validity or to reflect on how Paul is using them. As far as possible, within the limits of the commentary, the procedure for discerning allusions is generally twofold: to demonstrate the validity of various OT allusions and to discuss their significance. Neither of these tasks has been consistently carried out in past study of Colossians, except in Beale (2007) and Beetham (2008).

Commentators offer various definitions of "allusion" and "echo" and posit various criteria for discernment of both, sometimes defining an echo as unconscious and unintentional and sometimes as conscious and intentional. Whether OT references are referred to as "allusions" or "echoes," the purpose in the commentary is to argue the likelihood that Paul, to one degree or another, intended to make the reference. The goal is to point out, on a case-by-case basis, the clearest cumulative evidence for the presence of an intentional OT reference, regardless of how one wants to categorize it formally (i.e., as an echo or allusion; see excursus 2 for an elaboration of the criteria for discerning allusions).

Nevertheless, readers will make different judgments on the basis of the same evidence, some categorizing a reference to be "probable," and others viewing the same reference to be only "possible" or even so faint as not to merit analysis. Indeed, one wants to avoid being a "parallelomaniac." I have tried to include for study those OT allusions whose validity is attested by the best evidence and that I consider to be probable. However, some may still wonder whether Paul has intended to make a particular allusion, and they may ask, If Paul really intended to convey all the meaning from an OT text for which I am contending, why did he not make the links with that text more explicit? In such cases I would allow for the possibility that Paul may merely have presupposed the OT association in his mind, since he was such a deep and long-experienced reader of the OT Scriptures. This would not mean that there is no semantic link with the OT text under discussion, but rather that Paul perhaps was either unconscious of making the reference or more likely was not necessarily intending his audience to pick up on the allusion or echo. In either case, identification of the reference and the enhancement of meaning that comes from the context of the source text may well disclose the author's underlying or implicit presuppositions, which form the basis for his explicit statements in the text[27] (e.g., texts in

26. I am indebted to Beetham for cataloging the various allusions and echoes recorded by various commentators; of course, I have subsequently consulted the commentary literature myself to confirm these references and added others. For a large-scale discussion and analysis of allusions in Colossians, see Beetham 2008. As noted above, I have detected some new allusions not previously observed by commentators and Beetham, but for the most part the allusions that I discuss have been identified by one or another of the commentators.

27. The issues raised in the paragraph were posed to me as a possibility in a personal communication by D. A. Carson in response to Beale 2007.

the following discussion that may be susceptible to this kind of conclusion are Col. 1:9, 12b–14; 2:11; 3:1).[28]

Being sensitive to the presence of OT allusions in Colossians has important significance for some greatly debated issues in Colossians, which also concern the important biblical-theological themes in the letter. For example, as we will see, there are four specific allusions to specific OT texts about the temple that are applied to Christ and the church (1:9–10, 19; 2:9, 10). Why is Paul concerned to make so many temple allusions in the space of such a short letter? We believe the answer is that Paul wants to contrast the true temple in Christ, with which believers are identified, with the pseudo-claims of a heavenly temple experience by the false teachers. All the positive OT temple texts come before the most explicit piece of false teaching in the entire epistle (2:18). In fact, we think these preceding positive texts are key to recognizing that 2:18 concerns a false claim about heavenly temple experience. The "fullness" (1:19; 2:9–10) that so many commentators discuss and debate (whether it is a polemic against a gnostic teaching or some other kind of false teaching) is best understood, we believe, as the "fullness" of God in Christ as the new, end-time temple. Believers have all the "fullness" of Christ's presence in the temple that they need, in contrast to the empty "fullness" of temple experience offered by the false teachers. Accordingly, the OT background of the NT affects both the Christology of Colossians (Christ is the full divine expression of God's presence in the end-time temple) and the ecclesiology (the church is part of the latter-day temple, residing in the midst of the divine tabernacling presence).

Likewise some of the OT allusions are crucial to substantiating the notion of Christ as the last Adam and end-time image of God (1:15) and of believers being identified in union with the last Adam and his image (3:9–10; cf. similarly the Gen. 1 allusions in Col. 1:6, 10 also with respect to implications for Christians being in God's image).

Another important OT motif is the "mystery" (Col. 1:26–27; 2:2–3), which also is sometimes understood to be a polemic against proto-gnostic teaching. The "mystery" derives from the visionary prophecy of Daniel (Dan. 2:19–22, 28–30) and is best understood in the light of Christ fulfilling the "mystery" of that text. It is more viable that Daniel would have been an influence on Paul's mystery concept than the gnostic mystery notions, since the former clearly predates Paul, but the latter literature derives from the second, third, and following centuries.[29] Thus those arguing for a gnostic background of the mystery must posit a "proto-gnosticism" that existed in the first century AD, for which there is no written evidence.

An additional important theme is that of the relationship of the OT law to the present Christian epoch. Especially Col. 2:16–17 shows that the OT food laws and holiday (holy day) laws are no longer binding, as they were in

28. This discussion so far on the use of the OT is a revision of Beale 2007: 841–42.

29. See Finegan (1989: 218–19, 264–65, 283–84) on the dating of the various corpora of gnostic literature.

the OT period. The reason they are no longer valid as formerly is that they were all "foreshadowings" of the coming of Christ, who is the "substance" or fulfillment of these institutional laws. In particular, these laws revolved around worship of God at the temple, so that now Christ is the one who is the focus of worship in the new temple. Physical circumcision in Israel also foreshadowed believers being spiritually "circumcised with a circumcision made without hands, . . . by the circumcision of Christ" (i.e., union with his death that separates him and believers from the old, sinful world).

Similarly, the notion of new creation (e.g., see on Col. 1:15–23; 2:20; 3:1–11) is to be viewed against an OT background. For example, the first creation in Gen. 1 is seen to be recapitulated in a new creation and on an escalated scale through Christ's resurrection (see on 1:15–23).

Even Paul's explanation of the gospel is best understood against an OT background. Colossians 2:14 says God "cancelled out the certificate of debt consisting of decrees against us, which was hostile to us; and he has taken it out of the way, having nailed it to the cross." We will see that the "decrees against us" are best understood as the OT law that people have broken and for which they stand liable for judgment (i.e., their debt). Christ has paid this "debt" (judgment) at the cross and "taken it out of the way" for believers, so they do not need to suffer it.

There are other OT references in Colossians, which we will address as we come to them in the course of the commentary. Consequently, the use of the OT in Colossians plays a role in some of the most debated passages of the epistle.

Occasion: The False Teaching

It is commonly acknowledged that Paul did not personally know most of the Colossians, since the epistle tells us that Epaphras founded the church there (Col. 1:7–8). Paul's desire to visit the Colossians was probably fulfilled after his release from prison (Philem. 22), though he apparently already knew Onesimus and Archippus (Col. 4:7, 9, 17) as well as Apphia and Philemon (Philem. 1–2; C. E. Arnold, *ABD* 1:1089). But in the meantime, Paul wished to write to the Colossians before visiting them. The main reason he wanted to write to them is because of the false teaching beginning to make inroads within the church. He instructs them about wisdom in Christ (2:3) "in order that no one may delude [you] with persuasive argument" (2:4*). He warns them not to let anyone "take [them] captive through philosophy and empty deception, according to the tradition of men, according to the elementary principles of the world, rather than according to Christ" (2:8; so also 2:19: the false teachers are "not holding fast to the head [Christ]"). Thus, at stake is whether one bases faith on the false teaching or on Christ.[30] Paul elaborates more specifics about the false teaching in the remainder of chapter 2. He thus exhorts the hearers to be steadfast in their faith in the face of such false teaching (2:2, 8; cf. Pascuzzi 2013: 228). Is this a Jewish false teaching

30. D. Moo (2008: 48) has crystallized this conclusion in my own mind.

based on a distorted view of OT law, is it a pagan false doctrine, or is it a combination of both?

Jewish Elements of the False Teaching

The commentary analysis will argue that the false teaching is mostly of Jewish origin, though there are probably some pagan elements mixed in. A combination of the two makes sense even against an OT background. We will see that Paul identifies the doctrinal error as idolatry (see on 2:22, as well as 2:8). Idolatry in the OT often involved a syncretistic combination of a distorted view of Yahweh worship in which Baal worship (or worship of other pagan gods) was combined. So, against such a background, it is understandable that there might be some kind of combination of distorted OT notions together with pagan ideas in the false teaching at Colossae. The concept of idol worship was uniquely Jewish, since Jews were monotheists and Greco-Romans worshiped as many of the traditional gods as they wished. Accordingly, the very notion of idolatry is to be understood against an OT background.

The False Teaching: Old Testament Legalism and Apocalyptic Judaism in Relation to a Pagan Background

The first glimpse we get at some of the specifics of the erroneous teaching is in 2:16: "Therefore let no one act as your judge in regard to food or drink or in respect to a new moon or a Sabbath day."* Recall that the false teaching is "not according to [based on] Christ" (2:8), "in [whom] all the fullness of deity dwells in bodily form" (2:9). As we will argue, the contrast with the false teaching is that Christ is the true end-time temple of God's presence, and believers "in him have been filled"* with that tabernacling presence (2:10). Consequently the error includes some false teaching about how to experience God's presence in the true heavenly temple. The false teachers did not deem being in Christ to be a sufficient experience of the temple. According to 2:16, this deviant teaching affirmed that obedience to OT dietary laws and ordinances about holidays (holy days) was necessary in order to come into the presence of God in his heavenly temple. Colossians 2:21 repeats the food law requirement: "Do not handle, do not taste, do not touch!" Thus "Let no one judge you" in 2:16 (NKJV) is a further development of "Be careful not to let anyone captivate you"* in 2:8, which emphasizes the warning not to let the false "philosophy" dominate anyone (D. Moo 2008: 218).

Most commentators have mentioned only that these were dietary laws and decrees about holidays, the ongoing validity of which the false teachers were wrongly affirming. While this is true, the vast majority of Colossians commentators have not noticed that the primary purpose of these laws in the OT was to enable the Israelite to become clean and be able to enter into God's temple to worship him. The commentary analysis goes into detail about how these food laws in the present age were seen to have continuing validity for qualifying one for gaining an experience of heavenly temple worship. There is also a background for abstention from "food or drink" (dietary laws in 2:16;

cf. 2:21) in order to prepare for mystical experiences with the pagan gods in the mystery cults or for pagan priests to be qualified to serve in their temples.

Could both OT and pagan settings serve as relevant backgrounds here? Perhaps. But while there may be echoes of the Hellenistic setting, the OT background is much more explicit, especially when seen in direct connection to the phrase in 2:16, "a festival or a new moon or a Sabbath day." The Greek equivalents of these three words occur as a triadic formula in the LXX and early Judaism almost always inextricably linked to temple sacrifices or temple worship; or when the temple is not explicitly mentioned, it is likely assumed to be in mind to some degree since these feasts were held at the temple. While "feasts" and "new moons" and "Sabbaths" were observed by some Gentiles, the triadic formula is found elsewhere not in pagan Greek contexts but only within OT and Jewish contexts.[31] That the food laws are to be understood mainly against an OT backdrop is also confirmed from Col. 2:17: these laws and the OT holidays were a "shadow of what is to come, but the substance is of Christ" (cf. NKJV). Clearly the OT rites and institutions were the "shadow" that is in mind here. This false teaching about dietary laws and holidays is clearly rooted in a distortion of OT and Jewish ideas, especially related to the temple, which commentators have not previously recognized. When this is acknowledged, it begins to make sense why Paul has already alluded to four OT temple texts, affirming either that Christ is the temple (1:19; 2:9) or that believers are part of this temple (1:9–10; 2:10). Thus all the temple experience they need is in Christ; they do not need to pursue any other avenues to any other kind of temple involvement to have a fulfilling temple participation, such as that advocated by the false teaching. Therefore the Colossian believers should not fear being "judged" for not following such a false teaching. The observation that these positive references to the temple are clearly from the OT suggests a polemic against a false conception of the OT teaching about the temple.

Indeed, that the false teaching contains a clear strain of Jewish thought is explicitly in view in the further description of the false teaching in 2:18: "Let no one keep disqualifying you from your prize by delighting in self-abasement and the worship of the angels, taking his stand on visions he has seen, inflated without cause by his fleshly mind."* The notion of "self-abasement," like the food laws, was likely designed to prepare for and enhance a visionary heavenly experience, such as seeing visions of angels who are to be worshiped or of worshiping angels in heaven that are seen.

The most contested verse of the whole epistle concerns the phrase in 2:18: ἃ ἑόρακεν ἐμβατεύων (*ha heoraken embateuōn*). The most straightforward rendering is "which things he has seen [the "angels" in heaven] when entering."*[32]

31. Since Col. 2:21 is clearly developing the OT-Jewish laws of purity in 2:16, such is probably still the focus in 2:21, though it is true that some Gentile customs included laws about not touching unclean animals (e.g., see Lohse 1971: 123).

32. Alternatively, Arnold (1995: 123) suggests another possible straightforward translation of "because he 'entered the things he had seen.'"

The most viable renderings among English translations and commentaries, which are quite different, are the following: (1) "taking his stand on visions he has seen" (NASB); (2) "[going] into great detail about what he has seen" (NIV); (3) "entering into possession" of something (perhaps a heavenly inheritance); (4) "entering into the innermost sanctuary." The last option dominated commentaries during the last half of the twentieth century. All four translations are possible, but the last is most preferable, for which Arnold (1995: 110–31) argues and this commentary contends. However, some commentators have doubted that this translation and understanding of Col. 2:18 is correct because they see no reference elsewhere in the epistle to an idea of the temple. But this understanding of the difficult expression fits right into Paul's repeated positive emphasis on Christ and believers as the true temple, which these commentators have failed to see. Paul's prior underscoring of the positive temple idea is designed as a polemic against the false teachers' claim that one can obtain experience of the heavenly temple apart from Christ. Thus Col. 2:18 becomes the climax of Paul's presentation of the false teachers' position about having a heavenly temple experience that is "not based on Christ" (cf. 2:8b HCSB; 2:19a).

The false teachers' concept of the temple, as noted above, is probably best understood from an OT background, though we have seen some Hellenistic echoes in the food laws in Col. 2:16. However, with the clause in 2:18 a pagan background comes more into focus. Arnold has persuasively expanded on the argument by earlier commentators that the hapax legomenon ἐμβατεύω (*embateuō*) is an allusion to several inscriptions in nearby cities in Asia Minor. These inscriptions are found in Asia Minor mystery cults, where there were two stages of initiation: (1) an initial entrance into an oracle grotto, followed by (2) a climactic entrance into the inner sanctuary, where the presence of the god resided. Strikingly, the second and climactic part of the initiation is designated by ἐμβατεύω, which describes the "entering" of the initiate into the innermost sanctuary of the god. A total of four relevant inscriptions employ ἐμβατεύω in this manner.[33] In the commentary, I have tried to bolster Arnold's argument. The mention of "angels" in 2:18[34] further points to a temple-vision experience: in biblical literature, when angels are seen in heaven, they are typically portrayed around God's throne in the heavenly temple.

In this light, both pagan and distorted Jewish ideas about the temple appear to have been merged into the false teaching. The Christians in Colossae

33. See Arnold (1995: 110–13) for a convenient presentation of the full Greek and English translations of the four inscriptions.

34. Arnold (1995: 11–102) argues that in Asia Minor angels were invoked through magical rites for help and protection from evil heavenly forces, thus becoming the object of veneration by personal petitioners, and such angelic veneration became virtually the same as worshiping the angels. This was the case in Jewish, Christian, and pagan contexts (e.g., see Arnold 1995: 88). If so, this might also represent a syncretism of pagan, Jewish, and Christian ideas. See further on 2:18 in the commentary.

should not fear being "disqualified" from being first-class Christian citizens by the false teachers, because their teaching is false, and the genuine believers' union with Christ as the temple is true and all they need.

Conclusion: The False Teaching as a Combination of Pagan and Distorted Jewish Thought

Before their Christian conversion the false teachers in Colossae themselves may have gone through a mystery initiation like that in the mystery cults, or they may have heard about these mystery-cult initiations, or they may have been acquainted with the association of ἐμβατεύω with "entering a sacred place or temple" from these mystery rites as well as from broadly elsewhere, as attested in Classical and Hellenistic Greek literature. And they may have tried to integrate this dramatic, charismatic experience into their new Christian faith. Accordingly, the misguided teachers "may have understood humility followed by visions seen upon entering 'the heavenly temple' to be analogous to initiation followed by reception of oracles upon entering the Apollos sanctuary."[35] They appear to have found further justification for this in the OT dietary and holiday laws, which were preparatory for participation in temple worship. They wrongly believed that these laws were still valid, and they combined them with the pagan mystery background. What may also have played into this syncretism from the Jewish side is the fact that certain traditions in apocalyptic Judaism focused on various ways in which humans could ascend into the temple's throne room of God (see the second additional note on Col. 2:18). To whatever degree the pagan mystery cults are in view, Paul probably uses God's "revelation of the mystery" in this epistle as a polemic against the pagan cult's revelation of its mystery. That is, the true mystery is now fully revealed in Christ in contrast to the pseudo-mystery. Thus the false teaching was based on a combination of distorted Hellenistic and Jewish ideas. This syncretism is natural since, as we have seen above, there was a significant Jewish population in Colossae, while the majority of the population was Gentile.[36] Such syncretism is not new, as noted earlier, since false teaching in the OT arose from combining pagan idolatry with the worship of Yahweh.

35. Francis 1975b: 176. See on 2:18 for comment on the similar position of Francis 1975a: 203–4, as well 198–99.

36. Copenhaver (2018: 236–37) concludes that there were no specific opponents in the sense of a clearly defined group who were actively trying to deceive the Colossian Christians. Rather, Paul is aware of a broader opposition against people who have become Christians and have made the transition from out of the world to enter into the covenant community of the church. Copenhaver sees two distinct strands of false religion (Jewish and Hellenistic) from which the believers had come out. Thus there was not one specific awareness of a combined Jewish-Hellenistic false teaching but a broader awareness of one of two false religious backgrounds of which the believers had formerly been a part to some degree. Copenhaver's view is possible, but it does not affect the exegesis of this commentary, except that what is considered in this commentary to be a specific combined Jewish-Hellenistic false teaching would be considered a broader false religious influence.

Relationship of Colossians to Ephesians

Many commentators have discussed the relationship of these two letters. Theories abound about how they are related and were composed. The purpose here is only to make some general comments, especially with respect to the order of writing the letters and to their interpretive relationship. Some have viewed both epistles as Pauline, both as non-Pauline, or just one as Pauline (usually Colossians). Some have thought that Colossians was written first and that Ephesians followed in imitation of much in Colossians. Others have held the reverse, claiming that Ephesians was written first and that Colossians used Ephesians as the template. Still others have affirmed that the two letters were written around the same time by the same author and that there was a natural conceptual overlap at significant points.[37] One obvious difference between the letters is that Colossians has a fairly clear occasion (false teaching), while Ephesians has no obvious occasion, which is due to the likelihood that it was a circular letter ("in Ephesus" does not appear in the best and earliest manuscripts).[38]

Our view is agnostic about which was written first and which second; yet as stated above, we accept the Pauline authorship of Colossians as well as of Ephesians.[39] It is plausible to suppose that both epistles were written around the same time by the same author and that their resemblances are due to that fact.

What is most important about the resemblances or parallels is that they are likely to be seen as mutually interpretive. The context of a parallel in Ephesians can help illuminate a parallel in Colossians, even if there is not complete verbal exactness in the parallels.[40] This is based on the presupposition that Paul's thought is consistent between the two letters. The parallels may represent in one letter an interpretive development in comparison to the other letter, but this should be seen as a development and not as contradictory thought. It is best to allow the parallels "to interact and interlock with one another" (N. Wright 1986: 39). This will be the approach taken in the commentary, which at times will have significant interpretive and theological implications for Colossians.

The Outline and Argument of Colossians

Commentators differ over the outline and flow of thought of the epistle. Some examples will illustrate this.

37. See N. Wright (1986: 37–38) for a similar presentation of theories, who has led me to see the importance of stating these proposals held by a variety of commentators.

38. See Metzger (1994: 532) on the textual problem and his acknowledgment that commentators have therefore suggested that it was a circular letter directed to various churches. See likewise the NET Bible on Eph. 1:1.

39. The limits of the present commentary do not allow for argumentation of the Pauline authorship of Ephesians.

40. E.g., this is the interpretive approach of N. Wright (1986: 39) and Hendriksen (1967: 5–32); the latter includes an extensive synoptic chart of the parallels and discussion of some of the significant differences.

D. Moo (2008: vi–vii) sees the following main divisions (N. Wright 1986: 44–45 is very similar):

1. The letter opening (1:1–2:5)
2. The letter body (2:6–4:6)
3. The letter closing (4:7–18)

Garland (1998: 34–35) divides the major parts of the epistle differently:

1. Salutation and thanksgiving (1:1–23)
2. Letter body (1:24–2:23)
3. Ethical admonitions (3:1–4:6)
4. Final greetings (4:7–18)

Dunn (1996: 41–42) sees the following divisions:

1. Address and greeting (1:1–2)
2. Extended thanksgiving (1:3–23)
3. A personal statement (1:24–2:5)
4. The theme of the letter (2:6–4:6)
5. Conclusion (4:7–18)

Lincoln (2000: 584–85):

1. Letter opening (1:1–2)
2. Extended thanksgiving (1:3–23)
3. Letter body (1:24–4:9)
4. Letter closing (4:10–18)

Barth and Blanke (1994: vi–vii) see the following major segments:

1. Epistolary address (1:1–2)
2. Thanksgiving, intercession, and hymn (1:3–23)
3. Paul, servant of the Colossians (1:24–2:5)
4. The threat to the community (2:6–23)
5. Exhortations (3:1–4:6)
6. Conclusion of the epistle (4:7–18)[41]

Sumney (2008: vii–viii) splits the sections as follows:

1. Epistolary greeting (1:1–2)
2. Introductory thanksgiving and prayer (1:3–23)
3. Paul is the trustworthy bearer of the true gospel (1:24–2:5)
4. Remain faithful to the gospel you received (2:6–23)

41. Barth and Blanke (1994: 42) also present another outline: (1) letter opening (1:1–2); (2) thanksgiving and intercession for the gospel's spread and the spiritual growth of the congregation (1:3–2:5); (3) hymnic and didactic praise of God, Christ, and the apostolic ministry for reconciliation of all through Christ's blood (1:12–2:5); (4) opposition to human-made religion, proclamation of perfection and life in Christ alone (2:6–3:4); (5) general and special calls for true worship and participation in the church's mission (3:5–4:17). They do not mention 4:18 here but apparently see it as the final conclusion.

5. Granted holiness in baptism, live holy lives (3:1–4:6)
6. Final greetings and instructions (4:7–18)

There is overlap but also some differences in the way the commentators above divide up the subsections within the major segments that they see. It would take a dissertation to try to evaluate all of the various proposed divisions and subdivisions. I will content myself with presenting my own major divisions and subdivisions and the flow of thought among these various divisions as I see it. The following summaries of each unit are an expansion of the table of contents presented at the beginning of the commentary.[42]

I. Letter opening: Paul the apostle and Timothy desire that the *saints at Colossae have grace and peace from God* (1:1–2).

Transition: To what does the notion of grace and peace from God lead? Probably the entire letter is an explanation of this grace and peace, which may be pointed to by observing that the letter ends with "Grace be with you" (4:18).

II. Letter thanksgiving: *Paul thanks God for the readers' Christian lives and prays they will live for the Lord, the divine and sovereign last Adam, through whom God has reconciled them* (1:3–23).

A. *Paul thanks God for the readers* because he recognizes in them the genuine faith, love, and hope of God's end-time people (1:3–8).

Transition: To what does Paul's thanksgiving lead?

B. Paul prays continually that believers would understand God's will for them *to live with the purpose of pleasing the Lord Christ in every way* (1:9–14).

Transition: Who is Christ "the Lord" whom believers are to live for and please and what has Christ done for them?

C. Christ's supremacy over the first creation is a pattern recapitulated *for the new creation to bring about reconciliation of all creation*, especially in order to make believers acceptable before God (1:15–23).

The flow of thought in 1:3–23 climaxes with the christological section of 1:15–23.

III. Letter body: Christians should strive for maturity, not by keeping earthly legalistic laws but by faithfully seeking the heavenly Christ, which should result in putting off the old sinful lifestyle and living a new-creational lifestyle *with a view to prayer for the gospel's spread and witness* (1:24–4:6).

42. Italic type in the exegetical summary of each section of Colossians represents where the logical prominence is in each statement.

Summary of the section: Paul rejoices to bring believers to eschatological maturity and protect them from deception (1:24–2:5); on the basis of these two goals they are to live their lives by faith "in Christ" (2:6–15) and not according to legalistic laws (2:16–23). Consequently, Christians should seek heavenly things (i.e., the ascended Christ) and not earthly things (3:1–4), which should result in laying aside the old sinful lifestyle (3:5–11) and putting on a new-creational lifestyle with a Christocentric focus (3:12–17). This new-creational lifestyle is to be lived out in the family and workplace (3:18–4:1), *which should lead to prayer for the spread of the gospel and witness for Christ* (4:2–6).

The logical climax of 2:24–4:6 is living a life characterized by prayer for the spread of the gospel and witness for Christ.

A. Paul rejoices in his struggle to proclaim Christ as the revealed mystery of the OT, which leads to *rejoicing in his struggle to bring believers to eschatological maturity in Christ and to prevent their deception* (1:24–2:5).

Transition: On the basis of these two goals, how are believers to live their lives?

B. *Believers should live only on the basis of Christ* and not any other belief system, since Christ came in the fullness of deity in bodily form, resulting in his redeeming them through his death, resurrection, and triumph over their enemies (2:6–15).

Transition: Also, on the basis of the goals of maturity and protection from false teaching, in what further manner should the Colossians live their lives?

C. *Believers should not be required to submit to extraordinary religious practices of bodily discipline and holiday-keeping in order to experience the tabernacling presence of God*, since only faith in Christ is necessary for that (2:16–23).

Transition: Instead of seeking to live by old world laws, what should believers seek for?

D. *Believers should seek heavenly things and not old earthly things* because they have died to the old world and have been raised with Christ as a new creation in a new heavenly world (3:1–4).

Transition: Seeking Christ in heaven means that believers have died and have been raised with him. What should be the further effect of seeking the heavenly Christ?

E. Because saints must seek heavenly things as a result of having died to the old world and having been raised with Christ into a new heavenly world, *they must lay aside the sinful lifestyle of the old world* (3:5–11).

Transition: What should be the further effect of seeking Christ in heaven—Christ, with whom saints have died and been raised?

F. Since believers must seek heavenly things because they have become a new creation in Christ (3:1–11), *they should live according to a new-creational lifestyle that is instilled with a Christocentric focus* (3:12–17).

Transition: Where must this new-creational lifestyle be lived out?

G. This new-creational lifestyle (3:12–17) *should especially be lived out in the family and workplace* (3:18–4:1).

Transition: What should result from this new-creational lifestyle being lived out in the family and workplace?

H. The new-creational lifestyle (3:12–17), which is to be lived out in the family and workplace (3:18–4:1), *should lead to prayer for the effective spread of the gospel and to witness for Christ to unbelievers* (4:2–6).

IV. Letter closing: Paul progresses to the conclusion of the epistle; *he emphasizes his pastoral concern for the Colossians* by reminding them that not only he but also his coworkers have pastoral concern for them, and they should show the same concern for others (4:7–18). The purpose of this final section is to motivate readers to listen sympathetically to what he has said and to heed it.

Is it possible to highlight what is most logically and thematically prominent in Colossians? The main point and goal of the body of the letter appears to be at 4:2–6, on prayer for the spread of the gospel and actual witnessing for Christ. Since 1:3–23 leads to the letter body, the point of 4:2–6 appears still to stand as the main point of all of 1:3–4:6. The rhetorical function of 4:7–18 is to encourage readers to heed the message of 1:23–4:6. The whole letter may be an explanation of the "grace and peace" in 1:2 (perhaps pointed to by "grace" in 4:18). If so, the main point of the letter in 4:2–6, prayer for witness and actual witnessing, can occur only by means of God's grace and peace that believers already have with God. Prayer for witness and actual witnessing are the main imperatival goals of the letter, which are grounded in the indicative of the person of Christ and his work for his people and the various commands flowing out of his person and work (which are contained in 1:3–4:1).

➤ I. Letter Opening: Paul and Timothy Desire Grace and Peace for the Colossians (1:1–2)
II. Letter Thanksgiving: Paul Thanks God for the Readers' Christian Lives (1:3–23)
III. Letter Body: Christians Should Strive for Maturity (1:24–4:6)
IV. Letter Closing: Paul Emphasizes His Pastoral Concern for the Colossians (4:7–18)

I. Letter Opening: Paul and Timothy Desire Grace and Peace for the Colossians (1:1–2)

Just as most modern letters contain an opening address ("Dear . . ."), often an introductory wish ("I hope all is well with you"), a body that contains the main part of the letter, and a concluding farewell ("Sincerely," "With best wishes" + the sender's name), so Hellenistic letters had the similar basic structure. As we will see, Paul adapts this variant fourfold Hellenistic letter convention, especially by injecting Christian theology into it. For example, the opening address in Colossians of "Paul" is expanded to "an apostle of Jesus Christ by the will of God," a typical expression added in various ways in Paul's other letters. This is an adaptation of the Hellenistic letter, in which the letter replaces the writer's presence. Yet as we will see in the case of Paul, the letter represents not merely Paul's presence but also his apostolic authority over the recipients. This apostolic authority actually entails that the letter carries with it the authority of God and Christ, whom Paul represents in each letter, including that of the one sent to the Colossians. The second part of the ancient letter was a generic greeting, which Paul replaces with the theologically charged "grace and peace," typically followed by "from God our Father and the Lord Jesus Christ," which indicates further that behind Paul's letter-writing stand God and Christ. Colossians follows this pattern, though it has only "from God our Father," for some reason omitting "and from the Lord Jesus Christ."

Paul never structures the parts of his epistles as merely formal, stylistic formulas, but as we have already begun to see, he packs his letters with theological substance and means every word he says. He cares deeply about the people to whom he writes his epistles, and there is much feeling expressed in his letters, including his introductory greetings. This is certainly true of his Letter to the Colossians. The main point of verses 1–2 is in verse 2, which states the goal of the letter: that God would give "grace and peace" to the recipients, which they will need to stand against the false teaching and to persevere and grow in their faith, which the remainder of the epistle will make clear.

Exegesis and Exposition

[1]Paul, an apostle of Christ Jesus [through] the will of God, and Timothy our brother,
[2]to the saints at Colossae and [the faithful brothers] in Christ: Grace to you and peace
from God our Father ⸢ ⸣.

1:1 Paul's greeting first focuses upon his office as an "apostle" (ἀπόστολος, *apostolos*). He is an "apostle of Christ Jesus," which likely expresses that he belongs to Christ (a possessive genitive, though possibly also including the notion that he was sent out by Christ [a subjective genitive], as expressed explicitly in Gal. 1:1; on the two senses of the genitive here, see Wallace [1996: 82] as well as Harris [2010: 7]).[1] Paul was called as an apostle through "the will of God."[2] This call happened to Paul when the resurrected Christ appeared to him on the Damascus road and commissioned him (Acts 9:3–19; 22:6–16; 26:12–20; 1 Cor. 9:1; 15:7–9). Thus Paul's apostleship is grounded in the authoritative call of the resurrected Christ. He became an apostle through the working of God's powerful will and not through his own independent decision making (Melick 1991: 188). The initial mention of Paul himself as an "apostle" in this verse suggests that the letter ultimately carries his own apostolic authority. As an apostle, he represents the authority of the Messiah. Thus Paul's self-reference as an "apostle" refers to his unique office and is qualitatively different from other uses of "apostle" to designate mere human messengers (cf. NASB marginal readings at Phil. 2:25 and 2 Cor. 8:23) or approved missionaries (e.g., 1 Cor. 9:5–6; 15:7; cf. Gal. 2:9; on which see D. Moo 2008: 74).[3] Paul's mention of "Christ [Messiah] Jesus" is used so much by him (as is the word order of "Jesus Christ") that one might think it has become a mere name carrying little theological freight. However, the name probably at least evokes the OT expectation of a Messiah, who is now identified with Christ (likewise D. Moo 2008: 75; Bird 2009: 34).[4] This point is possibly enhanced by "Christ" being placed first, as in "Messiah Jesus."

The greeting is not only from Paul but also from Timothy (so also in the greeting sections of 2 Cor. 1:1; Phil. 1:1; 1 Thess. 1:1; 2 Thess. 1:1; Philem. 1). The mention of Timothy here and in the other introductions indicates, at least, that he is one of Paul's "fellow workers" in the ministry (Rom. 16:21; 1 Thess. 3:2; cf. 1 Cor. 16:10), but it may also imply that he is Paul's secretary (it is less likely that this implies multiple authorship). Paul and other NT writers used secretaries in other letters (he dictated Romans to Tertius: Rom. 16:22; Peter used Silvanus as a secretary: 1 Pet. 5:12). Besides being a "fellow worker," Timothy accompanied Paul in his travels (Acts 16:1–20:4; Phil. 2:19;

1. It may also merely be a genitive of relationship, describing Paul's apostleship to be bound up in some indefinable way with Christ (so D. Moo 2008: 75, though he mentions the subjective genitive possibility in light of Gal. 1:1).

2. See Rom. 1:1; 1 Cor. 1:1; 2 Cor. 1:1; Gal. 1:1; Eph. 1:1; 1 Tim. 1:1; 2 Tim. 1:1; cf. 1 Cor. 12:28; 1 Tim. 2:7; 2 Tim. 1:11.

3. See Bruce (1984: 38) for a good, though dated, bibliography on the notion of apostleship in Paul's letters and in the NT in general.

4. For the use of the "anointed one" or "Messiah" with reference to the coming end-time king in the OT, see Ps. 2:2 (cf. 2:7) and Dan. 9:25–26 (cf. Pss. 89:19–29 [88:20–30 LXX] and 132:10–12 [131:10–12 LXX], where David is the "anointed" one and is related to his descendants, who will rule forever). For the same use of "anointed" in Judaism, see 1 En. 48.10; 52.4; Pss. Sol. 17.36; 18.6, 8; in Qumran the same kind of eschatological use of "Messiah" occurs in, e.g., CD-A 12.23; 14.19; CD-B 19.10; 1Q28a (= 1QSa) 2.12, 20. See also Pokorný 1991: 35.

1 Thess. 3:6), preached alongside him (2 Cor. 1:19), and represented Paul's teachings to others (1 Cor. 4:17). Therefore it is natural that Paul calls him a "brother" at the end of verse 1,[5] and accordingly it is natural that Timothy would be one of Paul's secretaries.

Use of secretaries is also implied by the way Paul brings attention to his own unique signature at the conclusion of some of his epistles (with statements like "I, Paul write this greeting in my own hand, which is the distinguishing mark in all my letters. This is how I write": 2 Thess. 3:17 NIV; likewise 1 Cor. 16:21; Gal. 6:11). This is highlighted in Col. 4:18: "the greeting [is] by my hand, Paul."* This also indicates that Paul is the true author, even if writing through a secretary.

Furthermore, that Paul's secretaries did not have an independent hand in composing the letters is apparent from the way dictation took place in the ancient world. Cicero mentions two kinds of dictation: a looser dictation method, in which secretaries listened and wrote down "whole sections"; and a more strict method, in which secretaries wrote down "syllable by syllable" (Cicero, *Att.* 333, 13.25).[6] Even the looser manner of dictation would not have meant that Paul's secretaries had an autonomous role in writing, since it is highly probable that Paul would have read the letter himself before sending it off, or he would have had the letter read back to him, to ensure that what the letter finally said represented precisely what he wanted to convey.

In addition, the initial mention of Paul himself as an apostle before the comment about Timothy, who is not called an "apostle," suggests that the letter ultimately represents Paul's own apostolic authority (so also Lincoln 2000: 587). Moreover, Paul's authority behind the letter is also reflected by passages where the first-person pronoun (I/my), referring to Paul, is found (such as Col. 1:23–25, 29; 2:1, 4–5; 4:3–4, 7–8, 10, 13, 16, 18), which finds close and numerous parallels in the epistles unanimously accepted by all to be Pauline (e.g., Phil. 2:19–28; 1 Thess. 2:18; 3:5; 5:27; see Barth and Blanke 1994: 143). The same evidence points away from a disciple of Paul first composing a letter independently but in the name of Paul and with Paul's ultimate approval (as argued by Schweizer 1982: 15–24; Dunn 1996: 44, 47).[7]

Hence, with these qualifications in mind, it is appropriate that Timothy may have had some part in writing this letter as a secretary. It is possible, however, that mention of Timothy is merely Paul's way of commending him as a faithful "fellow worker" in the ministry, or the mention may merely indicate that he was formally commissioned by Paul to deliver his letter (so Doty 1973: 30). All of the above ideas are not mutually exclusive of one another and may be in mind. It is interesting that Timothy is likely referred to as among the "apostles" in 1 Thess. 2:6–7 (cf. 1 Thess. 1:1), but that was more

5. Yet we will see in Col. 1:2 that "brother" includes the notion of fellow believers being part of a family.

6. I thank Gordon Fee for first bringing this text from Cicero to my attention many years ago.

7. In agreement with Barth and Blanke 1994: 144.

likely a temporary designation by which he shared in Paul's representative authority, just as his time of serving as Paul's secretary and writing down Paul's authoritative words would have happened only on special occasions (see further additional notes).

1:2 Paul is writing to "the saints and faithful brothers." There is a question about whether "saints" (dative pl., ἁγίοις, *hagiois*) is to be taken as an adjective (which it is by form) or whether the adjectival form is being used as a noun (which is often also the case). Some think it is better to take it adjectively since the plural article "the" (τοῖς, *tois*) preceding ἁγίοις is missing before "faithful," so that the article is doing double duty. This would mean that the plural of ἅγιος (*hagios*) is to be taken together with "faithful," and since the latter is clearly adjectival, so must be ἁγίοις, with the meaning of "holy." The resultant translation would be "to the holy and faithful brothers," which is viable.[8] Since, however, ἅγιος in the plural always functions as a noun in the opening of Paul's Epistles (Rom. 1:7; 1 Cor. 1:2; 2 Cor. 1:1; Eph. 1:1; Phil. 1:1), it is perhaps more likely that the word functions that way here: "to the saints [or holy ones] and faithful brothers" (following O'Brien 1982: 3). Outside of Paul's introductory greetings, the adjective "saints," or "holy ones" (the pl. of ἅγιος), is also found to function as a noun ("saints") throughout the NT with reference to believers in Christ. What further points to the adjective "holy ones" being used as a noun is the observation that the phrase "in Colossae" is syntactically closer to and goes viably with the plural "saints" (ἁγίοις), "faithful brothers" is closer to and goes with "in Christ," and the two clauses are separated by the conjunction "and" (καί, *kai*). This syntactical pattern is especially found in Eph. 1:1, which is the closest parallel of all to Col. 1:2 and supports the position taken here (see further below). Thus the plural article can still be considered to be doing double duty without necessitating that ἅγιος functions as an adjective. The significance of the double duty is that the "saints" and "faithful brothers" are regarded to be a unified whole (see MHT 3:181).

There likely is continuity with the OT use of the word to describe the "saints" of Israel (Pss. 16:3 [15:3 LXX]; 34:9 [33:10]), especially those who will live in the dawning of the end-time age of the kingdom (Dan. 7:18, 21–22, 25, 27; 7:27 LXX reads "holy people"), a kingdom that Paul in this letter regards as having begun to appear (1:13; 4:11). Perhaps the Dan. 7 background is not out of mind, since "saints" (pl. of ἅγιος) together with close mention of "kingdom" (βασιλεία, *basileia*) occurs only in Dan. 7 in all of the OT (see the preceding references) and only in Col. 1:12–13 in the NT ("<u>saints</u> in Light . . . transferred . . . to the <u>kingdom</u> of His beloved Son"). Indeed, Paul appears already to have made allusion to Dan. 7:22 (KJV, "judgment was given to the saints of the most High") in 1 Cor. 6:2 ("the saints will judge the world"),[9]

8. As argued by Sumney 2008: 27; Slater 2006; and Campbell 2013: 2. Campbell argues that Paul's readers would have read it this way, since it is the natural order of the Greek.

9. Early Judaism developed the Dan. 7:22 notion of Israel judging the nations: Wis. 3:7–8; 1 En. 1.9; 1QpHab 5.4 (cf. 1 En. 95.3), and this exegetical tradition derived from Dan. 7 may be

though a Dan. 7 background is not as prominent in Col. 1:2 as in the 1 Corinthians text. The audience is composed not merely of "saints" but of "faithful brothers," which connotes Paul's understanding of Christians generically (brothers and sisters) as composing a family, with God as their "Father" (note the end of 1:2). The preceding reference to Timothy as a "brother" enhances this family notion. Christians are a family, and their spiritual ties transcend the bonds of the physical family (see further Matt. 10:37–38; Luke 14:25–33; Thompson 2005: 14–17).

At least part of the reason why the Colossians are considered to be "faithful" (πιστός, *pistos*) is that they have put their faith in Christ, as Paul immediately elaborates on in 1:4 ("We heard of your faith in Christ Jesus"). The word "faithful" (πιστός) in Paul can refer to an attitude of trust or to faithful works, and sometimes both ideas can be included (see BDAG 820–21, s.v. πιστός). The notion of "faithful" here is on remaining true to Jesus through an inward attitude of trust in Jesus as well as by outward acts of faithfulness to him arising from this trust (for inclusion of both ideas in the use of πιστός, see Col. 2:7 [though the noun form appears here]; 4:7, 9; cf. Davids 2008a: 243). Accordingly, the idea is not only that they are "faithful" in "Christ Jesus" in the sense of believing in Christ. Included also is the idea that just as they are "holy ones" who are "in Colossae," so they are "faithful ones" who are "in Christ Jesus." That a faithful and dependable character is also in mind is apparent from 1:7, where "faithful" (πιστός) is used to describe Epaphras: "a faithful servant of Christ on our behalf."

Thus their spiritual location is "in Christ" (cf. also MHT 3:263). The phrase "in Christ" occurs so much throughout Paul's Epistles that in each case it must be understood in light of its immediate context.[10] Only twice more does the phrase occur in Colossians (1:4, 28; cf. 2:5), and we must wait until later to see what it means there. Here the first use of the phrase likely indicates, at least, that the audience is intrinsically identified with Christ (similar statements occur in 1 Cor. 1:2; Eph. 1:1; Phil. 1:1; 1 Thess. 1:1; 2 Thess. 1:1). It has been observed that the expressions "in Colossae" and "in Christ" are finely balanced, being on either side of the middle phrase "the saints and faithful brothers." This helps to define more precisely in context what "in Christ"

in Paul's mind in 1 Cor. 6:2 (see Fee 1987: 233) and perhaps echoed here in Col. 1. The broader background for Paul's understanding of "saints" lies in Israel's call to be a "holy people" (λαὸς ἅγιος, *laos hagios*; Deut. 7:6; 14:2; 28:9; Isa. 63:18) and a "holy nation" (ἔθνος ἅγιον, *ethnos hagion*, Exod. 19:6), which they failed to be, but in the latter days they were finally to realize this calling (Isa. 62:12; Dan. 8:24; 12:7). See Dunn (1996: 48), for references to Israel as "saints" in early Judaism. Israel was to be "holy, set apart" because they were to be like their God, who was "holy, set apart" (e.g., Lev. 11:44; 19:2; on this last point, following Lohse 1971: 7, among others). Just as was true of OT Israel, the end-time Israel, of whom the Colossians were a part, were likewise to be holy to reflect their God, who was holy, so that their "election" could not be separated from the requirement that they be holy (see Deut. 7:6; 14:2; Col. 3:12; and cf. Col. 1:22, following Sumney 2008: 27).

10. See Barth (1974: 69–71) for a brief sketch of twentieth-century interpretations of the Pauline formula "in Christ."

means: since "in Colossae" identifies and locates the saints as members of an earthly community, "in Christ" shows them as "faithful ones" to be identified with and located "in Christ" as members of the true people of God (N. Wright 1986: 47).

This parallelism of "in Colossae" and "in Christ" implies that the Christians' spiritual location "in Christ" should affect how they live in their physical location (cf. Wall 1993: 37–38). As "faithful ones," their faith has brought them into union with Christ and set them apart from the world (hence, they are "holy ones"). This fits into one of the main purposes of the letter, which is to reassure the readers about the genuineness of their faith and the object of their faith (i.e., Christ) in the face of false teaching (see "Occasion: The False Teaching" in the introduction and my comments on 1:4–7 and 2:4–15). The Colossians have been "[delivered] from the domain of darkness," in which they were spiritually located, and "transferred . . . to the kingdom of His beloved Son" (1:13), which is their new location. Accordingly, they "have died" and their "life is hidden with Christ in God" (3:3). The spiritual identification of the saints being "in Christ" means that Christ represents them and that his redemptive work has paved the way for the predominately Gentile church at Colossae to become part of the latter-day "saints" of Israel (perhaps the καί, *kai*, in this first clause of v. 2 is epexegetical): "the saints in Colossae, <u>that is</u>, the faithful brothers in Christ" (so Pao 2012: 48).

What is the resulting benefit of the Colossians now standing "in Christ," that is, in the realm where Christ dominates? Paul's answer comes at the end of verse 2: "<u>grace</u> [should come?] <u>to you and peace</u>." Commentators have rightly noticed that the typical introductory "greeting" (χαίρειν, *chairein*) of the Hellenistic letter is replaced by the similar sounding "grace" (χάρις, *charis*), as a theological play on words (e.g., O'Brien 1982: 4). Paul injects a theology of grace into what was typically a default way of saying "hello." After the greeting in the Hellenistic letters, there was typically a wish about the recipient's health (or comment about the sender's health). Paul replaces this with his invocation of "peace" upon the readers (following Sumney 2008: 29).[11]

Paul pronounces such an introductory "grace" and "peace" to his audience in every one of his letters. The following context of each letter defines what he means by this twofold greeting. Is the "grace and peace" greeting a wish, a statement of fact, or a prayer? Perhaps it is best not to make these distinctions, since the context of Colossians makes clear Paul's belief that the readers now benefit in various ways from God's grace, and he also prays that God would continue to extend his grace to them in the future (for the present, e.g., see Col. 1:6, 12–14; cf. 2:12–13; and for the future, see Col. 1:9–11; cf. 1:28; 3:4). Hence, both their present blessed condition and their hoped-for future state are in mind in verse 2. From beginning to end, Paul sees that being in Christ is a work of God's grace, which fittingly concludes the epistle: "Grace be with

11. For the typical pattern of "greeting" followed by comments about health in Hellenistic letters, see Hunt and Edgar 1932: 269–395.

you" (4:18). That "Grace to you" begins the epistle (1:2) and "Grace be with you" concludes the epistle points to a highlighting of God's grace as a major theme of this letter.

True and ultimate "peace" also comes only "from our Father," for those who have been "reconciled" to him through Christ's work on the cross (Col. 1:19–22). The final tone of the letter opening is upon the audience receiving "grace and peace from God," which will be conceptually elaborated upon in the rest of the epistle. Though Paul uses these two words in each of his epistolary introductions, they are not merely polite throwaway terms but appear to be the goal of verses 1–2. The "grace and peace" greetings found at the conclusion of the letter openings of Paul's other letters are also presumably not perfunctory terms. The only way one can ever have grace and peace is if one is "in Christ Jesus." How can people enter into such a relationship? Col. 2:6–7 says that it is by "receiving Christ Jesus" by "faith" (so also cf. 1:4; 2:12). This "grace and peace" is to enable believers to live set-apart lives (i.e., to be "saints," "holy ones") and be "faithful" as they live "in Colossae" (cf. Wall 1993: 39).

The reason why only "God our Father" is mentioned and not also "the Lord Jesus Christ," which follows in most of Paul's other epistles, is that the double mention of brotherhood in these two verses has invoked the father-child side of this relationship and caused Paul to focus only on it (see further the note on 1:2 below).[12] This is highlighted by the observation that "brothers" (ἀδελφοῖς, *adelphois*) designates the recipients of a letter in Paul's epistolary greetings only here, as pointed out by Aletti (1993: 45), while acknowledging that in other greetings Paul does refer to his coworkers in the singular as "brother" (1 Cor. 1:1; 2 Cor. 1:1; Philem. 1; cf. Col. 1:1) and once in the plural (Gal. 1:2).

Additional Notes

1:1. Could Timothy have been considered by Paul to be an "apostle," since Timothy is mentioned so much in participating together with Paul in his work and since Timothy was likely Paul's secretary for Colossians, and 1 Thess. 2:6–7 includes Timothy as among the "apostles" (cf. 1 Thess. 1:1)? There is a problem in Paul referring to himself as well as to Silas and Timothy as "apostles" in this text, since the latter two were not a part of the official "apostolate." Possible solutions are proposed: (1) the implied "we" in 1 Thess. 2:6–7a is an epistolary "we," referring only to Paul; (2) this is a secondary group of apostles outside of the Twelve; (3) Paul was including only Silas in the "we," since he may have been on a prophetic par with the Twelve (Silas is mentioned as a prophet in Acts 15:32); (4) Paul did not have a clearly defined view of "apostleship" at this early point in his ministry or, perhaps, the concept was never clearly defined and could be used flexibly (see Marshall 1983: 69–70 for the options, though he prefers solution 3 above; cf. Acts 14:14: "the apostles Barnabas and Paul"). Possibly the best solution is through an understanding of corporate representation, whereby the authority of the representative can be extended to the ones being represented: Silas and Timothy temporarily enjoyed the authority of the apostolic circle since they were working under the authoritative aegis of Paul the apostle

12. Following Aletti (1993: 45–48), who appears to be the only commentator who has plausibly explained why Paul has referred to only "God our Father" and not included Christ directly afterward.

(following Beale 2003: 70–71, who also reviews the same above options for 1 Thess. 2:7). This notion is also applicable to Colossians, as is apparent from the "we" passages (e.g., 1:3, "*We* give thanks to God"), which are not merely an authorial plural but likely include Timothy (so also see Col. 1:4, 9, 28; Col. 4:3).

We have taken the adjectival form ἁγίοις (*hagiois*) to function not as an adjective ("holy ones") but as a noun ("saints"), which is followed by the phrase "and faithful brothers." If this is correct, it would then be an example of the Granville Sharp rule, which in the case of a preceding definite article governing plural nouns indicates either that the two nouns are to be identified in some overlapping or unified manner or that they are completely identical in every way, the latter of which is likely here; on this see Wallace (1996: 278–83), who takes the close parallel in Eph. 1:1, "to the saints who are in Ephesus and who are faithful in Christ Jesus," as an example of the Granville Sharp rule and as referring to identical groups.

1:2. A number of MSS, including several good ones (e.g., א, A, C, F, G, 075), add "and the Lord Jesus Christ" (καὶ κυρίου Ἰησοῦ Χριστοῦ, *kai kyriou Iēsou Christou*) after "God our Father" at the end of verse 2. This may be original, since the introductions of every other epistle by Paul, except for the Pastoral Epistles, follows "Father" by "and [the] Lord Jesus Christ." On the other hand, there is equally good MS evidence for the omission. It is harder to explain why a scribe would intentionally or accidentally omit the added phrase rather than why a copyist would add the clause to an original shorter text. In the latter case, it would be irresistible for a scribe to add "and [the] Lord Jesus Christ" in the light of the fact that the introduction to almost every other epistle includes the phrase.

The introductory "grace" and "peace" may have its broader background in the OT and early Judaism, though there not "grace" (χάρις, *charis*) but "mercy" (ἔλεος, *eleos*) and "peace" are found: e.g., Isa. 54:10; Ps. 85:11 (84:11 LXX); Tob. 7:12; compare also the Shemoneh Esreh; Jer. 16:5; 1QH 5.11 (= *olim* 13.5); Jub. 22.9; 2 Bar. 78.2 (see Beale 1999a: 204–23). However, Paul and other NT writers see "mercy" to be generally synonymous with "grace" (e.g., 1 Tim. 1:2; 2 Tim. 1:2; 2 John 3; cf. Jude 2). Note also Paul's conclusion of "mercy" and "peace" in Gal. 6:16.

II. Letter Thanksgiving: Paul Thanks God for the Readers' Christian Lives (1:3–23)

Here is a fuller statement of the main idea of this unit: *Paul thanks God for the readers' Christian lives and prays that they will live for God, who reconciled them through his Son, the divine and sovereign last Adam.*

In the introduction to Col. 1:1–2, we saw that Paul adapts the variant fourfold Hellenistic letter convention (opening address, greeting, body, and farewell), especially injecting Christian theology into it. Some Hellenistic letters had an introductory thanksgiving element in the pattern of letters, but most apparently did not (Pao 2012: 43). Paul often adopts this unusual thanksgiving element, though sometimes he adds an introductory blessing and a prayer (all three are found in Eph. 1:3–23). In our letter, Paul first pens a thanksgiving (1:3–8) and then follows it with a prayer (1:9–14), which specifically picks up the mention of "praying" in 1:3 (so Schweizer 1982: 32) and which concludes with another "thanks[giving] to the Father" (v. 12a), as in 1:3. Verses 12a–13a further identify the "Father" who is being thanked, and verses 13b–23 identify who the Father's Son is and his redemptive work, all of which are ultimately related back to the "thanks[giving] to the Father" (v. 12a). Thus the second thanksgiving extends all the way from verse 12 to verse 23. Everything from verse 12b through verse 23 is the basis for the thanksgiving of verse 12a, and all of verses 3b–23 ultimately support "thanksgiving" in verse 3a as the main point of the entire section. Whereas the thanksgiving sections of Hellenistic letters were addressed to some pagan god, Paul directs his thanks to the God of Jesus Christ. The themes found in this initial thanksgiving are developed throughout the letter, as is typical in Paul's other introductory thanksgivings.[1] How some of these themes are developed later will be explored in my comments on 1:3–8.

1. See, e.g., O'Brien 1977: 261–63. For the background of Hellenistic or Jewish thanksgivings in relation to Paul's thanksgivings, see the literature cited in Lohse 1971: 12–13; Barth and Blanke 1994: 147–48.

A. Paul Recognizes the Genuine Faith, Love, and Hope of God's End-Time People (1:3–8)

Here is a fuller statement of the main idea of this unit: *Paul thanks God for the readers because he recognizes in them the genuine faith, love, and hope of God's end-time people.*

In the introduction we discussed that Paul was inspired to write to the Colossians because he had heard of the false teachers, who were trying to lead the believers astray (2:4, 8). Therefore Paul begins by thanking God because of the Colossian believers' faith, love, and hope (1:3–5a), which are rooted in their acceptance of the gospel, which has increasingly borne fruit in them (vv. 5b–6) and which they learned from Epaphras (vv. 7–8). "Giving thanks" is the major point of the paragraph; everything else in the paragraph forms part of the logical basis to support that point. More specifically, the remainder of verses 5b–8 explains the "hope" (v. 5a) that was contained in the wide-spreading "gospel," which the Colossians had heard from faithful Epaphras. The "hope" itself is the inspiring cause for the hearers' "love" (v. 4b), which, together with "faith" (v. 4b), is the basis upholding thanksgiving as the main point of verses 3–8. The reason why Paul thanks God for these things is to assure the Colossians of the truth of their Christian faith by causing them to reflect upon the evidence of their faith working within them, which is based on the "word of truth, the gospel." Paul will amplify what that true gospel is at points throughout the epistle (e.g., 1:20–22; 2:12–15), especially in contrast to the false teaching.

Several commentators have observed that verses 3–8 form a chiasm:

A We give thanks to God, the Father of our Lord Jesus Christ, <u>praying always for you</u> (v. 3),
  B we heard of your faith in Christ Jesus and <u>the love which you have for all the saints</u> (v. 4);
    C of which <u>you previously heard in the word of truth, the gospel</u> (v. 5),
      D which has come to you (v. 6),
      D′ just as in all the world, also it is constantly bearing fruit and increasing, even as in you also
    C′ since <u>the day you heard and understood the grace of God in truth</u>; just as you learned it from Epaphras (v. 7),
  B′ and he also informed us of <u>your love</u> in the Spirit (v. 8).

A′ For this reason also, since the day we heard, we have not ceased to pray for you and to ask that you . . . (v. 9).[1]

The chiasm shows that “bearing fruit and increasing” is the central structural element. Many think that the central element of a chiasm is the main point of a literary structure, but the outermost parallels also may plausibly serve as the main points, depending on context and the logical development of thought. Since verse 9, which is the beginning of the next literary unit, is included in the chiasm, this is not a perfectly tidy literary example of a chiastic structure within a tight literary unit. We have tried to show that the tracing of the logical flow of thought locates the major point with thanksgiving in verse 3a. Nevertheless, there is a sufficiently recognizable chiasm that reveals the structural centrality of the universal fruit bearing and increasing of the gospel (v. 6a). Part of the reason for this central location may be to highlight verse 6a as an allusion to Gen. 1:28 (see on v. 6), whose importance is underscored by the same repeated allusion in verse 10. This also suggests that verse 6a is a vital element in the further explanation of the “hope” and of the “gospel” (v. 5).

As here, much powerful Pauline theology can be found packed into Paul’s opening thanksgivings throughout his letters.

Exegesis and Exposition

3We give thanks to God, the Father of our Lord Jesus Christ, praying always [concerning] you, 4[because] we heard [about] your faith in Christ Jesus and the love ⌜which you have⌝ for all the saints, 5[which is inspired by] the hope [that is] laid up for you in [the heavens, . . .] which you previously heard [by] the word of truth, the gospel[,] 6which has come to you, just as . . . also it is . . . bearing fruit ⌜and increasing⌝ [in all the world, just] as . . . in you . . . [from] the day you heard . . . and understood the grace of God in truth; 7just as you learned . . . from Epaphras, our beloved fellow . . . servant, who is a faithful servant of Christ on ⌜our⌝ behalf, 8and he also [made clear to] us . . . your love in the Spirit.

Thanksgiving arises out of a constant attitude of prayer. The main point 1:3
of verse 3 is “giving thanks” (εὐχαριστέω, *eucharisteō*), which is based on a prayerful consideration of the effect of God’s grace in the readers’ lives. Since both Paul and Timothy have just been mentioned in verse 1, it is natural that the “we” who gives thanks is both Paul and Timothy, despite the fact that Paul is the main author of this epistle (as discussed in v. 1; see D. Moo 2008: 82;

1. Here I have followed Dunn (1996: 54) and Lamarche (1975: 453–54) for the chiastic layout, the latter of whom is followed by D. Moo 2008: 87. See the similar structural proposal of Dibelius 1953: 5. Garland (1998: 44–45) likewise offers a persuasive chiasm of verses 4–8, which also has “constantly bearing fruit and increasing” (v. 6) as its center; so similarly Lohse (1971: 14) views verse 6a as the center of the structure of verses 3–8. Yet no proposed chiasm is perfectly fitted to the clear literary unit of 1:3–8.

Harris 2010: 13). However, since Paul is the author and since Timothy is not mentioned in the remainder of the epistle, it is best to view Paul as the primary referent of the "we" (accordingly, see Sumney 2008: 32), which is borne out by Paul's repeated self-references to "I" (1:23–25, 29; 2:1, 4–5; 4:3–4, 8, 13, 18 ["my"]; cf. Lohse 1971: 14). That Paul gives thanks "to God, the Father of our Lord Jesus Christ" is atypical, since at the beginning of most of his letters, when he links the Father and Jesus, usually it is in the phrase "God our Father and the Lord Jesus Christ." Not much should be made of this difference here, since sometimes the Colossians expression also occurs elsewhere at the commencement of Paul's Letters (2 Cor. 1:3; Gal. 1:1 ["God, the Father, who raised Him from the dead"]; so also 1 Pet. 1:3, virtually identical to 2 Cor. 1:3). The different expression results only from stylistic reasons.[2] Calling Jesus "Lord" is not a merely honorific title, sometimes applied to kings or masters, but a reference to "Lord" (κύριος, *kyrios*) in the Greek OT, which was the typical Greek translation of Yahweh in the LXX (cf. Fee 2007: 20–27, 179, 577–78, 631–38) and was a word also used by pagans of their gods. This is thus a reference to Jesus's deity.[3]

As typical in his other epistles, here Paul's introductory thanksgiving arises from a preceding attitude and activity of prayer: "We give thanks . . . when [i.e., at the times] we always pray for you." The prayers that come directly after the introductory thanksgivings elsewhere in his letters typically include some recollection of God's gracious work in the lives of the readers, followed by various expressions of concern that facets of their faith become increasingly established and grow (Rom. 1:8–11; Eph. 1:15–17; Phil. 1:3–6; Col. 1:3–11; Philem. 4–6; cf. 2 Cor. 1:11). These other introductory thanksgivings reveal the pattern that Paul first prayerfully meditates on the experience of divine grace in the lives of believers, and this then leads him to thank God for that grace. The same is true in Col. 1:3. It is not merely that Paul is praying at the time of his thanksgiving or that his thanksgiving is part of his prayer, but as in his other epistolary openings (Phil. 1:3–4; 1 Thess. 1:2; Philem. 4), his continual thanksgiving emerges because he is recalling in prayer how the believers have experienced the grace of God (notice 1:6, "You came to understand the grace of God in truth").

Paul's thanksgiving is not merely a onetime act by Paul but is something that arises repeatedly or continually, which may be the sense of "always" (πάντοτε, *pantote*) and that many see modifying "giving thanks." According to this view, Paul does not mean that he literally offers thanks every minute of the day but that he does so regularly at his times of prayer (O'Brien 1982: 10). However, since "always" appears directly before the phrase "praying

2. Though D. Moo (2008: 83) argues that, in a letter emphasizing the supreme position of Christ, the expression, together with the unique mention of "Father" in verse 2 and of "the Father" in verses 12–13, highlights that Christ is anchored to God the Father.

3. For the background and use of "Lord" (κύριος) in the pre-Christian Jewish and Greco-Roman world, as well as its use to refer to deity in the NT, see W. Foerster and G. Quell, *TDNT* 3:1039–95; and H. Bietenhard, *NIDNTT* 2:510–20.

concerning you," and the phrase "we do not cease praying [προσευχόμενοι, *proseuchomenoi*] and asking" in verse 9 appears to be a direct development of the wording about "praying" here in verse 3 (so Schweizer 1982: 32), it seems a bit more likely that "always" modifies "praying."[4] Thus the idea is not that Paul prays every second of the day but that he does so regularly, as he would have been used to doing as a Jew (following the prayer tradition of Dan. 6:10–11; cf. Acts 3:1; 10:30; see Garland 1998: 46). To the extent that Christians have a continual mind-set of prayer (see 1 Thess. 5:17), they will have a thankful mind-set. Spiritual impoverishment comes when believers do not prayerfully contemplate the experience of God's grace in their lives, and such impoverishment results in an unthankful perspective.

Part of what is packed into his prayer in verse 3 is explicitly elaborated upon in verses 4–8 and at subsequent points in the epistle (e.g., 3:9–11).

In verses 4–8 Paul says that thanksgiving arises out of recognizing in others **1:4**
the true marks of Christian existence. The apostle has used the participle "praying" in verse 3 to modify "giving thanks" by naming the occasion for thanking and, implicitly, the seedbed from which thanks emerges. Paul now adds another adverbial participial modifier of "giving thanks." This second participle is best translated "because we have heard [ἀκούσαντες, *akousantes*]," which gives another basis for why Paul is thanking God in verse 3.[5] Thus he is also thanking God because he has heard about their "faith [πίστις, *pistis*] in Christ Jesus and the love [ἀγάπη, *agapē*] which [they] have for all the saints." The vertical relationship with Christ (the attitude of "faith in Christ")[6] is

4. Some translations place "always" (πάντοτε, *pantote*) as a modifier of "giving thanks" (εὐχαριστέω, *eucharisteō*; RSV, NRSV, NIV, TNIV, HCSB, ESV, NET). However, it could modify "praying" (προσευχόμενοι, *proseuchomenoi*; so ASV, KJV, NASB, Douay, NLT, NJB): thus, "always praying concerning you." Eadie (1856: 6) prefers the first view and lists older commentators supporting one or the other of the views. Robertson (1934: 473) thinks it could easily go either way. However, "always" modifies "giving thanks" elsewhere both in the epistolary introductions (1 Cor. 1:4; 1 Thess. 1:2; 2 Thess. 1:3; Philem. 4 [?]) and outside (Eph. 5:20; 2 Thess. 2:13). In addition, that "always" could modify "giving thanks" in 1:3 is pointed to by the pattern that an adverb usually follows the verb (here the ptcp.) it modifies (so MHT 3:227–28). This is supported by the conceptual parallel in Eph. 1:16 ("I do not cease giving thanks in behalf of you"*; Lightfoot 1875: 133), since Ephesians has more parallels with Colossians than with any other epistle. On the other hand, in the letter openings, "always" can modify verbs expressing prayer (Phil. 1:3–4), as well as outside of the letter openings (Rom. 1:10; Col. 4:12; 2 Thess. 1:11). Our preference that "always" modifies "praying" is swayed by the immediate context, especially the mention of "ceaseless praying" in verse 9. Furthermore, that "always" modifies "praying" may be indicated since it is closer to it, even though it precedes "praying," and since "always" is directly placed before "concerning you" (περὶ ὑμῶν, *peri hymōn*), which also probably modifies "praying," as it does in verse 9. The resulting translation of the adverbial participial clause would be "We give thanks . . . while we are always praying concerning you."

5. See also, e. g., Robertson (1934: 1128), for the causal use in 1:4, though a temporal aspect of the participle is still in mind.

6. So BDAG (819–20, s.v. πίστις), showing that the word refers to an attitude of faith and not acts of faithfulness; yet see BDAG's ambiguous category of "true piety, genuine devotion, . . . which for our lit[erature] means being a Christian." Though it may be possible rarely to render the word as "faithfulness" in Paul (as perhaps in Gal. 5:22; 1 Tim. 5:12 marg.; Philem. 5),

inextricably linked with the horizontal relation with fellow Christians ("the love which you have for all the saints"; Dunn 1996: 56). The former always gives rise to the latter. "Giving thanks" of verse 3 continues to be the main point in verses 3–4a, since the attitudes of "faith" and "love" are the supporting cause of the thanksgiving.

There is ambiguity about whether "faith in Christ Jesus" (ἐν + Χριστῷ Ἰησοῦ, *en* + *Christō Iēsou*) indicates Christ as the sphere in which faith operates and in which those with faith exist (for the latter see Hübner 1997a: 45) or whether it indicates Christ as the object of faith. There are good commentators on both sides of the debate (see D. Moo 2008: 84 for a listing and who prefers that Christ is the object in contrast to Lightfoot 1875: 133; Bruce 1984: 41; and others, who prefer sphere).[7]

Paul's reference to "faith" looks ahead to his later awareness that their faith is threatened by false teaching in 1:23 and 2:4–8 (esp. vv. 5, 7), where in each passage "faith" is juxtaposed to false teaching. Apart from these passages, the only other time in the epistle where "faith" is used is in 2:12, where the object of faith is Jesus's resurrection, a continuing belief that will remind them of their identification with Christ's resurrection and prevent them from succumbing to the false teaching (cf. 2:16–23 with 3:1 and its introductory "therefore"). God's true people also have love and show love to each other. The term "saints" (pl. of ἅγιος, *hagios*), objects of the "love," refers to the same notion of "saints" discussed in 1:2 above: the people (i.e., Christians) of the new-covenant age who are inheriting the end-time promises made to Israel.

1:5 The "love . . . for all the saints" of verse 4 has its origin in the "hope" (ἐλπίς, *elpis*) that they have, as the beginning of verse 5 explains: their love has its *basis in* "the hope[8] that is laid up for you in the heavens." The more precise nuance

---

the typical rendering revolves around "faith" as an attitude or as that which is to be believed (contra apparently Thompson 2005: 19), which is confirmed from the only other uses of "faith" (πίστις, *pistis*) in Colossians, where the word refers to an attitude of "faith" in Christ or in his redemptive work (1:23; 2:5, 7, 12).

7. Lightfoot (1875) offers support for this by contending that if Christ were the object, then the prepositions ἐπί (*epi*) or εἰς (*eis*) would be used and not ἐν (*en*), which more typically indicates sphere and not an object. In further support, Lightfoot and Bruce appeal to syntactical parallels in 1 Tim. 3:13; 2 Tim. 1:13; and 3:15 (Bruce adds Gal. 3:26; 5:6; 1 Tim. 1:14), though D. Moo interprets these verses differently. Bruce notes that when Paul clearly refers to "Christ" as the object of "faith" in this letter, he uses πίστις + εἰς (*eis*): cf. Col. 2:5, τῆς εἰς Χριστὸν πίστεως ὑμῶν (*tēs eis Christon pisteōs hymōn*); in agreement regarding Col. 2:5, Harris (2012: 235) also adduces Philem. 5 as a parallel for faith with an object designated by πρός (*pros*) and not ἐν (*en*). Melick (1991: 197) contends that because Paul uses "unto" (εἰς) in the directly following clause about love being directed toward the object of saints, his different use of "in" (ἐν) likely connotes sphere, since he could have easily also used "unto" in the faith clause but did not. Davids (2008a: 245) argues that "Christ Jesus" is the object of "faith" since the following parallel clause clearly has "all the saints" as the object of "love." Sumney (2008: 34) thinks that it is difficult to make a "hard and fast distinction between" Christ as the object of faith and as the sphere in which faith operates. It is perhaps best to let this ambiguity stand.

8. Here διά (*dia*) + the accusative τὴν ἐλπίδα (*tēn elpida*) expresses basis or cause.

here is that love "spring[s] from" (NIV) or arises from hope.[9] Some, however, see the clause "because of the hope" to modify "giving thanks" of verse 3 and to be another reason for the thanksgiving ("We give thanks . . . because of the hope"; so, e.g., Eadie 1856: 9–10). But the "hope" clause is too far away from "giving thanks" for this to be probable. Most see the same phrase "because of the hope" to be the basis for both the faith and love in verse 4, since the two attitudes are both the parallel objects of the hearing.[10] While plausible, the singular relative pronoun "which" (ἥν, *hēn*) is followed by the verb "have" (ἔχω, *echō*), with the resulting rendering of "[the love] which you have"; this then is directly followed by the prepositional phrase "because of the hope" (διὰ τὴν ἐλπίδα, *dia tēn elpida*). Prepositional phrases typically modify the nearest verbs and not more distant verbal nouns (in this case like "faith" together with "love"; so, e.g., Wallace 1996: 357). This is especially the case with the preposition διά (*dia*) + the accusative in the NT (Wallace 1996: 357) and particularly in Paul. In fact, out of almost 90 uses of the preposition διά (*dia*) + the accusative in Paul and outside of Col. 1:4–5, there appears to be only one clear occurrence where it modifies a verbal noun rather than the nearest verb (Rom. 3:25).[11]

Thus "because of the hope" appears directly and most naturally to be related to the immediately preceding "love which you have,"[12] and the phrase is not an arbitrary restriction of the prepositional phrase to "love" (against the contention of Harris 2010: 15). The resulting sense is "the love that you have for all the saints because of [or "inspired by"] the hope." This focus on "love" as inspired by "hope" is also indicated by observing that this literary segment ending at verse 8 concludes with reference to the Colossians' "love" (v. 8) and not their "faith" (see also Callow 2002: 18; and love is also repeated in 1:7: "Epaphras the beloved [ἀγαπητοῦ, *agapētou*]"). In fact, as we saw in the introduction to this section, "love" forms a concentric circle (or serves as bookends) around the majority of this literary segment of verses 3–8. Thus this structure shows more of a focus on "love" than "faith" as a ground of the thanksgiving (see the structural overview in the introduction to verses 3–8 above and on verse 6b below). Likewise "love" occurs both at the beginning and end of the thanksgiving in Philem. 5 and 7 as probably a greater ground of it than "faith."[13] Furthermore, we will see that everything from verse 5b (beginning

9. Thus διά + the accusative of various words elsewhere can have the more precise notion of, e.g., "mercy" that arises from "love" (Eph. 2:4); cf. similarly Phil. 1:6–7 (confidence arising from heartfelt feelings); 1 Thess. 3:6–7 (comfort springing from faith, love, and kindness). The construction expresses other attitudes arising from other various conditions (e.g., see 2 Tim. 1:6, 12; 2:10).

10. So, e.g., Harris 2010: 15; 2012: 75–76; see likewise D. Moo 2008: 85; Barth and Blanke 1994: 148; Moule 1957: 49; Melick 1991: 197; and others.

11. Some of these prepositions modify clearly implied verbs, especially the verb "to be," which is directly linked to the preposition. Also, among the roughly ninety uses of the construction διά (*dia*) + the accusative, four form a question ("Why?").

12. So also Calvin (1972: 301–2), Peake (1970: 497), and Callow (2002: 18); the latter two cite others in agreement.

13. See Pokorný (1991: 37) for these last two points.

with the phrase "laid up for you in heaven") through to verse 8 ultimately is rooted in an explanation of the "hope" of verse 5a, which culminates in the readers' "love" in verse 8. This means that precisely in this context the "hope" gives rise only to "love" and not to "faith,"[14] though Paul would likely agree theologically with such a dual idea. In fact, Paul mentions "faith" and "love" each four times elsewhere in the epistle,[15] suggesting that he places an equal emphasis on both (indeed, he directly links "faith" with "hope" in 1:23).

Why is there a focus more on "love" than "faith" and "hope" in verses 5–8? It is hard to say, though it may be an anticipation of 3:12–14. There, after enumerating several godly attributes that Paul says believers should "put on," he concludes by affirming that "beyond all these things, put on love, which is the perfect bond of [complete] unity" (see the additional note on 1:5 for why "love" is singled out in 1:5 and 3:14). It may also be that, as in 1 Cor. 13:13, "love" is singled out as "the greatest" among "faith" and "hope" because it will last forever, in contrast to "faith and hope," which will end when the invisible that is believed and hoped for becomes visible in the new creation (Fee 1987: 649–52).

"Hope" does not refer to an inner attitude of hope but (by metonymy)[16] the object of hope,[17] as in Rom. 8:24 (the second occurrence), Gal. 5:5, and perhaps 2 Cor. 3:12 (Barth and Blanke 1994: 154). In this letter, that the "hope is laid up in the heavens" likely refers to "the things above, where Christ is seated at the right hand of God," and the "life" of believers in that upper realm, which "is hidden with Christ and God" (Col. 3:3). At his final coming, Christ will "be revealed," at which time believers "also will be revealed in glory" (Col. 3:1, 4), which probably alludes to their glorious resurrection bodies. Thus though "hope" refers to the object of "hope," it is implied that the readers' hope resides in their future glorious resurrection (see also Callow 2002: 18).

However, this resurrection existence has already begun in their union with Christ (see 3:1, "You have been raised up with Christ"), so that their "hope" lies in their *unseen present and future* resurrection existence[18] because of their identification with the resurrected Christ. This is likely what is referred to in Col. 1:26–27: "This mystery . . . is Christ in you, the hope of glory." Thus the resurrected Christ is the foundation of their hope in resurrection (following Aletti 1993: 60, for the most part). The beginning realization of their "hope"

14. Abbott (1897: 195–96) notes that most of the Greek fathers and modern commentators of the nineteenth century held the same view, though he disagrees with it. See Eadie (1856: 8–9) for commentators restricting the basis of "hope" to "love," as well as commentators holding that both "faith" and "love" are undergirded by "hope."

15. For "faith" (πίστις, *pistis*) see 1:23; 2:5, 7, 12; for "love" (ἀγάπη, *agapē*) see 1:8, 13; 2:2; 3:14, though 1:13 refers to God's love for his Son; see likewise the verbal form applied to God's love for his people in 3:12.

16. A figure of speech by which the attitude of hope is substituted for the object of that hope in order to connote that "hoping" is critical to inheriting what is hoped for.

17. Harris 2010: 15, along with many commentators.

18. In agreement with Wall 1993: 47; N. Wright (1986: 52) leans toward an emphasis on the inaugurated reality.

in their presently unseen resurrection life inspires even greater confidence[19] that the final phase of bodily resurrection will assuredly occur. The inaugurated aspect is underscored by noticing that "the hope" is said to be that "which is laid up for you in heaven" (following Lincoln 2000: 591). Many translations leave out the verb "is" and merely have "the hope laid up," which is temporally somewhat ambiguous. Other translations, however, rightly express the present notion by including "is" (KJV, NIV, NJB, Douay, Geneva). The phrase "which is laid up" is a rendering of the articular adjectival present passive participle τὴν ἀποκειμένην (*tēn apokeimenēn*), which, in light of the immediate context, expresses the present reality of the hope that is in heaven. That this participial expression does not refer exclusively to the future but includes the present is evident not only from 3:1–4 (where the heavenly inheritance is a present reality)[20] but also from the directly following context. That is, the "already and not yet" aspect of the hope is also expressed in 1:12 ("the one who has qualified us for a share of the inheritance," present and future) and 1:13 ("he transferred us into the kingdom of his beloved Son," past and present).

The implication of a verbal idea of hope together with an explicit notion of hope as an object is given some plausibility from the parallel in Rom. 8:24, where both ideas are explicitly mentioned. Paul also refers to "hope" with reference to confident expectation of a future resurrection in his other epistles (Rom. 4:17–18; 8:20–25; Titus 1:2; 3:7), an idea found elsewhere in the NT (Acts 2:26; in 23:6 and 24:15 Paul is the speaker; 1 Pet. 1:3, 21).

Peter similarly says that believers have been "born again to a living hope through the resurrection of Jesus Christ, . . . to obtain an inheritance, which is [incorruptible] and undefiled and will not fade away, reserved in heaven for you, who are protected by the power of God through faith for a salvation ready to be revealed in the last time" (1 Pet. 1:3–6; see also 2 Tim. 4:8). This "inheritance," which is based on Christ's own resurrection, is none other than the "new heavens and a new earth," of which the believers' resurrection body will be a part (cf. 2 Pet. 3:9–13). This parallel points further to Paul's expression, "the hope laid up for you in heaven," as a reference to hope in the resurrection on the last day.[21] The mention of this "hope . . . which you . . .

19. Likewise note that Heb. 11:1 understands "hope" as an expression of "faith" in the presently unseen things: "Now faith is the assurance of things hoped for, the conviction of things not seen."

20. Though the participial expression is not used in 3:1–4, the same conceptual heavenly reality is expressed.

21. See likewise 2 Macc. 12:45, where Judas "was looking to the splendid reward that is laid up [ἀποκείμενον, *apokeimenon*] for those who fall asleep in godliness" (NRSV), which refers to the reward of resurrection (12:43–44). Philo (*Rewards* 104) refers to "those men for whom that true wisdom is laid up in heaven" in contrast to "those persons who, by reason of their impiety or unrighteousness, have not a heavenly inheritance." Interestingly, here "wisdom" is a metonymy for the reward of "wisdom," which is the believer's heavenly inheritance, much like the use of "hope" in Col. 1:5 (cf. Dibelius 1953: 6, who cites these texts as parallels). For a future reward or inheritance laid up in heaven for believers, see 2 Esd. (4 Ezra) 7:14, 83 (cf. in relation to 7:96–98, 101, 120–23; 8:1); 2 Bar. 14.12–13; 24.1 (cf. likewise Gnilka 1980: 33). For "hope of

heard in the word . . . of the gospel" here clearly anticipates Paul's concern that they not be "moved away from the hope of the gospel that you have heard" in verse 23 (so similarly Abbott 1897: 197), another example of an objective use of "hope." This verbal parallel then already signals Paul's later unease about the threat of the false teaching that had the potential to "move" them away from their faith, and it shows that he is already giving them assurance about their Christian "hope" (see 2:1–4, 6–8; cf. Garland 1998: 47).

At this point and throughout the letter, the eschatology of Colossians has compatible spatial and temporal aspects. The end-time inheritance that Paul sees coming in the future is an actual place. As noted above, this end-time place of resurrection existence has also been inaugurated in time (Col. 3:1–4) but remains a hope to be consummated.

Despite the fact that "hope" (ἐλπίς, *elpis*) as an object of hoping is not exactly parallel with the verbal notions of faith (πίστις, *pistis*) and love (ἀγάπη, *agapē*), we saw (above) that the verbal idea of "hope" as a confident expectation was implied. Therefore the mention of "faith, love, and [implied] hope" together here recalls Paul's use of the triad elsewhere to summarize the essence of Christian existence, especially for protection against the threat of false teaching that marks the end-time tribulation (see the additional note on 1:4–5). "Giving thanks" in verse 3 continues to be the main point in verses 3–5, since not only are the attitudes of "faith" and "love" (v. 4) the supporting cause of the thanksgiving but so also is "hope."

Thus Paul does not thank the readers but thanks God for their reception of the gospel and its work in them, especially their faith, love, and hope. This indicates that it was not their independent, autonomous efforts that earned God's grace in their lives. Rather, everything about their Christian lives is a result of God's unconditional "grace" (χάρις, *charis*, v. 6). The Colossians also have "understood the grace of God in truth" from the beginning. Human significance does not reside in self-determination apart from divine influence. Rather, Paul sees that human self-worth has its foundation in the grace of God alone (see 1 Cor. 4:7). There is difference of opinion among commentators about whether salvation is based to a significant degree in human actions apart from God's working or in God's absolute unconditional work. This commentary affirms that the evidence of Colossians and the rest of Paul's writings reflects the latter perspective.

The "hope" that the Colossians had "previously heard" was "in the word of truth, the gospel." The expression "word of truth" (τῷ λόγῳ τῆς ἀληθείας, *tō logō tēs alētheias*) is an adjectival (or qualitative) genitive, focusing on the qualitative nature of the "word," "the true word" (likewise TNIV). The phrase τοῦ εὐαγγελίου (*tou euangeliou*) that modifies "the truthful word" is a genitive of apposition, so that the full clause should be rendered "the true word, which is the gospel." This is confirmed from Eph. 1:13, where "the gospel" is even

the world that was to be renewed," see 2 Bar. 57.2; for "hope" being "full of immortality," see Wis. 3:4 NRSV.

more clearly appositional to "the word of truth" (NRSV).[22] The "word" which is "the gospel" is "true" in that its content is absolutely dependable (cf. BDAG 42a, s.v. ἀλήθεια). In the OT the "word of truth" (forms of λόγος [*logos*] + the genitive of ἀλήθεια [*alētheia*]) refers to God's word, often identified with Scripture (Ps. 119:43 [118:43 LXX]; Prov. 22:21; Eccles. 12:10; see also T. Gad 3.1; Philo, *Heir* 143 [in light of 129–30, 140–41]; cf. Philo, *Dreams* 1.23; Pss. Sol. 16.10; Gos. Eb., frag. 2), thus underscoring here the authoritative nature of the gospel message (cf. Sumney 2008: 36). The same word combination occurs repeatedly in the NT also to highlight the authoritative nature of the gospel (2 Cor. 6:7; Eph. 1:13; James 1:18; Ign. *Phld.* 3.2) and sometimes appears to overlap with authoritative Scripture (2 Tim. 2:15 in relation to 3:14–17).

"Gospel" (εὐαγγέλιον, *euangelion*) occurs often throughout Paul. He likely chose the word under the influence of the verbal use ("preach, announce good news") in Isa. 40–60, where in context it refers to the announcement of God's coming restoration of Israel (Isa. 40:9; 60:6), especially through his messianic servant (Isa. 52:7; 61:1). Jesus himself drew from this OT background (Matt. 11:5; Luke 7:22), and this background became formative in summarizing his mission (Acts 10:36; following Dunn 1996: 60). Paul himself applies this Isaiah background to Christ's essential salvific mission.[23]

This "gospel" had "come" to the Colossians, "just as likewise [it had come] **1:6**
in all the world." "World" (κόσμος, *kosmos*) here refers to the entire world in its geographical sense with a focus on the gospel beginning to pierce into the world of Gentiles that lay outside of Israel. Κόσμος has the same frame of reference in Rom. 1:8[24] and 1 Cor. 4:9. Virtually the identical phrase is reiterated in Col. 1:23: "the gospel that you have heard, which was proclaimed <u>in all creation</u> [κτίσις, *ktisis*] under heaven." These Gentile regions to which the gospel had reached were representative of the entire Gentile world throughout the created order where the gospel would continue to spread (so N. Wright 1986: 35) and thus by association include the entire created earth in which humans live. The idea reflects an "already and not yet eschatological" sense in which the gospel has begun its universal spread, and it is implied that this extension will be completed at the very end of time (cf. Pao 2012: 55).[25]

That the entire animate and inanimate creation as the sphere in which humans live is in mind is apparent by observing that "all the world" (ἐν παντὶ τῷ κόσμῳ, *en panti tō kosmō*) is part of an allusion to "all the earth" in Gen.

22. See also Gal. 2:5, 14, where the same appositional relationship between "truth" and the "gospel" is observable, though not as clearly; see likewise Bruce 1984: 42.

23. See Isa. 52:7 and 57:19 in Eph. 2:17 (cf. NA[27] margin for the allusions); cf. Rom. 10:15 in application to Christian missionaries in solidarity with Christ.

24. Note, e.g., that Rom. 1:5 speaks of Paul bringing about "the obedience of faith among all the Gentiles" (cf. likewise Rom. 15:9–12; 16:26).

25. "All the world" can be seen as a hyperbole, an extreme exaggeration (such as "I waited *for a million years* at the doctor's office), which here refers merely to the extensive spread of the gospel. However, it is better to see it actually referring to all the geographical world in an "already and not yet" end-time sense, as noted above.

1:28 (LXX, πάσης τῆς γῆς, *pasēs tēs gēs*), which Adam was to fill with his created offspring (see additional notes below).

The "gospel" that the Colossians had received also had broken into other parts of the Gentile world ("in all the world") and had been "bearing fruit and increasing" there, as it similarly had been doing among the Colossians, "since the day [they] heard of it and came to know the grace of God in truth." This phrase refers to the gospel's growth in the world to include the Colossians when they first believed, but the "bearing fruit and increasing" of the gospel continues to affect the Colossians' lives as they persevere in their faith. This ongoing effect takes the form of "bearing fruit in every good work" and "increasing in the knowledge of God," as will be seen below (1:10).

Both in 1:6 and 1:10 there is the same OT allusion to "bearing fruit and increasing" from Gen. 1:28. The point of the allusion is to indicate that the Colossian Christians have begun to participate in the new creation and thus have commenced to carry out the commission to Adam and Eve in a more effective way than it had ever been done in the OT era.[26] As we will see, the reason they are able to carry out the Gen. 1:28 commission is because they are identified with Christ, the last Adam, who has already effectively carried it out. As seen in the introduction to verses 3–8, the growth of the gospel in the middle of verse 6 is actually also the literary centerpiece of the concentric structure of verses 3–8: the outer ring of prayer (vv. 3b and 9a), the next ring of "love" (vv. 4, 8),[27] the next inner ring of having "heard" the gospel (vv. 5, 6c), and the innermost central ring of "bearing fruit and increasing" (v. 6b).[28] However, this is not the main logical point of the segment's thought flow, since, as we have seen, the thanksgiving of verse 3a is the main point, being logically undergirded by everything else from verses 3b–8, of which verse 6 forms a crucial part in supporting the thanksgiving. Nevertheless, Paul has structurally highlighted this phrase in verse 6 literarily through the chiasm in order to draw more attention to the OT allusion, which unpacks how the gospel (vv. 5–6a) has become present to the readers.

Paul repeats that what the Colossians have believed is "true": "you came to know the grace of God in truth." "Knowing" in this context refers not only to the cognitive but also to the experiential aspect of human knowledge. "Grace" (χάρις, *charis*) is substituted here for the "gospel" in verse 5 ("what you heard through the truthful word, which is the gospel").[29] The substitution highlights that everything about the gospel is the result of God's grace, which is unmerited by humans (e.g., see Eph. 1:6–7; 2:5, 7–8; 3:2, 7–8). The word

26. See the additional note on 1:6 for the Gen. 1:28 background of "bearing fruit and increasing" and Paul's use of it.

27. Though "faith" is also mentioned in verse 4.

28. As also noted earlier, it may be hard to know where the emphasis is in chiasms or concentric structures, since the middle element or the framing elements may receive emphasis, depending on context and the logical flow of thought.

29. See Acts 20:24, where "the gospel" is equated with "grace" (Lightfoot 1875: 136); Paul elsewhere closely associates the "gospel" with "grace."

ἀλήθεια (*alētheia*) is used for the second time in the space of two verses. Some commentators have suggested that the word occurs in verse 5 to highlight for the readers that the gospel they believed is unswervingly true in contrast to the false teaching that existed among them, which emphasized human-centered teachings (e.g., 2:4, 8, 16–19; so e.g., Lightfoot 1875: 136). However, the mere mention of "truth" in verse 5 is likely not sufficient to establish the probability of such a connection. Nevertheless, the second mention of "truth" (v. 6) does point to the likelihood that this link, indeed, is in Paul's mind. This seems to be the best explanation of why Paul mentions "truth" twice in such close proximity. The phrase "in truth" indicates that the Colossians' "hearing" and "knowing" God's "grace" took place in the sphere of truth or, possibly, that they "truly heard and knew" (the latter argued by Harris 2010: 18), or that it is a reference to "true grace."[30]

Paul cannot think of true Christian faith, love, and hope (vv. 3–5) apart from the fruitful works that each of these three attitudes produces in the genuine Christian life (vv. 6, 10). Works are not the basis of salvation but are the telltale evidence that one has true faith, love, and hope. In verses 3–5 we saw that "thanksgiving" was the main point, supported by the notions of prayer and the triad of faith, love, and hope. Without the marks of faith, love, and hope *resulting in* fruitful works, there would have been no thanksgiving. For Paul, the attitudes of faith, love, and hope are inextricably linked to works. The increasing fruitfulness on a universal scale, "in all the world," is an inevitable sign of the gospel's truth over and against the parochial and unfruitful false teaching on which Paul will elaborate (so Patzia 1990: 19).

The "grace of God in truth" that the hearers "have come to know" (v. 6) was **1:7**
"just" exactly (καθώς, *kathōs*) what they "learned from Epaphras." Epaphras was a "beloved fellow servant" together with Paul and his circle of fellow workers. In fact, he was a "fellow prisoner in Christ Jesus" with Paul (Philem. 23). The reference to Epaphras as Paul's and Timothy's "fellow slave" (σύνδουλος, *syndoulos*) refers to them together as "slaves" of Christ, who is their master. Paul often refers to himself as Christ's "slave" (Rom. 1:1; Gal. 1:10; Phil. 1:1; Titus 1:1), which indicates his humility and absolute desire to carry out Christ's will, and so it does for Epaphras too.

Not only is Epaphras a "fellow slave," but he is also "a faithful servant of Christ on behalf" of the Colossian Christians.[31] The reference to Epaphras as a "servant" (διάκονος, *diakonos*) is not merely a general reference to his faithful Christian service but also identifies his special status as a servant in the "ministry," since every other use of διάκονος in Paul refers to some kind of special status of serving (so twenty other times in Paul, whether of Christ,

30. Though Barth and Blanke (1994: 162) contend that whether "in truth" modifies the verbs or "grace," it makes no real difference in meaning, since true knowing would have to be based in that which is true.

31. The genitive πιστὸς . . . διάκονος τοῦ Χριστοῦ (*pistos . . . diakonos tou Christou*) may be possessive or, better, objective: "faithfully serving Christ"; cf. Harris 2010: 20.

Paul, the apostolic circle, or the church office of deacon; see further D. Moo 2008: 91).[32] This special status of Epaphras is confirmed further by noticing that the preceding σύνδουλος occurs only one other time in Paul, and that in Col. 4:7 with reference to Tychicus. There Tychicus is another fellow slave together with Paul,[33] and he is also referred to there as a "servant" (διάκονος) who can be relied upon to bring the Colossians trustworthy information from the apostolic circle of Paul. According to Col. 4:12, Epaphras is a faithful "slave [δοῦλος] of Jesus Christ, always laboring earnestly for" the Colossians "in his prayers, that [they] may stand [complete] and fully assured in all the will of God." In this respect, Paul is assuring the Colossians that the apostolic gospel they have "heard and known . . . in truth" (v. 6) is what they have exactly[34] "learned from Epaphras," in contrast to the false teachings they are facing, as Paul will soon reveal (R. Lucas 1980: 27). In fact, Epaphras is a representative of Paul's apostolic good news, since he is ministering "on <u>our</u> [Paul's] behalf."[35] The genitive phrase "faithful servant of Christ" may be a possessive genitive (i.e., "Christ's faithful servant"; see NLT; cf. JB).[36]

1:8 It is likely that Paul had "heard" from Epaphras about the "faith, love, and hope" among the Colossians (1:4–5), since verse 8 now says explicitly that Epaphras "made known" to him the Colossian believers' "love inspired by means of the Spirit" (ἀγάπην ἐν πνεύματι, *agapēn en pneumati*). This is a love for Paul, Timothy, and other saints since, as we have seen, this verse itself is partly developing the reference to the Colossians' "love . . . for all the saints" (v. 4; so also see Aletti 1993: 65). Here πνεῦμα (*pneuma*) refers to the Holy Spirit and not the renewed human spirit of the readers (contra, e.g., Schweizer 1982: 37–38, who holds the latter). It is true that the only other use of πνεῦμα (*pneuma*) in Colossians may refer to the human spirit (2:5), though even there it could (and likely does) refer to God's Spirit (see further on 2:5). Furthermore, out of the fourteen uses of πνεῦμα in Ephesians, the letter having the most parallels with Colossians of all Paul's Letters, only one time does the word refer to the renewed human spirit and not God's Spirit (Eph. 4:23; possibly also Eph. 1:17). Furthermore, that the divine Spirit is in mind in the phrase ἀγάπην ἐν πνεύματι is apparent from observing that it is best translated as "love inspired by means of the Spirit" (an instrumental dative), which is parallel to other Pauline passages where God's Spirit is the means by which love is produced in Christians (so Rom. 5:5; 15:30; Gal. 5:22). Finally, in the very

32. Two of these uses refer to the special status of the state in its judicial role (Rom. 13:4).

33. The noun δοῦλος occurs in Paul with reference generally to Christians serving, and it can be used of an elevated Christian status.

34. Cf. this significance of "just as" (καθώς, *kathōs*) in often connoting that what follows is in exact correspondence with something that precedes (cf. BDAG 493); e.g., an event narrated that is then cited as a fulfillment of OT prophecy, the two being linked by καθώς.

35. See the additional note on 1:7 for the textual problem, where I prefer "our" (ἡμῶν, *hēmōn*) over "your" (ὑμῶν, *hymōn*).

36. Or it may be an objective genitive ("a faithful servant for Christ)"; see Pao (2012: 57), who prefers an objective genitive here, though most translations leave the genitive ambiguous.

next verse (Col. 1:9) Paul will use the adjective πνευματικός (*pneumatikos*) to refer to the Spirit in giving "wisdom and understanding." Paul habitually uses ἐν (*en*) + the dative of πνεῦμα to designate that something happens in the sphere of God's Spirit or by means of the Spirit (so at least 15× in Paul outside of Col. 1:8).

In verse 5 we spoke of the spatial and temporal aspect of eschatology: the end-time inheritance coming in the future is an actual place, the "new heavens and a new earth." As noted there, this is an end-time place of resurrection existence, which has also been inaugurated in time (Col. 3:1–4) but remains a hope to be consummated. Here in verse 8 the work of the "Spirit" is also eschatological, since the coming of the Spirit was one of the great eschatological promises of the OT and early Judaism, which the NT (including Paul) sees as beginning to be fulfilled (e.g., Acts 2:17, 33; 2 Cor. 1:20–22; Gal. 3:14; Eph. 1:13–14; see further Beale 2011: 559–91).

Additional Notes

1:4. The phrase "[love] which you have" (ἣν ἔχετε, *hēn echete*) is changed to only "which" (τὴν, *tēn*) by some later MSS (e.g., K, L) and is omitted by Codex Vaticanus (B), while the earliest and best MSS (excluding B) retain the full phrase "[love] which you have." While it is possible that a scribe was influenced to change an original "which" to "which you have" because of the parallel with Philem. 5, which has the full phrase, it is just as plausible that the Philemon parallel shows that Paul was perfectly capable of using the same phrase elsewhere, such as here. Therefore the earliest and best MSS favor retaining the full phrase, which is also the preference of NA^{28}.

1:4–5. It was noted above that "hope" (ἐλπίς, *elpis*) is not exactly parallel with the verbal notions of faith (πίστις, *pistis*) and love (ἀγάπη, *agapē*),[37] but that nevertheless the mention of all three together here recalls that Paul uses this triad elsewhere. Faith is probably Paul's most typical term for describing an attitude of true Christian existence (e.g., Col. 1:23; 2:5, 7, 12). Love for other believers in this epistle is focused upon, as here in verse 4 (1:8; 2:2; 3:14), though Paul also uses it elsewhere to refer to love for God (2 Thess. 3:5). The observation here that the triad concludes with "hope" is interesting, since the well-known formula in 1 Cor. 13:13 concludes with "love" ("faith, hope, love"). Is there a reason for the change of order? Perhaps. Or could it be due to merely stylistic reasons? Could it be that the reason the Corinthian triad climaxes with love is because one of the primary problems among the believers in Corinth was divisiveness and not loving one another? So Paul highlights it by putting it at the end. On the other hand, the triad ends with "hope" in Col. 1:3–4 because the problem at Colossae was false teaching, which undercut faith in Christ now and hope in his final coming and the final resurrection in the future (Col. 3:1–4, 24).[38] Likely for the same reason, Paul elsewhere sometimes concludes the mention of "faith" and "love" with "endurance" (ὑπομονή, *hypomonē*), a word closely associated with "hope" (1 Thess. 1:3; 1 Tim. 6:11; 2 Tim. 3:10; Titus 2:2; so also Barn. 1.4; Ign. *Phld.* 3.2–3).

However, whatever the real circumstances of the various addressees were, Paul always places "faith" first in the triad because it is the foundation of true Christian living (following R. Collins 1984: 349). Some commentators have observed that "faith, love, and hope" is a summary

37. That is, "hope," in contrast to the verbal ideas of "faith" and "love," does not have an explicit verbal notion of an inner attitude of hope but refers (by metonymy) to the salvific object of hope (see further below).

38. Though false teaching about the believers' final resurrection was also a problem in Corinth (see 1 Cor. 15:12–28).

of Christian existence: faith looks back to Christ's redeeming death and resurrection, love looks up to Christ (and around to fellow believers), and hope looks to Christ's last coming (e.g., cf. Wood 1952: 19). In the context of all of Colossians, the threefold formula encapsulates in logical order how the readers are to persevere in faith while facing the false teaching (cf. 2:4–8, 18–22).

Elsewhere Paul says these three qualities are necessary for Christians to be protected from the damaging consequences of teachers who twist the truth, which is a sign that the apostasy Jesus predicted would happen in the end times had commenced (see Mark 13:5–6, 21–23 and synoptic parallels). The eschatological nature of these three qualities is indicated by their close connection to expectation of Christ's imminent coming (1 Cor. 13:7–8 with 13:10–12; Col. 1:4–5 with 3:4; 1 Thess. 5:8 alongside 1 Tim. 6:11 with 6:14–15; 2 Tim. 3:10 with 4:1; Titus 2:2 with 2:11–13). The majority of the occurrences of the three-word combination appear in association with the notion that the end times had already started (see 1 Cor. 11:11 and 13:10; 1 Thess. 5:1–11 with Acts 1:6–8; 1 Tim. 4:1; 2 Tim. 3:1; cf. Titus 1:2–3). Not coincidentally, errant teaching is also discussed in most of the contexts of these passages (cf. 1 Tim. 4:1–3 and 6:20–21; 2 Tim. 3:1, 5–9; Titus 1:2–3, 9–16).[39] Thus, the Colossians need faith, love, and hope to weather the eschatological storms of false teaching that they face.

Yet, as we saw above, "love" receives more focus than "faith" and "hope" in Col. 1:4–5. We have argued above that this may be an anticipation of 3:12–14. There, after listing several godly characteristics that Paul says believers should reflect, he concludes by saying, "Beyond all these things, put on love, which is the perfect bond of complete unity." But why are "love" and "unity" so important? Colossians 3:15 explains this "unity" to be the "peace of Christ" to which they "were called in <u>one</u> body." Then 3:16 appears to give the means by which such loving "unity" is achieved and "oneness" maintained: "Let the word of Christ dwell in you richly, in all wisdom teaching and admonishing one another" (cf. KJV). Thus, focusing on the true teaching of Christ and not on the false teaching mentioned throughout the letter will bring about "love" and "unity." Even if this is not the precise relationship between 3:14–15 and 3:16, at the least "love" and "unity" are in some way closely linked to true teaching. This link is even closer in 2:2: "that their hearts may be encouraged, [as a result of] having been knit together in love and [knit together] for attaining to all the wealth that comes from the full assurance of understanding, resulting in a true knowledge of God's mystery, [which] is Christ" (and note the contrast with false teaching in 2:4). It appears that "love" here has the purpose of or results in "understanding" and "knowledge" (see further on 2:2). Whatever the exact link is of "love" and true teaching, the general connection is that doctrinal truth without "love" is hollow and "love" without "truth" is misguided. Only through faith in the true gospel, that God showed his love in sending Christ, can God's people show horizontal love to one another. Perhaps this is similar to John's "love in

39. Following in part Beale 2003: 47. This association of the latter days with false teaching occurs also in the Epistle of Barnabas and in Polycarp's *Letter to the Philippians*. The combination of the words "faith, love, and hope" in the former epistle appears twice (Barn. 1.4, 6) in direct connection with believers who have been given "the firstfruits of the taste of things future" (Barn. 1.7; cf. Heb. 6:4–5), which is to protect against the deception of the evil one, who works evil (Barn. 2.1), and the deceptive "works of lawlessness, lest the works of lawlessness overpower us" (Barn. 4.1). Such menacing evil is called "the error of the present time" (4.1) and the beginning fulfillment of Daniel's end-time prophecy that forces of evil would persecute and delude God's people (Barn. 4.3–5, quoting Dan. 7:7–8, 24). It is no wonder that, in the context of such apostasy, the author highlights "hope" by twice placing it last and seeing it as the ground for faith and love to endure ("great faith and love dwells in you through hope of the life which is His" [1.4]; "the hope of life, which is the beginning and end of our faith" [1:6]). The logical order of the triad in Polycarp's *Letter to the Philippians* (3.2–3) is faith, hope, and love again because of the threat of false teaching, which is evidence that the "antichrist" is already present (Pol. *Phil.* 7), though "hope" is not highlighted here. Later in this work, "hope" and "endurance" are highlighted and said to be needed to "hold fast" (Pol. *Phil.* 7.2–8.1) against such deceptive forces (Pol. *Phil.* 7–11). For looser forms of the triad in the NT, see Rom. 5:3–5; Gal. 5:5–6; Heb. 6:9–12; cf. Rev. 2:2–4.

truth" (1 John 3:18; 2 John 1; 3 John 1; cf. Eph. 4:15; 2 John 3). As we saw in our discussion of 1:4 above, "love" is likewise singled out as "the greatest" among "faith" and "hope," in 1 Cor. 13:13.

1:5. Why does Paul understand that "love" springs from "hope" in verse 5? Though Paul is not clear about this, the reason why hope inspires love appears to lie in his understanding that those who have begun to have true love (arising from true faith) have begun to participate in the redemptive-historical process that will culminate in the final coming of Christ,[40] when he will raise his people from the dead (cf. generally Phil. 1:6), the latter of which is the content of their hope. Apparently this hope of consummated resurrection inspires love in the present. That is, they have begun to be raised from the dead in the present and at the final coming of Christ their initial resurrection existence will be consummated in a new body. This may be borne out by comparing Col. 1:27 with 3:1–4. In the former passage, "Christ, . . . the hope of glory" is further elaborated on in verse 28 by reference to Paul's goal to "present every man complete in Christ." It is likely that 3:1–4 picks up on this hope and completion in Christ: "When Christ, who is our life, is revealed, then you also will be revealed with him in glory," in resurrection glory, which is the consummation of the inaugurated "[resurrection] with Christ" (3:1). Thus the "hope" of 1:5 is likely the hope of the resurrection, which has begun in the Colossians and will be consummated in the bodily resurrection of the entire person. A significant parallel (recognized by Wolter 1993: 52) is Barn. 1.3–4, where the author says he is "hoping to be saved" and that he is "compelled . . . to love you [the readers] . . . because great faith and love dwell in you, because of the hope[41] of his [Christ's] life." Note that the author's "love" is based on their "faith and love," which in turn are based on their "hope."

But why does the hope of an "already and not yet" resurrection become the basis for love? Paul is not explicit about the answer to this question. Calvin is probably correct to say that "the hope of eternal life will never fail . . . to produce love in us," since the person who is persuaded "that the treasure of life is laid up for him in heaven will aspire thither, despising the world," directing his "affections to the worship of God and to exercises of love" (Calvin 1972: 301–2). The clue to this may come from elsewhere in the NT: 1 John 4:9 affirms that love for God was "manifested" in believers through (or because of) God's sending his "Son into the world so that we might live through him." That is, apparently as believers contemplate God's work through Christ that has given them resurrection life, their love for God grows out of gratitude for this work (cf. Smalley 2007: 229; similarly see Jude 21).

Yet we find the simplest explanation: Paul understands that Christians will be inspired to love increasingly to obtain the future inheritance. Some may react against this by thinking it is a "works-salvation" notion, but Paul and other NT writers do see elsewhere that while works are necessary for salvation, they are not the ultimate cause, which is in Christ's redemptive work through which people are justified by faith (for elaboration of this idea, see Beale 2011: 469–526). True believers should have a desire to increase in faith and the fruits of faith, in this case love, in order to be found worthy of their inheritance at the end. Interestingly, in Rom. 5:5 Paul says that "hope does not disappoint, because the love of God has been poured out within our hearts through the Holy Spirit who was given to us." We can ask the same question about Rom. 5:5, though it is the other way around: why is love the basis for hope? The answer to this is not straightforward.

1:6. Only late MSS omit "and increasing" (καὶ αὐξανόμενον, *kai auxanomenon*) after "bearing fruit," which are also not of the quality of the earlier MSS supporting the inclusion of this

40. That is, they have begun to participate salvifically in union with Christ's death and resurrection and the next great redemptive-historical events are the destruction of the cosmos, the judgment, creation of a new cosmos, and the final consummate resurrection.

41. "Because of the hope" is a rendering of ἐλπίδι (*elpidi*) as a dative of cause, though it could well be a dative of means, "through the hope," but the difference in meaning is not great. "The hope of life" here likely includes Christ's resurrection life, since Barn. 1.7 refers to Christ having "given us a foretaste of things to come."

reading (e.g., ℵ, A, B, C, D [06], F [010], G [012]). Likely a scribe who finished writing "bearing fruit" (καρποφορούμενον, *karpophoroumenon*) glanced back at the MS he was copying and focused on the -μενον (*-menon*) ending of "increasing," which has the same ending as "bearing fruit," and he continued copying from there, thus omitting "and increasing."

1:6. The first OT allusion in the epistle occurs in 1:6 and is repeated in 1:10, the former a part of the thanksgiving and the latter a part of a prayer based on the thanksgiving (which will also be discussed here):

Genesis 1:28	Colossians 1:6, 10
"increase [αὐξάνεσθε, *auxanesthe*] and multiply [πληθύνεσθε, *plēthynesthe*] and fill the earth . . . and rule over . . . all the earth [πάσης τῆς γῆς, *pasēs tēs gēs*]" (LXX)	"in all the world [ἐν παντὶ τῷ κόσμῳ, *en panti tō kosmō*] also it [the word of truth, the gospel] is . . . bearing fruit [καρποφορούμενον, *karpophoroumenon*] and increasing [αὐξανόμενον, *auxanomenon*]" (v. 6)
"Be fruitful and multiply, and fill the earth . . . and rule . . . the earth" (NASB rendering of MT)[a]	"bearing fruit [καρποφοροῦντες, *karpophorountes*] in every good work and increasing [αὐξανόμενοι, *auxanomenoi*]" (v. 10)

[a]Note that Gen. 1:26 has "rule over . . . all the earth" in both LXX and MT (also "all the earth" appears in 1:29).

Several commentators have noticed that verses 6 and 10 are an allusion to Gen. 1:28 (and perhaps Gen. 1:22: see esp. Beetham 2008: 41–59; in addition, see R. Martin 1974: 49[42] and N. Wright 1986: 53–54, 59); while O'Brien (1982: 13) and more tentatively Schweizer (1982: 36–37) view it as an echo, and yet others have merely noted similarities to the Genesis passage. Ernst (1974: 158) believes the wording of verses 6 and 10 is too general to posit a probable allusion to Gen. 1:28. It appears that the Hebrew text may be the focus, since the LXX renders the Hebrew פָּרָה (*pārâ*, bear fruit) by αὐξάνω (*auxanō*, increase) and רָבָה (*rābâ*, multiply) by πληθύνω (*plēthynō*, multiply). The LXX is a viable rendering, since αὐξάνω can have the connotation of the "increase" of fruit or of some kind of organic growth (e.g., Isa. 61:11; 1 Cor. 3:6–7). The LXX may be combining both notions of "multiplying" and "bearing fruit" by its choice of αὐξάνω in order to anticipate the directly following reference to "multiplying." Paul appears to give perhaps a bit more of a literal rendering of the verbs by translating פָּרָה (*pārâ*) by καρποφορέω (*karpophoreō*, bear fruit) and רָבָה (*rābâ*, to multiply) by αὐξάνω (*auxanō*) as well as reproducing "all the earth" either from the MT of Gen. 1:26 or 1:29 or plugging the "all" from those two verses into the wording about "earth" in 1:28 (or perhaps he could have been influenced by the LXX rendering itself of 1:28).[43]

One might doubt that such an allusion exists in Col. 1 because, whereas Gen. 1 refers to the increase of humans on "all the earth" and their dominion over it, Col. 1:6 refers to the word of the gospel "in all the world . . . bearing fruit and increasing," and 1:10 refers to good works as "bearing fruit" and Christians' growth "in the knowledge of God" (i.e., in God's word). There does appear, however, to be sufficient linguistic evidence to posit a probable and conscious allusion to Gen. 1:28. The repetition of the wording in Col. 1:10 highlights the earlier identical phrase and points further to Paul's conscious awareness of alluding to Gen. 1:28. Therefore the question is whether Paul used the text to suit his own rhetorical purposes without being interested in the original meaning of Genesis. In order to answer this question, more analysis of Gen. 1:28 is needed. More discussion than elsewhere in our study will be dedicated to this first allusion in

42. R. Martin (1974) also includes Jer. 3:16 and 23:3 within the allusion, both of which are repetitions of Gen. 1:28 that are applied to Israel.

43. Could Mark 4:8, 20 stand in the background, as some have suggested? There "seed" is interpreted to be the "word" that is heard and accepted and "bears fruit." The lexical connection is not as great as in Gen. 1:28 and its reiterations, but the idea is quite similar to that in Col. 1:6, 10.

Colossians because it is repeated and our analysis is designed in part to set up the contextual framework for some of the following allusions.

It may be that Paul's use of the Gen. 1:28 language about the beginning of the old creation, despite its apparently different application, is intended to indicate merely the general notion that a new creation has been inaugurated with believers because of their identification with Christ. But more may be in mind than this. Elsewhere we have argued that Gen. 1:26–28 was a mandate to Adam to reflect God's image (the following extended discussion on Gen. 1:26–28 and its use elsewhere in the OT is based on a larger study in Beale 2004: 81–121, and secondary sources cited therein). This reflection was implicitly ontological and explicitly functional. God created Adam and Eve with the internal equipment (e.g., moral, spiritual, volitional, and rational attributes) to be able functionally to "subdue," "rule," and "fill" the entire earth with the presence and glory of God. The very notion of being in God's "image" likely included reflecting the divine glory since God himself is essentially a glorious being. See Ps. 8 for an underscoring of the Adamic role to glorify God; notice the use of Ps. 8:2 [8:3 LXX] in Matt. 21:16. Being in God's "image" also suggests that Adam is God's "son," just as when Adam's son is born, Adam is said to be the "father of [a son] in his own likeness, according to his image" (Gen. 5:3; Luke 3:38 supports this by referring to "Adam, the son of God"). Certainly part of "ruling and subduing" is to "be fruitful and multiply and fill" the earth with literal children who are to join Adam in reflecting God's image and in exercising kingly dominion over the earth.

Thus Adam and Eve and their progeny were to be vice-regents and act as God's obedient children, reflecting God's ultimate glorious kingship over the earth. Already in Gen. 1–3, and relevant for Col. 1:6, 10, it is apparent that obedience to God's word was crucial to carrying out the task of Gen. 1:26, 28 (and disobedience to it led to their failure: in Gen. 2:16–17 and 3:2–4 are three examples of Eve's misquotation or intentional twisting of the divine word in Gen. 2; see Ross 1988: 133–35). Included in carrying out the mandate likely was defeating and ruling over the evil serpent partly by remembering and trusting in God's word of command in 2:16–17 (note the emphasis on God "said" or "saying" with reference to 2:16; 3:1b, 3). Nevertheless, the serpent ended up ruling over Adam and Eve by deceiving them with his word.

Being "fruitful and multiplying" in Gen. 1:28 refers to the increase of Adam and Eve's progeny, who were also to reflect God's glorious image and be part of the vanguard movement, spreading out over the earth with the goal of filling it with divine glory. This assumes that essential to Adam and Eve's raising of their children was spiritual instruction in God's word that the parents themselves were to remember and pass on, since this would be crucial to them in order to reflect the divine image.

Paul has tapped into one of the most important veins of the redemptive-historical story line of Scripture, albeit allusively. In fact, the mandate of Gen. 1:28 is repeated throughout the OT, as in Gen. 9:1, 6–7; 12:2; 17:2, 6, 8; 22:17–18; 26:3–4, 24; 28:3–4; 35:11–12; 47:27; Exod. 1:7; Lev. 26:9; Pss. 8:5–9; 107:38; Isa. 51:2; Jer. 3:16; 23:3; Ezek. 36:10–11, 29–30 (most of which contain the actual dual terminology of "increase and multiply," and several of which have the phrase "all the earth" [πᾶς + γῆ, *pas* + *gē*]; Gen. 17:8; 26:4; Ps. 8:9 [8:10]; Isa. 54:2–5; Jer. 23:3), as also in Col. 1:6, though 1:6 has κόσμος (*kosmos*); cf. also 1 Chron. 29:10–12; N. Wright 1986: 53, and to a lesser extent, O'Brien 1982: 13; also see that the subsequent repeated mandate in the OT may be within Paul's purview.

It is possible that what we see in Col. 1:6, 10 is the collective impact of these restatements upon Paul's thinking. If Paul is consciously alluding to Gen. 1:28 in verses 6 and 10,[44] how could he be appropriating this material? He appears to be focusing on the role of God's word in Gen. 2–3 in relation to carrying out the Adamic commission. This is highlighted in Col. 1:5–6, where "the word of truth" has finally begun expansion "in all the world, . . . bearing fruit and increasing" in the way the first Adam should have spread it. This expansion is also taking place "in" the Colossian believers, who have been "delivered from the domain of darkness and transferred . . . to the kingdom" (v. 13), which should have happened earlier in the case of the successive

44. See below on Col. 1:10 for further echoes of Gen. 1:26–28 that may be heard in the nearby context of Col. 1:10.

recipients of the repeated Adamic commission but did not occur in the way it has with Christ's coming. As believers continue to "bear fruit and increase," the commission of Gen. 1 is growing in them, with the inevitable result that it will expand beyond them to others. Verse 10 shows in what they are "bearing fruit and increasing": they are "bearing fruit in every good work and increasing in the knowledge of God." Reference to "the knowledge of God" is conceptually synonymous in a general way with the earlier mentioned "word of truth." The more one gains a knowledge of God's word, the more one should "bear fruit" in good works.

Therefore, believers are the created progeny of the last Adam, who are beginning to fulfill in him the mandate given to the first Adam. The Gen. 1:28 language applied to them in 1:6, 9–10 indicates that they are a part of the inaugurated new creation and are beginning to fulfill in Christ what has been left unfulfilled in the primordial mandate throughout the ages.

The book of Acts refers three times to Gen. 1:28, and, like Col. 1:6–10, appears to refer collectively to the repeated commission later in Genesis and elsewhere together with an interpretative focus on the "word":

Acts 6:7	"And the word of God continued to increase, and the number of the disciples continued to multiply greatly in Jerusalem, and a great many of the priests were becoming obedient to the faith."*
Acts 12:24	"But the word of the Lord continued to grow and to be multiplied."
Acts 19:20	"So the word of the Lord was growing mightily and prevailing."

That the repeated commission is most likely in mind in these three verses is evident from noticing that Acts 7:17 actually quotes one of the repeated commissions from Exod. 1:7, 20 (Pao 2002: 167–69; this makes Pao think that the Exodus restatement of the commission is the focus in the other restatements in Acts). The two verbs for "increase and multiply" are identical to Gen. 1:28 LXX, except for "prevail" in Acts 19:20, which uses ἰσχύω (*ischyō*) instead of πληθύνω (*plēthynō*, to multiply), though ἰσχύω occurs in Exod. 1:20 and the prefixed form in Exod. 1:7. These passages are virtually identical in sense with Col. 1:6, which all view the literal commission about progeny to be interpreted in the new age as the increase of the reception of God's word in new believers and the multiplication of believers. And, as we have seen, the notion in Col. 1:10 is very similar.

The interpretation of Gen. 1:28 that we have discovered in Colossians becomes more plausible by observing that it has various kinds of precedents in early Judaism and is attested elsewhere in early Christianity, especially through a combination of the language of Gen. 1:28 together with growing-garden imagery from Gen. 2 (see Hel. Syn. Pr. 12.44–45, 49–52; Philo, *QG* 2.56; 1 En. 10.16–22; likewise 1 En. 5.7, 10; Jub. 36.6; Josephus, *Ant.* 4.112–17; T. Levi 18.9–10, 14; CD-A 2.11–13a; 4Q158 frags. 1–2.7–8; 4Q433a frag. 2; 1QH 14.11–19 [*olim* 6.11–19]; 4Q418 frag. 81 [= 4Q423 8 + 24?]; Odes Sol. 11–12 and 38; Barn. 6.11–19).

If one had to try to classify the particular category of the "use of the OT" here in Col. 1:6, 10, possibly it is merely an analogical use. However, the closest category might be typology: the continued failure to fulfill the Genesis commission pointed to an eschatological humanity who would finally be obedient to the Genesis command. The presupposition underlying such a use is likely the notion of the "last, eschatological Adam," Jesus Christ, who first came as the true "image of the invisible God" (1:15) and who initially carried out the commission, so that his people could be identified with him and walk in his steps in continuing to obey the mandate (for further elaboration on Paul's use of these two allusions in Col. 1:6, 10, as well as the use of Gen. 1:28 in Judaism, see Beale 2007: 842–46). In Col. 1:6 and 10 Paul has given us a corporate glimpse of the individual end-time Adam to be elaborated upon in verses 15–20 (so also N. Wright 1986: 54).

1:6–7. The precise translation of verse 6 is difficult because of the two uses of "just as" (καθώς, *kathōs*). The following would appear to be the best rendering: "which has come to be present among you, just as also it is bearing fruit and increasing in all the world, just as also [it is bearing fruit and increasing] among you." The first "just as" indicates in what manner the gospel has come to the Colossians. The second "just as" serves to emphasize the first: that for the Colossians the manner that the gospel has come to be present among them is in a fruit-bearing and increasing manner exactly as in the rest of the world, further identifying them with the gospel's spread throughout the world; the third "just as" in verse 7a underscores that Epaphras's teaching, which the Colossians received, was in precise accordance with this universally spreading gospel (so also Sumney 2008: 40).

1:7. Most of the textual variants in 1:3–8 result in insignificant changes in meaning. The one that comes closest to altering the meaning significantly is found in verse 7. Some MSS read that Epaphras was "a faithful servant of Christ on behalf of us" (ἡμῶν, *hēmōn*), referring to Paul and his coworkers, instead of "on behalf of you" (ὑμῶν, *hymōn*), the Colossians. The former reading is supported by the earliest and best MSS (𝔓[46], ℵ, A, B, D, F, G), though some think it was introduced by a later scribe in order to conform it to the preceding ἡμῶν (*hēmōn*, our) in verse 7a and to the following ἡμῖν (*hēmin*, to us) in verse 8a (so Metzger 1994: 552–53). Copyists commonly confused the sound of the η (*ē*) and υ (*y*) vowels in the first- and second-person plural pronouns (Harris 2010: 20). Even though NA[28] and UBS[5] prefer "your," the "our" (ἡμῶν, *hēmōn*) reading should be preferred because of the overwhelmingly better MS evidence (following the note in the NET Bible on 1:8). Furthermore, it appears likely that a scribe would have been influenced to change an original "our" to "your" to conform it to the parallel in Col. 4:12 ("Epaphras . . . laboring on behalf of you" [ὑμῶν, *hymōn*]); in the light of 4:12 "our" in 1:7 becomes the more difficult and, therefore, on internal grounds the preferred reading (following Gnilka 1980: 37, who also lists a number of commentators on both sides of the debate; so also Wolter 1993: 56). Accordingly, the idea is that Epaphras was doing work on behalf of Paul, labor that belonged to the sphere of Paul's calling to extend the gospel to the Gentiles (Peake 1970: 498).

Epaphras may be the same person as Epaphroditus (apparently the long form of Epaphras; cf. BDF §125.1) mentioned in Phil. 2:25 and 4:18, but since it was a common name in the ancient Hellenistic world, it is difficult to know if these references allude to the same person. However, all these references may point to the same person, since both are described similarly: the Epaphroditus in Philippians is called a "brother and fellow worker," and Epaphras in Col. 1 is a "beloved fellow bond-servant" and "minister."

B. Paul Prays Continually That Believers Would Understand God's Will (1:9–14)

Here is a fuller statement of the main idea of this unit: *Paul prays continually that believers would understand God's will to live with the purpose of pleasing him in every way.*

In the introduction I argued that Paul was motivated to write to the Colossians because he had heard of the false teachers, who were attempting to lead the believers astray (2:4, 8), and that perhaps as early as 1:3–8 Paul was addressing the Colossians with the problem of false teaching in his peripheral vision. Therefore, at least partly in response to the false teaching, Paul begins by thanking God because of the Colossians' perseverance in faith, love, and hope (vv. 3–5a), which is rooted in their acceptance of the gospel, which has increasingly borne fruit in them (vv. 5b–6) and which they learned from Epaphras (vv. 7–8). We also saw that "thanksgiving" is the major point of the paragraph and that everything else forms part of the logical basis to support and uphold that point.

In addition, we observed that verses 3–9 form a literary chiasm or concentric circle (with inner circles like an archery target), and that the second outer circle of that structure or second parallel of the chiasm is Paul's prayer in verses 3b and 9a. In verse 3 we argued that Paul's thanksgiving arises during and out of his constant times of prayer. Now Paul focuses on that habitual prayer in verses 9–14. Numerous words are repeated from verses 3–8 and appear in verses 9–14, some of which will be pointed out below. These repetitions show that these two segments are closely linked (O'Brien 1982: 18; Harris 2010: 28).

The syntactical structure of verses 9–14 is as follows:

Asking
  that you may be filled with the knowledge . . .
        in wisdom . . .
    in order to walk . . .
      in order to please God . . .
    bearing fruit . . .
      increasing . . .
      being strengthened . . .
      giving thanks to the Father
        who has
          qualified . . .

He has rescued
and transferred[1]

But how are these syntactical expressions logically related to one another? Verse 9 commences the segment by unpacking the prayer that Paul only briefly mentioned earlier in verse 3. "For this reason also, since the day we heard" (v. 9a) refers back to verses 3–5, where Paul says that he thanks God because "we heard about the faith . . . and the love . . . based on the hope." Likewise now Paul prays because "we have heard" about your faith, love, and hope. The content of the prayer is that the readers would "be filled with the knowledge of His will" (v. 9b). The purpose (or intended effect) of being filled with such knowledge is that the believers live "worthy of the Lord" (v. 10a), which itself is to achieve the purpose of "pleasing" him "in every way" (v. 10b). Some of the ways by which Christians can walk worthily to please the Lord are elaborated on in a fourfold manner in verses 10c–12a: (1) by "bearing fruit" (v. 10c); (2) by "increasing in the knowledge of God" (v. 10d); (3) by being "strengthened with power" to be "steadfast and patient" (v. 11); and (4) by "thanking the Father" (v. 12a). The remainder of this paragraph (vv. 12b–14) is a description of who the "Father" is whom Paul is thanking: he has "qualified" believers to "share in the inheritance" (v. 12), and he has "rescued" them and "transferred" them "to the kingdom of His beloved Son" (v. 13). Verse 14 then says that in the Son believers "have redemption" and "forgiveness." Verses 12b–14 ultimately support or ground the idea of "thanksgiving" in verse 12a, since they elaborate on God, who is being thanked and who has provided redemption.

The content of the prayer in verse 9 focuses on the purpose of "walking worthy of the Lord" with the greater purpose of "pleasing" him (v. 10a). "To walk worthy of the Lord to please him in all respects" is supported by the fourfold manner of how to please God. That the last way of pleasing God is by offering thanks returns to the earlier notion of the same thing (v. 3a), but this time ultimately in support of "pleasing" God (v. 10b). Thus "pleasing" God is the main idea of the paragraph and is supported by all the other ideas in this literary unit.

Some commentators see a new paragraph break beginning with "giving thanks" in verse 12, but there is no exegetical basis for this (see the good assessment of O'Brien 1982: 19–20).[2]

1. See Harris (2010: 25) for a very similar structure, though I have veered from it in some minor ways.

2. In particular, some see the participle "thanking" to have an imperative thrust and to begin a new section of thought (so R. Martin 1974: 53; Schweizer 1982: 47), but this would break it off from its parallelism with the preceding three adverbial participles of manner that modify "walk" in verse 10; in addition, the use of anarthrous participles in an imperatival sense is rare in Paul (see further Dunn 1996: 68) and in the NT generally (Wallace 1996: 650).

Exegesis and Exposition

[9]For this reason . . . , since the day we heard of it, we [also] have not ceased to pray for you and to ask that you may be filled with the knowledge of His will in all spiritual wisdom and understanding, [10]so that you will walk in a manner worthy of the Lord, to please Him in all respects, bearing fruit in every good work and increasing in the knowledge of God; [11]strengthened with all power, according to His glorious might, for the attaining of all steadfastness and patience; joyously [12]giving thanks to ⌜the Father⌝, who has ⌜qualified⌝ ⌜us⌝ to share in the inheritance of the saints in Light, [13][who] . . . rescued us from the domain of darkness, and transferred us to the kingdom of His beloved Son, [14]in whom we have redemption ⌜ ⌝, the forgiveness of sins.

1:9 *As a result of hearing about the readers' faith, love, and hope, Paul constantly prays that they will understand God's will.* Paul's thanksgiving in verse 3 arises out of his frequent times of prayer. Now in verses 9–14 Paul elaborates on the content of that constant prayer. Verse 9 begins by explaining the reason ("for this reason") for the prayer that Paul merely mentioned in passing in verse 3.[3] Most commentators rightly see this as referring to verses 3–8 giving the "reason" he has in mind. That is, Paul's prayer now arises out of the thankful acknowledgment of their faith, love, and hope. He thus prays that they will increase in their spiritual fruits.

The phrase "since the day we heard" (ἀφ' ἧς ἡμέρας ἠκούσαμεν, *aph' hēs hēmeras ēkousamen*, v. 9a) pinpoints the particular reason Paul has in mind in the preceding segment, since the phrase refers back to verses 3–5, where Paul says that he thanks God because "we heard [ἀκούσαντες, *akousantes*] about the faith . . . and the love . . . based on the hope." This is the corollary development to the readers' initial hearing of the gospel, reported in verse 6: "from which day you heard" (ἀφ' ἧς ἡμέρας ἠκούσατε, *aph' hēs hēmeras ēkousate*). Similarly in verse 9, in addition to thanking God (v. 3), Paul "also" (καί, *kai*) prays[4] because "we have heard" about your faith, love, and hope. The content of Paul's "praying" includes not only thanksgiving (v. 3) but also "asking" (αἰτούμενοι, *aitoumenoi*) God for particular things.

The specific content of his request is "that" (note the declarative ἵνα, *hina*) the readers be "filled with the knowledge of his [God's] will." The word "be filled" (πληρόω, *plēroō*) does not refer to some kind of spatial filling of the Christian, but it figuratively indicates that by which one is characterized. For example, the verb elsewhere refers to people being characterized by various attributes, such as unrighteousness (Rom. 1:29), joy and peace (15:13),

3. Thus, the διὰ τοῦτο (*dia touto*) refers back to verses 3–8 and not forward to "that" (ἵνα, *hina*) in verse 9 and the following content of the prayer (see Callow 2002: 25). While the διὰ τοῦτο (*dia touto*) refers back to verses 3–8, it is also an adverbial modifier of the verbs ("we do not cease praying and asking"), which is always the way Paul syntactically uses διὰ τοῦτο (*dia touto*) elsewhere.

4. The καί (*kai*) here is adverbial, modifying the verb ("praying"), which is the way the word functions in its only other uses where it follows διὰ τοῦτο in Paul (Eph. 1:15; 1 Thess. 2:13; 3:5), as well as elsewhere in the NT (Matt. 24:44; Luke 11:49; John 12:18).

goodness (15:14), and so on (see likewise 2 Cor. 7:4; Phil. 1:11). Here Paul asks that the Colossians be characterized by knowing God's "will." God's "will" (θέλημα, *thelēma*) in Pauline usage can often refer to his decretive will (i.e., his unalterable redemptive-historical plan; e.g., Eph. 1:1, 5, 9, 11) or to his preceptive will (i.e., his commands for his people to obey; see, e.g., Rom. 2:18; 12:2; Eph. 6:6; 1 Thess. 4:3). Here God's commanding "will" is in mind, as is clear from the directly following purpose of "knowing God's will" so that the Colossians would live in a godly way (e.g., "walking worthy of the Lord," "bearing fruit").

Some commentators view the phrase "in all spiritual wisdom and understanding" to reflect a broad OT-Jewish tradition in which the phrase is often found. More probably, however, the wording alludes only to Exod. 31:3; 35:31–32; and 1 Kings 7:14 (7:2 LXX), and possibly secondarily to Isa. 11:2–3. These are the only texts where (1) the "Spirit" and (2) "filling" (though different verbs in the Exodus and Isaiah texts) are (3) directly linked to "wisdom and understanding" and "knowledge." First Kings 7 lacks explicit mention of the "Spirit," but it does use a form of the very same verb "fill" (πληρόω, *plēroō*), and it uses it in the same passive voice "filled" (πεπληρωμένος, *peplērōmenos*). Exodus and 1 Kings are more prominent in the allusion, since, like Col. 1:9, it sees the effect of the filling to be that of doing God's will "in every work" (Exod. 31:3; 35:31–32; 1 Kings 7:14 [7:2 LXX]), a phrase not found in Isa. 11:2–3. The Exodus passages say that God filled Israelites (Bezalel, Oholiab, and others) with his Spirit to have skill in building the tabernacle (cf. Exod. 31:1–11). First Kings 7 says the same thing with reference to building Solomon's temple, but the "filling" applies only to one person (Hiram), and there is no explicit reference to the "Spirit." Isaiah 11:2 refers to the future king on whom God's "Spirit will rest, . . . the spirit of wisdom and understanding, . . . the spirit of knowledge." Then Isa. 11:2–3 culminates in a central focus on the temple: "my holy mountain" (11:9), a development of "the mountain of the house of the Lord" in Isa. 2:2. Thus all four of the texts from Exod. 31; 35; 1 Kings 7; and Isa. 11 (if the last is in mind) enforce the theme of the temple (see additional notes for textual comparisons and further discussion of the allusions).

The point of the allusion in Col. 1:9 is that Paul is praying that God would fill believers with the Spirit in order that they would build their ethical lives skillfully, as verse 10 will make clear ("to walk, . . . bearing fruit in every good work"). But since "every good work" in Col. 1:10 is still part of the Exod. 31:3; 35:31–32; and 1 Kings 7:14 allusion referring to temple building, the believers' "bearing fruit in every good work" is part of the process of them contributing to building up the body of Christ (as evident also from 1:6), which, as we will see, is the new spiritual temple. That God is the one who will do the filling is also apparent, since Paul is praying *to God* that the believers will "be filled" (Harris 2010: 30). The combination of "knowledge" (ἐπίγνωσις, *epignōsis*), "wisdom" (σοφία, *sophia*), and "understanding" (σύνεσις, *synesis*) in verse 9b is carefully chosen to anticipate the use of the very same three Greek words in 2:2–3,[5] where they are focused on Christ and are immediately contrasted with false yet "persuasive argument" (2:4), which is later referred to as having "the appearance of wisdom in self-made religion" (2:23). That Paul would allude to the same three words in specific OT passages suggests that he is already contrasting true Israelite wisdom and knowledge with false Jewish understanding (recalling that the false teaching of Colossians has a partly Jewish origin). Later we will see that part of that false understanding had to do with a wrong view of the temple.

The content of the "knowledge" (ἐπίγνωσις) is defined as consisting "in all spiritual wisdom and understanding": ἐν (*en*, in) plus the dative (πάσῃ σοφίᾳ καὶ συνέσει, *pasē sophia kai synesei*) modifies the verbal noun "knowledge" (ἐπίγνωσις) and indicates content.[6] It is possible that the prepositional phrase modifies "filled," so that "in all spiritual wisdom and understanding" is the instrumentation by which God will "fill."[7] However, that "wisdom and understanding" modifies and unpacks the content of the verbal notion of "knowing" (i.e., "knowledge") is apparent from our preceding observation that this phrase is part of an allusion to Exod. 31 and 35 and 1 Kings 7, as well as perhaps secondarily Isa. 11:2, where "knowledge," "wisdom," and "understanding" are placed in synonymous parallelism, and all convey the general notion of "effective understanding."[8] This is a "wisdom and understanding" about God's will, especially how he wants them to live. The adjective "spiritual" (πνευματικός, *pneumatikos*) refers to God's Spirit, who imparts the "understanding," as well as the "wisdom,"[9] which is also clear from the Exod. 31 and 35 allusion (see further the additional notes and see the same use of πνευματικός in 3:16: "spirit-given psalms, hymns, and songs"). "In all" (ἐν πάσῃ, *en pasē*) refers to every kind of spiritual wisdom and understanding (Harris 2010: 31), especially since the wisdom and understanding in the Exodus, 1 Kings, and Isaiah texts are so inextricably linked and synonymous.

What is the source of the "knowledge," "wisdom," and "understanding" of God? Paul would say it is the word of God in Scripture and nothing else.[10]

5. Note the additional synonym of γνῶσις (*gnōsis*, knowledge) in 2:3, which emphasizes the idea of the other three words, and notice that 3:16 directly develops the same wealth of "wisdom" in Christ from 2:3 with respect to "teaching and warning." In addition, the "wisdom" of 4:5 is directly related to the Colossians' "answering" people about their faith. Lightfoot (1875: 137) also sees a link between the mention of true "wisdom" versus false wisdom (in 2:23) but apparently on the basis only of the common use of the word "wisdom" (cf. similarly R. Martin 1974: 51).

6. See Moule (1957: 53), followed by O'Brien (1982: 21); and cf. Wallace 1996: 170–71.

7. It is also possible that "in all spiritual wisdom and understanding" modifies the following "to walk" in verse 10 instead of modifying the verbal noun "knowledge" (so Harris 2010: 30–31). Although D. Moo (2008: 94) notes this possibility, he does not prefer it and rightly takes the passive verb as a divine passive, so that God is the subject of the filling.

8. Cf. similarly Sumney (2008: 46–47), though he does not see a conscious allusion to any specific OT passage.

9. Abbott (1897: 202) notes the parallel of 1 Cor. 12:8 for the "Spirit" giving "wisdom."

10. Following Calvin (1972: 304), whose view is borne out by the following texts: Rom. 2:17–21; 3:2; 9:6; Col. 3:16. Note the wording in Col. 3:16 of "in all wisdom teaching and

The fact that Paul derives his view of Spirit-given wisdom and understanding from Exod. 31 and 35 and implicitly 1 Kings 7, as well as possibly Isa. 11, further shows that his source for apprehending such things is Scripture. The greater focus in Colossians is that Christ is the ultimate source of wisdom (Col. 2:3) and thus the source of the divine word through his Spirit (see Col. 3:16, where Christ, the Spirit, and word are inextricably linked).

The main point of the prayer in verse 9 builds toward readers being "filled with the wise and perceptive knowledge of his [God's] will."*

The purposes of knowing God's will are to live worthy of him and to please **1:10a**
him. Paul now sets forth the purposes of knowing God's will.[11] The first purpose is that the believers "walk worthy of the Lord." Knowing God's will should engender godly conduct (D. Moo 2008: 94), since this is a fruit of the Spirit, recalling that the "knowledge" and "wisdom and understanding" in verse 9b are given by the Spirit. In fact, the following references to "bearing fruit and increasing" (v. 10b) fit naturally as results of the Spirit's work (Gal. 5:22–23, "the fruit of the Spirit"), as does the mention of "patience" and "joy" (v. 11b), which are part of the Spirit's fruit in Gal. 5:22–23 (following R. Martin 1974: 52–53). Of course, "walk" is figurative for "live" or "conducting" one's life. "Worthily" (ἀξίως, *axiōs*), the adverbial form of the verb "to be worthy" (ἀξιόω, *axioō*), together with the adjectival form "worthy" (ἄξιος, *axios*) can convey notions of "deserving, suitable or fitting" (BDAG 94). The adverb occurs six times in the NT, five of which are in Paul. Every time the adverb occurs outside of Col. 1:10, it refers to Christian behavior being "fitting" with or "suitable to" being a "saint" (Rom. 16:2), to Christian "calling" (Eph. 4:1), to the "gospel" (Phil. 1:27), or to God (1 Thess. 2:12; 3 John 6). The use in Col. 1:10 has the last sense, though the reference is to living in a way that is "fitting" not to God the Father but specifically to the "Lord" Jesus, since 1:3 has just distinguished "God the Father" from "our *Lord* Jesus Christ," and this distinction occurs in the directly following context of the epistle (2:6; 3:17; the other eight uses in the letter presumably have the same reference). That is, the ethical character of the believer is to be fitting with or matching the character of Jesus. For example, in 3:13 believers are commanded to "forgive each other," and then the basis for that command is given: "Just as also the Lord forgave you, in the same manner should you."*

Thus the believer's ethical lifestyle is to reflect that of Jesus. The purpose of living in a manner that matches Jesus's lifestyle is "in order that" they would "please him <u>in every way</u>" (cf. NIV). The εἰς (*eis*) preceding "please him in every way" modifies the infinitive "walk," indicating the purpose of walking (though it could represent the intended result, which is very similar).

---

admonishing one another with psalms and hymns and spiritual songs," the latter of which likely include OT psalms.

11. This is the function of the epexegetical infinitive "walk" (περιπατῆσαι, *peripatēsai*), which indicates the purpose of being "filled" in verse 9 (Robertson 1934: 1086–87), though possibly it indicates an intended result (so Lightfoot 1875: 137), which is virtually the same idea.

Even this purpose matches Jesus's own character, as found in Rom. 15:1–3: believers are not to "please themselves" but "each . . . is to please his neighbor. . . . For even Christ did not please himself" but God. The word ἀρεσκεία (*areskeia*) in Hellenistic Greek can refer to one who gains favor by performing "exceptional public service" or by exhibiting a behavior of "devotion" (BDAG 129, s.v. ἀρεσκεία).[12] Believers serve the Lord by pleasing him. The purpose of believers pleasing the Lord or God occurs elsewhere in Paul, which shows how important this is for Christian living (see the verbal form of ἀρεσκεία in 1 Cor. 7:32; 1 Thess. 2:4; 4:1; cf. Gal. 1:10 and 2 Tim. 2:4). Everything (εἰς πᾶσαν, *eis pasan*) a follower of Jesus does is to be "pleasing" to him, which is the main point so far in verses 9–10a.

1:10b *Paul elaborates on a fourfold manner by which believers walk worthily, to please the Lord.* Now Paul uses the first two of four adverbial participles that all modify the infinitive "walk" and explain the manner or way in which saints are to walk, though the participles may express the means by which the "walk" is carried out[13] (there is a fine line between these two uses).[14] That "manner/way" is uppermost in mind is apparent from the directly preceding phrase "please him in every way" (following NIV),[15] which introduces the four participles (Pao 2012: 71). Thus these participles define what is "walking worthily."

First, they are to "walk" by "bearing fruit [καρποφοροῦντες, *karpophorountes*] in every good work" (= all kinds of good works)[16] and, second, by "increasing [αὐξανόμενοι, *auxanomenoi*] in the knowledge of God." The dative phrases modifying each participle indicate either the sphere in which or the manner by which they are growing, though it could be the means by which they multiply (the latter proposed by Abbott 1897: 203; Lohse 1971: 29; Dunn 1996: 72; Sumney 2008: 49). The dative phrase ἐν παντὶ ἔργῳ ἀγαθῷ (*en panti ergo agathō*, in every good work) does not refer specifically to the sphere of the action (though that is generally true) nor does it indicate a separate instrument or means by which the action is accomplished. More likely the

12. The verbal form of ἀρεσκεία is used in Philo (*Unchang.* 23) to refer to God being "pleased" by a person who "desires tranquillity."

13. Pao 2012: 67, suggests this option.

14. An observation made by several commentators (e.g., O'Brien 1982: 19). Since the participles modify the infinitive περιπατῆσαι (*peripatēsai*), they should be accusative (as subjects of infinitives usually are) instead of nominative, but perhaps these are nominative because they more loosely modify the infinitive (D. Moo 2008: 96; cf. Schweizer 1982: 43), and as such they may be considered adverbial nominative absolutes. Perhaps the simplest solution is that since the infinitive itself is dependent on πληρωθῆτε (*plērōthēte*, in 1:9), the subject of which is the nominative "you," the following four nominative participles carry forward descriptions of this subject (so Lenski 1961: 36).

15. "In every way" is a rendering of εἰς πᾶσαν (*eis pasan*), which other translations render similarly as "in all respects" (NASB; likewise Geneva, NJB, NET); others translate the phrase as "fully" (NRSV, ESV, HCSB) or "unto all" (KJV).

16. Paul refers to "good works" (ἔργον + ἀγαθός, *ergon* + *agathos*) often elsewhere and even several times "every [πᾶς, *pas*] good work," but as here, he is not explicit about what those good works are.

dative defines the action of "bearing fruit" (thus, a dative of manner), and consequently it is likely that the following parallel τῇ ἐπιγνώσει τοῦ θεοῦ (*tē epignōsei tou theou*, in the knowledge of God) is the definition or manner of the "increasing."[17]

This language of "bearing fruit and increasing" is a repetition of the clear allusion to "bearing fruit and increasing" from Gen. 1:28 in 1:6 (καρποφορούμενον καὶ αὐξανόμενον, *karpophoroumenon kai auxanomenon*).[18] Paul is again applying the Adamic commission to expand throughout the earth to the believers and focusing here on the "good works" and "the knowledge of God" that are one of the ways they are fulfilling that commission. In fact, "increasing in the knowledge of God" here is further unpacked in 3:10, where believers are "being renewed [un]to a knowledge [ἐπίγνωσις, *epignōsis*] according to the image of the one who created him." This parallel indicates that the genitive "of God" in verse 10b is an objective genitive, "knowledge about God" (so also D. Moo 2008: 97, though he does not appeal to 3:10). Later we will contend that 3:10 is part of another allusion to Gen. 1–3, where "knowledge" (γινώσκειν, *ginōskein*) was crucial to whether Adam would be faithful in carrying out his mandate (cf. Gen. 2:17; see on 3:9–10).

Colossians 1:5–6 has highlighted "the word of truth" as expanding, which alludes to the role of God's word in Gen. 2–3 that was crucial for Adam to execute his commission. Verse 10 now similarly concentrates on how "the knowledge of God" is essential for the fulfillment of the commission. And if there is true "knowledge," then it will inevitably be accompanied by "good works," which arise from the knowledge. Whereas the "word of truth, the gospel," is "bearing fruit and increasing" in 1:6, now it is the Colossian Christians themselves who are "bearing fruit in every good work and increasing in the knowledge of God." The Gen. 1:28 commission is portrayed as growing within the believers, with the implied effect of an expansion beyond themselves to others, who will also share in their "knowledge" and do "good works." These are two sides of one coin: "good works" are inextricably linked to the "knowledge of God." The "bearing fruit and increasing" happen at the same time,[19] as in 1:6 and Gen. 1:28, and are thus parallel.

If one truly knows God, then good works will inevitably follow in contrast to "the evil works" that have characterized one's former life of unbelief and false knowledge (Col. 1:21; see Lohse 1971: 30). Notice that Paul begins praying that the Colossians will be given "knowledge" of God in verse 9, and then sees that it will issue into doing "good works" (v. 10b), which itself is parallel

17. For this distinction between the dative of means and that of manner, see Wallace 1996: 161.

18. There is probably no significant difference between the active participle καρποφοροῦντες here and the middle form (καρποφορούμενον, *karpophoroumenon*) in 1:6 (so MHT 3:55). Accordingly, the middle participial form of αὐξάνω (*auxanō*) in both 1:6 and 10 likely expresses an active sense.

19. Meyer 1885: 216. We have seen that they are adverbial present participles of manner, which includes a time element contemporaneous with the action of the preceding verb πληρωθῆτε in verse 9 and the infinitive περιπατῆσαι in verse 10.

to and thus directly linked to "knowledge of God" (v. 10b, i.e., "knowing God," an objective genitive). This is not circular reasoning but more like a spiral: knowledge of God leads to good works and to even greater knowledge of God (cf. N. Wright 1986: 58).

Consequently, Christians are the offspring of the last Adam, who has begun to carry out the Gen. 1:28 mandate, on which Col. 1:15–20 elaborates. By identification and union with Christ, his progeny are a part of the beginning new creation and are continuing to carry out this Adamic commission, which had not been successfully fulfilled throughout the ages until Christ came. The ongoing failure to carry out the mandate pointed to a latter-day humanity who would finally be obedient to the primal commandment.[20]

Thus the two adverbial participles in verse 10 describe the Adamic and new-creational[21] manner in which believers are to "walk worthy of God" in order to "please" him.

1:11 The third adverbial participle explaining the manner of "walking" is "strengthened" (δυναμούμενοι, *dynamoumenoi*) "for all steadfastness and patience" (the "all" [πᾶς, *pas*] doing double duty for both nouns, all of which are in the same gender). God is certainly the unmentioned subject of the strengthening. This "strengthening" is emphasized by adding two prepositional modifiers expressing strength: "with all power" and "according to his glorious might." The first modifier likely indicates the means by which the strengthening occurs—"by means of" (ἐν, *en*) God's power.[22] The second modifier "according to" (κατά, *kata*) explains the basis or origin of the believers' strength:[23] it comes from God's "glorious might." Hence, Paul prays almost identically in Eph. 3:16 that God would "grant" to believers, "according to the richness of his glory, to be strengthened with power." "Glory" in this Ephesians parallel represents the richness of God's attributes that are being given to believers "so that Christ may dwell in them" (Eph. 3:17). The same notion of "glory" is likely in mind here, though either Christ (as Lord) or God could be the antecedent of "the might of his glory," since both are mentioned in verse 10. Nevertheless, since God is the subject of the strengthening in the Ephesians parallel, presumably it is the case here.

"Of the glory of the might" is best rendered as "glorious might," either an adjectival or qualitative genitive,[24] and the following "of him" designates that God is the possessor of this "glorious might." In Eph. 3:16 the strengthening

20. On the use of Gen. 1:28 in Col. 1:6 and 19, see further on the additional notes on 1:6 above.

21. Recall that "new-creational" here and throughout the commentary refers to the inaugurated end-time new creation.

22. The ἐν (*en*) plus the dative may indicate the means of the "strengthening" (Meyer 1885: 217; Harris 2010: 33), the sphere in which it takes place, or the content of the strengthening (Pao 2012: 72).

23. In addition to basis or cause, Harris (2012: 159) suggests the possibility of "in conformity with," referring to the amount of resources available for the strengthening (this is close to the notion of "by the standard of," another meaning of the preposition).

24. D. Moo (2008: 98) and Pao (2012: 72) prefer a qualitative genitive.

from God is imparted "through his [God's] Spirit," which is also implicitly in mind here. Paul applies the same noun "power" (δύναμις, *dynamis*) to himself in Col. 1:29 to show that his own "labor" and "striving" is based on "[God's] energy, which works mightily [ἐν δυνάμει, *en dynamei*] in [him]"* (similarly cf. Eph. 3:20).[25]

Interestingly, some might think that such a theology results in an attitude of spiritual laziness: "I don't need to be motivated to obey God, since God's power will work through me as a believer regardless of whether I am motivated to obey; I can just sit back and do nothing, and God will nevertheless work through me." On the contrary, genuine saints should be motivated to carry out God's precepts because they understand that God has provided the power for them to do so. In fact, such a theology of divine sovereignty actually provides motivation to "labor" and "strive," as Paul says it did for him (e.g., 1 Cor. 15:10). It is not coincidental that this divine power at work within Paul is what gives him ongoing strength to do all he can "to encourage" the Colossians in the face of false teaching to have "full assurance" of a true "knowledge of God's mystery, that is, Christ himself" (1:29–2:5). This concern for the threat of false teaching in the first segment of the epistle's introduction (1:3–8) has already been repeatedly observed.

The purpose (or intended result) of the "strengthening" (note the εἰς [*eis*] directly following the participial clause) is that the readers possess "all endurance and patience" (πᾶσαν ὑπομονὴν καὶ μακροθυμίαν, *pasan hypomonēn kai makrothymian*).[26] That is, God's strengthening empowers his people to have "endurance and patience" in the midst of trials (Barth and Blanke 1994: 181–82), which includes confronting false teaching.

"Patience" (μακροθυμία, *makrothymia*) is also a mark of those who are truly "elect ones" (3:12), thus providing assurance that one really does know and believe the truth even in the face of false teaching. While there may be a difference in nuance between ὑπομονή (*hypomonē*) and μακροθυμία (*makrothymia*),[27] they are generally synonyms that can overlap with the notion of "patience," so that the point here apparently is to emphasize that overlapping notion (e.g., see James 5:10–11, and possibly 2 Tim. 3:10).[28] The "unto all" (εἰς πᾶσαν, *eis pasan*) indicates that this is "endurance and patience" of every kind (Harris 2010: 33), which is suited for various kinds of situations as needed. This is now the fifth use of πᾶς (*pas*) in verses 9–11, which appears to emphasize that God will "fill" the Colossians with everything they need to know and do God's will (v. 9b; cf. Hay 2000: 45).

25. Elsewhere Paul sees that God's "power" (δύναμις, *dynamis*) is the basis of, the source of, or the means of the believers' ability to live godly lives (Rom. 15:13, 19; 2 Cor. 4:7; Eph. 1:19; 3:7, 16, 20; 2 Tim. 1:8).

26. Again, it is possible that the εἰς (*eis*) modifying the participle indicates intended result, which is virtually the same as purpose.

27. See N. Wright (1986: 60), who finds a distinction in meaning between the two words.

28. See BDAG (612–13, s.v. μακροθυμία; and 1039–40, s.v. ὑπομονή) for the overlapping notion of both nouns in terms of steadfastness or endurance.

1:12 The fourth adverbial participle describing the manner of "walking" is "thanking" (εὐχαριστοῦντες, *eucharistountes*), which is to be done "joyously"[29] (vv. 11b–12). "Joyously" (μετὰ χαρᾶς, *meta charas*) is placed as a preceding modifier of "thanking" for emphasis (Abbott 1897: 205). The "Father" is the object of the thanks. Since "thanking the Father" occurred also in verse 3, several commentators think that Paul may be indicating that he is finishing the introductory thanksgiving (e.g., Callow 2002: 13). This becomes less likely by the observation, however, that in verse 12 "giving thanks" is parallel to the preceding three adverbial participles, all of which are logically supportive of "walking worthily" in verse 10a. Indeed, as we have seen, these four participial descriptions in 1:10b–12 of how to "walk" have the aim of "pleasing" God (v. 10a). It is true that "thanking" repeats the thanksgiving of verse 3. But this time, together with the prior three adverbial participles, it is ultimately in support of "walking worthily, to please God" as the main point so far, whereas in verses 3–8 thanking was the main point itself. So it is not so clear that this second repetition of "thanksgiving" is an *inclusio* parallel to that of verse 3 and signals the end of the introductory thanksgiving. Our view is that the initial thanksgiving concluded in verse 8.

The rest of the paragraph (vv. 12b–14) is an elaboration of the Father being "thanked," which also implicitly entails the notion of why he is being thanked (so also Hendriksen 1964: 55), so that this elaboration is subsumed under and undergirds the thanksgiving, which is the main point of verses 12b–14.[30] Accordingly, there is implicit thanks for the Father's qualifying of the saints (v. 12), his redemption of them (v. 13), and thanks for the person of the Son (v. 14), the latter of which is expanded upon in verses 15–23 (cf., e.g., Melick 1991: 205).

The Father is described in terms of what he has done. First, verse 12 says that he "has qualified" believers for a great "inheritance." The Greek verb ἱκανόω[31] (*hikanoō*, and adjective form, ἱκανός, *hikanos*) in the NT and LXX convey notions of being "worthy," "fitting," "appropriate" (each of the three renderings with nuances of being "adequate" or "qualified") and various nuances of being "sufficient" (see BDAG 472–73). The first two meanings overlap in meaning with "worthily" (ἀξίως, *axiōs*) in verse 10, the adverbial form of "to be worthy" (ἀξιόω, *axioō*), which, together with the adjectival form

29. Some commentators think "joyously" modifies the verbal notion of being "steadfast and patient" (e.g., Barth and Blanke 1994: 183; likewise Lightfoot 1875: 138). This is possible, but following D. Moo 2008: 100, since the prior three participles have adverbial modifiers, it suits that pattern to have one here also. And Sumney (2008: 51) notes that the first and third participles also have the modifying prepositional phrase preceding them. Furthermore, prepositional phrases typically modify verbs or adverbial participles rather than nouns, although they can sometimes modify nouns with a verbal sense. Thematically, "with joy" as a modifier fits with either the preceding or following wording.

30. Similarly, Pao (2012: 74) takes the first adjectival participle τῷ ἱκανώσαντι (*tō hikanōsanti*, the one having qualified) to indicate the reason for the thanksgiving.

31. See the additional note concerning ἱκανώσαντι (*hikanōsanti*) versus the textual variant καλέσαντι (*kalesanti*).

"worthy" (ἄξιος, *axios*), we saw can convey notions of "deserving, suitable or fitting." In fact, the Synoptic Gospels use the two words synonymously with the meaning of "worthy" or "fitting" (see Luke 7:4–6). We concluded that "suitable" or "fitting" is the meaning in Col. 1:10, with respect to believers living in a manner that matches Christ's character. Here we find that it is God who has caused the saints to be "worthy," "qualified," or "fitting" to receive "the inheritance,"[32] which develops the earlier reference to "the hope laid up for you in heaven" (v. 5). In contrast to the "worthiness" of the saints' ongoing lifestyle in verse 10, this refers to a decisive once-for-all "redemption" and "the forgiveness of sins" (cf. v. 14), by which God has caused them to be "worthy" or "qualified" for this inheritance.

As the Israelites were "delivered from" bondage in Egypt, were called "saints," and received "a share of the inheritance" in the land of Canaan, so likewise the new-covenant community had been "rescued from" a larger-scale slavery (i.e., satanic "darkness," v. 13) and had been "qualified . . . to share" in a grander "inheritance of the saints in Light." Literally, believers have been qualified to have a "share of the inheritance." "Of the inheritance" is not a partitive genitive ("a share in the inheritance"; so Harris 2010: 34); it is probably an appositional genitive ("share [or portion], which is the inheritance"). The reason for this is because the combination of the words μερίς [*meris*] and κλῆρος (*klēros*) occurs seven times in the LXX of Numbers, Deuteronomy, and Joshua as synonyms to refer to the promised land (e.g., Deut. 10:9: "Therefore the Levites have no portion nor inheritance"*).[33] Thus "share" (or "portion") is not a subset of the "inheritance" but is another way of referring to the inheritance. The same background shows that the εἰς (*eis*) preceding "share of the inheritance" expresses destination or purpose, since after God delivered Israel at the exodus, his purpose was that they gain possession of the promised land as an inheritance.[34] The resulting paraphrase would be "the one who qualified you in order that you would receive a share, which is the inheritance."[35] The dual idea of sphere and destination is confirmed from verse 13 ("He . . . transferred us to the kingdom").

"Of the saints" indicates that the "inheritance" is possessed by the latter-day Israelite saints, the church (as we saw in 1:2, echoing here and likely also there Dan. 7:18, 22), which has experienced a grander exodus than that of

32. The only other use of the verb in the NT refers to God "qualifying" Paul to be an apostolic servant (2 Cor. 3:6). Though 2 Cor. 3:6 has "made *us* adequate," Paul is likely the focus, even if Timothy and Sylvanus (cf. 2 Cor. 1:19) are secondarily included.

33. Lightfoot (1875: 139) and D. Moo (2008: 101) argue similarly.

34. Possibly the εἰς has the notion of the inheritance to be possessed by God's people, though such a usage of εἰς is rare (see BDAG 289 for both notions of destination/purpose and "focus on the area within the point reached").

35. Note that 1QapGen ar 16 refers to land given as a "lot" and "an everlasting inheritance" (synonymously), which was given to Japheth and Shem. So also 1QS 11.7–8: "To those whom God has selected he has given them as [an] everlasting possession; until they inherit them in the lot of the holy ones . . . an everlasting plantation" (cited by Dunn 1996: 76).

Israel from Egypt.[36] Plural "saints" was first used of Israel, directly after God delivered them from Egypt, as in Lev. 11:45 LXX: "For I am the LORD who brought you up out of the land of Egypt to be your God: and you shall be holy ones [saints, ἅγιοι, *hagioi*], for I the LORD am holy" (see also Lev. 11:44; 19:2; 20:7, 26; 21:6; Num. 15:40; 16:3).[37] Somewhat similar to Col. 1:5 ("the hope laid up . . . in heaven"), the gaining of this inheritance has begun with Christ's first coming and will be consummated at his final coming. In particular, in verse 5 we saw that this hoped-for inheritance had begun in the believers' participation in Christ's resurrected status. If this is going in the correct direction, then "the share of the inheritance" has begun in their participation in Christ's resurrection. Consequently, Paul sees the promised land in the OT as a foreshadowing of the new creation, which has begun in Christ's resurrection (Col. 1:15–18 will expand on Christ's resurrection as the beginning of new creation). Paul argues the same thing about the promised land in Eph. 1:13–14 and elsewhere (see the additional notes).

That the "saints are in the sphere of the light"[38] is part of the exodus redemption background, since Isaiah's second-exodus prophecies portray Israel as being delivered from "darkness" to "light" (e.g., Isa. 42:6–7, 16). "Light" also echoes the light of the first creation (Isa. 60:1–3), of which the exodus itself was a recapitulation and of which the promised land was an adumbration (see the additional notes below for expansion of the background involving exodus / second exodus and new creation). In keeping with this OT

36. Some commentators prefer that "saints" refers to angels, especially because of some parallels in Qumran (e.g., 1QS 11.7–8, where believers are given an "eternal possession . . . [and] made heirs in the legacy of the Holy Ones [saints]; with the Angels has he united their assembly"; Wise, Abegg, and Cook 2005). Accordingly, for an identification of "saints" with angels, among others, see R. Martin (1974: 54), Pokorný (1991: 52), as well as MacDonald (2000: 50), who adduces other Jewish texts in favor of the notion. Bird (2009: 43) observes that not only can "saints" refer to angels but "light" is sometimes associated with angels and the heavenly realm; he then suggests that in view of the mention of worship with angels in Col. 2:18, "Paul might be suggesting that believers have been qualified to inherit the rights and privileges normally given to angelic beings." Some also adduce 1QM 12.7 and 1QH[a] 11.23, among other DSS texts, in support of angelic identification. However, as we will see directly below, Acts 26:18, a very closely related passage, contains uniquely common themes ("light," "darkness," "authority," forgiveness of sins," "inheritance"). One additional common theme is "holy ones," which clearly refers to believers and not angels ("those who have been made holy by faith in me"; following O'Brien 1982: 26). In addition, the pl. of ἅγιος (*hagios*, saints) is used elsewhere in Colossians only with respect to believers (1:2, 4, 22, 26; 3:12; following Schweizer 1982: 47; in Ephesians the word in the pl. is used ten times to refer to believers). Benoit (1982: 83–101) contends that "holy ones" refers to both human saints and angels.

37. Fee (2006: 206) contends that this usage has its source in Exod. 19:6, where Israel at Mount Sinai is called "a priestly kingdom and a *holy nation* (ἔθνος ἅγιον, *ethnos hagion*).

38. Here ἐν [*en*] + the dative τῷ φωτί (*tō phōti*) indicates sphere or destination, which is in keeping with the above Isaiah background of God delivering Israel and the nations from darkness into light: the Isaiah context refers to God restoring them (and the nations along with them) from exile back into their land, where the light of God's salvific presence resides. D. Moo (2008: 102) and Pao (2012: 75) opt for the notion that it is specifically the "inheritance" that is "in the light," but the Isaianic background points toward those restored being in the light.

background, then, "in the light" primarily refers to "saints" who are "in the light" and not primarily "the inheritance," though this would be included, since the saints possess it.

After referring to the continued exodus-redemption background about God "who rescued us from the authority [NASB marg.] of darkness," this redemption in verse 13 is now further explained there as God "transferring us into the kingdom of his beloved Son."

Verse 13 begins to give the basis for verse 12 (note the interpretative rendering 1:13
"for" in the NASB, NIV, TNIV, and NLT; cf. NJB). God's "qualification" of believers "for a share in the inheritance of the saints in light" is grounded in his "rescuing us from the authority of darkness, and transferring us to the kingdom of his beloved Son." Again, the exodus background is important for determining that 1:13 is not a mere general elaboration of verse 12 (as argued by D. Moo 2008: 102), but is the precise basis for verse 12: just as God's delivering Israel from Egypt, "the house of bondage" (e.g., Exod. 20:2 KJV), was a crucial basis for enabling them then to be able to possess the land, so God's delivering people from "the authority of darkness" (v. 13) is the basis for them to be able to be qualified for the inheritance (v. 12).[39]

"Authority of darkness" has its antithetical parallel in "kingdom of his Son," so that "authority" parallels "kingdom," and "darkness" parallels "Son." Accordingly, "darkness" may be a metonymy whereby something (i.e., darkness) is substituted for something else (i.e., the person of Satan in antithetical parallelism to the person of the "Son"). The phrase then may be a genitive of source, which would be rendered "the authority arising from darkness (i.e., Satan). Alternatively, the clause may be a possessive genitive, "the authority held by the darkness." It is hard to know which option is best, but either is consistent with the phrase "the authority of Satan" found in the parallel of Acts 26:18 (cited just above).[40] Thus, in mind may be two kingdoms ruled over by two personal authorities (Callow 2002: 41).

39. The second-exodus prophecies in Isaiah portray the same logical pattern. D. Moo (2008: 103) rightly cites Exod. 6:6–8 as a good summary of this Exodus background, but does not draw the conclusion that the deliverance from Egypt is a basis for Israel to be able to inherit the land, and that the same logic is reflected in Col. 1:12–13. Additionally, Paul's awareness of the second-exodus restoration background in Isaiah is apparent from his description of his own call by the second exodus language of Isa. 42:7, 16 (noted above) together with wording uniquely similar to Col. 1:12–14: "to open their eyes in order that they may turn from darkness unto light and from the authority of Satan to God, in order that they should receive forgiveness of sins and an inheritance among those who have been made holy by faith in me"* (Acts 26:18). Here also it is clear that believers must first go from *darkness and Satan's authority* (both of which refer to the same reality) to God before they can receive an "inheritance." In fact, it is probable that Paul is reflecting on his call recorded in Acts 26:18 in Col. 1:12–14 (cf. Moule 1957: 56; Hendriksen 1964: 62, the latter who sees Paul echoing the Acts passage here).

40. Here Eph. 2:2 is a good parallel: the believers had "walked formerly . . . according to the one ruling over the authority of the air."* Ephesians 6:11–12 refers to the demonic "world powers of this darkness" over and through which the "devil" rules. Another parallel with the exodus background may point further to a personal identification of "darkness":

It is also quite possible and perhaps preferable, however, to understand "authority" (ἐξουσία, *exousia*) as referring to Satan and take "the darkness" as indicating the kind of realm over which Satan has authority (in this case "of darkness" would be an objective genitive).[41] This is pointed to by the use of "authority" elsewhere in Colossians and Ephesians, where without exception "authority" refers to personal cosmic evil beings (Col. 1:16; 2:10, 15; Eph. 1:21; 3:10; 6:12). In context, part of the point would be that they have been "delivered from the power of darkness" because Christ's redemptive work has subjected these "authorities" to himself (1:20; 2:10, 15), and verse 14 begins the explanation of how that occurred. Likewise, Christ had the power to subject the evil authorities because he is the one as Creator who brought them into being in the first place (1:16).[42]

God's "delivering" may be identical to the "transferring" (so D. Moo 2008: 102), but it appears more to focus on what "qualifies" his people to be "transferred into the kingdom,"[43] again in keeping with the parallel of the Egyptian deliverance, where removal from Egypt would bring Israel to God at Sinai and bring about Israel's formal constitution as a "kingdom" (see Exod. 19:1–6).[44] "Kingdom" in Col. 1:13 is a further interpretation of the preceding "inheritance" in verse 12.

This "kingdom" belongs to God's "beloved Son" (lit., "the son of the love of him"), "of the love" being an adjectival genitive (so likewise Robertson 1934: 496) and "of him" a subjective genitive: God is the subject of the loving, though of course he possesses such love.[45] This appears to be an

In Exod. 6:6 LXX, God says, "I will lead you out from the *power* [δυναστεία, *dynasteia*] *of the Egyptians*" (observed by Fee 2006: 206). Likewise, Qumran typically uses the phrase "Sons of Darkness," which expresses a clear personal element related to the darkness (e.g., 1QM 1.1, 10, 16; 3.6, 9; 13.16; 14.17; 16.11), though note also the phrase "rule of darkness," where the subject of the "rule" is "Belial" (1QM 13.11–12). Some take the phrase in Col. 1:13 to be an appositional genitive ("the authority, which is the darkness"; Wallace 1996: 100), or a qualitative or descriptive genitive ("the dominion that is characterized by darkness"), which Harris (2010: 32) and D. Moo (2008: 104) prefer, seeing no evidence for a personal reference to Satan.

41. Possibly this may be an epexegetical genitive: "the dominion which is characterized by darkness"; cf. Pao 2012: 76.

42. See Fee (2006: 206–7) for this connection to 1:16 and 1:20.

43. For the same focus of the verb "transfer," see 2 Macc. 11:23: "Since our father was <u>transferred</u> [or <u>translated</u>] unto the gods, we want those from our kingdom to be quiet."* Lightfoot (1875: 141–42) says the verb was used of the "wholesale deportation of peoples" by their conquering kings, and as an example he cites Josephus (*Ant.* 9.235), who uses the verb to refer to Tiglath-Pileser removing the Transjordanian tribes: "He transported them to his own kingdom"; others cite also *Ant.* 12.149, though a different verb than in Col. 1:13 is used.

44. Exodus 19:1–3 portrays Israel going out of Egypt and then coming to God at Sinai; 19:4–6 reads: "I bore you on eagles' wings <u>and</u> [i.e., <u>with the purpose that I</u>] brought you to myself. . . . Now then, if you will indeed obey my voice and keep my covenant, . . . you shall be to me a kingdom of priests."

45. D. Moo (2008: 105) prefers a genitive of possession as the focus ("love that belongs to God"). It is possible that the genitive αὐτοῦ (*autou*) modifies "son," so that the precise idea may be that Jesus is the possession of God.

allusion to 2 Sam. 7:12–16, where God promises that one of David's seed would be a "son" to God, would have an eternal kingdom, and that God's "lovingkindness" would be with this descendant. The apostle views this as having its ultimate fulfillment in Christ and his kingdom (see further in the additional notes). That God "transferred" people that he "delivered" into "the kingdom of his beloved Son" is yet another expression of inaugurated eschatology, since this refers to the end-time kingdom prophesied in the OT, especially in 2 Sam. 7 (see also O'Brien 1982: 26). Elsewhere, just as here, Paul also refers to the inaugurated end-time kingdom (Rom. 14:17; 1 Cor. 4:20; apparently also Col. 4:11), though he sometimes refers to the future coming of the kingdom in its final form (1 Cor. 6:9–10; 15:24, 50; Gal. 5:21; Eph. 5:5[?]; 1 Thess. 2:12; 2 Thess. 1:5; 2 Tim. 4:1, 18; see Beale 2003: 75; cf. 185).

But how does God's deliverance of his people in verse 13 provide the basis for 1:14
God "qualifying" people for the "inheritance" in verse 12? This qualification is based on or accomplished through God's "deliverance," which is effected by means of the Son's "redemption, the forgiveness of sins," the latter further defining what is entailed in "redemption" (so also Hay 2000: 49). Recalling the exodus background already in mind in verses 12–13, God's redemption of Israel out of Egypt involved "delivering" them out of bondage, which itself was based on the prior identification with the blood of the Passover lamb. Thus God "qualifies" saints for the inheritance of the kingdom on the basis of or by means of the redemptive work of God's Son in forgiving the sins of his people. The lexical combinations "deliver from" (ῥύομαι + ἐκ, *rhyomai* + *ek*) and "redemption/redeem" (ἀπολύτρωσις/λυτρόω + ἐκ, *apolytrōsis/lytroō* + *ek*) occur uniquely in Exodus and Col. 1:13–14, which points strongly to an exodus allusion here (see again the additional notes below for expansion of this exodus background). Thus, whereas the saints' ongoing lifestyle of godliness makes them "worthy" of God in verse 10, here it is not their own work but God's work through the Son's "redemption" that makes them "worthy" of receiving "the inheritance" of the "kingdom." The godly fruit of God's people, however, flows inevitably from God's work of redemption that has been applied to them. In fact, the "in whom" of verse 14 expresses the notion of the saints' identification or union with Christ.

The phrase "the forgiveness [ἄφεσιν, *aphesin*] of sins" is in apposition to "redemption," and is roughly synonymous with it. As "redemption" expressed "deliverance from bondage," so ἄφεσις (*aphesis*) connotes "release" from some kind of debt or bondage in the LXX and likely retains that sense here, with the debt or bondage being to sin: "release from sins."[46]

46. The term ἄφεσις translates יוֹבֵל (*yôbēl*, jubilee) more than any other Hebrew word: e.g., Lev. 25:10, 11, 12, 13, 28, 31, 33. ἄφεσις (*aphesis*) also is a rendering of דְּרוֹר (*dərôr*, release) and שׁמט (*šmṭ*, release) in the LXX (see Hatch and Redpath 1954: 1.182). The word in Hellenistic Greek means "release" (MM 96), and in the LXX has notions of "remission, the act of

Here Paul does not state how that union accomplishes their "redemption" and "forgiveness of sins," but he does elaborate on more of these details in 1:20–22 and 2:10–15, especially with respect to the believers' identification by faith with Christ's death and resurrection (see further on 1:20–22 and 2:10–15). The "in whom" (ἐν ᾧ, *en hō*) thus indicates that believers have been placed into union with Christ, but the notion of agency is likely included ("by means of whom"), since the following context of verses 16–17 also uses ἐν αὐτῷ (*en autō*) with an idea of agency[47] (cf. also explicit phrases expressing agency in 1:20).

"We have" (ἔχομεν, *echomen*) plus an abstract noun in Paul can indicate that believers are in some kind of condition or state, such as of "peace" (Rom. 5:1), "confidence" (2 Cor. 3:4), or "boldness" (Eph. 3:12).[48] The more exact idea then in Col. 1:14 is that saints in union with Christ are in a condition of "forgiveness," as well as "redemption," which has resulted from Christ's work of redeeming and forgiving them.

Thus, in this paragraph, Paul prays that the Colossians will know God's will (v. 9) in order to "walk worthy of God," which is aimed at obtaining the goal of "pleasing" him (v. 10a), and this is the zenith point of the segment, since it is the idea supported by all the other following ideas in verses 10b–14, with verses 10b–14 giving four ways that believers can "walk worthily," to accomplish the aim of "pleasing" God.

Additional Notes

1:9. Some commentators (e.g., N. Wright 1986: 58; MacDonald 2000: 48; Ernst 1974: 161) view the concluding phrase, "in all wisdom and spiritual understanding," to reflect a broad OT-Jewish tradition in which the phrase is repeated: e.g., Exod. 31:3; 35:31; Deut. 4:6; 1 Chron. 22:12; 2 Chron. 1:10–12; Job 12:13; 28:20; 39:17; Pss. 49:3; 111:10 (LXX: 48:4; 110:10); Prov. 1:7; 2:2, 3, 6; 9:10; 24:3; Isa. 10:13; 11:2; Jer. 51:15 (28:15 LXX); Dan. 1:17; 2:21; Sir. 1:4; 14:20; 15:3; 39:6; Bar. 3:23; cf. Deut. 34:9; 1QS 4.3–7; 4Q213a frag. 1.14; 4Q504 frag. 8.4–5; cf. CD-A 2.3; 1QS 4.22; 11.6; 1QH 9.19 (*olim* 1.19). More probably, however, the wording alludes to only a few specific OT passages: Exod. 31:3; 35:31; 1 Kings 7:14 (7:2 LXX); Isa. 11:2 (see Fee 1994: 642, who sees the Exodus and Isaiah texts as uppermost in mind among other possible LXX parallels; cf. also Dunn 1996: 70–71, who sees that "wisdom and understanding coming only from the Spirit" occurs in the Exodus and Isaiah passages, as well as Wis. 9:17–19; Sir. 39:6; Philo, *Giants* 22–27; 2 Esd. [4 Ezra] 14:22, 39–40, but he sees no specific allusion to any of these passages). Exodus 31:3; 35:31; 1 Kings 7:14 (7:2 LXX); Isa. 11:2 are the only texts where the (1) "Spirit" (though only implied in 1 Kings) and (2) "filling" (though a different verb in LXX of Exodus and Isaiah) (3) is directly linked to "wisdom and understanding" and "knowledge" (though a different noun for "knowledge" is used in the Exodus texts); cf. also Sir. 39:6; 1QS 4.3–7; and 4Q213a frag. 1.14, which themselves probably allude to these OT passages:

---

sending away, . . . release of captivity, . . . cancellation of a debt, . . . letting go, release" (LEH 48). Almost without exception, elsewhere in the NT the word refers to the "remission" of sins, which is likely a better translation here than "forgiveness."

47. Though the phrase in verse 17 may include a spheric sense.

48. The same construction has the same idea in 1 John 1:6, 7, 8; 3:21; 5:14.

Exodus, 1 Kings, Isaiah	Colossians 1:9–10a
Exod. 31:3 LXX: "I have filled [πίπλημι, *pimplēmi*] him with a divine Spirit [πνεῦμα, *pneuma*] of wisdom [σοφία, *sophia*] and understanding [σύνεσις, *synesis*] and knowledge [ἐπιστήμη, *epistēmē*] in every work [ἐν παντὶ ἔργῳ, *en panti ergō*]."[a]	"that you should be filled [πληρωθῆτε, *plērōthēte*] with the knowledge [ἐπίγνωσιν, *epignōsin*] of his will in all wisdom [σοφία, *sophia*] and spiritual understanding [συνέσει πνευματικῇ, *synesei pneumatikē*] in order to walk about . . . in every good work [ἐν παντὶ ἔργῳ ἀγαθῷ, *en panti ergō agathō*]."*
1 Kings 7:2 LXX (7:14 MT): "He was filled [πεπληρωμένος, *peplērōmenos*] with skill (or wisdom) and understanding and knowledge [τῆς τέχνης[b] καὶ συνέσεως καὶ ἐπιγνώσεως, *tēs technēs kai syneseōs kai epignōseōs*] in order to do every work [ποιεῖν πᾶν ἔργον, *poiein pan ergon*]."	
Compare also Isa. 11:2–3 LXX: "The Spirit [πνεῦμα, *pneuma*] of God will rest upon him: a spirit of wisdom [σοφίας, *sophias*] and understanding [συνέσεως, *syneseōs*], . . . a spirit of knowledge [γνώσεως, *gnōseōs*]; . . . the spirit of the fear of God will fill [ἐμπλήσει, *emplēsei*] him."	

[a]Exod. 35:31–32a LXX is virtually identical.

[b]The MT has "wisdom" here. Some LXX MSS likewise have "wisdom" (σοφία, *sophia*).

Colossians is clearly closer to Exod. 31; 35; and 1 Kings 7, since, in contrast to Isa. 11, they also view the purpose of the filling of the Spirit to be accomplishing God's will "in every work" (cf. Exod. 31:3 // 35:31–32 and 1 Kings 7:14 [7:2 LXX][49] with Col. 1:10a; Exod. 31:3 and Col. 1:10 read ἐν παντὶ ἔργῳ for this last phrase, though Exod. 35:31–32a reads πάντα τὰ ἔργα [*panta ta erga*] and 1 Kings 7:14 [7:2 LXX] reads πᾶν ἔργον [*pan ergon*]).[50] Furthermore, the Exodus and 1 Kings 7 texts more closely match the order of Col. 1:9–10a: "fill" + the three nouns for knowledge + "every work," whereas in Isa. 11:2–3 LXX "fill" comes last in the list (v. 3) and refers only to "filling" by "the spirit of the fear of God"; also, in Isa. 11:2 LXX "spirit of knowledge [γνώσεως]" does not directly follow the other synonymous nouns for knowledge (separated from σοφίας and συνέσεως by four words).[51]

The Exodus and 1 Kings texts assert that God filled people with the Spirit in order to have skill to be able to build the tabernacle or temple and make its inner contents (cf. Exod. 31:1–11; 36:1–39:43; 1 Kings 7:14 [7:2]).[52] Accordingly, Paul sees God as filling Christians with his Spirit

49. First Kings 7:14 (7:2 LXX) and to a lesser degree Exod. 35:35 are virtually verbatim with 31:3 and 35:31–32, though both lack reference to the divine "Spirit." However, it is clear that the phrase "He filled them with wisdom and understanding of mind to understand all things" in 35:35 LXX assumes, in the light of Exod. 31:3 and 35:31–32, that it is the Spirit that does the filling. The same is true of the phrase "he was filled with skill [or wisdom] and understanding and knowledge" in 1 Kings 7:14 (7:2 LXX), especially since this text is an inner-biblical development of the Exod. 31 and 35 texts (Hiram's task is a recapitulation of Bezalel's and Oholiab's task).

50. Barth and Blanke (1994: 175–76, 180) repeatedly compare the Exod. 31 and 35 passages to Col. 1:9 but do not refer to them as allusions.

51. The phrase "every good work/deed" occurs also in the Pastoral Epistles five times without allusion to the OT (1 Tim. 5:10; 2 Tim. 2:21; 3:17; Titus 1:16; 3:1; also in 2 Thess. 2:17).

52. Josephus (*Ant.* 3.105, 200) presumably alludes to Exod. 31 and 33 when naming "Besallel" (Bezalel) and "Oholiab" as those who were the main builders of the tabernacle. Philo

in order that they live skillful godly lives. Except for the clear allusion to Exod. 31 and 35 and 1 Kings 7, the immediate context may not appear to reflect the notion that Christians are being equipped to construct a spiritual temple, though the following context will indeed support that such an idea is already in mind here through the Exodus and 1 Kings allusion (see comments on 1:19 below, as well as on 2:9–11 and on a false view of the temple in 2:16–18).

Colossians 1:9–10a refers not so much to a quality of mere human "spiritual understanding" but more primarily to an "understanding" that comes from God's Spirit, since Exodus explicitly refers to God's Spirit as the originator of the "wisdom and understanding" (see further Fee 1994: 642). Paul uses the adjective πνευματικός (*pneumatikos*) twenty-four times with the sense of something being "of, from, given, or inspired by the Holy Spirit," so that the best rendering in Col. 1:9 is "in all Spirit-given wisdom and understanding" (see fuller analysis of this point in Beetham [2008: 72–79], who follows and builds on BDAG 837, s.v. πνευματικός; and Lohmeyer 1964: 33; as well as, e.g., E. Schweizer, *TDNT* 6:436–37; J. D. G. Dunn, *NIDNTT* 3:706–7; J. Kremer, *EDNT* 3:122–23). That πνευματικός (*pneumatikos*) modifies not only σύνεσις (*synesis*) but also σοφία (*sophia*) is apparent from the OT allusions, where the Spirit gives both "wisdom" and "understanding."

On the other hand, Isaiah does have in common with Colossians virtually the same Greek word for "knowledge" (Isaiah: γνῶσις, *gnosis*; Colossians: ἐπίγνωσις, *epignōsis*; while Exodus has ἐπιστήμη, *epistēmē*). And like Exod. 31 and 35, Isa. 11:2–3 also views God's Spirit as the originator of the "wisdom and understanding and knowledge," though using the language of the Spirit "resting" on the coming king. Judaism repeatedly applied Isa. 11:2–3 to the coming Messiah and the end-time community, and it is natural that the early Jewish-Christian community, including Paul, would have utilized it in like manner (T. Levi 18.7, 11; 1 En. 49.1–4; 61.11; see further references below).[53] Especially noteworthy is that one of the main instruments used by the anointed leader in establishing his rule is "the word of his mouth" (Isa. 11:4 LXX), a crucial element also picked up from Genesis in Colossians (T. Levi 18.6–11 also applies Gen. 1:28, as well as Adam and Eden motifs, to the Isa. 11:2–3 figure). The climax toward which Isa. 11:1–3 works is the final revelation of God's "holy mountain" sanctuary in Isa. 11:9 (as observed also by Beetham 2008: 64), so that Isa. 11:1–3 is likewise vitally linked to God's sanctuary, as are the Exodus and 1 Kings texts, though the latter are so more explicitly.

In the light of the above, it appears that both the Exodus tabernacle and the 1 Kings temple texts are uppermost in mind in Col. 1:9–10a (and the Gen. 1:28 allusion in Col. 1:10b) and that Paul develops both. Isaiah 11 may secondarily be echoed, recalling that it also is inextricably linked to a temple expectation. Beetham (2008: 65) thinks Isa. 11:2 would have more likely been in mind for three reasons: (1) Isa. 11:2 was a well-known text in early Judaism in contrast to the obscure Exod. 31 and 35 texts. He cites five early Jewish texts in support (Beetham 2008: 67–72). (2) The following context of Isa. 11:2–3 refers to a universal filling of the earth (11:9), which is also a theme of Col. 1:6; (3) Isa. 11:6–9 contains new creation imagery, as does Col. 1:10b.

In response to reason 1 above, Exod. 31:3 is repeated in Exod. 35:31–32 and then cited in 1 Kings 7:14 (7:2 LXX), and as noted above, Judaism makes allusion to the Exodus texts.[54] Furthermore, the building of the tabernacle was not an obscure event in Israel's history. In

(*Plant.* 26) refers to Bezalel as "summoned up" to Sinai, just as Moses was, to see the vision of the tabernacle, since he was to make the "sacred furniture" of the tabernacle.

53. Indeed, Paul himself alludes to Isa. 11:2 in Eph. 1:17 ("a spirit of wisdom and revelation in the knowledge of him"; so Fee 1994: 675, and more loosely, cf. Hendriksen 1967: 97).

54. See again Josephus, *Ant.* 3.105, 200, with respect to Bezalel and Oholiab; Philo, *Plant.* 26; see further in this respect, Philo, *Giants* 23–28a, 47; *Alleg.* 3.95–96, 102–3; *QG* 1.90; see likewise later Jewish texts citing Bezalel from Exod. 31:3 or 35:31–32: b. Ber. 55a; Midr. Pss. 50.1; Pesiq. Rab. 5.6; Exod. Rab. 1.16; Num. Rab. 12.10; Pirqe R. El. 3, which cites Exod. 31:3; 1 Kings 7:14; and Isa. 11:2 on the basis of the common mention of "wisdom, understanding, and knowledge"; so likewise Midr. Tanh. 10.6 on Exod. 35: esp. 35:3–35, part 6, cites Prov. 3:19–20; Exod. 31:3; and 1 Kings 7:14 on the basis of the common mention of "wisdom, understanding, and knowledge; Eup. 34.1 (158/157 BC) cites and discusses Hiram from 1 Kings 7:14 (7:2).

response to Beetham's second point about universal filling, it is not insignificant that Philo relates the "divine Spirit filling" Bezalel with "wisdom and understanding and knowledge" (also shared by Moses and the seventy elders), which is "diffused in its fullness everywhere and through all things" (*Giants* 23–28).[55] Finally, in response to Beetham's third point concerning new creation, Philo interprets Bezalel's work in constructing the temple to have been ultimately done by "the creator and maker of the holy work of the creation" (*Giants* 23), thus understanding the building of the tabernacle as another work of creation like the creation of the world in Gen. 1.[56] Recall too the general recognition that the tabernacle and temple were designed to be microcosmic symbols of the entire cosmos (e.g., Beale 2004: 31–60). In addition, a reference to the temple in Col. 1:9–10 fits into and prepares for the temple references we will see in Col. 1:19; 2:9, 10, and 18.

Colossians, however, goes one step further than Isaiah, if indeed Isaiah is in mind: the "spiritual wisdom and understanding" is now applied not to just one person but to all of God's people who participate in temple building and the new creation. This wider application has possibly been sparked by the presence of the context of the Gen. 1:28 allusion in Col. 1:6, 10, which was intended to be applied to all of Adam's progeny. Now all of the last Adam's progeny have the "spiritual wisdom and understanding" that is needed "to walk worthy of the Lord" and to "bear fruit in every good work" in the new creation. Recall, however, that already what was true of Bezalel and Oholiab in Exod. 31 and 35 was also said to be true of other Israelites in building the tabernacle (cf. esp. Exod. 31:3–6 with Exod. 35:31–36:2). Thus, this may have been reason enough to apply to all believers what was true of Hiram in 1 Kings 7:14 and of the Messiah in Isa. 11:2–3. Consequently, all the Colossian believers can grow in these attributes only as they continue to hear (and heed) God's "word of truth" (1:5), which Adam should have heeded, and which their true Adamic forerunner, Jesus Christ, did heed (Matt. 4:1–11; Luke 3:38–4:13).

Thus, when saints identify with Christ by faith, they begin to possess the attributes of their messianic representative, since "in [Christ] are hidden all the treasures of wisdom and knowledge" (σοφίας καὶ γνώσεως, *sophias kai gnōseōs*, Col. 2:3). The application to God's eschatological people of what would be true of their king had a precedent already in earlier Jewish interpretation of Isa. 11:1–10 (for focus on the individual king or Messiah, see 4Q161 frags. 8–10 3.9–25; 1 En. 49.1–4; T. Levi 18.7, 11; Pss. Sol. 17.35–43; Gen. Rab. 2.4; 97; Num. Rab. 13.11; Ruth Rab. 7.2; Pesiq. Rab. 33; Pirqe R. El. 3; Tanh., Gen. 9.13; and with respect to application to the corporate people, see 1 En. 61.11 [cf. 61.8–9]; 1QS 4.3–7; and Sir. 39:6; cf. 4Q213a frag. 1.14, 17; see also quotation of Exod. 31:3 in 4Q365 frag. 10.4 [= DJD 13:276]). Note that T. Levi 18; T. Jud. 24; and 1 En. 49; 61 combine both notions (application to king and people).

Therefore Paul may merely apply the Exodus, 1 Kings, and Isaiah texts (if the latter is in mind) analogically to the Colossians; since Isa. 11 is a prophecy, then believers may be seen as continuing to fulfill it by virtue of their identification with Christ (cf. 1:18, 24, 2:10, 19), who has inaugurated the fulfillment of Isa. 11:2–3. If the latter is included in the thought, then in Jesus's first coming Paul saw the fulfillment of the Isa. 11:2–3 prophecy, which he is assuming as the basis for the readers' partaking of the Spirit (following Beetham 2008: 78). The fulfillment sense of Isa. 11:2–3 in combination with the Exodus texts points to the Exodus allusions as being typological and not merely analogical. If one were to conclude that there is no explicit link with Isa. 11:2–3 in

55. Note reference to the "divine Spirit" and "wisdom, understanding, and knowledge" from Exod. 31:2 and 35:31–32 in Philo, *Giants* 24 and in 27–28a.

56. Note that b. Ber. 55a further associates Exod. 31:3 and 35:31 with the creation of the cosmos by saying that Bezalel's "wisdom, understanding, and knowledge" for constructing the tabernacle included his ability "to combine the letters by which the heavens and earth were created"; the same talmudic passage puts this in parallel with Prov. 3:19: "The Lord by wisdom founded the earth; by understanding he established the heavens." In Philo (*Alleg.* 3.96), Bezalel's name is interpreted to be "in his [God's] shadow," meaning God's word, "which he used like an instrument when he was making the world." Midrash Tanhuma 10.6 on Exod. 35, esp. 35:30–35, part 6, cites Prov. 3:19–20; Exod. 31:3; and 1 Kings 7:14 on the basis of the common mention of "wisdom, understanding, and knowledge," thus comparing God's creation of the world (in Prov. 3:19–20) with the creation of the tabernacle and temple.

Paul's mind, it may have still formed an underlying foundation for the statement that he makes about the readers' "spiritual wisdom and understanding" in 1:9.

1:12. Some MSS read "to God" (θεῷ, *theō*) or "to God and" (θεῷ καί, *theō kai*) before "the Father." The earlier and better quality MSS (𝔓[46, 61], A, B, C*, D) support only "the Father" (τῷ πατρί, *tō patri*) and consequently should be preferred. In further confirmation of this is that "the Father" is an unusual construction by itself, usually occurring with a following reference to "Christ," so that scribes would have been tempted to add "to God" or "to God and" to "the Father," since the phrase "to God the Father" or "to God and the Father" is a phrase occurring elsewhere (1 Cor. 15:24; Eph. 5:20; Phil. 4:20; James 1:27; Rev. 1:6) and the phrase τῷ πατρὶ (*tō patri*) by itself occurs nowhere else in Paul apart from Col. 1:12 (cf. Metzger 1994: 553 for somewhat similar reasoning).

1:12. Instead of ἱκανώσαντι (*hikanōsanti*) some MSS read καλέσαντι (*kalesanti*, in D*[,c], F, G, 33, 1175, pc it, sa; Ambst, Spec); Vaticanus (B) has both verbs. While D*, F, G, and B are good MSS (and B is early), the reading only of ἱκανώσαντι is preferred on the basis of better MS attestation (date and quality of MSS, among which are 𝔓[46], 𝔓[61vid], ℵ, A, C, D[2], I, Ψ, 075, 1739). In addition, it is likely that an early scribe mistook the similar-looking τῷ ἱκανώσαντι for τῷ καλέσαντι—with uncials and no spaces between words, it would have appeared as ΤΩΙΚΑΝΩΣΑΝΤΙ, which the scribe read as ΤΩΚΑΛΕΣΑΝΤΙ—and then B picked up that corruption (following Abbott 1897: 206).

1:12. Good and early MSS support both "you" (ὑμᾶς, *hymas*) and "us" (ἡμᾶς, *hēmas*). The latter is most likely merely a scribal attempt to conform to the "us" (ἡμᾶς, *hēmas*) of the directly following verse 13a ("he delivered us").

1:12–14. While a specific OT passage is not likely in mind, the broad biblical tradition portraying Israel's exodus appears to have influenced the wording of verses 12–14 (cf. generally MacDonald 2000: 51). "In Christ" the believers "have redemption" (ἀπολύτρωσις, *apolytrōsis*, Col. 1:14), and they have been "delivered from" (ῥύομαι + ἐκ, *rhyomai* + *ek*) bondage to evil (1:13). Likewise Israel was "delivered from" the bondage of Egypt (see λυτρόω + ἐκ, *lytroō* + *ek*, in Exod. 6:6 [ῥύομαι ἐκ + λυτρόω, *rhyomai ek* + *lytroō*]; Deut. 7:8; 13:5 [13:6]; 24:18 [with ἐκεῖθεν, *ekeithen*, instead of ἐκ, *ek*]; 2 Sam. 7:23; 1 Chron. 17:21; Ps. 106:10 [105:10 LXX]; Esther 13:16 NETS [= 4:17g Rahlfs LXX]).[57] Interestingly, the second-exodus prophecies of Israel's deliverance from exile also employ the terminology of "redemption" (Isa. 44:22, 23, 24; 51:11; 52:3; 62:12; cf. 41:14; 43:1, 14) and forgiveness of sins (see Isa. 40:2; 44:22 ESV, "I have blotted out your transgressions; . . . your sins are like mist").[58]

In addition, echoed in Col. 1:12 are the Isaiah prophecies of a second exodus that use the language of "bringing [Israel] out of darkness" (σκότος, *skotos*; cf. Ps. 107:10–14 [106:10–14 LXX], where in verse 2 the synonym for "lead" is "redeem" [λυτρόω, *lytroō*]; Isa. 42:7; cf. 42:16; 49:9). These prophecies also picture Israel as being restored from the "darkness" (σκότος) of exile into "light" (φῶς, *phōs*) (referring to the Exodus background, see Isa. 42:6b–7, 16; 58:10), which may be a development of contrasting "darkness" (σκότος) and "light" (φῶς) that was part of the first exodus narrative (Exod. 10:21–23; 14:20).[59] Israel's deliverance from Egypt also had qualified them to become "saints" (ἅγιοι, *hagioi*; Exod. 22:31 [22:30 LXX]; Lev. 11:44–45; 19:2; 20:7, 26; 21:6; Num. 15:40; 16:3) and to receive "a share of the inheritance" in Canaan. Also behind Col.

57. Ten other times the LXX also uses *lytroō* to refer to Israel's redemption out of Egypt; see also Exod. 14:30, ῥύομαι + ἐκ (*rhyomai* + *ek*); see Caird 1976: 171–74; Dunn 1996: 77, 80; Wall 1993: 57–61; Hübner 1997a: 53; MacDonald 2000: 51; Thompson 2005: 26–27; and Davids 2008a: 256, who also see Israel's deliverance from Egypt as background.

58. Pao (2012: 78) says that the word for "forgiveness" in Col. 1:14 points to the new-exodus background of the following Isaiah references, which predict God's end-time deliverance of his people (Isa. 58:6; 61:1–2); he also includes in the background Isa. 44:22 (connecting redemption with forgiveness of sins) and Isa. 40:2 (NIV, Israel's "sin has been paid for").

59. In Col. 1:12 there may also be an echo of the Genesis new-creation background in view of Isa. 9:2 [9:1 LXX]; 60:1–3.

1:12 is the μερίς, *meris*, word group + the κλῆρος, *klēros*, word group, occurring over ten times in the LXX of Numbers, Deuteronomy, and Joshua, often with respect to the Levite who had "no portion" or "inheritance" in the land along with the other tribes who did. The actual combination of the words μερίς and κλῆρος occurs seven times in the above corpus, as in Deut. 10:9 LXX: "Therefore the Levites have no portion nor inheritance" (cf. also Eadie 1856: 32; Melick 1991: 205–6; Dunn 1996: 80; Garland 1998: 66; Sumney 2008: 53).[60]

Just as Israel had been "delivered from" Egyptian slavery and had become "saints," and then these tribes received "a share of the inheritance" in the promised land, so likewise has the church been "delivered from" (ῥύομαι + ἐκ and ἀπολύτρωσις) a greater bondage than that of Egypt (satanic "darkness," σκότος) and has become "qualified . . . for a share" in a greater "inheritance of the saints in Light" (μερίς + κλῆρος + ἅγιοι + φῶς).[61] This inheritance is none other than "the kingdom of [the] beloved Son" (Col. 1:13). Believers have begun to participate in this inheritance and kingdom, but its consummation is yet future (cf. Col. 1:24). Furthermore, Yahweh's "redemption" (cf. λυτρόω, *lytroō*) of Israel out of Babylonian captivity has escalated significance in comparison to the release from Egypt, since it is equated with "wiping out [their] transgressions" (Isa. 44:22; likewise Isa. 40:2), which is strikingly comparable to Col. 1:14: "in [him] we have redemption, the forgiveness of sins" (Barth and Blanke 1994: 192, who also see the above Exodus and Isaiah's second-exodus background as relevant [1994: 186–88, 190–93]).

What would have fueled Paul's application of exodus imagery to the church's salvation?[62] Presumably, he sees the people of God in Christ as undergoing an exodus like that out of Egypt but on an escalated scale, beginning spiritually in this age and culminating in physical resurrection (on the latter see 1 Cor. 15:52). Paul was also more probably directed to such an application because of Isaiah's second-exodus prophecies, which utilized and developed some of the same language as the first exodus. Elsewhere in his epistles, Paul views the restoration prophecies of Israel and of its second exodus as having begun fulfillment in Christ's first coming and in the formation of the earliest Christian churches.[63] Indeed, in Col. 1:9 Paul has just made a combined allusion to significant events associated with the first and second exodus (respectively, Exod. 31:3 and possibly Isa. 11:2–3; cf. 11:4–16). Paul's consciousness of OT restoration themes is apparent from the Acts 26:18 portrayal of his own call and commission by the second-exodus language of Isa. 42:7, 16 together with wording uniquely similar to Col. 1:12–14 (quoted above and discussed in the commentary section).

Paul either uses the exodus images analogically or typologically; if the latter, then Israel's redemptive history prefigures that of eschatological Israel, the church. A typological use is pointed to by Paul's awareness elsewhere and in the nearby context of Isaiah's second-exodus prophecies (Dunn 1996: 81, also prefers a typological use here). These prophecies were fertile ground from which Paul's typological understanding of the first exodus easily could have grown. It may be more precise to say that Paul presupposes a typological approach to the first exodus (so Beetham 2008: 94–95). In fact, there appears to be a mixing of the first-exodus (historical)

60. Fee (2006: 205–6) has also observed the Exodus background in Col. 1:12–14 for the themes of "deliverance," "inheritance," and "saints"; likewise N. Wright 1986: 61–63; Shogren 1988: 177–80; Sumney 2008: 53, 56–57; Garland 1998: 68; cf. likewise Hübner (1997a: 52–53), though not mentioning "saints"; and cf. Moule (1957: 55), and Davids (2008a: 253), who see the background of the inheritance of the promised land.

61. For this background of Israel's redemption and inheritance for Col. 1:12–14, see Patzia 1990: 24; N. Wright, 1986: 61; Wall 1993: 55–61 (who also includes "saints" as part of the Exodus background); Hübner 1997a: 52–53. For the background only of Israel's inheritance in the land behind the wording "share of the inheritance" in Col. 1:12, see Lightfoot 1875: 141; Masson 1950: 96; Callow 2002: 30–31; Melick 1991: 205–6; E. Martin 1993: 49; Vaughn 1978: 179; and R. Martin 1974: 53–54 (Melick and Martin also include "saints" as part of the OT background). Lindemann (1983: 22) cites only the "share" and "portion" of the land promise as a parallel.

62. See Foster (2016: 168–69), who says the proposal of "a New Exodus theology standing behind" Col. 1:13 is "overblown."

63. E.g., see Beale 1989; J. Scott 1992: 167–71, 179; Keesmat 1994: 29–56.

and second-exodus (prophetic) material in verses 12–14 since, as seen above, to some degree the combination of "light and darkness" recalls Isaiah (see above; 1 Pet. 2:9 does likewise, combining Exod. 19:6 and 23:22 LXX with Isa. 42:6–7, 12, 16 and 43:20–21). Paul would have viewed Isaiah's second-exodus prophecies as beginning to be fulfilled, to the degree that he was conscious of them. Even if it is concluded that the first-exodus and second-exodus prophecies were not used expressly and consciously by Paul, his mind surely held some affinity with such prophecies so that by association they became the underlying trigger in his thinking, inspiring his description of the readers' salvation.

Paul does not appear to be the only one of his time to have conducted such a typological exegesis. Early Judaism applied the promise about Israel's "share of an inheritance" in Canaan to an eternal, end-time reward, which likely also was done according to a typological rationale.[64]

1:12. The notion that Christ's resurrection and the Christian's identification with that resurrection in this life is the beginning fulfillment of Israel's land promises and of the new creation occurs not only in this verse but also elsewhere in Paul and the NT (see Beale 2012: 760–72, e.g.). Thus Eph. 1:13–14 affirms that the possession of this "inheritance" is evident from believers having been "sealed in him [the resurrected Christ] by means of the Holy Spirit of promise," who is "a down payment of our inheritance."* The Spirit's work in Christians likely includes their inaugurated resurrection existence, since Paul sees the Spirit elsewhere as the agent of the resurrection, and in Eph. 1:13 the Spirit "seals" believers in Christ, meaning the resurrected Christ (see Eph. 1:20–22). Thus part of the "inheritance" that God's people are receiving now is a beginning share in resurrection existence, which will be consummated at the very end of time in bodily resurrection in the completeness of the new creation. The language of "inheritance" in Eph. 1:13–14 alludes to the inheritance of the promised land, so that Paul sees Israel's inheritance as pointing to the inheritance of the new creation that begins in Christ's resurrection and in those who participate in that resurrection during the church age. The same concept can be found in Rom. 8:23, where Christians have the "firstfruits of the Spirit" (NIV), which includes the Spirit's operation of raising them spiritually from the dead, a resurrection to be completed physically at the very end of history according to Rom. 8:18–23 (see Beale 2012: 581–82, 763; for discussion of Eph. 1:13–14, see Beale 2012: 581, 763; cf. also 252–54).

1:13. Some commentators have suggested that "the kingdom of his beloved Son" is an allusion to 2 Sam. 7:12–16 (Barth and Blanke 1994: 190; Fee 2006: 211, seeing it as an echo; cf. also Mark 1:11, 9:7; Eph. 1:6). In the 2 Samuel text, God promises to David that he "will establish" a descendant's "kingdom . . . forever," and that this descendant would be a "son" to God. The Hebrew text of 2 Sam. 7:15 says that God's "lovingkindness [חֶסֶד, *ḥesed*; LXX: ἔλεος, *eleos*] shall not depart from him." In this light, David's statement in 2 Sam. 7:18 LXX that this promise shows how much God has "loved [ἀγαπάω, *agapaō*] him" implies that 2 Sam. 7:15 indicates that such love would continue with his descendant (see Beetham 2008: 99–102, who views "love" in the LXX passage as part of the 2 Sam. 7 allusion in Col. 1:13).

Thus in Col. 1:13 the notion of God's "beloved Son" with an eternal "kingdom" has unique affinity with the 2 Samuel text and likely alludes to it. Since exodus themes have been interwoven throughout Col. 1:12–14, it is possible that Hosea 11:1 (NIV, "When Israel was a child, I loved him, and out of Egypt I called my Son") was the underlying link between the Exodus and 2 Samuel passages. So N. Wright (1986: 63) sees the Hosea passage as "fitting well with the rest of our

64. E.g., see 1QS 11.7–8 (God "has given them an inheritance in the lot of the saints" as a striking parallel to Col. 1:9–12; similarly 1QH 19.10b–12a = *olim* 11.10–12); see the combination of words in CD 13.12, which refers to faithful members of the community who had a "share in the allotment of light." So also 4Q418 frag. 81 3–20; 1QapGen ar 16.12; cf. likewise 4Q511 frag. 2.4–8, where also "light" is repeatedly referred to. See Wis. 5:5 ("his inheritance is among the saints"). Most of these OT and Jewish parallels have been acknowledged by several commentators, especially Dunn 1996: 76; 1995: 158; T. Ab. (rec. A) 13.13; see Pokorný 1991: 52, who gives additional references.

passage"; several commentators such as Lenski (1961: 43) also see an echo of Matt. 3:17, "my beloved Son" (as do some MSS of Luke 9:35). Lohmeyer (1964: 50) observes that Col. 1:13 may also have been influenced by the repeated reference to Israel as a "son" (υἱός, *huios*) whom God "loves" (ἀγαπάω, *agapaō*), as in Ps. 28:6 LXX (clause missing in MT, Eng.); Ps. Sol. 13.9, in parallelism with "firstborn"; 18.3–4, with ἀγάπη, *agapē*, and "firstborn son"; and Wis. 16:26, with the plural "sons."

Again, presuming Paul's consciousness of the 2 Samuel allusion, we must ask whether he perceives an analogical, a typological, or a prophetic relationship underlying his linking of the Exodus and 2 Samuel texts. The context of the 2 Samuel passage points to a typological or prophetic-fulfillment connection. Clearly 2 Sam. 7:10–16 is a prophetic promise. The question is whether it was completely fulfilled in Solomon or whether only partially, so that part of the prophecy remained to be fulfilled at a later point. If the former, then the fulfillment itself could become a typological event pointing forward to Christ.

It appears, however, that the prophecy was fulfilled only partially by Solomon. That the promise certainly has Solomon in mind is evident since the text says that the promised king would commit "iniquity" and be "corrected" for it. On the other hand, however, 2 Sam. 7:10–16 says that the coming kingdom and temple will last forever, which was not true with Solomon's temple and kingdom nor that of his descendants. Likewise Exod. 15:17–18 affirms the eternal character of the coming kingdom and, implicitly, of the temple, to which allusion is made in 2 Sam. 7:10, 12–13. Sometimes the Hebrew word עוֹלָם (*ʿôlām*) may connote a long time or an "eternal" period. Though there is debate, when considered in the light of the context of the canon, the word in 2 Sam. 7:12–16 likely refers to an eternal epoch because of its links with the purposes of Eden that are developed with the patriarchs and because of the links with the eternal eschatological temple and kingdom later in the OT and NT (e.g., cf. Heb. 1:5; similarly Acts 2:30; 13:23; 2 Cor. 6:18; Rev. 21:7; also Luke 1:32; John 1:49; 7:42; for further support in these respects, see Beale 2004: chap. 3).

Hence the Colossians reference sees that what was promised in 2 Sam. 7, and partially fulfilled by Solomon, was finally fulfilled in Christ, though the consummation even of Christ's fulfillment still remains. The prophesied eternal kingdom of 2 Sam. 7 is also seen elsewhere in the NT to have begun fulfillment in Christ (see the Hebrews and Acts references directly above; allusion to 2 Sam. 7 in Acts 13:23 and 2 Cor. 6:18 comes from Paul himself). Thus Hübner (1997a: 53–54) rightly contends that "the eternal dominion of Christ in 1,15 [*sic*; read 1:13] is . . . the *messianic fulfillment from 2 Sam. 7,16*." Qumran (4Q174 1.17–12) also understood 2 Sam. 7:11–14 to be a prophecy of the coming eschatological Messiah, who will deliver "the sons of light" from the onslaughts of Belial (cf. Col. 1:12, "the saints in Light").

It is possible that Ps. 2:7, "You are my Son, today I have begotten you," is also echoed in the Colossians expression. As part of the background here, Wolter (1993: 67) sees 2 Sam. 7:14//1 Chron. 17:13//Ps. 2:7; likewise Ps. 89:27–28. Nevertheless, perception of the psalm's presence may only be an impression created by the fact that the psalm itself alludes to 2 Sam. 7 (see Delitzsch 1970: 96). That a possible echo of the psalm could be heard may be pointed to by Heb. 1:5, where the psalm is quoted and then is directly linked to a quotation of 2 Sam. 7:14. If there is any trace of such an echo, it would support a prophetic use of 2 Sam. 7 since the psalm is probably directly prophetic of a coming messianic king (which is the way Paul understood the psalm in Acts 13:33; likewise Heb. 1:5; 5:5; see Beetham 2008: 104–12, for survey of 2 Sam. 7:12–14 in Judaism, elsewhere in the NT, and in the early fathers).

1:14. There is debate over whether in the NT ἀπολύτρωσις (*apolytrōsis*) means merely "release" or "release by a price." In Classical and Hellenistic Greek, it almost always has the latter connotation, often in contexts of slaves being released by a price. While it is true that there are some NT contexts which seem to emphasize only release, even here the idea of "payment" is compatible and could be in mind (so Rom. 8:23; 1 Cor. 1:30; Eph. 4:30; Heb. 11:35). The dual idea of "release by a price" is seen more clearly in Rom. 3:24–25[65] and Heb. 9:15, and even in

65. Several commentators understand there that "by his blood" (ἐν τῷ αὐτοῦ αἵματι, *en tō autou haimati*) is a "dative of price" (e.g., BDF §219.3).

the OT-Exodus context where the "price" could be construed as the lamb's blood, although as a secondary idea. Though 1 Cor. 6:20 does not contain the word or its cognate word group, it expresses the concept of redemption by a price: "for you have been bought with a price." In Eph. 1:7, virtually the identical phrase as in Col. 1:14 occurs: "In him we have redemption through his blood, the forgiveness of our trespasses." The primary difference in the Ephesians parallel is that the price of release is explicitly stated as being Christ's "blood" (= death; see the next additional note), though this is explicitly mentioned in Col. 1:20 ("the blood of his cross"), which is interpreted to mean Christ's "death" in 1:22. See further Morris (1955: 37–48, e.g.), who supports the notion of "redemption" connoting "release by a price" and cites others who affirm in contrast only the idea of release.

1:14. A few later and lesser quality MSS insert διὰ τοῦ αἵματος αὐτοῦ (*dia tou haimatos autou*, "through his blood"), but this was surely added by a later scribe under the influence of Eph. 1:7: "we have the redemption *through his blood* [διὰ τοῦ αἵματος αὐτοῦ, *dia tou haimatos autou*], the forgiveness of trespasses." The vast preponderance of extant MSS, including early and good MSS, omit this phrase.

C. Christ's Supremacy over the First Creation Is a Pattern for the New Creation (1:15–23)

Here is a fuller statement of the main idea of this unit: *Christ's supremacy over the first creation is a pattern recapitulated for the new creation to bring about reconciliation of all creation, especially in order to make believers acceptable before God.*

The famous so-called poem of Col. 1:15–20 has been written on by commentators more than many other texts in the NT and certainly more than any other particular passage elsewhere in this epistle. Here we are able to give only a brief analysis of the recent interpretative history of this passage and some of the main lines of past interpretation. Many believe that Paul has adopted a preexisting hymn (so, e.g., Schweizer 1982: 55–56 and literature cited there). This is typically based on the following observations about 1:15–20: (1) that verses 15–20 contain balanced rhythmic units; (2) the section could appear to stand alone and make sense apart from its context; (3) frequently repeated words, (4) non-Pauline phraseology and hapax legomena; (5) the use of literary devices such as chiasm (or *inclusio* or parallel or antithetically parallel expressions);[1] (6) the unusually numerous relative pronouns; (7) the shift in pronouns: verses 13–14 are in the first person, and verses 21–23 are in the second and third person, while verses 15–20 are consistently in the third person (see Mitchell 2000: 65; Garland 1998: 82, summarizing most of these observations by others). More recently Gordley (2007: 32–39) defines Col. 1:15–20 as "an example of a hybrid of Jewish and Greco-Roman expressions of praise that can be considered a philosophical prose hymn" (2007: 39), which has been adopted by the author of Colossians (2007: 170–230).

Others are doubtful that such a hymn can be detected. If the conclusion of most scholars that Paul has alluded to such a preexisting hymn is correct, then Paul has adapted it to fit into the context of what he is writing.[2] Since we do not have the context of the preexisting hymn against which to interpret Paul's use, we must remain doubtful about whether it really existed as a hymn and concentrate only on how Paul is using the wording in

1. On observations 1 and 5 especially, see Reyes 1999.

2. For further discussion of the poem, its background, its meaning, and the considerable amount of literature written on the passage, cf. Moule 1957: 60–62; R. Martin 1974: 61–66; Caird 1976: 174–75; Barth and Blanke 1994: 227–42; O'Brien 1982: 31–40; Bruce 1984: 5, 63–80; Barclay 1997: 56–68; Sappington 1991: 171–73; Wolter 1993: 70–71; Dunn 1996: 83–104; Hübner 1997a: 55. For a convenient list of bibliography on the hymn, see Pokorný 1991: 56–74; Lohse 1971: 41; D. Moo 2008: 107–16; Harris 2010: 48. Fee (2007: 298) cites secondary sources summarizing the most significant literature on this passage.

its context.[3] For example, Caird (1976: 174) says that a poetic form in Col. 1:15–20 can be discerned "only by the excision of words which do not fit, on the grounds that they are a gloss by the final editor." Though a minority viewpoint, it is possible and even probable that Paul himself created the section perhaps as a hymn or poem, since parts of his other epistles reveal that he was skilled in liturgical style.[4] Yet whether it is a hymn or a poem or some creedal confession is difficult to know. As we investigate the purported hymn, we will see how its themes are developments of the preceding context. The so-called hymn probably includes verses 12–14 (though most doubt this)[5] and fits into the overall context well as part of the thanksgiving given earlier, in verse 3 (cf. also v. 12). Thus, while there is a massive amount of literature written on this supposed hymn, much of it will not be summarized here. The reason for not doing so is because, even if verses 15–20 were based on an earlier preformed hymn, no significant light is shed on the meaning of verses 15–20, since we do not know the original context and historical setting of that hymn. Thus this commentary has nothing new to offer on this debated issue, though we agree with those who are doubtful about a preformed hymn being the basis for this passage. Even if there were a preformed hymn, it would not affect our exegesis of the Colossians text.

Most directly, verses 15–20 (together with vv. 21–23) are an explanation of the directly preceding verses, that is, who Christ is as "the son of his love, in whom we have the redemption, the forgiveness of sins"* (vv. 13b–14). Recall that verses 13b–14 concerning Christ are part of verses 12b–13a concerning the Father's work in salvation, so that all of verses 12b–14 provide the basis for "giving thanks to the Father" in verse 12a. Recall also that all of verses 12–14 are ultimately supportive of the main point in verses 3–14 of Paul's prayer that believers "walk in a manner worthy of the Lord to please <u>him</u>" (v. 10a), pleasing the Lord being the climactic goal of verses 3–14. Thus, verses 15–20 (along with vv. 21–23) are also part of the ground, together with verses 12b–14, for the thanksgiving (v. 12a) and are also ultimately supportive of walking "in a manner worthy of the Lord to please <u>him</u>" (v. 10a). Accordingly, verses 15–23 are vital in understanding how believers are to "walk worthily to please <u>him</u>." They need to know who Christ really is and what he has done for them to know who they really are and to act out of that knowledge. Verses 15–20 are also an amplification of "the <u>kingdom</u>

3. For significant qualifications about this passage being based on a preformed hymn, see Moule 1957: 60–62; Caird 1976: 174–75; O'Brien 1982: 32–37; and N. Wright 1986: 64. Barth and Blanke (1994: 227–42) conclude that the author of Colossians composed the hymn ad hoc; cf. similarly Bruce 1984: 56–57.

4. So Garland (1998: 82–83), citing others in agreement. See similarly Pao 2012: 89–91.

5. In this respect, some commentators have noticed the liturgical ring of verses 12–14, which bring it close to the more overt liturgical nature of verses 15–20; cf., e.g., Sumney (2008: 56), who sees liturgical elements in verses 12–14 that prepare the reader for verses 15–20. See also Davids (2008a: 256), who sees verses 13–14 as a bridge between verses 3–12 and verses 15–20, with verses 13 (12?)–14 being a praise to the Father, which is a transition leading to praise of the Son.

of the . . . Son" (v. 13), highlighting Christ's sovereign rule over not only the church but also all of creation (so likewise Melick 1991: 210). Verses 15–20 are treated as a new paragraph not only for literary reasons[6] but also because of the new subject matter. Whereas Christ was only introduced in verses 13b–14, now there is an expanded description of who he is, especially as the sovereign king over all things (picking up "the kingdom of the Son" in v. 13). We include verses 21–23 as part of a larger segment together with verses 15–20 because of its close logical connection with verses 15–20 (see on v. 21). Nevertheless, verses 21–23 are a subdivision within verses 15–23 and literarily distinct from verses 15–20.

The verses in this segment can be broadly divided into three thematic sections: (1) Christ's supremacy over the first creation (vv. 15–17), which is the basis for (2) Christ's supremacy over the new creation (vv. 18–20), all of which results in (3) Christ's supremacy in reconciling sinful creation (vv. 21–23), which is the main point of verses 15–23. The emphasis on Christ's supremacy over the cosmos is to strike an initial blow to those among the Colossians who think there are other cosmic spirit authorities who should also be appealed to in order to find spiritual "fullness."[7] Furthermore, it underscores that the "rescue" from the "authority of darkness" (v. 13) and the "redemption, the forgiveness of sins" (v. 14), has certainly taken place because it was accomplished by none other than Christ, who is the sovereign deity over the entire cosmos.[8] Thus, while verses 13–14 conclude Paul's prayer begun in 1:9, they are also transitional to the segment of 1:15–20 (so also Sumney 2008: 44, 56, 58).

Exegesis and Exposition

[15]He is the image of the invisible God, the firstborn of all creation. [16]For by Him all
things were created, both in the heavens and on earth, visible and invisible, whether
thrones or dominions or rulers or authorities—all things have been created through
Him and for Him. [17]He is before all things, and in Him all things hold together. [18]He
is also head of the body, the church; and He is the beginning, the firstborn from the
dead, so that He Himself should come to have first place in everything. [19]For it was
the Father's good pleasure for all the fullness to dwell in Him, [20]and ⌜through Him⌝ to

6. D. Moo (2008: 108) makes three observations in this respect: (1) adverbial participles dominate verses 3–8, verses 9–14, and verses 21–23, whereas in verses 15–20 indicative verbs in main clauses occur much more; (2) there is a piling up of second-person and first-person pronouns that focus respectively on the readers or the writer and first- or second-person pl. verbs in verses 3–8, verses 9–14, and verses 21–23 (though only two pronouns focusing on reader or writer in vv. 21–23), but these features do not occur in verses 15–20; (3) in the verses surrounding verses 15–20 are complex sentences that form arguments, whereas in verses 15–20 are short statements about Christ. Also, the tight literary chiastic structure in verses 15–20 reveals its encapsulated nature (below see the structural parallelism from N. Wright 1992a: 104).

7. D. Moo 2008: 111. See similarly Witherington (2007: 130) for this role of the hymn for the entire epistle.

8. Cf. D. Moo (2008: 111), who focuses mainly on the link to verse 13; cf. also Sumney 2008: 56.

reconcile all things to Himself, having made peace through the blood of His cross;
through Him, I say, whether things on earth or things in heaven.

[21]And although you were formerly alienated and hostile in mind, engaged in evil
deeds, [22]yet He has now ⸢reconciled⸣ you in His fleshly body through death, in order
to present you before Him holy and blameless and beyond reproach—[23]if indeed you
continue in the faith firmly established and steadfast, and not moved away from the
hope of the gospel that you have heard, which was proclaimed in all creation under
heaven, and of which I, Paul, [became] a minister.

1. Christ Is Supreme over the First Creation as the Divine Preexisting Adam-Like Being (1:15–17)

1:15 Paul begins with an interpretive elaboration upon the initial description of Christ in verses 13b–14 that continues all the way through verse 23. The initial ὅς (*hos*) has its antecedent in ᾧ (*hō*) in verse 14 ("in whom we have the redemption"), which refers to Christ's redemption of his people. Christ, God's "beloved Son" (v. 13b) and the redeemer (v. 14), is now called "the image of the invisible God" and "the firstborn of all creation."

An Adamic background for the portrayal of Christ as the preexisting "image of God." A number of commentators rightly understand that the reference to Christ as the "image of the invisible God" is, at least in part, an allusion to Gen. 1:27: "God created man in His own image, in the image of God He created him" (LXX: "God made man according to the image of God"; see additional notes below). Paul's language here is virtually identical with his reference elsewhere to "man" being in "the image of God" (1 Cor. 11:7, where clear allusion is made to Gen. 1:27; e.g., on 1 Cor. 11:7, see Fee 1987: 515). A clear link to Gen. 1:26–27 in 1:15a (ὅς ἐστιν εἰκὼν τοῦ θεοῦ, *hos estin eikōn tou theou*) is also indicated by recognizing that precisely the same phrase "who is the image of God" (ὅς ἐστιν εἰκὼν τοῦ θεοῦ) occurs in 2 Cor. 4:4, where it focuses on Christ in his incarnate and especially glorified state as the pristine image in which the first Adam should have been.[9] In 2 Cor. 4:4 the "is" (ἐστίν, *estin*) refers to the ongoing truth of Christ in his exalted state as "the image of God," which likely has some overlap with the idea in Col. 1:15.[10]

Paul's thought may have been led to this Gen. 1 background, not only because of the repeated allusion to Gen. 1:28 in the preceding context (Col. 1:6, 10) but also because of the mention of "son" in verse 13.[11] "Sonship," as we saw earlier, is inextricably linked to the Gen. 1 notion of God's "image." For example, Gen.

9. Indeed, 2 Cor. 4:6 quotes Gen. 1:3 ("Light shall shine out of darkness") in further explanation of 4:4; cf. also Abbott 1897: 210; Phil. 2:6–7 apparently has the same significance as 2 Cor. 4:4: Christ "existed in the form of God . . . and [was] made in the likeness of men."

10. If the verb "is" here in Col. 1:15 is atemporal, then it would include Christ being in "the image of God" in eternity past, present, and future, though the focus in 2 Cor. 4:4 is on his being the image in his exalted state.

11. The relative pronoun ὅς (*hos*) in Col. 1:15, like ᾧ (*hō*) in verse 14, has its antecedent in "the son of his love" in verse 13.

5:1–4 implies that Adam's being in God's "image" means that Adam was God's "son": when Adam's son was born, Adam was said to be the "father of [a son] in his own likeness, according to his image" (so also Luke 3:38 speaks of "Adam, the son of God"). Thus image language is sonship language.

Colossians 3:10 also points to a Gen. 1:26–28 background, where the Christian is said to be "renewed . . . according to the image of the One who created him." Here "image" is most likely connected with "image" in Col. 1:15, since it is also an allusion to Gen. 1:26–27 and the two passages are so close together. Obviously Col. 3:10 refers to something in this age and not in eternity past.[12] Also strikingly similar to Col. 1:15 is Rom. 8:29, which echoes Gen. 1:27 (note the allusion to Gen. 3:17–19 in Rom. 8:20): Christ is both "the image of His Son" (to which believers become "conformed") and the "firstborn." This passage also refers to the historical Christ as being in God's image. But does "image" in 1:15 refer to the incarnate and exalted Christ?[13]

In contrast to Rom. 8:29; 2 Cor. 4:4; and Col. 3:10, here Col. 1:15a refers not to Christ as the "image" in his human incarnational and exalted form. Rather, as we will see in verses 15b–17, Christ's preexistence as God's divine "image" is the focus, though his status as the divine image still applies to his incarnational state and eternal exalted status. The reason for this widely temporal understanding is found in ἐστίν (*estin*, is) in verse 15a, which is a timeless or gnomic[14] present in that Christ is eternally and originally the "image of the invisible God" (cf. Tipton 2008: 187). This eternal status in God's image refers to eternity past (the focus here), the incarnation and exaltation and Christ's exalted status into eternity future. In support of this ongoing sense of Christ as the "image," as we will see, the perfect verb in the clause "all things have been created" in 1:16b highlights a stative idea, referring to the very beginning of creation and to its continuing existence on into the new cosmos. The genitive "image of God" should be taken as an objective genitive (Jesus "imaging God") instead of a genitive of relationship or a possessive genitive (cf. Harris 2010: 39), since the tone in the context is on Jesus reflecting God both before and in his incarnation and exaltation and into eternity future. In this respect, in Col. 1:15 Christ as the "image" includes notions of "representation of," "similarity to," and "likeness to" God (so Callow 2002: 43).

Early Judaism also closely associated the notions of Adam's sonship and his being in God's image, sometimes even referring to his being the image of the "invisible" God (see the additional notes below). Paul either independently interprets the OT notion of the Adamic image along the same lines as does Judaism or he follows the interpretative trajectory begun in earlier Judaism.[15]

12. Likewise 2 Cor. 3:18 refers to Christians becoming "transformed" into Christ's incarnational exalted "image" in this age and consummated in the future.

13. See Caird (1976: 177), who sees the connection between 1:15 and 3:10 as partial support for "image" in 1:15 having reference to the incarnate and exalted Christ.

14. On which cf. Wallace 1996: 523–25.

15. Lohse (1971: 47) cites as possibly relevant some texts from the Hermetic Corpus that speak of the cosmos or humanity being in the "image of God," but these texts come from the

Either way, he sees that Christ was in the divine image of God before creation and that he is (ἐστίν, *estin*, referring to a timeless truth) still in the divine image throughout redemptive history and on into eternity: the eschatological image of Christ in his resurrected estate is the manifestation of his eternal ontic status as the divine archetypal image in its eschatological significance in light of Christ's incarnation, death, and resurrection. Christ has come in human form and accomplished that which the first Adam did not (as apparent from Col. 1:18). The incarnate Christ is the perfect ectypal image reflecting his preincarnate archetypal image.[16] The incarnation brings something truly new in terms of Christ's eschatological image bearing: it is not something contradictory to his divine preincarnate existence as the archetypal Adam-like image but is a manifestation of it in a mode that is conditioned by Christ's work in redemptive history. Consequently, as the preexisting and divine image, Christ reflects in eternity past, present, and future the archetypal image that Adam and others should have reflected in an ectypal manner but did not.[17] Accordingly, Ridderbos (1975: 73) rightly affirms that "Christ's power and glory, already in his preexistence, are defined in categories that have been derived from his significance as the second Adam."[18]

In contrast, a number of commentators have concluded that Christ as the visible incarnate revelation of the invisible God appears to be the main focus of verse 15 (see also Calvin 1972: 308; Mitchell [2000: 58] cites John 1:18; 12:45; 14:9 as parallels to this idea in Col. 1:15). The incarnational revelatory emphasis is also pointed to by Col. 1:12–14, where the exodus-redemption background has been applied to God's redemption of people through his Son; indeed, verse 15 continues to describe the "Son," who accomplished redemption and forgiveness for his people (vv. 13–14; so also N. Wright 1992a: 109). Likewise, 1 Cor. 15:45–49 portrays Christ as possessing the heavenly image of the last Adam, which Christians will fully reflect at his final parousia. Thus, to see Col. 1:15 referring to Christ in his redemptive-historical role and primarily against the background of Genesis is a line of interpretation followed by many commentators, though a few resist it (especially the Adam background).[19] Many might say that not to see "image" in Col. 1:15 as having the same background and

second and third centuries AD, too late to have had any influence on the first-century text of Colossians.

16. "Archetype" (lit., "first" plus "impress, stamp, type") may be defined as "the original or model from which copies are made; a prototype" (*OED* 1:108–9); "ectype" is "an impression . . . of a seal or medal" (*OED* 1:108–9). The German synonyms are "Urbild" and "Abbild."

17. I am grateful to my research assistant William Wood for his comments in helping me refine my discussion of "archetypal" (with respect to the preexistent Christ) and "ectypal" image (with respect to the first and last Adam) throughout this analysis of Col. 1:15.

18. Likewise, Ridderbos (1975: 78) says, "[Paul] delineates even the glory of Christ in his preexistence and in his divine exaltation with features drawn from redemptive history, and the image of the second Adam."

19. See, e.g., Aletti 1993: 94–116; Schweizer 1982: 66; Dunn 1996: 87–88, though he sees an Adamic background in Col. 1:18; Talbert 2007: 187.

redemptive-historical meaning of "image" in Rom. 8:29; 2 Cor. 4:4; and 1 Cor. 15:45–49 would seem unlikely.

But in light of the observation that verses 16–17 affirm Christ as the preexisting Creator and sustainer as the ground for verse 15, it is clear that the main thought in verse 15 is of Christ being in God's image *before* creation began. This "image" is certainly described with Adamic contours from Gen. 1, but the image refers to Christ in his preexistence. Paul is speaking of the eternal relationship of the Son to the Father.[20] Recall that ἐστίν (*estin*) refers to a timeless truth of Christ being in the divine image not only before creation but also in that archetypal image in his incarnation and exaltation. Christ being in the perfect Adamic image in his incarnation is but the expression of his eternal existence as the divine archetypal Adam-like image in his preexistence.

This implicit pattern of preexistent archetypal image and incarnational ectypal image appears to be present in Phil. 2:6–7, where Christ is said to have "existed in the *form of God*" before his incarnation, and then he "came to be in the likeness of men,"* both phrases which many commentators now view rightly to have an Adamic identification (e.g., cf. N. Wright 1992a: 56–98, esp. 57–62, 90–97). Wright declares it appropriate that Christ in his preincarnate divine state could be said to be in God's image, since the mission of the perfect man who would represent Israel and save the world is a task that the OT also attributes to God; indeed, the glorious authority of the ideal or perfect man (in fulfillment of Gen. 1:26–28; Ps. 8; and Dan. 7:13–14) is (according to Isa. 45) thoroughly suitable for God himself (N. Wright 1992a: 95). It may well be that describing Christ's preincarnate condition with the word "image" is a way of portraying him "as being, so to speak, a potential man" (N. Wright 1992a: 95, a conclusion Wright makes about Christ being in "the form of God" in Phil. 2:6). However, "potential man" is language that in this context is ambiguous and could be misleading, since one must ask, In what sense was Christ a "potential man" in his divine preexistence?

But if by "potential man" Wright means that Christ preexisted as the divine archetypal image that the first Adam was to reflect ectypally, then the notion is consistent with Paul's thought. In a similar vein, Wright also mentions that just as 2 Cor. 8:9 can refer to the preexistent Messiah by his subsequent incarnate name of "Lord Jesus Christ," so the same is the case with calling the preexistent Christ the human "image" of God, "much as we might say 'the Queen was born in 1926'" (N. Wright 1992a: 116) or that "'the Prime Minister studied economics at Oxford'" (N. Wright 1992a: 96). I was initially attracted to the helpfulness of these examples, though after further reflection they express a view in which Christ as the *human* image of God is cast back

20. See Ridderbos (1975: 70–71), who also says that Col. 1:15 refers to the preincarnate Christ as God's image, which distinguishes him from God and, on the other hand, he is "identified with God as Bearer of the divine glory," so that "in him . . . God becomes manifest." Ridderbos's last comment makes good sense in light of the fact that "glory" and "image" are sometimes synonymous in Scripture (e.g., Ps. 106:20 [105:20 LXX]; in Paul see, e.g., Rom. 8:29–30; 1 Cor. 11:7; 2 Cor. 3:18; 4:4). For such references in Judaism, see Beale 2011: 443n12.

upon the preincarnate image and could potentially compromise that preexistent divine ontic existence. Before the incarnation Christ was not identified as a human but existed only as the Second Person of the Trinity, even if his divine image reflected features of the first and last Adam.

The preexistent Christ is being described in the language portraying his historical revelation; "the author is merely ascribing to Christ in *protology* what is true of him in *eschatology*" (Dunne 2011: 6–9), though this must be understood respectively as Christ preexisting in the archetypal image and coming eschatologically in the perfect incarnate ectypal image. The one who brought redemption (Col. 1:14) and reconciliation (1:20, 22) to the world is the same one who existed as a ruler in God's divine image before the creation of the world.[21] Paul can conceive of the manifestation of Christ's ontic image in his economic image-bearing as incarnate Son without confusing the two.

With regard to the ontological aspect of the image, Jesus is an exact representation of God, especially in the light of Col. 1:19 and 2:9; the latter reads, "In him [Christ] dwells all the fullness of deity in bodily form" (so Harris 2010: 39). Some also think that Christ as the image of God in his incarnational form is the focus of 1:15a, since Christ is the expression of the "invisible God" (so, e.g., O'Brien 1982: 43), and his existence as God's image before his incarnation was in an invisible sphere. But, on the other hand, Christ's imaging of "the invisible God" does not have to be and probably is not a visible imaging of the invisible deity. Rather, as we have seen above, in the light of "glory" and "image" being synonymous in the OT and Paul, one can easily conceive that Christ as God's image reflects the glory of God, which before creation presumably would have been a nonphysical reflection of the glory. This is similar to Heb. 1:3: Christ "is the radiance of His glory and the exact representation of His nature," which focuses on Christ's existence before creation (see Heb. 1:2),[22] though this is set in the context of the redemptive-historical revelation of Christ (see Heb. 1:1–4).

Philo's repeated references to a nonphysical and eternal Adam-like figure and a physical Adam created after the pattern of the incorporeal Adamic-figure are a striking parallel to Col. 1:15, where Christ is portrayed as the true Adamic archetype who existed before creation. It is similarly implied in Col. 1:15 that the earthly Adam was created after the image of this preexisting invisible Adam, since the Gen. 1:27 allusion to Adamic "image" language is applied to the preexisting Christ. This is a precedent indicating that a being could be thought to be in the image of God and not have a physical, visible existence before the creation of the corporeal Adam in Gen. 1–2.

21. Cf. O'Brien (1982: 44), who says that Christ as the image in Col. 1:15 refers to the "revealing of the Father on the one hand and his preexistence on the other—it is both functional and ontological," though what O'Brien means by "functional" is unclear.

22. The participle ὤν (*ōn*) in Heb. 1:3 is probably timeless like ἐστίν (*estin*) in Col. 1:15. In terms of systematic theology, the eternal generation of the Son from the Father, wherein the Son reflected his Father, did not entail before his incarnation that the Son be in a visible form.

Thus, in summary, the concept of "image" here does not originate ultimately from Paul's view of Christ as the second or last Adam in Rom. 5 or 1 Cor. 15, where Christ follows after the historical first Adam. Rather, Christ as "image" is "antecedent to the first [Adam], and in this respect the first Adam cannot be regarded as his 'type,' as is the case in Romans 5 and 1 Corinthians 15."[23] We think it best that Christ "in the image of God" is the original and perfect archetypal image, likeness, representation, and revelation of God, after which the human Adam was to be patterned ("in" or "according to the image," Gen. 1:26) as the ectypal image.[24] The first "Adam was a *creaturely replica* of the eternal Son of God" (Tipton 2008: 193), thus "an earthly sketch of the eternal, preexistent Son of God" (Tipton 2016). As such, "Adam manifests something of the glory of the eternal Son" (Tipton 2008: 193). Adamic "image" language from Gen. 1:27 is applied to Christ even as the preexisting invisible image, since this was the image after which the human Adam was to be created and was to reflect. In his nature, from eternity past, Jesus was "the image of God," perfectly mirroring the life and character of his Father. *Therefore, it was suitable for him later to be "the image of God" as man, since from eternity he had maintained the same relation to his Father that humanity, at the time of creation, had been designed ectypally to bear* (following N. Wright 1986: 71), *though no human would ever do it perfectly, as the incarnate God-man Jesus has done.* Being in the essential image of the Father in his divine person was a presupposition for him becoming the ectypal representative image in his incarnate person unto the world (Eadie 1856: 45, citing Owen 1867: 78). Thus the preexistent Christ being in the perfect ontological image enabled him in his incarnate form to function perfectly in the Adamic image of God.[25] The following chart expresses this relationship of Christ and the first Adam as both being in God's image (this chart is from Tipton 2016):

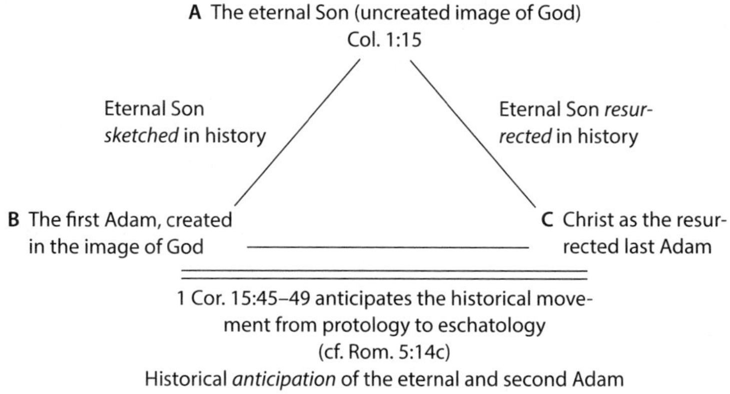

23. In this paragraph thus far following Ridderbos 1975: 84.

24. See likewise D. Moo (2008: 118–19), who also cites others in agreement.

25. Col. 1:18 expresses this, especially with respect to Christ being "firstborn" and "preeminent" (ESV), traits of the first historical Adam as an ectype of the preexistent Son.

The *A-B* and *A-C* coordinates refer to the revelation of the eternal Son and his image-bearing glory; Adam bears the glory of the preexisting Son's image via his creation (the *A-B* coordinate), and Christ does so via his resurrection (the *A-C* coordinate). Just as the creation of the human Adam as the son of God temporarily manifested the eternal glory of the uncreated Son of God, so also the historical resurrection of the last Adam reveals the eternal glory of the incarnate Son of God (following Tipton 2016). Christ as the resurrected Adamic image is the typological fulfillment of the first Adam's failure to reflect the image (the *B-C* coordinate). Christ began to become the incarnate last Adam even in his earthly ministry (see Beale 2011: 385–429), though this is not depicted as clearly in the chart.

An Adamic background for the portrayal of Christ as "the firstborn." In the second line of Col. 1:15, the reference to Christ as the "firstborn [πρωτότοκος, *prōtotokos*] of all creation" highlights further the idea that he is an Adamic figure and "Son" of God, the latter of which expands further on what it means that Christ is God's "beloved Son" (v. 13b). Is the "firstborn <u>of all creation</u> [πάσης κτίσεως, *pasēs ktiseōs*]" to be translated "all creation" or "every creature" (KJV)? Either rendering is viable lexically, but the first is probable for three reasons: (1) The parallel "in all creation" (ἐν πάσῃ κτίσει, *en pasē ktisei*) in 1:23 does not mean "among every creature" but "in all creation," because of its clear parallel with "in all the world" in 1:6 (ἐν παντὶ τῷ κόσμῳ, *en panti tō kosmō*; see additional notes on 1:23b). (2) Paul clearly has in mind the entire animate and inanimate creation in 1:16a ("in him was <u>created all things in the heaven and on the earth</u>"*), 1:16b ("<u>all things have been created</u> through Him and for Him"), and in 1:17 ("in Him <u>all things</u> hold together"). (3) Paul's typical use of κτίσις (*ktisis*) refers to the animate and inanimate created "world" as a complete creation (Rom. 1:20; 8:19, 20, 21, 22, 39 [?]; 2 Cor. 5:17 [?]; Gal. 6:15 [?]), though it can sometimes mean "creature" (Rom. 1:25; 2 Cor. 5:17 [?]; Gal. 6:15 [?]).[26] Nevertheless, the focus is probably more on animate beings, as Col. 1:16 indicates ("whether thrones or dominions or rulers or authorities"), though they are singled out as a part of the larger creation, since Paul wants to focus on them more later,[27] just as he focuses on the humans within the sphere of the whole creation in verses 6 and 23.

What precisely does "firstborn" mean? The meaning cannot be that Christ was the first of other beings that were created, since verse 16 says that the entire creation came into being by him (Bruce 1984: 59). The OT repeatedly asserts that the "firstborn" of every Israelite family gains authority by virtue of being given a double share of inheritance rights (e.g., Deut. 21:17). This notion was projected back upon the first Adam by early Judaism, since Adam was

26. Elsewhere in the NT, κτίσις can refer to the entire creation of the "world" (Mark 10:6, 13:19; Heb. 9:11; 2 Pet. 3:4; Rev. 3:14 [?]) or to particular "creatures" in the world (Mark 16:15, probably all human creatures living throughout "all creation"; Heb. 4:13; cf. 1 Pet. 2:13).

27. Some think that the anarthrous construction πάσῃ κτίσει (*pasē ktisei*, as in 1:23) should be "every creature" (as in KJV, NRSV, NIV, etc.) rather than "the whole of," but such uses of πᾶς (*pas*) often express the whole of something (D. Moo 2008: 120).

the "firstborn" of all human creation.[28] By a similar application, this feature of Adam as "firstborn" is projected back upon the preexistent Son, who in reality is the prototype of the first historical Adam. Christ is the "firstborn," not only of all humanity in the new creation (see on 1:18 below) but also of "all [things in the old] creation" (1:15b).[29]

Even Israel was called God's "firstborn" (πρωτόγονος, *prōtogonos*, Sir. 36:17 [36:11 LXX]) and his "very first [πρώτιστος, *prōtistos*] offspring" (e.g., Philo, *Post.* 63). Both the law of primogeniture and Israel as "firstborn" are part of the background for Paul's expression (so Wall 1993: 67; see additional notes on Col. 1:15b for further references to Israel as "firstborn" in Judaism). The reason Israel was assigned this name was probably because the nation was given the same mandate to "rule and subdue, multiply and fill the earth" (cf. Gen. 1:28) as Adam and Noah, the latter a second Adam figure (see comments on Col. 1:6, 10 above). Thus Israel was a corporate Adam figure and thus was to accomplish the same purposes of supremacy over creation as Adam, and Col. 1:15a–b show Christ in his preincarnate state having this feature of supremacy over the first creation.

In the light of the above, it is understandable that Ps. 89 (88 LXX) refers to David and (typologically) to the coming eschatological messianic king as having God as his "Father," being "firstborn" (πρωτότοκος, *prōtotokos*), and inheriting a position "higher than the kings of the earth," with a "throne" that lasts "forever" (Ps. 89:27–29, 37 [88:28–30, 38]).[30] The emphasis on ruling instead of on temporal priority in Psalm 89 is apparent from recalling that David was the youngest among his brothers (1 Sam. 16:11), yet in this psalm he is called "firstborn" (see Pao 2012: 95). "Firstborn" in Col. 1:15 probably includes allusion to this psalm passage.[31] Allusion to the psalm develops the notion in the immediate context of Colossians that Christ as the preexistent Adam is the archetypal king and ruler over the creation (Gen. 1:26–28; see further Beale 2011: 30–33). There will come a time when the archetypal king will become incarnate and fulfill in history the psalm's typological prophecy (with David pointing to the Messiah within the psalm itself).[32] What points further to a Ps. 89 allusion is the use of χριστός (*christos*) twice in the psalm

28. E.g., cf. Num. Rab. 4.8, where the "firstborn" Israelites were redeemed by Levites and received the "birthright" because "Adam was the world's firstborn," who served as a priest, as did his representative progeny until the Levites were established.

29. Hugedé (1968: 53–54) sees the first Adam in Gen. 1 as the background for understanding the last Adam, Christ, as the "firstborn."

30. In Heb. 12:23, "church of the firstborn" likely connotes the church as being in an exalted position of inheriting eschatological blessings (cf. Lightfoot 1875: 147) because of its identification with Christ the "firstborn" (Heb. 1:6; Hay 2000: 56).

31. Cf. Abbott 1897: 210–11; Simpson and Bruce (1957: 194), O'Brien (1982: 44), and Fee (2007: 301) see an echo of the psalm in Col. 1:15.

32. Later Judaism understood that Ps. 89 [88] could refer to the coming eschatological king on analogy with Exod. 4:22, where God says of the nation, "Israel is My son, My firstborn" (Exod. Rab. 19.7, the context of which primarily identifies the patriarch Jacob with "Israel," who then is compared by analogy to the coming Messiah).

(89:38, 51 [88:39, 52 LXX]) to refer to Israel and the use of the verbal form χρίω (*chriō*) to refer to David being "anointed" and, implicitly, to the coming Davidic seed who will be the eschatological representative king of the nation (see 89:19–28, 34–36 [88:20–29, 35–37]). Though "Christ" as a name does not occur in the poem of Col. 1:15–20, it does appear repeatedly in the nearby context (1:1–4, 7, 24, 27–28).

The subsequent reference to Christ as "before all things" (Col. 1:17a) further highlights his role as "firstborn" of all creation (1:15). The three descriptions of Christ in verses 15–17 ("image of God," "firstborn," "before all things") are thus different ways of referring to Christ, the Son, as the archetypal Adamic-like figure. This highlights how the Second Person of the Trinity is what Adam was patterned after, since they were common ways of referring to the first Adam or to those who were Adam-like figures and were given the first Adam's task to rule over the creation, whether this be Noah, the patriarchs, or the nation Israel. In this respect, "image" is superbly fitting, since in Gen. 1:26–28 it refers to Adam as reflecting God's image, partly as the king of creation who is to rule over it (following Barth and Blanke 1994: 249–50).

And just as Adam's temporal priority was not the main point of his purpose but contributed to his ultimate design to be a world ruler, so these names of "firstborn" and the one "before all things" in Colossians were not merely intended to indicate Christ's *temporal priority* to the old creation but primarily underscored his *sovereignty* over it, as most commentators acknowledge.[33] The pretemporal connotation does not indicate that Christ was the very beginning part of the creation but that he was "born before it" (rightly, according to Moule 1957: 76, in the sense of the "eternal generation of the son"), which places Christ as separate from the rest of the creation; Christ's separateness from creation and existence before that creation are underscored by the affirmation that he is the agent of creation (and thus the Creator), which the next verse (16) underscores.

As we saw above, it is this point of world sovereignty that Ps. 89 [88 LXX] emphasizes about the "firstborn" messianic king. In particular, "I shall make him a firstborn" in Ps. 89:27 [88:28 NETS] is directly followed by the phrase "high among the kings of the earth," showing, at the least, that the two notions are inextricably linked, if not the latter being a further explanation of the former.[34]

As we will see in Col. 1:16, this position of authority is also grounded in the acknowledgment that Christ is the sovereign Creator of the world (v. 16, with an introductory ὅτι, *hoti*) and sovereignly maintains its ongoing existence (v. 17b). Therefore Christ perfectly embodies in his preexistence the ruling

33. Likewise the significance of "firstborn" Israelites was that they gained authority over the household and inheritance, and each of Philo's references to the highest ranking angel called "firstborn" also emphasize this (except for *Dreams* 1.215); see the additional notes on 1:15b.

34. As suggested by Theodore of Mopsuestia, cited in Abbott 1897: 211; Rev. 1:5 also alludes to Ps. 89:27, 29, 37 (88:28, 30, 38 LXX), to highlight that Christ's resurrection has placed him in a position of rule.

position that Adam and his flawed human successors should have imitated in an ectypal manner. He is, at the same time, the perfect divine Creator of all things, who is separate from and sovereign over that which he has created, especially underscored by the phrase "all things have been created through Him and for Him" at the end of 1:16 (on the latter, see Dunn 1996: 90–91).

As widely recognized, while Col. 1:15–17 refers to Christ's sovereignty over the first creation, verses 18–20 affirm his sovereign position in the second, new creation that has been launched by his resurrection. In this respect, the identical title of "firstborn" is reapplied to Christ in verse 18 in order again to indicate Christ's rule over the new order by virtue of his resurrection from the dead (v. 18c). His priority in the new creation entails his kingship over it (see also Heb. 1:2–5 and 2:5–9 for a relevant parallel).

As we will see, the reasons given for Christ's position of rule in the new redemptive-historical age are stated in Col. 1:19–20: (1) Christ is the full expression of deity, amplified in 2:9, "In Him all the fullness of Deity dwells in bodily form"; and (2) he has inaugurated the process of bringing creation back into harmonious relation to itself and to God (i.e., "reconciling"). In verse 18 Paul portrays Christ as God and end-time Adam in the flesh in order to affirm that "Jesus fulfills the purposes which God had marked out *both* for himself *and* for humanity" (N. Wright 1986: 70–71). The design for humanity originally reaches its completion in the last Adam. The first Adam's failure to obey God and rule under him left a gap of needed obedience for humanity to reach its eschatological completion, so that even the first Adam's disobedience typologically pointed to another Adam's obedience and ultimate rule. But in 1:15 Christ is the preexistent perfect Adam-like image, who is the model for the later earthly Adam and who would himself become the last Adam as a manifestation of his preexisting divine image (as v. 18 affirms). The Second Person of the Trinity in his preexistent state is being depicted in language that is like the first Adam in order to (1) set up the archetype-ectype relation of the preexisting Son to the first human Adam (the *A-B* coordinate in the above chart) while simultaneously (2) providing a context for the first Adam–last Adam typology (the *B-C* coordinate) and (3) the redemptive-historical coming of the Son as second Adam (in the *A-C* coordinate).

A number of commentators think that the figurative portrayal of "wisdom" in Judaism and in Prov. 8:22–27 (as "the beginning of His [God's] way" prior to the creation, who helped bring creation about) is reflected in Col. 1:15–17. This is possible, and to some extent this may be discernible, though the background of Adam-like features applied to the preexistent Christ is uppermost in mind (see the additional notes below on 1:15–17 for elaboration of the possible wisdom background, which we will argue is related to an Adamic notion). If so, wisdom—considered to be an attribute of God, existing before creation, and helping to create—is now identified with the person of Christ.

What is the significance of portraying Christ as a divine preexistent Adam-like figure? Christ as God's "Son" (v. 13b) and as "redeemer" (v. 14) is also to be understood as the very image of God, which Adam should have consummately and eternally reflected, but did not. Perhaps, as suggested earlier, the conceptual link between Christ as God's "Son" (v. 13b) and the last Adam is supplied by Gen. 5:1–3, where Adam and Eve are said to have been made "in the likeness of God," and then Adam "begot a son in his own likeness, according to his image" (NASB). Thus, to be in the "likeness and image" of someone is to be that one's son. Consequently, in the light of Gen. 5:1–3, Adam was also a "son" of God in Gen. 1:26–27. Likewise, Christ as preexisting with Adamic features is also God's Son yet so much so that he is divine. Christ later had to become incarnate as the perfect Adam in order to be God's perfectly faithful human "Son" and in order to be a human representative to take sin upon himself and to accomplish redemption (so see Col. 1:13–14!). But only a divine being could be perfectly faithful in every way. Consequently, Christ became a divine incarnate last Adam in conformity with his preexisting Adam-like image as the eternal Son.[35] Romans 8:29 refers to Christ as "the image of his Son" (in his incarnation and exaltation) and as "the firstborn" (as the first to rise from the dead), both of which refer to the Son's relationship to redeemed humanity.

But, as we observed in verse 15, these identifications of Christ with Adam are also projected back before creation, so that now the focus is not on Christ's incarnate relationship to humanity but on his relationship to creation (here following Fee 2007: 298). He is the perfect divine expression in eternity past of God's image, the archetype behind God's design for Adam to reflect God's image in an ectypal manner and likewise for his people in the new creation to reflect God's image. As "firstborn" Christ is also prior to and especially divine ruler over the first creation, which became the pattern for him to be the incarnate "firstborn" of the new creation in order to have "supremacy over all things" in the remaining old and emerging new creation. The pattern inherent in Christ as the preexisting divine king of the first creation was the blueprint for him to become the divine-human king of the new creation (cf. likewise Garland 1998: 100). This is part of the pattern reflecting the notion that God "makes the last things like the first things" (Barn. 6.13; see further on 1:18).

The genitival clause "firstborn of all creation" does not likely indicate a partitive genitive[36] (i.e., Christ as the actual first part "of [among] all the creation"). This is unlikely since, as we will see in verses 16–17, Christ is portrayed as the divine Creator, which has already been intimated in verse 15a with Christ as the preexistent "image of the invisible God." Thus Christ as the divine Creator is distinguished from "all creation" in verse 16 (Harris 2010: 40). In the light of the emphasis of "firstborn" being on "supremacy

35. Nevertheless, some commentators do not believe that there is an Adamic idea behind "firstborn" (e.g., Schweizer 1982: 67–68), which is improbable in the light of the preceding evidence.

36. So MHT 3:210. It would be more precise to speak of this option as a "wholative" genitive, "among all the creation," the whole of creation of which Christ would be part. Meyer (1885: 225–26) takes it as a genitive of comparison: "first-born in comparison with every creature," which means he was born before every creature, implying his unique divine origination from eternity. But this is unlikely, since such genitives "almost always" come after a comparative adjective (cf. Wallace 1996: 110 on comparative genitives).

over," the genitival phrase "firstborn <u>of all creation</u>" is best taken as a genitive of subordination ("firstborn <u>over</u> all creation") instead of more generally as a genitive of reference ("firstborn with reference to all creation"; so Wallace 1996: 238). Besides the sovereign sense that we have seen "firstborn" to have, this genitival option is further confirmed from the following phrase in Col. 1:16a ("by Him all things were created"), which would make little sense in supporting Christ as the first of creation in only a chronological sense. Rather, Christ as the sovereign Creator (v. 16a) supports his role as the supreme sovereign "over all creation" (v. 15b, or "over every created thing"; so Robertson 1934: 772).[37] The universal idea is supported from 1:16a by observing that the neuter plural τὰ πάντα (*ta panta*) is a description of "the universe," as common in the NT, which further elaborates on the "all creation" of 1:15 (so Robertson 1934: 653–54, who observes that neuter plurals of other words are used with a collective meaning for "the sum total" of something).

That "firstborn" focuses on sovereign rule is borne out from Col. 1:18, where the same word is an explanation of "head," "beginning," and is further explained by "have supremacy" (see on v. 18 for the "ruling" sense of all these words).[38]

In summary of the theological significance of the two Adam-like portrayals in Col. 1:15, two theological conclusions may be drawn. First, it is apparent that "image of the invisible God" indicates Christ's "preexistent consubstantial relation to the Father" (Tipton 2008: 188), which the parallel in 1:19 (and 2:9) clarifies[39] (see the table at my comments on 1:18–20 titled "Preeminence of Christ in the First Creation and in the New Creation"). Second, "firstborn of all creation" explains Christ's preexistent relation to creation as its ruler and ultimate cause.

This verse gives the basis (note the introductory ὅτι, *hoti*) for verse 15's af- **1:16**
firmation that Christ "is the image of the invisible God and the firstborn of all creation." Verse 16 now explains the reason for Christ's preceding titles of divine preexistence, which underscore his sovereignty over the cosmos: Christ is the divine image and ruler over all things *because* he is the agent of all creation and as such he existed before the creation. Verse 16 makes clear that the Adamic contours of the "image of the invisible God" and "firstborn of all creation" refer not to Christ's incarnational state but to his preexistent

37. So also Wallace 1996: 104, 128; likewise MHT 3:210; Zerwick and Grosvenor 1981: 604.

38. Could "firstborn" in Col. 1:15 mean that Christ was a part of the first creation, since "firstborn from the dead" in verse 18 includes the idea that he was the very first part of the new creation? This is not likely, since the phrase in verse 18 is not completely parallel with that in verse 15: the relation between the two is that the eternal Son of God (v. 15) became incarnate as part of the old physical creation, and then his resurrection meant that he would be the very beginning of the new physical creation. Christ's body was dead and was "among the dead ones," so that when he rises and exits alive from "among the dead ones," he is the first "among the dead ones" to rise, i.e., "firstborn" (cf. Meyer 1885: 234).

39. Harris (2010: 99) says that the parallel in Col. 1:19 and 2:9 "signifies that Jesus is an exact, as well as a visible, representation of God."

status. First, "all things were created by Christ," so that he is the agent of creation. That agency is in mind is pointed to by the end of the verse, where it is clearly referred to ("through him"), as well as 1 Cor. 8:6 ("all things . . . through" Christ were created) and John 1:3 ("all things came into being through Him [Christ], and apart from Him nothing came into being that has come into being"). Yet most of the uses of ἐν (*en*, in) with Christ as the object of the preposition in Colossians clearly refer to the idea of sphere.[40] On this viable basis, D. Moo prefers the likelihood that sphere is in mind in verse 16.[41] In further support of this is Eph. 2:10 ("for we are his creation, having been created in Christ Jesus"*). But what would it mean for "all things" to have been created in the "sphere" of Christ? Would it suggest that his sovereign presence held sway over everything that was brought into being? It is not clear exactly what such a spheric use could mean here.[42] Foster (2016: 182–83) has offered a viable explanation of the spheric use: Christ "constitutes the domain and locus of power in which the cosmos can be brought into existence." He rightly concludes that one seeks too much precision by choosing only one or the other of these options and thus concludes that both notions of agency and sphere are included.

Perhaps relevant to Col. 1:16a is Eph. 2:15, "in order that he [Christ] should create the two in himself."* Here ἐν αὐτῷ (*en autō*, in himself) certainly designates the sphere within which Christ created, but the fact that Christ is doing the creating shows that he is the agent of creating Jew and Gentile "in himself." It is thus better to take the phrase in Col. 1:16a to be a thicker reference that includes Christ as both the agent of creation and the sphere in which all things were created. The translation would be something like "with respect to Christ all things were created," but the reference would mainly be to both agency and sphere together.[43] The idea of agency may also be more in focus if this phrase about old creation in 1:16a is a parallel with the phrase that expresses part of the new creation in verse 20 ("and through Him to

40. See 1:14, 19; 2:6, 7, 9, 10, 11; 3:18, 20; 4:7, 17; the uses in 1:4 and 17 could be spheric, though this is not clear.

41. Though he finally adopts a very general use of the dative here without a focus on agency or sphere or even both (D. Moo 2008: 121).

42. O'Brien (1982: 45) proposes the idea that creation occurs "in Christ" and not separately from him. Campbell (2012: 180, 182) prefers only a locative (i.e., spheric) use.

43. Foster (2016: 182–83) agrees that both agency and sphere are likely in mind here. Lincoln (1990: 21–22) and O'Brien (1999: 97–98) conclude with respect to Eph. 1:3b that God's "blessing" of believers that came "in Christ" (ἐν Χριστῷ, *en christō*) has both a representative-incorporative idea and a notion of agency ("through Christ") on the basis of usage in the immediate context and elsewhere in Ephesians. The difference in Col. 1:16a is that this is not talking about believers but of unseen powers, including evil ones. The sense then of Christ as the one who brought these powers into being would seem to be the focus, since this would mean that, just as he was sovereign over them at the inception of their being, so he is now. Perhaps Col. 1:16a is similar to 3:1, where συνηγέρθητε τῷ Χριστῷ (*synēgerthēte tō christō*), though lacking the preposition ἐν (*en*), has the notion of both "You were raised by means of Christ" and "You were raised in Christ." Wallace (1996: 434) argues for only "intermediate agency" in Col. 1:16.

reconcile all things to Himself").[44] As noted on 1:15, that he is the sovereign agent of creation also further indicates that the affirmations about Christ in verse 15 focus on his supremacy *over* all creation. By associating Christ with an activity typically considered to be a divine prerogative or attribute, his proximity to God is highlighted (Foster 2016: 183). This is tantamount to a divine-identity Christology, whereby an activity of God is attributed to Christ.

"All things" comprises every animate and inanimate thing that has been created.[45] Included among these created things are "the visible things and the invisible things" (τὰ ὁρατὰ καὶ τὰ ἀόρατα, *ta orata kai ta aorata*). There are realities in the creation that can be seen and those that cannot be seen with the naked eye.[46] The latter is especially pointed to by the directly following enumeration of heavenly sovereign forces that cannot be seen with the human eye, so that at least part of the "heaven" in verse 16 overlaps with the "heavenlies" in Ephesians, where the evil powers of Satan reside (Eph. 1:21; 3:10; 6:11–12).

Also among all created things are "thrones," "dominions," "rulers," and "authorities." The focus is upon invisible heavenly sovereignties, though secondarily earthly rulers are in mind to the degree that they are represented by the heavenly potentates (as, e.g., in Dan. 10:20–21; 12:1; Rev. 2:1, 8, 12, 18; 3:1, 7, 14; on which, e.g., see Beale 1999a: 217–19).[47] But that both heavenly and earthly powers are in mind is apparent from the observation that the list of these various kinds of powers is a further explanation of the preceding

44. See the chart of parallels between 1:15–17 and 1:18–20 at the beginning of comments on 1:18–20 below.

45. For further rationale see the additional notes on 1:23b; in agreement, e.g., see Furter 1987: 100 in contrast to Hugedé 1968: 59, the latter who sees reference only to animate personal beings.

46. Philo uses the two Greek words together often, referring sometimes to God who is not visible but invisible (e.g., *Migr.* 183; *Emb.* 310), and alluding generally to the parts of the seen and unseen creation (e.g., *Spec.* 1.302); cf. also T. Reu. 6.12.

47. The angelic authorities in Daniel are both good and evil. Synonymous with "rulers and authorities" is "thrones" in Col. 1:16. Note that the only places where "thrones" (θρόνοι, *thronoi*) in the nominative case is found in the LXX is in Dan. 7:9 and Ps. 121:5 (122:5 Eng.), the first referring to heavenly thrones of good angels and the second to David's throne. But the only place in all of the Greek OT where θρόνοι (*thronoi*) occurs with ἀρχή (*archē*) and ἐξουσία (*exousia*) is in Dan. 7:9, 12, 14, referring to both good and evil earthly and angelic authorities (cf. also the use of ἄρχων, *archōn*, in Dan. 10:13 and 20 [Theod.] with reference to heavenly powers, as well as ἀρχή [*archē*] together with ἐξουσία [*exousia*] in Dan. 7:27 LXX, focusing on earthly powers but possibly including heavenly ones). Thus, this combined wording in Col. 1:16 reflects Dan. 7:9–14, especially since the "Son of Man" there is sovereign over these powers, as is Christ here as Creator, and in Col. 2:10 as ruler, as implicitly also in 1:18, where Christ is the "head" and "beginning"/"ruler." Further parallel in Dan. 7:27 is the reference to "all rulers" (πᾶσαι αἱ ἀρχαί, *pasai hai archai*, Theod.) / "all authorities" (πᾶσαι αἱ ἐξουσίαι, *pasai hai exousiai*, OG), who are "subjected" to God or the Son of Man or both, which has unique analogy with Col. 2:10 NET, "every ruler and authority" (πάσης ἀρχῆς καὶ ἐξουσίας, *pasēs archēs kai exousias*), which expands on the phrases in Col. 1:16 (cf. Stettler 2000: 190). The other word in verse 16 that is also used synonymously for "rulers or authorities" is "lordships"* (κυριότητες, *kyriotētes*), found elsewhere in the NT only in 2 Pet. 2:10a and Jude 8 (in both referring to good heavenly authorities in light of the following context) and in Eph. 1:21 (focusing on evil heavenly authorities, as we will see below).

"things created in heaven and on earth, visible and invisible" (Sumney 2008: 67–68). Texts in Judaism use the same kinds of expressions for the various types of angelic powers that God created (see Arnold 1995: 253–55; Garland 1998: 89). Probably evil authorities in heaven are primarily in mind (though all unseen good angels are in the peripheral vision of Paul), since the same "rulers and authorities" are mentioned in 2:10 and 15 and are malevolent there (e.g., see τὰς ἀρχὰς καὶ τὰς ἐξουσίας, *tas archas kai tas exousias*, in Col. 2:15 and the same nouns in 2:10).[48] It is obvious in 2:15 that the "rulers and authorities" are evil and unseen, but perhaps it is not so clear in 2:10. Nevertheless, we shall see that 2:10 also alludes to evil invisible powers over whom Christ is sovereign. And we shall see there that Christ's rule over these powers is related to the Colossians' protection from false teaching (see on 2:8–10).

Consequently, the reference to such powers in 1:16 anticipates part of Paul's argument against the false teaching besetting the Colossians, though this reference itself has been anticipated earlier by the singular reference to "the authority of darkness"* (τῆς ἐξουσίας τοῦ σκότους, *tēs exousias tou skotous*) in 1:13, which confirms the malevolent nature of these beings in verse 16 (following Talbert 2007: 187). The point is, as will become more evident in 2:4, 8, and 10, that the hearers should not be deceived, because Christ is the ruler over the invisible powers that are inspiring this wrong teaching through the false teachers.

This is probably why Paul does not focus on other parts of "all" the creation in verse 16 (e.g., trees, seas, mountains, rivers, forests). Rather, he immediately focuses on the invisible authorities that were created, since he is going to say more clearly later that Christ has defeated them and is their king. Some object that the forces in 1:16 can only be good, since evil principalities were not created evil but became sinful later (Callow 2002: 45). However, verse 17 affirms that every single part of creation ("all things," which occurs twice in v. 16) is preserved or "held together" by Christ's sovereign power, so that even if the above objection were relevant for verse 16, Christ is still seen as absolutely sovereign even over evil angels in the light of verse 17 (see on v. 17). In 2:10, that Christ "is head over all rule and authority" gives part of the reason why the Colossians are not to be taken in by false teaching but are to hold to the truth of Christ (2:8). The point accordingly is that the hearers should not be deceived because Christ is the ruler over the invisible powers that are inspiring this teaching by the false teachers. As long as the Christians stay planted on

48. In Eph. 1:20–21 Christ is said to be ruler "in the heavenlies" over "all rule and authority," which is the very same phrase as in Col. 2:10 and virtually the same expression as in Col. 2:15. While the phrase refers to all authorities without exception, the focus is likely on evil authorities, since Ephesians, like Colossians, uses the same or virtually same expression later in the epistle to refer only to evil authorities (so clearly 2:2, "ruler of the authority of the air"; 6:12; and likely 1:22 and 3:10, though the latter two cannot be argued here [though see further Thielman 2010: 108–9, 216–17]). Likewise, 1 Pet. 3:22 says that "angels and authorities and powers" have been "subjected" to Christ, as a result of his resurrection (cf. Moule 1957: 66), which likely are evil heavenly powers.

the foundational "principles" of Christ, they will be protected from the evil "principles of the world" (2:8; see further on 2:10).

Colossians 1:16 ends as it began by repeating that "all things have been created through [διά, *dia*] Him."[49] This emphatically shows that Christ at the first creation is not the first of created reality nor in any way a part of the creation but is the means or agent of creation (cf. Thompson 2005: 32). At the end of verse 16 is the addition that "all things have been created . . . for [εἰς, *eis*] him." According to this use of εἰς (*eis*), Christ has designed that he himself be the goal of his own creation (see Harris 2012: 88). The idea from the immediate context is that the past act of creating has effects that continue into the present; that is, the ongoing existence of the creation is the effect of his past creating activity. Thus ἔκτισται (*ektistai*, have been created) carries what many consider the traditional sense of the perfect tense because of the context of verse 16a, where an aorist tense refers to the initial act of creating; then the focus of the perfect tense in verse 16b is on the ongoing *state* of the creation.[50] The creation must have an ongoing existence in order to accomplish its future end-time goal in Christ, which is his glorification, as Rom. 11:36 clarifies: "For from Him and through Him and to Him are all things. To Him be the glory forever. Amen."[51] It is amazing to think that the one who was crucified as a criminal and offered "the body of his flesh through death"* (Col. 1:22) is the goal of the entire creation's existence.[52]

The thought of verses 15–16 continues here. In particular, this verse expands **1:17**
on verse 16 as the basis of and explanation for verse 15. Verse 17a further explains the divine side of Christ as "the image of the invisible God" and "the firstborn of all creation" in verse 15. The last part of verse 17 is a summary of the end of verse 16 ("All things have been created through Him and for Him"), which affirms that the ongoing existence of the creation is maintained by Christ.

The reference to Christ being "before all things" is a near-synonymous expression for "firstborn of all creation" in verse 15, where both phrases were discussed. And, just as we saw in verse 15 that the phrase includes the idea

49. Zerwick (1963) rightly suggests that the διά (*dia*) at the end of verse 16 expresses "instrumental causality" (38) or "efficient cause" (36, 97): "all things through him." See virtually the same expression applied to Christ in 1 Cor. 8:6 as the creator.

50. Cf. Zerwick 1963: 97. See Campbell (2008: 47–52) for this stative notion of the perfect and the debate about the perfect in relation to the ongoing development of verbal aspect theory. Campbell (2013: 12) views this specific verb in Col. 1:16 to be stative. Cf. Porter 1989: 260–63. Turner (MHT 3:70) sees the perfect in verse 16 carrying the sense of an aorist, which has just been used earlier in the verse, though Robertson (1934: 844, 894) disagrees.

51. Though this could refer to Christ (note the use of "Lord" in Rom. 11:34, which in 10:9, 12–13 refers to Christ, as elsewhere in Romans), it presumably here refers to the Father. Nevertheless, the parallel is helpful, since Christ's divine identity is being expressed in Col. 1:15–16. A striking parallel occurs in Marcus Aurelius, *Med.* 4.23: "All things are from you, all things are in you, and all things are for you"; see further Pao 2012: 96.

52. Cf. O'Brien 1982: 47; perhaps reflected in Judaism by b. Sanh. 98b: "The world was created only . . . for the sake of the Messiah."

of temporal priority, so it does here.[53] We concluded there, however, that the expression refers to Christ as a preincarnate Adam figure, who not only was in existence before the rest of the creation, but whose temporal precedence also entails that he was sovereign over all things, since in the Gen. 1–3 context temporal priority entails rule over something.[54] And just as Adam's temporal priority to the rest of human creation was not the main point of his purpose but contributed to his ultimate design to be a world ruler, so this idea is projected back onto the preexisting Christ. Psalm 89:27 (88:28 LXX) enforced this idea of world sovereignty, referring to the messianic king as "firstborn" ("I will make him a firstborn"), which is directly followed by the phrase "highest of the kings of the earth." This indicates that the two notions of kingship and firstborn are inextricably linked and overlapping in sense. Thus Christ's temporal priority as "firstborn of all things" entails his sovereign position over all things,[55] which expands upon the initial description of him as "firstborn of all creation" in Col. 1:15.

But why is the notion from verse 15b restated here? It is to explain the undergirding reason for the ongoing preservation of "all things [that] have been created" until they find their eschatological goal in Christ (v. 16b). That is, Christ's sovereign rulership will superintend all of creation to its final goal. The present tense ἐστίν (*estin*) could merely refer to Christ's "existence" (Christ "exists before all things"), or perhaps preferably, ἐστίν indicates not only that Christ was sovereign over creation at its beginning, but also that he is in control of it throughout time until the end of history.[56] As in verse 15, the ἐστίν is probably timeless in the sense that it includes eternity past, present, and eternity future. The truth of Christ's sovereign existence occurs before, during, and after the creation and in eternity future.

The second half of Col. 1:17 clarifies this very point about the ongoing preservation of creation: "in Him all things hold together."[57] Here the ἐν (*en*, in) plus the dative αὐτῷ (*autō*, him) is ambiguous. It could connote sphere (so most translations) or agency (the latter being preferred by Douay, KJV, and HCSB), though both might be in mind. Yet since Christ as the agent of creation has been repeated twice in verse 16, it may be that this is more of the focus here. It is by Christ's sovereign rule that creation is maintained, as it was created from the beginning.

53. In line with Paul's other eleven uses of the preposition πρό (*pro*, before), all of which refer to temporal priority, which leads Hanna (1983: 368) wrongly to think that this excludes the idea of superiority in rank. Similarly, Robertson (1934: 622) sees only a temporal idea with the phrase and not also superiority.

54. See Dunn (1996: 93) for a list of scholars holding to the notion of temporal precedence, on the one hand, and those on the other hand who hold to a view of superior status.

55. See also Harris (2012: 42, 187), who argues that the preposition πρό (*pro*) has a dual sense of priority of time and of supremacy of rank, especially in light of the immediate context (including the potentates mentioned immediately before in verse 16 over which Christ is clearly superior).

56. Cf. Moule 1957: 66; and Barth and Blanke 1994: 204.

57. See similarly Heb. 1:3 for Christ as the "exact representation of His nature" (cf. Col. 1:15), who "upholds all things by the word of His power."

The word συνέστηκεν (*synestēken*) is rendered primarily in two ways by the translations: "hold together" (NASB,[58] NRSV, ESV, NIV, HCSB, NJB) or "consist" (Geneva, KJV, ASV, Douay). The first option is a good translation; the latter is questionable. The verb form συνίστημι (*synistēmi*) is used elsewhere in Paul and numerously in the Greek OT, Philo, and the Jewish Greek pseudepigrapha. There are many ranges of meaning, but in the NT three notions stand out, especially in Paul: (1) to demonstrate something; (2) to commend someone or something; (3) to refer to God or Christ's sovereign rule over the creation, though apart from Col. 1:17 this idea occurs only in 2 Pet. 3:5. These ranges of meaning occur also in the Greek OT, Philo, and the Jewish Greek Pseudepigrapha. Obviously the word in Col. 1:17 fits into a creation context and does not fit into the first two above ranges of meaning. For example, 2 Pet. 3:5 says, the "earth was formed out of water and by water." Here the word is virtually synonymous with "created,"[59] referring to the initial creation by God. Yet the verb in creation contexts can also refer to the ongoing sustaining of the creation's existence instead of the initial creation itself.[60] The word in Col. 1:17 could refer to the initial creation but, like the phrase "all things have been created" in verse 16b, this one too is in the perfect tense, so that while the first act of creation could be in view, the focus is on a stative notion, the ongoing state or existence of the creation, which by implication in the context is the effect of the initial creation.[61] Christ "holds together" the creation by his providential power. "Hold together" is a better rendering than "consist" since the clause "All things consist by Christ" is a bit awkward; yet if the ἐν αὐτῷ (*en autō*) is taken in a spheric manner, then it makes sense: "All things consist in him."[62] Furthermore, "consist" would be a rare rendering of the

58. The marginal note of the NASB has "endure."

59. See likewise the use of συνίστημι in 1 En. 101.6; Philo, *Creat.* 17, 26, 63, 67; *Migr.* 135; *Etern.* 8, 25; T. Ab. (rec. A) 9.6. E.g., Philo (*Creat.* 63) says that God "commanded all kinds of fish and sea-monsters to take shape" at the Gen. 1 act of creation.

60. For example, Philo (*Heir* 58) says that the bodies of humans "hold together . . . by the providence of God," since the human race could not exist "for a single day" otherwise; likewise see Philo, *Mos.* 2:132–33: "It is impossible for anything that is to subsist without invocation of Him, for it is His goodness and gracious power which join and compact all things. . . . Reason [of God] . . . holds together and administers all things" (see also Philo, *Creat.* 29b; cf. Philo, *Heir* 152, 281, 311). Some commentators compare Sir. 43:26 ("By his word all things are composed"*), but σύγκειμαι (*synkeimai*) is used there (among the relevant ranges of meaning is "composed, compounded") instead of συνίστημι, and it is not clear that the meaning is the same. See also Philo, *Flight* 112: "The word of Him who is living is the bond of all things . . . and holds [συνέχω, *synechō*] all things together and binds all the parts, preventing them from being dissolved and separated," though συνέχω is used here instead of συνίστημι. Several commentators also cite Ps.-Aristotle, *Univ.* 6 (397b): "Everything exists from God and is held together [συνέστηκεν, *synestēken*] through God." Cf. Plato, *Tim.* 41A: "Those works whereof I [God] am framer and father are indissoluble save by my will," which is the "bond" that preserves creation from being dissolved (see Hay 2000: 59). Thus Paul's general idea in Col. 1:17 was known in the Greek world outside OT and Jewish circles.

61. See the discussion above of the perfect ἔκτισται (*ektistai*) in verse 16 for the rationale for understanding the perfect tense in this manner; see likewise Campbell 2013: 14.

62. Campbell (2012: 180, 182) prefers that only the locative (or spheric) use is in mind.

verb. There is little change in meaning, but since we have concluded here that the ἐν αὐτῷ focuses on agency and only secondarily connotes sphere, it is better to go with the "hold together" translation.

That "all things hold together" in Christ is a reference to the old creation that continues into the overlap of the inbreaking new creation narrated in Col. 1:18–20, and by implication it includes all things in the new creation and its consummation in the final, eternal new heavens and earth.[63] Thus the subsection on the old creation in verses 15–17 does have overlapping ideas with the age of the new creation, which we see at the end of verse 17. We have also seen Christ as an archetypal Adam-like ruling figure in verse 15, which focuses on his preexistence but includes[64] within its purview redemptive history and eternity future, so that Christ as such a prototype is true before history and throughout history and onward. This means that Christ continues to be sovereign over the unseen spiritual forces of evil already mentioned as a part of creation (v. 16), which were a spiritual threat to the readers.

2. Christ Is Supreme over the New Creation (1:18–20)

Now the focus changes from Christ as the divine sovereign king over the first creation to Christ as the divine sovereign over the new creation. The thematic and linguistic parallels between verses 15–17 and verses 18–20 are striking in showing Christ's dual divine kingship over the old and new creations:[65]

Preeminence of Christ in the First Creation and in the New Creation[66]

In the First Creation	In the New Creation
He is the image of the invisible God, (1:15a–b)	For it was the Father's good pleasure for all the fullness to dwell in Him. (1:19)
the firstborn of all creation. (1:15c)	He is also the firstborn from the dead/ (1:18)
He is before all things. (1:17a)	head/beginning, so that He Himself will come to have first place in everything. (1:18)
For by Him all things were created, both in the heavens and on earth. (1:16a; cf. v. 16f)	The Father's good pleasure [was] . . . through Him to reconcile all things to Himself, . . . whether things on earth or things in heaven. (1:19a, 20)

Christ's sovereignty over the first creation in his preincarnate existence is stated first in verses 15–17, since it is the basis and blueprint for the recapitu-

63. Robertson (1934: 773–74) notes that τὰ πάντα (*ta panta*) is a common NT expression for "the sum of things, the all," and includes the use in 1:17 in this category, though he does not specify whether this refers to both the old creation and the new creation.

64. By the timeless present-tense verb "is."

65. See Harris (2010: 38) for other ways to divide up verses 18–20. Some see verse 18a and b ("and he is the head, . . . the firstborn of the dead"*) to form the climax to the first part of the poem (vv. 15–17), but verse 18a–b would still be parallel to verse 15 (cf. the discussion of O'Brien 1982: 48), as they would be, at least partially, if they begin the second part of the so-called poem.

66. I am grateful to my former student Tim Sweet for constructing the following parallel chart.

lating idea of Christ's sovereignty in his incarnation over the second or new creation. This reflects the biblical principle that God "makes the last things like the first" (Barn. 6.13).[67] The first things of the old cosmos point to, and thus become, the basis and pattern for the recapitulating pattern of the last things of the new cosmos, inaugurated by Christ. The main point in the comparison is that just as the preincarnate Christ was the divine sovereign over the temporary first creation, *so certainly he will be the divine-human sovereign over the new*, everlasting creation inaugurated by his resurrection, his defeat of evil powers (see on 2:15), the establishment of the "church," and his "reconciling" work (1:20, 22) and consummated in the entirety of the new heavens and earth (cf. Rom. 8:18–25). Christ's historical work of bringing about the new creation in his resurrection is not to cause us to lose sight of his preexistence before history, since the former is but the revelation of the latter.[68] Each of the four parallel themes indicates that what Christ was before the first creation (left-column parallels) is manifested in what he became in the new redemptive-historical creation (corresponding right-column parallels). For example, (1) Christ's being the "image of the invisible God" (v. 15) is revealed in "all the fullness [of Deity] dwell[ing] in Him" (1:19). (2) Likewise, his being "the firstborn of all creation" (v. 15) is manifested in his being "firstborn from the dead" (v. 18). (3) "He is before all things" (v. 17) is made evident in his being head/beginning, "so that He Himself will come to have first place in everything" (v. 18). (4) The reality that "by Him all things were created, both in the heavens and on earth" (v. 16) is made observable in his task "to reconcile all things, . . . whether things on earth or things in heaven" (v. 20; likewise Tipton 2008: 189).

If this is correct, then it means that verses 18–20 of the so-called poem are the main point, and the beginning of the poem (vv. 15–17) is the important supporting basis that upholds this and highlights this as the main point (see similarly Dunn 1996: 99). These four parallels above will be addressed as they are found in the order of the verses, so that the first parallel will be discussed below with verse 19.

I have followed several scholars (see below) who divide the so-called hymn into two sections: verses 15–18b and verses 18c–20. The parallel structure of the two main sections of the poem can also be discerned through a more in-depth literary analysis, which confirms also most of the parallels observed in

67. The Barnabas statement is introduced by "and the Lord says," which likely means that Barnabas is drawing from the OT. The most likely source, of which Barnabas is an interpretative paraphrase, is Isa. 41:22: "Tell us what things were of old, and we will apply our understanding, and we shall know what are the last things."* The next closest parallel is Isa. 43:18–19: "Remember not the former things, nor consider the things of old" (v. 18 ESV). "Behold, I will do new things, which shall presently spring forth, and you shall know them: and I will make a way in the wilderness, and rivers in the dry land"* (v. 19). A future exodus will occur (v. 19), certainly a recapitulation of the first exodus, which is narrated in 43:17 in comparison to another prophecy of a future exodus in 43:16. This is not far away from the exodus typology that we have found earlier, in Col. 1:13–14.

68. Ridderbos 1975: 68; see the entire discussion there.

the above chart of verses 15–20. The following is a broad chiastic version of a very viable threefold division.[69]

Colossians 1:15–20

A **ὅς** ἐστιν εἰκὼν (15a)
τοῦ θεοῦ τοῦ ἀοράτου, (15b)
πρωτότοκος πάσης κτίσεως, (15c)
ὅτι ἐν αὐτῷ ἐκτίσθη **τὰ πάντα** (16a)
ἐν τοῖς οὐρανοῖς καὶ ἐπὶ τῆς γῆς, (16b)
τὰ ὁρατὰ καὶ τὰ ἀόρατα, (16c)
εἴτε θρόνοι εἴτε κυριότητες (16d)
εἴτε ἀρχαὶ εἴτε ἐξουσίαι· (16e)
τὰ πάντα **δι' αὐτοῦ καὶ εἰς αὐτὸν** ἔκτισται· (16f)
B καὶ αὐτός ἐστιν πρὸ πάντων (17a)
C καὶ τὰ πάντα ἐν αὐτῷ συνέστηκεν, (17b; center of the chiasm)
B′ καὶ αὐτός ἐστιν ἡ κεφαλὴ (18a)
τοῦ σώματος τῆς ἐκκλησίας· (18b)
A′ **ὅς ἐστιν** ἀρχή, (18c)
πρωτότοκος ἐκ τῶν νεκρῶν, (18d)
ἵνα γένηται ἐν πᾶσιν αὐτὸς πρωτεύων, (18e)
ὅτι ἐν αὐτῷ εὐδόκησεν (19a)
πᾶν τὸ πλήρωμα κατοικῆσαι (19b)
καὶ **δι' αὐτοῦ** ἀποκαταλλάξαι **τὰ πάντα εἰς αὐτόν**, (20a)
εἰρηνοποιήσας διὰ τοῦ αἵματος (20b)
τοῦ σταυροῦ αὐτοῦ, [δι' αὐτοῦ]
εἴτε τὰ ἐπὶ τῆς γῆς εἴτε τὰ ἐν τοῖς οὐρανοῖς. (20c)

A **who** is the image (15a)
of God, the invisible, (15b)
firstborn of every creature, (15c)
because in him were created **all things** (16a)
in the heaven and in the earth, (16b)
the seen things and the unseen, (16c)
whether thrones or lordships (16d)
whether rulers or authorities; (16e)
all things **through him and to him** were created; (16f)
B and he is before all things, (17a)
C and all things hold together in him, (17b; center of the chiasm)
B′ and he is the head (18a)
of the body, the church; (18b)

69. The following analysis is based for the most part on N. Wright (1992a: 104), who himself builds on the work of others, and which is similar to other literary analyses (e.g., see D. Moo 2008: 116), though there have been various proposals of the structure of the so-called hymnic section (for discussion of some of these proposals, see additional notes below).

A′ **who is** the beginning, (18c)
firstborn from the dead ones, (18d)
so that he might become in all things himself preeminent, (18e)
because in him was pleased (19a)
all the fullness to dwell (19b)
and **through him** to reconcile **all things to him**, (20a)
making peace by the blood of his cross [through him], (20b)
<u>whether things on the earth or things in heaven</u>.* (20c)

The chiasm is broad only with *A-A′* and *B-B′* parallels and a middle *C* element. But within each *A* section are four subordinate parallels. As Wright contends, these parallels show that there is poetic structure in verses 15–20 (N. Wright 1992a: 105–6). This literary analysis supports three of the four parallels seen in the earlier chart. Rather than verse 15 ("He is the image of the invisible God") being parallel with verse 19 ("For it was the Father's good pleasure for all the fullness to dwell"), Wright's more detailed literary structure instead has verse 15 being parallel with verse 18c ("who is the beginning"). This fits better with the detailed literary parallels in Wright's analysis, but it does not make as much conceptual sense. How is Christ being "the image of the invisible God" parallel with Christ "who is the beginning"? Now, one could say that Christ as the Adam-like image of God was the beginning (i.e., ruling creator) of the first creation (as we argued earlier, on v. 15), and therefore it makes parallel sense that he is "the beginning" of the new creation. Or one could say that "image of the invisible God" and "beginning" are parallel conceptually because they both refer to attributes of "wisdom." But it might make even better conceptual sense to see verse 15 being parallel with verse 19: Christ as "image of the invisible God" (v. 15a–b) in the first creation is the one in whom "all the fullness" of deity "dwells" in the new creation (1:19; 2:9). In both cases, Christ is the *full expression* of deity.

It is probably best to let this tension between the thematic and structural parallels stand and to appreciate, to one degree or another, both vantage points. As noted, the main point of the twofold thematic approach would be on verses 18–20, with verses 15–17 as the supporting basis of that main point (and within vv. 18–20, the main point is in v. 18, with vv. 19–20 being the supporting basis ["because"] of that main point). On the other hand, the main point or focus of the threefold chiastic approach would appear to be on verse 17b ("all things hold together in him"), which is the central part of the chiastic threefold structure.[70] In appreciating both perspectives, I see verse

70. See D. Moo (2008: 125), who also sees verse 17b ("In him all things hold together") as the center line in the literary structure. There are twenty-one lines in the poetic structure: the first ten lines are about the first creation; the last ten lines are about the new creation; and the line in the middle, the eleventh line, is verse 17b, "And all things hold together in him." Though verse 17b is the formal conclusion of the "first-creation section," its perfect (stative) tense ("hold together") indicates that it is by Christ's sovereign rule that creation is maintained now and will be in the future, as it was first created from the beginning. The past, present, and future

17b as a highlighted transition between the two sections leading to the main point of verse 18,[71] though the main comparison and contrast of verses 15–20 is between verse 15 (the preincarnate Christ as divine sovereign over the first creation) and verse 18 (the incarnate Christ as divine-human sovereign over the new creation).

1:18 Verse 18 is part of the second and third parallels noted above (see the table titled "Preeminence of Christ in the First Creation and in the New Creation"). Part of the third parallel comes first in verse 18. Just as Christ existed "before all things" created in the first creation and was sovereign king over its continued existence (1:17), so he became in his incarnation "the head" and the "beginning" so that "he himself should come to have first place among all things" in the new creation (1:18) as the ruler of it. Christ as "head" indicates his rule over "the church" (which is his "body"). There has been much debate over whether "head" (κεφαλή, *kephalē*) means a position of authority or a source from which something derives.[72] But these positions are not necessarily mutually exclusive. The notions, for example, of the head being in control over the body and yet being the source of nourishment for the body can be complementary. An example of this may be Eph. 4:15–16: "But speaking the truth in love, we are to grow up in all aspects into Him who is the head, even Christ, from whom the whole body, being fitted and held together by what every joint supplies, according to the proper working of each individual part, causes the growth of the body for the building up of itself in love." Here Christ, as "head," authoritatively directs the development of the body and causes its growth (so Col. 2:19).[73] The idea of unity is probably also in mind in Eph. 4 and Col. 2. That "head" clearly means "authority over" in Ephesians is clear from 1:22–23: God "put all things in subjection under His feet, and gave Him as head over all things to the church, which is His body, the fullness of Him who fills all in all." Here in Col. 1:18 headship is a further explanation of "all things in subjection" to Christ, so that "head" expresses his authority. Yet, that Christ also "fills all in all" is probably an echo of God filling the earth with his creation, which is not only an authoritative task but one that also sees Christ as the source of the church's growth in the sense of being the cause of that

---

reference of verse 17b makes it suitable as a transition to the reference to the present-and-not-yet new creation of 1:18–20.

71. Remember that in the logical development of thought, verse 17 is part of a basis (together with v. 16) for verse 15, the latter of which (v. 15) is the logical main point of verses 15–17.

72. E.g., see Grudem (1985) for the notion that κεφαλή (*kephalē*) means only "authority," and, e.g., Bedale (1954), who believes that it means primarily "source" (granting the possibility that it means "over-lordship" in Eph. 1:22 and that included in the meaning of uses in 1 Cor. 11:3–12 are both authority and source). See also Grudem's article for his contention that κεφαλή never means "source" in Classical, Hellenistic, or NT Greek; he also refers to other scholars who argue only for the idea of "source," some of whom explicitly cite Bedale in support. See Harris (2010: 48–49) and Garland (1998: 91) for further secondary sources on the debated meaning of κεφαλή.

73. Though Grudem's point (1985) is viable that, since no text in the ancient Greek world clearly expresses that κεφαλή means source, then the focus on its use in the Eph. 4 and Col. 2 texts may well be on "authority over."

growth. Again, here the head connected to a body suggests both authoritative direction and cause of growth, *as well as unity*.[74] Likely the same thing is in mind in Eph. 5:22–24, where again the notion of "being subject to" and "head" are combined: wives are to "be subject to" husbands, which is followed by the husband being "the head of the wife, as Christ also is the head of the church." Thus, as in Eph. 1, "head" again expresses authority, but likely the image of the husband as head of the body, his wife, is presumably a picture that is in mind. If so, then the notion of headship would suggest again one who directs and causes growth; hence the notion of source would be included secondarily,[75] as well as unity.

That Col. 1:18 says Christ is "the head of the body, the church" ("church" in apposition to "body") likewise conveys the notion of his position of authority. But perhaps also included, as in Ephesians, is his position as the causative source of the church's growth.[76] Since there are many parallels between Colossians and Ephesians, it should not be surprising that the meaning of "head" in Colossians is like that in Ephesians. Likely included in the picture of the head-body relationship is Christ as the "one" who is the corporate ruling representative of the "many" (so O'Brien 1982: 50). Accordingly, τοῦ σώματος (*tou sōmatos*) is a genitive of subordination (Campbell 2013: 14): "head over the body."

"Church" here refers likely to the so-called church universal, though, of course, the local church in Colossae would be included (this is in parallel with the same universal sense of "church" in Eph. 1:22; 3:10, 21; 5:24–32). The universal reference of the church is indicated by the saturation of universal cosmic language throughout Col. 1:15–23. Since "head" and "body" language is used, here the church is likely understood to be the corporate body of Christ (see further on the background of ἐκκλησία in the additional notes, where the church is seen to be the continuation of Israel as God's "assembly" or "church," ἐκκλησία, *ekklēsia*). As Christ is the source of the new creation, the church is "the visible locus of the renewal of creation" (Davids 2008a: 259).

The second and third parallels in the initial chart introducing Col. 1:18–20 are taken from the remainder of verse 18. Christ as the "beginning" (ἀρχή, *archē*), while including a reference to temporal priority, focuses more on his position of rule (for the latter usage, see BDAG 138, s.v. ἀρχή). At least partly in mind is Gen. 1:1 ("In the beginning [ἀρχή] God created the heavens and the earth"), which indicates that Christ as the "beginning" in Col. 1:18 is the commencement of the new creation. Proverbs 8:22–23 LXX also alludes to Gen. 1:1 in referring to "wisdom" (8:11–21) as "the beginning [ἀρχή] of his

74. Cf. Lightfoot 1875: 157; see also Rom. 12:4–5 and 1 Cor. 12:12–27 on the unifying significance of the body metaphor; note that in 1 Cor. 12:21 "head" is mentioned, not with respect to Christ but only as one among other body parts; cf. Bruce 1984: 67–68.

75. On the inclusion of both ideas of authority and source, cf. Witherington 2007: 135.

76. A striking parallel is found in Orphic frag. 21a: "Zeus is the head [κεφαλή, *kephalē*]," and all things are dependent on this "head"; see further Pao (2012: 99), who notes that some manuscripts of the fragment include "beginning" (ἀρχή, *archē*) as a name for Zeus.

[God's] ways": "Before eternity he established me [wisdom], in the beginning [ἀρχή, *archē*]." Since we have seen that "wisdom" is in mind to some extent in Col. 1:15–17 above, likely both Gen. 1 and Prov. 8 are echoed here in verse 18 (see Pao 2012: 100 for these two allusions).

Ἀρχή is further explained by Christ being "the firstborn [πρωτότοκος, *prōtotokos*] of the dead," and both these expressions amplify what "head" means. Just as Christ was "the firstborn of all [in the first] creation" (v. 15b), so he is the "firstborn" of the new creation through having been raised "from among the dead ones" (1:18; on Christ's resurrection as new creation, including Col. 1:18, see Beale 2012: 298–316).

This is one of the clearest texts in the NT that Christ's resurrection is understood to be the beginning of a new creation, with more to come (i.e., of more resurrected ones from the dead to come; on which see almost identically 1 Cor. 15:20–23). Paul views Christ's resurrection from the dead "as a manifestation of the one great movement of God in raising his people from the dead" (Tipton 2016). Revelation 1:5 refers to Christ as "the faithful witness, the firstborn [ὁ πρωτότοκος] of the dead, and the ruler of the kings of the earth," showing the appropriateness of "firstborn" for Christ's resurrection and that it is inextricably linked to a ruling position, which is also an allusion to Ps. 89:27–29, 36 (88:28–30, 37 LXX). And then Rev. 1:5 is expanded in Rev. 3:14 by referring to Christ as "the faithful and true witness, the Beginning [ἡ ἀρχή] of the creation of God," which refers not to the first creation in Gen. 1 but to the new creation, as a result of Christ's resurrection (on Rev. 1:5 and 3:14, see Beale 1999a: 190–92, 297–303).[77] Not only is this a new-creational[78] expression: it also indicates Christ's rulership, just as we saw that Christ being firstborn of the old creation indicates his rule over it (Col. 1:17a). For example, recall that πρωτότοκος, the word also used of Christ being "firstborn of all [the old] creation" in verse 15, includes the idea of him being ruler over the first creation. In particular, we saw that just as the historical Adam's temporal priority included the notion that a part of his ultimate design was to be a world king (as mandated in Gen. 1:28), so these names in Colossians about Christ's *temporal priority* to the old creation entail his *sovereignty* over it (esp. as developed by Ps. 88 LXX = 89 Eng.). So πρωτότοκος indicates the same notion of authority here in Col. 1:18. The combination of ἀρχή with

77. Likewise, Jesus calls himself "the first [ὁ πρῶτος, *ho prōtos*] and the last" in Rev. 1:17 and the "Alpha and the Omega, the first [ὁ πρῶτος] and the last, the beginning [ἡ ἀρχή] and the end" in Rev. 22:13. These references are applied to Christ in his incarnate and exalted condition because of his death and resurrection (esp. in Col. 1:17), and they identify him with God, who calls himself "the Alpha and Omega" in Rev. 1:8; 21:6, and "the beginning and the end" in 21:6 (see also Hay 2000: 61, who reminded me of these parallels). These expressions are based on Isa. 41:4; 44:6; 48:12, originally referring to Yahweh (see Beale 1999a: 213–14, 1138). The polar temporal opposites in these expressions indicate that God and Christ were present and sovereign in the beginning, will be present and sovereign at the end of history, and are present and sovereign over all things in between.

78. Recall that "new-creational" here and throughout the commentary refers to the inaugurated end-time new creation.

πρωτότοκος points to Christ being the authoritative founder of the new redeemed humanity ("firstborn of the dead") and of the new creation in general (since the new humanity is also part of the beginning of the new creation, sparked off by Christ).[79] This is further pointed to by the fact that when Christ rose from the dead, he achieved power over death as the last enemy of death (cf. Acts 2:24–36; Rev. 1:18), and when he ascended to the right hand of the Father, he received an escalated position of kingship, greater than during his ministry (as expressed in Col. 3:1 and more clearly in Eph. 1:20–22; cf. also Acts 2:30–36). Thus the resurrection placed Christ at God's "right hand" and into an even greater stage of redemptive-historical kingship over death and evil heavenly rulers.

The final phrase of Col. 1:18 appears to highlight the meaning of sovereign rule even more than the preceding three clauses. Thus it may be in apposition to or a further explanation of them: "so that He Himself should come to have first place in everything." However, this last clause of verse 18 is not a mere interpretative restatement of what precedes but more likely expresses the purpose or result of Christ being the "head," the "beginning," and the "firstborn of the dead."[80] The new added element in the last clause is "in everything." Christ's rule over the church and being himself the beginning of the new creation is designed to demonstrate that he is supreme over the entire creation (the first creation and the new creation) at the consummation of history.[81] Thus the logical weight of the verse supports Christ having "first

79. And note that the parallel of 1 Cor. 15:20–22 strikingly sees Christ as a last-Adam figure in his resurrection, which was the "first fruits of those who are asleep." Philo (*Cher.* 54) calls Adam a "firstborn [πρωτότοκος, *prōtotokos*], who was the beginning [ἀρχή, *archē*] of the generation of men from one another." This refers to Adam as a founder of the human race and probably alludes to more than merely the idea that he was source but also some aspect of authority, as we have argued just above and earlier in verse 15 on Adam as a "firstborn," which is alluded to in verse 15. See the use of the two Greek words in Gen. 49:3 LXX: "Reuben, you are my <u>firstborn</u>, my power and the <u>beginning</u> of my children," where not only the idea of source but also an authoritative position is in mind: note the use of "power," which alludes to some aspect of rule or authority (likewise Deut. 21:17; both texts cited by O'Brien 1982: 50). Likewise, interestingly, 1 Chron. 26:10 LXX uses the same two Greek words: "Merari had sons who kept <u>office</u> [or rule, ἀρχή], even though he was not the <u>firstborn</u> [πρωτότοκος], but his father made him <u>chief</u> [ἄρχων, *archōn*]" anyway. The last word, ἄρχων, shows that the notion of firstborn entails rule, as does the first use of ἀρχή (*archē*), which does not mean "beginning" but authoritative "office " or "rule." According to O'Brien (1982: 50–51), even though Merari was not firstborn but received authority, this exception proves the rule that the authority is usually bestowed on the firstborn son.

80. Sometimes purpose and result in these ἵνα (*hina*) clauses with the subjunctive are not clearly distinguished and may shade into one another, especially to express divine purpose together with result; see Wallace 1996: 472–74.

81. "Everything" (πᾶς, *pas*) could be dative masculine referring to the "dead ones" (τῶν νεκρῶν, *tōn nekrōn*), but it is better taken as dative neuter referring to the entirety of the creation (Harris 2010: 45), since the entirety of the first creation (vv. 15–17) is set in parallel to the entirety of the new creation (vv. 18–20); the former points to the latter as its climax. Likewise, πᾶς has been used repeatedly in verses 15, 16a, 16b, 17a, and 17b, so that the use of πᾶς (*pas*) again here in verse 18 most naturally continues the previous references to the word.

place" among all things. Verses 19–20 give a ground or reason in support of this last clause of verse 18, thus making it the main point upheld by the first three clauses of verse 18, as well as verses 19–20.[82] Furthermore, as we have seen, the literary structure indicates that verse 17b is the precise center of the chiasm forming the conclusion to the first section about the old creation and being a transition to the second section, on the new creation. Verses 17–18 are a broader center of the chiasm. Just because verse 18a is a broader part of the chiastic center does not mean (contrary to common opinion) that it is the logical or even conceptual center of the section on new creation. Our above analysis shows that it is supportive of the main point at the end of verse 18, which is the purpose clause, itself supported by verses 19–20.

Rendering πρωτεύω (*prōteuō*) as "supremacy" (TNIV, NIV), "supreme" (NJB, NLT), "preeminence" (ESV, RSV, KJV, ASV, Geneva), or "primacy" (Douay) is likely better than "have first place" (NASB, HCSB, NRSV), since the latter does not express authoritative position as clearly. The word πρωτεύω has the notion of supreme importance, which usually carries with it the notion of greatest authority. Though the word is used only in Col. 1:18 in all of the NT, it occurs in the LXX and Josephus, as well as other early Jewish writings. An example of this meaning for the word is in the book of Esther, where it says that Haman showed his friends his "wealth, and the glory with which the king had invested him, and how he had caused him to take precedence and bear chief rule in the kingdom" (Esther 5:11 LXX). Here the notion of "taking precedence" is not only that of being "most important" but also carries with it the idea of "bearing chief rule in the kingdom." Likewise Josephus uses the word a number of times to indicate supreme importance and rank, usually with authoritative connotations (e.g., in *Ant.* 16.383 he speaks of a "whole army and the officers [πρωτεύω]" over that army). Thus the idea of the word generally is that of being first in rank, along with authoritative overtones (cf. also W. Michaelis, *TDNT* 6:881–82). An example of this would be that King Henry VIII in sixteenth-century England was the *preeminent* person in all of the country not only with reference to his paramount importance but also to his authority.

This is not a restatement that Christ would be the "first" of the ensuing new creation in chronological order (though that is partly expressed by "firstborn from the dead") but that he would hold the "preeminent" position in the new creation, from its inception until its consummation. Thus he is preeminent in "all things" (ἐν πᾶσιν, *en pasin*)[83] pertaining to the old cosmos and the new

82. D. Moo (2008: 125) says that verse 18a is perhaps the "center" of the whole purported poem (vv. 15–20). If he means literary center, then this is not quite precise according to his own literary analysis (2008: 116), as well as our own nearly identical analysis (above, following N. Wright 1992a: 101–6), since it reveals that verse 17 together with verse 18a is the central part of the structure. If by "center" D. Moo means logical center, then this misses the observation that the main logical point in verse 18 is the purpose clause, which is supported both by verse 18a and by verses 19–20.

83. The phrase ἐν πᾶσιν is rendered "all things" in various kinds of contexts in the NT, where each context limits the reference in some way: 1 Cor. 15:28; 2 Cor. 11:6; Gal. 6:6; Eph. 1:23; 4:6;

cosmos. However, this last phrase does draw out the idea of rule from the preceding "firstborn from the dead" by indicating that he would hold absolute authority over everything as the divine-human Messiah from the point of his resurrection onward until the final completion of the age, which means that Christ as the incarnate Messiah even has primacy over the old creation (on the latter point, see Bruce 1984: 72–73).[84] This is not sovereignty only over "all things" that God "re-creates within the faith community" of the new age (as Wall 1993: 73 contends), but he is ruler even over all forces that do not acknowledge his rule. This notion of "preeminence" in Col. 1:18b also is supported by the other expressions of sovereignty in verses 15–17.

Verse 18 in relation to verses 15–17 needs brief reflection at this point. Jesus's resurrection brought him a "preeminence" (v. 18) that he did not previously have during his redemptive-historical manner of existence with regard to his human nature. But the Son of God (cf. Col. 1:13) came to have no greater "preeminence" (v. 18) in his resurrection than he had always possessed as the eternal, divine Son. The preeminence that the Son of God came to have through his resurrection entails not only a transformation of the human nature that he took on, but also a new redemptive-historical manifestation of what is always true of his eternal person.[85]

This verse now completes the first parallel about the old creation and the new **1:19**
creation noted above between verse 15 and verse 19 (see the table titled "Preeminence of Christ in the First Creation and in the New Creation"). That is, just as Christ was already the "image of the invisible God" before and at the time of the first creation (1:15), so in the beginning of the new creation the "fullness" of deity "dwelt in him," so that he is the perfect representation of God "in bodily form" (1:19 and 2:9, on which see below).

The initial ὅτι (*hoti*, for) indicates that this verse explains why Christ should "come to have first place in everything" (v. 18b), which itself is a further explanation of the similar words and phrases in verses 15–17. The reason is that Christ is God incarnate. But before elaborating upon this explanation, the OT background needs to be uncovered, since it is essential to understanding how verse 19 supports the goal of Christ coming to "have first place in everything" (v. 18).

Verse 19 can be translated in two different ways: "because in him [ἐν αὐτῷ, *en autō*] all the fullness [of deity] was well-pleased [εὐδοκέω, *eudokeō*] to dwell [κατοικέω, *katoikeō*]"; or "in him he was well-pleased for all the fullness [of deity] to dwell." The conceptual difference between the two renderings is not significant, though the first is perhaps slightly better (see additional notes). It

Col. 3:11; 1 Tim. 3:11; 2 Tim. 2:7; 4:5; Titus 2:9; Heb. 13:18; 1 Pet. 4:11. Here, as in 1 Cor. 15:28 and Eph. 1:23, "all things" refers to all things in the cosmos.

84. Which has been anticipated even in the first half of the segment by the two present tenses in 1:15a and 1:17a, as well by the perfect tenses, indicating an ongoing condition in verse 16b and verse 17b. All of these parts of the preceding verses are to a degree temporally overlapping with the present age and not completely limited to the time before creation, though that is the focus.

85. Following Tipton 2008: 190 in this paragraph.

is "all" of God the Father's divine fullness that was "well-pleased" to dwell in his Son ("in him"), which is borne out by the allusion to Ps. 67 LXX (68 MT; see below). The parallel with 2:9 ("all the fullness of Deity dwells [in Him] in bodily form") also supports this first rendering (following O'Brien 1982: 51). It is important to clarify theologically that it is not God the Father's divine nature that gives the Son his divine nature when he became incarnate, but they are both fully divine from eternity past (see 1:15–17). The point is to identify Jesus with Yahweh's divine identity in the psalm. Colossians 2:9 reinforces how Christ, even in his estate of humiliation, possesses a fully divine nature ("in Him all the fullness of Deity dwells in bodily form"). The preincarnate divine Son took on human flesh.

A number of commentators have observed that the combined wording of "well-pleased" and "dwell" in Col. 1:19 is traceable to Ps. 67:17 LXX (68:17 MT; 68:16 Eng.; see additional notes):

Psalm 67:17–18 LXX; 68:17–18 MT; 68:16–17 Eng.	Colossians 1:19
"God was well-pleased [εὐδοκέω, *eudokeō*] to dwell [κατοικέω, *katoikeō*] in it [ἐν αὐτῷ, *en autō* (Zion)]; . . . the Lord will dwell [there] forever, . . . in the holy place [קֹדֶשׁ, *qōdeš*]."[a]	"because in him [ἐν αὐτῷ, *en autō*] all the fullness [of deity] was well-pleased [εὐδοκέω, *eudokeō*] to dwell [κατοικέω, *katoikeō*]"[b]

[a]Most translations render קֹדֶשׁ (*qōdeš*) as "holy place" or "sanctuary" (KJV, NIV, HCSB, NJB, NLT, RSV, NRSV, ESV; so also 3 En. 24.6–7), though a few translate it as "holiness" (e.g., NASB, NEB). What confirms the rendering of "holy place" instead of "holiness" is that the ב preposition is followed by the article "the" (indicated by a short "a" vowel under the ב and a dagesh forte in the ק). On the other hand, "in the holiness" would result in a rather awkward rendering.

[b]Alternatively, "in him he was well-pleased for all the fullness [of deity] to dwell."

The unique wording in common between Ps. 67 (68 MT) and Col. 1 points to the probability of such an allusion: Ps. 67:17b is the only place in the LXX where the verbs "well-pleased" (εὐδοκέω, *eudokeō*) and "dwell" (κατοικέω, *katoikeō*) occur together. "Dwell" in Ps. 67:17b LXX and "dwell" (κατασκηνόω, *kataskēnoō*) in 67:17c and 19c LXX refer to God "dwelling" in his temple. Psalm 67:18c LXX makes this explicit: "The Lord is among them, in Sinai, in the holy place." Most English translations of the Hebrew text of the verse (Ps. 68:17) see a reference to the temple in the last line of the verse (see the chart above). That Paul often quotes from the Psalms (twenty-four times) throughout his letters further enhances the viability of a Ps. 68 (67 LXX) allusion here.[86]

There are other OT passages that are very similar to the Ps. 67 LXX (68 MT) passage and could be echoed together with the psalm allusion (see the additional notes below). The temple of the psalm is now applied to Christ in Col. 1:19. The notion of Christ as the temple of God's presence occurs elsewhere in the NT (e.g., John 2:19–21; Rev. 21:22) and in Paul (Eph. 2:20–22), though Paul usually highlights the church as the temple, no doubt because

86. M. Silva (*DPL* 631), cited also by Beetham (2008: 144), made me aware of the reference.

of its identification with Christ (as in Eph. 2:20–22 and 1 Cor. 3:17; for the church as a temple, see also 1 Cor. 6:19; 2 Cor. 6:16; Rev. 3:12; 7:15; 11:1–2).

Beasley-Murray (1980: 177) explains that the temple background in Col. 1:19 has often been overlooked because there has been too much narrow focus only on πλήρωμα (*plērōma*, fullness), though consideration of the language of the whole verse reveals that "Christ is portrayed as fulfilling the role assigned to the temple in the Old Testament," particularly Ps. 67:17 LXX (68:17 MT; 68:16 Eng.; so virtually identically see N. Wright 1986: 78; 1990: 463; and 1992a: 117).[87] While seeing only possible allusion to the psalm text, Pao (2012: 102) affirms, on the basis of other relevant background, that "Christ fulfills the role of the temple in which one finds the full presence of God" (see further additional notes). If the allusion is intentional, as some rightly think, then the point would be that God's presence on earth is no longer in the earthly temple (the holy of holies) but is now in Christ, who eschatologically instantiates and typologically fulfills all that the temple represented[88] (the subject of "well-pleased" could be God or "all the fullness [of deity]," which amounts to the same thing; cf. discussion in Harris 2010: 45). God's tabernacling presence on earth has now been more fully expressed in Christ's incarnation than in the old architectural temple, and God was "well-pleased" to do so. The Spirit of Jesus continues that earthly presence in the church as the true form of the temple, since Christ's ascension.

But the Ps. 68 background does not appear to provide the language of "fullness" that is integrated into the psalm allusion. However, the repeated idea of divine "glory filling the temple [or tabernacle]" is found in the LXX,[89] and πλήρης (*plērēs*, full)[90] is used in some of these LXX texts, where the temple is "full of the glory" of God (Isa. 6:1; Ezek. 43:5; 44:4; cf. Isa. 6:3). This background likely supplements the Ps. 67 LXX (68 MT) temple allusion. That this is God's "fullness" is clear from the development of this passage in Col. 2:9: "For in Him all the fullness of Deity dwells in bodily form."

The presence of God's holy of holies on earth was the most preeminent reality in all of Israel. So also the reason (ὅτι, *hoti*, 1:19) Christ should "come to have first place in everything" (v. 18b) is that he is the inaugurated end-time temple in which God's fullness has begun to dwell. He is the escalated form of

87. Beasley-Murray (1980: 177) also says that Ps. 67:17 LXX is a "parallel that is more than a matter of vocabulary."

88. Beetham (2008: 143–56) also sees clear reference to Ps. 67:17 LXX (68:17 MT; 68:16 Eng.) in Col. 1:19 and likewise views it to be understood typologically. He also cites other scholars seeing Ps. 67:17 LXX as an allusion or parallel and relevant Jewish background on the exegetical tradition of Ps. 68:16 Eng. Stuhlmacher (2018: 435–37) sees the divine "fullness" (= the rabbinic *shekinah*) dwelling in Christ in verse 19 to indicate that "Christ takes the place of the temple in Zion," to which he compares Exod. 29:43–46; Ps. 68:17 (68:16 Eng.); and Ps. 74:2 with Jub. 4.26.

89. In this respect, see uses of πίμπλημι (*pimplēmi*, a synonym of the πλήρωμα/πληρόω [*plērōma*/*plēroō*, fullness/fill] word group) in Exod. 40:34–35; 1 Kings 8:10–11; 2 Chron. 7:2; Hag. 2:7; Ezek. 10:3–4; cf. Isa. 6:4.

90. Πλήρης (*plērēs*) is part of the same word group as πλήρωμα/πληρόω in Col. 1:19 and 2:9 and almost synonymous with it.

God's presence in the holy of holies, and as such he himself is identified with God and is the most preeminent one together with God in the church and in all the cosmos. The idea is not that God's presence is in Christ but "that all that God is dwells in Christ" (Sumney 2008: 74). The point is that God should be the preeminent one in all of his creation. Since Christ is divine, he also is the preeminent one in the entire creation.[91]

This statement about God's tabernacling divine fullness in Christ is an anticipation of a response to the false teaching in Colossae, since this verse is taken up again in 2:9 ("In Him all the fullness of Deity dwells in bodily form") and is given as a reason the hearers are not to be "take[n] captive" by false teaching (2:8a) in contrast to holding true teaching about Christ (v. 8b).[92] Then 2:10 continues to give a reason for not holding to the false teaching: the readers have "been made full in" (2:10a NASB marg.) Christ's tabernacling presence, and "He is the head over all rule and authority" (2:10b), which is another reference to Christ's sovereignty over evil demonic beings who inspire the false teaching alluded to in 1:16. We will see that Paul wants to underscore Christ as the true temple here in order to contrast it with a false view of the temple in 2:18.

1:20 The fourth and last parallel between the former creation (vv. 15–17) and the new creation (vv. 18–20) introduced at the beginning of this segment is now picked up. Specifically, just as "all things were created . . . in the heavens and on earth" by Christ in the first creation (1:16), so in the second creation Christ "reconcile[s] all things to <u>Himself</u>,[93] . . . whether things on earth or things in heaven" (1:20). The parallelism of "created" (v. 16) and "reconcile" (v. 20) indicates that Christ's reconciling work is part of the creating of a new creation in which "peace" dwells, a connection found in the OT and elsewhere in Paul and the NT (see Beale 2012: 527–55). Christ thus has begun to restore the disorder, disharmony, and lack of peace of the first creation (so Dunn 1996: 104), and this will be consummated in the future.

Verse 20 continues the thought of verse 19 in explaining the effect of Christ becoming the escalated temple of God's revelatory presence, which continues to fill out the reason given in verse 19 for why Christ is "preeminent in everything"* (v. 18b). Israel's old temple was the place of God's mediating presence, where sinful people could come and have their sins atoned for (though not ultimately). Since Christ is God's incarnate tabernacling presence, he is able definitively to mediate that peacemaking presence through atonement to the alienated creation in the inaugurated phase of the eschaton, especially to sinful humans. That a rupture has occurred between God and his creation

91. It is then hard to understand why Sumney (2008: 79) goes on to say that "the point of this liturgical piece" in 1:15–20 "is not to declare Christ's equality with God but to identify Christ as the mediator of all God's acts." While Christ is certainly a mediator, he is more.

92. I am following MacDonald (2000: 62–63, 96–99), who is among commentators who see 1:19 in relation to 2:8–10 as an anticipation of a polemic against the false teaching.

93. Fee (2007: 309–13) identifies "himself" (αὐτόν, *auton*) with Christ instead of God.

is apparent at points in the epistle, especially as this fracture has occurred through the work of the devil and his spiritual forces (1:13), who have been defeated at the cross (2:15). In this light, Christ as their Creator (1:16) is in a position of sovereign rule over them (2:10; following generally Dunn 1996: 102–3). But the break between creation and Creator also occurred through sinful human agency, as 1:14 and 1:21 make clear, though this was under the influence of evil powers (1:13).

This reconciliation to God from the rupture was accomplished by Christ,[94] who has "made peace through . . . His cross." The way this peace came about for believers is expanded upon later, in Col. 2:14: "having canceled out the certificate of debt consisting of decrees against us, which was hostile to us; and He has taken it out of the way, having nailed it to the cross." To emphasize in 1:20 that it was the very Christ who accomplished this, Paul abruptly repeats the phrase "through him" (δι' αὐτοῦ, *di' autou*; see the first additional note on 1:20) from the first part of the verse and then completes it by expanding on the initial "all things:" "whether things upon the earth, whether things in [the] heaven[s]," the latter phrasing highlighting again the complete cosmic effect of Christ's work.

This does not indicate "universal salvation," but that at the consummation Christ will bring about a harmony of all things in the new, eternal creation, after decisively judging evil and putting it in its judicial place (as 3:6 indicates; cf. also 3:25). Thus the idea of "reconciliation" in this passage is a reference to the restoration of all things. Indeed, I have argued elsewhere that "reconciliation" is virtually equivalent to the OT concept of the restoration of Israel (see Beale 2012: 527–48). Given that Israel was a corporate Adam and was representative of humanity, here the idea is broadened to a restoration of all humanity (including evil angelic realities), whether by forced or faithful submission. Therefore, this is a "pacification" of *all* hostile and friendly forces (human and angelic), which has begun and will be consummated at the very end of history.[95] Just as Christ created all things in the first cosmos (Col. 1:15–17), so his re-creation and reconciling work must also include every single thing of the new creation (vv. 18–20; cf. Sumney 2008: 77, 79). The hostile forces (evil

94. It is possible that God is "reconciling all things to him [αὐτόν, *auton*, Christ]" instead of "to himself [αὐτόν, *auton*, God]" (so D. Moo 2008: 133–34; Fee 2007: 309–13). But this is improbable, since everywhere else in Paul's references to reconciliation, sinners are being reconciled to God through Christ's work. This is especially the case in the Eph. 2:15–17 parallel: "establishing peace, [so that He/Christ] might reconcile them both in one body to God through the cross, by it having put to death the enmity, and . . . He preached peace" (emphasis added); cf. the parallel in Col. 1:19–20: "It was the Father's good pleasure . . . through Him [Christ] to reconcile all things to himself, having made peace through the blood of [Christ's] cross" (emphasis added). As far as I can discover, all English translations render the pronoun αὐτόν (*auton*) as "himself," referring to God and not Christ.

95. This implies that even so-called good angels benefit from Christ's peacemaking work (so Calvin 1972: 313), even if only they now have a new relation to the cosmos in that they are no longer at war with evil angelic powers (so Lenski 1961: 66). Nevertheless, evil angels are more of the focus in verses 16 and 20.

angelic beings) have been decisively defeated at the cross and resurrection (so 2:15). Though they continue to exist (both angelic and human enemies) to the end of the age, they cannot stop the culmination of the pacification process.

Thus Col. 1:20 is a parallel to Eph. 1:10: "the summing [or heading] up of all things in Christ, things in the heavens and things on the earth." There Christ is portrayed as overseeing a household management of the cosmos (οἰκονομία, *oikonomia*), putting into order the disordered creation. Christ's reordering of the chaotic creation includes bringing humanity into a peaceful relationship with itself and with God, partly as a result of defeating the "rulers and authorities" (cf. Paul's elaboration of Eph. 1:10 in Eph. 1:20–23; 2:2; 3:10). Indeed, this restoration at the very end likely involves bringing about a harmonious restoration of the entire animate and inanimate creation (e.g., see D. Moo 2006: 137). Romans 8:19–21, for example, affirms that "the anxious longing of the [non-human material] creation waits eagerly for the revealing of the sons of God, . . . [and] the creation itself also will be set free from its slavery to corruption into the freedom of the glory of the children of God" (on which, e.g., see J. Moo 2008). Accordingly, the OT refers to eschatological peace involving peaceful harmony between antagonistic humans, hostile animals, and the fertility of creation as a sure sign that peace has come.[96] This is not a mere restoration of all things in some nebulous way but a restoration of peace in a new, consummate creation (note Isa. 11; 65; 66). The close linkage of reconciliation with new creation is evident from the parallel with Col. 1:16 ("all things were created . . . in the heavens and on earth") and the parallel language here ("to reconcile all things, . . . whether things on earth or things in heaven"). To enhance this inextricable connection between reconciliation and new creation is the observation that Paul's other uses of the reconciliation word group are also interconnected with new creation.[97] It is likely not coincidental that the temple idea of verse 19, which appears to be carried over into this verse and related to reconciliation and peace, is also connected with a coming new creation in both the OT and the way it is developed in various texts of the NT, including elsewhere in Paul (see the additional notes on 1:20).

Thus there is a reconciliation of the alienation that has occurred in the spirit world, the human world, and the material world (see Melick 1991: 225). Everything in these three spheres that compose the entire cosmos are put into their proper order in relation to and by Christ, which means everything will be rightly subordinated by Christ (Melick 1991: 227).

96. A passage such as Isa. 11 (though omitting the word "peace") shows that in the new creation there will be peaceful harmony not only between formerly antagonistic people groups (Jews and Gentiles) but also among formerly antagonistic animals and between animals and humans (for the latter idea, see also Isa. 65:17–25). In the eschatological future God would defeat the cosmic dragon, which would result in peace for his people (Isa. 27:1–5). The abundant fruitfulness of the new creation would be a sure sign of the peace that God would bring about (Isa. 55:12–13; Jer. 33:9–13; Ezek. 34:25–29); Zech. 8:10–23 indicates peace for Jew and Gentile and fertility of land as a certain sign of peace (cf. conceptually Joel 2:18–3:21).

97. See 2 Cor. 5:17–21; Eph. 2:13–17; Rom. 5:10–11; 11:15; see further Beale 2004: 528–48.

3. The Effects and Purpose of Christ's Cosmic Supremacy for Sinners Is to Reconcile Them to God and Make Them Acceptable in His Holy Tabernacling Presence (1:21–23)

This subunit is discernible from the change of topic: the effects and goal of **1:21–22**
Christ's cosmic sovereignty are immediately stated to apply to the redemption of sinners. The unit is also recognizable by the change from the focus on Christ to the repeated emphasis on "you." The verse starts with "and," which is a loose connector, likely indicating a further explanation of Christ's reconciling work in verse 20. Immediately, a concessive idea is introduced, which serves to highlight the contrasting statement in verse 22:[98] despite the fact that the Colossians ("you") were "alienated and at enmity in mind in their evil works, nevertheless" (δέ, *de*, BDAG 213) Christ "reconciled"* them to God. This reconciliation has occurred "in the body of his flesh through death."* "In the body" (ἐν τῷ σώματι, *en tō sōmati*) is ambiguous. Does it refer to the means ("by") of reconciliation or the sphere ("in") in which reconciliation takes place? The focus is likely on the means of reconciliation, since verse 20 has clearly said twice that "through [or by, δι', *di'*] him" he "reconciled all things." Nevertheless, that reconciliation has been achieved in the sphere of Christ's body is probably not out of mind. But it is not merely by Christ's body that reconciliation has occurred; it is also "by the death" of that body.

The hearers were formerly in a condition of alienation (the significance of the perfect ptcp., enhanced by the preceding ptcp. ὄντας, *ontas*, being).[99] They were also "at enmity by means of the mind [τῇ διανοίᾳ, *tē dianoia*; thought]" and "by means of evil deeds" (ἐν [*en*] + dative).[100] What does Paul mean by saying that Christ's death has "reconciled" (on this reading, see the additional note on 1:20, 22) people who are "alienated" and at "enmity" with God? Paul's use of reconciliation language elsewhere refers to the OT background of Israel's restoration out of the exile from God's presence, especially restoration from Babylonian exile. In fact, reconciliation for Paul is the equivalent of the concept of Israel's hope for restoration from exile (see the additional note on 1:20, 22). The placement of reconciliation in verses 20–22 is appropriate against the OT background, since these verses are the direct

98. On the concessive syntactical relation of verse 21a (ποτε ὄντας ἀπηλλοτριωμένους, *pote ontas apēllotriōmenous*, although formerly alienated) to verse 22, see the additional notes.

99. Burton 1898: 72; likewise BDF §352.

100. The first dative and the second preposition plus dative can plausibly be taken as instrumental rather than locative or referential. D. Moo 2008: 140 (and the NJB) takes the second phrase as a dative of means; D. Moo also suggests that the evil works are the result of a hostile mind (see likewise O'Brien 1982: 67). Harris (2012: 120) views ἐν (*en*) + τοῖς ἔργοις τοῖς πονηροῖς (*tois ergois tois ponērois*, your evil deeds) as a dative of cause: "enemies in your minds because of your evil deeds" (so also HCSB, NIV; Mitchell 2000: 71, though she says it may express the manner of the alienation). Apparently "because" in this view expresses the notion that "evil works" are the evidence of a hostile "mind" (so Melick 1991: 231) or express what is in such a mind (NET). Eadie (1856: 80) views the mind as "the seat of enmity" and the following phrase as designating the sphere of the mind's development, where it is embodied.

result of Christ becoming the end-time temple of God's presence in verse 19. According to OT restoration prophecies, one of the expectations was that there would be a latter-day temple built in Israel, at which returning Israelites could worship and experience God's intimate presence and peace. At his death on the cross, Christ as the summation of true Israel has gone through the ultimate exile from the Father, and his resurrection has restored him as Israel into the Father's peaceful presence, where Christ sits at the right hand of the throne in the heavenly temple. All who identify with Christ's exile and his restoration experience restoration or reconciliation to God.[101] This OT prophetic background of restoration is then seen as fulfilled in Christ and all who identify with him.

"But" (δέ, *de*) introduces a contrast and reversal to the prior alienated and hostile condition of the readers. Together with this, the introductory "now" (νυνί, *nyni*) in verse 22 is not the "now" of logical deduction but an eschatological "now."[102] "Now," at the turn of the ages, the great eschatological restoration promised for true Israel, the church, has begun to take place. This reconciliation came by means of "the body of his [Christ's] flesh through death"* (v. 22). Christ offered his body as a sacrifice to accomplish "reconciliation." This entails that the "alienation and enmity" of the sinful Colossians (v. 21), which blocked a peaceful relationship with God, was wiped away by Christ's death, "the blood of his cross" (v. 20). Christ suffered the "alienation" and death in place of sinful humans, so that their alienation and punishment of death would be removed and they could be "reconciled" to God (see further 2:13b–14). This is how the Colossians have experienced "the redemption, the forgiveness of sins"* (1:14). God is the subject of the verb "he reconciled" (1:22) and not Christ (as according to some commentators, e.g., Pao 2012: 107), since he was the subject of "reconcile" in verse 20 (see our argument),

101. For this notion of Christ representing true Israel in his death as exile and his resurrection as restoration, see, e.g., N. Wright 1992b: 387–90, 396–403; and 1996: 592–611.

102. Here we are concerned with both νυνί (*nyni*) and the alternate form νῦν (*nyn*). The use in Rom. 8:18 refers to the time period when resurrection existence for God's people is beginning (8:10–11), as is their experience of the end-time Spirit (8:5–17, 22–23); Rom. 13:11–12a is fairly straightforward in this respect: "Do this, knowing the time, that it is already the hour for you to awaken from sleep; for now salvation is nearer to us than when we believed. The night is almost gone, and the day is near"; 2 Cor. 6:2 refers to the present time, when the latter-day Isaiah prophecy about God helping his servant was beginning realization (Isa. 49:8), which continues the earlier reference to the "now" of the inaugurated resurrection life and new creation, when proper evaluative judgments about Christ will be made (2 Cor. 5:14–18); the "now" of Rom. 3:21, 26 is likely eschatological; the "now" of 2 Thess. 2:6 refers to the same time when "the mystery of lawlessness is already at work" (2:7), which is a beginning fulfillment of the end-time opponent prophecy of Dan. 11:36. For the discussion of resurrection and the Spirit in Rom. 8, see Beale 2011: chap. 9; for further discussion of 2 Cor. 5:14–6:2, see Beale 2011: chaps. 10 and 16; for additional discussion of 2 Thess. 2, see Beale 2011: chap. 7. The uses in Rom. 11:5 and 2 Cor. 8:14 are not explicitly eschatological but are susceptible to such a meaning. The more obvious examples of this eschatological use of "now" (νῦν) are Rom. 16:26; Eph. 3:5, 10; Col. 1:26; and outside of Paul, see John 4:23; 5:25; 12:31; 1 John 2:18; 4:3; with respect to the alternate form of "now" (νυνί), see Rom. 7:6; 1 Cor. 15:20; Eph. 2:13; Col. 1:22; outside Paul, see Heb. 9:26.

which is also in line with all of Paul's reconciliation discussions in his other epistles, where he always has God as the subject of reconciliation.

The second part of verse 22 gives the purpose of Christ's reconciliation: "in order to present you holy and blameless and beyond reproach." That Christ has "reconciled" the Colossians "in His fleshly body" (adj. genitive) implies that "both before and after his resurrection Christ possessed a body" (Harris 2012: 128), since Christ had to "present" them to God after his sacrifice. Colossians 2:9 confirms this by affirming that "all the fullness of Deity dwells in bodily form," since context suits the idea that "dwell" (κατοικεῖ, *katoikei*) is a gnomic present, which cannot be limited to only one point in Christ's earthly ministry or heavenly session at God's right hand (likewise, for the same reason κατοικῆσαι [*katoikēsai*] is a gnomic aorist used in the same way in 1:19). Christ "presenting" the believers as "holy and spotless and blameless"* (1:22) is the language of acceptable sacrifices, which OT priests were to offer in the temple.[103]

The three words "holy" (ἅγιος, *hagios*), "spotless" (or "blameless," ἄμωμος, *amōmos*), and "blameless" (ἀνέγκλητος, *anenklētos*)[104] are generally synonymous, indicating that which is set apart as pure or "holy." In the LXX ἅγιος is employed especially in Leviticus to designate sacrifices (of grain or animals) as that which is "holy" to the Lord (Lev. 7:1 [6:37 LXX]; 27:9, 10; Num. 18:17) or first holy to the Lord and then holy for the priests (Lev. 2:3, 10; 6:17 [6:10 LXX]; 10:17; 14:13). The word ἄμωμος is used often in Exodus, Leviticus, and Numbers to refer to "spotless" or "unblemished" animal sacrifices offered at the tabernacle (e.g., Exod. 29:1, 38). The "unblemished" nature of the sacrifices made them "acceptable to the Lord."[105] Some of these "unblemished" sacrifices were "peace offerings" (e.g., Lev. 3:6, 9), and some were for "sin offerings" (e.g., Lev. 4:3, 14, 28, 32), to appease by atonement God's wrath about sin committed by Israelites (e.g., Lev. 5:18; Ezek. 43:22; 45:18).

Probably, all of these associations of "unblemished" offerings are included in Paul's purview to one degree or another. Thus ἄμωμος here is best translated as "spotless" or "unblemished," referring to Christians as holy and "acceptable" sacrifices "before him [God]." The combined use of "holy" and "blameless" likely then reflects the sacrificial nuances of the words in Leviticus and Numbers (though when the words are used separately later in the OT, they refer merely to moral purity of the saints). Christ is apparently viewed as the priest in the new temple who performs his reconciling work through his own priestly, acceptable sacrifice ("through the body of his flesh,"* v. 22; and "through his blood," v. 20)[106] to make holy and acceptable sacrifices to God of

103. See Lightfoot (1875: 162), who views "present . . . spotless" to have an OT sacrificial background.

104. The latter is a very close synonym of ἄμωμος.

105. E.g., Lev. 1:3; cf. likewise Lev. 22:21; the following present "a soothing aroma to the Lord" (virtually the same phrase): Lev. 23:18; Num. 28:27; 29:2.

106. Thus in verses 19–22 Christ is portrayed as the temple, a priest serving in the temple, and the sacrifice the priest offers.

those who were sinful and tainted with sin (cf. Caird 1976: 182). The phrase "to present you before Him [κατενώπιον αὐτοῦ, *katenōpion autou*]" following "holy and blameless" likely also reflects part of the sacrificial terminology of the tabernacle (= temple), where ἄμωμος is used. The "blameless" sacrifice was to be presented as "acceptable before the Lord [ἐναντίον κυρίου, *enantion kyriou*]" in the temple (Lev. 1:3; so also 9:2; cf. similarly 4:14; 5:15).[107] Christ's cultic offering resulted in "peace" with God for those formerly "alienated" and at "enmity," as also was the case with the OT unblemished sacrifices.[108]

1:23 "If" the Colossians "remain" or "continue in the faith" in Christ's work just narrated in verses 18–22, then they will benefit from it (the conditional clause should not be restricted only to verse 22 or only a part of verse 22, though it is uppermost in mind). It is possible that "faith" refers to the doctrinal content of what Christians believe, but it seems perhaps better to view it as a reference to the act of faith on the part of the readers (the word has this sense everywhere else it occurs in Colossians [1:4; 2:5; 2:12; esp. see the parallel of 2:7]). Furthermore, elsewhere in Paul ἐπιμένω (*epimenō*, continue) plus the dative (as in Col. 1:23) can designate the disposition of people (e.g., Rom. 6:1; 11:22, 23, following Sumney 2008: 87). Persevering in faith is thus the basis for benefiting from Christ as supreme over the new creation and as the end-time temple, which mediates reconciliation to sinful and alienated people. Paul likely has confidence that they will finally persevere in their salvific condition (in light of 1:28b; 2:5 [cf. O'Brien 1982: 69]; 3:12), or at least the majority will.[109]

Nevertheless, despite his confidence, this is a real condition: if the Colossians do not persevere, then they will not benefit from Christ's work described in verses 19–22. This is developed further in 2:6: "Therefore as you have received Christ Jesus the Lord, so walk in Him." If they do not persevere, does it mean that they will lose the benefits of Christ's redemptive work that have been applied to them as the "elect of God"* (3:12) in 1:21–22 (and elsewhere in the epistle)? Or does it mean that they were pseudo-believers all along and never really benefited from that work? We think the latter is the case.[110] However, this classic theological problem involves tensions between election and

107. In the LXX see Lev. 4:14: an "unblemished" (ἄμωμος, *amōmos*) animal sacrifice is brought to the "doors of the tabernacle"; in 4:17 the blood of that sacrifice is "sprinkled . . . before [ἔναντι, *enanti*] the Lord, in front of [κατενώπιον, *katenōpion*] the holy veil." Thus here ἔναντι is in parallelism with the following κατενώπιον (cited by BDAG 531a).

108. See additional notes for those who reject an OT sacrificial background and propose that "present" and "blameless" refer to a context of avoiding the final judgment.

109. This is in line with his caveats in his other epistles: e.g., 1 Cor. 11:19; 2 Cor. 5:20; 11:13–15; 13:5; and Eph. 4:20–21 indicate that he is not sure about the genuineness of all who profess faith in his churches. This is a first-class condition in Greek in Col. 1:23, in which the "if" clause (in the indicative mood) is assumed to be true for the sake of argument (Wallace 1996: 690–94). Here the context shows that Paul does assume the truth of the "if" clause in the way we have qualified it above.

110. It is unlikely that this is a perseverance related only to a mature Christian's positive evaluation before Christ's judgment seat, while nonperseverance still results in salvation for less mature believers but without such a positive evaluation (so Bing 2007). Among the problems with

accountability in relation to warnings, which cannot be fully elaborated on here.[111]

The means by which they are able to continue in the faith are "by being founded" and being made "steadfast." "Founded" (τεθεμελιωμένοι, *tethemeliōmenoi*) is an adverbial participle modifying the verb "continue" by giving the means or instrumentation by which the believers are able to maintain their ongoing faith.[112]

It is likely not coincidental that "founded" and "steadfast" are usually architectural terms that refer to the stability of a structure (see below). Accordingly, the best translation is "with your foundation established and your structure immovable."[113] The structural concept here is their sure maintenance as a part of the temple in Christ, with whom they are identified.[114] Accordingly, these two words convey architectural language of the temple. What points further to the continuation of the temple idea from 1:19–22 is the generally acknowledged parallel with Eph. 3:17–18: "so that Christ may dwell in your hearts through faith; and that you, being rooted and grounded [τεθεμελιωμένοι] in love, may be able to comprehend with all the saints what is <u>the breadth and length and height and depth</u>."[115] Likely Eph. 3:17–18 develops the temple portrayal of Eph. 2:20–22 (see further in the additional note on 1:23a): "Having been built on the foundation of the apostles and prophets, Christ Jesus Himself being the corner stone, in whom the whole building, being fitted together, is growing into a holy temple in the Lord, in whom you also are being built together into a dwelling of God in the Spirit."

If Eph. 3:17–18 continues the temple portrayal of Eph. 2:20–22, and if Col. 1:23 is truly its parallel (as broadly recognized), then it makes good contextual sense that Col. 1:23 continues the temple idea laid out in the immediately preceding text of 1:19–20.[116] The Ephesians and Colossians passages also

---

such an unusual view, it must presuppose that all professing believers in Colossae are genuine believers, yet some would experience a greater reward at the eschaton than others.

111. But see further Beale (1999a: 518, 868, 1102–3); Volf (1990), who is in line with my own conclusion.

112. Possibly the participle is an adjectival modifier of the pl. "your" of the preceding verb "remain," as would be the following participle "not moved." The intervening adjective "steadfast" (ἑδραῖοι, *hedraioi*) might point to these adjectival uses.

113. This is an alternative rendering proposed but rejected by Harris (2012: 54–55), since he does not see architecture imagery here; Callow (2002: 56–57) sees both words as "dead figures" of speech "taken from the semantic domain of building."

114. This is a notion similar to Rev. 3:12, "He who overcomes, I will make him a pillar in the temple of My God, and he will not go out from it anymore"; likewise 1 Pet. 2:5, "You also, as living stones, are being built up as a spiritual house for a holy priesthood." For Col. 1:23a O'Brien (1982: 70) cites conceptual parallels to temple language from elsewhere in the NT.

115. See Thielman (2010: 243–37) for alternative identifications of these four dimensions, among which the temple is one, though not preferred by Thielman.

116. Instead of "rooted" (ῥιζόομαι, *rhizoomai*) in Eph. 3:17, the Col. 2:23 parallel uses ἑδραῖος (*hedraios*, steadfast), which among its rare uses can be employed as an architectural metaphor (e.g., see 4 Bar. 1.2: "For your prayers are a firm pillar in her midst"). In Col. 2:23 the noun has a verbal sense of "being steadfast," since it is sandwiched between and parallel to

have in common the link between "reconciliation" and the temple (Eph. 2:16; Col. 1:20–22), the identically common use of the aorist infinitive κατοικῆσαι (*katoikēsai*, to dwell: Eph. 3:17; Col. 1:19), and the same use of the perfect passive participle τεθεμελιωμένοι (Eph. 3:17; Col. 1:23).

Christ being the temple (Col. 1:19) was the basis for his being supreme over the new creation (1:18), and the Colossians' identity with Christ as the temple here thus continues to provide part of the basis for Christ's new-creational supremacy.

The following participle μὴ μετακινούμενοι, (*mē metakinoumenoi*, not moved away) is adverbial, like the preceding τεθεμελιωμένοι, and thus likewise indicates the means by which they "continue in the faith." If they are "founded and steadfast" as a part of God's temple in Christ, it means they will also be immovable (again, see the conceptual parallel in Rev. 3:12a). To be a permanent part of the temple in Christ is to be "not moved away from the hope of the gospel," since the gospel is about Christ.

The last phrases of verse 23 are a repetition of the almost identical wording in verses 4–7:

Colossians 1:4–7	**Colossians 1:23b**
Since we heard of your faith . . . because of the hope laid up for you in heaven, of which you previously heard in the word of truth, the gospel, which has come to you, just as in all the world, . . . just as you learned it from Epaphras, our beloved fellow bond-servant, who is a faithful servant of Christ	From the hope of the gospel that you have heard, which was proclaimed in all creation under heaven, and of which I, Paul, became a servant.

Note: Dotted underlining in both columns indicates synonyms and not identical wording in Greek, whereas solid underling indicates the same words in Greek.

The repetition has, at least, a twofold purpose. First, it forms an *inclusio* around virtually the entire broad literary unit of 1:3–23 (though the parallel at the start of the unit begins at v. 4 instead of v. 3). Both verses 4–7 and verses 21–23 contain four references to "you" (either as the pronoun or as the second-person pl. verb), which points to the abrupt change to "and you" (καὶ ὑμᾶς, *kai hymas*) in verse 21 as signaling the start of a new and concluding subunit within verses 3–13. This is further evidence that the broad literary unit ends at verses 21–23 (esp. concluding with v. 23).

Second, by concluding the same way the segment began, Paul is underscoring three things: (1) the importance of the gospel that the Colossians have heard and in which they have put their hope; (2) the gospel's arrival among the Colossians as just one example of its spreading to humans throughout the whole created world order (see the additional note on 1:23b); (3) Paul as the human, apostolic authority behind this gospel, of whom Epaphras "is a faithful

"founded/established" and "not moved" and likely is to be recognized as part of the means to "continue in the faith." However, "rooted" (ῥιζόομαι) is used in conjunction with θεμελιόω (*themelioō*) in Col. 2:7 ("having been rooted and founded in Him"*), which shows ἑδραῖος as a near synonym with "rooted" (ῥιζόομαι).

servant of Christ on our [Paul's!] behalf" (v. 7). Epaphras is a worker under Paul's authority, who himself was commissioned as an apostle to the Gentiles by God. The concluding phrase "of which I, Paul, became a servant"* in verse 23 is a shorthand reference to Paul's Damascus road Christophany experience, where he was both converted and appointed a prophetic apostle to go to the Gentiles. This is apparent from noticing the unique parallel between Col. 1:23 (and 1:25, which repeats "of which I became a servant"*) and Eph. 3:7 ("of which I became a servant"*).[117] It is clear that Eph. 3:7 continues (from earlier in chap. 3) one of Paul's clearest autobiographical accounts of the commission to Gentiles at his Damascus road experience: "If indeed you have heard of the stewardship of God's grace which was given to me for you; that by revelation there was made known to me the mystery, as I wrote before in brief, . . . that the Gentiles are fellow heirs and fellow members . . . and fellow partakers of the promise in Christ Jesus" (Eph. 3:2–3, 6).

Additional Notes

1:15a. Several commentators correctly understand that the reference to Christ as the "image of the invisible God" is, at least in part, an allusion to Gen. 1:27, "God created man in His own image, in the *image of God* He created him": seeing Gen. 1:27 as an echo are G. Kittel, *TDNT* 2:395–96; Simpson and Bruce 1957: 193; Yates 1993: 22; and Wall 1993: 66–67. Seeing the Genesis passage as part of the background are O'Brien 1982: 43; Masson 1950: 98–99; and Hugedé 1968: 52–54. Abbott (1897: 210) sees Col. 1:15a rooted in Gen. 1:26. Pokorný (1991: 74) sees allusion to Gen. 1:26–28; a possible variant of this is Burney's 1926 article ("Christ as the ΑΡΧΗ of Creation"), in which he argues that Paul exegeted Gen. 1:1 ("in the beginning") via Prov. 8:22, on which see our discussion of Proverbs below (for expansion of Burney's complicated view, see Caird 1976: 175); cf. Fee 2007: 299–301, who sees reference to Adam as the image of God.

Early Judaism viewed Adam to have been created in God's image. This was a corporeal Adam composed of body and mind, who "was fashioned after the image of his Maker" (Philo, *Heir* 56, citing Gen. 1:27; 2:7)[118] and who was "the faithful impression of the divine image" (Philo, *Heir* 57; so also *Heir* 231, citing Gen. 1:27; *Virt.* 204, where Adam is said to be in the "image" of the "eternal God"). Philo (*Plant.* 18–20) also underscores that the corporeal Adam was created "to be a genuine coinage of that dread Spirit, the Divine and Invisible One" who "breathed into his face a breath of life" (Gen. 2:7), and this Adam "has been made after the Image of God [Gen. 1:27], not however after the image of anything created"; likewise Philo (*Worse* 86) says "the invisible Deity stamped on the invisible soul the impress of Itself, to the end that not even the terrestrial region should be without a share in the image of God." Noah, as a second Adam figure, is viewed as being given the original Adamic commission from Gen. 1:28 and, accordingly, is said to be "born to be the likeness of God's power and image of his nature, the visible of the invisible [εἰκὼν τοῦ ἀοράτου, *eikōn tou aoratou*]" (Philo, *Mos.* 2.65; cf. Col. 1: 15, εἰκὼν τοῦ θεοῦ τοῦ ἀοράτου, *eikōn tou theou tou aoratou*).[119] Here Noah is a physically visible image of God (composed of mind and body), as was the corporeal Adam.

117. The parallel is further enhanced by noticing the common use of οἰκονομία (*oikonomia*, stewardship, household management) in both Col. 1:25 and Eph. 3:2, 9.

118. Translations of Philo in this additional notes section are from the Loeb Classical Library edition.

119. Lightfoot (1875: 144–46) sees "image" in Col. 1:15 to be partly linked to Philo's similar uses.

On the other hand, Philo also sees that there was an Adam-like figure who was pure mind and incorporeal. In *QG* 1.4, Philo in commenting on Gen. 2:7 distinguishes "the sense-perceptible man and a likeness of the intelligible type." But there is also one who "is [made] 'in accordance with the image [of God]'" and "made in accordance with [God's] form," who is the "intelligible and incorporeal and a likeness of the archetype," after which the "sense-perceptible man" is made. This incorporeal Adam figure is here called the "Logos of God, . . . the Archetypal idea." Since the corporeal Adam is "a likeness of the intelligible type" in this passage, he appears to be made after "the Archetype" of the incorporeal Adam.[120] Here and elsewhere Philo conceives of two Adam-like figures, one being a Platonic and genderless intelligible type (the figure created in Gen. 1:26–27) and the other a mixture of the corporeal and intelligible (the one created in Gen. 2:7), though Philo is not always consistent in how he makes the contrasts (e.g., sometimes he sees Gen. 1:26–27 and Gen. 2:7 to refer to the creation of the same being). In alluding to Gen. 1:27, Philo in *QG* 1.8 refers to the "molded man," composed of mind and body, and contrasts him with the "man made in his image," who is "the intelligible and invisible, . . . in the class of incorporeal species" (likewise *QE* 2.46). So also in *QG* 2.56, Philo says that Gen. 1:27–28 refers to the Adam-like figure "who was [made] in the form and likeness of the truly incorporeal Being," who is the purely intelligible ideal in contrast to the Adamic "molded and earthy man."[121] Israelite saints can become "sons of His invisible image . . . [who] is the eldest-born image of God," the latter of whom is the incorporeal Adam-like figure (*Conf.* 145–47). Accordingly, Philo can conceive of an Adam-like figure being in the image of God, but not existing in a visible body. Especially notable with respect to the two Adamic figures is *Alleg.* 1.31:

> There are two types of men; the one a heavenly man, the other an earthly. The heavenly man, being made after the image of God, is altogether without part or lot in corruptible and terrestrial substance; but the earthly one was compacted out of the matter . . . which Moses calls "clay." For this reason he says that the heavenly mind was not molded, but was stamped with the image of God; while the earthly is molded work of the Artificer, but not his offspring.

A classic example of these two kinds of Adam figures in Philo is found in *Creat.* 134:

> "God formed man by taking clay from the earth, and breathed into his face the breath of life" [Gen. 2:7]. By this also he shows very clearly that there is a vast difference between the man thus formed and the man that came into existence earlier after the image of God: for the man so formed is an object of sense-perception, . . . consisting of body and soul, . . . by nature mortal; while he that was after the (Divine) image was an idea or type or seal, . . . incorporeal.

Philo's repeated reference to an incorporeal and eternal Adam-like figure and a subsequent corporeal Adam is a striking parallel to Col. 1:15, where Christ is portrayed as existing before creation yet with Adamic features. This is a precedent showing that one could be thought to be in the image of God and not have bodily, visible existence before the creation of the earthly Adam in Gen. 1–2. However, there appears to be no direct dependence of Paul on Philo at this point, though presumably Paul may have been aware of Philo's writings.

Occasionally other Jewish writers referred to a physical Adam being the image of the "invisible" God, but they did not distinguish between two Adam-like figures in the way Philo did. Thus LAE 35 (ca. 100 AD) refers to God as Adam's "unseen Father" because "he is your image."

1:15b. Early Judaism closely associated the notions of Adam's sonship and his being in God's image. Philo refers to "God forming man" from clay and God's own breath (Gen. 2:7), which is a contrast to "the man that was born earlier [than the earthy Adam] according to the image of

120. Similarly, the corporeal Adam is said to be "the stamp of the Eternal Word" and his "soul has been made after the image of the Archetype, the Word of the first cause," the latter of which Philo (*QG* 1.4) identifies with the incorporeal Adamic figure.

121. On this distinction between these two Adam-like figures, see Hay (2004), who has greatly influenced my understanding of this distinction; cf. also Sterling 2013: 41–56.

God"[122] (*Creat.* 134; cf. 135–39),[123] and "the firstborn . . . imitating the ways of the Father" and being in the "divine image" (*Conf.* 62–63).[124] Israel was called God's "firstborn" (πρωτόγονος, *prōtogonos*, Sir. 36:11) and his "very first πρώτιστος [*prōtistos*; e.g., Philo, *Post.* 63] offspring." See also Jer. 31:9 (38:9 LXX): "Ephraim is my firstborn [πρωτότοκος, *prōtotokos*]"; Jub. 2.20 (though the Greek text is not extant at this point); Philo, *Flight* 208: "Israel, the son free-born and firstborn" (πρωτόγονος); Israel was also God's "firstborn, only begotten" (2 Esd. [4 Ezra] 6:58), his "beloved son and . . . firstborn" (Pss. Sol. 13.9), and "a firstborn, only begotten son" (18.4). Thus Israel as "firstborn" and the law of primogeniture are part of the background for "firstborn" in Col. 1:15b.

Similarly, Philo further strikingly refers to the highest ranking angelic figure as one "who holds the eldership among the angels, an archangel as it were," who is also "God's First-born, the Word, . . . 'the Beginning,' . . . the Word, and the Man after His image, . . . that is, Israel," and people who want to be represented by this angelic figure can become "sons of God" (citing Deut. 14:1; 32:18) and "sons of His invisible image, the most holy Word. For the Word is the eldest-born image of God" (*Conf.* 145–47); see also Philo, *Dreams* 1.215 (heavenly "High Priest, Firstborn, the divine Word" of whom the human priest is the "visible image"); see likewise Philo, *Agr.* 51 ("true Word and Firstborn Son," who is identified as an "angel"); *Conf.* 62–63 ("Son . . . firstborn" in the "divine image"). The angel probably was conceived to be Israel's heavenly representative.[125]

Similar to the use of Ps. 89:27 (88:28 LXX) in Colossians is Ps. 2, which underscores a similar idea: the Lord enthrones the "Messiah" (2:2), the end-time "king," and declares that he is "begotten" as God's "Son" (2:6–7). The result of this enthronement is the "Son's" rule over the entire world (2:8–12). Thus "begotten" (γεννάω, *gennaō*) in Ps. 2 does not refer to a time when the king was conceived or born biologically but rather when he was enthroned. The idea is that the king was born to rule at some point, so it is natural that when that point comes, he can be said to be "begotten." When the main purpose of his birth is reached, he can be said to be truly "born." It is likely not coincidental, in light of our discussion so far in Col. 1:15–17, that the Messiah's "inheritance" in Ps. 2 includes the "nations" and "the ends of the earth [as] your possession" (2:8), which likely develops the Adamic Gen. 1:28 mandate reiterated throughout the OT.[126] This background may enhance even more the notion that "firstborn" in Col. 1:15 has a clear sense of "sovereignty over."

1:15–17. To one degree or another a "wisdom" background for the portrayal of Christ is probably included in verses 15–17 in the background but not the foreground (see Caird 1976: 177). Many commentators believe that the figurative portrayal of "Wisdom" in Judaism and in Prov. 8:22–27 LXX (as "the beginning of his [God's] ways" before the creation) lies behind Col. 1:15–17. For example, some commentators (Lohse 1971: 47–56; N. Wright 1986: 66–71; Simpson and Bruce 1957: 197; and Wall 1993: 68) mention Gen. 1 and OT Wisdom, especially Proverbs (comparable to Proverbs, see further Sir. 24:9 LXX, "From eternity, from the beginning [ἀρχή, *archē*], he created me [Wisdom]"). In the case of Prov. 8, the personification of "Wisdom" as being in God's presence directly preceding his creation of the world is to indicate that God's Wisdom enabled him to be the perfect craftsman in accomplishing this marvelous work. Such a background is certainly plausible, but the allusion is not as clear as so often indicated.

Fee (2007: 300–301, 317–25, 595–630) has made the strongest case against the presence of any verbal allusions in Col. 1:15–17 to Prov. 8 or to the Hellenistic Jewish background of

122. LCL has who "came into existence earlier after the image of God." Again, this is the Adam-like figure who was incorporeal.

123. Once again in *Creat.* 134–39 Philo makes the same distinction between the two Adam-like figures.

124. This refers to the purely incorporeal Adam-like figure.

125. All of the references in this paragraph appear to refer again to the incorporeal Adam-like being.

126. See the above discussion on Col. 1:6 in the additional notes. On how Ps. 2:8 fits into the biblical theology of these Gen. 1:28 reiterations, see Beale 2011: 76–77, 754–55.

"wisdom" (so similarly Fowl 1990: 118–21). While Fee's analysis is plausible, at certain points he places too much emphasis on the lack of linguistic parallels. For example, in contrast to Col. 1:16, which has the preposition "through" (διά, *dia*) for creation "through" Christ, this preposition does not occur in the OT or Jewish texts; rather, "in" (ἐν, *en*) appears or no preposition at all. On this basis, he sees none of the Jewish texts affirming that creation came "through" so-called Wisdom. But these texts do speak of "Wisdom" *conceptually* as the agent (if there is personification) or means of creation (even if wisdom is conceived of as a divine attribute, i.e., conveying the notion that God through his own wisdom created; see Wis. 7:22 [7:21 LXX]; 8:4–6; 9:1–2; cf. also Prov. 8:28–30 and the use of ἐν σοφίᾳ [*en sophia*] in Ps. 104:24 [103:24 LXX] and Prov. 3:19–20, where in each passage both sphere and instrumentation may be in mind, as in Col. 1:16).

Another example adduced by Fee is that the Jewish literature does not use the precise word "firstborn" (πρωτότοκος, *prōtotokos*) for "Wisdom." Nevertheless, such strikingly similar expressions about "Wisdom" as the following are used: Prov. 8:22–24 LXX: "the Lord created me <u>the beginning of his ways</u>, . . . <u>before the ages he established me</u> in the beginning, before he created the earth"; likewise, see Sir. 1:4, "Wisdom was created <u>before all things</u>"; and 24:9, "He created me [Wisdom] from the beginning, before eternity." In addition, Philo (*QG* 4.97) speaks in linguistic terms close to the language "firstborn of all creation" in Col. 1:15: "Wisdom, who is the firstborn mother of all things" (in *Flight* 50–51, Philo holds that "Wisdom" is also a "father" and possesses "the powers and activities of consummate men"). Since this section of Philo is based on an Armenian translation, we cannot be sure if the Greek word being translated "firstborn" is πρωτότοκος (*prōtotokos*) or πρωτόγονος (*prōtogonos*). Whichever it is, the two are essentially synonymous; yet it needs to be remembered that the logos or wisdom in Philo is created by God and not coexistent with him in eternity past (see Caird 1976: 177), as is true of Christ in Col. 1:15–17, though this might not preclude Paul from being influenced by this background, going from the lesser to the greater. Again, as in the preceding example, Fee's argument about the absence of "firstborn" in Judaism seems to be too narrow a distinction, bordering on the "word-concept" fallacy.

From another perspective, Fee says that the parallels of OT-Jewish "wisdom" are not strong, since these texts do not speak of "wisdom" as a "hypostasis" or "personification," but only as an attribute of God. On the other hand, Fee says, the purported application of "wisdom" to Jesus is not conceived as an attribute but the instantiation of wisdom in Christ as a person. But could Paul not be identifying Christ with what was a divine attribute in the OT and Judaism and then be going from the lesser to the greater, thereby seeing that what was only a divine attribute was now to be identified as a divine person? Thus Fee seems to be drawing very thin descriptions from OT-Judaism, when some of these expressions seem "thicker" conceptually than he allows. Part of the problem is that Fee distinguishes a "wisdom tradition" from the use of "wisdom" as a divine attribute, which not all scholars would do. On the other hand, the word "wisdom" (σοφίᾳ, *sophia*) does not occur in Col. 1:15–17, which should caution us against seeing direct allusions, though echoes may be detected. Pizzuto (2006: 241) pays heed to Fee's caution yet still sees that the "Colossians author" has taken over themes and language from the "conceptual reservoir of Jewish wisdom speculation."

Though further discussion of this issue is not possible here, it appears that, in addition to various OT influences noted above (esp. Gen. 1), among plausible Jewish backgrounds that may have influenced Paul to one extent or another throughout Col. 1:15–17 is a pastiche of passages about wisdom from Wisdom of Solomon:[127]

127. Perhaps also influential together with this may be Philo's description of "wisdom" as "the beginning" and "the image" in *Alleg.* 1.43 and as "the image of God" in 1.31–32 (in connection with 1.43); cf. also Philo, *Conf.* 97 (cf. Moule 1957: 63), where God's "image" is his "most holy word." See likewise possibly the following Philo texts noted earlier with respect to "image" and "the Word": *Conf.* 145–47; *Dreams* 1.215; *Agr.* 51 (though "image" does not occur); also *Conf.* 62–63 (though "Word" does not occur, it is likely in mind). See the relevant wording of these Philo passages above in the additional notes to Col. 1:15–17; also see Hay

1. Wisdom, identified with God's Spirit (in light of 1:6), "holds all things together" (1:7 NRSV).
2. Wisdom is the "reflection of the everlasting light, the unspotted mirror of the power of God, and the image of his [God's] goodness"* (7:26).
3. Wisdom "makes all things new"* (7:27); "sweetly does she order all things"* (8:1), and "she works all things"* (8:5).
4. Wisdom is above "scepters and thrones" (7:8 NRSV; cf. 6:21).[128]
5. "Wisdom . . . was present when you made the world" (9:9 NRSV); "I will trace her [Wisdom's] course from the beginning of the creation" (6:22 NRSV).[129]
6. Wisdom was the agent or instrumentation through which God created the world (7:22 [7:21 LXX]; 9:1–2; so also Philo, *Heir* 199; *Names* 137).
7. "You formed man through your wisdom that he should have dominion over the creatures"* (Wis. 9:2), and wisdom "guarded the first-formed father of the world, who was created alone, and brought him out of his own transgression [i.e., his "fall" into sin], and gave him power to rule all things"* (10:1–2).

Boring, Berger, and Colpe (1995: 483–84) mention most of these passages from Wisdom as forming part of the background for Col. 1:15–17. Whereas the fullest manifestation of earthly wisdom in the OT was the Torah, now the Messiah is the greatest expression of divine wisdom on earth, the former pointing to the latter.[130]

Such a wisdom background is not necessarily mutually exclusive of a Gen. 1 Adamic background (so also D. Moo 2008: 118), though others are adamant that only the "wisdom" background is in mind and not Adam in Genesis (so, e.g., as noted above, see Aletti 1993: 94–116; Schweizer 1982: 66; Dunn 1996: 87–88). That the two backgrounds are compatible (so Pokorný 1991: 68) is evident from recalling that Philo applies Gen. 1:27 allusions to a preexistent Adam figure being in God's image, which Philo sometimes associates with "Wisdom."[131] Likewise, we saw in the Wisdom of Solomon that the preexistent "wisdom" "guarded" the earthly Adam, so that there is close connection between the two (See Wis. 9:2 with 10:1–2). Furthermore, an Adamic background in Col. 1:15 is apparent from recalling that one of Wisdom's key roles was to come to dwell in Israel (cf. Proverbs, Sirach, and Wisdom of Solomon),[132] the corporate representative of humanity, to enable them to be truly wise humans and to rule over the creation. This became connected to messianic expectation focused around a coming eschatological king (e.g., Ps. 89:27 [88:28 LXX]; following N. Wright 1992a: 112–13). In addition, the attributes of "Wisdom" were necessary for someone to be truly wise and were "required if humans are to *be* truly human" (N. Wright 1992a: 113), which Wis. 9:2 (noted just above) comes very close to affirming about wisdom in relation to Adam ("You formed man through your wisdom that

2000: 54, who says that Philo, Sirach, and Wisdom of Solomon speak of the same thing when they use "wisdom" or "word," which are equivalent to God's law and are a way of explaining God's transcendence and immanence.

128. On this element, see Witherington 2007: 130.

129. The Old Latin version of Sir. 24:3 indicates that wisdom as "firstborn" is categorically distinct from the rest of creation: "I went forth out of the mouth of the Most High, firstborn before every creature" (see Glasson 1969). This Latin variant clarifies the vaguer Greek variant of πρωτότοκος πάσης κτίσεως (*prōtotokos pasēs ktiseōs*, "firstborn of all creation"), which likely was added by a later Greek scribe under the influence of the same phrase in Col. 1:15b. Witherington (2007: 134) has also pointed out the same thing in Philo (*QG* 4.97) about wisdom, though with a maternal metaphor: "Wisdom, who is the firstborn mother of all things . . ." These two texts indicate an even closer parallel between the Jewish view of wisdom and Christ in Col. 1:15.

130. Witherington (2007: 130) gives a list similar to the above seven parallels, though they are somewhat looser.

131. See the references to Philo directly above, esp. *Alleg.* 1.43, where "heavenly wisdom" is "the beginning" and "the image" of God and as the image of God is the "archetype" for earthly wisdom, which is its "copy." Cf. also Philo, *Conf.* 97.

132. E.g., see Sir. 24:1–17; Wis. 8:17–9:11.

he should have dominion over the creatures"*). Likewise Sir. 24:28–34 says that "the first man knew her [wisdom] not perfectly," but nevertheless "wisdom" continued to "send forth her light afar off . . . to all ages forever . . . for all them that seek wisdom,"* so that wisdom's knowledge was to be an attribute of truly wise humans. Thus wisdom Christology and Adam Christology are very close, since they are both Israel Christologies (N. Wright 1992a: 113). Recall that the preexistent Christ, as Wisdom, is primarily in view in Col. 1:15a, so that what was true about the earthly Adam's wisdom would certainly be true of his precreational archetype (at least from Paul's and Philo's perspective). Nevertheless, we saw in 1:15 that the timeless present tense "is" (ἐστίν, *estin*) includes Christ not only being in the Adam-like image of God before creation, but also remaining in that archetypal "image" through to his incarnation, exaltation, and onward forever.

The Gen. 1 kingship background is dominant throughout in Col. 1:15, and Christ as a ruling figure continues throughout Col. 1:16–20 (see also Dunne 2011). That a wisdom background may well be included to some degree is pointed to by the description of the incarnate Christ as the repository of true wisdom in Col. 2:3: "in whom [Christ] are hidden all the treasures of wisdom and knowledge," which, as we will see, is important in countering the purported wisdom of the false teachers (see on 2:3). A wisdom background is also suggested by the idea that one of "wisdom's" dwelling places on earth was the temple; Col. 1:19 says God's dwelling place now is in the new temple of Christ (see comments and notes on 1:19).

If Hellenistic Jewish wisdom is part of the background behind Col. 1:15–17, then there would also be included some reference to Christ as the perfect revelation of the invisible God.

1:15–20. *The Structure.* There have been various proposals for the structure of the so-called hymnic section. In addition to dividing the passage into two parts (for scholars holding this view, see Baugh 1985: 229), there are several who hold to a tripartite structure (1:15–16; 1:17–18a; 1:18b–20; cf. the summary of views by Mitchell 2000: 65). Pizzuto (2006: 118–205) offers his own chiastic analysis, as well as surveying and evaluating other structural analyses. Pizzuto's own chiasm has verse 17b ("and all things hold together in him") as the center, verse 17a ("and he is before all things") and verse 18a ("and he is the head of the body, the church") as the inner ring and verses 15–16 and verses 18b–20 composing the outer ring. Virtually identically, Reyes (1999: 139–46), following Baugh (1985) among others, proposes the following viable threefold structure: (A) verses 15–16; (B) 17–18a, and (C) verses 18b–20. Sections A and C serve as the two main outer rings, section C is the central matrix, and verse 17b is the core of that matrix and the pivot point of the hymn. Thus verse 17b ("In Him all things hold together") is the focus of the entire hymn. If this is correct, then the point of the hymn is that everything in the sphere of creation and redemption finds its cohesion in Christ. This structural analysis is attractive, is certainly viable, and may indeed be a refinement of the twofold approach. In addition to D. Moo 2008: 116, another survey of various past structural analyses of Col. 1:15–20 is given by Baugh (1985: 228–35) and Gordley (2007: 5–16).

1:18. There has been debate about the background and origins for Paul's use of the word ἐκκλησία. Trebilco (2011), building on the arguments of others, thinks the word (ἐκκλησία, *ekklēsia*, church) is to be understood mainly from its Septuagint background, where it refers to Israel, often in its congregated form. Van Kooten (2012) has responded to Trebilco by contending that the word is best understood, not against an LXX background, but from the Greco-Roman background, where it refers to gathered public assemblies of a political nature. Trebilco (2011: 445–46, 486n84) acknowledges that there may be Greco-Roman influence but affirms that it is slight. Similarly, Van Kooten (2012: 537) recognizes some degree of LXX influence but argues throughout his essay that the Greco-Roman impact is far more dominant.

Of course, there cannot be thorough discussion here. We believe the LXX background to be a greater influence than the Greco-Roman.[133] If this is going in the right direction, then it points

133. For more thorough analysis of this, see Beale (2015), of which this entire section on ἐκκλησία is a summary.

to the conclusion that the church is the Israel of God in the new-covenant age.[134] Sometimes, however, the Greco-Roman background is implicit, so that the church is viewed as the true assembly of the heavenly commonwealth in contrast to the assembly of the world.

Nevertheless, the OT background of ἐκκλησία exercises a dominant influence on Paul. Paul refers sixty times to ἐκκλησία as the Christian "church," among which are twelve references to "the church of God" (ἐκκλησία + θεός, *ekklēsia* + *theos*; including once in Acts 20:28, where Paul is the speaker, and once in the plural). Some commentators have asserted that these uses are likely allusions to the repeated references to "the church [assembly] of the Lord" in the LXX (ἐκκλησία + κύριος, *ekklēsia* + *kyrios*; seven times),[135] including presumably "the church [assembly] of God" (Neh. 13:1).[136] Commentators have also observed that ἐκκλησία by itself occurs seventy-three times in the LXX as a translation of the Hebrew קָהָל (*qāhāl*, congregation), which refers to Israel assembled to hear God's law from Sinai or from Joshua, or it can refer to the nation gathered together for festive occasions.[137]

The point has not been formerly made, however, that the references to "church of God" (ἐκκλησία τοῦ θεοῦ, *ekklēsia tou theou*) in Paul appear to focus most specifically on Neh. 13:1. The Nehemiah passage is the only place in all of the Septuagint where the phrase ἐκκλησία τοῦ θεοῦ occurs. Nehemiah 13:1 actually quotes Deut. 23:2, "assembly of the Lord," but renders it "assembly of God."

But even if Neh. 13 is not always the focus, if the proposal by some (e.g., Marshall 1973, noted earlier) is accepted that Paul abbreviates "church of God" in his other numerous single references to ἐκκλησία by itself, then it is possible that Paul also viewed the single uses of ἐκκλησία in the Greek OT to be abbreviations of "assembly of God" and "assembly of the Lord." In this respect, Paul may have assigned an even wider scope of reference to ἐκκλησία throughout the LXX, triggered initially by the "assembly of God" and "assembly of the Lord" references. Whether this is the exact pathway of associations in Paul's mind may be hard to prove, but something roughly similar to it seems likely. Did Paul always have centrally in focus the OT references to "assembly of God" and "assembly of the Lord" behind all of his own multiple "assembly of God" uses, or did he even have clearly in mind the OT uses of ἐκκλησία by itself in his own single uses of the Christian ἐκκλησία? The likelihood is that the OT was uppermost in his mind at times, though at other times it was just in his peripheral cognitive vision. Nevertheless, even when not the central focus, he probably had the OT tacitly or latently in mind to some degree, being in what we might call his cognitive peripheral vision.[138] Whichever is the case, the above analysis points to the probability that the LXX uses of ἐκκλησία τοῦ θεοῦ and ἐκκλησία κυρίου and ἐκκλησία by itself are the quarry from which Paul in some way drew for his understanding of the "church," including his reference in Col. 1:18. The saturation of OT and Jewish allusions in Col. 1:15–22 also points to ἐκκλησία having an OT background. The upshot is that the Christian church is the continuation of true Israel of the OT.

1:19. This verse may be rendered in two different ways: "because in him [ἐν αὐτῷ, *en autō*] all the fullness [of deity] was well-pleased [εὐδοκέω, *eudokeō*] to dwell [κατοικέω, *katoikeō*]" (RSV, ESV); or "in him he was well-pleased for all the fullness [of deity] to dwell" (NASB, KJV, NIV, Douay, HCSB, NJB). In the first, "all the fullness" is taken as a nominative clause as the subject of "well-pleased." In the second, "all the fullness" is taken as an accusative clause as the subject

134. E.g., see, among others, not only Trebilco (2011) but also earlier works by Marshall (1973) and O'Brien (1982: 57–61).

135. Four times in Deut. 23:2–4, 9 (23:1–3, 8 Eng.), 1 Chron. 28:8, and Mic. 2:5. From here on versification in Deut. 23 is given according to the Hebrew and LXX versification, which are the same.

136. However, on Neh. 13:1, see directly below.

137. Marshall 1972–73: 359; twenty-three more occurrences of ἐκκλησία (*ekklēsia*) appear in Judith and Sirach but not as a translation of קָהָל (*qāhāl*), most of which refer to Israel.

138. On this concept of "tacit" or "latent" knowledge, among others see Polanyi 1966; and Polanyi and Prosch 1975. See also Beale 2014.

of the infinitive "dwell." Two observations support the first rendering: (1) it is more awkward to add "for" (or other words) to make the second translation work; (2) the allusion to Ps. 68:16–17 (67:17–18 LXX; see below) points to the first translation, since it more directly expresses the structure of the psalm reference to *God* being *pleased* to *dwell* in the temple (the psalm has "be pleased" [εὐδοκέω, *eudokeō*] followed directly by the infinitive "to dwell" [κατοικεῖν, *katoikein*]; so also D. Moo 2008: 131). The second rendering is supported by Col. 2:9, where "all the fullness of Deity" is the subject of the verb "dwell," but the first translation also reflects the same thing ("all the fullness was well-pleased to dwell"; complementary infinitival clause). The first translation could seem awkward: "all the fullness was well-pleased to dwell and to reconcile." Perhaps this awkwardness is intensified by recognizing that a neuter (πᾶν τὸ πλήρωμα, *pan to plērōma*) is joined with a masculine participle in verse 20 (εἰρηνοποιήσας, *eirēnopoiēsas*). But this awkwardness is softened if this is taken as a "construction according to sense" (Barth and Blanke 1994: 210–11) and is paraphrased as "God in all his divine fullness was well pleased to dwell and to reconcile"[139] (a paraphrase supported by the parallel of 2:9; cf. Barth and Blanke 1994: 212–13). However, the difference in meaning between either translation is not significant.

In addition to Beasley-Murray 1980: 177; N. Wright 1986: 78; 1990: 463; 1992a: 117; Pao 2012: 102; and Beetham 2008: 143–46, several other scholars have seen an allusion to Ps. 68:16–17 (67:17–18 LXX; 68:17–18 MT). So Pizzuto 2006: 228–29; Münderlein 1962: 266–70, seeing an undoubted connection between Ps. 67:17 LXX (68:17 MT; esp. the targumic version) and Col. 1:19; D. Moo 2008: 131–33, admitting a "probable echo" of Ps. 67:17 LXX (68:17 MT); Abbott 1897: 219, hearing an echo of the psalm text; Barth and Blanke (1994: 212) include Tg. Ps. 68:17 and Tg. 1 Kings 8:27 in the echo; cf. likewise Lona 1984: 127–28. Pao (2012: 102) sees a "possible allusion" to Ps. 68:16 (Ps. 67:17 LXX); Stettler (2000: 254) takes the wording of Col. 1:19 to be a "close analogy" to the psalm verse and cites similarly Ps. 132:13–14 (131:13–14 LXX); MacDonald (2000: 63) says the wording "calls to mind Jewish Scripture, . . . LXX Ps. 67:17, for example"; Wolter (1993: 85) argues that the wording comes from the Jewish OT background, especially Ps. 68:16–17 (and secondarily from Ps. 132:13–14; 2 Macc. 14:35; 3 Macc. 2:16); likewise Lona (1984: 127–28) includes Tg. Ps. 68:17 and Tg. 1 Kings 8:27 in the echo; Talbert (2007: 194) says "the image comes from" Ps. 67:17 LXX or 2 Macc. 14:35; Gnilka (1980: 71) affirms that "especially near in the formulation" of the wording in Col. 1:19 is Ps. 67:17 LXX; O'Brien (1982: 52) says only that the combination of the two verbs in both Ps. 68:16 (67:17 LXX) and Col. 1:19 "is of special significance" (see Hay 2000: 62, more tentatively); Wall (1993: 75) sees a reference to the OT temple but does not adduce convincing parallels.

Haggai 1–2 contains language and concepts quite close to those of Ps. 67:17 LXX (68:17 MT) and Colossians: "Build the house, and I will take pleasure in it [εὐδοκήσω ἐν αὐτῷ, *eudokēsō en autō*], and I will be glorified" (Hag. 1:8); "I will fill [πλήσω, *plēsō*] this house with glory" (2:7); Tg. Zech. 3:2 similarly has "the Lord who has been pleased to make his Shekinah dwell in Jerusalem." Likewise 2 Macc. 14:35 affirms, "O Lord of all, who has need of nothing, you were pleased [ηὐδόκησας, *ēudokēsas*] that there be a temple for your habitation [σκηνώσεως, *skēnōseōs*] among us."

The Targum to 1 Kings 8 also repeatedly links God's "good pleasure" with his "dwelling" (Shekinah) in Solomon's temple (Tg. 1 Kings 8:13–15, 23–24, 27–30; 2 Chron. 6:4–5, 20; 7:16); it also twice says that God's glory cloud "*filled* the house of the sanctuary" (Tg. 1 Kings 8:10–11), language having further affinity with Col. 1:19.[140] Similarly to Col. 1:19, the LXX also reads forms of κατοικητήριον (*katoikētērion*) in 1 Kings 8:39, 43, 49 with reference to the heavenly temple in relation to its extension to the earthly temple; so also see κατοικέω (*katoikeō*) and κατοίκησις (*katoikēsis*) in 2 Chron. 6:18, 21, with reference to the earthly temple, and see κατοικητήριον

139. Following D. Moo 2008: 131 on this point.

140. The LXX of 1 Kings 8:10–11 and the parallel in 2 Chron. 7:1–2 reads ἔπλησεν (*eplēsen*) for "filled," though the latter reads πληρόω (*plēroō*) for "filled" in two MSS (MSS c and e), similar to πλήρωμα in Col. 1:19; see repeated statements about God's glory "filling" (πίμπλημι, *pimplēmi*) the tabernacle and temple in Exod. 40:34–35; Ezek. 10:3–4; see likewise ἐμπίπλημι (*empiplēmi*, fill) in 2 Chron. 5:13–14.

(*katoikētērion*) in 2 Chron. 6:30, 33, 39 with respect to the heavenly temple in parallel to that of 1 Kings 8:39, 43, 49; so also Pao (2012: 102) sees this language of temple "dwelling" in 1 Kings and 2 Chronicles to lie behind the use in Col. 1:19. Linguistically, among all the above parallels outside Ps. 67:17–18 LXX, the closest is 3 Macc. 2:15–16, which affirms, "for, indeed, your dwelling place [κατοικητήριον, *katoikētērion*], the heaven of heaven, is unapproachable to men; but since you were well-pleased [εὐδόκησας, *eudokēsas*] to set your glory in the midst of your people Israel, you sanctified this place [the temple]." This passage itself may likely also be an allusion to Ps. 67 LXX.

Thus Ps. 68:16–17 (67:17–18 LXX) appears to be alluded to in Col. 1:19. But, even if one doubted it, at the very least Col. 1:19 reflects this general background of God being well-pleased to dwell in and fill the temple. In particular, Colossians may resonate with interpretative rings of the Targum (or perhaps the exegetical tradition that it reflects) together with Ps. 68 (67 LXX); and the 1 Kings background at least shows that Paul's allusive language of Ps. 68 is about God's dwelling in the temple.[141] Also cf. Tg. Ps. 132:13: "For the Lord is pleased with Zion; he has desired it for his habitation"; the MT has "For the Lord has chosen Zion, he has desired it for his habitation" (NJPS), and verse 14b reads, "Here I will dwell, for I have desired it"; the LXX renders the MT's "desired" (אִוִּתִי, *ʾiwītî*) with "choose" (αἱρετίζω, *hairetizō*).

Another intriguing observation is possibly related to Col. 1:19. There appears to be some relationship between "wisdom" and the temple in early Jewish understanding of these OT notions, and this might also stand in the background of Col. 1:19. It appears significant, in the light of the generally acknowledged allusion to "wisdom" in Col. 1:15–18, that early Judaism viewed "wisdom" as having its "headquarters" in the temple, as, for example, Sirach affirms: "So the Creator of all things gave me [wisdom] a commandment, and he that made me caused my tabernacle to rest, and said, 'Let thy dwelling be in Jacob, and thine inheritance in Israel. He created me from the beginning before the world, and I shall never fail. In the holy tabernacle I served before him; and so I was established in Sion'" (Sir. 24:8–10 KJV).[142] Likewise, Philo says that "God's dwelling-place, the tabernacle," is symbolic of "wisdom," which "is the court and palace of the All-ruler" (*Prelim.* 116–17).[143] Very similarly, Philo also says, "Do you not see that also when he received the tabernacle from God, and this tabernacle is wisdom, in which the wise man tabernacles and, dwells, he fixed it firmly and founded and built it up strongly. . . . 'And it was called the tabernacle of testimony'; that is to say wisdom was borne witness to by God. For every one who seeks the Lord went forth out of his house" (*Alleg.* 3.46).

141. Barth and Blanke (1994: 212) see Ps. 67:17 LXX (68:17 MT; 68:16 Eng.); Tg. Ps. 68:17; and Tg. 1 Kings 8:27 as "especially close parallels" to Col. 1:19, while also seeing echoes from the LXX: 2 Sam. 7:6; 2 Chron. 6:18; Pss. 21:4; 131:14; 134:21 (MT: 22:4; 132:14; 135:21; Eng.: 22:3; 132:14; 135:21); Isa. 8:18; Lohse (1971: 58) briefly discusses some of this background but never comments on the bearing of it for Col. 1:19.

142. For further analysis holding that all of Sir. 24:1–27 focuses on "wisdom" as being in the temple, see further Hayward 1999; see likewise Wis. 9:4–9; cf. 1 En. 42.1–2 with 39.6–13.

143. In a context about the "holy tabernacle," Philo (*Dreams* 1.208) says, "Its [knowledge's] most holy [cultic] image will be enshrined in all the house of Wisdom both in heaven and on earth" (LCL, brackets added). Elsewhere in Philo, "image" (ἀφίδρυμα, *aphidryma*) refers to erecting images in temples: e.g., *Decal.* 7; *Virt.* 102; cf. *Emb.* 310, 317). Similarly, Philo (*Migr.* 4–6) says that the "word" is God's "abode" and equates this abode with "the House of God" (see Beetham 2008: 155). This is significant, since Philo sometimes either equates the "word" (λόγος, *logos*) with "wisdom" (σοφία, *sophia*) (e.g., *Alleg.* 1.65; *Prelim.* 174; *Dreams* 2.245) or very closely associates the two (*Flight* 97; 137; *Dreams* 1.66; 2.242). Note also Hel. Syn. Pr. 12.9–11, which appears to be an allusion to Col. 1:13–18: "The one who brought everything into being . . . through your only Son, and gave him birth before all ages, . . . an only Son, . . . a living Wisdom, a firstborn of all creation, . . . your high priest, . . . the one before all things, through whom are all things; . . . you . . . have made all things through him." The mention of the "Son," who is "Wisdom," being a "high priest" is fitting with the temple theme of Col. 1:19.

This background about the association of "wisdom" and the "temple" points further to a temple reference in Col. 1:19 and may even make more sense of why Col. 1:9 alludes to Exod. 31:3 and 35:31, where God filled people with the Spirit in order to have "wisdom" to be able to build the tabernacle. In verse 9 Paul may already subtly be anticipating the OT temple allusion of verse 19. Verse 9 significantly mentions "wisdom" of the believer, which ultimately is related to one's identity with Christ, presented as "wisdom" in verses 15–18, since only by growing in "wisdom" can one be "complete in Christ" (1:28), "in whom are hidden all the treasures of wisdom" (2:3; likewise Col. 3:16).

1:20. Some MSS (e.g., B and D*) omit the phrase "through him" (δι' αὐτοῦ, *di' autou*), but it is certainly the harder reading because of its abruptness, and most of the earliest as well as best MSS support the insertion (e.g., 𝔓[46], א, A).

1:20. The connection between Christ's reconciling and peacemaking work as part of a new creation and his identification with the end-time temple of God's presence observed above in verse 20 finds striking parallel in Eph. 2:14–22:

> For He Himself is our peace, . . . by abolishing in His flesh the enmity, . . . thus establishing peace, and might reconcile them both in one body to God through the cross, by it having put to death the enmity. <u>And he came and preached peace to you who were far away, and peace to those who were near</u>. . . . So then you are no longer strangers and aliens, but you are fellow citizens with the saints, and are of God's household, having been built on the foundation of the apostles and prophets, Christ Jesus Himself being the corner stone, in whom the whole building, being fitted together, is growing into a holy temple in the Lord, in whom you also are being built together into a dwelling of God in the Spirit.

Since Christ is the new temple of the divine presence, he is able to mediate that presence to the alienated cosmos, especially sinful humans in the inaugurated eschatological epoch (for the same connections, see 2 Cor. 5:17–7:1, on which see Beale 1989). Stuhlmacher (2018: 437) thinks the background of verse 20 is the atonement executed in the temple, which was oriented to the renewal and preservation of the cosmos and which brought about reconciliation.

1:20, 22. Discussed above was the notion that Paul's view of reconciliation in Christ is the beginning fulfillment of the OT promises of Israel's restoration from exile. We have already explained how this is related to the restoration hopes of the end-time temple, which verse 19 says is Christ. But there is more.

Contrary to the apparent near consensus that there is no OT background for Paul's reconciliation language (καταλλάσσω, *katallassō*, word group), there does appear to be a specific OT background in some of the key passages where Paul explicitly discusses reconciliation. These crucial passages are 2 Cor. 5:14–21 and Eph. 2:13–17. After one determines the background and meaning of reconciliation in these two passages, Paul's other "reconciliation" texts (Rom. 5:1–6:11; 11:11–31; Col. 1:15–22) should be analyzed in their respective contexts, and then the relation of these texts to 2 Cor. 5 and Eph. 2 should also be discussed. We have done this study elsewhere, so only the results can be summarized here.[144] The primary OT background is Isa. 40–65. One of the crucial Isaiah texts alluded to in the new-creation-reconciliation passage of 2 Cor. 5:14–21 is Isa. 43:18–19, which closely connects the hope of new creation to restoration (a connection we have also seen in Col. 1:18–22 above). The Isa. 43 context is only one of a series of sections in the so-called Book of Consolation (Isa. 40–55) that *explains the restoration of exiled Israel as a new creation or at least integrally associates the two concepts of restoration and creation.*[145] Isaiah 60:15–22; 65:17–25; and 66:19–24 continue the same thematic emphasis. God's act of new creation as restoration

144. See Beale (2012: 527–48), also more fully interacting with supporting secondary literature.

145. Isa. 40:28–31; 41:17–20; 42:5–9; 44:21–23, 24–28; 45:1–8, 9–13, 18–20; 49:8–13; 51:1–3, 9–11, 12–16; 54:1–10 (esp. v. 5); 55:6–13.

is also described outside of Isa. 43 as his "redemption" of Israel (e.g., 44:1–8; 44:24–45:7; 54:1–10) and as a new exodus.[146]

Moreover, Isa. 40–66 describes Israel's exile as an expression of divine "wrath" (51:20; 60:10), "anger" (47:6; 51:17, 22; 54:8; 57:16–17; 64:5, 9), "forsakenness" (49:14; 54:6–7; 62:4), "rejection" (54:6), "hiddenness" (54:8; 57:17; 59:2; 64:7), and consequent "separation" between God and the nation (59:2). All these texts assume that sin or iniquity is *the* cause of Israel's forsaken condition, and this cause is sometimes explicitly stated for the sake of emphasis (cf. 50:1; 51:13; 57:17; 59:1–15; 64:5–9). God's restoration of Israel from this estrangement is described not only as a redemptive new creation, but also as a time when the nation will "not be forsaken" (62:12) and will be reunited with God (45:14) and "know" him (43:10) because of his gracious initiative in regathering them (54:6–8; 57:18). And God "wipes out their transgressions" (43:25) and frees them from the bondage resulting from sin (42:6–9; 49:8–9) by the sacrificial death of the servant, who becomes the guilt offering for the people (53:4–12). Therefore, the return from exile is a period in which there is a cessation of anger, when "peace" is reestablished between the nation and its God (cf. 48:18; 52:7; 57:19). This is a peace that results from and is characteristic of the new creation, modeled on the original paradisial conditions.[147] In fact, in the context of Isa. 43, restoration and new creation are to be viewed as brought about through the payment of a ransom (43:3–7.) and the forgiveness of sins (43:22–25). The vicarious suffering of the servant in Isa. 53 probably has the same function.

Therefore the complex of ideas found in 2 Cor. 5:14–21 can already be seen in Isa. 40–66. The same ideas appear to be present in Col. 1:18–22, especially in connection to the temple idea in verse 19. In light of the thematic overview of Isa. 40–66, it is plausible to suggest that in Col. 1:20, 22 *"reconciliation" in Christ is Paul's way of explaining that Isaiah's promises of "restoration" from the alienation of exile have begun to be fulfilled by the atonement and forgiveness of sins in Christ.*[148] The believer's separation and alienation from God because of sin has been overcome through the divine grace expressed in Christ, who has restored the believer into a reconciled relationship of peace with God.

1:21. The periphrastic participial clause in the phrase "and you being alienated [ὄντας ἀπηλλοτριωμένους, *ontas apēllotriōmenous*]" is best rendered concessively ("though you were formerly alienated"), apparently with the sense of an adverbial or circumstantial accusative-absolute construction, modifying the verb "reconciled" in verse 22 ("nevertheless, now he has reconciled"). This is parallel to the same kind of construction in Eph. 2:1 (see Wallace 1996: 191) in relation to the main verb in 2:4, and the construction is repeated in Eph. 2:5 (which picks up on the beginning of 2:1). The initial ὑμᾶς (*hymas*) in Col. 1:21 serves as the object of the following verb ἀποκατήλλαξεν (*apokatēllaxen*) in verse 22 (in agreement, Pao 2012: 106; cf. Lightfoot 1875: 161).

1:22a. Most of the earliest and best MSS read the third-person active verb "he reconciled" (ἀποκατήλλαξεν, *apokatēllaxen*), though a few early and quality MSS (𝔓[18] and B) read a second-person passive verb "you were reconciled" (αποκατηλλάγητε, *apokatēllagēte*). The latter is certainly the more difficult reading for two reasons: (1) it clashes with the "you" in verse 21, which should be nominative to harmonize with the subject of "you were reconciled" (so Callow 2002: 55); (2) it is followed by an infinitive with a different subject (God) than the preceding verb and better explains the other minor variants, as well as the aorist reading. With respect to the latter, the passive reading is not impossibly difficult, since the subject of the infinitive could well be conceptually Christ, the subject of the preceding phrase: "in the body of his flesh through death." Though this is a hard textual decision to make, in the end it seems slightly better to side with the majority of the earliest and best MSS and see the passive variant as having arisen in some accidental way early in the transmission of the text. See further accordingly Lohse 1971: 64;

146. Cf. Isa. 40:3–11; 41:17–20; 44:24–28; 51:1–13; 52:7–10; see also 43:16–21.

147. Cf. Isa. 26:11–19; 27:1–6 (cf. Targum Isaiah); 32:15–18; 45:7–8 (cf. Targum Isaiah); 45:18–25 Sym.; 55:12 MT; 60:15–22; 66:12–14, 19–23.

148. See my fuller explanation of this OT background in Col. 1:18–22 in Beale 2012: 543–46.

O'Brien 1982: 64; Metzger 1994: 554–55, here citing the majority opinion of the UBS editorial committee, though Metzger himself favors the passive; Fee (2007: 314–16) and Lincoln (2000: 606) also prefer the passive, the former providing more explanation than others in support.

1:22b. D. Moo (2008: 142–43) rejects the idea that "holy and blameless" allude to the OT sacrificial background and says that the verb "present" (παρίστημι, *paristēmi*) together with "blameless" (ἀνέγκλητος, *anenklētos*) indicates presenting believers as innocent before the judgment seat of God. Abbott (1897: 226–27), Lohse (1971: 65), and O'Brien (1982: 68–69) agree with D. Moo; though they acknowledge that in the LXX ἅγιος (*hagios*) and ἄμωμος (*amōmos*) describe sacrificial animals set apart to the Lord, they deny that such thoughts are carried over into the Colossians expressions, claiming that the words have only a judicial sense (somewhat similarly, Mitchell 2000: 72; Sumney 2008: 85–86; Sumney contends that the judicial sense is primary). Among the parallels adduced by D. Moo and containing some of this judicial language, however, only one clearly refers to a judgment context (Rom. 14:10); he cites Eph. 1:4 and 5:27, but these could just as easily fit into an OT sacrificial context. One could add 2 Pet. 3:14 (ἄσπιλοι καὶ ἀμώμητοι, *aspiloi kai amōmētoi*), which is clearly part of a final judgment scene (cf. 3:10); though only one of the two words from Colossians occurs in 2 Pet. 3:14, the phrase appears to be synonymous with that of Col. 1:22. The word παρίστημι (*paristēmi*) is used in a variety of ways and only rarely refers to a judgment context (Acts 27:24; Rom. 14:10). Significantly, there is a striking parallel in Rom. 12:1, which refers to the OT sacrifices: "Present your bodies a living and holy [ἁγίαν, *hagian*] sacrifice, acceptable to God, which is your spiritual service of worship" (likewise the verb παρίστημι is used in Luke 2:22 in a temple context for "presenting" Jesus "to the Lord"). In fact, ἵστημι (closely related to παρίστημι) in the LXX can refer to "presenting" a sacrifice "before the Lord" (Lev. 14:11; 16:7, 10). Also, Paul's use of παρίστημι a few verses later (Col. 1:28) is not judicial but refers to people becoming progressively "complete in Christ" (Pao 2012: 108).

A sacrificial context in Col. 1:22 is also suggested by the observation that the first part of the verse portrays God as reconciling "in the body of [Christ's] flesh through death"; a similar sacrificial picture is given in verse 20: "to reconcile . . . through the blood of His cross." In this light, it is surprising that Mitchell (2000: 72) can say, "The immediate context does not suggest a primary interest in sacrifice." However, to boost the proposal of a judgment context, D. Moo (2008: 142–43) contends that ἀνέγκλητος (*anenklētos*) is a legal term (Col. 1:22). However, its other uses by Paul do not have a context of judgment *clearly* in mind; the majority of his uses refer to candidates for the office of elder or deacon being "above reproach" as one of the necessary qualifications (1 Tim. 3:10; Titus 1:6, 7), although 1 Cor. 1:8 could include a judgment scene. Harris (2012: 247) also sees κατενώπιον αὐτοῦ (*katenōpion autou*) as expressing a judicial atmosphere (Col. 1:22). In support, he cites Eph. 1:4 and Jude 24, neither of which clearly allude to a juridical context (though Jude 23 is set in a context of judgment).

So it is possible that such a judgment context is echoed here with the word, but it is not clear. Yet if so, it would be a legal metaphor combined with the sacrificial background (as, e.g., Dunn 1996: 109–10), much as Rom. 3:24–25 combines a legal background ("justification") both with slave-market language ("redemption") and sacrificial language ("propitiation" or "mercy seat"). In fact, the sacrifices in the OT temple system carried both notions of purity and a legal sense of "not guilty." The Hebrew word for "atone" (כִּפֶּר, *kipper*) conveys the notion of "ransom," which is a payment that delivers a guilty party from a just punishment by the offended party (God) and appeases the offended party, thus restoring peace to the relationship. But the idea of "purify" is likely also included in the word's meaning, since this is sometimes seen to be the effect of the "atoning" (e.g., see Lev. 16:33a; Ezek. 43:20–26). In reality, in all of the contexts where the verb (*kipper*, atone) occurs, it is very difficult to choose one idea over another, since one notion may be the focus but the other may still be implied or echoed secondarily (see Beale 2011: 486–90). So the word ἀνέγκλητος (*anenklētos*) is also not inappropriate for the sacrificial context already suggested by "holy and spotless" (Col. 1:22). Pokorný (1991: 92) likewise sees the idea here of presenting sacrifices acceptable to God to be similar to the forensic notion of ἀνέγκλητος, "beyond reproach"; Garland (1998: 67) recognizes both a sacrificial background that leads to "lawcourt imagery." Moule (1957: 73) and Caird (1976: 182) understand the words "present," "unblemished," "holy," and "before him" to be sacrificial language, though they do not comment specifically on ἀνέγκλητος. Pao (2012: 108–9) also sees that a sacrificial idea is dominant in Col. 1:22b for some of the same reasons as noted above; he does not see an exclusively future reference to "before [κατενώπιον, *katenōpion*] him," since Paul frequently uses the word with reference to the present age.

1:23a. On the viability of the parallel temple imagery of Col. 1:23a with Eph. 3:17–18, note the following, which points to Eph. 3:17–18 being the development of the temple portrayal of Eph. 2:20–22: (1) κατοικέω (*katoikeō*) of Eph. 3:17 probably develops κατοικητήριον (*katoikētērion*) of 2:22, clearly referring to God's "dwelling" in his temple of the church. (2) In both texts such "dwelling" occurs through the "Spirit" (πνεῦμα, *pneuma*, Eph. 2:22; 3:16). (3) Both passages speak of Christ providing a "foundation" for believers: "having been built on the foundation [θεμέλιος, *themelios*] of the apostles and prophets, Christ Jesus Himself being the corner stone" of the foundation (Eph. 2:20), "so that Christ may dwell in your hearts" and thus you may be "grounded [τεθεμελιωμένοι, *tethemeliōmenoi*] in love" (3:17). (4) The purpose of this indwelling through the Spirit and resulting "grounding/founding" is so that believers "may be able to comprehend . . . what is the width and length and height and depth." What are these dimensions about? Likely they are about believers' understanding the amazing scope of Christ's indwelling in them as his temple. It is not coincidental that these dimensions are sometimes descriptions of God's temple in the OT. For example, 1 Kings 6:20 LXX affirms with the same three Greek words as Eph. 3:18 that the "length . . . and the width . . . and the height" of the inner sanctuary (the holy of holies) were all of equal measurement. Indeed, the same three Greek words are used for the ark in the tabernacle (Exod. 25:10), for the equal measurements of the "ten brazen bases" in the temple courtyard (1 Kings 7:27 [7:14 LXX]), for the bronze wash basins in the temple courtyard (Eup. 2.17), for the measurements of "the portico in front of the house [temple]" (2 Chron. 3:3–4 LXX), for the "four tables of hewn stone" for the whole-burnt offerings in the temple courtyard (Ezek. 40:42), for the foundation of the temple (Eup. 2.13),[149] and for the measurements of the walls surrounding Israel's temple in the Second Temple period (Let. Aris. 84).[150]

(5) The word "rooted" (ῥιζόομαι, *rhizoomai*) found in conjunction with "founded" in Eph. 3:17 is not typically an architectural metaphor, but the verb is used in association with the temple

149. In Eup. 2.13, though, the word πλάτος (*platos*) is used for "width" and is also used again, enigmatically, for "height." Interestingly, the aorist active infinitive of θεμελιόω (*themelioō*) is rendered here "laid the foundation," which is similar to Eph. 3:17–18, where the same verb is used in the perfect tense together with the three Greek words for "width and length and height." θεμελιόω is also found with reference to laying the foundation of the temple (LXX: 1 Kings 7:47 [7:10 Eng.]; 2 Chron. 8:16; 1 Esd. 5:55; 6:11; Ezra 3:6, 10; Ps. 77:69 [78:69 Eng.]; Hag. 2:18; Zech. 4:9; 8:9; Isa. 44:28) or of the temple walls (Sir. 50:2), though the verb can be used for laying the foundation of various kinds of other structures. The noun form θεμέλιος (*themelios*) can also be used for the "foundation" of the temple (1 Esd. 6:19; Ezra 5:16), though it also can refer to the foundation of other things as well.

150. Though a different word is used for "height" in the Aristeas text. See also the same three words as above used of the measurements of Noah's ark in Gen. 6:15, the measurements of Solomon's temple (1 Kings 6:2; cf. 7:14 [7:27 Eng.]), and for the measurements of walls built around a city (Jdt. 1:2). Two of the four words in Eph. 3:17 are found in different kinds of contexts, including temple contexts. The word for "depth" (βάθος, *bathos*) in Eph. 3:18 is rarely used in temple contexts, though in Ezek. 43:13 it refers to "the measurements of the altar, . . . a cubit deep [βάθος], and a cubit shall be the breadth [εὖρος, *euros*] . . . and the height [ὕψος, *hypsos*] of the altar." Likewise Ezek. 43:14 refers to the measurements of the mercy seat (which appears to be the same object as the "altar") as "from the depth [βάθος] . . . to this great mercy seat, four cubits, and the breadth [εὖρος] was a cubit." Job 11:8–9 refers to God's wisdom as "high," "deeper" than other things, "longer than the . . . earth and broader than the sea." However, only two of the Greek words found in Eph. 3:18 appear in Job 11:8–9. So likewise 1 En. 93.11–14 and 2 Bar. 54.1–4 (though there is no extant Greek text of these sections of 1 Enoch or of 2 Baruch).

(Sir. 24:10–12), and so is the noun form: the "Lord . . . left us a root and a name in the place of thy sanctuary" (1 Esd. 8:78 KJV [8:75 LXX]). While it may seem odd to have an agricultural metaphor used with an architectural metaphor to describe the temple, it is not unprecedented in Paul, since the arboreal garden of Eden was a sanctuary, whose various garden-like features were replicated in design in Israel's later temple (see Beale 2004: 66–80, e.g.). This explanation of such apparently mixed metaphors appears best to account for Paul's abrupt shift from speaking about "God's field" and "God's building" in one breath (1 Cor. 3:9), and then elaborating on this in terms of the church being a temple (1 Cor. 3:10–17; Beale 2004: 245–52). We find both agricultural and architectural words in the temple passage of Eph. 2:21: "the whole building, being fitted together, is growing into a holy temple in the Lord" (emphasis added; Beale 2004: 263). Thus "rooted and grounded/founded" in Eph. 3:17 is consistent with the agricultural and architectural language of the temple in the OT and elsewhere in Paul (see Eph. 2:20–22, which appears to be developed in 3:17–18).

1:23b. Some translations have "to every creature under heaven" (e.g., RSV, KJV, NIV), which for those favoring this rendering would mean "to all humankind."[151] Other translations have "in all creation under heaven" (e.g., ESV, NASB, HCSB), which would refer to all animate and inanimate creation. The verbal parallel with 1:4–7 favors the latter as an all-inclusive reference to creation (so also Zerwick and Grosvenor 1981: 605; Robertson [1934: 772] renders this "every created thing"). The all-inclusive meaning is confirmed from the reference to "in all the world" in 1:6, to "all creation" in 1:15 (cf. Wall 1993: 85; though human creation is likely the focus here), to "all things" being created in 1:16, and "all things" being "held together" in 1:17, all of which refer to the original creation of all things, which has its background in the Gen. 1 creation account.[152]

The use of κτίσις (*ktisis*) in the NT (including Paul) can refer to all "creation" or particular "creatures" (the latter possibly even in 2 Cor. 5:17 and Gal. 6:15), though when Paul uses κτίσις and κόσμος (*kosmos*) together, they refer to the entire created world (Rom. 1:20, "the creation of the world"). The same two words are used together in Mark 16:15: "Go into all the world and preach the gospel in all of creation"* (though the last phrase could also be translated "to all creation" or "to every creature"). What may suggest that here in Mark the "world" and "creation" also refer to the entire creation is the observation that κτίσις has this reference elsewhere in Mark (10:6; 13:19; and 14:9 suggests the same: "wherever the gospel is preached in [the sphere of] the whole world [κόσμος]").

What points further to κτίσις in Col. 1:23 being a reference to the entire creation and not merely human creatures is that, as we have seen in verse 20, restoration at the very end of time involves bringing about a harmonious restoration of the entire animate and inanimate creation (see Rom. 8:19–21). Thus the gospel is preached throughout the sphere of the whole created order to humans who inhabit that order (for further support of this idea and "in all creation under heaven" possibly being a hyperbole, see on 1:6 above). It is possible to see the expression of cosmic universality in 1:23 and its parallel in 1:6 to be a synecdoche of the whole for the part (so Bullinger 1968: 620). The purpose of such a figure is to emphasize the significance of the part for which the whole is substituted. The point would be that the gospel has begun to penetrate into part of the Gentile world outside of Israel, and it will inevitably spread throughout every part of the earth by the consummation of time. Thus it is better to take the expression literally in an "already and not yet" eschatological sense rather than as hyperbole (see Pao 2012: 110). Christ's divine sovereignty over every part of creation demands that he will eventually have absolute dominance over that creation at the eschaton (cf. 1 Cor. 15:24–28; see Pao 2012: 111–13).

151. E.g., O'Brien (1982: 70–71), who then interprets this to mean "the cities and towns from which the gospel moved further afield."

152. The Gen. 1 background is alluded to in 1:6 and certainly echoed in 1:15–17; see further under "An Adamic background for the portrayal of Christ as 'the firstborn,'" on 1:15 above.

III. Letter Body: Christians Should Strive for Maturity (1:24–4:6)

Here is a fuller statement of the main idea of this unit: *Christians should strive for maturity, not by keeping earthly legalistic laws but by faithfully seeking the heavenly Christ, which should result in putting off the old sinful lifestyle and living a new-creational lifestyle with a view to prayer for the gospel's spread and witness.*

Now Paul comes to the main part of the letter. This largest segment of the letter is divided into eight sections. (1) Paul takes joy in his struggle to proclaim Christ (1:24–2:5); (2) Christians should base their lives only on Christ (2:6–15); (3) it is not necessary for saints to submit to extraordinary religious rituals (2:16–23); (4) believers should concentrate on things in heaven and not things on earth (3:1–4); (5) saints should put off the sinful lifestyle characteristic of the old world (3:5–11) and instead (6) put on a new-creational lifestyle with a focus on Christ (3:12–17); (7) this new-creational living should especially take place in the workplace and family (3:18–4:1); (8) such new-creational living should result in prayer for the spread of the gospel (4:2–6). The first section (1:24–2:5) focuses on Paul's rejoicing in his struggle to proclaim Christ and his rejoicing in his ministry to the Colossians to bring them to maturity in Christ and to prevent them from falling into deception.

A. Paul Rejoices in His Struggle to Proclaim Christ (1:24–2:5)

Here is a fuller statement of the main idea of this unit: *Paul rejoices in his struggle to proclaim Christ as the revealed mystery of the OT, which leads to rejoicing in his struggle to bring believers to eschatological maturity in Christ and to prevent their deception.*

This unit circles back to the main point of 1:3–23, which is to "walk worthy of the Lord to please him" (v. 10a). The goal of 1:24–2:5 is that believers be "complete in Christ" (1:28), which is achieved by them not being "deluded" by false teaching, so they can maintain "good discipline" and "stability of faith" (2:4–5). And this becomes the basis of "walking in" Christ in 2:6 (the beginning of the next section), which explicitly expands on "walking" worthily in 1:10a.

The focus of 1:3–14 was on God the Father, which leads to a focus on Christ the Son (1:15–23), and this leads to Paul, the minister of Christ (1:24–2:5; Pao 2012: 119).

Paul begins this section by rejoicing in his sufferings on behalf of the Colossian Christians (v. 24a), especially because his suffering "fills up" some of "what is lacking" in the amount of decreed "afflictions" for the body of Christ, the church (v. 24b). This suffering is explained to be what is entailed in being a "servant" appointed as a steward by God to announce "the word of God" (v. 25). God's "word" is the formerly hidden "mystery," which has now been revealed (v. 26). Paul defines this declared "mystery" to be "Christ," "the hope of glory," "among the Gentiles" (v. 27). In response, Paul "announces" this revealed mystery about Christ in order to "present every [hu]man complete in Christ" (v. 28). It is in view of this goal that Paul rejoices to "suffer" (v. 24) or "struggle," and he is spurred on to do so because of the power that God imparts to him (v. 29). The aim of "presenting every man complete in Christ" is the main point of verses 25–29, since everything else in the paragraph supports it.

Colossians 2:1–5 elaborates on how the goal of "presenting every man complete in Christ" (1:28) is to be accomplished. Paul wants all in the region of Colossae to know his joyous struggle in the goal of bringing them to completion in Christ (2:1). The purpose of imparting this knowledge is "that their hearts may be encouraged" (v. 2a). The grander purpose of such knowledge is that the Colossians would attain "to all the wealth," and this is immediately explained to be "a true knowledge of God's mystery, which is Christ"* (v. 2b). Christ is the content of this "true knowledge of God's mystery" because "in him are hidden all the treasures of wisdom and knowledge" (v. 3). Paul underscores that Christ is the content of "a true knowledge of God's mystery" to achieve the goal for the readers not to be "deluded with" false teaching (v. 4). To accomplish this goal, Paul rejoices in wanting to bring the readers to "stability of . . . faith" (v. 5), and to achieve the goal to "present" the believers "complete in Christ" (1:28). Thus "presenting every man complete in Christ" (1:28b) is also the main point of 2:1–5, since that section undergirds it.

The boundaries of this new literary unit are apparent from the new topic introduced in 1:24, which extends through 2:5. This new topic is Paul's suffering servanthood in making known the mystery. The boundaries of this segment are also observable from its broad chiastic structure, where the parallels are formed not merely by concepts but also by the very same Greek terms[1]:

A "Rejoice" (1:24)
    B "make known," "riches," "mystery" (1:27)
        C "struggling" (1:29)
        C′ "struggle" (2:1)
    B′ "knowledge," "riches," "mystery" (2:2)
A′ "rejoicing" (2:5)

1:24–29 and 2:1–5 are also each loosely structured chiastically, revealing them as literary subsections of this larger literary unit (see below).

Exegesis and Exposition

[24]Now I rejoice in my sufferings for your sake, and in my flesh I do my share
on behalf of His body, which is the church, in filling up what is lacking in Christ's
afflictions. [25]Of this church I was made a minister according to the stewardship from
God bestowed on me for your benefit, so that I might fully carry out the preaching
of the word of God, [26]that is, the mystery which has been hidden from the past ages
and generations, but has now been manifested to His saints, [27]to whom God willed
to make known what is the riches ⌜of the glory⌝ of this mystery among the Gentiles,
which is Christ in you, the hope of glory. [28]We proclaim Him, admonishing every
man and teaching ⌜every man⌝ with all wisdom, so that we may present every man
complete in Christ. [29]For this purpose also I labor, striving according to His power,
which mightily works within me. [2:1]For I want you to know how great a struggle I
have on your behalf and for those who are at Laodicea, and for all those who have
not personally seen my face, [2]that their hearts may be encouraged, having been knit
together in love, and attaining to all the wealth that comes from the full assurance of

1. See Aletti (1993: 130) followed by Dunn (1996: 128), though sometimes the Greek may vary in verb or noun form: e.g., the first parallel in 1:24 is the finite verb "rejoice" (χαίρω, *chairō*), and its counterpart in 2:5 is the participle "rejoicing" (χαίρων, *chairōn*).

understanding, resulting in a true knowledge of ⌜God's mystery, that is, Christ Himself⌝, [3]in whom are hidden all the treasures of wisdom and knowledge. [4]I say this so that no one will delude you with persuasive argument. [5]For even though I am absent in body, nevertheless I am with you in spirit, rejoicing to see your good discipline and the stability of your faith in Christ.

1. Paul Rejoices in His Struggle to Proclaim Christ as the Revealed Mystery of the Old Testament (1:24–29)

Colossians 1:24–29 reflects a loose thematic chiastic arrangement, which identifies it as the first subsection of 1:24–2:5:[2]

A The apostle's suffering (v. 24)
  B The apostle's commission (v. 25)
    C The mystery (vv. 26–27)
  B′ The carrying out of the commission (v. 28)
A′ The apostle's toil and struggle (v. 29)

1:24 The introductory νῦν (*nyn*, now) is not primarily temporal (as it can be elsewhere) but indicates in context further explanation of something that precedes ("now, at this point in my argument, I want to elaborate").[3] Paul begins to expand on what it means in the directly preceding verse that he was "made a servant" in "proclaiming" the "gospel" (v. 23b). This link with the preceding is clear from the verbatim repetition of "I became a servant"* in verse 23 and in verse 25. His servanthood entails "sufferings for your sake" (v. 24a), that is, "for your benefit,"[4] though precisely "for your sake" modifies "I rejoice," which means his "rejoicing in sufferings" is for the benefit of the readers. The reason for his "rejoicing" in suffering and the explanation of his suffering[5] is that he "fills up what is lacking in the tribulations of Christ,"* which are said again to be "for the benefit of" (ὑπέρ [*hyper*] + genitive) not only the Colossians but also the wider corporate body of believers (Christ's "body"). This repetition highlights that Paul's labors in ministering to the Colossian church are for their benefit and intended to reveal the mystery of Christ (1:25–27; 2:2) in order to "present [them] complete in Christ" (1:28), which is the main point of all of 1:24–2:5. It is hard to know

2. Following generally Zeilinger 1974: 44–46.

3. For similar views, see Dunn (1996: 113), who opts for a resumptive use, much as in everyday speech today, following Moule (1957: 75), who renders it as "and so." Alternatively, Campbell (2013: 21) says the focus is not so much on present time "as the situation at any given moment." Sumney (2008: 98) and Pao (2012: 123) think νῦν has an eschatological nuance, which is quite possible. If they are right, then this anticipates the clear eschatological use of the same word in 1:26 (see on 1:26). Here it would indicate the latter days as a time of tribulation and suffering.

4. See Harris (2012: 209, 215–16) for this significance of ὑπέρ + genitive.

5. Harris (2010: 59) argues that among the possible renderings for καί (*kai*) here is "in that," indicating an explanation of the sufferings just mentioned.

if these are sufferings due to Paul's imprisonment or some other kind of sufferings.

In Ephesians, Paul likewise directly links his revelation of "the mystery of Christ" (3:2–11) to his imprisonment "on behalf of the Gentiles"* (3:1) and his "tribulations on behalf of" believers (3:13). This suggests that the "sufferings" in Col. 1:24, indeed, also refer to imprisonment. References to "being bound"* in Col. 4:3 and "my chains" (NRSV) in 4:18 further point to Paul's sufferings being imprisonment (Foster 2016: 213). Also in Eph. 3:1 is the repetition of ὑπέρ (*hyper*) + genitive, which underscores that Paul's manifestation of the mystery through his ministry is for the "benefit of" the believers, especially Gentiles. This benefit is explicitly said in Ephesians to be the readers' "glory" (3:13).

Assuming that the notion of glory from Eph. 3 carries over, how does Paul's suffering relate to the readers' glory? When believers persevere in the midst of weakness, God causes his glorious strength to shine through them (2 Cor. 4:16–18; 12:9–10; 13:4). At least part of what appears to be entailed in the "glory" in Eph. 3:13 is that Paul's suffering for the readers "is producing" even in the present "an eternal weight of glory" (2 Cor. 4:17) not only for Paul but also for them, since both they and he are corporately identified together as Christ's body and share common core realities that are part of that "body." Since they share the same sufferings as the body of Christ, so they share the same glory. This notion from Eph. 3 is likely in mind in Col. 1:24, since in the following verses several specific parallels with Eph. 3 can be observed (see below). Furthermore, as in Eph. 3:13, so Col. 1:27 mentions "glory" twice: "the richness of the glory of this mystery among the Gentiles, which is Christ in you, the hope of glory." Here the focus on "glory" is on "Christ in" the Gentiles. It is Paul's suffering ministry (1:24) that has resulted in the revelation of this mystery to the Gentiles and their sharing in the glory of Christ, in which Paul also shares.

That Paul "fills up what is lacking in the tribulations of Christ" does not mean that there was an insufficiency in Christ's atoning work at the cross, to which some other human could make addition, since everywhere else Paul is convinced of the sole and complete sufficiency of Christ's atoning work for sinful people. Furthermore, if Paul were contending that Christ's death was not completely sufficient, it would support the false teachers' contention (later in the letter) that something more than Christ is required to receive divine blessings (Sumney 2008: 99). According to this perspective, these are not the "afflictions" of the historical Christ but the "afflictions of Christ" in "His body (which is the church)," part of which Paul experiences ("fills up") in his own "flesh." Since the "church" is explained to be Christ's corporate "body" at the end of the verse (so also in Eph. 1:23), Paul's "filling up" of Christ's trials means that he does his part ("in my flesh") as a fellow member of God's new covenant people in enduring the trials (patterned after Christ's sufferings) destined throughout the interadvent age for the benefit of[6] Christ's corporate

6. This prepositional phrase modifies the verb "fill up."

body, the church.[7] This is in line with Christ's apostolic commission of Paul in which he wanted to show to Paul "how much he must suffer for my sake"* (Acts 9:16; following O'Brien 1982: 76).

Thus, "what is lacking <u>of the tribulations</u> of Christ"* could well be a wholative genitive, indicating all the decreed suffering of the universal church, a part of which Paul himself suffers[8] (for alternative ways to take the genitive see Schweizer 1982: 103; Barth and Blanke 1994: 254). Revelation 6:11 could express this a little more clearly: deceased saints in heaven are told to continue to "rest . . . until the number of their fellow servants and their brethren who were to be killed even as they had been, would be completed [πληρωθῶσιν, *plērōthōsin*] also" (so NASB, RSV, NRSV, ESV, HCSB, NLT, NIV [cf. NJB] rightly insert the notion of a "number to be completed"). In the light of Rev. 6:9–10, the final judgment will begin when all believers whom God has decreed to suffer finally fulfill their destiny. Paul is among the number of those who are in the process of fulfilling part of the decreed suffering destiny of the corporate body of Christ. The idea is not so much that Paul's suffering is part of the decreed afflictions of the corporate body of Christ so that other Christians will have to suffer less (so Caird 1976: 184) but that all have their allotted portion of suffering to endure.[9]

The church is destined for suffering because of its identification with Christ, who went through inaugurated end-time tribulations during his own earthly ministry. In Acts 26:15, Jesus says to Paul at the Damascus Christophany, "I am Jesus whom you are persecuting." But Paul was persecuting Christians and not the very person of Jesus on earth. Jesus's statement indicates that he corporately represents those who trust in him. Consequently, when his followers suffer, he can speak of himself as suffering.[10] The reason believers suffer,

7. Pauline teaching is that all believers in union with Christ are identified with his past suffering and suffer in conformity after the pattern of and subsequent to Christ's earthly suffering (e.g., Rom. 8:17; 2 Cor. 1:5, 7; Phil. 3:10; cf. Rom. 8:29); so also 1 Pet. 2:21: "for you have been called for this purpose, since Christ also suffered for you, leaving you an example for you to follow in His steps"; so also 1 Pet. 4:13. And it is Christ's resurrection presence that empowers believers to persevere through suffering (so Phil. 3:10; Col. 1:23) for God's glory.

8. Another version of this view is that Paul is speaking about a lack of Christ-sufferings exhibited in his (Paul's) own flesh, so that he is affirming that he is completing the sufferings that he has already begun to suffer, in line with Acts 9:16, where Christ says to Ananias about Paul, "I will show him how much he must suffer for My name's sake." Thus, when Paul dies, he will have completed all the sufferings appointed for him by Christ. For explanation of this option, see J. White (2017: 97–98), who cites commentators holding this view and notes, among other problems with the view, that such an idea cannot be found elsewhere in Paul and that the meaning of ἀνταναπληρόω (*antanaplēroō*) does not support such a view; see further below.

9. See 2 Esd. (4 Ezra) 4:33–43 in association with trials, as in 4:36, "when the number of those like yourselves is completed"*; cf. also 1 En. 47.1–4 (following Davids 2008a: 263–64) and 2 Bar. 21.19–30.5 for the notion of a predetermined amount of end-time tribulation for both unbelievers and saints. Similarly see Mark 13:19–20 and Luke 21:24 (on the latter see Gustafson 1963: 34).

10. "Afflictions <u>of Christ</u>" may be a possessive genitive ("Christ's afflictions"), an objective genitive ("afflictions imposed on Christ"), or a subjective genitive ("afflictions suffered by

however, is that they are first identified with Jesus and his earthly suffering destiny. Revelation 1:9 testifies to this: "I, John, your brother and fellow partaker in the tribulation and kingdom and endurance in Jesus."* This threefold self-description in verse 9a is modeled on that of Christ's in Rev. 1:5a because John views Christians as corporately identified with Jesus.[11] This corporate identity is the basis for the latter-day tribulations that confront them, as well as for their strength to endure such trials and to participate in the kingdom as kings[12] (cf. Luke 24:46; Acts 14:22; Phil. 1:29).[13] Corporate identity with Jesus's suffering is a theme found elsewhere in Paul (Rom. 8:17; 2 Cor. 1:5; 4:10–12; Phil. 3:10; following Schweizer 1982: 104).

Another less probable version of this view is that Paul's sufferings being "for you," that is, "for his body, the church," means that the greater amount of destined suffering Paul incurs, the less other believers (including the Colossians) will endure and the sooner the messianic glories of the age to come will materialize.[14]

While we believe the above corporate view is viable, there is another view of "filling up Christ's tribulations" that is more persuasive and fits better with the meaning of ἀνταναπληρόω (*antanaplēroō*). Some affirm that Paul sees his "filling up that which is lacking in Christ's afflictions" to be something unique only to him and his apostolic role on behalf of the church. But a difficulty with this view is the recognition that the apostolic circle's experiencing "the sufferings of Christ" is not unique to them but is shared by the Corinthian Christians (2 Cor. 1:5–7; cf. also 2 Cor. 4:10, "carrying about in the body the dying of Jesus," which seems to refer to sufferings of the apostolic circle that are extended to the Corinthian believers [4:14–18]). Accordingly, it would seem unlikely that Paul portrays himself as the only one suffering and "filling up Christ's afflictions" for the sake of the church, which does not share in the apostle's unique suffering.

Christ"). Perhaps even a qualitative genitive is included, referring to Christlike afflictions. In addition to the above, other genitival ideas are possible (see Harris 2010: 59), so it is best to leave the genitive ambiguous here. Whatever genitive is in mind, it is not Christ himself but the body of Christ, the church, that is the primary focus. However, it is possible that Christ himself is included secondarily in the genitive in the sense that he began to suffer these tribulations that others must complete. That both Christ and his body, the church, may be in mind is suggested by the concept of corporate identification (where, e.g., in Isa. 40–53 the suffering servant refers at times to Israel as a whole nation, Israel as the faithful remnant, as well as to the individual servant). See further Gustafson (1963) for the inclusion of the corporate body of Christ and the individual Christ in understanding the genitive.

11. The preposition ἐν (*en*) in Rev. 1:9 likely designates both incorporation and sphere with respect to Christ, as it does in Rev. 14:13.

12. See Beale (2011: 191–94; 1999a: 200–202) for further discussion of Jesus as the Son of Man who represents the saints both as king and as a sufferer of end-time tribulation, in the light respectively of Dan. 7 and Rev. 1:9. See Beale (2011: chap. 7) for the concept of Christ and the church enduring the eschatological tribulation.

13. See O'Brien (1982: 77–81) for interpretive alternatives for understanding "what is lacking in Christ's afflictions," whose own view is in line with our interpretation.

14. See J. White (2017: 98–99) for discussion of this view, which he subsequently rejects.

But elsewhere Paul can refer to things about his apostolic role that are unique to him and to things that he holds in common with all believers. The question is which is the case here. We think the scales are tipped in the direction of his unique apostolic role. The following considerations favor this perspective. (1) Col. 1:15–23 highlights the unique redemptive-historical person and work of Christ and how that affects believers in the inaugurated era (being reconciled, v. 22) and at the eschatological consummation ("presented before Him holy and blameless"). (2) Col. 1:25–29 also focuses on the unique redemptive-historical role of Paul as an apostle. Accordingly, 1:24 fits naturally into this unique redemptive-historical context. In fact, Col. 1:24–29 presents Paul in his unique suffering role as a mirror image of the unique Christ in his suffering role (his death, 1:18, 22; his "blood," 1:20; Clark 2015: 107–27).[15]

Also, (3) recent lexical study of ἀνταναπληρόω has clarified the meaning of the word here in Col. 1:24. A consensus about the meaning previously was generally "filling up something that is lacking." Clark (2015) has investigated every use of ἀνταναπληρόω in extrabiblical Greek literature (twelve relevant uses, including the noun form; Clark 2015: 14–50). He found a pattern of meaning that is more specific than the above-cited general notion: (a) that which achieves fullness comes from a source other than the beginning contribution of the original source and *in place of its lack* (this is the semantic significance and contribution of the prefix ἀντί [*anti*]); (b) seven of the uses have the idea of "add so as to bring to completion in place of another."[16] Furthermore, what adds is similar or identical to what originally contributes. In fact, six of the uses exhibit the syntagmatic pattern of verb + direct object + genitive, which is identical to the pattern in Col. 1:24. Furthermore, of the remaining six uses, four have the direct object clearly expressing the notion of "lack," as also in Col. 1:24 (using words such as ὑστερέω, *hystereō*; ἐνδέω, *endeō*; or λείπω, *leipō*). Two other uses have the idea of a "filling" that brings "balance or proportion," which does not appear to be an idea included in Col. 1:24. Clark (2015: 42) concludes, "The contribution made in the action of ἀνταναπληρόω in Col. 1:24 is probably one that is similar/identical to the former contribution, so that it has a completing (versus balancing) effect." The first contribution failed to bring completion (for whatever reason), and in the action of the verb ἀνταναπληρόω, a second or subsequent "contribution is made in addition to (or in place of) the original contribution" to bring about fullness (Clark 2015: 42). The point is that a *final* completion is achieved or desired.

Specifically, according to this meaning, the afflictions could be either those that Christ had suffered (or in some way was still suffering) or that the church was enduring (and was continuing to suffer). But the latter possibility is ruled out by the meaning of ἀνταναπληρόω referring to a second contribution from

15. Contra Foster (2016: 214), who finds it doubtful whether "ἀντί retains any of its lexical meaning" like "in place of."

16. I count nine such uses with this meaning (unless I am missing something). But two of these seven come from mid-fourth century uses, questionable in terms of their chronological relevance (see second additional note on 1:24).

another source, which added to the first and fully completes what the first began to do. That is, the notion cannot be that the church began to suffer (as the first contribution) and that Paul and later people in the church continue to "fill up" the afflictions, since the second contribution (in this case, Paul) fully completes what began with the first. There are no further contributions of suffering after the second is added.[17] Also, that Paul and later generations of the church do the "filling up" would mean that the second contribution comes from the *same* source (the church), and we have seen the word as indicating that the second contribution comes from a *different* source.[18] Likewise ruled out is the notion that Christ made the first contribution of suffering on earth and then continued to suffer as the exalted Lord, since the ἀνταναπληρόω refers to the second contribution being added from a different source.[19]

Rather, the most viable view is that Christ made the first contribution of suffering, which was incomplete, and that Paul necessarily had to suffer additionally in place of Christ's incomplete sufferings in order to bring those sufferings to definitive completion. This conclusion is based on seven (at most nine) uses in extrabiblical writings (and four of these from only one writer, Apollonius Dyscolus, 2nd cent. AD). Is this enough to establish a pattern of usage to be determinative for Col. 1:24? Probably, especially if the context also fits with the meaning, which it does.

Paul is doing this completing "on behalf of the church." Thus Paul is completing the prophesied suffering of the Messiah. This does not mean that Christ's unique atoning sufferings were incomplete or inadequate but that the general, imitative sufferings of Christ in fulfilling the prophecy of Israelite and Gentile salvation were incomplete. We saw above that all Christians share in and are destined to be conformed to the exemplary sufferings of Christ.[20] So Col. 1:24 is applying this general concept in a unique way to Paul as Christ's

17. However, use in Clement of Alexandria (*Misc.* 7.12.4) does not appear to fit well with Clark's definition of it as "to complete/fulfill (a role/function) in place of another," which is a final, onetime completing. The passage speaks of the generic "gnostic" whose godly lifestyle "fills the apostolic absence." Thus an innumerable group of gnostics may successively "fill up" the apostolic absence. This would appear to be comparable to the notion of Paul (and later the generic church) "filling up" the sufferings that the earlier generic church had begun to endure.

18. But one could reply here that the first contribution of suffering was endured by the ethnically *Jewish* churches of "Judea," and the added contribution of subsequent sufferings was from a different source, being done by the predominately *Gentile* churches outside of Judea (so, e.g., see 1 Thess. 2:14: "For you, brethren, became imitators of the churches of God in Christ Jesus . . . in Judea, for you also endured the same sufferings at the hands of your own countrymen, even as they did from the Jews").

19. Some believe the word refers to sufferings that the exalted Christ endures through mystical union with Paul (or even with all believers; so Peake 1970: 514–15, who appears to limit the suffering to Paul in mystical union with Christ). It is not Christ who continues to suffer because of the believers' suffering, since Christ "now in heaven is not suffering any such thing" (Augustine, *Serm.* 341.10, translated by Gorday 2000: 25).

20. See, e.g., Rom. 8:17; 2 Cor. 1:5, 7; Phil. 3:10, "that I may know Him and the power of his resurrection and the fellowship of His sufferings, being conformed to His death"; cf. Rom. 8:29; so also 1 Pet. 2:21; 4:13.

suffering apostle. Paul does not suffer in an atoning manner for the church as Christ did, but he suffers as an apostle *like* Christ in completing the task of reconciliation that Christ began. It is very important to remember that the contribution in the use of the verb ἀνταναπληρόω (*antanaplēroō*) completes either in an identical or similar manner as the original contribution. It is clear that Paul's completing sufferings are not identical to Christ's (they are not atoning), but they are similar or imitative.

In this respect, Paul likely would have noticed that his own sufferings were similar to the Messiah's nonatoning sufferings, especially as portrayed in the suffering servant of Isaiah.[21] The servant was "despised and rejected by men" (Isa. 53:3 ESV), and Paul gives testimony that he was likewise treated (1 Cor. 4:9–14; 2 Cor. 4:8–9; 6:4–10; 11:23b–27). The servant is depicted as having a marred appearance, to which people reacted with shock (Isa. 52:14); Paul reports that the Galatians and Corinthians had similar responses to his visage (Gal. 4:14; 2 Cor. 10:10). The servant was afflicted and stricken by God (Isa. 53:4); Paul likewise suffered bodily afflictions (2 Cor. 12:7; Gal. 4:13). The servant was punished with stripes (Isa. 53:5 KJV); Paul also was flogged with whips and rods (2 Cor. 11:24–25). Just as Paul would have seen these prophesied sufferings of Christ as comparable to his own, so would he have seen his own as predestined.[22] Both the sufferings of Christ and of Paul further the act and message of reconciliation (Clark 2015: 154).

Christ began to fulfill the Isaianic prophecy to Israel, and Paul completed the fulfillment in his mission to the Gentiles. The understanding of prophesied Jewish and Gentile salvation as integral to understanding "the filling up" will be elaborated on further below. Paul's unique and definitive redemptive-historical "completing" of Christ's sufferings is also pointed to by the parallel of Christ as "the head <u>of the body, the church</u>" (1:18), with Paul "filling up the afflictions of Christ . . . on behalf <u>of the body, which is the church</u>" (cf. 1:24; Clark 2015: 109). Similarly, just as Christ's reconciling work is to "present you holy and blameless and without reproach" (1:22), so Paul as Christ's apostolic agent is to "present every man[23] . . . complete in Christ" (1:28). Accordingly, Christ fulfills his part of the prophecy about reconciling the church (1:18, 20, 22), and Paul completes this reconciling ministry as Christ's apostolic agent. This is in line with Paul's unique apostolic role in being given the message of reconciliation in 2 Cor. 5:14–21 (as argued by Clark 2015: 133–57).[24] In fact, in the 2 Cor. 5 context Paul affirms that if the Corinthians do not reject him but are reconciled to him, it is evidence that they have been reconciled through

21. See additional notes for the argument that Paul viewed himself as completing the prophesied sufferings that Jesus began to fulfill as the prophesied Isaianic servant.

22. See J. White (2017: 105–6) for this list of sufferings in common between the suffering servant and Paul, which he contends Paul would have recognized.

23. We shall see that "every man" focuses on Gentiles throughout the world (see on 1:28), as does the revelation of the "mystery" (see on 1:26–27).

24. See especially the seven unique thematic and lexical parallels between the two passages offered by Clark 2015: 161.

Christ to God (see Beale 1989: 579). Thus reconciliation to Paul is not identical to but closely associated with reconciliation to God through Christ.

Not all Christians (but only Paul) have been given "the ministry of reconciliation" (2 Cor. 5:18), nor is every Christian (except Paul) given the unique apostolic "word of reconciliation" to proclaim (2 Cor. 5:19), nor are all believers (only Paul) serving as "ambassadors for Christ" in giving the message "Be reconciled to God" (2 Cor. 5:20). Just as Isaiah proclaimed himself as unclean as all other Israelites and was provided with an atonement that would be required for any other Israelite (Isa. 6:5–7), this does not suggest that his subsequent commission as a prophet (Isa. 6:8–10) was not uniquely applicable to Isaiah alone. And so it is with Paul.[25]

Consequently, Paul's and Christ's "afflictions" are (1) qualitatively different from the sufferings of saints in general; (2) the "afflictions" have the same general goal in that they both achieve reconciliation, especially in "presenting" saints to God at the eschaton (Col. 1:22, 28); (3) the "afflictions" are qualitatively distinct in that their roles are not the same: Christ's suffering in his life and his atoning work led to reconciliation, and Paul's suffering led to that reconciliation being uniquely proclaimed. Paul, says the Lord, "is a chosen instrument of Mine, to bear My name before the Gentiles and kings and the sons of Israel, for I will show him how much he must suffer for My name's sake" (Acts 9:15–16).[26] Therefore, Paul's completion of the Messiah's suffering "for your sake" and on "behalf of his body, the church" consists in the fact that Paul brought the message of reconciliation to the Gentiles for their great benefit, a ministry that did not occur through the earthly Christ's ministry. The unique apostolic role of Paul will continue to be seen in 1:25–29.

Paul now explains that his suffering for the benefit of the Colossians and **1:25**
the broader "church" (v. 24)[27] is expressed through him being a "servant" (διάκονος, *diakonos*). The Greek word can refer to one who is an authorized agent to transmit an important message. But the word also can refer to one who "serves" another who is a superior. Both ideas are in mind here.[28] Thus Paul is an apostle commissioned faithfully to convey the gospel and to do so as a servant of God. Both these nuances of the word occur elsewhere in Paul (1 Cor. 3:5; 2 Cor. 3:6; 6:4; Eph. 6:21), including elsewhere in Colossians (Col. 1:23; 4:7). In fact, Paul here is elaborating on what he has just said in 1:23, that he "became a servant" (CEB) of the gospel that he has proclaimed to the readers and others: note the virtual verbal repetition of οὗ ἐγενόμην ἐγὼ . . . διάκονος (*hou egenomēn egō . . . diakonos*) from 1:23 here in verse

25. Following Clark (2015: 139) in this paragraph. See also Lohse (1971: 70–72), who limits the "completing of the afflictions" to the uniqueness of Paul's apostolic office.

26. Following Clark (2015: 26) in this paragraph, though points 2 and 3 are stated differently here in an attempt to clear up some ambiguity. I have found that J. White (2017: 94–96) agrees with the overall thrust of Clark's study.

27. The relative pronoun ἧς (*hēs*) at the beginning of verse 25 refers to the "church" at the end of verse 24.

28. See BDAG 230, s.v. διάκονος, for the range of meaning that includes the two ideas.

25 (ἧς ἐγενόμην ἐγὼ διάκονος, *hēs egenomēn egō diakonos*). The point of the repetition is now to emphasize this servanthood and to show that it involves suffering on his part for the sake of God's people.

Paul became a "servant [minister]" because he has been commissioned for a "stewardship" from God ("of God" in v. 25a being a genitive of source, though many take it as a subjective genitive). The word οἰκονομία (*oikonomia*) can be rendered "stewardship" or "household management." The idea is that one who manages the affairs of a household (οἰκονόμος, *oikonomos*) for the owner is one who has received a stewardship (οἰκονομία). This is its typical use in classical and Hellenistic Greek (cf. BDAG 697–98, s.v. οἰκονομία; in rabbinic writings the "son of the house," a slave, is the household manager). In the LXX, οἰκονόμος can refer to a manager of the Israelite king's palace or household.[29] Closely linked, οἰκονομία indicates the office of such a management (Isa. 22:19, 21). Likewise in the NT, οἰκονόμος can refer to one who manages the affairs of a household for the owner.[30]

In Ephesians οἰκονομία occurs three times (1:10; 3:2, 9), each time implicitly or explicitly referring to Paul's stewardship of announcing the "mystery" of Christ and the gospel, which focuses on the unity of Jew and Gentile (cf. Eph. 2:11–22 with 3:1–10, esp. 3:6). That Paul was "a servant according [κατά, *kata*] to the stewardship from God given to him"* (Col. 1:25; cf. Eph. 3:2–3; 3:7–9) indicates that his servanthood was to be carried out by performing the responsibilities entailed by the stewardship (or his servanthood came about because of the stewardship).[31] The nuance of God's plan is included in οἰκονομία in that Paul's calling was part of God's planned management of the latter days, which was determined long ago (cf. O'Brien 1982: 81) and kept hidden as a mystery, but now has been revealed. Thus οἰκονομία in Colossians (and Ephesians) expresses the ideas of an office of management and the execution of the management, both of which concern management of God's revealed end-time mystery or plan (cf. similarly Reumann 1967: 165; BDAG 697–98).[32] That Paul is a "servant" commissioned for such a management reflects the typical picture of a slave or servant who was appointed to manage a master's household affairs.[33]

Paul's stewardship of the mystery in Ephesians, as in Colossians, also entails him suffering "tribulations on behalf" of the readers. Thus, here in Col. 1:25, Paul has been given the responsibility as a servant to manage the affairs of the

29. See 2 Kings 18:18, 37; 19:2; 1 Chron. 29:6; Isa. 36:3, 22; 37:2; sometimes the word refers generally to a wider range of responsibilities, e.g., Esther 1:8–9.

30. In Luke, four times; likewise οἰκονομία refers to such a management three times in Luke; Rom. 16:23 refers to one who manages the financial affairs of a city.

31. For both notions of "norm" and "cause" being included in κατά, *kata*, see BDAG 512, s.v. κατά B.5.δ).

32. So also 1 Cor. 4:1–2, where Paul is also a "steward [οἰκονόμος, *oikonomos*, 2×] of the mysteries of God."

33. So also 1 Cor. 4:1–2, where Paul refers to himself as a "servant" (though ὑπηρέτης [*hypēretēs*] is used instead of διάκονος [*diakonos*]); even the notion of the "trustworthiness" of the steward is included here, as further reflective of the household responsibility.

church by faithfully proclaiming the gospel despite and through suffering. In line with Ephesians, the very next verse labels the "word of God" from verse 25 as a "mystery" (v. 26) whose content concerns Gentiles (v. 26) and Christ (v. 27; the significance of the Ephesians parallels will be brought out in vv. 26–27).

Paul explains that his "stewardship from God which has been given"* to him is "for the benefit [of]" (εἰς ὑμᾶς, *eis hymas*; cf. Harris 2010: 61) the readers, underscoring again the same idea already repeated twice in verse 24 and reflecting further the parallel in Eph. 3:13, noted above.

Paul defines his stewardship as the commission to "fully carry out the preaching of God's word" of the gospel (v. 25b). It is viable to translate this as "to fulfill" (so numerous translations), which can be understood in the sense of "fulfilling the word [i.e., promise or prophecy] of God" from the OT (see the additional note on 1:25). However, this rendering may not be best since the closest verbal parallel is with Col. 4:17: "Take heed to the ministry [διακονίαν, *diakonian*] that you have received in the Lord in order that you should fulfill it [πληροῖς, *plērois*],"* which does not appear to have a prophetic nuance. Both verses have in common the διακονία/διάκονος (*diakonia*/*diakonos*) word group, a ministry received from God, and the use of πληρόω (*plēroō*). Since the idea of "fulfilling" without a prophetic sense in 4:17 is clearly that of faithfully executing or completing a ministry, it appears quite plausible that the same sense is to be found in 1:25.[34]

But in light of the immediate context of Col. 1:15–24 and 1:26–29, there appears to be a prophetic notion in πληρόω in 1:25, even if it is best understood here in the sense of execute or "fully carry out" the (prophesied) task of preaching the gospel (e.g., NASB). A better translation than any of the above may be prophetically "completing" (cf. NJB, NET) the commission of preaching God's word or "fulfilling the word [prophecy] of God" (see the additional note on 1:25). If so, the idea would be that of Paul "completing" the prophesied task of announcing God's end-time salvation, a task that was begun by Jesus as the predicted Isaianic servant. There is the very same prophetic idea in a very close parallel use in Rom. 15:19 (see the additional note on 1:24).[35]

"The word of God" at the end of verse 25 is now identified as "the mystery" **1:26–27**
(τὸ μυστήριον, *to mystērion*). The Greek word is sometimes translated with such renderings as "secret," "secret purpose," "hidden truth," or "secret plan of salvation" (cf. Harris 2010: 62 for the options), though all connote the same idea. "Secret" could be misleading, since as we will see, the Greek word does not express something that was completely unknown but a notion of making much clearer something in the OT that was to some small degree partially

34. BDAG 828 (s.v. πληρόω 3) categorizes the use of πληρόω in Col. 1:25 as "to bring to completion that which was already begun."

35. In agreement with Dunn 1996: 118–19. Some translations render πληρόω as "fulfill" (Geneva, KJV, ASV, Douay), which could be understood as "fully carry out," "complete," or "fulfill" in the sense of fulfilling a prophetic decree. Other translations have "make fully known" (NRSV, ESV, HCSB) and "present in its fullness" (NIV).

understood in the OT itself. Accordingly, "mystery" may be more preferable a rendering, since it is more susceptible of referring to something that may not be completely unknown.[36] The word "mystery" occurs again in 1:27 and 2:2, where the "mystery" is identified to be "Christ." "Mystery" appears finally in 4:3, where Paul asks for prayer that he would be given opportunities to "speak forth the mystery of Christ." This could be rendered "the mystery which is Christ" or "the mystery about Christ." Though "mystery" is not defined in 1:26, the three remaining uses in the letter define it to be "Christ," which is likely also the case in 1:26. Verse 26 concludes by saying that this "mystery [was] hidden from [former] ages and generations, but now has been manifested to His saints [holy ones]."

The word "mystery" (τὸ μυστήριον in the LXX and רָז, *rāz*, in the MT), with a prophetic and eschatological sense, occurs in the OT only in Dan. 2 (2:18–19, 27–30, 47).[37] There the revelation of the "mystery" refers to the *hidden* interpretation of the king's dream, the content of which was a giant statue representing four world kingdoms. A rock is cut out without hands and smashes the statue, and the rock grows into a mountain and fills the earth. The rock is understood to represent God's kingdom, which will defeat the evil kingdoms of the world in the end time. The primary point of the dream was that in the end times God will destroy the kingdom of evil and establish his own eternal kingdom (2:44–45).

The use of "mystery" elsewhere in Jewish apocalyptic and Judaism is associated with eschatological issues in general, and sometimes with the end-time coming of a messianic figure in particular, occasionally in association with Dan. 2 (e.g., 2 Esd. [4 Ezra] 12:37–38; 1 En. 46; 52; 71; Qumran, e.g., 1QS 9.18–19; 1QpHab 7.5–14).

"Mystery" (τὸ μυστήριον) occurs twenty-eight times in the NT, where it is linked to eschatological issues, often with respect to the prophesied kingdom. A feature noticeable in many of the occurrences is that the word is directly linked with OT quotations or allusions (sometimes from the book of Daniel itself). In almost all of these cases, at least, "mystery" appears in order to indicate two things: (1) OT prophecy is beginning fulfillment, and (2) this fulfillment is unexpected from the former OT vantage point. With respect to this last point, it is apparent that various NT authors understand OT texts in the light of the Christ event and under the guidance of the Spirit, leading to new interpretative developments though still not out of line with the OT idea. Thus, though Daniel may not always be in mind in all of these NT uses, the notion of an eschatological prophecy needing further inspired interpretation is. While such a notion appears not always to be directly alluding to Dan. 2, this idea of "mystery" probably has its ultimate origin there.

36. Like a "mystery" novel in which there are hints early on about who committed the murder, a notion with ancient analogies, as we will see.

37. "Mystery" also occurs in Dan. 4:6 MT (4:9 Theod.) with reference to the hidden interpretation of the king's prophetic dream, which Daniel makes known to him.

There is not space to elaborate on the uses in Judaism or the majority of uses elsewhere in the NT nor to defend the thesis just laid out, though I have done that elsewhere, especially with respect to Qumran and the NT uses.[38] How do these uses of "mystery" in Daniel, Judaism, and especially elsewhere in the NT relate to those in Col. 1? The wording of the "mystery" phraseology in Col. 1:26–27 appears to be based on the verses in Dan. 2.

Daniel 2:19–22, 28–30 (Theod.)	Colossians 1:26–27
19–21The mystery [μυστήριον, *mystērion*] was revealed, . . . [the one] giving wisdom [σοφίαν, *sophian*] to the wise and knowledge to ones knowing understanding [σύνεσιν, *synesin*]. 22He makes known . . . the hidden things [ἀπόκρυφα, *apokrypha*]; 28the one revealing mysteries [μυστήρια, *mystēria*], and he made known [ἐγνώρισεν, *egnōrisen*]. (so virtually identically v. 29 and similarly v. 30)[a]	the hidden mystery [τὸ μυστήριον τὸ ἀποκεκρυμμένον, *to mystērion to apokekrymmenon*] . . . manifested to his saints, to whom God willed to make known [γνωρίσαι, *gnōrisai*] what is the richness of the glory of this mystery [μυστηρίου τούτου, *mystēriou toutou*][b]

[a]The Theodotion tradition reads in Dan. 2:29–30 "the one revealing mysteries made known . . . this mystery was revealed." MS 230 of the Theodotion tradition reads in verse 30, "He made known this mystery [ἐγνώρισεν τὸ μυστήριον τοῦτο, *egnōrisen to mystērion touto*]"; the same phrase without τοῦτο is read in MSS of Alexandrinus and the Armenian. The Old Greek (LXX) differs somewhat from Theodotion.

[b]For some of these text comparisons, see Hübner 1997b: 530. In addition to these parallels, note the use of "wisdom" (σοφία, *sophia*) and "understanding" (σύνεσις, *synesis*) in direct relation to "mystery" in Col. 2:2–3 and Eph. 3:3–10.

The above underlined five lexical combinations ("this mystery,"[39] "hidden," "made known," "wisdom," and "understanding") are found in biblical and Hellenistic Greek only in Dan. 2; Eph. 3:3, 9; and Col. 1–2. For example, the phrase "this mystery he [God] made known" occurs only in Dan. 2:30 Theod. (MS 230, ἐγνώρισεν τὸ μυστήριον τοῦτο, *egnōrisen to mystērion touto*)[40] and Col. 1:26–27 (γνωρίσαι . . . τοῦ μυστηρίου τούτου, *gnōrisai . . . tou mystēriou toutou*).[41] This last phrase from Dan. 2:30 by itself may be an allusion.

These combined unique verbal correspondences go beyond mere general apocalyptic terminology.[42] Most commentators, however, do not see an allusion

38. See Matt. 13:11; Rom. 11:25; 16:25; 1 Cor. 4:1; 13:2; 14:2; Eph. 1:9; 3:3, 9; 5:32; Col. 1:26–27; 2:2; 4:3; 2 Thess. 2:7; Rev. 1:20; 10:7; 17:5, 7. See Beale 1999a: 215–72; Beale and Gladd 2014: passim.

39. Note that "mystery" is repeated in both Dan. 2:19–22, 28–30 and Col. 1:26–27; 2:2.

40. See Beale (1996: 139–40) for the likelihood of a pre-first century AD date for proto-Theodotionic readings of Daniel, some of which are clearly attested elsewhere in the NT.

41. In addition, the infinitive γνωρίσαι (*gnōrisai*) also follows μυστήριον (*mystērion*) in Dan. 2:30 Theod. as in Col. 1:26–27. Ephesians 3:3 almost identically has "the mystery was made known" (ἐγνωρίσθη μοι τὸ μυστήριον, *egnōristhē moi to mystērion*), which is also an allusion to Dan. 2.

42. This an example of what Beetham (2008: 17) refers to as an allusive "word cluster," where several "words, phrases, and/or images from a section of an older text are incorporated and scattered in a paragraph or section of a new text." However, Beetham says this combination of words should be "uncommon words," and one could argue that is not the case here. Nevertheless, "mystery" is an uncommon word in the OT, found only in Daniel in OT canonical literature,

to Dan. 2, apparently not detecting the unique verbal parallels. Therefore, they do not discuss the context of Dan. 2 as background for this passage. However, there is sufficient basis for positing an intentional allusion without the danger of parallelomania, which then warrants asking how Paul might have seen the Daniel background informing his exposition here. As in Eph. 3, so also here the unique combination of wording expresses eschatological realities that are thematically likewise in line with the end-time focus of the Dan. 2 "mystery."[43]

Daniel concerns the establishment of the eschatological kingdom, and Ephesians and Colossians focus on the end-time messianic king (*christos*) and the eschatological nature of the "mystery"[44] revolving around him. The explicit identification of the "mystery" in Col. 1:27 as "Christ in you [the Gentiles],"and the similar identification of the "mystery" as Christ in 2:2, points to the same kind of mystery as in Eph. 3: Jews and Gentiles are fused together on a footing of complete equality by means of corporate identification in Jesus the Messiah, the true Israel:[45] they are in Christ and Christ is in them (presumably through the Spirit). This is a "mysterious" fulfillment of Daniel's prophecy[46] because it is not clear in the OT that Israel's theocratic kingdom would be so thoroughly transformed that it would find its continuation only in the sphere of the end-time, Israelite messianic king himself.[47] This

and it is the key word here, so that together with the other words that occur in Dan. 2 with it, it should be viewed as an allusive cluster here.

43. E.g., Dan. 2:28–29, 44–45; see Aletti (1993: 156–57), who sees Dan. 2 as the "obvious" background for "mystery" in Col. 1:26–27, since it refers to (1) a "mystery" (2) that occurs in the latter days (Dan. 2:20–30), (3) which is revealed to some but not to the wise of the world (Dan. 2:27–28, 47–48 LXX). Hübner (1997a: 70) sees the idea of the Dan. 2 mystery to be "near" to that of Col. 1:26 and sees the language of ἀπεκαλύφθη (*apokalyphthē*) in Dan. 2:19, 30 Theod. to "correspond" to ἐφανερώθη (*ephanerōthē*) in Col. 2:26. Bruce (1984: 84) views "mystery" in this passage and elsewhere in Paul and the NT to have its background "in the Aramaic part of the book of Daniel." Johnson (1962a: 232) sees the word in Paul to have "its roots in the OT and is found frequently in" Dan. 2 LXX. Wolter (1993: 104) understands "mystery" here generally against the background of Jewish apocalyptic and Qumran.

44. As we shall shortly see, "now" (νῦν, *nyn*) in Col. 1:26 is an overt reference to the notion that the "mystery" here has been revealed in the latter days, as Dan. 2 also prophesied (see Dan. 2:28, 29, 45 LXX); e.g., Daniel "revealed the mysteries" about "what must come to pass in the latter days"* (Dan. 2:28), which concern the establishment of the eternal, worldwide kingdom (Dan. 2:44–45).

45. Hendriksen (1967: 154–55) makes a similar conclusion, which I have revised and built on and applied here to Colossians.

46. Aletti (1993: 157) refers to the Dan. 2 prophecy as "finding . . . an unexpected confirmation" in the NT events.

47. In Ephesians, Jew and Gentile are one because they are now incorporated and identified with the risen Messiah (which is also clear from comparing Eph. 1:20–21 with 2:5–6). Gentiles can be "fellow inheritors and fellow members of the body and fellow partakers of the promises in Christ Jesus"* (Eph. 3:6) along with Jewish Christians (see the contrast of these three ideas in Eph. 2:12) because the promises and inheritance of Israel have been inaugurated in Messiah, the Israelite king who represents all true Israelites. Christ's resurrection has launched the beginning of the new creation, wherein there can be no nationalistic distinctions. Some commentators have seen the mystery as consisting of complete equality, but as far as I can determine, none have recognized that the basis for such equality lies in the one resurrected person, "Christ Jesus," *as*

may well have been hinted at by the four-kingdom parallel in Dan. 7, where the Son of Man's reign replaces the image of the stone of Dan. 2. There in Dan. 7, the Son of Man represents the saints of Israel, so that what is true of him is also true of them and vice versa (see further Beale 2011: 393–96). This link between the Dan. 2 stone and the Dan. 7 Son of Man is explicitly made by 2 Esd. (4 Ezra) 13:3–7, where the Dan. 7 Son of Man figure "carved out for himself a great mountain [grown from a stone] and flew up upon it."

Is this revealed mystery something that was completely hidden in Daniel and the OT, or was it partly revealed? Colossians 1:26 might seem to indicate that it was entirely hidden: "the mystery which has been hidden from the past ages and generations, but has now been manifested to His saints." It is best, however, to see this as parallel to Eph. 3:4–5, where "the mystery of Christ . . . in other generations was not made known to the sons of men, as [ὡς, *hōs*] it has now been revealed to his holy apostles and prophets." The ὡς directly preceding "now" (in Greek) indicates that Ephesians views the revelation of the mystery there as one of degree. The content of the mystery was evident to some small degree in the OT, but "now" it is fully revealed. There is no reason not to see the same transition from partial to full revelation in Col. 1:26, especially since we have seen that the inclusion of the Gentiles in verse 27 was something partly revealed in Dan. 2. In fact, even in Dan. 2 and 4, Daniel's revealed interpretation of the mystery about Nebuchadnezzar was a clarification or fuller revelation of something about which the king had some partial knowledge (see the additional notes on 1:26–27). But what does not appear to have been revealed at all is how Gentiles become members of the end-time Israelite kingdom on the same footing as Jews through identification with the Messiah and not the nationalistic tags of the law. However, even this may have arisen from some seedlike ideas in the OT (see the additional notes on 1:26–27).

The mention of "now" (νῦν, *nyn*), in contrast to former "ages and generations," indicates that the revelation of the mystery is part of the inauguration of the latter days. Paul elsewhere uses "now" (νῦν) with an inaugurated end-time sense (Rom. 8:18; Rom. 13:11–12; 2 Cor. 6:2; 2 Thess. 2:6).[48] The above-mentioned parallel with Eph. 3:5, as well as 3:9, and its use of "now" is significant since the word in Eph. 3:5 and 10 is developing an inaugurated sense of "the fullness of the times" from Eph. 1:10, which is the time when the "mystery" there was "made known."[49] This use of "now" continues the

the true Israel, since there can be no distinguishing marks in him but only unity. The same notion from the parallel in Ephesians carries over to Col. 1:26–27, where also believers' unity with Christ, the Israelite king, is highlighted (1:27; 2:10–13, 19–20; 3:1–4). For fuller discussion of this conclusion and of the use of Daniel's "mystery" in Eph. 3, see Beale 1998: 242–47; Caragounis 1977: 123–26; Beale and Gladd 2014: 159–74.

48. See other inaugurated eschatological uses elsewhere of "now" (νῦν/νυνί) in Paul on the comment on "now" in Col. 1:22 above. See further Beale 2011: 480–83.

49. Here cf. Eph. 1:9; see also Rom. 16:25–26, "Revelation of the mystery which has been kept silent for long ages past, but now is manifested."

"now" (νυνί, *nyni*) in Col. 1:22, where "reconciliation" is part of the commencement of the latter days.[50]

Colossians 1:27 explains the mystery, only briefly introduced in verse 26. Several genitival phrases here are difficult to define precisely (see the third additional note on 1:27). Despite this difficulty, the point of verse 27 is that "the glory of this mystery among the Gentiles" is "Christ," who is "the hope of glory." Is this to be understood as the "mystery [Christ] [preached] among the Gentiles" or more straightforwardly as "the mystery [Christ] [displayed] among the Gentiles," since they have accepted him by faith? There is not much difference of meaning here, but the directly following phrase "Christ in you [the predominant Gentile church]" favors the notion of a focus on Christ's actual presence being among the Gentiles and the translation "the mystery [Christ] [displayed] among the Gentiles."[51] But this is not a mere presence among the Gentiles as a corporate group but "in" the Colossian Gentile Christians in particular and in each believing person among these Gentiles, as verse 28 highlights by expanding on the plural "you" (ὑμῖν, *hymin*) with three repetitions of "every [hu]man" (πάντα ἄνθρωπον, *panta anthrōpon*). "Christ in you" thus emphasizes that the mystery of Christ has *included* the Gentiles along with believing Jews,[52] whereas Gentiles had been excluded from the OT covenant community where God's promissory revelation was experienced (cf. Calvin 1972: 322). Of course, a remnant of believing Jews are included in the new covenant community, along with Gentiles, to whom the mystery is being revealed (v. 26). Formerly Gentiles were "separate from Christ" and "having no hope" (Eph. 2:12), but now Christ "is in" them, and they possess "the hope of glory," which is Christ (Col. 1:27; so Eadie 1856: 101). Such presence of Christ in individual Gentiles occurs through the Spirit (see Eph. 2:21–22; cf. Rom. 8:9). Thus "every [hu]man" focuses on Gentiles but certainly includes a remnant of believing ethnic Jews.

Thus, while it is true that the above Ephesians parallels in context highlight the Gentile-focused mystery more than Colossians,[53] the idea of the mystery being concerned with Gentiles still carries over into Colossians at this point. The earlier references to the worldwide effect of the gospel (1:6, 20,

50. Dunn (1996: 120) has also recognized that the νῦν is eschatological.

51. Contra D. Moo (2008: 158), who thinks the former option points to a de-emphasis on a focus on the Gentiles and a more non-Gentile definition of the mystery.

52. Which Bruce (1984: 86) expresses with the rendering "Christ is even in you Gentiles."

53. D. Moo (2008: 158), e.g., notes that Ephesians uses ἔθνος (*ethnos*) five times as opposed to only once in Colossians, in 1:27. However, the significance of the use of this word should be qualified to some degree, since pronouns for the predominate Gentile church at Colossae are used throughout; e.g., note the use of "world" and three uses of "you" being a part of the "world" in Col. 1:6 (cf. similarly Col. 1:23b); likewise note the Gentile tone of the pronouns four times in Col. 2:13, especially in the light of Eph. 2:1, 5 (cf. likewise Col. 1:21–22). The threefold repeated phrase πάντα ἄνθρωπον (*panta anthrōpon*), "all men," also is an unmistakable Gentile sphere of reference, emphasized by its threefold repetition (see the footnote below on πᾶς + ἄνθρωπος). An explicit Gentile note is also struck in Col. 3:11 (as with the very similar phrase in Gal. 3:28); see directly below.

23) have been leading up to this explicit statement about Gentile inclusion. And Col. 3:11 later highlights the same thing: the renewal of people occurs in the sphere of Christ "in which there is no . . . Greek and Jew, circumcised and uncircumcised, barbarian, Scythian, slave and freeman, but Christ is all and in all" (see on 3:9–11).

Christ is "the hope of glory" for the believing Gentiles. The phrase is an objective genitive, "hoping in the glory." Colossians 3:4 is the nearest parallel that illumines the idea here: since "Christ . . . is [the] life" in which believers are bound up, when "he should be manifested" at his final coming, so will they "be manifested in glory."* Thus their present trust in and union with Christ's resurrection life and "Christ in you" is what gives them "hope" to share "glory" with Christ at the consummation.

Paul's focus on Christ as the specially revealed mystery probably counters the false teachers' claim that special revelatory visions of heaven justify their view that self-effort supplements faith in Christ, which comes by grace (Sumney 2008: 105–6).

In response to the revelation of Christ as messianic king among the Gentiles **1:28**
and "the hope of glory," Paul "announces" this mystery, since it is his "stewardship" to fulfill as a "servant" of God (cf. 1:25). This verb "announce/declare" (καταγγέλλω, *katangellō*) refers to Paul's preaching, as in Acts, and is used only by Paul in his writings to refer to his or others' proclamation of the gospel (so, e.g., O'Brien 1982: 87). The adverbial participles "admonishing" and "teaching" explain the manner by which Paul announces the mystery of Christ. He admonishes "all men" and teaches "all men." The repetition of "every [hu]man" (πάντα ἄνθρωπον, *panta anthrōpon*) after each participle and a third time at the end of the verse underscores that the revelation of Christ in the latter days (cf. the eschatological "now" of v. 26) has been designed to extend the kingdom of Christ and his salvation to the Gentiles throughout the world.[54] In this respect, "all men / every human" develops the preceding mention of Christ being "among the Gentiles" (v. 27) and the earlier note that the gospel has been "proclaimed in all creation" (1:23; so likewise in 1:6, "in all the world"). This emphasis on universality and "wisdom" for all may be a contrast to the notion of the local mystery religions, in which the esoteric mysteries were reserved for an elite informed group and which may even have been a feature of the false teaching and pseudo-wisdom in Colossae (see Lightfoot 1875: 169–71; see on 2:4; cf. O'Brien 1982: 88).

On the other hand, "every man" also includes within it reference to that remnant of Jews who came to faith in Christ, along with Gentiles.

Paul has prayed that the readers would be "filled with the knowledge of His [God's] will <u>in all</u> . . . <u>wisdom</u> [ἐν πάσῃ σοφίᾳ, *en pasē sophia*]"

54. Paul elsewhere uses "all men" (πᾶς + ἄνθρωπος, *pas* + *anthrōpos*) to refer to Jews and Gentiles throughout the world (Rom. 5:12, 18; 1 Tim. 2:1; 4:10 [?]) or to focus on Gentiles (1 Thess. 2:15; 1 Tim. 2:4; 4:10 [?]; Titus 2:11), and that is the focus here.

(1:9), and now he likely sees his efforts of "admonishing" and "teaching . . . with all wisdom [ἐν πάσῃ σοφίᾳ]" in 1:28 as one of the ways his prayer will be answered.[55] The same verbatim expression from 1:28 is used again in 3:16, presumably because Paul thinks his prayer will also be answered if the believers "let the word of Christ richly dwell within . . . , with all wisdom teaching and admonishing one another [ἐν πάσῃ σοφίᾳ διδάσκοντες καὶ νουθετοῦντες ἑαυτούς, *en pasē sophia didaskontes kai nouthetountes heautous*]." The "wisdom" of 3:16 is found in OT "psalms and hymns and spiritual songs," which are OT psalms or based on such psalms,[56] part of the Bible of the early church.

The "wisdom" of 1:28 likewise originates from the same sources, though, as we will see, Christ is the zenith point of the OT revelation (2:3), so that this older revelation must be seen through a Christ-centered lens (just as Col. 3:16 says that the "word of Christ" is expressed in the OT "psalms and hymns and spiritual songs"). He is the full source of wisdom. The verb νουθετέω (*noutheteō*) probably specifies part of what the wise "teaching" is about: "counsel about avoidance or cessation of an improper course of conduct" (BDAG 679, s.v. νουθετέω). This definition is relevant, given the directly following references to cautions about false teaching in 2:4 and 2:8. "Stand perfect [τέλειος, *teleios*]" in Col. 4:12 confirms that this "wise" teaching and counsel is a condition of the believer being "fully assured" about and following "all the [true] will of God" (see Lohse 1971: 78), despite being confronted with falsehood.

The purpose of Paul's task to "announce" this mystery to "all men in all wisdom" is in order to "present all men complete in Christ." The word for "complete" is τέλειος (*teleios*), which Paul uses elsewhere to refer to believers who are "mature" (1 Cor. 2:6; 14:20; Phil. 3:15; so also Heb. 5:14). The use in Eph. 4:13 is closest to that here: "until we all attain to the unity of the faith, and of the knowledge of the Son of God, to a mature man, to the measure of . . . the fullness of Christ." Both in the Ephesians text and here the idea is that of an eschatologically consummated "full-growth" or "maturity" (cf. BDAG 995, s.v. τέλειος 2). This end-time growth to maturity in Christ is explained further

55. As in 1:9 ἐν (*en*) plus the dative πάσῃ σοφίᾳ indicates content, and here it is the content of his "admonishing and teaching" (though in both verses a dative of manner is possible).

56. See on 3:16 for the close syntactical combination of "psalm" (ψαλμός, *psalmos*), "hymn" (ᾠδή, *ōdē*), and "song" (ὕμνος, *hymnos*) within the space of one verse, which occurs also within the space of one verse only two times in the psalter of the LXX (Pss. 66:1; 75:1 [Eng.: superscriptions for Pss. 67 and 76]). The theme of the two psalms is also compatible with the context in Col. 3 (see 3:11) and here in 1:27–28, since both contexts highlight Gentile salvation and both psalms relate the hymnody to end-time Gentile salvation. Thus Col. 3:16 likely makes allusion to these two psalms, which shows that it concerns Christ's word as expressed in OT psalms or based on such psalms. All the verbal parallels between Col. 1:28 and 3:16 are so close that "the announcing" of Christ through "admonishing . . . and teaching . . . in all wisdom" is here also linked, as in 3:16, to OT revelation being related to Christ. And this, as we have seen, is the point of Christ being the revelation of the OT mystery in the context (1:25–27).

in Eph. 4:15: "We are to grow up in all aspects into Him" (cf. also Eph. 4:16). Believers have begun to be identified with Christ in the inaugurated end-time phase of the revelation of the mystery, and at the completion of the latter-day epoch, they will be fully identified with or conformed to him (cf. Rom. 8:29), that is, "fully grown" in him. This goal of Paul's latter-day "presentation" (παρίστημι, *paristēmi*) of believers "fully grown in Christ" (Col. 1:28) further explains 1:22, where Christ's reconciliation was designed "in order to present [παρίστημι, *paristēmi*] you before Him [God] holy and blameless and beyond reproach." In verse 22 we saw that this was sacrificial language, which may be continued with the use of τέλειος (*teleios*), since it can have that nuance in the OT (Exod. 12:5). Paul's apostolic efforts are crucial in accomplishing Christ's work of presenting believers before God on the last day. This full consummate eschatological maturity as an acceptable sacrifice likely includes the notion of moral and spiritual perfection (O'Brien 1982: 89).[57]

How can Paul fulfill such a task of "presenting" believers "complete in Christ" **1:29**
at the eschaton? He does it by "strenuous labor," literally, "I labor, struggling" (κοπιῶ ἀγωνιζόμενος, *kopiō agōnizomenos*) or, more paraphrastically, "I labor in a struggling manner" ("struggling" being an adverbial ptcp. of manner). Paul can use the verb (κοπιάω, *kopiaō*) and the cognate noun "labor" to refer to work done in service to God (see Beale 2003: 46–47, 161). This is a further explanation of verse 24, what it means that Paul suffers (so D. Moo 2008: 159). Paul's fellow servant Epaphras also "struggles" to achieve the same goal as Paul (Col. 4:12, where ἀγωνίζω + τέλειος, *agōnizō* + *teleios*, also occurs). The two colleagues worked hard toward the same purpose.

Paul's struggle, however, is not an autonomous effort on his part. He is able to continue this hard labor only by God's power: "on the basis of [κατά, *kata*] his working, which works in power in me"* (κατὰ τὴν ἐνέργειαν αὐτοῦ τὴν ἐνεργουμένην ἐν ἐμοὶ ἐν δυνάμει, *kata tēn energeian autou tēn energoumenēn en emoi en dynamei*). The repetition of the synonyms "working," "work," and "power" emphasizes that Paul's struggle for his readers is not rooted in his own ability but in God's power working in him. Almost the same phrase is used in Eph. 3:7 (κατὰ τὴν ἐνέργειαν τῆς δυνάμεως αὐτοῦ, *kata tēn energeian tēs dynameōs autou*; cf. also Phil. 4:13), which is referred to as "the gift of [or which is] the grace of God." God's grace is how Paul is able to perform his ministry. Paul's ministry is not performed by a synergistic activity involving his own independent contribution together with the help of God's grace. Rather, as he says in 1 Cor. 15:10, "By the grace of God I am what I am, and His grace did not become empty in me, but I labored more than all of them, <u>yet not I</u>, but the grace of God with me."*

57. Barth and Blanke (1994: 268) contend that τέλειος here has the more typical LXX idea of undivided commitment to the one God, so that the idea in Col. 1:28 connotes undivided commitment to the one Christ, in contrast to any degree of loyalty to the "rulers and authorities" (cf. Col. 2:10) or, it could be added, to other avenues of truth in addition to Christ offered by the false teachers.

2. Paul Rejoices in His Struggle to Present Believers Complete in Christ, the Revealed Mystery, to Prevent Their Deception (2:1–5)

As mentioned in the introduction to the 1:24–2:5 segment, 2:1–5 is a part of the larger section begun at 1:24. Nevertheless, it is a discernible literary subsection within the overall segment of 1:24–2:5. This is recognizable through both a change in thematic focus and literary arrangement. With regard to the former, Paul shifts from a focus on a description of his own apostolic ministry to the effects of that ministry on the Colossians (D. Moo 2008: 163). With respect to the latter, 2:1–5 appears to reflect a thematic chiasm: Paul's concern for the readers (vv. 1 and 5), Paul's expected response from the readers to his concern (vv. 2 and 4), and the center of the chiasm being that the readers know the "mystery" (v. 3).[58]

2:1 Paul now repeats that he has "struggled" (cf. ἀγωνίζω, *agōnizō*, in 1:29 with ἀγών, *agōn*, in 2:1) to present them complete in Christ (1:28); he expands on the details of that struggle and clarifies it (thus γάρ, *gar*, is best rendered here as "for, you see"; cf. BDAG 189d, s.v. γάρ). Accordingly, he wants to highlight for them "how great a struggle" it has been, which he has exerted on their behalf and for others in the region who had never met him. Though Paul's struggles were due to a wide range of circumstances revolving around his ministry to churches (Sumney 2008: 111), the focus here is on a "struggle" against opponents to the Christ-centered gospel, since the combination of the verb (ἀγωνίζω, *agōnizō*) and noun form elsewhere in Paul has struggling against doctrinal opponents in mind (so 1 Tim. 6:12; cf. esp. 6:3–5, 20–21; and 2 Tim. 4:7; cf. esp. 4:3–4, 10, 14–16).[59] Thus Paul is already anticipating the opponents of the Colossians who are trying to deceive them (on which he is about to elaborate in 2:4), though he has not yet met them face to face.

2:2 The goal of struggling to present everyone complete in Christ (1:28–2:1) is that "their hearts may be encouraged." "Heart" in the NT, and here, likely has the same notion as in the OT: it represents the inner spiritual center of one's relationship with God, which is inextricably linked to the volitional, intellectual, and emotional aspects of a person, all of which form a psychical unity (cf. Beale 1984a: 132, which see for further nuancing). Their hearts, the core of their life, are to be encouraged by them "having been knit together in love" (συμβιβασθέντες, *symbibasthentes*, being an adverbial ptcp. of means, manner, or perhaps cause or result, but not imperative, as argued by Hanna 1983: 369). As they are increasingly confident of being on the pathway to becoming "complete in Christ," Paul wants their love for one another to grow.

58. So Aletti 1993: 147–48; cf. D. Moo 2008: 163. See also Sumney (2008: 119) for verses 1 and 5 forming an *inclusio* of parallels regarding Paul's relationship with those whom he does not know or those with whom he is not present.

59. Note the use of the noun elsewhere in contexts of Paul struggling against opponents to his ministry (Phil. 1:30; 1 Thess. 2:2).

In addition, their knowledge that Paul is struggling on their behalf is encouraging in the midst of whatever struggles they are undergoing, knowing they are not alone in their suffering (Sumney 2008: 114). The only other use of συμβιβάζω (*symbibazō*) in the letter appears in 2:19. There it is part of a warning against false teaching continuing from verse 18 up through verse 23: the readers are to beware of "not holding to the head [Christ], from whom the whole body, being supplied and <u>knitted together</u> [also a participial form of συμβιβάζω] through the joints and ligaments, grows with a growth from God."*[60] Likewise, in verse 4 Paul is about to affirm that the reason he is saying what he does in 2:1–3 is to help protect the readers from false teaching. Continuing to progress in becoming "complete in Christ" (1:28–2:1) is likely equivalent to "holding to the head [Christ]" and "growing" up into him as a result (2:19; so likewise Eph. 4:15–16, which is also a remedy to false teaching and clarifies that in Col. 2:19 the "growth" is in Christ). Thus 2:19 points to the notion that Christ is the one who "supplies" the believers in 2:2 with the ability to have their "hearts knit together in love" for one another.[61] Paul's motivation is to "present" the church "complete in Christ" (1:28) in order to strengthen them against a false teaching that would take the focus off their complete commitment to and sole worship of Christ (see further on 2:16–23).

Paul's purpose or intended result (εἰς, *eis*) in so encouraging the Colossians[62] is that they may obtain "all the riches of the full assurance of understanding"*[63] (v. 2).

The last clause of verse 2 gives a second purpose or intended result of Paul's "encouragement": "resulting [εἰς, *eis*] in the knowledge of the mystery of God, <u>which is Christ</u>."* Χριστοῦ (*Christou*) is an appositional genitive, explaining that Christ is the mystery, not that Christ is God, though that point is made elsewhere in Colossians and Paul. That is, the content of the revealed "mystery of God" is Christ. It is possible that this second εἰς (*eis*) clause repeats and elaborates on the first εἰς (*eis*) clause (so D. Moo 2008: 168) or that it gives

60. Some, like O'Brien (1982: 93), think that συμβιβάζω means "teach" (with the rendering, "having been taught in love"), since it has this meaning elsewhere in the NT (Acts 19:33; 1 Cor. 2:16) and always has this meaning in the LXX (so 8×). But that meaning is unlikely here for three reasons: (1) the clear meaning of "knit together," which occurs not far away, in 2:19; (2) the directly following mention of "love" seems more suitable for an organic-growth notion than a purely cognitive idea, especially in the light of Col. 3:14: "love, which is the bond of completeness"*; (3) its meaning flows out of the notion of Jew-Gentile unity in 3:11 (for the latter two ideas, see Barth and Blanke 1994: 278).

61. See also Col. 1:4, 8; and 3:14, where ἀγάπη (*agapē*) refers to "love" of believers for one another; cf. the verb likewise in 3:19.

62. Possibly but less likely, the εἰς modifies Paul's "struggle" in verse 1, giving another purpose for it, as Harris 2010: 74 prefers.

63. Πληροφορία (*plērophoria*) could mean "full assurance" or merely "fullness" (see BDAG 827d, s.v. πληροφορία). If the former, the focus is on the assurance "that comes from understanding" (so, e.g., NASB), while the latter would focus on the "fullness of understanding" (cf. NIV). It is difficult to know which is best here, though in the only other place outside Colossians where Paul uses the word, 1 Thess. 1:5, it clearly means "full assurance [conviction]" (yet the word occurs as a variant in Rom. 15:29, where either of the two above meanings is possible).

the purpose of the first clause. However, these options are less likely, since prepositional phrases typically function to modify verbal forms and not other prepositional phrases.[64]

2:3 Verse 3 explains that "in" Christ, who is the "mystery" (2:2), are "hidden all the treasures of wisdom and knowledge."[65] We will consider "the mystery" of 2:2 here, since it is combined with another allusion that follows in 2:3. We have already seen that the "mystery" has its background in Dan. 2 (see discussion on 1:26–27 above). The same background continues here but, as we will see, is supplemented by Proverbs:

Daniel 2 (Theod.)	Colossians 2:2–3
[19–21]the mystery [μυστήριον, *mystērion*] was revealed . . . [the one] giving wisdom [σοφίαν, *sophian*] to the wise and knowledge to ones knowing understanding [σύνεσιν, *synesin*]; [22]he makes known the deep and hidden things [ἀπόκρυφα, *apokrypha*]	unto all the richness of the full assurance of understanding [συνέσεως, *syneseōs*], unto a knowledge of the mystery [μυστηρίου, *mystēriou*] of God, which is Christ, in whom are hidden [ἀπόκρυφοι, *apokryphoi*] all the treasures of wisdom [σοφίας, *sophias*] and knowledge.

The above underlined four lexical combinations ("this mystery," "hidden," "wisdom," and "understanding") are found only in Dan. 2 and Col. 1–2. This is likely a continued allusion to Daniel's "mystery" from 1:26–27, where it was even more clearly alluded to. It is best, however, to see the Dan. 2 allusion now merged with Prov. 2:3–6 and leading Paul to focus on the latter text in verse 3:

Proverbs 2:3–6	Colossians 2:2–3
For if you should call upon wisdom [σοφίαν, *sophian*], utter your voice for understanding [συνέσει, *synesei*], and if . . . you should search for her as treasures [θησαυρούς, *thēsaurous*],[a] then you will understand [συνήσεις, *synēseis*] . . . and find the knowledge [ἐπίγνωσιν, *epignōsin*] of God. For the Lord gives wisdom [σοφίαν, *sophian*], and from his presence is knowledge [γνῶσις, *gnōsis*] and understanding [σύνεσις, *synesis*].*	unto all the richness of the full assurance of understanding [συνέσεως, *syneseōs*], unto a knowledge [ἐπίγνωσιν, *epignōsin*] of God's mystery, which is Christ, in whom are hidden [ἀπόκρυφοι, *apokryphoi*] all the treasures [θησαυροί, *thēsauroi*] of wisdom [σοφίας, *sophias*] and knowledge [γνώσεως, *gnōseōs*].*[b]

[a]In place of "treasures" in Prov. 2:4, Sym. and Theod. read "hidden things," τὰ ἀπόκρυφα, *ta apokrypha*.
[b]For some of these text comparisons, see Hübner 1997b: 532, 534.

Though "wisdom" (σοφία, *sophia*) and "understanding" (σύνεσις, *synesis*), and rarely even the additional word "knowledge" (γνώσις, *gnōsis*), occur together throughout the LXX (see above on 1:9), the addition of θησαυρός

64. Though exceptions can occur where a verbal noun appears in a prepositional phrase, which a following prepositional phrase could modify. If one were to try to conceive of σύνεσις as a verbal noun, then the second εἰς clause in verse 2 could modify the first εἰς clause.

65. "Of wisdom and of knowledge" are appositional genitives: "treasures consisting of wisdom and knowledge."

(*thēsauros*) and ἀπόκρυφος (*apokryphos*),[66] in close conjunction with these three words, yields a fivefold word combination that is unique in all the OT.[67] Furthermore, the validity of the Proverbs reference is to be seen in the prior emphasis on Christ as epitomizing true "wisdom" in Col. 1:15–17 (recall that Prov. 8:22–31 was seen as part of the possible background in Col. 1:15–17). That identification emerges again here. It may even be that the preceding description of the "mystery" in 1:26 anticipates the clearer reference to the "mystery" as "wisdom" here, since "mystery" and "wisdom" occur so closely together in Dan. 2:19–21 Theod.; compare also the loose link between "mystery" in Col. 1:26–27 and "wisdom" in 1:28.[68]

Believers are able to have genuine "knowledge of the mystery of God, which is Christ,"* because it has been revealed to them (1:26–27; 2:2). Since Christ is the true fount of "wisdom and knowledge" (2:3), the saints also share in such understanding by virtue of their identification and union with him (likewise see 2:3–8). Whereas the Torah was the epitome of "wisdom" in the OT epoch,[69] the Messiah is now the grandest expression of divine "wisdom." In this light, Torah was the typological precursor of the fullest expression of "wisdom," which was to come in the person of the Messiah. This relates to our discussion on 1:26–27, where we concluded that the focus of the revealed mystery was on how Gentiles become members of the latter-day Israelite kingdom through identification with the Messiah and not the nationalistic tags of the law. Colossians 2:2–3 clarifies further why this is the case: Jesus

66. Yet τὰ ἀπόκρυφα (*ta apokrypha*) is a textual variant in Prov. 2:4 (Sym., Theod.) for θησαυρός (*thēsauros*), which may represent a first-century reading (see Beale 1996: 139–40), of which Paul may have been aware; or it shows that in Proverbs Paul already had a precedent for expanding "treasures" by "hidden things." It is also possible that "hidden things" comes only from Dan. 2:22 as Paul merged elements from it with Prov. 2:3–6.

67. N. Wright (1986: 95) says Prov. 2:1–8 LXX is "echoed several times" in Col. 2:2b–3; R. Martin (1974: 76) says "the whole train of ideas and words suggests a conscious indebtedness to the figure of wisdom in Prov. 2:3ff."; Moule (1957: 87) affirms that reference to Prov. 2:3–4 "is suggestive enough," especially in light of the directly following context. Wolter (1993: 111–12) sees Paul's "treasures of wisdom" to be reflective of a common metaphor used for "wisdom" in early Judaism, though he includes Prov. 2:3–4 among the list of references he adduces for this background; some commentators see a parallel to Isa. 45:3 LXX ("I will give you dark treasures [θησαυρούς, *thēsaurous*], hidden [ἀποκρύφους, *apokryphous*] invisible things I will open to you"), but the Proverbs passage is closer in wording (though recall that Symmachus and Theodotion substitute "hidden things" for "treasures" in the Proverbs passage). Also cf. Sir. 1:25, "treasures of wisdom" (θησαυροῖς σοφίας, *thēsaurois sophias*); and 1 En. 46.4, "The Son of Man . . . will open all the hidden storerooms." Lohse (1971: 82) sees no quotation or allusion to any OT passage in Col. 2:3, and Beetham (2008: 271–74) considers the possibility of an allusion to Prov. 2:2–6 in Col. 2:2–3 but concludes against it (see also his list of other scholars who, in addition to the ones noted above, favor some degree of allusion to the Proverbs passage together with other OT influence, as well as those who see no influence at all from Proverbs).

68. Cf. "the mystery hidden from the ages [ἀπὸ τῶν αἰώνων, *apo tōn aiōnōn*]" in 1:26; and Sir. 24:9, God "created me [Wisdom] before the age [πρὸ τοῦ αἰῶνος, *pro tou aiōnos*], from the beginning"; together with Sir. 24:29, wisdom's "counsels [are] profounder than the great deep."*

69. A view that Judaism also held; e.g., cf. Sir. 24:23–27; Bar. 3:15–4:4; 2 Bar. 44.14; 54.13–14; on which cf. Dunn 1996: 132.

Christ is what Israel's old law pointed to, so he is the fullest expression of the law's revelation and wisdom. Consequently, membership in the new-covenant community must come now by identifying with Jesus "in whom are hidden all the treasures of wisdom and knowledge." That "all . . . wisdom and knowledge" is found in Christ rules out the possibility that any true wisdom can be found in any other source (O'Brien 1982: 95), such as from the false teachers. Consequently, the Colossians should not see wisdom in any other source but in Christ.

2:4 Paul introduces verse 4 with "this I say." Since it is unlikely that he is referring to what follows in verse 4 (so O'Brien 1982: 97), to what in the preceding context is he referring as the content of "this"? The reference could be to all that Paul has said so far in the epistle (cf. D. Moo 2008: 172), but more probably 1:26–2:3 is the focus, where he has said that Christ is the content of the knowledge of the mystery, especially with respect to being the ultimate and sole identification tag for Gentiles to participate in true eschatological Israel. The purpose (ἵνα, *hina*) of Paul revealing this to the Colossians is that "no one deceive you by means of enticing argument"* (so also see on 2:8).[70] Thus Paul presses the point that they are to be completely focused, committed to Christ for their salvation, and distracted by no other teaching that would take the sole focus away from Christ. That is, what Paul has said in 1:26–2:3 is crucial for them to know in order not to be sidetracked by false teaching. At least part of this false teaching is that believers still need to identify not only with Christ but also with the identification signs of the old law (see on 2:16–17, 20–22) and must give some allegiance also to worship of angels together with Christ (see on 2:18–19).

2:5 No one should delude the hearers with false teaching (v. 4), Paul says, because (γάρ, *gar*) he is with them "in spirit," though "absent [from them] in body." Paul states the contrastive condition of being "absent in body" in order to highlight the main point: he is with them "in spirit." It is now well known that Paul considered his own letters to represent his authoritative presence among those to whom he wrote. His rejoicing is partly because he has confidence that the teaching he is imparting to them will counter the false teaching. But the focus is on the fact that since both Paul and the Colossian believers live in union with Christ (note their existence "in Christ" in vv. 5b, 6, and 7), Paul is present in his renewed human spirit with them (Campbell 2013: 30). This makes clearer and emphasizes the same idea in 2:1, where Paul has said that many had not "seen his face in the flesh,"* but nevertheless he was present through his letter, encouraging them in their faith (v. 2). Accordingly, because of the contrast with "in body" (or "flesh"), πνεῦμα (*pneuma*) refers neither specifically to the Holy Spirit nor merely the human spirit in general but to the regenerated human spirit in union with Christ (cf. Johnson 1962b: 304).

70. Though Moule (1959: 145) argues for an imperatival sense of ἵνα (*hina*), it does not appear to have such a sense.

Paul is confident about the genuineness of their faith in what he has just told them about Christ as the sole object of their faith and as the only identification marker for their membership in the new covenant community. And he is confident that their faith in this will continue: they will maintain "order and the stability of faith in Christ." His response to their present and persevering faith in the future leads to him "rejoicing and seeing" such order and stability. The two participles joined by "and" (χαίρων καὶ βλέπων [*chairōn kai blepōn*]) likely form a hendiadys, with the resultant translation of "rejoicing to see," as most translations so render (following D. Moo 2008: 173–74).

The word τάξις (*taxis*) has been translated "discipline" (NASB; TNIV reads "disciplined"), "order" (Geneva, KJV, Douay, RSV, ESV), "well-ordered" (NJB, HCSB), "orderly" (NIV 1984), and "morale" (NRSV, NET). The word likely has to do with a "doctrinal order" since it is directly juxtaposed to the threat of false teaching (2:4) that looms over the Colossians. In this respect, it is very similar to the doctrinal "unruliness" (ἀτακτέω, *atakteō*; and ἀτάκτως, *ataktōs*), against which Paul warns the Thessalonians (2 Thess. 3:6, 7, 11; see Beale 2003: 249–58). In facing the threat of false teaching, which has begun to make inroads into the church community, Paul wants them to maintain the good doctrinal order of their faith in Christ and only Christ. That good doctrinal order of their faith is in mind is clarified in the directly following clause of verse 5: "the stability of your faith in Christ Jesus." Maintaining the doctrinal order of their faith means that their faith in Christ will be stable. The firm or unwavering condition of their faith has already been touched upon in 1:23 and will be alluded to again in 2:7. This shows Paul's concern for challenges to the constancy of the hearer's faith, which verse 4 has already expressed and will come through again at points throughout the remainder of chapter 2 (cf. Barth and Blanke 1994: 288–89).

Additional Notes

1:24. *Biblical-theological background for "the afflictions of Christ."* The "Son of Man" in Dan. 7 was a corporate representative for the saints of Israel, with respect to both suffering trial and to ruling, and this title was uniquely used only by Jesus in the Gospels to indicate his veiled, inaugurated kingship amid suffering (Beale 1999a: 201). Indeed, only in Dan. 7 do we get a concept of a suffering messianic figure ("Son of Man") who also rules and who represents Israel in doing so (cf. Dan. 7:13–25). Jesus begins to fulfill these Dan. 7 prophecies by enduring end-time tribulation during his earthly ministry, climaxed at the cross; yet all the while he also ironically inaugurates the Dan. 7 prediction of the reign of the Son of Man (see Beale 2012: 189–99). Daniel 7 appears to be the best background here for understanding Christ as an absolute messianic ruler (Col. 1:15–20) together with the ideas of "the tribulations of the Messiah (the messianic king)" and of an end-time ruler who represents his people in these roles (Col. 1:24). As in Dan. 7 and the Gospels' use of Dan. 7 (see again Beale 2012: 189–99), these "tribulations" of Col. 1:24 are the continuation of the eschatological tribulation that Jesus himself began to undergo. Outside of Dan. 7 in the OT and Judaism, there is no other place where both the Messiah's prophesied sufferings and kingship are combined. Of course, Isa. 53 refers to the servant's sufferings, but not his kingship (so also Dan. 9:26; Zech. 12:10; 13:7). While other OT passages and texts in Judaism generally mention a coming latter-day tribulation for Israel, none except Dan. 7 see a messianic figure included in that suffering along with Israel. The word θλῖψις (*thlipsis*) is used in Dan. 12:1 to refer to faithful Israel's coming "tribulation," which develops the notion of end-time suffering for righteous Israel from Dan. 7:21, 25. Then Matt. 24:21 (//Mark 13:19) alludes to this Dan. 12 text and calls it a "great tribulation" (θλῖψις μεγάλη, *thlipsis megalē*); Rev. 7:14 also alludes to Dan. 12:1 with the same Greek phrase, "great tribulation." In all of the OT, Dan. 12:2 is the only passage that uses θλῖψις to refer to the "tribulation" of *faithful* Israel in the end time. Thus the end-time background of Dan. 7 and 12 appears to stand behind the "tribulations [τῶν θλίψεων, *tōn thlipseōn*] of the Messiah"* (Col. 1:24), who in his sufferings represents those of "his body, the church," the true Israel (for the notion that ἐκκλησία [*ekklēsia*] has its LXX background in Israel as the "congregation" [ἐκκλησία, *ekklēsia*] of God, see additional note on 1:18 above).

Thus Paul's sufferings in carrying out his apostolic ministry are part of Daniel's prophesied tribulation to come upon Israel and its king in the latter days, a notion that was further developed in Jewish thought with respect to saints but not to the Messiah (on the latter, see further, e.g., Lohse 1971: 70–72; O'Brien 1982: 78–79).

Yet together with the Daniel background is that of Isaiah's suffering servant (cf. esp. Isa. 52:13–53:8). That Paul does his "share on behalf of his body (which is the church) in filling up that which is lacking in Messiah's afflictions" likely includes some echo of this suffering servant. Dunn (1996: 116), following a suggestion by Bruce (1984: 82–83), proposes that Paul views himself as completing the prophesied mission of the suffering servant from Isa. 53, which is likely correct in light of the passages Dunn adduces in support: see Acts 13:47 (= Isa. 49:6); 26:18 (= Isa. 42:7); Gal. 1:15–16 (= Isa. 49:1–6); and 2 Cor. 6:2 (= Isa. 49:8), *where Isaianic-servant prophecies are viewed as continuing fulfillment in Paul's ministry* (so subsequently also Lincoln 2000: 614–15), *as Paul was corporately identified with the Isaianic servant's suffering ministry*. Paul's reference to himself as a "servant" (διάκονος, *diakonos*) appears to enhance this background all the more (so Lincoln 2000: 614), though it is not the same Greek word (παῖς, *pais*) for the "servant" in Isaiah. Nevertheless, διάκονος (*diakonos*) is the word Paul uses as the apparent equivalent to παῖς (*pais*), since he styles Christ and himself with this word in describing their role elsewhere as fulfilling the Isaianic servant's prophetic task (see discussion of Rom. 15:8–21 directly below; see also 2 Cor. 6:2–4; though the LXX of Isaiah sometimes uses δοῦλος [*doulos*] to render the Hebrew "servant"). Thus, in this respect Paul's "filling up that which is lacking in Messiah's afflictions" has to do not only with his corporate identification with the prophesied suffering mission of the Son of Man but also, above all, of the suffering servant, which Paul is prophetically completing.

In corroboration of the preceding point, Paul uses πληρόω (*plēroō*) similarly in Rom. 15:19, a very close parallel to Col. 1:25, to indicate that preaching is part of the fulfillment of Isa. 52:15 (see Rom. 15:21): "I have fulfilled the gospel of Christ"* (Rom. 15:19). According to Lincoln (2000: 614–15), when Rom. 15:8–9 says that Christ became a "servant" (διάκονος, *diakonos*) to Israel to confirm the patriarchal promises and to cause the Gentiles to glorify God, Christ himself only carried out the first goal and not the second; rather, Rom. 15:16–21, especially Paul's citation of Isa. 52:15, shows that Paul sees himself to be carrying out the mission to the Gentiles, thus "completing" the prophecy of the gospel that Jesus began to fulfill and continued to fulfill through Paul (i.e., "what Christ has accomplished through me"). The most plausible background against which to understand this two-part prophetic fulfillment respectively to Israel (through Jesus) and then to Gentiles (through Paul) is the two-part prophetic mission of Isa. 49:1–6.[71]

Accordingly, πληρόω (*plēroō*) may best be rendered "completed" with a sense of prophetic fulfillment: in Rom. 15:19 "completed the promised preaching of the gospel of the Messiah,"* and Col. 1:25, "to complete the preaching of the promised word"* of the gospel. Thus both passages do not entail a preaching of the gospel in general, as some suppose, but the specific preaching of it to Gentiles (in Col. 1:27), which was prophesied in the OT (Eadie 1856: 95). This fits nicely with our view of "filling up" in 1:24, where we argued that Christ first began to fulfill (contributed

71. I have subsequently found that J. White (2017: 100–106) has come to the same conclusion.

to fulfilling) his prophesied sufferings and that Paul completed those predicted sufferings. This is probably to be understood within the framework of Christ's suffering ministry to Israel, which was completed by Paul's suffering ministry to Gentiles.

Comparable to Paul rejoicing in sharing in Christ's sufferings for the benefit of his readers is 2 Cor. 1:5–7, where "comfort" replaces "rejoicing":

> For just as the sufferings of Christ are ours in abundance, so also our comfort is abundant through Christ. But if we are afflicted, it is for your comfort and salvation; or if we are comforted, it is for your comfort, which is effective in the patient enduring of the same sufferings which we also suffer; and our hope for you is firmly grounded, knowing that as you are sharers of our sufferings, so also you are sharers of our comfort.

Another similar parallel is 2 Cor. 4:10–12 (so D. Moo 2008: 152).

A number of commentators (e.g., Pao 2012: 126) see that when Paul's suffering does its part in filling up the quota of the decreed church's sufferings, it hastens the fulfillment of God's work in history and thus explains how his suffering could benefit the church. But this latter idea is not at all clear in this text.

1:24. *Further lexical reflections on "filling up that which is lacking."* The ἀντί (*anti*) prefixed to αναπληρόω (*anaplēroō*) may express the notion that the "fullness replaces that which is lacking," or may in some way anticipate the ὑπέρ (*hyper*, on behalf of) that follows (so Moule 1959: 71); Porter (1994: 144–45) prefers the former option. Either of these nuances is possible for the preposition here, since both are typical meanings of the preposition. Similarly Lightfoot (1875: 163) says that ἀντί (*anti*) in this compound verb indicates "that the supply comes from an opposite quarter to the deficiency," which is in line with typical meanings of the preposition such as "opposite," "instead of," or "in place of," though it can also indicate equivalent correspondences (BDAG 87–88, s.v. §§1–2). It is difficult to be overly confident about the precise meaning of the verb because of its rarity, though the following meaning is probably preferable: "'I am filling up in order to complete' what is lacking in regard to Christ's afflictions" (D. Moo 2008: 150–51, who also gives other options for expressing the preposition's significance).

Extrabiblical Greek usage of the verb ἀνταναπληρόω (*antanaplēroō*), which occurs nowhere else in biblical Greek and only ten times elsewhere in classical and Hellenistic Greek (up through the 3rd cent. AD), is supportive of the basic notion of "something filling up what is lacking in place of another." Note the following:[72] Demosthenes, *On the Naval Boards* 17 (4th cent. BC); Dio Cassius, *Roman History* 44.48 (3rd cent. AD); Epicurus, *Epistle to Herodotus* 48 (4th cent. BC; with the noun form ἀνταναπλήρωσις, *antanaplērōsis*, in Diogenes Laertius, *Lives* 10.48 [3rd cent. AD]). Four references are from Apollonius Dyscolus, *About Syntax*[73] 1.19; 2.44; 3.111; 4.64. In a music context, see Claudius Ptolemaeus, *Harmonics* 1.11 (2nd cent. AD).[74] Finally, see Clement of Alexandria, *Misc.* 7.12.77 (2nd to 3rd cent. AD). I had examined these uses before reading Clark, and I have found Clark's clarifications helpful. Clark (2015: 32–37) adds two more later references from Eusebius (*Commentary on Isaiah* 2.50; and *Supplemental Questions to Marinus* E) and one from Basil of Caesarea (*Epistles* 92.2), all of which are from the mid-fourth century AD and thus questionable with respect to their chronological relevance.

Garland proposes that the combined use of αναπληρόω (*anaplēroō*) and ὑστέρημα (*hysterēma*) in 1 Cor. 16:17 and Phil. 2:30 are the key to the combined use in Col. 1:24 (though the verb has an extra prefixed preposition in Colossians!). Paul suffers as the representative of Christ's suffering bodily presence, which is now "lacking," since Christ has died. "'What is lacking' has nothing to do with some measure that must be filled but is an idiom for representing

72. These are all the verbal uses found in the *TLG*, plus one noun form.

73. Translations and book and section numbers in these references can be found in Householder 1981.

74. See the English translation of Claudius Ptolemaeus, *Harmonics*, by Solomon 2000: 38.

Christ's bodily" presence in his suffering (Garland 1998: 122). This may well be a fairly simple yet ingenious solution to this infamously problematic passage.[75]

However, among the several problems with this view is that the uses adduced by Garland are only the shorter verbal form αναπληρόω and not the full prefixed form ἀνταναπληρόω (*antanaplēroō*) as in Col. 1:24.[76] Garland never discusses whether there might be a difference of meaning in the different verb forms themselves or whether they are synonymous. Second, in both the Corinthians and Philippians passages it is the presence of the people that is "lacking" and is represented by Paul's coworkers (though the Philippians passage is less clear about this in the light of Phil. 4:10–20, which focuses on material needs that must be provided). But "what is lacking of the afflictions of Christ"* in Col. 1:24 puts focus not first on Christ but on "afflictions," and it is these "afflictions" that "are lacking," and there is not a focus on Christ's presence that is lacking. This focus on "afflictions" is enhanced by the article "the" before "afflictions," which several commentators believe suggests the force of something well known (e.g., Lohse 1971: 71; O'Brien 1982: 80): the expected coming end-time suffering and tribulation linked to the Messiah's coming. An eschatological view of "the tribulations of Christ" adduced above is further supported by the context of Col. 1:25–27, which contains words expressing "already and not yet" eschatological concepts ("fulfill the prophetic word of God," "mystery," "now," and "Gentile" salvation), as well as the background of Daniel's Son of Man and Isaiah's suffering servant.

Thus, in Col. 1:24 the focus is not on Christ's presence with eschatological "afflictions" being only secondary, but the focus is on the "afflictions."

1:25. In contrast to "fully carry out announcing the word of God," an alternative translation of the phrase πληρῶσαι τὸν λόγον τοῦ θεοῦ (*plērōsai ton logon tou theou*) is "to fulfill the word of God" or "to complete the promised preaching of the word [gospel] of God," with a sense of prophetic fulfillment.[77] This phrase could viably mean that Paul's servanthood in being commissioned for a stewardship is a fulfillment of OT prophecy. Pointing to this prophetic idea of the word is the above observation that Paul is identifying himself corporately with the ongoing completion of the prophesied suffering Danielic Son of Man and especially the prophesied Isaianic suffering servant. Our conclusions about ἀνταναπληρόω strikingly fit with this idea of ongoing fulfillment of prophecy, first by Christ and then by Paul. Sumney (2008: 103) says, "The language of fulfillment [in 1:25] has an eschatological orientation," since verse 26 is so overtly eschatological (see on 1:26). Thus "Paul's commission is a part of the eschatological acts of God, and his proclamation to Gentiles facilitates the advancement of God's plan for the world" (Sumney 2008: 103). In addition, other reasons supporting this prophetic sense of πληρόω (*plēroō*) are the following:

1. "Word" (λόγος, *logos*) in the LXX can have or include a prophetic meaning (1 Kings 2:4; 8:56; Neh. 9:8). In the Hebrew OT, דָּבַר (*dābar*) refers to speaking God's promises, and the noun form refers to God's "word" or "words," which are promises (singular or plural, as in Josh. 21:45; 1 Kings 2:4; Neh. 5:13).
2. While Paul mostly uses the phrase "word of God" to refer to divine revelation, including often the gospel (1 Cor. 14:36; 2 Cor. 2:17; 4:2; 1 Thess. 2:13; 1 Tim. 4:5; 2 Tim. 2:9; Titus 2:5), he can use λόγος (*logos*) in the phrase "word of God" on occasion to refer to a prophetic promise from the OT (Rom. 9:6, 9). Thus, if the context warrants it, the phrase could include reference to OT prophecy here in Col. 1:25.

75. Though note that BDAG 87 appears to come close to supporting this conclusion. "After receiving his apostolic assignment, Paul assumes the burden of sufferings that would befall Christ were the latter to undertake the apostolic mission in person."

76. Clement of Alexandria (*Misc.* 7.12.77) is the only use among the nine earlier above-cited extrabiblical uses of ἀνταναπληρόω that could possibly support Garland's view, and it is the latest among those references (2nd to 3rd cent. AD).

77. In either rendering, "word of God" would likely be both a genitive of source ("word from God") and an objective genitive ("word about God"); so Sumney 2008: 103–4.

3. Pao (2000: 147–76) argues that the repeated phrase "the word of God" (or "of the Lord," over twenty times, plus other variants with "word") in Acts has its roots in the new-exodus prophecies of Isa. 40–66 and is used by Luke in inextricable association with such prophecies that are beginning to be fulfilled in the church. This shows that the early Christian community within which Paul moved used λόγος in close association with prophetic fulfillment, even though usually referring to the gospel. Pao's view here also is corroborated by the background discussed above about the prophesied suffering servant of Isaiah (see additional notes on 1:24 above).[78]
4. The phrase "fulfill the word of God" (πληρῶσαι τὸν λόγον τοῦ θεοῦ) in Col. 1:25 could be an echo of 2 Chron. 36:21 LXX, where Israel's captivity in Babylon occurred "in order that the word of the Lord should be fulfilled" (τοῦ πληρωθῆναι λόγον κυρίου, *tou plērōthēnai logon kyriou*), the only passage in the entire Septuagint where this phrase occurs, though cf. 2 Chron. 36:22, "after the saying [ῥῆμα, *rhēma*] of the Lord was fulfilled," referring to the same event as in 36:21 (likewise almost identically, 1 Kings 2:27, also referring to fulfillment of prophecy). Paul may not have any of these OT contexts specifically in mind but might be influenced generally by the language of fulfillment there.[79] However, it appears to be beyond coincidence that the two references in 2 Chron. 36:21 and 22 are viewed as including not only the full time of Israel's captivity in Babylon but also the very beginning of their restoration from captivity under Cyrus, as 2 Chron. 36:23 shows: Cyrus says, "He has appointed me to build Him a house in Jerusalem, which is in Judah. Whoever there is among you of all His people, may the Lord his God be with him, and let him go up!" This may be relevant, since Cyrus and the servant (discussed above) in Isa. 40–53 are both agents of Israel's prophesied restoration. In this light, allusion to 2 Chron. 36:21–22 appears to be viable.
5. Five out of six uses of πληρόω (*plēroō*) with λόγος (*logos*) elsewhere in the NT refer to prophecy (the "word") from the OT or from Jesus being "fulfilled" (Luke 1:20; John 12:38; 15:25; 18:9, 32).[80]
6. The directly following reference in Colossians, "the mystery," is appositional to "word of God" and is typically used by Paul and the NT elsewhere to refer to end-time prophetic fulfillment (see the discussion below at 1:26–27; 2:2). Likewise, the words in the immediate context of "administration" (οἰκονομία, *oikonomia*) and "now revealed" (1:26) are charged with the sense of eschatological prophetic fulfillment (see on 1:26–27; Melick 1991: 241).

In the light of these above six points, it may be best to translate Col. 1:25 as "to complete the prophesied preaching of the word [gospel] of God" or "to complete the preaching of the promised word [gospel] of God" instead of "to fully carry out the preaching of the word of God," though even this could be understood to include a prophetic sense (see directly below). The insertion of the word "preaching" may be warranted from the context, especially 1:28, where Paul says he has "preached" the mystery of Christ.

Therefore, contrary to protestations otherwise (Barth and Blanke 1994: 260–61), Paul may well be viewing his preaching in Col. 1:25 to be part of "fulfilling prophecy."[81] How does Paul see himself doing this? As noted above, he believed that Christ had begun to fulfill the prophecy about

78. In the LXX, "word of God" refers to a revelation from God (7×), prediction (1 Kings 13:5; Jer. 9:2), or both (Jer. 1:2). In the Gospels, "word of God" refers either to a revelation from God (4×) or Jesus's teaching about God (3×).

79. Cf. Lightfoot (1875: 167), who acknowledges the parallel to the Chronicles and Kings passages but denies any influence.

80. The other use refers to "the whole Law" being fulfilled in one word, in the statement "You shall love your neighbor as yourself" (Gal. 5:14). Here the idea is that of carrying out the law by carrying out the love command, which is more compatible with the alternative translation of "fully carry out the preaching of the word of God," which has no necessary prophetic sense.

81. Moule (1957: 80) similarly says there is the "implication that to proclaim the Gospel is part of the *fulfilling* of God's plan."

Isaiah's servant, Israel. Presumably, he considered that he was continuing to fulfill and complete the OT prophecy, particularly, the prophecy that God's end-time salvation would be proclaimed among the nations by God's Son of Man and "servant," who would suffer in the process. The traditional translation of "fully carry out the preaching of the word of God" may still convey an idea included within the prophetic sense argued for above, since it was prophesied that the servant was to have people announcing "good news" and "salvation" (Isa. 52:7; cf. 53:1), which elsewhere Paul sees himself together with other authoritative apostles and preachers fulfilling (Rom. 10:15–16). All of this fits admirably with our conclusions in 1:24 that Paul was uniquely completing the prophesied sufferings that Christ had first begun to endure.

1:26–27. That the revelation of the mystery in verses 26–27 is not completely new, with no hint from the OT, is apparent from noticing that the origin for Paul's view of mystery comes from Dan. 2 and 4, where Daniel's interpretative revelation of the mystery was a clarification and fuller explanation of the king's dream. The dream in Dan. 4 was about a giant tree under which all animals of the earth found shelter and sustenance. The tree was cut down. But in the dream itself, before Daniel's revealed interpretation, an angel declares that the tree is a human who has had dominance over the earth: "Let him be drenched with the dew of heaven, and let him share with the beasts of the field in the grass of the earth. Let his mind be changed from that of a man, and let a beast's mind be given to him, and let seven periods of time pass over him." This would be to show that God bestows kingship "on whom he wishes" (Dan. 4:15–17). Thus, even before Daniel fully interprets the dream, the king already knows that some of the dream's symbols represent a king's sovereignty and subsequent judgment, and the king likely suspects that the dream is about him, since he is "fearful" and "alarmed" by the dream.[82] If Paul is using the concept of mystery in line with that in Dan. 4, then his revealed interpretation of the prophesied mystery in Dan. 2 is not completely new but a fuller revelation of what was already known to some degree.

While the revealed mystery that Gentiles become members of the latter-day kingdom of Israel by identification with the Messiah and not the nationalistic tags of the law was not verbalized in the OT (our conclusion in the comments on 1:26–27), it does not seem to be absolutely unanticipated. The revelation may have grown from the notion that the OT views the messianic servant to be one who sums up faithful Israel in himself (e.g., Isa. 49:3). Even from the OT perspective (e.g., from Isaiah's vantage point), all those who would be redeemed in the eschaton would not only need to trust in the servant's redemptive work (Isa. 53) but also identify with the servant. This appears to be the reason why, after Isa. 53, for the first time in the book faithful Israelites corporately are repeatedly referred to as "servants" (eleven times), presumably because they identify with the servant.[83] One could surmise then that the messianic servant is the key eschatological marker of being a true Israelite. Paul then plausibly develops this further and sees that Gentiles do not need to take on the nationalistic identity markers of Israel's law to become true Israelites but need only to identify with the key identity marker of the Messiah, Jesus. This makes even more sense when it is seen that Paul sees Jesus as typologically fulfilling that to which the identity markers of Israel's law ultimately pointed: he represents the epitome of the wisdom of the law (see on Col. 2:3 above), he is the true temple (see on 1:19 above), the true circumcision (see on 2:11–12 below), the true Sabbath (2:16–17), and everything to which the dietary laws truly pointed (2:11–12).[84] Some of these developments by Paul even are intimated in the OT itself. For example, the comments above show that the "stone" of Dan. 2 is parallel to the "Son of Man" in Dan. 7, which means that the "kingdom" of Dan. 2 (interpreted in 2:44–45 to be what the "stone" represents) is to be identified with the Son of Man. But I have argued elsewhere that the stone represents not only the kingdom of Israel but also its end-time temple (see Beale 2004: 144–53). If so, the Son of Man is not only seen to be the king who represents

82. Daniel 4:5 and the language of his sovereignty in the dream itself (Dan. 4:12) are developments of Dan. 2:38, describing Nebuchadnezzar's sovereignty.

83. I am grateful to my former research student, Daniel Brendsel, for this observation.

84. On these last two ideas, see on 2:16–17 below.

Israel's kingdom (as is also apparent by comparing Dan. 7:13 with 7:17–27) but also is essentially identified with its temple.

1:27. Among the MSS, 𝔓[46] omits "of glory" (τῆς δόξης, *tēs doxēs*) after "riches" (πλοῦτος, *ploutos*); others (D*, F, G, b, vg[mss]; Ambst) add "of God" (τοῦ θεοῦ, *tou theou*) after μυστηρίου, thus reading "the riches of the glory of the mystery of God." It is difficult to discern whether these changes were accidental or intentional.

1:27. This verse is fraught with syntactical ambiguities. There are several genitives here in the phrase literally rendered "the wealth of the glory of this mystery," each of which can be understood in different ways. First, "the wealth of the glory" (τὸ πλοῦτος τῆς δόξης, *to ploutos tēs doxēs*) could express source ("wealth arising from the glory"), an adjectival idea ("the glorious wealth"), a possessive notion ("wealth possessed by the glory"), an attributed genitive ("the wealthy glory"), or an epexegetical genitive ("riches consisting in the glory"). Genitive of source or, even better, possession seems best in light of other Pauline parallels. The "wealth of his glory" refers in Rom. 9:23; Eph. 1:18 (though without "his"); and Eph. 3:16 to God's glory, from which his rich attributes arise or, better, the rich attributes that his glory possesses (glory appearing to be a reference to God's character or rich attributes in general). In line with this is Phil. 4:19: "My God will supply all your needs according to His riches in glory in Christ Jesus." In this text, wealth possessed by God's glory is revealed in Christ. Colossians 1:27 is close to the use in Philippians, since the "glory" in verse 27 is to be identified with the "mystery," whose content is "Christ."

Similar to the preceding genitive, the genitival phrase δόξης τοῦ μυστηρίου τούτου (*doxēs tou mystēriou toutou*) could express source ("glory arising from this mystery"), attribution ("this glorious mystery"), or most likely possession. That is, the revealed "mystery" possesses glory, which is to say, Christ possesses glory, since he is the content of the mystery ("the glory of the mystery, . . . which is Christ"). Or just as plausibly, "of this mystery" is appositional to "glory": the glory is (or consists in) the mystery. D. Moo (2008: 157) prefers this option, based on verbal genitival parallels elsewhere in Paul: "the glorious riches that are the mystery." However, only two of the parallels clearly are examples of this (2 Cor. 8:2; Eph. 2:7); the other examples can perhaps just as easily be taken as genitives of source or possession (see the Pauline references in the preceding paragraph).

The genitival phrase "the hope of glory" is a further explanation of the preceding reference to "Christ." Specifically, "glory" appears to be an objective genitive, which can be paraphrased as following: "Christ is the believers' basis for hoping in their participation in future end-time glory with him." This appears to be an anticipation of Col. 3:4: "When Christ should be manifested, who is our life, then also you with him should be manifested in glory."*The phrase ἐλπίδι τῆς δόξης τοῦ θεοῦ (*elpidi tēs doxēs tou theou*) in Rom. 5:2 is almost the same, except that it refers to God's and not Christ's glory (though the latter is likely not out of mind): "hope of [sharing in] the glory of God"; here "glory" would be an objective genitive, and "of God" a possessive genitive, thus meaning "glory possessed by God." In light of Rom. 3:23 ("All . . . fall short of the glory"), "glory" in 5:2 probably refers to the state of likeness to God, distorted in Adam and to be restored at the end of time (cf. Rom. 8:17, 18, 21, 30; following for the most part D. Moo 1996: 301–2). Titus 2:13 is similar ("awaiting the blessed *hope* and appearing of the *glory* of our great God and Savior, Jesus Christ"*), where Christ is equated with "hope" and closely associated with "glory."

There is one last significant syntactical problem in verse 27. It is difficult to ascertain what the phrase "among the Gentiles/nations" (ἐν τοῖς ἔθνεσιν, *en tois ethnesin*) relates to. Does the phrase relate to the infinitive "to make known" (γνωρίσαι, *gnōrisai*; TNIV, HCSB) or the phrase "this mystery" (μυστηρίου τούτου, *mystēriou toutou*; NASB, NRSV, ASV, NJB, NET)?[85] If the prepositional phrase modifies "this mystery," then the emphasis falls on the significance of the mystery as it relates to "the Gentiles" (see Lightfoot 1875: 169). That is, the mystery

85. A good case can also be made for the phrase to modify "what is the riches of the glory" (Harris 2010: 64).

largely entails that the Gentiles are part of the mystery. If, on the other hand, it relates directly to "to make known," as several commentators and translations suggest, Paul is highlighting the proclamation of the mystery "among" or "to the Gentiles."

Relating "among the Gentiles" to "mystery," while not betraying the *precise content* of mystery, underscores the significance of the mystery *as it relates* to the Gentiles. It would lend further credence to the view that the revealed mystery concerns, to a large extent, something about the Gentiles, for which we argued above. If, however, "among the Gentiles" modifies "make known," it places emphasis not so much on the Gentiles being part of the mystery but the extent to which the mystery has been heralded—the unveiled mystery has reached *even* to the Gentiles. I prefer the former rendering: the disclosed mystery concerns the Gentiles.[86] If I am correct in the construal of verse 27, the first part of the verse could be rephrased as follows: "to whom God willed to make known what is the riches of the glory of this mystery [as it is demonstrated or expressed] among the Gentiles."[87] Either syntactical option, nevertheless, relates Gentiles in one way or another to "the mystery."

1:28. The second occurrence of "all men" (πάντα ἄνθρωπον, *panta anthrōpon*) directly after διδάσκοντες (*didaskontes*) is omitted by some MSS (D*, F, G, 0278, 33, 614, 629, *pc*, it, vg^{mss}, (sy^{p}); Cl Ambst (L 81, 1241^{s}, 1505, *pc*: *h.t.*) due to the scribe's eye skipping back to the first occurrence of the same phrase and coming back and continuing to copy with "in all."

2:2. To agree with "hearts," the participle συμβιβασθέντες (*symbibasthentes*) should be a feminine nominative instead of a masculine nominative. Among the possible ways to understand the lack of concord is that this is a nominative absolute (a so-called hanging nominative) or a nominative "according to sense" (i.e., the masculine instead of feminine does not change the sense of the adverbial participial construction). But neither of these options or others offered explain satisfactorily why the masculine nominative is used here (cf. Harris 2010: 73, for several options; see also Campbell 2013: 28).

The genitive phrase "the full assurance of understanding" (τῆς πληροφορίας τῆς συνέσεως, *tēs plērophorias tēs syneseōs*) is likely a genitive of source or product: "the full assurance derived from understanding" (also cf. MHT 3:211, taking it as a genitive of result: "conviction which is the result of insight"; BDAG 827d, s.v. πληροφορία, viewing it as a subjective genitive: "a wealth of assurance, such as understanding brings"). This whole genitival phrase stands in apposition to "the riches" ("the riches consist of the full assurance of understanding," Rienecker 1980: 225). D. Moo (2008: 167) prefers to view πληροφορία as meaning "fullness" and understands the complete phrase to be an attributive genitive, "complete [full] understanding" (on the concept of this kind of genitive, see Wallace 1996: 89–91).

There are a bewildering number of textual variants (fourteen) as alternatives to the preferred reading of NA^{28} (τοῦ θεοῦ, Χριστοῦ, *tou theou, Christou*), but the reading of NA^{28} is likely the original for two reasons: (1) all the other variants can be explained as corruptions of it but it

86. What perhaps may tip the scales in favor of this rendering ("this mystery [demonstrated] among the Gentiles") is the relative pronoun "whom" at the beginning of verse 27. As is quite evident, verse 26 largely focuses on those who have been privileged to receive the mystery, the believers (a remnant of Jewish believers and a majority Gentile Christians): "the mystery . . . has now been manifested to his saints." The antecedent of the pronoun "whom" (οἷς, *hois*) of verse 27 is the saints (τοῖς ἁγίοις, *tois hagiois*) in verse 26 and specifies the group who has received the mystery: "*to whom* [οἷς, *hois*] God willed to make known . . . this mystery." In other words, to affirm that "among the Gentiles" modifies the infinitive "to make known" renders the phrase somewhat redundant, since Paul has already specified that Gentiles are among the recipients of the mystery in verse 26 and in his use of "whom" in verse 27, which repeats reference to the recipients (i.e., Jewish and Gentile believers). See D. Moo 2008: 157–58, for reasons supporting "mystery" as a modifier of "make known."

87. On this conclusion and its interpretive implications, see further Beale and Gladd 2014: 201–7.

cannot easily be seen to be a corruption of any of these other readings; (2) the character and age of the MSS supporting this reading are better than the others (𝔓[46], B, Hilary of Poitiers; see Metzger 1968: 236–38). Consequently, the full expression most probably read "the mystery of God, of Christ," with "of Christ" designating the content of the "mystery of God."

2:3. The two genitives in the phrase "all the treasures of wisdom and knowledge" are genitives of content: "treasures consisting of wisdom and knowledge" (Wallace 1996: 93).

Here, together with 1:26, is a striking parallel with 1 Cor. 2:7: both have in common the mention of "mystery," "hidden wisdom," "the ages," all within a context about "mature" believers and the revelation of God's glory (cf. Pao 2012: 129). This further enhances the teaching that Christ is the revelation of the mystery in 1:26 and 2:3, since the same is the case in 1 Corinthians. It is preferable to view the "hiddenness" to be generally referring to the "wisdom and knowledge" having been mostly "hidden" in Christ in the OT but now fully revealed (in line with the earlier idea of the mystery about Christ in 1:26). If, however, there is emphasis on the present hiddenness, it may refer to unbelievers for whom the mystery is still hidden, though revealed to believers (as in 1 Cor. 2:6–8; a view preferred by Sumney 2008: 118).

In the same way that the mystery about Christ was largely hidden in the OT but now revealed, so Col. 3:3–4 says that believers' resurrection "life is hidden with Christ in God" in the present but will be "manifested in glory"* at the very end of the age. Though there is some revelation about the present invisible spiritual reality of the Christians' resurrection existence, at the consummation that existence will be fully manifested in full spiritual and physical resurrection life.

2:4. Translations render πιθανολογία (*pithanologia*) by "persuasiveness of speech" (ASV), "persuasive argument/s" (HCSB, NASB), "plausible arguments" (NRSV, ESV), "beguiling speech" (RSV, Douay), "enticing words" (Geneva, KJV), "specious arguments" (NJB), or "fine-sounding arguments" (NIV). All of these are reasonable translations. Philo uses the word πιθανός (*pithanos*) often to refer typically to "convincing, persuasive, or plausible" (even "probable") statements of sophists or those who are affirming untrue things but trying to make them appear true or wrongly believing them to be true (e.g., see Philo, *Decal.* 3). Sometimes the word is used in a courtroom setting, where a lawyer's persuasive arguments and their power influenced the audience toward an unjust verdict. Accordingly, the word's notion is close to the modern English expression "to talk someone into something" (Johnson 1962b: 304). This is the idea in Col. 2:4.

B. Believers Should Live Only on the Basis of Christ (2:6–15)

Here is a fuller statement of the main idea of this unit: *Believers should live only on the basis of Christ and not any other belief system, since Christ came in the fullness of deity in bodily form, resulting in his redemption of them through his death, resurrection, and triumph over their enemies.*

This section, anticipated by 1:24–2:5, circles back to the main point of 1:3–23, which is to "walk . . . worthy of the Lord" (v. 10a). The goal of 1:24–2:5 is that believers be "complete in Christ" (1:28), which is achieved by them not being "deluded" by false teaching (2:4), so they can maintain "good discipline and the stability of faith" (2:5). And this is the basis of "walking in" Christ in 2:6, which explicitly expands on "walking" worthily in 1:10a. This expansion is observable from noticing that both 1:10–12 and 2:6–7 have a series of four adverbial participles (beginning with an agricultural metaphor) that modify "walk" and conclude with a mention of thanksgiving (D. Moo 2008: 179–80; likewise O'Brien 1982: 106; Sumney 2008: 128; Pao 2012: 156). Here in 2:6–15 we will see that Paul refers back in other ways to 1:10–2:5 to elaborate on what he has said in that context.

Paul begins this section by commanding the listeners to "walk" in Christ in the same way (by faith) that they received Christ. They are able to "walk" in Christ because they have been initially "rooted . . . in Him" at the inception of their belief, and on that foundation they continue to be "built up in Him and established" (v. 7a). When they first believed, they were taught these truths and "overflowed with thanksgiving"* (v. 7b) for them.

They are to "walk worthily" (1:10a; 2:6) not only by focusing on the truth (2:7) but also by not being led astray by "philosophy and empty deception," which is based on false worldly views and not on Christ (v. 8). Instead, they should base their lives (their lifestyle "walk") only on Christ (or be "captivated" by Christ instead of false teaching; v. 8b). From various angles everything else in the remainder of verses 9–15 supports this proposition of "walking only on the basis of Christ" (vv. 6b and 8b) as the main logical point of all of verses 6–15.

The readers are to found their lives on Christ because he is the only one in whom "Deity dwells in bodily form" (v. 9). Verses 10–11 explain the threefold effects of Christ being the one in whom "all the fullness of Deity dwells in bodily form" (v. 9b): (1) believers "have become filled in Him"* (v. 10a), (2) "He is the head over all rule and authority" (v. 10b), and (3) "in Him [they] were also circumcised" (v. 11a).

Then the entire remainder of the segment (vv. 11b–15) flows out of the last effect of being "circumcised."[1] Christians were circumcised "by the circumcision of Christ, which occurred by "having been buried with Him in baptism" (vv. 11b–12a). By means of this baptism they were also "raised up with" Christ (v. 12b). Then the next verse adds that, despite their sin, their resurrection (being "made alive") was a direct result of God "having forgiven them" their "transgressions" (v. 13) and "having canceled out the certificate of debt" against saints (v. 14a). Verse 14b explains further what it means that this "certificate of debt" has been "canceled": God "has taken it out of the way [by] having nailed it to the cross." Verse 15 concludes the segment by progressing on to mention an effect of forgiveness at the cross (vv. 13–14), explaining also an effect of the earlier point from verse 10b that Christ "is the head over all rule and authority": because Christ is over all rulers, through the cross he was able to defeat and triumph over the evil, satanic "rulers and authorities."

Thus everything in Col. 2:6–15 revolves around the main point of "walking only in Christ" (v. 6b, reiterated in v. 8b). The "in Him" (Christ) in verse 6 sets the tone of the Christ-centered discussion throughout verses 6–15 (generally observed by commentators), where the phrases "Christ" (v. 8b), "in Him" (vv. 6, 7, 9, 10, 11), "in whom"* (vv. 11, 12 [?], 15b [?]), and "with Him" (vv. 12 [2×], 13; and three σύν [*syn*] verbs)[2] occur. These references are a strand that links all of these verses together, not only to focus on Christ but also on the believers' corporate identity with Christ. This emphasis on Christ is set in antithesis to the non-Christ-centered false teaching.

Exegesis and Exposition

[6]Therefore as you have received Christ Jesus the Lord, so walk in Him, [7]having
been firmly rooted and now being built up in Him and established in your faith, just as
you were instructed, and overflowing with gratitude. [8]See to it that no one takes you
captive through philosophy and empty deception, according to the tradition of men,
according to the elementary principles of the world, rather than according to Christ.
[9]For in Him all the fullness of Deity dwells in bodily form, [10]and in Him you have been
made complete, and He is the head over all rule and authority; [11]and in Him you were
also circumcised with a circumcision made without hands, in the removal of the body
of the flesh by the circumcision of Christ; [12]having been buried with Him in ⌜baptism⌝,
in which you were also raised up with Him through faith in the working of God, who

1. D. Moo (2008: 193–94; cf. 212) says that Col. 2:9–15 interpretatively "elaborate" or "explain" what it means that the false philosophy is "not according to Christ" (v. 8) by positively explaining Christ and his work. Sumney (2008: 135) views verses 11–15 to be the means by which Christians come to possess the "fullness" of Christ in verse 10. These views are viable and close to the view adopted here.

2. On the meaning of the σύν (*syn*) verbs and the preposition by itself, see my comments on 2:13.

raised Him from the dead. 13When you were dead ⌜in⌝ your transgressions and the uncircumcision of your flesh, He made ⌜you⌝ alive together with Him, having forgiven ⌜us⌝ all our transgressions, 14having canceled out the certificate of debt consisting of decrees against us, which was hostile to us; and He has taken it out of the way, having nailed it to the cross. 15When He had disarmed the rulers and authorities, He made a public display of them, having triumphed over them through Him.

2:6 The initial "therefore" (οὖν, *oun*) indicates that the preceding context provides the basis for the command to "walk." The focus of this basis is Paul's desire that the Colossians become "complete in Christ" (1:28) by disregarding false teaching and maintaining "stability of faith" (2:5) in true Christian teaching. They have "received Christ Jesus the Lord." The word "receive" (παραλαμβάνω, *paralambanō*) often has the idea of believers receiving a Christian tradition that has been "delivered" to them (e.g., 1 Cor. 11:23; 15:1, 3; Gal. 1:9, 12; Phil. 4:9; 1 Thess. 2:13; 4:1; 2 Thess. 3:6; following Bruce 1984: 93). Many commentators insist that this is the thought here.[3] On this basis, some contend that the idea primarily is not "referring to receiving Christ Jesus as one's personal Lord" (Pao 2012: 155). The "receiving," however, does seem to include committing themselves personally to Christ as their Lord (so also O'Brien 1982: 105). The element of personal commitment is reflected by 1:10, where "to walk worthy of the Lord" is "to please him in all respects," though 1:7 says that they "learned" the gospel tradition "from Epaphras," teaching that has come indirectly through Paul (cf. 1:23–28). The giving of "thanks" in 1:12 and 2:7 also focuses on a personal relationship with Christ. Of course, in the context of Col. 1–2 (e.g., 1:6–7, 23, 28), what they believed about Jesus has been passed on to them and is part of the apostolic tradition about Jesus (as confirmed from such parallel passages as 1 Cor. 15:1–2; Phil. 4:9; 1 Thess. 4:1, on which see further below). That in "receiving Christ," they were also receiving the "tradition" about him is evident from 2:7, where reference to their "faith" is directly followed by "just as you were taught."* And this received tradition is set in immediate contrast to the false "tradition of men" (2:8; cf. Abbott 1897: 244). Thus, "receiving Christ" is equally a personal and an intellectual commitment (cf. Schweizer 1982: 124–25; MacDonald 2000: 88), though the notion of a passed-on tradition is "subordinated to the . . . idea that what the missionaries had passed on to their converts was Christ himself" as a person (Caird 1976: 189; likewise Barth and Blanke 1994: 300–301, 311; Lincoln 2000: 620).

As we concluded in 1:1, "Christ Jesus" is no mere name without interpretative significance but reflects to some degree the OT expectation of a Messiah (cf. also Barth and Blanke 1994: 302), who is now identified as Jesus of Nazareth (the article before "Christ" may enhance this point; Harris 2010: 80; contra Sumney 2008: 127n1). Some think that the words "the Lord" that

3. E.g., O'Brien 1982: 105; Bruce 1984: 93, 105; Dunn 1996: 138–39; Sumney 2008: 126–27; Pao 2012: 154–55; so also Barth and Blanke (1994: 299–301), who show that this is in line with OT and Jewish tradition.

immediately follow receive greatest emphasis in this verse. It is argued that when the title comes after a transitive verb, it tends to function predicatively: "Christ Jesus as Lord" (so O'Brien 1982: 106; D. Moo 2008: 178–79; followed by several translations: NLT, NIV, NET; HCSB; cf. NJB). The parallels of 2 Cor. 4:5 and Phil. 2:11 are offered in support (though the latter has a different order of words and both lack the article before "Lord"). Some translations, however, render merely "Christ Jesus the Lord" (KJV, RSV, NRSV, ESV).[4] Regardless of which translation is best,[5] it is likely correct to identify this name for Christ as part of a reference to the early confession "Jesus is Lord." Colossians so far has identified this confession as Christ being "the image of the invisible God" (1:15), "the firstborn of all creation" (1:15), the creator of "all things" (1:16), the sustainer of "all things" (1:17), "[the] head of the body, the church" (1:18), "the firstborn from the dead" (1:18), the new temple (1:19), the "reconcile[r]" of all (1:20, 22), and "God's mystery" (2:2; following in part D. Moo 2008: 179).

This early Christian confession is based on "Jesus" being the Messiah ("Christ") and being the divine "Lord." In 1:3 we have already observed that referring to "Jesus" the "Lord" is not a mere title of respect, applied to kings or masters, but to some degree a reference to "Lord" (κύριος, *kyrios*) in the LXX, which was the usual Greek translation of Yahweh in the Greek OT (cf. Fee 2007: 20–27, 179, 577–78, 631–38) and was a word also used by pagans of their gods. This is thus a reference that includes identifying Jesus with Yahweh of the OT.[6] In other explicit NT expressions of "Christ" as the "Lord," the emphasis also is on confessing Christ as Yahweh,[7] so that he is identified with the unique God of the OT. "For Paul, to confess that Jesus is Lord is to confess that he is Yahweh" (Wallace 1996: 188). This part of the early confession is important to observe here, since most of what has been mentioned about Jesus in 1:15–2:2 has focused on his divine identity, and his deity will again be developed in 2:9 below. In light of this preceding and following context, it is probably correct to see "Lord" as the emphasis in 2:6.[8] This emphasis on Jesus's deity is likely a counter to the false teaching (mentioned in 2:4, 8), which focuses on other religious elements in addition to Christ in order to find and experience true wisdom and knowledge. Authentic wisdom and knowledge can be found only in the inexhaustible "fullness" of the divine Christ (see 2:3), which trumps all other philosophies, which are "empty" (2:8).

4. Accordingly, "the Lord" is best viewed as an accusative in apposition to "Christ Jesus" (Campbell 2013: 32).

5. Wallace (1996: 183) says it is debatable whether the phrase should be translated as "Christ Jesus as Lord" ("Lord" taken predicatively) or as "Christ Jesus the Lord" ("Lord" taken in apposition to Christ Jesus).

6. For the background and use of "Lord" (κύριος, *kyrios*) in the pre-Christian Jewish and Greco-Roman world, as well as its use to refer to deity in the NT, see W. Foerster and G. Quell, *TDNT* 3:1039–95; and H. Bietenhard, *NIDNTT* 2:510–20.

7. See Rom. 10:9–13 and 1 Pet. 3:15, where the confession is based on OT texts about Yahweh, which are applied to Jesus (see Wallace 1996: 187–88).

8. A conclusion reached by D. Moo (2008: 179) but on other grounds.

"Walk" is an obvious figurative expression for "lead one's life" (a marginal reading in the NASB). The manner by which (ὡς, *hōs*) they must continue to "walk" is by the same faith in "Christ Jesus the Lord" by which they began their Christian existence ("as you have received"). Their initial trust in Christ brought them into union with him, and they are to continue to "walk in him," that is, continue to live by faith in union with him (the ἐν, *en*, focuses on sphere).[9] Thus the faithful manner by which they "received" Christ is the manner by which they are to continue to live. This continues the theme from earlier, where Paul repeatedly says that his readers have begun by "faith" (Col. 1:2, 4; 2:12) and continue to live by "faith" (Col. 1:2, 4, 23; 2:5, 7). Paul's only other imperative of περιπατέω (*peripateō*, 4:5) in the epistle may indicate that part of the way believers are to "walk" is by having "wisdom toward outsiders," "so that they may know how they should respond to each person" (4:6), including unbelieving false teachers.

As we have suggested, this verse is a direct development of 1:10a, where Paul exhorts believers to "walk in a manner worthy of the Lord." The point there is that the saint's ethical character is "to be fitting with" or matching the character of their "Lord" (Jesus) in order to "please" him. This enforces the notion that the manner of the "walk" in 2:6 is also the focus, which we have seen to be the function of the introductory ὡς (*hōs*). The manner by which Christ's followers are to continue their lives is by the same faith as they began with Christ. The same notion of encouraging Christ's followers to live now in line with the way "you" first "received [second-person aorist active indicative, παρελάβετε, *parelabete*] Christ" appears in Paul's other epistles.[10] The closest of these parallels (outside of Col. 1:10) is 1 Thess. 4:1, which calls believers "to walk" in the manner of faith they have exercised earlier. The parallel of Phil. 4:9 includes the same notion. These parallels reinforce that Col. 2:6 expresses the idea of walking in the same manner of faith. Perhaps not coincidentally, the parallel of 1 Cor. 15:1–2 is part of a defense against false teaching (15:12–19), which is also part of the context here.

2:7 That the hearers must be "firmly rooted and now being built up in him and established in . . . faith" reiterates that "stability of . . . faith" in true Christian doctrine (2:5) is the basis for the "walk" of verse 6.[11] They have been "rooted" (perfect passive participle) in their Christian faith in the past (a past yet ongoing condition), and they are continuing to be "built up in him

9. In addition to sphere, the ἐν could be a packed expression and secondarily may include basis ("Walk on the basis of faith in him") and instrumentation ("Walk by means of faith in him"). Campbell (2012: 183–84; 2013: 32) prefers "under the control of, under the influence of, in close association with" (see BDAG 327, s.v. ἐν 4.c).

10. 1 Cor. 15:1–2; Phil. 4:9; 1 Thess. 4:1, the latter of which follows with the second-person περιπατεῖτε, *peripateite*, as in Col. 2:6.

11. The four adverbial participles in Col. 2:7 indicate the basis of the "walk" in verse 6, though instrumentation may be included (the latter favored by Campbell 2013: 32–33). Harris 2010: 81 says the participles are attendant circumstance, but this is unlikely (see the necessary criteria in Wallace 1996: 641–42, which are lacking here).

and established (present participles) in their faith."[12] "Rooted," "built up," and "confirmed" reflect a continuation of temple imagery from 1:23 ("firmly founded and steadfast and not moved"*; see the additional note on 1:23a).[13] This may also anticipate the temple reference in 2:9 (see below). The point appears to be close to that in Rev. 3:11–12: "I am coming quickly; hold fast what you have, so that no one will take your crown. He who overcomes, I will make him a pillar in the temple of My God, and he will not go out from it anymore; and I will write upon him the name of My God, and the name of the city of My God, the new Jerusalem, which comes down out of heaven from My God, and My new name." The point in Revelation, and here, is that the person who "overcomes" by faith becomes a part of the end-time temple and will be eternally secure in the salvific presence of God and Christ (see Beale 1999a: 294–96). The passive mood forms of the first three participles in verse 7 shows that it is God, not the Colossians, who is making them part of his temple, as in Rev. 3:12.[14]

There is also development of 1:23, where if the Colossians "continue in the faith firmly established and steadfast, and not moved away from the hope of the gospel," they will be presented "holy and blameless and beyond reproach"

12. So also several commentators, among whom are Abbott 1897: 244; Garland 1998: 140; MacDonald 2000: 88; Harris 2010: 81; Sumney 2008: 128; Pao 2012: 157.

13. "Rooted" (ῥιζόομαι, *rhizoomai*), found in conjunction with "founded" (θεμελιόω, *themelioō*) in Eph. 3:17, is not typically an architectural metaphor, but the verb is used in association with the temple (Sir. 24:10–12), and so is the noun form ("O Lord, . . . [you] left us a root and a name in the place of thy sanctuary," 1 Esd. 8:78 KJV). "Being built up" (ἐποικοδομέω, *epoikodomeō*) is another temple-related word for Paul; he uses the same word in Eph. 2:20 to speak of Christians "having been built on the foundation" of the new temple, and he uses the same word four times in 1 Cor. 3:10–14 to speak of the same thing (on the 1 Corinthians text, see Beale 2004: 245–50; likewise see Eph. 2:22; so also οἰκοδομέω [*oikodomeō*] refers to building the temple in Matt. 21:42; 26:61; 27:40; Mark 12:10; 14:58; 15:29; Luke 20:17; John 2:20; Acts 7:47, 49; 1 Pet. 2:5, 7; in 1 Macc. 5:1 KJV: "The altar was built and the sanctuary renewed"). Likewise, βεβαιόω (*bebaioō*) can be used of temple imagery; e.g., Philo says, "Do you not see that also when he [Moses] received the tabernacle from God, and this tabernacle is wisdom, in which the wise man tabernacles and dwells, he fixed it firmly and founded [ἐβεβαιώσατο, *ebebaiōsato*] and built it up strongly" (*Alleg.* 3.46, trans. Yonge 1993: 55). While it may appear strange to have an agricultural metaphor combined with architectural metaphors to portray the temple, it is not unparalleled in Paul (see Eph. 2:21, "growing"; 3:17, as well as 1 Cor. 3:9 with 3:10–17). The origin of such a combination of metaphors is Gen. 2–3, which conceives of the garden of Eden as a sanctuary, as explicitly expressed in Ezek. 28:13–18 (see Beale 2004: passim). Perhaps not coincidentally, Philo combines agricultural metaphors ("God plants a paradise)" with an architectural temple picture ("the altar of the Lord") and partial allusion to the paradise in Eden (*Alleg.* 1.46–50). So also 1QS 8.5–9 and 11.8 make the same kind of combination of agricultural and architectural metaphors to depict the Qumran members as a temple.

14. Following in part D. Moo 2008: 181; and Harris 2010: 81, though not including the notion of the temple. It is possible that all four participles are in the middle voice rather than passive, since they modify an imperative verb ("you walk"; for which Campbell 2013: 32–33 argues). But if the image of the temple is in mind, then the passive would seem more appropriate, since it is God and Christ who build and establish the temple. The only commentator I have found in agreement with viewing "rooted and built up" as references to the temple is Pao 2012: 156–57, who alerted me to repeated uses of ἐποικοδομέω (*epoikodomeō*) in 1 Cor. 3, also used in Eph. 2:20.

on the last day (1:22). This anticipates the onslaught of the false teachers now explicitly mentioned in 2:4 and 2:8, by which the readers are not to be "moved" away from the truth, since the "gospel" is "truth" (1:5) in contrast to the false gospel of "deception" (2:8; on this latter contrast, see D. Moo 2008: 186). While "faith" here could well refer to the object of belief (O'Brien 1982: 108), it is perhaps preferable, as in 1:23 and 2:5 (on which see), to view "faith" here to refer to the exercise of a person's own faith, and yet, of course, that faith is in true Christian doctrine about Christ.

The phrase "just as you were taught" refers not only to the directly preceding participles of 2:7 but also includes verse 6. Paul reminds the hearers that they were "overflowing with thanksgiving" in response to their "instruction." This continues the theme of "thanksgiving" from 1:3 and 12, a theme that will be reprised in 3:15 and 17 and 4:2. This is thus a major idea in Colossians, conveying the notion of gratitude to God, especially because God is the source of their faith (e.g., 1:3–4; 2:6–7), their inheritance and redemption (1:12–14), and the other blessings that they possess.

2:8 In contrast to the reliable instruction summarized in 2:6–7, the hearers are to be wary ("see," "be on the lookout for") of anyone espousing any teaching or "philosophy" that contradicts the true teaching they "have received."[15] They are not to be "taken captive" by such people. They have been "delivered from the authority of darkness"* (1:13), and they are to guard against being taken captive again (Wall 1993: 105; likewise Garland 1998: 141–42). "Take captive" is probably the best translation of συλαγωγέω (*sylagōgeō*), since this verse is so parallel with Gal. 4:3, where people are said to have been "held in bondage under the elemental things of the world." This last phrase also occurs in Col. 2:8 (Barth and Blanke 1994: 308). Commentators agree that Paul is not condemning all "philosophy" but only that which does not base itself on and line up with[16] this faithful teaching. Such "philosophy" is "empty deception"[17]

15. As here, βλέπετε + μή (*blepete* + *mē*) occurs in the Gospels (Matt. 24:4; Mark 13:5; Luke 21:8) as a warning to watch out for false teaching. In Acts 13:40; 1 Cor. 8:9; 10:12; Gal. 5:15; and Heb. 12:25, the phrase is a warning of danger about sin (following Pao 2012: 158 on the Pauline texts). In Phil. 3:2 Paul also uses βλέπετε when exhorting the hearers to watch out for false teachers.

16. The three uses of κατά (*kata*) in 2:8 indicate both the ground of why the teaching is false and the conformity of the teaching to false standards of truth (cf. BDAG 512, s.v. κατά B.5.δ, who says that "often" this preposition is the "norm" and "at the same time the reason, so that" the two "are merged.").

17. The "philosophy" and "empty deception" are parallel genitive substantives governed by only one article, which indicates a unity of the two (Robertson 1934: 787) or a close association of the two, so that the "philosophy" is considered to be "empty deception" (cf. D. Moo 2008: 185), though the TNIV's rendering of "hollow and deceptive philosophy" is not precise enough, since "vain" is a genitive that modifies "deception" and not "philosophy." Perhaps better is Calvin (1972: 330), Lightfoot (1875: 178), Caird (1976: 189), Sumney (2008: 130), and Pao (2012: 159), among others, who take the connecting καί (*kai*) to be epexegetical, perhaps expressing paraphrastically "philosophy that is empty deception." It is well known that at the time of Jesus the word "philosophy" could be applied to Greek philosophy or to such biblical

for three reasons: (1) because it is based on "the tradition of men" and not on the "word of God" (1:25) or true "instruction" (2:7), which they have "received" (2:7); (2) because it is based on worldly doctrine ("the elements of the world") and not on that which proceeds from heaven (cf. 3:1–2); (3) because it is not based on Christ. Rather, all knowledge is to be seen through the lens of Christ and him alone (Garland 1998: 159).

The content of this "philosophy" is "in conformity with" and "based on" (κατά, *kata*)[18] "the tradition of men" and "the elementary principles of the world." These sources of knowledge are now, at the end of verse 8, defined by what they are not: they are not based on and do not conform to the content of the teaching about Christ (not "according to Christ"). But what more can be said specifically about the content of these two sources of false knowledge? Paul stops short of further description in verses 9–15, where instead he wants to concentrate on the basis of the true teaching: Christ and his redemptive work. Then in verses 16–23 he returns to the deceptive philosophy that he has begun to introduce here in 2:8. In this concluding section to chapter 2, Paul will explain what he means by "the tradition of men" and "the principles of the world," which are both mentioned again verbatim. We will find that the first phrase is part of an OT allusion (see on 2:22), and the second is best understood against an extrabiblical Hellenistic background (see on 2:20). Both backgrounds will unfold the defective content of the "philosophy" that Paul has introduced here.

Thus the verse ends by highlighting that this false teaching is not "in conformity with" nor "based on" (κατά, *kata*) the true teaching about "Christ." This means it is a "distortion of the gospel" (Gal. 1:7) and is ultimately a "different gospel," like the false gospel taught in Galatia (Gal. 1:6; so also 1:9; cf. Dunn 1996: 136). The vain philosophy based on "the tradition of men" and "the elements of the world" has replaced Christ as the source of truth, which, as we will see, is idolatry (see on 2:22).

The verse starts with "because" (ὅτι, *hoti*) to indicate that a reason is now **2:9**
beginning to be given about what the philosophy lacks by not being based on Christ. Positively, verse 9 implies an explanation of why believers should "walk in Him [Christ]" (v. 6) and be "captivated by" Christ instead of the false philosophy. In this respect, verse 9 introduces the remainder of the segment up through verse 15, which is distinct in that it contains either repeated reference(s) to Christ or the cross, thus showing the centrality of Christ in this explanation (O'Brien 1982: 111). The implicit repetition of "walk" from verse 6 at the end of verse 8 (walk "according to Christ" in contrast to walking according to the false teaching) is the main logical point of verses 6–15. This main point in verses 6 and 8 is supported by the large section of grounding in verses 9–15.

---

notions as the Mosaic law or to Jewish sects (Essenes, Sadducees, and Pharisees; see Lightfoot 1875: 179; Barth and Blanke 1994: 309).

18. Note again BDAG (512, s.v. κατά B.5.δ), who affirm both notions.

The main reason given for why the "philosophy" is so deficient and, implicitly, why believers should "walk" not according to that philosophy but "according to Christ" is that "in Him all the fullness of Deity dwells in bodily form" (v. 10). This clause has been the subject of much discussion.

The first observation in verse 9 is that the wording builds on Col. 1:19, most of which is word-for-word reproduction in Greek of 1:19:

Colossians 1:19	Colossians 2:9
because in Him He was well pleased for all the fullness to dwell*	because in Him all the Divine fullness dwells in bodily form*
ὅτι ἐν αὐτῷ εὐδόκησεν πᾶν τὸ πλήρωμα κατοικῆσαι	ὅτι ἐν αὐτῷ κατοικεῖ πᾶν τὸ πλήρωμα τῆς θεότητος σωματικῶς
hoti en autō eudokēsen pan to plērōma katoikēsai	*hoti en autō katoikei pan to plērōma tēs theotētos sōmatikōs*

We saw that 1:19 was an allusion to Ps. 67:17–18 LXX (68:16–17 Eng.): "God was well pleased [εὐδοκέω, *eudokeō*] to dwell [κατοικέω, *katoikeō*] in it [ἐν αὐτῷ, *en autō* (Zion)]; . . . the Lord will dwell [there] forever, . . . in the holy place [קֹדֶשׁ, *qōdeš*]."[19] This allusion was applied to Christ in 1:19. The Ps. 67:17–18 LXX allusion carries over from 1:19 to 2:9.[20] God's holy of holies presence on earth was the most preeminent reality in all of Israel. So also the reason (ὅτι, *hoti*, 1:19) why Christ should "come to have first place in everything" (1:18b) is that he is the inaugurated end-time temple in which God's fullness has begun to dwell (1:19). He is the escalated form of God's presence, the true holy of holies, and as such he himself is identified with the unique tabernacling presence of God and is the most preeminent one together with God in the church and in all the cosmos. Now Paul applies this truth about Christ's preeminence as the temple from 1:18–19 and places it in contrast to the false teachers, who do not base their pseudo "philosophy and vain deception"* on Christ. This is the first suggestion that the false teaching in Colossae has to do with not focusing on Christ as the true temple. We shall see that this will soon become explicit.

The idea in 1:19 is not that God's presence is in Christ but rather "that all that God is dwells in Christ" (Sumney 2008: 74); and in 2:9, "it is not merely godlikeness that dwells in Christ, but actually the divine nature itself" (Sumney 2008: 133). In this light, since 2:9 is so verbally parallel with 1:19, the point of 2:9 is a reiteration of the point that Christ is the end-time temple in[21] whom

19. See on 1:19 and the additional notes there for arguments for the validity of this OT reference and commentators who affirm it.

20. D. Moo (2008: 193–94) and Beetham (2008: 154) also see the allusion from 1:19 carried over into 2:9 here; more recently Pao (2012: 161) sees that 2:9 "may" continue to "allude to Ps. 68:16 (67:17 LXX)." Likewise Stuhlmacher (2018: 435–37) also sees the notion that Christ taking the place of the temple in Zion is being carried over from 1:19 to 2:9.

21. The dative construction ἐν αὐτῷ (*en autō*) designates that it is the sphere of Christ's body in which the "fullness of Deity dwells," though this may be refined as designating union between Christ and God (see further below).

"the fullness of Deity dwells." Whereas "Deity" was not mentioned in 1:19, it is expressed explicitly here to make more explicit "the fullness" referred to in 1:19. The phrase πλήρωμα τῆς θεότητος (*plērōma tēs theotētos*) is an attributive genitive: "Divine fullness" (possibly a genitive of content, "fullness which is deity").[22] And it is not just part of the "Divine fullness" that dwells in Christ, but "all" of it dwells in him (BDAG 829, s.v. πλήρωμα 3, renders the phrase as "the full measure of deity"). There is a complete "union between God and Christ" (Campbell 2012: 432). This is not only an *ontological* union but also a full *identity* with the unique God of the OT who inhabited Israel's temple and would fully fill the end-time temple,[23] the latter of which is the focus here. Christ is so identified with the complete tabernacling divine presence that he must be considered to be fully Deity himself. The repeated notion of God's "glory filling the temple [or tabernacle]" is found in the Greek OT,[24] and πλήρης (*plērēs*, full)[25] is employed in some of these passages, where the temple is "full of the glory" of God (Isa. 6:1; Ezek. 43:5; 44:4; cf. Isa. 6:3). This background probably supplements the above-noted Ps. 67 LXX (68 MT, Eng.) temple allusion.[26]

The reference to "bodily form" also highlights that Christ's divine presence has not taken up abode in a physical architectural structure, as in the OT, but in Christ's own body as the new form of the temple (so D. Moo 2008: 193–94). Thus the reason why the false teaching of 2:8 is so defective is that it leaves out Christ, who is "the complete Divine fullness in bodily form." That Christ is the one in whom "Deity dwells in <u>bodily form</u>"[27] is also the reason why the Colossians should not pay attention to the false teaching and should "walk" (lead their lives) only on the basis of Christ. The false teaching is "empty," in contrast to "all the <u>fullness</u> of Deity dwelling in" Christ. The present tense "dwells" underscores the enduring reality and condition of the tabernacling divine presence that is fully expressed in the incarnate Christ (cf. D. Moo 2008: 196), both during his earthly ministry, at his death, and in his resurrection and exalted state. The focus here, however, is on the latter state, since that

22. Many have argued that θεότης (*theotēs*) is to be distinguished from θειότης (*theiotēs*), the former referring specifically to the divine being and the latter to a divine attribute. However, the two words are nearly synonymous (see Barth and Blanke 1994: 312, 361–63).

23. See Bauckham (2008: passim) for the distinction between a focus on the being of God and the unique identity of God, and the emphasis in the NT being on the latter with respect to Christ's identification with the God of the OT.

24. In this respect, see uses of πίμπλημι (*pimplēmi*, a synonym of the πλήρωμα/πληρόω [*plērōma*/*plēroō*] word group), in Exod. 40:34–35; 1 Kings 8:10–11; 2 Chron. 7:2; Hag. 2:7; Ezek. 10:3–4; cf. Isa. 6:4.

25. Πλήρης (*plērēs*) is part of the same word group as πλήρωμα/πληρόω (*plērōma*/*plēroō*) in Col. 2:9 and almost synonymous with it.

26. Wall (1993: 110) sees "fullness" here to be broadly understood against the background of God's glorious presence in the OT temple (he cites Isa. 6:3 for this), which now completely fills Jesus as the new "temple," though he sees no allusion to the Ps. 68 (67 LXX) text.

27. Here σωματικῶς (*sōmatikōs*) is adverbial, modifying the verb "dwells," and could be rendered "in him all the divine fullness dwells bodily" or "in him dwells bodily all the divine fullness."

is the time referent of all the "in him" statements in verses 9–12 (though it is true that Christ began to be the temple during his earthly ministry, this was escalated in his death and especially in his resurrection).[28] This also means that the divine Christ, the Son of God, will forever exist in a human body (Harris 2010: 89). In contrast to the errorists' denigration of the physical body (see 2:16–23), the point here is that Christ's physical body was and is the sacred abode of deity and not a detriment to his divine status; in fact, his fleshly body was necessary for the eschatological presence and power of God to be expressed, especially in reclaiming people from sin and the malevolent powers that held them captive (which is part of the point in v. 10a; Gupta 2013a: 92).

It is possible to translate σωματικῶς (*sōmatikōs*) as "substantially," which would indicate that Christ as the divine presence in the new temple is the fulfillment of the partial presence of God in Israel's old temples, which pointed forward to the "full measure" of the divine presence in the end-time temple. The use of σῶμα (*sōma*) in Col. 2:17 could support such a use here, since there it refers to Christ being the "substance" (or "reality") of what the OT types of the OT law foreshadowed.

On balance, the translation of "bodily" (referring to the incarnation) may be preferable over "substantially" (referring to typological substance replacing the shadows), though the latter is a viable option because of its fit with a concept of temple typology, especially in line with the typological use of σῶμα (*sōma*) in 2:17.[29]

2:10a Now in verses 10–11, three effects or results of Christ being the very tabernacling presence of God are stated. The first part of verse 10 says that Christ's divine temple presence has resulted in believers "in him" (possibly "through him")[30] having "been made full" or "having become filled" (for the latter, see ESV, NET). Viable also is the NIV 1984's rendering, "You have been given fullness in Christ." The perfect tense focuses on the "full" condition that believers are in. Some have acknowledged the possible problem if this means that Christians "have all the fullness of deity within them, just as Christ does" in 2:9–10 (Lincoln 2000: 623; cf. Peake 1970: 524). But commentators generally

28. Campbell (2013: 35) views the present tense as indicating a stative notion, but views it as referring only to the "post-incarnational state."

29. O'Brien (1982: 112–13) makes the same preference but sees the typological view as a close second, though those affirming this second view (such as Calvin 1972: 331; Caird 1976: 191–92; Garland 1998: 146) do not relate it to temple typology. Some have proposed that σωματικῶς (*sōmatikōs*) refers to deity "expressing itself through the Body [of Christ, i.e., the Church]" (cited by Moule 1957: 92, who lists commentators holding the view, though he does not prefer it). This view can appeal to σῶμα (*sōma*) as referring to the church within this epistle (1:18, 24; 2:19; 3:15). The problem with this view, however, is that it makes 2:10 redundant, and it seems strange to express such a view through the adverbial form. See Barth and Blanke (1994: 312–15) for review and evaluation of all the major alternative identifications for σωματικῶς.

30. Most translations express a spheric sense of ἐν (*en*), "in him," while the HCSB has an instrumental idea ("by him"), though the NLT combines both, "you are complete through your union with Christ" (cf. Campbell 2012: 181, who affirms the idea of "union"). It is possible that the spheric or incorporative sense is the focus and the instrumental is secondarily in mind.

equate the "filling" here with the reality that the fullness of salvation is only in Christ (e.g., O'Brien 1982: 113) or that it meets all their spiritual needs in contrast to the false teachers' proposals (Peake 1970: 524). These general, vague proposals are understandable, since Pauline theology would not let the interpreter think the believer could be divine like Christ! But these proposals are too general and do not satisfactorily answer the problem just addressed. However, if the "fullness" that is "in Him" (v. 9) expresses Christ's divine presence as the true temple, then it is likely that "[believers who] have been filled in him"* (2:10) has something to do also with the filling of the temple by Christ, which is borne out by the verbal parallelism in Greek between verse 9 and verse 10a:[31]

Colossians 2:9	Colossians 2:10a
because in him all the divine fullness dwells in bodily form*	and in him you have been filled*
ὅτι ἐν αὐτῷ κατοικεῖ πᾶν τὸ πλήρωμα τῆς θεότητος σωματικῶς	καὶ ἐστὲ ἐν αὐτῷ πεπληρωμένοι
hoti en autō katoikei pan to plērōma tēs theotētos sōmatikōs	*kai este en autō peplērōmenoi*

Believers' union with Christ means that, just as Christ has become the divine temple presence of God, so they have *begun* to be identified with and to experience the effect of being "filled" with that tabernacling presence of Christ's divine "fullness,"[32] just as their union with him in verses 11–13 means they have been circumcised in him, buried with him, and raised with him (Campbell 2013: 35–36). Thus verse 10a is to be understood in line with other Pauline passages about the church being identified with the temple because believers are in Christ. This is similar to 1 Cor. 3 and Eph. 2, where Christ is the foundation of the new end-time temple and believers are built on him as a part of that temple (cf. 1 Cor. 3:10–17; Eph. 2:19–22). In Eph. 1:22–23 "the church" is "the fullness [τὸ πλήρωμα, *to plērōma*] of Him [Christ] who fills [τοῦ . . . πληρουμένου, *tou . . . plēroumenou*] all things [not only the church] in every way."* This is developed in Eph. 3:16–19, where God's "glory" is given to believers, and "the Spirit's" work in them results in Christ "dwelling," which leads to saints "comprehending" that they are part of the temple in Christ (v. 18) and "know[ing] . . . the love of Christ, in order that you should be filled [πληρωθῆτε, *plērōthēte*] unto all the fullness [τὸ πλήρωμα, *to plērōma*] of God."* Ephesians 3:16–19 is a development of the temple text in Eph. 2:20–22, so that, in light of its parallel with Col. 2:9–10, it should not be surprising that the "filling" language in the latter passage should also be about Christ

31. Following O'Brien (1982: 103), who notes the lexical parallelism but does not mention the theme of the temple.

32. A similar pattern is apparent in Ps. 64:5 LXX: "Blessed is he whom you have chosen and adopted; he shall dwell in your courts; we shall be filled [πλησθησόμεθα, *plēsthēsometha*] with the goodness of your house, your holy temple" (see similarly Ps. 65:4 MT).

filling the temple of believers[33] and that this "filling" is equivalent to the glory of deity filling the church.

Many translations of verse 10 have "You have become *complete* in him," but this conveys the possible notion of final eschatological perfection. Instead, the idea here is that of the church beginning to be identified with and thus filled with Christ's tabernacling divine presence as the end-time temple,[34] as is the case in the 1 Cor. 3 and Eph. 2 passages. In the light of the Ps. 67 LXX temple allusion in 1:19, the continuation of that idea in 2:9 and on into verse 10 here suggests that the church has begun to be identified with the latter-day temple because of its union with Christ, being "in Him."[35] Accordingly, this does not refer to an eschatologically consummate completeness, as does Col. 1:28 ("that we may present every man complete in Christ").

2:10b I think there is solid footing for discerning the temple notions in verses 9 and 10a, which continue the temple idea from 1:19, itself already subtly continued in 1:22 (temple sacrifices); 1:23; and 2:7; yet a link with believers and the temple has occurred early on already in 1:9 (see my comments, including the additional note, on that verse). We will now speculate a bit further on the possible continuation of this idea into 2:10b–11. But at this point let us ask, Why would Paul be concerned with this theme and why is it worth investigating the possible continuation of this idea in verses 10b and 11? We believe that Paul has been focusing on the true temple of Christ, of which believers are a part, in order to counter the errorists' claims that they experience visions of and participate in the worship of the heavenly temple. These purportedly elite so-called Christians are claiming to have unique experiences of the heavenly temple that enhance their religion in a way that leaves other Christians disenfranchised. They believe that ascetic practices prepare them for such temple experiences and visions, which they regard as necessary to be a part of the true temple. It is this false claim on which verses 16–23 elaborate. And it is this claim that 2:9–15 (esp. vv. 9–11) is countering by affirming

33. For connection of Eph. 3:16–19 to the concept of the temple, see the additional note on 1:23a. Macaskill (2013: 152–53) declares, "The dimensional language of verse 18 has obvious associations with the measuring of the temple in Ezekiel 47–48." Macaskill (2013: 149–51) also thinks Eph. 1:23 pertains to filling the temple with divine glory. Even the references to "His fullness" in John 1:16 and "the fullness of Christ" in Eph. 4:13 are linked to temple portrayals (on John 1:16, see Carson 1991: 126–34). Note that Eph. 4:13 has its purpose in 4:14–15, which concludes with Christ, who is then associated with the church as a temple (4:16). Note the parallel wording between the temple portrayal in Eph. 2:21–22 and 4:16, which shows that the latter passage continues the temple portrayal from 2:21–22: οἰκοδομή + συναρμολογέω + αὔξω or noun form + πᾶς, *oikodomē* + *synarmologeō* + *auxō* + *pas*. (I am indebted to my student Brandon Levering for this observation.) Note also the identification of Christ and his followers as both a part of the same temple in 1 Pet. 2:4–8; cf. also John 2:19–22 with John 7:37–39.

34. The perfect tense πεπληρωμένοι (*peplērōmenoi*) conveys the idea of a condition or state of "filling."

35. Beetham (2008: 154) likewise argues that the "echo" of Ps. 67:17 LXX at Col. 1:19 informs the interpretation of Col. 2:9–10a. He says the Colossians' being "filled in him" suggests that they "in a derivative fashion have become a locus of the presence of God, a temple."

that believers have already achieved eschatological fullness in the new, true temple in Christ, which fullness will be consummated at Christ's return (cf. 3:1–5). It is important to recall that 2:6–23 is the heart of the epistle, so it is significant that the focus on true versus false temple worship occurs in this crucial section of the epistle. The burden of this proposal will be to show that false heavenly temple worship is, in fact, what is primarily in mind in verses 16–23. Thus the point of verse 10a is not merely that "fullness" (defined in various vague ways) can be found only in Christ and not in the false teachers' extra regulations (so many commentators), but that their participation in Christ as the true temple is all they need to experience the eschatological tabernacling presence of God.

The second part of verse 10 expresses a second result of Christ's divine presence as the true temple: "He is the head over all rule and authority." This develops two earlier notions from chapter 1. First, 1:16 has affirmed that because Christ is the divine Creator (v. 16a) of "all things" (v. 16c), then it is deducible that "thrones or dominions or rulers or authorities" (whether good or evil) are part of the creation, which is not equal to him but under him as Creator. The same words for "rule" (ἀρχή, *archē*) and "authority" (ἐξουσία, *exousia*) found in 2:10 also appear in 1:16 as part of what Christ has created. Now, what was implicit in 1:16 is brought to the fore: since Christ is the divine Creator, he is ruler "over all" the creation, including "all rule and authority." In 1:15 we have found that, in light of the emphasis on "firstborn" being about "supremacy over," the genitival phrase "firstborn <u>of all creation</u>" (πρωτότοκος πάσης κτίσεως, *prōtotokos pasēs ktiseōs*) was best taken as a genitive of subordination, "firstborn <u>over</u> all creation," instead of more generally as a genitive of reference, "firstborn with reference to all creation." Here also in 2:10 the phrase ἡ κεφαλὴ πάσης ἀρχῆς καὶ ἐξουσίας (*hē kephalē pasēs archēs kai exousias*) is the same kind of genitive and should be translated, "head <u>over</u> all rule and authority." We shall see in verse 15 below that "the rulers and authorities" there are evil spiritual forces, which Christ defeated at the cross. Here the same reference anticipates verse 15 by generally saying that because Christ is divine (v. 9), he is the absolute ruler even over evil, unseen heavenly powers.[36] Then verse 15 shows how in particular he exercised that

36. As noted in 1:16 (see my comments there), 1:13 has already anticipated that the "authorities" include evil powers: God "delivered us from the authority of darkness" (τῆς ἐξουσίας τοῦ σκότους, *tēs exousias tou skotous*). See on 1:16 for references in Ephesians expressing that the "rulers and authorities" include evil heavenly forces (esp. Eph. 2:2; 3:10; 6:12) and for references from Daniel (OG and Theod.) which contain relevant references. The only place in all of the Greek OT where θρόνοι (*thronoi*) occurs with ἀρχή (*archē*) and ἐξουσία (*exousia*) is in Dan. 7:9, 12, 14, referring to both good and evil earthly and angelic authorities. And Col. 1:16 is the only place in the NT where the threefold combination occurs. Further parallel with the prophecy of Dan. 7:27 is found in the reference to "all rulers" (πᾶσαι αἱ ἀρχαί, *pasai hai archai*, Theod.) or "all authorities" (πᾶσαι αἱ ἐξουσίαι, *pasai hai exousiai*, OG), who are "subjected" to God or the Son of Man or both, which has unique analogy with Col. 2:10 (πάσης ἀρχῆς καὶ ἐξουσίας, *pasēs archēs kai exousias*), which expands on the phrases in Col. 1:16. In this light, Col. 1:16 and 2:10 echo the expressions in Dan. 7, affirming Christ as the fulfillment of that prophecy.

divine rulership when he came as “the fullness of deity in bodily form” to earth and conquered these powers at the cross.

Not surprisingly, the reference to “head” (κεφαλή, *kephalē*) is connected to the meaning of the same word for “head” in Col. 1:18: “He is also head of the body, the church.” In 1:18 we concluded that Christ as “head” indicated primarily the notion of headship, yet suggesting that the authority was expressed through directing and causing growth of the church body into a unified whole. However, here in 2:10 only the idea of authority is expressed, as confirmed from 2:15, since Christ is “head over” evil forces as a victor and the church is not in mind, as it was in 1:18. Accordingly, Christ is in a position of authority over what is good, the church, and over what is evil, the invisible satanic powers. Of course, 1:15–17 has affirmed his divine authority over every single thing in creation.

Verse 10 is parallel to Eph. 1:21–23, where also Christ is said to be “above all rule and authority” and “head” (though of the church), and the church is “His body, the fullness of the one filling all things in every way.”* There, in context, it is through Christ’s sovereignty over the bridgehead of the church that the evil heavenly powers will continue to be subdued.

But how could Christ as the “head” relate to the central temple notion in Col. 2:9–10a, which we have been proposing? Since Christ has become the divine ruler in the end-time temple, he has authority not only over his people but also over pseudo-members of the covenant community, the false teachers, behind whom stand the evil angelic “rulers and authorities” (2:15). In fact, the continuation of the Ps. 67:17–18 LXX (68:16–17 Eng.) allusion from 1:19 in 2:9 also suggests this, since in the psalm the climax of God’s tabernacling in the temple occurs directly following his defeat of the enemy (in LXX: Ps. 67:19; also 67:21–25, 29–30; in Eng.: 68:18, 20–24, 28–29).[37] The same connection occurs here in Col. 2:10b.

Generally the OT mention of God dwelling in his temple includes the idea that he is the king enthroned there in a victorious position over his people, after defeating all enemies (cf. Exod. 15:1–16 with 15:17–18; cf. also Pss. 78:65–69; 132:13–18).[38] Some of these temple portrayals include God enthroned above angelic or heavenly powers.[39] In this light, it is natural that Paul sees Christ in his latter-day temple as the “head” of the evil powers.

2:11a *Overview of the verse.* Could the idea of the temple still be in mind? Perhaps it is an overreading to think so. But even if the temple is not in mind, the third

37. See esp. the use of the victory text of Judg. 5:12 in Ps. 67:19 LXX.

38. See the additional notes about why Christ as “head” relates to his authoritative position in the end-time temple, which entails his defeat of evil powers and reign over them.

39. Psalm 67:18–19 LXX (68:17–18 Eng.) also envisions Yahweh, with whom Christ is now identified, as enthroned in the heavenly temple amid myriads of angels. Likewise Isa. 6:1–7 and Ezek. 1 picture God enthroned above the angels, which Rev. 4–5 also portrays by way of allusion to Isa. 6 and Ezek. 1 and where Christ is also enthroned with God (e.g., see allusion to Isa. 6:2 in Rev. 4:8 and allusion to Ezek. 1:10 in Rev. 4:7). These passages in Isaiah, Ezekiel, and Revelation are all visions of the heavenly temple.

result is now given of what "all the Divine fullness dwelling bodily" in Christ entails. But if this is so, then Christ's "fullness" as the new temple may still be in mind, and the verse explains one more result that Christ being the temple has brought about. In particular, Christ as the divine presence of the temple may continue in the introductory phrase "in whom [Christ] also" (ἐν ᾧ καί, *en hō kai*). The καί (*kai*) could be translated here as "also" or "likewise" (cf. BDAG 495–96, s.v. b2) and functions adverbially to modify the verb "circumcised." The adverb may advance on to a completely new and unexpected thought beyond that of 2:9–10, as some contend (e.g., O'Brien 1982: 115), or it may continue the thought of verses 9–10:[40] "in Him [Christ]" may thus continue to refer to Christ as the new temple, as in 2:9 and 2:10, which would be best expressed by "in whom likewise you were circumcised" (note that 2:9 and 2:10 each refer to the thought of Christ ["in Him"] as the temple, and verse 11 likewise begins with "in Him").

If the thought of Christ as the temple continues on into Col. 2:11a in this manner, then the background against which to understand verse 11 may be that of circumcision taking place in the temple, which was the custom in Israel (as evident in Luke 2:22–39). In fact, "made without hands" (ἀχειροποίητος, *acheiropoiētos*) always refers elsewhere to the new, end-time temple (sometimes the temple in Christ),[41] which was built not by humans but by God. The very same word occurs in Col. 2:11, which is the only place where the word is not explicitly accompanied by a word for the temple. The point, at the least, is that circumcision in Christ was done by God and not by humans. The observation, however, that the word elsewhere in the NT (two times) and its synonymous

40. Pao likewise argues that the adverbial καί (*kai*) connects verse 10's positive "filling" metaphor with the negative picture of "stripping off." If so, the two metaphors are two sides of one coin. Nevertheless, Pao (2012: 164), like O'Brien (1982: 115), says the introduction of circumcision is unexpected. Other commentators say that spiritual circumcision is introduced here as a polemic against the false teachers, who were saying that physical circumcision was necessary to be truly initiated into the Christian faith (e.g., Caird 1976: 192); though this may be speculation, since nowhere does Colossians say this, we believe there may be merit to it.

41. In Dan. 2:34, 45 the "stone cut without hands" (though not using the precise word ἀχειροποίητος) that smashed the statue, representing evil nations, indicated that the stone was of divine, not human origin. It represented not only God's end-time kingdom (Dan. 2:44–45) but also the kingdom conceived as a growing eschatological temple (see further Beale 2004: 144–53). This very passage is applied to Christ as the new temple in Matt. 21:42–44//Luke 20:17–18, where Christ who defeats his enemies is in the immediate contexts of those passages (Beale 2004: 183–88). Note likewise the use of ἀχειροποίητος to refer to an end-time temple "made without hands" in the NT: in Mark 14:58 a "temple . . . made without hands" is contrasted with a temple "made with hands," the former referring to a temple built by God and not humans. So likewise 2 Cor. 5:1 (see Beale 2004: 256–58). Virtually identical is Heb. 9:11, 14, referring to a temple "not made with hands" (οὐ χειροποιήτου, *ou cheiropoiētou*). Similarly, Acts 17:24 speaks of "God" who "does not dwell *in temples made with hands*" (οὐκ ἐν χειροποιήτοις ναοῖς, *ouk en cheiropoiētois naois*) and Acts 7:48, "the Most High does not dwell in handmade houses"* (οὐχ ὁ ὕψιστος ἐν χειροποιήτοις κατοικεῖ, *ouch ho hypsistos en cheiropoiētois katoikei*; see Beale 2004: 230–32 and 216–29). Similarly cf. Barn. 6.14–15 and 16.1–10 (cf. Schweizer 1982: 141); Philo, *Spec.* 1.66–67. Interestingly, the word "handmade" (χειροποίητος, *cheiropoiētos*) refers to an idol's temple in Isa. 16:12 LXX.

equivalents (only twice in Daniel, twice in Acts, and twice in Hebrews) refer only to a God-built temple may suggest an association with the temple in our present text. The point would be that now spiritual circumcision has taken place "in Christ," the temple, and since the temple of Christ is "made without hands" (ἀχειροποίητος), so is the "circumcision" that takes place in this new temple "made without hands" (ἀχειροποίητος). This would also fit well with the typology of the physical temple pointing to the spiritual temple in Christ (in the background in 1:19 and 2:9) and the typology of physical circumcision pointing to spiritual circumcision, which we will argue is in mind in 2:11 and 13.

Interestingly, in this respect, Luke 2:21–39 is the only passage in the Bible (and, as far as I can tell, in Judaism) that says that it was a "custom" that a child should be *circumcised in the temple* "eight days" after the child's birth. Indeed, in this passage Luke says that Jesus's parents followed this "custom of the Law" and had him circumcised in "the temple" (2:27), after the prescribed period, "according to the Law of the Lord" (2:39; also 2:22–23). This is not only the sole reference to "circumcision" in the "temple" (cf. 2:27, 37) as a "custom," but it also is the only reference to "Jesus," identified as "Christ" (see 2:26), undergoing "circumcision" in the "temple." This event of Christ's *presence at the time of his circumcision in the temple* (2:27) was immediately interpreted to indicate Jesus's future role in accomplishing "salvation" (2:30), vindication (2:34), and "redemption" (2:38) for Israel. The unique wording and theme (even including the idea of redemption) in common between Luke 2 and Col. 2:11 suggests that Colossians at this point is echoing the Luke passage (in its oral form). For this reason O'Brien (1982: 117), following Bruce (1984: 234), says that Christ underwent circumcision at the cross, "of which his literal circumcision [in Luke 2] was at best a [typological] token by way of anticipation,"[42] though Bruce and O'Brien do not comment on the possible common temple theme. At first glance, the phrase "circumcision of Christ" sounds like it could refer to the account of Christ's infant circumcision in the temple. Apparently because of this, some commentators immediately discount this impression, since they believe it to be obvious that Paul is not referring to this event.[43] However, these commentators do not reflect on whether this early event could be a foreshadowing of a greater event in Christ's career, his death.

The circumcising occurred "in Him" (ἐν ᾧ, *en hō*, Col. 2:11), which either means by the *instrumentation* of Christ or *in the sphere* of Christ, though the focus is on the latter, in the sense of union with Christ (cf. Campbell 2013: 36). This is union with Christ as the temple. Thus the third result of Christ's being the full latter-day divine presence of God in the temple (v. 9)

42. Similarly the Catholic Church (1994: 133) also views Christ's circumcision in Luke 2:21 as "prefiguring that 'circumcision of Christ' which is Baptism" (citing Col. 2:11–13). The collect for January 1 ("The Circumcision of Christ") in the Book of Common Prayer (BCP 2012) compares the infant Christ's circumcision to "the true circumcision of the Spirit" of the believer. Foster (2016: 264), without explanation, says that "the circumcision of Christ" "is not a reference to the story of the physical circumcision of Jesus as narrated in Luke's Gospel (Luke 2:21–24, 39)."

43. E.g., see Peake 1970: 525; Talbert 2007: 214.

is his "circumcising" his people in that temple and making them clean to be in that temple.

Exodus 12:48 establishes an ordinance to be observed in following generations: "If a stranger [Gentile, LXX = "proselyte"] sojourns with you, and celebrates the Passover to the LORD, let all his males be circumcised, and then let him come near to celebrate it; and he shall be like a native of the land. But no uncircumcised person may eat of it" (cf. Num. 9:14). The "drawing near" is coming to the temple, where the Passover lamb was sacrificed throughout Israel's generations.[44] Thus Gentiles had to be "circumcised" in order to be clean, to be qualified to enter into the temple courts, and to celebrate the Passover sacrifice.

Intriguingly, Ezek. 44:7–9 says that part of Israel's sin was to allow Gentiles who were "uncircumcised in heart and uncircumcised in flesh" to enter Israel's old "sanctuary." In the future, however, the Ezekiel passage says that no Gentiles "uncircumcised in heart and uncircumcised in flesh"[45] will be allowed to enter God's eschatological "sanctuary." This text is not saying that no Gentiles will be allowed to enter into the end-time temple, but rather only those who are circumcised will enter. This is the only OT passage suggesting that Gentiles need to be spiritually circumcised in the latter days, and especially circumcised to be clean to enter in the new, end-time temple,[46] which I am contending is the point of Col. 2:11 (cf. 2:13). This is the same latter-day temple that the "LORD God" and the "prince" of Israel[47] will also enter (Ezek. 44:2–3).

Strikingly, Qumran (1QS 5.5) says that a faithful Israelite must "circumcise the foreskin of his sinful inclination and of his stiff neck in order to lay a foundation of truth," which is referred to as "the house of truth" (1QS 5.6) that is "founded on truth" and is a "foundation of the holy of holies for Aaron, . . . the precious cornerstone, . . . the most holy dwelling" (1QS 8.5–8). This is a spiritual view of circumcision for members of the end-time covenant community;[48] its goal is to establish a spiritual temple for "holiness" (1QS 5.6) and "perfection" (1QS 9.6), in order to form a corporate "holy of holies" (1QS 9.6), much like that in Col. 2:10–11 (following García Martínez 1996).

44. So Deut. 16:2, 5–6; 2 Chron. 30:5, 15–19; 35:8–11, 16; the Passover sacrifice will also take place in the latter-day temple (Ezek. 45:21).

45. The phrase "uncircumcised in flesh" (ἀπερίτμητος σαρκί, *aperitmētos sarki*) is synonymous with the phrase "uncircumcison of flesh" (τῇ ἀκροβυστίᾳ τῆς σαρκός, *tē akrobystia tēs sarkos*) in Col. 2:13. If the Ezekiel text contributes any background, then only the spiritual circumcision would be in mind, since, as we will see, spiritual circumcision in Christ fulfills the type of physical circumcision.

46. Philo (*QG* 3.48) asserts that one of the purposes of circumcision in Israel was "with a view to cleanliness, . . . [to be able to] enter into the courts of the temple" (cf. Deut. 23:1 [23:2 MT, LXX]), which likely refers to one who is emasculated as not being able to enter into the temple in "the assembly of the LORD."

47. Cf. Ezek. 34:24 and 37:25, where there will be an eschatological "David," who is called a "prince" (same Hebrew word for "prince" as in 44:3).

48. Interestingly, the edition of Qumran documents by Wise, Abegg, and Cook (2005) includes "Gentile proselytes" as part of the community and thus among those needing this "circumcision."

As noted above, it shall be found in Col. 2:16–23 below that the false "philosophy" was a fundamentally wrong understanding of the meaning and application of OT law for the new age. This appears to be part of the erroneous Jewish doctrine that focused on the continuing validity of the law and its institutions instead of Christ as the epitome of divine revelation (e.g., see N. Wright 1986: 23–30). In response to such false teaching, Col. 1:1–2:11 expresses at various points that Christ is the fulfillment of OT prophecy, types, and the wisdom of the law, so that one should see no need to go back to practicing aspects of the law that have now found their full realization in Christ. In their identification with Christ, believers share in this fulfillment. We have seen in verses 9–11, in particular, that Christ's divine presence in the end-time temple is the NT reality to which the OT physical temples pointed. If we are correct in tracing the temple theme in these verses, we want again to ask, How might this add further to understanding how Paul is responding to the false teaching? It is likely that 2:18 is referring to people who "delight in asceticism and worship of angels, which things he has seen by entering [into the heavenly temple?], puffed up by his fleshly mind."* If this translation that includes the "temple" is correct (see further on 2:18), then Paul's emphasis is a contrast with imperfect heavenly temple worship of angels, with the true temple being completely filled by Christ's presence, in which believers are sufficiently "filled" also as a part of the temple.[49] It is the fullness of Christ's tabernacling presence only that should be worshiped.

The fulfillment of what the temple institution pointed to is not only introduced in 2:9–11 but also verses 11–13 introduce circumcision as an OT institution that is a type, which finds its fulfillment in Christ and believers. "In Him [they] were also circumcised <u>with a circumcision made without hands</u>," which is an implied contrast to "circumcision . . . by human hands" in Eph. 2:11, the latter of which refers to ethnic Jews. "A circumcision made without hands" expresses the manner in which the circumcising took place.[50] The word "handmade" (χειροποίητος, *cheiropoiētos*) always refers to idols in the Greek OT and is without exception a negative reference, with overtones of idolatry, in the NT (see further Beale 2004: 224–25). Thus the implied reference to "circumcision made with hands" in Col. 2 indicates that to continue

49. See on 2:17 and 21 for suggestion of a temple context. Part of the false teaching may have required circumcision (which is debated among commentators) in order to be qualified for participation in temple worship, since this was an OT requirement, and one particular strain of Judaism affirmed that angels were circumcised from the beginning, and for Israel to be in the presence of God and "his holy angels," they had to be circumcised (Jub. 15.27, following in part Gupta 2013a: 93, 118n7). Recall that Philo (*QG* 3.48) asserts that one of the purposes for circumcision was to be clean in order to enter into the temple courts for worship.

50. "With a circumcision" (περιτομῇ, *peritomē*) following "you were circumcised" (περιετμήθητε, *perietmēthēte*) is a cognate dative, which typically emphasizes the action of the verb, usually expressing the manner of the verb (so Wallace 1996: 168–69). Thus the full dative phrase περιτομῇ ἀχειροποιήτῳ (*peritomē acheiropoiētō*) likely expresses manner, though it possibly could indicate the means by which the "circumcising" takes place.

to affirm circumcision as the true identity marker of God's new-covenant people is idolatrous (Pao 2012: 165 agrees). This further enforces the notion that it is idolatrous to continue to trust in the OT "shadows" once their fulfillment has come.[51] Thus the aberrant teaching confronting the Colossians is not only false but also idolatrous. Hence the Colossians should not follow such teaching. Verses 16–23 give further details of the "shadows" (cf. v. 17) in which trust should no longer be placed (see, e.g., dietary laws, special cultic feast days, Sabbaths).

These external rites of the law, of which circumcision is a classic representative, are no longer necessary because their redemptive-historical purpose was to function as a "shadow of things about to come, that is, the [substantial] body of Christ"* (Col. 2:17). In one way or another, Paul understood that the various external expressions of the OT law pointed to the coming Messiah, who has now arrived. Therefore, the law's preparatory adumbrating function has come to an end, since the messianic "substance" to which it points has arrived. The idea here is very similar to that in Matt. 5:17: Jesus "fulfill[s] . . . the Law [and] the prophets" by fulfilling in his actions and words the OT's direct verbal prophecies, foreshadowing events (e.g., the Passover lamb) and institutions (e.g., sacrifices and temple), the ultimate meaning of the law, and the true and enduring authority of the OT (for the full argument, see Carson 1995: 140–45).

Accordingly, in 2:11–13 Paul views the external rite of circumcision, where a piece of flesh is stripped off, to be a typological pointer to the greater redemptive reality of the entire body of Christ and his followers being "circumcised" or "cut off" from the old sinful world and set apart to a new one.[52] Saints have been "circumcised with a circumcision made without hands, <u>in the putting off of the body of the flesh</u>." The "circumcision <u>without hands</u>" (ἀχειροποίητος, *acheiropoiētos*) refers either to Christ as the agent of the circumcision or, more probably, implies God (through the Spirit) as the agent,[53] especially in light of Rom. 2:29, "Circumcision is that which is of the heart, by the Spirit and not by the letter."

"The removal of the body of flesh." The word ἀπέκδυσις (*apekdysis*) in the **2:11b**
dative explains the further manner in which the circumcising was done[54] and conveys the notion of unclothing, stripping, or undressing, which will become clearer in 2:15 and 3:9–10, where the verbal form of the word occurs (see my

51. This identification with idolatry is developed further in Col. 2:18, 22–23; see Beale 2007: 860–62.

52. See Pao (2012: 166) on the notion of going from the lesser rite of circumcision, in which a piece of flesh is removed, to the full body of Christ being stripped.

53. We noted above that divine agency was part of the point of the four uses of the same word in the NT and the other six synonymous uses in Dan. 2, Acts, and Hebrews.

54. Ἐν + τῇ ἀπεκδύσει (*en* + *tē apekdysei*) is parallel with the directly preceding dative clause, "circumcision made without hands," also modifying the verb "circumcised," probably indicating the "manner" of how the verbal action is carried out; yet as with the preceding phrase, it could express the instrumentation of the verb.

comments on those verses; also cf. BDAG 100, s.v. ἀπέκδυσις). The clothing that is taken off is "the body of the flesh" (τοῦ σώματος τῆς σαρκός, *tou sōmatos tēs sarkos*).

Is it Christ's followers who are the objects of the stripping, or is it Christ himself at the cross? Commentators differ on the answer, since the identification is not clear. The answer is that both are stripped. Christ was stripped in his death, but since he was a corporate representative for believers, they were stripped "in Him" (cf. "in Him" at the start of 2:11 and in 2:10, 12). It is apparent that Christ is the object of the stripping, though with believers secondarily in mind. This is evident from the following observations: (1) the phrase "body of flesh" occurs in the NT only in Col. 1:22, where it refers to Christ's old, earthly, and preresurrection body. The phrase occurs elsewhere in Hellenistic Judaism, where it also refers to a physical body of flesh, pointing further to the reference to Christ's earthly "fleshly body" in 1:22.[55] Paul is referring back to this phrase in 1:22 in order to develop its implications further (so Dunn 1996: 157).

Colossians 1:22	Colossians 2:11
He reconciled [you] <u>in the body of</u> his <u>flesh</u> through death.*	You were circumcised . . . in the stripping off of <u>the body of flesh</u>.*
ἀποκατήλλαξεν <u>ἐν τῷ σώματι τῆς σαρκὸς</u> αὐτοῦ διὰ τοῦ θανάτου	περιετμήθητε . . . ἐν τῇ ἀπεκδύσει τοῦ <u>σώματος τῆς σαρκός</u>
apokatēllaxen <u>en tō sōmati tēs sarkos</u> autou dia tou thanatou	*perietmēthēte . . . en tē apekdysei tou <u>sōmatos tēs sarkos</u>*

Also there is a parallel in both texts of a redemptive action by Christ: "he reconciled" and "you were circumcised." In Col. 1:22, it was by means of and in the sphere of his old body "through death" that he "reconciled" the hearers. Now this reconciliation from 1:22 is to be explained by means of the removal of Christ's old-world body from this world through his death, which makes way for his new, resurrection body. Thus Christ's death is implied because of the parallel of 1:22 with 2:11. (2) Focus on Christ as the object of the stripping could also be pointed to by its parallelism with the immediate following phrase, "the circumcision of Christ," which we will see refers to Christ being circumcised in his death (i.e., the flesh of Christ being stripped away at the cross, as O'Brien [1982: 117] contends). Note that both phrases begin with ἐν (*en*) + the dative article τῇ (*tē*) + a dative noun + a genitive noun, which shows the parallel syntactical nature, suggesting that they are parallel in content: either both phrases refer to believers or both refer to Christ (the latter we

55. The same phrase in Greek (τῷ σώματι τῆς σαρκός) occurs in 1 En. 102.5, where it refers to the fleshly body of people. So likewise in Sir. 23:16 (17 LXX) the almost identical phrase appears with the same meaning, though missing the articles. Very close also is Prov. 5:11 and Job 41:23 (41:15 LXX), where the same combination of the two Greek nouns is rendered "flesh of your [or his] body," which also refers to the physical body (the latter referring to an animal body).

prefer).[56] (3) While some think the lack of a pronoun after "flesh" differentiates it from 1:22 and suggests a reference to believers and not Christ, Paul can easily omit it here, since he has repeatedly used pronouns (three times) in the preceding verses to refer to Christ and can assume a pronoun here (these last two observations are from Pao 2012: 166).

As we have said, in Christ's corporate representative stripping, his followers are also secondarily to be seen as the object of the stripping. Instead of "body of flesh," some translations have "sinful nature" (NIV 1984, NLT) or "natural self" (NJB) or "body of the sins of the flesh" (KJV, among others, which follow MSS with a scribal addition of "sins" before "flesh"). A more straightforward reading of "the body of the flesh" is preferable because of the parallel with 1:22 and its Jewish parallels, though the genitive construction is best taken adjectivally or, more precisely, attributively, "fleshly body" (note in NET; Wallace 1996: 87).

The point in both 1:22 and here is that the "body of flesh" refers to that which is a part of the old, corrupt world. This clause in 2:11 affirms that it was such a body that was stripped from Christ at his death, and it was such a body in which he died for his people (so also Garland 1998: 147–48; Lincoln 2000: 624), and it is such a body that is "stripped off" the saints through their corporate identification with him, though this is a secondary but included idea in verse 11 (an inaugurated spiritual stripping of saints followed by a consummative spiritual and bodily unclothing at the end of the age). Referring to virtually the same thing, Rom. 7:4 says, "[Brothers], you also were made to die to the Law through the body of Christ, so that you might be joined to another, to Him who was raised from the dead" (cf. Moule 1957: 95, citing also the parallel of 1 Pet. 4:1). We will see that dying to the requirements of the law is a major issue also in Colossians (see on 2:16, 20–23).

"The circumcision of Christ." The "circumcising" of 2:11a also occurred **2:11c**
according to the manner of (ἐν, *en* + dative) "the circumcision of Christ."[57] The "circumcision of Christ" could be an objective genitive ("circumcising Christ") or a subjective genitive ("circumcision by Christ") or a possessive genitive ("Christ's circumcision" or "Christian circumcision"), though the third alternative does not preclude the second one: the circumcision belongs to and is carried out by Christ.[58] It is difficult to choose which is best. The first option is pointed to by the following (against the objections of Harris 2010: 92): (1) the initial clause of verse 11 tells the readers that they were

56. This parallelism makes it unlikely that the first phrase could refer to Christians and the second to Christ or vice versa.

57. Another cognate dative, as with "a circumcision made without hands" directly above, though it is possible to take it as "by means of." Harris (2010: 91) also suggests a dative of time or an epexegetical dative ("in a circumcision"). "The circumcision of Christ" could possibly designate the manner of the directly preceding "stripping off [of the body of the flesh]," which is a verbal noun.

58. A possessive genitive (perhaps together with a subjective genitive) is preferred by Salter (2010: 24–25), who discusses both options.

circumcised in union with Christ. That is, they were corporately identified with Christ's circumcision, so that what is now made explicit is that they were also considered to have been "circumcised" in the circumcision that happened to Christ, who was their representative in receiving this circumcision (the passive verb indicates that God is the subject performing this circumcision). (2) An objective genitive also may be suggested by observing that Christ's death is referred to twice in the directly following verse 12. That is, "having been buried" and "death" (end of v. 12) is something that happened to Christ, and not something he performed. Especially the initial phrase of verse 12, "having been buried with him in baptism," appears to be a further explanation of "the circumcision of Christ," where again Christ's "having been buried" corporately represents the saints. Since Christ is the object of being "buried" in verse 12, as are believers who are identified with him, so it is likely that Christ is the object of "circumcision" in verse 11, as are believers who are identified with him. (3) An objective genitive is also pointed to by the observation that in the twelve other occurrences in the Greek of Hellenistic Judaism and the NT, the genitive that follows περιτομή (*peritomē*) is always objective.[59] It is significant that among these objective genitive uses, two are in Paul (Rom. 2:25, 29). (4) Christ being the object of the circumcision, referring to his death, best explains the unexpected redemptive-historical "progression from circumcision to burial to resurrection in 2:11–12; . . . the sequence summarizes the essential affirmations of Christianity: Christ died, was buried, and was raised (see 1 Cor. 15:1–4)."[60]

Consequently "the circumcising of Christ" refers to his death,[61] which Paul could conceive of as taking place in the temple, according to Rom. 3:25.[62] Thus, there as here, the new temple is inaugurated in Jesus's death, not only in his resurrection, as other NT texts affirm (e.g., John 2:19–22), and which is likely included in Col. 2:9–10. Also, the "circumcising of Christ" means that he himself was stripped of his old, corrupt body, so that his part in the old world was removed (as we have seen in the preceding phrase "stripping of the fleshly body").[63] The believers' union with Christ's death means the same thing for them (so also Peake 1970: 525), though they are also set apart from the corrupt world's sin, in which they had participated, but Christ had not.[64] The old-world realm of the "flesh" includes not only the "body" of a person

59. Beetham (2008: 177) cites Exod. 4:25–26 (2×) LXX; Jer. 11:16 LXX (MT wording differs); Rom. 2:25, 29; Josephus, *Ant.* 1.192; 8.262; 12.241; 13.319; *Ag. Ap.* 2.137–38; Philo, *Spec.* 1.2. See also Odes Sol. 3 (= 11.3); Artap. 3.10. Cf. Philo, *Spec.* 1.9 (?).

60. Garland 1998: 148–49; likewise Barth and Blanke 1994: 364–65.

61. So also Moule 1957: 95–96; Lincoln 2000: 624; Garland 1998: 148.

62. In Rom. 3:25, Jesus is "displayed publicly as a mercy seat in his blood"* in the heavenly temple; see further Beale 2011: 486–92.

63. See also Moule (1957: 94–96), who takes both the "stripping of the flesh" and the "circumcision of Christ" to refer to Christ's own death.

64. Romans 8:3 states Christ's identification with the old world similarly and very carefully: God sent "His own Son in the likeness of sinful flesh and <u>as an offering</u> for sin," and as such "He condemned sin in the flesh."

but also the "mind."[65] The old "body of flesh" in itself does not necessitate that one be sinful, since Christ had such a body that was physically corruptible but was not inextricably linked to sin, though all fallen humans are under the domination of sin/flesh.[66] Christians have "stripped off the old man" from themselves (see on Col. 3:9, using the verbal form of ἀπέκδυσις, *apekdysis*), and, as we will see, have "clothed themselves with the new man"* (Col. 3:10; see below). It is because they have already been corporately stripped in Christ that they are able to strip themselves. The stripping means that the power of the old sinful world over Christians has been broken (see further on the verbal form of ἀπέκδυσις, *apekdysis*, in 2:15; so also D. Moo 2008: 200–201). As we will see on Col. 3:9–10, the "old man/self" is their identity with the fallen Adam, who corporately represented them in his action of sinning and with his subsequent condemnation. The "new man/self" is their identity with Christ, the new Adam,[67] who has corporately represented them in his act of being put to death (the focus of 2:11c here and v. 12a) and being raised from the dead (the focus of the next two verses, 2:12b–13), resulting in their forgiveness (2:13b–14) and justification (Rom. 5:17–18).[68] The stripping of Christ's fleshly body also involved the removal of his subjection to the corruptible Adamic body, which made way for him as the new Adam, with a new-creational body (cf. Dunn 1996: 158, who makes a similar point).

Also, whereas Christ immediately received a new body, they have not. As noted earlier, their circumcision by Christ has an "already" dimension, by which their spiritual identification with the old world has been stripped off, yet also the full stripping off of their physically corrupt body must await the final resurrection at the end of the age, when also their inaugurated spiritual resurrection existence will be perfected.[69]

65. Accordingly cf. "the body of the flesh" in 2:11 and "the mind of his flesh"* in 2:18.

66. Following D. Moo (2008: 200), who also cites in support the parallels of Rom. 6:6 ("body of sin"), Rom. 7:24 ("body of . . . death"), and Phil. 3:21 ("body of humiliation"*).

67. We will see that Col. 3:9–10a alludes to Adam in Gen. 1:26–28, and Col. 3:10b to the clothing of Adam and Eve in Gen. 3:7, 21. Beetham (2008: 175) also sees that Col. 3:9–10a's allusion to Gen. 1:26–27 indicates that the stripping off of the old Adam is likewise in mind in Col. 2:11. Similarly Dunn (1996: 158) and Arnold (1995: 296) see a "stripping off" of believers' solidarity with the old Adam in Col. 2:11 (cf. esp. Arnold 1995). Note Adamic allusions also in 1:6, 10, 15.

68. Even the saints' justification was something that happened first to Christ because of his resurrection (see 1 Tim. 3:16a; cf. Rom. 4:25) and because of his corporate representation of them (see further, Beale 2011: 469–97). See Rom. 5:14–19 for the parallel representative acts of disobedience by and condemnation of the first Adam and the representative obedience by and resulting justification through Christ as the last Adam (cf. also 1 Cor. 15:20–23). D. Moo (2008: 200) generally applies the first-last Adam corporate concept from Rom. 5 and 1 Cor. 15 to Col. 2:12–13 as an illustration. However, we see it actually to be implicit in Paul's mind in Col. 2:11–13, especially in the light of the parallel in 3:9–10.

69. Cf. Rom. 7:25, saying that those dwelling in the realm of the "flesh" serve "the law of sin." See Rom. 8:13, where also "living according to the flesh" is parallel with the sinful "deeds of the body." In Rom. 8:3–12 the "flesh" and the "Spirit" are opposite realms: the flesh represents the old world, sin, and death; the Spirit represents the new world and resurrection

Before leaving this discussion of circumcision, it is necessary to anticipate and address the following phrase in Col. 2:13, "in . . . the uncircumcision of your flesh." In verses 11 and 13, we have only briefly discussed how the external rite of circumcision was a pointer to the greater redemptive reality of Christ and his followers being "circumcised" or "cut off" from the old sinful world and set apart to a new one. In verse 11 we have seen that believers' redemption consists of being "circumcised with a circumcision made without hands," which has occurred by means of the "circumcision of Christ" (i.e., his death). The clause "uncircumcision of your flesh" (v. 13) appears to represent sinful unbelief, from which one needs to be "circumcised." This phrase also helps us understand how physical circumcision in the OT foreshadows the circumcision of Christ and believers (for further discussion, see excursus 4).

2:12 After explaining that the "circumcising" of verse 11a was a third result of Christ's authoritative divine status (v. 9) and having described the manner of the "circumcising" (v. 11b–c), now Paul explicitly explains the primary means or manner by which the Colossians were "circumcised" (v. 11a): they were "buried." The adverbial participle συνταφέντες (*syntaphentes*) modifies the verb "circumcised" of verse 11 and, besides being generally contemporaneous with the main verb, appears more specifically to express the manner in which the circumcising took place, though the means of the circumcising could also be in mind. Manner is pointed to by recalling that the focus of the last three adverbial dative clauses indicates the manner of the circumcising.[70] Though this may seem a fine point of Greek grammar, it makes a significant exegetical and theological difference in the way this passage understands baptism in relation to circumcision. For example, D. Moo (2008: 201) sees that the participle "burying" in baptism expresses *only* a separate but temporally contemporaneous act alongside the "circumcising." On the other hand, if the participle more specifically conveys the means or manner of the circumcising, then "buried in baptism" is part of the action or concept of the circumcising. Context is the ultimate determiner of how adverbial participles function. We have tried to understand this participle's function in connection with the way the preceding three adverbial clauses function. In addition, the following adverbial participles in verses 13b, 14a, 14b, 15a, and 15b all are generally contemporaneous but also specify some logical modification of the verb (or an action that overlaps with or explains the concept of the verb) that they modify.[71]

That saints were "buried with Him [Christ]" again shows their union with Christ.[72] Their belief in Christ means that they are identified with Christ's

---

existence. The same contrast is in Col. 2:11–13. Likewise cf. 2 Cor. 5:16–17; Gal. 4:29; 5:16, 19, 24; 1 Tim. 3:16 (on these references, see the Scripture index and corresponding discussions in Beale 2011).

70. For further elaboration of this adverbial participle, see the additional notes on 2:11–12.

71. An observation with which D. Moo (2008: 207–9) agrees in his following commentary discussion of some of the participles in verses 13–14.

72. Thus the dative αὐτῷ (*autō*) indicates that the sphere of the burying is "in" Christ.

death. Their identification with Christ's burial has occurred in "a baptizing manner" or was "by means of baptism" (the preposition + dative, ἐν τῷ βαπτισμῷ, *en tō baptismō*). Possibly both may be in mind.

In the manner of or by the instrumentation of baptism (ἐν ᾧ, *en hō*), the saints were not only "buried" but also "were raised."[73] Their resurrection also came about by "faith in the working of God,[74] who raised Him [Christ] from the dead." As their baptism identifies them with Christ's death, so it also identifies them with his resurrection. The mention of the believers' resurrection followed by Christ's resurrection probably alludes again to his representative role: because Christ has first been raised, their union "with Him" means that they also are "raised up with Him." This double mention of resurrection also reflects the intensely eschatological nature of what has happened to believers in Christ. Eschatology in the OT and Judaism was inextricably linked to resurrection. The end-time resurrection has begun in Christ, and with it the new creation (see further Beale 2011: 225–354). This notion of resurrection is highlighted even further in Col. 2:13 through mention of God "[making believers] alive together with [Christ]" (see also John 5:21; 6:63; Rom. 4:17; 8:11; 1 Cor. 15:22, 45; 2 Cor. 3:6; 1 Pet. 3:18, where ζῳοποιέω, *zōopoieō*, also occurs, though σύν [*syn*, with] is prefixed to the verb in Col. 2:13).

A number of commentators think that highlighting the idea of an inaugurated resurrection (here; 2:13; and 3:1–4) indicates non-Pauline authorship, but several scholars have rightly pointed out that such an idea is found in Paul's so-called authentic epistles (e.g., see Rom. 6:4, 11, 13; 2 Cor. 5:14–17), and so is the idea of resurrection as new creation.

Though some see βαπτισμός (*baptismos*) or βάπτισμα (*baptisma*)[75] to be an explicit reference to the physical sacramental rite of water baptism (e.g., D. Moo 2008: 202), it is probable that since the "circumcision" in Col. 2:11 is clearly spiritual, so is the "baptism" in verse 12a (so also Pao 2012: 167).

73. The dative clause ἐν ᾧ (*en hō*) in verse 12 likely refers to the directly preceding dative "in baptism" (τῷ βαπτισμῷ), so that it is baptism "in which you were also raised," though it is possible that its antecedent is the more distant "with him" (αὐτῷ), which would then mean the dative phrase in question means "in whom you were raised." On this, see the third additional note on 2:12.

74. This translation interprets the phrase πίστεως τῆς ἐνεργείας τοῦ θεοῦ (*pisteōs tēs energeias tou theou*) to be an objective genitive, "faith in God's work" in raising Jesus from the dead. It is possible that it could be a subjective genitive, "faith by God's working" in them, i.e., God's work in them brought about their faith, which could be supported by Col. 1:29, where Paul "strives according to <u>His working</u> [ἐνέργειαν αὐτοῦ, *energeian autou*], <u>which</u> mightily <u>works</u> [τὴν ἐνεργουμένην, *tēn energoumenēn*] within me"* (the parallel of Eph. 1:19 may also support a subjective genitive). The objective genitive is more probable, since the genitive after πίστις (*pistis*) in Paul typically describes the object of faith and not its source (Lightfoot 1875: 185). Sumney (2008: 140) understands πίστις (*pistis*) to mean not the believers' "faith" but "the <u>faithfulness</u> of the working of God," so that "of the working of God" would be a possessive genitive. This is possible, but if Paul had this in mind, would he not say more directly and less awkwardly "the faithfulness of God"?

75. See the second additional note on 2:12 about which of the two words is the original reading.

Nevertheless, the visible sacrament is probably in the background, since it signifies spiritual baptism.[76]

That the rite of water baptism can be explicitly said to stand in the background of spiritual baptism is apparent throughout the NT (Luke 3:16; John 1:33; Acts 1:5;[77] 11:16). Also, even closer to our passage is Jesus's statement that his suffering of death is "the baptism with which I am baptized" (Mark 10:38; so likewise Luke 12:50), which he then applies to his disciples: "You shall be baptized with the baptism with which I am baptized" (Mark 10:39).[78] If the "circumcision of Christ" (Col. 2:11) is his own death, which represents the believers' spiritual circumcision, the same spiritual reality seems to apply to the believer being "buried with [Christ] in baptism." Paul refers to believers who "by one Spirit . . . were baptized into one body" (1 Cor. 12:13). That Paul likely has a spiritual view of baptism in mind in 1 Cor. 12:13 is pointed to by 1 Cor. 10:2, where he says that Israel was "baptized into Moses in the cloud and in the sea." Here identification with Moses, Israel's leader, is primarily in mind. Particularly relevant is Gal. 3:27: "For all of you who were baptized into Christ have clothed yourselves with Christ," though one could debate whether this is spiritual or water baptism, or whether the latter stands in the background of the former, as we have argued for Col. 2:12. That Spirit baptism is the focus is apparent from the observation that Col. 2:12a speaks of actually being "buried" with Christ "in baptism, in which you were also [actually] raised up with Him through faith." One would have to have a supernatural sacramental view of water baptism to see it as the focus.[79] If the sacrament is in the background, however, then, as with John's baptism in relation to Spirit baptism (Luke 3:16; John 1:33; Acts 1:5; 11:16), so here it is a merely symbolic act signifying—not actually conveying—the reality of dying and rising with Christ in Spirit baptism.

2:13 There is now further progression (note the "and," καί, *kai*) in explaining the circumcising of believers in verse 11, which we saw was a third effect of Christ possessing "all the fullness of Deity . . . in bodily form" (v. 9). We have observed that the OT background of circumcision included a setting apart from death,

76. D. Moo (1996: 359) takes the opposite view in Rom. 6:3–4 (he sees v. 4 as an organic parallel to Col. 2:12), that water baptism is primarily in mind and a spiritual or metaphorical view of baptism is in the background (citing those holding primarily a spiritual or metaphorical view).

77. In this respect, note the close association of water baptism and "receiving the gift of the Holy Spirit" in Acts 2:38, the latter of which in context is likely equivalent to being "baptized with the Holy Spirit" in Acts 1:5 (esp. in the light of the parallel to 1:5 of receiving the Holy Spirit in 1:8).

78. Recall that βάπτισμα (*baptisma*), which may represent the original reading in Col. 2:12, is used in these Mark and Luke texts.

79. The way D. Moo (1996: 366) avoids this "supernatural sacramental" view, as held, e.g., by Catholics, is to say that Paul assumed that the believer's faith, conversion, and gift of the Spirit preceded the water rite of baptism. D. Moo's is not an exegetical judgment but a biblical-theological decision (so likewise Schreiner 1998: 305–10). D. Moo (2013: 251) draws the same conclusion about Gal. 3:27, where he also says "baptism" is "'shorthand' for the entire conversion experience" (citing in agreement those holding primarily a spiritual or metaphorical view).

sin, and the old world and a setting apart to new life (see excursus 4, "The Old Testament Background of 'the Uncircumcision of Your Flesh' in Colossians 2:13"). Verses 11–12 explicitly focus on setting apart from death, though the setting apart to life is likely implied. The conclusion of verse 12 makes explicit that circumcision, as one aspect of its meaning, signifies setting apart to life. Verse 13 continues to focus on the giving of life.

The "you being dead"* introduces a concessive idea whereby the contrary proposition of "being dead in trespasses and in the uncircumcision of your flesh"* underscores the strength of the following statement: "He made you alive with Him." This results in the following rendering: "And <u>though</u> you were dead, . . . <u>nevertheless</u> he made you alive with him"* (see further in the first additional note on 2:13).

"In trespasses" and "in the uncircumcision of your flesh" are parallel expressions. Thus they explain one another. For example, to be in the condition of the "uncircumcision of flesh" is to be dominated by the realm of sin. This confirms our earlier discussion of the phrase (see excursus 4), which is likely an analogical allusion to Gen. 17:10–27 LXX, where "the flesh [σάρξ, *sarx*] of your/his uncircumcision [ἀκροβυστία, *akrobystia*]" appears four times. As we saw, the point in Gen. 17 is that those who are in covenantal relationship with God should express that relationship through being "circumcised in the flesh of his uncircumcision [foreskin]" (e.g., Gen. 17:11). This is a symbol expressing that a true Israelite is one whose heart has been cut apart from a condition of cursing, unbelief, and actual sin, and is set apart to God. "The flesh of your <u>uncircumcision</u> [foreskin]" in Gen. 17 is likely best rendered as "your fleshly foreskin" (an attributed genitive) or "your uncircumcised flesh" (adjectival or attributive genitive). Paul's phrase, "the uncircumcision [foreskin] of your flesh" could also be respectively understood as "your uncircumcised flesh" (attributed genitive) or "your fleshly uncircumcision [foreskin]" (adjectival or attributive genitive).[80] The latter is probably best, since there appears to be a parallelism with "the body of the flesh" in Col. 2:11, which is best seen as an adjectival genitive ("fleshly body"). Thus "fleshly <u>body</u>" in 2:11 and "fleshly <u>foreskin</u>" in 2:13 are synonymous (contra Harris 2010: 95) and refer to the old, corrupt Adamic body. Paul compares physical circumcision to the spiritual reality of the new covenantal relationship with Christ. When believers are identified by faith with Christ's death, which "cut him off" (= "the circumcision of Christ") from his portion in the old world and led to his resurrection, they are likewise "cut off" from the old world and subsequently raised (the point of 2:11–13). Paul's reference to the "removal of the fleshly body"* in 2:11 anticipates the allusion to Gen. 17 in Col. 2:13, where also "fleshly foreskin" is part of the description of the symbolic corruptible condition directly preceding circumcision.

If verse 13 is parallel with the similar concessive clause in 1:21–22, then the reference here to "trespasses and the uncircumcision of your flesh"* also

80. See Wallace (1996: 86–91) for the distinction between an "attributed" and "adjectival (or attributive)" genitive.

appears to include "being alienated and hostile in mind" and dominated by "evil deeds" (1:21). "Trespasses" are the likely reason for the "dead" state, since Paul elsewhere explicitly states this (Rom. 5:15, 17). The ἐν (*en*) before the dative τοῖς παραπτώμασιν (*tois paraptōmasin*) probably does double duty with the dative τῇ ἀκροβυστίᾳ (*tē akrobystia*): actual acts of "trespasses" and the condition of the "uncircumcision of the flesh" are both not only the reason for their dead condition but also indicate the sphere in which the "dead" live (Harris [2010: 95] prefers a causal use). This condition of deadness in "uncircumcision" is likely the spiritual condition from which actual "trespasses" arise and which enhance their dead state.

In contrast to the readers' former dead condition, God "made [them] alive together with Him" (the preposition σύν [*syn*, with] prefixed to the verb intensifies the following σύν). "Made alive" is synonymous with "resurrected."[81] Because Christ was raised from the dead and believers are in union with him, they also are considered to be resurrected: "made alive together with him" or "along with him" (Harris 2010: 201). The σύν- verb and following σύν preposition highlight union with the resurrected Christ.[82] It is not their doing but God's doing. This is a true resurrection from the dead, which begins spiritually in this age and is consummated both spiritually and physically at the end of the age. This resurrection is also the beginning of the latter-day new creation, which will be completed when believers receive new-creation bodies and live in the new cosmos (see further Beale 2011: 249–316). Christians thus are now in union *with Christ's* own resurrection life, which will be consummated in union with him at the end of the age: "Your life is hidden with [σύν] Christ in God. When Christ, who is our life, is revealed, then you also will be revealed with [σύν] Him in glory" (Col. 3:3–4).[83] This beginning new creation is none other than regeneration.

The saint's resurrection occurred as a result of God "having forgiven[84] [them] all [their] trespasses" when Jesus died. The historical forgiveness at the cross is a necessary condition for existential regeneration. Or possibly the point may be less precise; perhaps Paul merely wants to show that in some manner forgiveness is closely linked to saints being made alive (D. Moo 2008: 207–8).

81. See the nonprefixed form of ζῳοποιέω (*zōopoieō*, "make alive") in John 5:21; 6:63; Rom. 4:17; 8:11; 1 Cor. 15:22, 45.

82. Lohse (1971: 104–5) rightly contends that these σύν verbs have almost the identical meaning as the "in him [Christ]" phrases, all connoting union with Christ. Campbell (2012: 220, 225, 235, 330, 336, 355–66, 372) sees the σύν verbs (and that preposition by itself) in 2:12–13 as focusing on participation in Christ's death and resurrection.

83. See likewise W. Grundmann (*TDNT* 7:785), who also sees Col. 2:13 at this point being developed in Col. 3:3–4.

84. The aorist adverbial participle χαρισάμενος (*charisamenos*) modifies the aorist indicative συνεζωοποίησεν (*synezōopoiēsen*) and appears to give the cause for being "made alive." When an aorist adverbial participle modifies an aorist main verb, the time element is often generally contemporaneous to the action of the main verb, though there is usually some logical modification, as here (cf. Wallace 1996: 624–25). See the additional notes on 2:11–12 for further discussion of the function of the adverbial participle "having been buried" in verse 12 and the accompanying footnote there.

In the light of Col. 2:11–13, the question presses upon us about how Christ's historical death and resurrection for his people relate to the believer's identification and union with those two events during the lifetime of the believer. Paul is clearly focusing on a person's faith as that which has brought a believer into union with Christ's death and resurrection (so 2:12, as well as "receive" in 2:6 and "faith" in 2:7; cf. also "faith" in 1:4, 23; 2:5). But in the background is the notion that Christ's historical death and resurrection entail that those who will believe are already identified with him in his redemptive work. Their union with him by faith in their own time is an outworking of their identification with his redemptive work in his historical time. This is evident sometimes from the near blurring of the two in such expressions as "You [have] been buried with him" (2:12) and "having forgiven us [at the historical event of the cross]" (2:13). Colossians 2:14 makes this historical forgiveness at the cross even clearer: "having nailed it [our debt] to the cross."

In addition to being "made alive with" in verse 13 being the result of (or neces- **2:14**
sary for) forgiveness, it is also the result of God's historical "cancel[ing] out[85] the certificate of debt . . . against us, which was hostile to us." This phrase about canceling debt at Christ's cross is natural here, since it may be generally synonymous with the preceding participle, "forgiving" (χαρισάμενος, *charisamenos*) in verse 13, and elsewhere this word can refer to canceling out debts (Luke 7:42–43; Philo, *Spec.* 2.39; see Lohse 1968: 108). The document contained "the charge of our legal indebtedness, which stood against us" (so NIV) because of sinful violation of God's law.[86] Some have summarized the "handwriting" (χειρόγραφον, *cheirographon*) as an IOU, which was typically written by the one who owed the debt.[87] This meaning is likely in mind, since it occurs often throughout contemporary papyri, sometimes in contemporary Hellenistic Judaism and in classical and Hellenistic writings.[88] The content of the IOU is "in decrees" (τοῖς δόγμασιν, *tois dogmasin*), which likely is a dative of content, though a dative of cause could be in mind ("because of decrees").[89]

85. This adverbial aorist participle modifies "made alive" in verse 13 and functions in the same way as the directly preceding aorist participle.

86. "The certificate of debt/indebtedness" is the rendering by the NASB, NET, and HCSB (so similarly NJB, ESV) of the more straightforward "the handwriting" (the latter read by Geneva and KJV). E. Lohse (*TDNT* 9:435), Harris (2010: 96, 103), D. Moo (2008: 208–12), and BDAG (1083, s.v. χειρόγραφον) refer to it as "a note" or "a certificate of indebtedness."

87. There are uses where an IOU is in mind but not written and signed by the debtor (Barth and Blanke 1994: 371, citing Apoc. Paul 17 and Apoc. Zeph. 3.6–9). Thus, the main idea of an IOU can still be in mind here without the notion of being signed by the debtor.

88. Some see it explicitly as an IOU; see the additional note on 2:14 for further nuances of meaning.

89. The dative phrase τοῖς δόγμασιν (*tois dogmasin*) modifies the verbal idea of γεγραμμένον (*gegrammenon*) involved in the noun χειρόγραφον (*cheirographon*; Abbott 1897: 255); D. Moo (2008: 211) takes the clause as a dative of cause (likewise MHT 3:242). However, every English translation takes it as a dative of content (so also Moule 1957: 45), since it is natural to have a "handwritten" document contain something, in this case "decrees": "certificate of debt consisting of decrees" (NASB); "certificate of indebtedness expressed in decrees" (NET);

If this were a dative of cause, then the "certificate of debt" is "against us because of the decrees" written in it that have been broken. That the "decrees" (pl. of δόγμα, *dogma*) here are part of the OT law of God is apparent from 2:20, where "submitting to decrees" (δογματίζω, *dogmatizō*) refers to ordinances of the OT law, especially the dietary laws (see on 2:20–21; so also Pao 2012: 171), which the errorists have distorted.[90] Ephesians 2:15 makes this even clearer: "abolishing in His flesh the enmity, which is the Law of commandments contained in ordinances [decrees, pl. of δόγμα, *dogma*]."[91] The NJB well paraphrases Col. 2:14 by "He has wiped out the record of our debt to the Law." This document of legal debt likely existed in the heavenly realm (see the additional note on 2:14), and its being wiped out probably occurred not only in the earthly but also the heavenly dimension, since the "disarm[ing of] the rulers and authorities" in 2:15 has occurred at the earthly cross but certainly also in the invisible heavenly realm, where those evil powers reside (cf. Eph. 6:11–12; cf. Col. 1:16).[92] As with the temple in the OT, Christ's cross was the place where heaven and earth intersected. God's law condemned Jews, who had contracted with God to obey his law but broke it (Deut. 27:9–26; 30:15–20).[93] Gentiles also stood guilty because they violated the law's moral commands, which would have been known through their

"certificate of debt, with its obligations" (HCSB); "record that stood against us with its legal demands" (NRSV). Similarly Bruce (1984: 106) views it as a dative of accompaniment. The parallel phrase in Eph. 2:15 (τῶν ἐντολῶν ἐν δόγμασιν, *tōn entolōn en dogmasin*) also points to a dative of content in our passage. Could a dative of cause be compatible with the broader idea of dative of content?

90. Sappington (1991: 219) also holds that this distorted Jewish notion of the law may be in mind and cites others who see the δόγμα (*dogma*) as to one degree or another referring to the Mosaic law.

91. The term δόγμα (*dogma*) in Hellenistic Judaism refers to Mosaic law, laws, or often "doctrine": Josephus, *Ant.* 15.136; *Ag. Ap.* 1.42; 3 Macc. 1:3; 4 Macc. 10:2 (cf. Lohse 1968: 110, on these four references); Philo, *Plant.* 62; *Migr.* 131; *Names* 32, 168, 202, 210; *Spec.* 1.345; 2.61; *Virt.* 99; the following references in Philo refer also to "doctrine" but that which has been allegorically deduced from OT law: Philo, *Creat.* 25; *Alleg.* 2.55; 3.1; 3.194, 229; *Sacr.* 19; *Worse* 133; *Unchang.* 88 [?]; *Agr.* 44; *Post.* 129; *Plant.* 77, 98; *Prelim.* 167 (cf. 166 and 168); *Flight* 45, 173; *Dreams* 1.181; 2.256; *Spec.* 2.29. Other references in Philo are not as explicit and are a bit more contextually ambiguous but still are also likely to be identified generally with OT law (some perhaps with allegorization and others without): see *Cher.* 85–86, 121; *Worse* 135; *Post.* 24; *Plant.* 70; *Drunk.* 212 (cf. 213); *Conf.* 51; *Migr.* 53 (cf. 54–55); *Mos.* 2.66; *Spec.* 2.63; 4.140–41; *Etern.* 2. Josephus (*Ant.* 4.210) and Tob. 4:19 use ἐξαλείφω (*exaleiphō*) to indicate the "blotting out" of the Mosaic "laws" from a person's mind. The legal nature of the "decrees" is also reflected elsewhere in the NT (e.g., both Luke 2:1 and Acts 17:7 refer to legal requirements imposed by Caesar). See Harris (2010: 97) for numerous interpretive alternatives for τοῖς δόγμασιν (*tois dogmasin*); he agrees that the expression refers to the "demands of the Mosaic law"; so also G. Kittel, *TDNT* 2:231; cf. also Dunn 1996: 165.

92. Colossians 1:20 says Christ's reconciling work at the cross had both earthly and heavenly effects.

93. Note esp. Neh. 10:29: Israel was "taking on themselves a curse and an oath to walk in God's law, which was given through Moses, . . . and to keep and to observe all the commandments," which they did not then keep, as is clear from the subsequent context (cf. Neh. 13:4–29, esp., e.g., 13:25). Also cf. Exod. 19:8.

conscience (cf. Rom. 2:14–15).[94] In fact, Israel was a corporate Adam figure who represented all humanity in their obligation to obey God.[95] Thus all humanity needed forgiveness for breaking the divine law.

That the legal "certificate of debt" was "against us" (καθ' ἡμῶν, *kath' hēmōn*) indicates that it contained testimony against all people for violating the laws of God. That the "certificate of debt" is also said to be ὑπεναντίον ἡμῖν[96] (*hypenantion hēmin*) emphasizes this even more by explaining that the condemnatory testimony was "hostile to us" (the Greek word appears often in the LXX and always refers to "enemies" or "adversaries"; cf. O'Brien 1982: 126). This opposition of "the certificate of debt consisting of decrees" broken by people is highlighted by observing that the expressions of opposition surround the phrase like bookends, which some English translations obfuscate (NASB, KJV, NIV), or in some cases one of the phrases is omitted because of purported needless redundancy (NRSV, NLT).

The "wiping out of the certificate of debt in decrees against us"* (2:14) is an explanation of "forgiving them all their trespasses"* (v. 13b). What is "wiped out" precisely are not human sins but the written record of sins that testify to the guilt of humans.[97] Forgiveness is the wiping out of the "debt" that must be paid or the legal penalty of sins that people deserve to suffer because they have violated God's OT "decrees" or legal requirements. Galatians 3:10 expresses the same thought: "For as many as are of the works of the Law are under a curse; for it is written, 'Cursed is everyone who does not abide by all things written in the . . . Law, to perform them'" (following Gupta 2013a: 96). In 2:16–23 Paul says that believers are not subject to the OT ceremonial "decrees," and the reason for this is given here in 2:14: Christ has taken the penalty for breaking all of God's law, including the cultic and ceremonial decrees (see esp. 2:14b, on which see below). We must wait, however, until

94. Here following Lightfoot (1875: 187), who says the primary reference is to the Mosaic law; O'Brien 1982: 12; Pao 2012: 171. Similarly, Dunn (1996: 165) says the thought is close to Rom. 1:32: Gentiles "know the ordinance [τὸ δικαίωμα, *to dikaiōma*] of God, that those who practice such things are worthy of death." Sumney (2008: 144) denies that the "decrees" here have any association with the Mosaic law, since "Colossians has no discussion of the place of the Mosaic law in the life of the believer." However, in addition to the above-mentioned relevance of the moral law in Gentile consciences, the main aspect of the false teaching is to get the Colossian believers to submit to various aspects of the Mosaic law. The Colossians, therefore, have acquaintance with the Mosaic law and are in a position to understand Paul's view of it as condemning all, both within and outside the covenant community, apart from Christ's redemptive death.

95. On this concept of Israel as a representative Adamic figure, see, e.g., Beale 2011: 46–58.

96. That this phrase precisely modifies "certificate of debt" and not "decrees" is apparent from observing that ὅ (*ho*) preceding ὑπεναντίον is neuter singular, like χειρόγραφον (*cheirographon*), whereas τοῖς δόγμασιν (*tois dogmasin*) is neuter pl. (see Harris 2010: 97; Sumney 2008: 145).

97. Following D. Moo 2008: 209. For example, Rev. 3:5 uses the verb ἐξαλείφω (*exaleiphō*) for the promise "not [to] erase" the record of one's "name from the book of life." So also Exod. 32:32–33; Num. 5:23; Ps. 68:29 LXX (69:29 MT; 69:28 Eng.); Philo, *Heir* 20; Josephus, *Ant.* 4.210. Josephus also uses the verb to refer to "blotting out" a son from a written "will" (*Ant.* 17.78; *J.W.* 1.600); see also Jos. Asen. 15.4 (3).

that section to explain why the ceremonial laws are the focus of that to which Christians are no longer obligated.

This context does not explain what that penalty is, though it is clear that the penal debt is "against" people, since they must suffer it. However, since forgiveness results in Christ's followers being "made alive" from their "dead" condition, not to be forgiven and to remain in that "deadness" would likely be entailed as part of the judicial penalty. That being "dead" in 2:13 is a legal condemnation is apparent from Rom. 5:15–18, where trespasses lead to both "death" and "condemnation." The penalty also entails "the wrath of God [coming] upon the sons of disobedience" (Col. 3:6), at which time "he who does wrong will receive the consequences of the wrong which he has done, and that without partiality" (3:25).

The last clause of 2:14 gives a yet further explanation of "forgiveness" (v. 13b) and, in particular, what it means that God "canceled out the certificate of debt against" his people (v. 14a): "He has taken it out of the way, having nailed it to the cross."[98] The cross is a metonymy whereby it stands in association with Jesus. Accordingly, "cross" is substituted here for Jesus's suffering in order to place more emphasis on the suffering itself.[99] That is, the penal debt against sinners was removed because it was placed on Jesus at the cross (so also Moule 1957: 98). He suffered the penal debt of his peoples' sin. He was "nailed" for the sinners' sin. Once the penal wrath (cf. 3:6) was removed "by the blood of His cross," then "peace" and "reconciliation"* between the sinner and God result (see Col. 1:20), and the "enmity" between God and humans is "put to death in him"* (Eph. 2:16). Could there be allusion to attaching to the cross the writing (ἡ ἐπιγραφή, *hē epigraphē*) describing the crime of the one being crucified, as was the case with Jesus (Mark 15:26)? If so, "God nails the accusation against us to the cross of Jesus, just as his accusation had been nailed there" (O'Brien 1982: 126; cf. N. Wright 1986: 113, with a different twist).

2:15 While believers were affected positively by the forgiving work of Jesus at the cross, Paul now progresses on and states that the satanic powers were negatively affected by the cross: "by unclothing the rulers and authorities, he made a public demonstration of them."* The specific link between verses 14 and 15 may be that "the stripping" of these evil powers, "whose possession of the damning indictment" kept people in their grip, is what released their fiendish grip on those who believed (Bruce 1984: 110, followed by O'Brien 1982: 126–27). This may be suggested by the close juxtaposition earlier of "forgiveness of sins" through Christ (1:14) and "delivering us from the authority of darkness and transferring us to the kingdom of his beloved Son"* (1:13). There is a similar juxtaposition here of "forgiveness of trespasses"* (2:13b) through

98. Again, an aorist adverbial participle modifies the main aorist verb "he took," which focuses on either the means of the "taking" or the cause of it.

99. Cf. 1 Pet. 2:24, expressing this explicitly: "and He Himself bore our sins in His body on the cross, that we might die to sin and live to righteousness; for by His wounds you were healed."

Christ's death, "the wiping out of the certificate of debt" at the "cross"* (2:14) and defeating "rulers and authorities" (2:15). What could be the connection? Could it be that in both sets of juxtapositions Christ's forgiveness of saints' sins relinquished the dominant hold of satanic powers over them? Therein may lie the essence of the victory: that believers' sins were forgiven through the weakness of the cross, which vanquished the devilish forces' powerful grasp over their former unbelieving lives and "stripped" the satanic foes of their power over the redeemed. This is in line with Eph. 2:2, where believers formerly "walked on the basis of . . . the prince of the power of the air, of the spirit that is now working in the sons of disobedience."* This satanic power over people because of sin's dominance over them was broken through the forgiveness at the cross.[100] Thus Christ's forgiveness of our sins (mentioned in 2:13b) and "wiping out the certificate of debt"* (2:14) appears here to be the lever releasing us from the "authority" of the powers of darkness, which appears to have included their authority in keeping us in bondage to the condemnatory accusations of that "certificate of debt" (2:14).[101]

God is most likely the subject of the verb and participle, though it could possibly be Jesus. However, the subject of the verb "circumcised" in 2:11 appears to be God, who is also the subject of the "raising" of Christ and believers in verse 12 and of the "making alive" and "forgiving" of saints in verse 13, as well as being the subject of the verbs "nailing" and "taking out of the way" in verse 14. Thus, in light of the preceding verses, God again appears to be the subject of the verb forms in verse 15.[102]

Many versions translate ἀπεκδύομαι (*apekdyomai*) as "disarmed" (ESV, HCSB, NASB, NIV, NLT, NRSV, RSV; NET, "disarming"), though some have "stripped" (NJB) more in line with "unclothed" (KJV has "spoiled"). All of these translations render the middle voice of the verb with an active sense, and with God as the subject. It is possible though improbable to see Christ as the subject and rendering the verb with a middle sense: Christ stripping himself of his fleshly body or in some sense stripping himself of evil powers (see the additional note on 2:15 for these views).

The translation of "stripped" or "unclothed" is preferable to "disarmed," since it is in line with translating the same verb with "stripping" in 3:9 and the noun form with the same translation in 2:11. This translation also preserves the intended background picture here of a conqueror who has vanquished the enemies, shamed them by stripping them of their weapons and armor, and leads them in a victory parade, which typically concludes in their death. One can, however, see how the translation of "disarmed" conveys the same notion, but it is a secondary and derived idea (as D. Moo [2008: 214] admits, though he still

100. Cf. similarly D. Moo (2008: 215–16), who has helped clarify my thinking on this main point of "power."

101. Sappington (1991: 211–13, 221–23) also sees the same kind of organic parallel between 1:12–14 and 2:13–15.

102. Sumney (2008: 146) and Pao (2012: 172) have made the same point; likewise MacDonald 2000: 103.

favors the translation of "disarmed"). It is more precise to keep the background picture and to see it as metaphorically conveying the idea of removing power or disarming, so that this idea is derived from the picture. This was a common picture in Roman victories over their enemies, and Paul is likely drawing on that background here. The Roman triumph parade, which we will see is in mind, always assumed that the enemies being led in it had been decisively defeated in a previous battle or war. So, if the full Roman picture is in mind, then portrayed here are the satanic powers that have been "stripped" of their battle attire (i.e., their power) and "publicly exposed" (with connotations of mocking and disgrace) "through God leading them in his triumphal parade by means of the cross."[103] The "stripping" can refer to the prior defeat of the evil powers preceding the triumphal parade, or it can be part of the triumphal process itself. The consummation of this parade will be the consummate defeat (death) of these powers at the very end of time (in line with the background picture that the victory parade typically concluded in the death of the humiliated enemy). The NJB is the only translation that expresses this picture: "he has stripped the sovereignties and the ruling forces, and paraded them in public, behind him in his triumphal procession." Recall that these "rulers and authorities" are satanic powers (see on 1:16 and 2:10), so that they are the ones being stripped here. Their apparent triumphal stripping of Christ (2:11) was ironically their own stripping. Accordingly, verse 15 explains how Christ expresses his victorious headship over the evil "rulers and authorities" in 2:10b.

In the light of the Roman victory image, NJB's "paraded them in public" conveys the intention of the more straightforward translation of the Greek, "made a public display of."[104] These spiritual enemies were put on display in their defeated and unclothed form, which carries notions that they were "exposed," "mocked," or "disgraced."

However, the NJB renders the last phrase of the verse, ἐν αὐτῷ (*en autō*), as "behind him," which is possible but may be too paraphrastic. This phrase may better be translated "through him [Christ]" or "through it [the cross]."[105]

103. See Hafemann (2000: 16–34) for discussion of the Roman background of leading captives in a victory procession, upon which my discussion is dependent.

104. The verb form δειγματίζω (*deigmatizō*) is used only once elsewhere in the NT and is not found in Hellenistic Jewish writings, though the noun form often occurs. The verb can be rendered "make an example of" or "make a show of" (LSJ 372) in the sense sometimes of "expose" or "disgrace" or "mock" (BDAG 214, s.v. δειγματίζω, who prefer the latter two ideas on Col. 2:15). In Matt. 1:19 Joseph did not "expose" or "disgrace" Mary when he discovered that she was pregnant, though they had not yet consummated their marriage. The noun form δεῖγμα (*deigma*), often translated as "example" or "demonstration," can be used in various kinds of contexts with shades of this meaning in Philo and Josephus, as well as other Hellenistic and Classical Greek sources. In Col. 1:15 the phrase following the verb, ἐν παρρησίᾳ (*en parrhēsia*) can be rendered "in public" or "openly," intensifying the "public" nature of the exposure or, possibly, it may be rendered "boldly," since the verb already contains the public idea (Harris 2010: 99).

105. So likewise NIV, HCSB, and NET view this as a dative of instrumentation. Some translations render ἐν αὐτῷ (*en autō*) as a dative of sphere, "in it" (KJV, NRSV). The following translations also understand ἐν αὐτῷ to refer to the cross: NLT, NIV. See MHT 3:265, for the possibility of an instrumental or local meaning of ἐν (*en*) here.

It is difficult to determine which is best. If ἐν αὐτῷ (*en autō*) refers to Christ (as in 2:9–10; cf. 2:13), then it is focusing on God as the one who stripped the evil powers in public display and who won the victory through Christ. If the last phrase refers to God, which is unlikely, then Christ is the one who stripped the enemy in public display and triumphed "through God's" power. If the concluding clause refers to the "cross," then either God or Christ can be viewed as the subject of the preceding actions, accomplishing them through the "cross."[106]

It seems that ἐν αὐτῷ refers to the "cross," since the nearest preceding nominal antecedent is "the cross" (also in the dative) at the end of verse 14 (τῷ σταυρῷ, *tō staurō*; so NET note). Furthermore, a reference to the cross would express the irony of the victory: God or Christ overcoming the opponent through the death and weakness of the cross. This ironic idea may be pointed to further by observing that Paul uses the same verb θριαμβεύω (*thriambeuō*) in 2 Cor. 2:14: "God, who always leads us in triumph in Christ." This time the verb refers to Paul's suffering ministry in Christ against the same Roman background picture of triumph over enemies (see Hafemann 2000: 16–34). Paul is now the one who has been defeated (at his Damascus conversion), and now in his ministry God is leading him in a triumphal parade as a captive slave to death. The point in the context of 2 Corinthians is that God brings a deathlike suffering onto Paul in order ironically to show his power and glorify himself through the weakness of Paul. It is true that the suffering captives being led in the triumphal parade in Col. 2:15 are the evil powers and not Paul or other saints, but a positive ironic element may still be included in the picture: victory through the defeat of the cross. In this respect, "the cross on which Christ died is compared to the chariot in which the victor rode in triumph" (E. Scott 1930: 49; also cited by Dunn 1996: 168); "the convict's gibbet is the victor's car" (Lightfoot 1875: 192).

Even if ἐν αὐτῷ (*en autō*) refers to Christ ("in him" or "by means of him") and not precisely the cross, the same idea of victory through Christ's death at the cross is probably still in mind. However, some think that, if Christ is in mind, then it is the victory of his resurrection that is the focus, so that the last phrase of the verse represents a temporal order going from death (v. 14) to resurrection (v. 15). Such a view is certainly possible and would be in line with other NT passages affirming that it was Christ's resurrection that defeated the "rulers and authorities." For example, Eph. 1:20–21 says God raised Christ from the dead and seated him in the heavenlies, "far above all rule and authority and power and dominion."[107] Yet the only parallels to Christ's relation to the "rulers" and "authorities" in Colossians are in 1:16, where he is ruler over them in

106. NASB, HCSB, and ESV have "Him [Christ]" but add a marginal reading, "it" (= the "cross"); others (NET, TNIV) have "the cross" but add a marginal reading, "him" (= "Christ").

107. So D. Moo (2008: 215), who cites additional parallels, but Eph. 1:20–21 is the only explicit supporting text; so also Pao (2012: 173) and Schweizer (1982: 152), who appeals to Ps. 68:18 (67:19 LXX) and its use in Eph. 4:8 to indicate that Christ "led captive his captives" (= leading prisoners in the triumphal procession in Col. 2:15) at the time of his resurrection. So

creation because he is the sovereign divine creator, and 2:10, where he is their "head" because of his incarnate sovereign divinity. There is no clear mention of Christ's resurrection in 1:16 or 2:10, and it is likely not intended in either of these parallels.[108] Such an identification is problematic: nowhere is it explicitly mentioned in 2:15. Only Christ's death has been in mind since verse 14, and as noted earlier, "the cross" at the end of verse 14 is the closest clear antecedent to ἐν αὐτῷ (*en autō*) at the end of verse 15. However, that the resurrection is secondarily in mind is likely, since verses 11–15 are ultimately to be viewed as a third effect of Christ's divine temple presence (v. 9). And 2:9 is based on 1:19, which gives the basis for Christ's preeminence as the resurrected Lord. This is plausibly part of the reason why the resurrection has been mentioned explicitly in 2:12–13.

Probably the best translation of the verb θριαμβεύω both in 2 Cor. 2:14 and Col. 2:15 is "lead in a triumphal procession."[109] Furthermore, God "lead[ing] us in [his] triumph in [through] Christ" in 2 Cor. 2:14 leaves open that in Col. 2:15 either God or possibly Christ is the subject of the "making a public display by stripping" and "triumphing." Nevertheless, since it is God's "triumph" in the 2 Corinthians text, it points to God as the subject of the verbs in our text, which we have also argued for in the light of the preceding verses.

Colossians 2:15 concludes a section (vv. 10–15) that gives the effects of Christ's sovereign deity (v. 9), and verse 9 is the basis for the audience's "walking" in line with Christ and not the false teaching. Verses 11–13 give an extended explanation of the third effect of verse 9. Verses 14–15 are linked to a development of the third effect of "circumcision," introduced in verses 11–13, but especially indicate the result of Christ being "head over all rule and authority" in verse 10. Could it be that Paul concludes with the evil powers being led in a triumphal captive train by God as a counterpoint to the warning to the Colossians in verse 8 not to be "taken captive" by the false teaching, which is empowered by the forces of darkness?[110]

Additional Notes

2:7. If βεβαιόω (*bebaioō*) is not part of an explicit temple picture, it may carry connotations of "establish" and include the idea of "confirm," in the sense of "put something beyond doubt"

---

also Arnold (1995: 286) believes it is too restrictive to limit Christ's work to his forgiving death but that the resurrection must especially be emphasized in verse 15.

108. Though "head" is used in 1:18a with reference to Christ's redemptive relationship over the church, neither Christ's death or resurrection is directly related to it, though there is reference to Christ's resurrection in 1:18b.

109. For a number of alternative translations for the verb, including "lead in a triumphal procession," see BDAG 459, s.v. θριαμβεύω.

110. Though συλαγωγέω (*sylagōgeō*, "carry off as booty, lead captive" or "rob, despoil"; LSJ 1671; BDAG 955, s.v. συλαγωγέω) in verse 8 is not a semantic synonym of θριαμβεύω in verse 15 (one range of its meaning is "lead in triumph, of conquered enemies": LSJ 806), the pictures portrayed in some contexts may convey ideas that partially overlap.

(BDAG 172–73, s.v. βεβαιόω). For example, the word can be used of Christ's verification of the patriarchal promises by fulfilling them (Rom. 15:8) or the verification of Paul's testimony through miracles performed by the hearers (1 Cor. 1:6–8) or of Christ's teaching by miracles performed through the apostles (Heb. 2:3–4). Perhaps the idea is that the Colossian believers' "rootedness" and being "built up in" Christ leads to their having great assurance about their faith, a development of 2:2, where "having been knit together in love" led to "full assurance of understanding" the "mystery" of Christ.

2:7. The phrase τῇ πίστει (*tē pistei*) may be a dative of means ("by means of faith") or sphere ("in faith") or a dative of reference ("with reference to faith"; see Harris 2010: 82). However, since the context does not favor clearly the first and second uses, the more ambiguous dative of reference is preferable.

2:10. Christ's resurrection has exalted him to be "head of the corner" (ASV) or "chief corner stone" of the temple, a repeated quotation of Ps. 118:22 (117:22 LXX, κεφαλὴν γωνίας, *kephalēn gōnias*) in the NT. Macaskill (2013: 149–54, 163–71) makes the novel contention that the use of this passage in the NT may be the origin of Paul's view of Christ as the "head" (κεφαλή, *kephalē*) of the church, which is his "body." Christ is an actual organic part, the chief part, of the temple, which includes his corporate people. But what Macaskill does not note is that in every quotation of Ps. 118:22, Christ as "the head of the corner" of the temple, which occurred by his death and especially resurrection, *has its direct effect in defeating his enemies within the covenant community* (so Matt. 21:41–46; Mark 12:9–12; Luke 20:16–19; Acts 4:8–28; 1 Pet. 2:4–8)! This idea of defeat of the enemy is explicit in these quotations, and the idea of believers as part of the temple is, at best, only implicit in these quotations, though 1 Pet. 2:4–8 also applies Ps. 118:22 explicitly both to the demise of unbelievers and to believers as part of the temple with Christ. If Macaskill is correct in linking Paul's use of "head" to Ps. 118[111] while viewing Christ and believers as part of the temple, then the use of "head" may also entail the idea that Christ as "head" of the temple also represents his defeat over enemies, over "all [evil] rule and authority." This would further explain why Paul could see Christ's headship over evil powers to be an effect of his becoming the incarnate divine temple at his resurrection in Col. 2:9. As noted in the commentary section, this also is in line with the allusion to Ps. 67:17–18 LXX (68:16–17 Eng.) from Col. 1:19 that is continued in 2:9, since the climax of God's tabernacling in the temple in the psalm happens immediately after he defeats the enemy (see Ps. 67:19 LXX [68:18 Eng.]). Christ's redemptive work in establishing his people as a temple and as his body is also what decisively defeated the evil powers, and it is through the body of the church that this victory will be consummated (on the latter idea, see O'Brien 1982: 114).

2:11–12. *The relationship between circumcision and baptism.* The inextricable link or overlapping reality between spiritual "circumcision" and spiritual "baptism" is evident in verses 11–12a:

> And you were circumcised
>   also
>   in him
>   in the manner of a circumcision made without hands
>   in the manner of the removal of the body of flesh
>   in the manner of the circumcision of Christ
>   in the manner of having been buried with him in baptism.*

The main verb in this long sentence is "you were circumcised" (περιετμήθητε, *perietmēthēte*), and this verb is modified by six following Greek adverbial clauses. The first modifier ("also") merely explains that verses 11–12 are progressing on from verse 10 to give another result of Christ's divine authority (v. 9). The second modifier ("in him") explains that believers are in

111. See also Eph. 2:20, where Ps. 118:22 is probably echoed in referring to "Christ Jesus" as "the corner stone" (but without use of the word "head"), where only focus on believers as part of the temple occurs and no reference to enemies is mentioned.

union with Christ, thus being corporately "circumcised in him."[112] The following four clauses of verses 11–12a explain something about the concept that believers "were circumcised" in Christ. All four adverbial clauses focus on describing in what *manner* the action of the verb "circumcised" occurred.[113] That is, they "were circumcised" (1) in the manner of a spiritual circumcision ("without hands," i.e., by God or Christ), (2) in the manner of "removing the body of flesh [from Christ at the cross]" (which representatively takes away people from their old identification with the sinful world), (3) in the manner of being made to identify with Christ's own death (which is referred to as "the circumcision of Christ"), and (4) in the manner of being "buried with him in baptism" (which also refers to identification with Christ's death).

Or plausibly, we saw that these last four adverbial clauses in the layout above could indicate, instead of manner, the *means* by which saints "were circumcised." It is hard to know whether manner or means is best, though they are very close in meaning. Perhaps both are included, though we have concluded that the greater focus is on these being adverbial of manner. Whichever is the case, the phrases would be qualifying the action of the verb "circumcise," so that they would not be seen as a separate concept from the circumcising action but overlapping with it.

At the risk of overanalysis, we suggest the following two points.

1. What is the ruling idea, if any, between the verb "circumcised" at the beginning of 2:11 and the following last series of four modifying clauses? It is likely that "You were circumcised" is the dominant or main point. The four last clauses logically support the verbal notion of "circumcised" by indicating the manner, or possibly means, by which this verb's action was carried out. These supporting phrases are piled one upon another, the first three pertaining to spiritual circumcision and the last to spiritual baptism. Therefore, since the three adverbial phrases following the "in whom also" clause (of v. 11a) are explained to be the manner or means by which they "were circumcised,"[114] it is probable that the directly following adverbial participial phrase, "buried with him in baptism," is also the manner or means of "were circumcised."[115] Furthermore, since these same three adverbial clauses of

112. Though we saw that "in him" could indicate "means," i.e., "circumcised through him."

113. The phrase "by [or in] the removal of the body of flesh" could modify the preceding "circumcision made without hands," indicating the means or manner of that preceding phrase; also, the phrase "by [or in] the circumcision of Christ" could specifically modify and indicate the means or manner of the preceding phrase, "by the removal of the body of flesh." These alternatives do not affect our overall argument in this section, which will focus on the relationship of the adverbial participle "having been buried" to the main verb "were circumcised."

114. Salter (2010) concludes that even though circumcision is to be considered conceptually a subordinate part of baptism (against my view that they are equivalent or virtually equivalent), he wants to be "cautious" in applying this to the church for all times and places, since the Colossians passage is "polemical," being "concerned primarily with addressing false teaching, not with providing the church with a theology of baptism" (2010: 28–29). In fact, he sees this polemical aspect as a partial basis for seeing the "circumcision" = "baptism" view to be an illegitimate position, not applicable to the contemporary church. This approach suffers from not appreciating that the false teaching in Colossae is part of the latter-day tribulation that extends throughout the church age. Consequently, Paul's solution to the problem also extends throughout the church age (see Beale 2012: 187–224, 819–23, including on the office of elder in relation to the eschatological tribulation of deception).

115. The phrase "having been buried" is a rendering of the adverbial aorist passive participle συνταφέντες (*syntaphentes*) in 2:12. It is possible that the participle indicates time and action antecedent to the main verb ("were circumcised"), but more likely it points to a generally contemporaneous action (which typically occurs when an aorist adverbial participle modifies an aorist indicative verb; on this see Wallace 1996: 624–25). However, along with this general contemporaneous time element, the participle likely also more specifically indicates the means or manner by which the action of the main verb is carried out (on which, again, see Wallace 1996: 624: "Even if a participle is labeled as temporal, this does not necessarily mean that such

2:11 appear to be semantic equivalents conceptually ("circumcision made without hands... in the removal... in the circumcision") to the initial "were circumcised," then, in line with these three preceding clauses, "buried in baptism" (v. 12a) likely designates the same thing as the spiritual notion of "were circumcised" in verse 11a. Syntactically, if "having been buried" is a qualification of the verb "were circumcised," then it is an aspect of that verbal action and essentially equivalent to it. Or alternatively, "buried in baptism" could perhaps be seen to be a subordinate logical notion included within the larger concept of spiritual circumcision, since it is the manner of such circumcision or the means to achieving it.[116] Thus spiritual baptism is likely equivalent to spiritual circumcision in this passage, or at least considered to be an integral though subordinate part of such circumcision.[117] In the latter case, one could conclude that spiritual baptism and spiritual circumcision are not precisely equivalent. Even in this case, there is significant conceptual overlap between the two (both representing death and resurrection).[118]

2. In the commentary section and in excursus 4 ("The Old Testament Background of 'Uncircumcision of Your Flesh' in Colossians 2:13") we concluded that OT physical circumcision as a type has been fulfilled in eschatological spiritual circumcision and is no longer relevant for entrance into the new-covenant community. Instead, spiritual "circumcision made without hands" and spiritual "baptism" are ongoing realities designating entrance into the covenant community.[119] Since spiritual circumcision in Christ is the fulfillment of the type of physical circumcision, and since spiritual circumcision is virtually equated here with spiritual baptism, then it appears plausible that such spiritual baptism is also seen as the fulfillment of the physical type of circumcision. This is still a step removed from saying that the physical rite of baptism for entrance into the covenant community is the equivalent of the physical rite of circumcision, since spiritual baptism is the focus in this passage. But if behind spiritual baptism lies the physical rite of baptism (as some commentators hold),[120] then physical circumcision can be seen to have its typological

is its only force. Often a secondary notion is present, such as means or cause"; yet I maintain that sometimes also the temporal element can be secondary). Context is one of the main clues in determining how an adverbial participle functions, and since the participle here is structurally parallel to the preceding adverbial phrases that indicate the manner or means of the main verb, so likewise probably does the participle συνταφέντες function. If a participle of means is in mind, then the participle would define how the action of the main verb is carried out (Wallace 1996: 629). It is possible that this is a participle of purpose, but this would be exceedingly rare in the aorist (1996: 636). Other logical uses of the participle are also not as likely here as manner or means. Salter (2010: 25–28), like D. Moo (2008: 201; see above) too narrowly categorizes the participle as only temporally contemporaneous.

116. The same is true of the preceding three adverbial phrases of verse 11, though they are also more obviously conceptual equivalents to "were circumcised."

117. Salter (2010: 26–28) concludes that circumcision is subordinate to and a part of baptism on the basis that in verses 11–12 baptism includes both death and resurrection, whereas circumcision connotes only death. However, our position on the equivalence or overlapping (i.e., subordinating) aspect of baptism to circumcision is based not only on the syntactical structure of all four adverbial clauses but also on the background of OT circumcision as connoting both separation from a sinful condition and a setting apart to a condition of life, as discussed above: Gen. 17; Deut. 10:16; Josh. 5:8–9; Jer. 4:4; 9:26; Ezek. 44:7, 9, including Paul's specific allusions to the OT, which associate *spiritual circumcision with life* (Gen. 17; Deut. 30), though it is likely that he would have held as well to that aspect of circumcision signifying being set apart from the sphere of cursing or sin (e.g., as in Deut. 10:16a; Jer. 4:4b).

118. Contra the conclusion of Salter (2010), who denies such an equivalence.

119. "Baptism" here is probably a reference to spiritual identification with Christ, though, as we will see below, the physical rite of baptism likely lies in the background.

120. Though, as we have seen in the commentary section, some like D. Moo (1996: 359) think physical baptism is in mind, with spiritual baptism in the background.

> fulfillment also in the physical rite of baptism. And, further, if it is true that physical baptism stands in the background behind spiritual baptism here, then even the liturgy of baptism is secondarily seen to function equivalently to the OT physical rite of circumcision, since physical circumcision probably stands behind spiritual circumcision in this passage.

Circumcision (physical and spiritual) and its equivalent in baptism (physical and spiritual) represent another example of the transformation of one of Israel's most explicit distinguishing marks.[121]

2:12. It is difficult to know whether βαπτισμῷ (*baptismō*) or βαπτίσματι (*baptismati*) is the original reading, since both are supported by MS evidence of roughly equivalent quality. Metzger (1971: 623), followed by O'Brien (1982: 118) and other commentators, speculates that βαπτισμῷ is the harder reading and therefore preferred, since it is less common than βαπτίσματι, the former occurring only three times outside Colossians and the latter nineteen times, and two of its three uses refer to Jewish washing rituals (Mark 7:4; Heb. 9:10) and not Christian baptism. It is hard to be confident that βαπτισμῷ is the harder and original reading, since one of its uses likely refers to Christian water baptism (Heb. 6:2), and Josephus (*Ant.* 18.117) uses βαπτισμός (*baptismos*), of which βαπτισμῷ is the dative form, to refer to John the Baptist's "baptism," which may represent a wider usage in reference to John's baptizing. Both words can refer to the ceremonial rite of water baptism, therefore, though βάπτισμα can indicate a metaphorical baptism (Mark 10:38–39; Luke 12:50; cf. Matt. 20:22; see BDAG 165, s.v. βάπτισμα). There seems to be no reason why βαπτισμός could not have the same metaphorical connotation, if context warrants, especially since one of its three NT uses likely refers to Christian water baptism (Heb. 6:2). Lightfoot (1875: 184) sees the two words as being almost synonymous, so that it does not matter which word was original in terms of the meaning.

2:12. It is not clear what is the antecedent of the ἐν ᾧ (*en hō*) phrase. It could refer to the preceding ἐν ᾧ (in him, i.e., Christ) in verse 11a, especially since the very same phrase clearly refers to Christ in verse 11, and ἐν αὐτῷ (*en autō*, in him) in verses 9–10 also refers to Christ, and Christ is the central strand throughout verses 9–15 (as argued well by O'Brien 1982: 118–19; Sumney 2008: 139; Campbell 2013: 37–38). However, the phrase may just as well refer to "in baptism," since βαπτισμῷ is the nearest antecedent. Furthermore, it would be easy to see that συνηγέρθητε (*synēgerthēte*) would be understood to have a following implied "him" (αὐτῷ, *autō*) carried over from its explicit mention at the beginning of the verse. Otherwise, to attach "<u>in</u> whom" to "you were raised <u>with</u>" is awkward, redundant, and overweights the verb, especially the rendering of "with" as a part of the verb becomes redundant with "<u>in</u> him." Thus "in which [baptism] also you were raised up with him" is preferable to "in whom [Christ] also you were raised up with." But whichever is the antecedent, the overall meaning of the verse remains little altered (e.g., see Sumney 2008: 139).

2:13. The phrase "and <u>you being dead</u>" (ὑμᾶς νεκροὺς ὄντας, *hymas nekrous ontas*) is best rendered concessively ("though you were dead"), and the participle may be an adverbial accusative-absolute construction, modifying the following verb "he made alive" ("nevertheless, he made alive"). However, Campbell (2013: 38) views the participle ὄντας (*ontas*) as adjectival, modifying the accusative "you" (ὑμᾶς, *hymas*), which seems preferable. This is parallel to the same kind of construction in Eph. 2:1, ὑμᾶς ὄντας νεκρούς (*hymas ontas nekrous*), and 2:5 (see Wallace 1996: 191, who sees the participle there to be concessively adverbial, modifying the following verb "made alive"). The initial ὑμᾶς in Col. 2:13, as in Eph. 2:1, would then serve as the object of the following verb, "he made alive" ("You . . . he made alive"), with the "you" then being repeated from the beginning of the verse for emphasis; O'Brien (1982: 123) also sees the "you" as being repeated by Paul for the sake of emphasis. The parallel with Eph. 2:1 is strengthened by observing that in both Eph. 2:1 and Col. 2:13 "you being dead" is followed by "in transgressions" and "made alive together" (cf. Eph. 2:5). Colossians 1:21 is a parallel to 2:13 and Eph. 2:1, since the same phrase καὶ ὑμᾶς ὄντας (*kai hymas ontas*) also occurs (though "alienated" of Col. 1:21 replaces "dead"

121. See Beale (2011: 812–16) for further argument that circumcision equals baptism.

in Eph. 2:1 and Col. 2:13), and the participle in Col. 1:21 likely forms a periphrastic participial clause "and you being alienated" (ὄντας ἀπηλλοτριωμένους, *ontas apēllotriōmenous*). Thus Col. 1:21 is best rendered concessively because of context ("though you were formerly alienated"), apparently as an adjectival participle and functioning as the object of the verb "reconciled" in verse 22 ("nevertheless you being dead, . . . you he now has reconciled").

Since the distinction between "you" and "we" in Eph. 2:1 and 2:5 likely indicates a distinction between Gentiles and Jews, the same may be the case with "you" and "us" in Eph. 2:11–13 (note the repetition of the second-person form also in Col. 2:10–12; so also MacDonald 2000: 101). Bruce (1984: 108), Sumney (2008: 143), and Pao (2012: 169) express more certainty about this. The following reference to "the uncircumcision of your flesh" (2:13) may further point to Gentiles being addressed at this point, even though the phrase has a primarily spiritual meaning (among others, see Calvin 1972: 333–34; Lightfoot 1875: 180; Caird 1976: 194; likewise Sumney 2008: 142; Pao 2012: 169). MacDonald (2000: 101) observes that "uncircumcision" is one of the ways Paul refers to Gentiles elsewhere (Rom. 3:30; Gal. 2:7). Of course, the spiritual significance of the expression would apply equally to Jewish Christians in their former unbelief.

2:13. The ἐν (*en*) in the first clause of verse 13 is barely favored by NA[28], since equally good MSS support its presence and its omission. If the omission were original, then a scribe may have been influenced to add ἐν, since it has been used repeatedly in verses 9–12. But the problem does not affect the meaning of the verse, since the directly following datives may function with the same sense as ἐν.

2:13. Instead of "you" (ὑμᾶς, *hymas*) after "he made alive," which is read by NA[28] (and supported by good and early MSS), some good quality and early MSS have "us" (ἡμᾶς, *hēmas*), which was likely changed by a scribe in order to harmonize with the following "us" (ἡμῖν, *hēmin*) near the end of the verse; some MSS also omit this ὑμᾶς in order to remove the redundancy created by "you" at the beginning of the verse. Thus "you" is the more difficult reading, which best explains how the other readings could have come into being. O'Brien (1982: 123) and Metzger (1994: 556) agree with this explanation.

2:13. The reading "us" (ἡμῖν, *hēmin*) has strong manuscript support. Metzger (1994: 556) thinks that the variant ὑμῖν (*hymin,* you) came about through a copyist's error in hearing, since the letters η and υ were pronounced alike in later Greek.

2:14. Some see the "handwriting" or "certificate of debt" (χειρόγραφον, *cheirographon*) explicitly as an IOU. So *TLNT* 3:508–10, e.g., notes that in the papyri it typically refers to an "'acknowledgment of debt,' i.e., the receipt signed by a debtor, who acknowledges that he owes a certain sum . . ."; e.g., one papyrus document says, "merchandise for which you have signed a receipt [χειρόγραφον]," so that the "receipt" is a document testifying to money owed for the merchandise, which has not yet been paid (*TLNT* 3:509, citing P.Oxy. 745.2 and adducing like papyrus examples). So also O'Brien (1982: 125), Harris (2010: 96, 103), and D. Moo (2008: 208–12) opt for the IOU meaning. For this sense of "certificate of debt," see also Plutarch, *Borrow* 4 (*Mor.* 829A); *Life of Aesop* G, sect. 122, line 5[122] (1st cent. AD). A number of commentators cite uses in Tob. 5:3; 9:5; and sometimes T. Job 11.11 (e.g., Dunn 1996: 164; cf. Davids 2008a: 272) that line up with this meaning, though the notion that this is a heavenly book, as Dunn (1996: 164) argues, is possible but not clear. Some commentators cite Philem. 18–19 as expressing the concept of this IOU, yet this term is not used there (e.g., MacDonald 2000: 102). See also Artemidorus, *Dreams* 3.40 (R. White 1975), where the word means "a note of hand," recording a loan that is owed. Polybius, *Hist.* 30.8 (3rd–2nd cent. BC) uses the word to refer to letters of alliance against Rome that condemned people who had written them in the presence of Roman authorities and their allies; likewise Dionysius of Halicarnassus, *Rom. Ant.* 5.8.2 (1st cent. BC), applies the word

122. From e Codex 397 Bibliothecae Pierponti Morgan (recensio 3; *TLG*). See Daly 1961: 85 for the English translation.

similarly to "letters" of conspiracy against a Roman consul that became a basis of accusation against the letter writers when the letters were discovered.[123]

After a thorough search of the word in the papyri, K. Kim (2017: 233–39) contends that χειρόγραφον merely refers to a document that contains a declaration or oath that the Colossians had sworn to observe religious obligations (i.e., those listed in Col. 2:16, 18). He argues that Christ has set them free from their previous declaration. He sees no reference in the papyri or in Colossians to a certificate of debt (though he acknowledges that sometimes the word does indeed refer in the papyri to a debt certificate, as we have argued). This is a possible view, which would fit with our following analysis of Col. 2:16–17 (i.e., that Christ has nullified the validity of the OT obligation to observe rituals; on which see). However, in light of the following considerations we still think the document referred to in Col. 2:14 is a document of debt: (1) the word can sometimes have this contextual meaning in the papyri; (2) the directly preceding phrase, "having forgiven us all our trespasses" appears to be further explained by "having canceled out the handwriting consisting of decrees against us, which were hostile to us." (3) The double reference to the "decrees" being "against" the Colossians fits much better with cancelling out a debt of sin that was "against" the Colossians than with Christ freeing them from the observance of religious rituals. K. Kim never addresses how the double reference fits into his view or how it relates to "forgiveness" at the end of verse 13.

Some appear to be correct to see here in Col. 2:14 some association with the Jewish and early Christian background of a heavenly book in which sins have been recorded (cf. Sappington 1991: 100–107, 208). See Apoc. Paul 17 and Apoc. Zeph. 3.6–9, which refer respectively to a heavenly "document" (Eng. rendering of the Latin *graffum*, a transliteration of Greek γραφή, *graphē*) and to a "manuscript" (Eng. rendering of the Coptic) in which sins have been written, which are the basis of a person's condemnation by God (cited also by Dunn 1996: 164; and Sumney 2008: 144; both of them say that the Latin and Coptic equivalents of χειρόγραφον are used respectively in these two documents). Sappington (1991: 215–17) also sees striking points of contact between Apoc. Zeph. 7.1–8 and Col. 2:14–15: (1) the transliterated word χειρόγραφον appears seven times in the Coptic text (also in chap. 3) and refers to sins written down as a record in heaven for judgment; (2) the "wiping out" of this record of shortcomings (see Col. 2:14) (3) leads to "triumph" and "prevailing over the accuser" (though the one triumphing is the sinner and not Christ, as in Col. 2:15); (4) as a consequence, the seer "crosses over" into the heavenly region of the "righteous ones."

Some cite the relevance of a saying from the Jewish prayer Avinu Malkeinu: "Our Father, our King, erase through your great mercy all our letters of transgression / entries of transgression" (cited by Str-B 3:628; followed by Barth and Blanke 1994: 369).

2:15. In addition to the position taken in the commentary section, two other translations and consequent interpretations of the phrase ἀπεκδυσάμενος τὰς ἀρχὰς καὶ τὰς ἐξουσίας (*apekdysamenos tas archas kai tas exousias*) were held by many church fathers and others up until modern times but now are not held by the majority of commentators: (1) "he [Christ] divested himself of the powers and authorities,"[124] and (2) "he divested himself of his flesh and made a show of the rulers and authorities" (so that "rulers and authorities" become the object of the verb "make a show of" and not of the participle "strip off").[125] Instead of taking the middle verb in an active sense, as preferred in the commentary section, these two renderings attempt to give full force to the reflexive sense of the middle voice of the verb, which it can sometimes carry.

The problem with the first translation is that God is the probable subject of both the participle "stripped" and the verb "made a show of" (see the footnote accompanying my comments

123. Sometimes χειρόγραφον (*cheirographon*) refers merely to "handwriting" as we might refer to it today (Artemidorus, *Dreams* 1.42 [2×]). Quite different from the above-cited uses, Clem. Hom. 45 employs χειρόγραφον to refer to God's created work of the sun and stars in "heaven"; see *ANF* 8:247.

124. So the Greek fathers, and more recently Moule 1957: 101–2.

125. Thus the Latin fathers, and more recently, e.g., Robinson 1952: 41.

on 2:15). It would be an unexpected change of subject from the previous verses to introduce Christ as the subject of the verb. Furthermore, this view entails the idea that Christ in his pre-resurrection body was subject to the demonic "rulers and authorities" but at his death cast off their authority over him. This is a problematic view, since Jesus was not always subject to the power of Satan but showed decisive power over him at various significant points throughout his earthly ministry (e.g., at the wilderness temptation and when he cast out demons from people; cf. further Luke 10:17–22). In support of this view, however, one could say that the cross was the consummative point where the devil and his powers were defeated, consummating what was begun in Jesus's ministry.

The problem with the second rendering, like the first, is that God is the probable subject of both the participle "stripped" and the verb "made a show of." Another weakness is that the idea of "flesh" has to be added, which is nowhere found in the Greek. The justification for this, however, is appeal to verse 11, where the noun form of the verb "strip off" occurs and which some understand (including this commentator) to refer to the "stripping off of the fleshly body" of Christ, who corporately represents believers in having their "fleshly body" stripped off. This is a possible link but not certain. This link is even more tenuous for commentators who see this phrase in verse 11 referring not to Christ but only to believers. As an additional problem with this position, it may imply that Jesus's flesh was inherently evil and/or that Jesus's resurrection body was not a body of flesh.

But most contemporary English translations provide a third and more probable view by which the middle-voice participle has active force (which can often be the case with middle-voice verbs; see, e.g., MHT 3:55; Zerwick 1963: 76). That this is the case is likely because when the related verb "strip off" (εκδύω, *ekdyō*) occurs with a following personal object, it is that personal object that receives the action of the stripping: one person strips clothes off another person (so D. Moo 2008: 213–14, who cites as LXX examples Gen. 37:23; 1 Sam. 31:9; 1 Chron. 10:9; Ezek. 16:39; 23:26; Hosea 2:5 [2:3 Eng.]; 2 Macc. 8:27; Matt. 27:28, 31; Mark 15:20; Luke 10:30; though in all these examples the verb is in the active and not the middle voice; Moo [2008: 214] claims that there are no examples of this verb in the middle voice followed by a personal object). The middle voice may still be expressed in this active translation with the sense that the action is done in the interest of the subject acting (following MHT 2:310; and Harris 2010: 98). The preposition ἀπό (*apo*) prefixed to the verb εκδύω likely intensifies the meaning of the verb but does not change its meaning.

For helpful summaries of the three above views of ἀπεκδυσάμενος (*apekdysamenos*) in Col. 2:15, see Lightfoot 1875: 189–91; Abbott 1897: 258–59; Moule 1957: 101–2; Bruce 1984: 107; O'Brien 1982: 127; Barth and Blanke 1994: 332–34; D. Moo 2008: 213–14.

C. Believers Should Not Be Required to Submit to Extraordinary Religious Practices (2:16–23)

Here is a fuller statement of the main idea of this unit: *Believers should not be required to submit to extraordinary practices of bodily discipline and holiday-keeping in order to experience the tabernacling presence of God, since only faith in Christ is necessary for that.*

This is the most debated section of the epistle. At the same time, it is the most important segment, since it gives more description of the false teaching. Is the description of the error quoted from the false teachers virtually verbatim by Paul, does it represent Paul's own interpretive polemical summary of that teaching, or is it a combination of the two?[1] The last option appears likely. But to whatever degree Paul is interpreting the errant teaching, it had to correspond to that teaching, since the readers would have been very aware of the content of this teaching (cf. Sumney 2008: 149). There is also much debate about the contextual background of the errant teaching: is it Jewish, Hellenistic, or a combination of the two?[2] My conclusion will be that it is primarily Jewish yet with some Hellenistic pagan elements. Recall that even in the OT, false teaching within the Israelite community entails some imbibing of pagan ideas (especially teaching proposing that pagan idols could be worshiped and integrated into Israel's religion without involving compromise).

The goal of Col. 1:24–2:5 was that believers be "complete in Christ" (1:28), which is achieved by them not being "deluded" by false teaching, so they can maintain "good discipline and stability of faith" (2:4–5). And this is the basis of "walking in" Christ in 2:6 (and 2:8b–9), which explicitly expands on "walking" worthily in 1:10a. The main point of 2:6–15 is that believers should live ("walk") only on the basis of faith in Christ and not by any other belief system (2:6–9). The reason for living only on the basis of Christ is that he came in the fullness of deity in the flesh as God's temple (v. 9). In doing so he thereby redeemed people by his death and resurrection (2:10–14), which accomplished victory over spiritual enemies (v. 15). This

1. See Barclay (1997: 50–53) for discussion of this thorny issue.

2. I will not interact with the various scholars who offer alternatives that see the main source of the teaching to be found only in some aspect of Hellenistic philosophy (though even these acknowledge varying degrees of some Jewish influence). See Barclay (1997: 45–47) for a summary of these views.

emphasis on living only by faith in Christ was set in antithesis to the non-Christ-centered false teaching (2:4, 8).

The "therefore" in 2:16 indicates that it is based on the idea of living only on the basis of Christ, the main point of 2:6–15. Saints cannot be "judged" by keeping extraneous and outdated OT temple laws because we are to live only by faith in Christ. We have already been judged through identification with Christ's death, who suffered judgment on our behalf (2:14). Furthermore, the cleanliness required for entrance into God's presence comes through being in Christ and not through keeping OT laws dealing with diet or special holidays. The emphasis on Christ as the only necessary focus for Christian living continues in verse 17. The reason why Christians do not need to keep these OT laws is that they are outmoded in the light of Christ's coming: these OT laws are a "shadow" of Christ, who has come and has brought these laws to material fulfillment (he is the "substance" to which these shadows pointed). As will be seen, these OT laws concerned ways to be acceptable for worshiping God in the OT temple. Now, however, these laws no longer apply because Christ is the temple and we are acceptable in him for worshiping God. We are clean to enter into temple worship because Christ has circumcised us (see on 2:11).

Verses 18–19a return to another extraneous requirement of bodily discipline for which Christians should not be judged or "disqualified" from entry into God's tabernacling presence. But, just as verse 17 focused on Christ as the reason for not following certain OT laws in verse 16, so verse 19 returns to that Christ-centered focus as a reason for not submitting to the requirements of verse 18.

On the basis of identification with Christ the head (v. 19), believers have died with him (cf. 2:11–12, 14) to the old world (v. 20a). And because they have died to that old world, they should not submit to outmoded OT commandments that belong to the old age (vv. 20b–21). There are three reasons one should not abide by these laws: (1) all of them are part of the old corrupt world, which will pass away (v. 22a); (2) these laws have their origin in human tradition (v. 22b); (3) and these laws about self-made religion and bodily discipline express only a superficial wisdom but are of no value against sin (v. 23).

The main point of verses 16–23 is that saints should not be required to submit to extraneous laws of bodily discipline in order to experience God's tabernacling presence. The reason for this is because only faith in Christ brings us into God's holy presence. In this respect, verses 16–23 are an amplification of the false teaching in 2:8, which is apparent from observing the following parallels (generally following D. Moo 2008: 217): (1) warning not to let the false teachers influence them (cf. 2:8 with 2:16 and 18); (2) the false teaching is based on "human" tradition (cf. 2:8 with 2:22); (3) the false teaching is based on "the elements of the world" (cf. 2:8 with 2:20); the false teaching is "empty deception" (2:8) and "inflated in vain" (2:18); (4) the false tradition is not based on Christ (cf. 2:8 with 2:19).

Exegesis and Exposition

[16]Therefore [let] no one . . . act as your judge in regard to food or drink or in respect to a festival or a new moon or a Sabbath day—[17]things which are a mere shadow of what is to come; but the substance belongs to Christ. [18]Let no one keep defrauding you of your prize by delighting in self-abasement and the worship of the angels, . . . [which] he has ⌜ ⌝ seen [upon entering into the temple], inflated without cause by his fleshly mind, [19]and not holding fast to the head, from whom the entire body, being supplied and held together by the joints and ligaments, grows with a growth which is from God. [20]If ⌜ ⌝ you have died with Christ to the [elements] of the world, why, as if you were living in the world, do you submit yourself to decrees, such as, [21]"Do not handle, do not taste, do not touch!" [22](which all refer to things destined to perish with use)—in accordance with the commandments and teachings of men? [23]These are matters which have, to be sure, the appearance of wisdom in self-made religion and self-abasement ⌜and⌝ severe treatment of the body, but are of no value [with respect to the full satisfaction of the flesh].[3]

2:16 The "therefore" (οὖν, *oun*) at the beginning of the verse refers back to the main point of 2:6–15 as the ground for the rest of the verse: Christian living should be centered only on Christ. Such living focused squarely on Christ is the basis for Paul saying, "Let no one judge you" (μὴ . . . τις ὑμᾶς κρινέτω, *mē . . . tis hymas krinetō*) by OT laws concerning diet and special holidays.* The believing readers have already been judged for their sin in Christ (2:11–12, 14), so that the judgment about diet and holidays is nothing compared with the decisive judgment in Christ on their behalf. This redemptive judgment has reconciled them to God (1:20) and given them inaugurated entrance to the very presence of God in Christ (on this see 1:19 and 2:9–10, where Christ as God's tabernacling "fullness" is shared by believers).

They need nothing else besides Christ and his forgiving work to help them be closer to God. They do not need to obey the extraneous laws cited in the remainder of verse 16 to draw them closer to God. Also, no one should "judge" them as being incomplete in their spiritual fullness if they do not obey these laws, since their final eschatological "completion" in Christ (1:28; cf. 3:3–4) has already begun through their "having been filled in him"* (2:10). As we concluded in 2:9–10, this "filling" pertains to them being identified with Christ as the end-time temple and being filled with his glorious presence in that temple. But, as we will see especially in 2:18, the false teachers are affirming that obedience to OT dietary laws and ordinances about holidays are necessary requirements in order to come into the presence of God in his heavenly temple. "Let no one judge you" is a further development of "Be careful not to let anyone captivate you"* in 2:8, which emphasizes the warning not to let the false "philosophy" dominate anyone (D. Moo 2008: 218).

3. The phrases in brackets represent adjustments I have made to the NASB translation.

Most commentators have mentioned only that these are dietary laws and decrees about holidays, the ongoing validity of which the false teachers are wrongly affirming. While this is true, the vast majority of Colossians commentators have not noticed that the primary purpose of these laws in the OT is *to enable the Israelites to become clean and be able to enter into God's temple to worship him*.

For example, the phrase "in food and in drink" (ἐν βρώσει καὶ ἐν πόσει, *en brōsei kai en posei*) refers to a part of the OT laws concerning how people can become clean or unclean. The commands "Do not handle, do not taste, do not touch!" in verse 21 refer to the same thing. There are various purposes for the clean and unclean OT laws. For example, it is possible that they are for hygiene, to promote ethical behavior (such as forbidding indiscriminate killing of animals for recreation), and to distinguish life and wholeness associated with God from death and disorder. But it is much clearer that one of the purposes is to make a separation from things contaminated by pagan idolatry (including immoral sexual activity associated with pagan worship) and especially to show a separation between unclean Gentiles and clean Israelites (which includes separation from idolatry). The latter is highlighted in Lev. 20:25–26:

> You are therefore to make a distinction between the clean animal and the unclean, and between the unclean bird and the clean; and you shall not make yourselves detestable by animal or by bird or by anything that creeps on the ground, which I have separated for you as unclean. Thus you are to be holy to Me, for I the LORD am holy; <u>and I have set you apart from the peoples to be Mine</u>.

Of course, the law in general separates Israel from its Gentile neighbors. The abolition of the food laws in the NT symbolizes that the barrier between Gentiles and Jews has been broken down (above all, see Acts 10–11, esp. 10:15 and 11:9, as well as Mark 7:19 and Rom. 14:14). We have already seen that this function of the law has been abolished, so that believing Jews and Gentiles can become one in Christ, which is part of the "mystery" in Col. 1:26–27 (see my comments on these verses). And we will see this point to be relevant again (see on 2:20 and 3:11). In the OT, observing these laws is evidence of being part of God's true people in contrast to unbelieving nations. The misguided teachers, however, continue to affirm the validity of these laws, despite the fact that the new age has been inaugurated with the coming of Christ (see N. Wright 1986: 119).

But, above all, the purpose of the clean and unclean laws is to make a person clean for worshiping the holy God in the temple (tabernacle) and to preserve the temple as a clean place. God is holy, and so his people are commanded to be holy. This is especially true with respect to God's holiness in the temple, and the Israelites are to be holy in drawing near to him in worship (cf. Lev. 20:25–26; Lev. 10, on the death of Nadab and Abihu; Lev. 11–15, on laws of purity). The unclean are to be separated from the tabernacle (Num. 5:3; Lev.

15:31) in order to protect the holiness of the tabernacle (Lev. 12:4; 15:31; Num. 19:13; Neh. 13:7–9, 29–30).[4]

Thus the main purpose of the unclean and clean laws is to preserve the sanctity of the temple by excluding any uncleanness from entering into it.[5] This means likewise that one must abide by these laws in order to be clean to worship God in the sanctity of the temple (in the courtyard for the ordinary Israelite, in the holy place for the priests, and in the holy of holies for the high priest).[6] Significantly, the purpose of the food laws showing a separation between unclean Gentiles and clean Israelites is also ultimately related to Israel being holy and clean from the uncleanness of the nations in order to be able to worship God at his sanctuary and to keep that sanctuary clean and holy (so Morales 2015: 162–64). Thus, to be clean is to allow entry into varying degrees of the life-giving presence of God in the sanctuary and the order of that sanctuary, but to be unclean is in varying degrees to be separated from the life of God and to be associated with death and disorder (so Morales 2015: 157–59, 166).

4. This summary of the purpose for the clean and unclean laws is based partly on Sprinkle (2000), who especially summarizes scholars' views such as Houston and D. Wright in support of the main purpose of the dietary laws being to preserve the holiness of the temple and to enable people to be clean to worship there: see Houston 1993: 123, 245–46; D. Wright 1987: e.g., 231–47, 273, 276, speaking of a graduated system of purity, with the allowance of some impurity in the courtyard but none in the holy place or holy of holies; blood had to be applied to parts of the tabernacle to purify them from the peoples' impurities (D. Wright 1987: 18, 130). See also especially Morales 2015: 153–67; likewise J. E. Hartley, *DOTP* 424–30; R. K. Duke, *DOTP* 650–51; Schiffman 1985: 843. Kohler (1903) contends that the dietary laws were extended from the priests and applied to the whole nation, so that the whole nation has a "priestly sanctity." Milgrom (1991: e.g., 724–26) discusses various purposes of the dietary and clean/unclean laws, including the goal of setting Israel apart from the nations. However, Milgrom also sees that one of the purposes is to show that Israel is to be clean because God's tabernacle is in its midst, yet Israel is also to be clean elsewhere in the land, since the sanctuary is potentially endangered by uncleanness arising from any source outside of itself (1991: 1005–7). He sees the purported Holiness Code in Leviticus as affirming that the sanctuary is the center of the community and is the only sacred sphere in it and that any kind of impurity happening anywhere in the Israelite community (whether by priest or layperson) "will pollute the sanctuary." But he sees the supposed Holiness Code to affirm that all Israel's land is sacred, not just the sanctuary, so that one must maintain the purity laws not to defile the land or the temple (Milgrom 1990: 85–86). Milgrom contends that the Temple Scroll applied the purity laws of the priests to all Israelites (i.e., "true Israel," the members of the Qumran community), so that all Israelites had to maintain the purity laws to enter the eschatological city-temple (1990: 88–89).

5. In Qumran the laws of purity were applied to the temple: 11QT 47.3–4 ("The city that I shall sanctify, in order to cause my name and temple to dwell in its midst, will be clean and holy") and 4Q400 frag. 1 1.14 ("Nor is there any unclean thing in their holy places [i.e., the heavenly holy places of the temple]"*; cited by Dunn 1996: 192). So also 11QT 47.12–18; T. Levi 15.1. Speaking of unclean people, CD 5.6–7 says, "They also defile the sanctuary, for they do not separate clean from unclean according to the Law, and lie with a woman during her menstrual period."

6. See Philo, *Plant.* 164: "It is impious for polluted things to come near to the altar" (trans. Yonge 1993: 205). Aaron and his sons could not take polluted drink in order to approach the altar and serve there (Philo, *Drunk.* 127, 131, 138). With respect to priests, see likewise Jub. 21.16. For people in general, see also Philo, *Spec.* 3.39, 205.

The false teaching identified in Col. 2:16 entails, therefore, not merely a wrong assertion that these dietary laws continue to be valid but also that one must abide by them to be clean to worship God in his end-time heavenly temple (so also Dunn 1996: 191–92, commenting on Col. 2:21; for the notion of a *heavenly* temple, see below on 2:18). Verse 21 has underscored the importance of these dietary laws by repeating them.

When the actual phrase "food and drink" is studied elsewhere in the NT, it typically refers to part of a preparation for worshiping God in the temple. Hebrews 9:8–14 says, "The [ultimate] way into the holy place has not yet been disclosed" during OT times (9:8). However, "gifts and sacrifices" pertaining to "food and drink [βρώμασιν καὶ πόμασιν, *brōmasin kai pomasin*][7] and various washings [and] regulations for the body" were required in the OT era (9:9–10) in order for one to be "sanctified" and "cleansed" to approach the temple (9:10, 13). Nevertheless, such things "cannot make the worshiper perfect in conscience" (9:9). Only "the blood of Christ" (9:14), the "high priest" (9:11), who "entered through the greater and more perfect tabernacle" (cf. Heb. 8:1–2), can "sanctify" defiled people "for the cleansing of your conscience"* (9:14). "Food and drink" (βρώμασιν καὶ πόμασιν, 9:10) is part of what formerly cleansed one to qualify for temple worship. These old food and drink laws appear to be the very thing that the false teachers in Colossae are still urging Christians to obey to be prepared for heavenly temple worship.[8] But, as Hebrews says, and Paul will soon say in verse 17, such laws are now outmoded for worship of God in his temple, which has come about in Christ's advent.

In a context of instructions for priests serving in the temple, Philo refers to the appetite as "a profane, and impure, and unholy thing," but temperance is "a pure and unblemished virtue, neglecting everything which relates to eating and drinking [βρῶσιν καὶ πόσιν, *brōsin kai posin*]," being "superior to the pleasures of the belly, [it] may be allowed to approach the sacred altars" in the temple (*Spec.* 1.150, trans. Yonge 1993: 548). Philo uses the very same phrase "food and drink" as in Col. 2:16 to refer to what is to be avoided in disciplining oneself to be able to be clean in order to approach the temple altars. This is Philo's only use of this phrase, which occurs in the context of the temple. Philo also says, with very similar language, that Moses "purified" himself from "meat and drink" (σιτίων καὶ ποτῶν, *sitiōn kai potōn*) and "neglecting meat and drink" (σιτίων . . . καὶ ποτῶν) in order to be qualified for his "fulfilling of the office of the priesthood" (*Mos.* 2.66–68) and for approaching God at the top of the "most sacred mountain" (*Mos.* 2.70), which was considered a sanctuary (see the additional notes on 2:18) and where he was instructed about "the building of the temple" (*Mos.* 2.71).

7. This is the only use of the combination of βρώμα and πόμα (*brōma* and *poma*) in the NT, which is almost identical to βρῶσις καὶ πόσις (*brōsis kai posis*) in Col. 2:16.

8. Similarly, 1QH 11.20–23 (*olim* 3.20–23) asserts that God had to "cleanse the perverse spirit from great sin that he [the sinner] might . . . enter into communion with the congregation of the Sons of Heaven . . . and that he might praise" God "in joyful concord" with the angels (trans. Dupont-Sommer 1962: 209).

In a context of discussing the Sabbath, fasting, full moons, and feasts (*Mos.* 2.21–24), Philo also says, "It is not lawful to take any food or any drink [οὐ σιτίον, οὐ ποτόν, *ou sition, ou poton*]" in order that people may think clearly in "propitiating the Father of the universe with holy prayers, by which they are accustomed to solicit pardon for their former sins" (2.24). This may also pertain to a temple context.

Josephus refers to "how the purity of it [the temple] was never to be profaned" (*Ag. Ap.* 2.102). For example, "all the Jews went into the second court, as well as their wives, when they were free from all uncleanness; into the third [court] went the Jewish men when they were clean and purified" (*Ag. Ap.* 2.104). There were also to be no "vessels" that "related to [unclean] food or drink being carried into the temple,"[9] so that the purity of the temple would be maintained (*Ag. Ap.* 2.106–8).[10]

This combined use of βρῶσις καὶ πόσις with a view to temple purity is found only in the NT, OT, and Judaism. The same combination frequently occurs in classical and Hellenistic sources but only with mundane reference to "food and drink" being the typical means of bodily nourishment. As far as I can tell in the sources I have checked, except for one instance, there is no cultic use of this specific phrase outside of biblical and Jewish sources.[11] This further

9. The Greek text of *Against Apion* is lacking at this point, yet see the Latin.

10. O'Brien (1982: 138) says Paul was likely "not referring directly to the OT food laws, since the Torah contained no prohibitions respecting drinks, except in a few special cases." But these cases, in addition to a few others, are significant. Recall that the idea of priesthood is applied to the whole nation (Exod. 19:6). In this respect, part of the dietary laws required priests not to "drink wine or strong drink" in the tabernacle in order "to make a distinction between . . . the unclean and the clean" (Lev. 10:9–10). This appears to have been more broadly applied to all Israelites, who were forbidden to drink water that became unclean through contamination with other impure objects, which is among other dietary prohibitions dealing with the clean and unclean (Lev. 11:34). Haggai 2:11–13 also affirms that one can become unclean through "wine." Likely Heb. 9:10 refers to Lev. 11:33–34 and Hag. 2:11–13 (L. Goppelt, *TDNT* 6:145). Likewise Israel did not drink "wine or strong drink" during their wilderness wanderings (Deut. 29:6). In addition to the above references to Philo and Josephus, the following texts support the notion that drinks were considered clean and unclean: 11QT 49.5–9; T. Lev. 8.3–5; 2 Bar. 66.2.

The phrase "food and drink" (βρωτῶν καὶ ποτῶν, *brōtōn kai potōn*), synonyms for the words in Col. 2:16, is used in the Let. Aris. 128, 142, 162 to refer to what is unclean for Israelites. The fuller phrase "food and drink and *touch*" (ἁφή, *haphē*) occurs in Let. Aris. 142, and similarly in 162, which is virtually identical to Col. 2:16 together with 2:21 (note ἅπτω, *haptō* in 2:21). See further Beetham (2008: 197–200) on the OT and Jewish background for unclean water as being part of the purity laws.

11. In this respect and with regard to this specific combination of βρῶσις καὶ πόσις, I have checked all the sources in the *TLG* that are available in English translation in order to be able easily to scan the broader context: in Homer, *Il.* 19.210; *Od.* 1.191; 13.72; Hesiod, *Shield* 395; Plato, *Laws* 6 (782A); Hippocrates, *Acute* 28; *Reg.* 1.18; *Dis.* 4.12; Xenophon, *Mem.* 1.3.15; Polybius, *Hist.* 6.7; T. Reu. 2.7; T. Ab. 13.6 (rec. B); Diodorus of Sicily, *Hist. Lib.* 1.45; Dio Chrysostom, *Envy* (77/78.30); and in Plutarch's *Moralia*: *Well* 8 (*Mor.* 126C); *Spart.* 5 (*Mor.* 226E); *Peace* 3 (*Mor.* 465E); *T. Talk* 5 (*Mor.* 673A); *Old Man* 5 (*Mor.* 786B); *Beasts* 6 (*Mor.* 989B). Restrictions about food and drink (though not using the precise words of Col. 2:16), including fasting, were a necessary preparation for mystical experience in the mystery cults of Eleusis in Greece and of Cybele and Attis in Phrygia, as well as in the cult of Isis (see Sumney 2008: 150).

confirms the OT and Jewish nature of this precise expression. The Colossian false teaching might have referred to fasting from all food and drink or from only some. That "food and drink" in 2:16 refers to Jewish dietary laws for cultic cleanness is apparent from the observation that the roughly synonymous wording of "do not handle, do not taste, do not touch" occurs in 2:21 and serves to highlight 2:16 as referring to such dietary laws. Furthermore, that Jewish dietary laws are in mind is confirmed by the immediately following phrase "a festival or a new moon or a Sabbath day" in verse 16b, which clearly refers to Jewish holidays (on which see below). Thus it is highly improbable that "food and drink" in verse 16a refers to common, everyday meals or to Hellenistic cultic purification practices.

The false teaching associated with the topic of the temple continues in the second part of verse 16. The verse states what believers are further not to be judged by: "in respect to a feast[12] or a new moon or Sabbath days."* These three words (ἑορτή, νεομηνία, σάββατον, *heortē, neomēnia, sabbaton*) occur as a triadic formula in the LXX and early Judaism, almost always inextricably linked to temple sacrifices or temple worship;[13] or when the temple is

---

The combination of βρῶμα and πόμα (*brōma* and *poma*), near synonyms of the words used in Col. 2:16, does occur; e.g., see Chaeremon (1st cent. AD), frag. 10, in Porphyry, *Abst.* 4.7, which refers to Egyptian priests not being able "to touch [ἅπτεσθαι, *haptesthai*] foods or drinks produced outside of Egypt" in order to be pure for their service in the temple (cf. also with Col. 2:21). Typical Hellenistic temple practices of washings and dietary practices to achieve purity are summarized by Diogenes Laertius, *Notes* 8.33: "Purification is by cleansing . . . and the other abstinences prescribed by those who perform mystic rites in the temples" (cited by DeMaris 1994: 108). The combination of βρῶμα and πόμα/πῶμα (*brōma* and *poma*/*pōma*) also occurs typically in noncultic contexts of ordinary food and drink: e.g., among a number of uses in Hippocrates, see *Anc. Med.* 15, 20 (the combination with the same sense occurs about fifteen other times in Hippocrates's works); see Plato's following works: *Rep.* 4 (437E); *Critias* (115B); *Laws* 11 (932E); also Plutarch: *Well* 26 (*Mor.* 136F); *Bus.* 13 (*Mor.* 521F); *Spart.* 24 (*Mor.* 210C); and Epictetus, *Ench.* 33.2; Galen, *Art* 7 (493K); Athenaeus, *Banq.* 3 (123D) and 4 (152E); Dio Cassius, *Hist.*, Epitome 68 (31); Xenophon, *Mem.* 4.9; *Cyr.* 5.17. The pursuit of purity in Platonic tradition entailed self-restraint in many matters, including "food" and "drink" (DeMaris 1994: 110). That many ancient peoples had customs pertaining to dietary issues is attested by Epictetus, *Diss.* 1.11.12: "Is it possible at this present time that all the opinions which Jews, and Syrians, and Egyptians and Romans hold on the subject of food are rightly held?" (cited by Hay 2000: 103).

12. "Feasts" can also be translated "festivals," which include the Festival of Tabernacles or Booths and the Festival of Passover or Unleavened Bread (see further D. Moo 2008: 220). The word ἑορτή (*heortē*) can refer to Hellenistic pagan holidays (Plutarch, *T. Talk 4* 6.2 [*Mor.* 671D], where Plutarch refers to the Jews' Feast of Booths as a feast to Dionysius); "new moon" and "feast" also can refer to pagan holidays (Plutarch, *Is. Os.* 43; and *Rom.* 12); sometimes the celebration of feasts and new moons together with fasting was part of cultic rituals performed in conjunction with mystery religions (so Plutarch, *Def. Orac.* 13–14); and Plutarch (*Is. Os.* 42–43) on Egyptian religion uses ἑορτή (*heortē*) with νουμηνία (*noumēnia*), the latter a variant form of νεομηνία (*neomēnia*; see MHT 2:91). However, pagan holidays are not likely primarily in mind in Col. 2:16, as we will argue.

13. See LXX: 1 Chron. 23:31; 2 Chron. 2:3 (2:4 Eng.); 8:13 (though "months" replaces "new moons"); 31:3; 1 Esd. 5:51–53 (held at the site where the second temple was to be built); Neh. 10:33; Isa. 1:13–14 (though more loosely; cf. also 1:12); Ezek. 45:17; Josephus, *Ant.* 11.77 (held at the altar on the site for the second temple); Josephus, *J.W.* 5.230 (though "seventh days" replaces

not explicitly mentioned, it is likely assumed to be in mind to some degree, since these feasts were held at the temple.[14] While "feasts," "new moons," and "sabbaths" were observed by some Gentiles,[15] this triadic formula is not found elsewhere in pagan Greek contexts but only within OT and Jewish contexts.[16] Therefore, the triadic formula in the LXX is the framework for understanding the threefold mention of the holidays of Col. 2:16 and shows the clear Jewish context and association with the temple there. Not only were the false teachers demanding obedience to dietary laws for cleanness to prepare for heavenly temple worship; they were also requiring that people observe the traditional Jewish holidays (perhaps through fasting,[17] "self-abasement" [vv.

"Sabbaths"); Philo, *Spec.* 1.168 (though "seven days" replaces "sabbaths"). In some texts only two of the holidays are mentioned similarly with some link to the temple: see in this respect, Ezek. 44:24 (e.g., "feasts" and "Sabbaths"); 46:3; 1 Macc. 1:39; 1:45; Philo, *Spec.* 1.182; 2.140, 144–45. The group at Qumran believed that on each Sabbath, worship and sacrifices were performed by the angelic priests in the heavenly temple (see, e.g., Davila 2000b: 83–167); in the Qumran Songs of the Sabbath Sacrifice, human worshipers were brought progressively to the heavenly temple vestibules, then through the veil of the sanctuary, to the foot of the throne, and lastly to the vision of the throne itself, where climactically the Sabbath sacrifice occurred (Baumgarten 1988: 201). Sacrifices offered "on the new months," on "the festivals," and on "the Day of Atonement" "effected atonement for a clean person who has eaten something unclean," and all such sacrifices "are offered up to effect atonement for imparting uncleanness to the sanctuary and its Holy Things" (m. Shevu. 1.4–5, trans. Neusner 1988). Also, 1QS refers to "new moons arriving" and that "their being renewed" is "a great day for the Holy of Holies" (10.3–4), and this is likewise directly linked to "holy days" (10.5) and a "feast [appointed time] of harvest . . . [and] feasts [appointed times] of their weeks [sevens] of years" (10.7).

14. Hosea 2:11; Jdt. 8:6; 1 Macc. 10:34. In some LXX texts only two of the holidays are mentioned, likewise with no explicit mention of temple, as in 2 Kings 4:23 (e.g., "new moon" and "sabbath"); Ps. 80:4 [81:3 Eng.]; Ezek. 23:34 [not in Eng.]; Lam. 2:6. See also Jub. 6.37, where "months and Sabbaths and feasts" occurs also in no explicit connection with the temple, but there is no extant Greek for this (likewise Jub. 6.38).

15. So Wilson 2005: 216–18. With respect only to Gentiles keeping the Sabbath, see Suetonius, *Tib.* 32.2 (cited by Pokorný 1991: 143), but, as the LCL note says, this may merely be a reference "to the seventh day of the week (Saturday)," using the Jewish term (cf. Suetonius, *Aug.* 76.2). Arnold (1995: 216) cites evidence that in Colossae there was worship of moon-gods, which likely would have occurred at various phases of the moon; similarly, there were mystery initiation rites in Asia Minor that took place on a "new moon."

16. The pl. "sabbaths" mentioned by itself and not part of the triadic formula in the LXX refers not merely to the one-day Sabbath each week (e.g., Exod. 16:23, often used; sometimes viewed as kept throughout the year) but also to the whole sabbatical system of not only sabbath "days" but also of sabbath "months and seasons and years" (Gal. 4:10). This would include the observance of the Sabbatical Year (every seventh year the ground was to rest; often used, as in Lev. 25:2) and likely sometimes included the Jubilee Year (after seven weeks of years came prescribed restoration of property that had been lost; see the pl. "sabbaths" of the land in Lev. 25:2 and 6 and cf. with 25:8–13, which links this with the Jubilee Year after seven weeks of years, as in 25:8 "seven sabbaths of years" = ἑπτὰ ἀναπαύσεις ἐτῶν, *hepta anapauseis etōn*, where ἀναπαύσεις is synonymous with σάββατα [*sabbata*]; cf. 1 Macc. 10:34). The same multiple meaning of "sabbaths" may be included in the triadic formula in the LXX and in Col. 2:16, though MHT 3:27 sees it as a Semitic pl. indicating a singular sabbath, which is possible.

17. "Fasting" appears to be associated in some way with these holidays (e.g., see Philo, *Spec.* 1.169; cf. 1.186) and was associated with gathering at the temple court (e.g., Josephus, *Ant.* 10.93) or with the Yom Kippur sacrifice made at the temple (Josephus, *J.W.* 5.236; Philo, *Emb.*

18, 23], "severe treatment of the body" [v. 23], and other regulations) in order to be eligible for such temple worship.

It is beyond coincidence that the dietary and holiday requirements of verse 16 are inextricably linked with worship at the temple.[18] The temple is not a new theme emerging here for the first time. As we have seen, it has been popping up at various points throughout the epistle. However, thus far the references have been either to Christ as the temple or to believers identified with him as the temple. This is the first time that a false view of the qualifications for temple worship has appeared in Colossians. Here is but the beginning of an explanation of a false view of the temple, an antitemple detour, in contrast to the true temple, which will reach its climax in verse 18.[19] This false teaching about dietary laws and holidays is clearly rooted in a distortion of OT and Jewish ideas, especially related to the temple, which commentators have not previously recognized.[20]

Now Paul says that the Colossian Christians should not be judged by the OT **2:17**
requirements of verse 16 because they are "a shadow [σκιά, *skia*] of what was about to come [μελλόντων, *mellontōn*],"[21] and "Christ" is the "substance" of those foreshadowings.* Since the shadows have found their substantial

---

306). Philo, *Mos.* 2.23 relates "fasting" to it being "not lawful to take any food or any drink" (so also Philo, *Decal.* 159; *Spec.* 2.197). There was even a holiday only for fasting, called "a Sabbath of Sabbaths" (Philo, *Spec.* 2.194).

18. An observation also made by Pao (2012: 195), though he uses the word "cultic" instead of "temple" or "tabernacle." *EDEJ* 636–45 notes that before the AD 70 destruction of the temple, all the festivals and holy days (Passover [Unleavened Bread], Festival of Weeks [Pentecost/Firstfruits], Tabernacles, Day of Atonement, Trumpets [marking holidays celebrated at the temple: e.g., Lev. 23:23–25; Num. 10:10; 29:1–6], new moons, Hanukkah, and other festivals) were celebrated in worship at the temple, usually through sacrifice. Apparently Purim and a few minor feasts of the Second Temple period were the only holidays not celebrated in the temple. The only public fast established by the Torah was for the Day of Atonement, which was centered in the temple. Other fasts of the Second Temple period were instituted, but it is not clear whether they were observed regularly.

19. Strikingly, Rom. 14:1–23, the only occurrence in the NT of the very same language as Col. 2:16, says that Christians are not to be "judged" (κρίνω, *krinō*) by what was formerly (in the OT) considered to be "unclean" "food and drink" (βρῶσις καὶ πόσις, *brōsis kai posis*, Rom. 14:17) and by religious holidays because of the death and resurrection of Christ, whom Christians serve above all else (14:6–9, 18). The same phrase "the meat and the drink" (τὴν βρῶσιν . . . καὶ τὴν πόσιν, *tēn brōsin . . . kai tēn posin*) occurs in Dan. 1:10 (OG, Theod.) to refer to "defiled" food and drink that Daniel and his friends would not ingest (1:8–9). Daniel was certainly trying to obey the purity laws of Israel while in exile. Note also the use of "food and drink" (using varying cognate forms of βρῶσις [*brōsis*] and πόσις [*posis*] found in Col. 2:16) in Ezra 3:7 (βρώματα καὶ ποτά, *brōmata kai pota*) and in 1 Esd. 5:53 (5:54 Eng.; βρωτὰ καὶ ποτά, *brōta kai pota*), which do not refer to temple laws of cleanness. Except for John 6:55, as far as I can tell, the above are the only uses of the phrase "food and drink" in the NT and LXX.

20. Except in the passing and peripheral comment above by Dunn 1996: 191–92.

21. Most translations render μελλόντων (*mellontōn*) something like "of what is to come" (e.g., NASB). But μελλόντων, a present tense participle, is probably better translated in a past-tense manner as above (NEB, NIV, NJB, HCSB), since it is in the context of an OT perspective looking toward the coming new age.

fulfillment in Christ, it is not necessary to obey them anymore. Hebrews 10:1 expresses almost the identical idea: "For the Law, since it has only a shadow [σκιά, *skia*] of the good things to come [μέλλω, *mellō*] and not the very form of things, can never, by the same sacrifices which they offer continually year by year, make perfect those who draw near." In the following verses of Hebrews, Christ as the supreme sacrifice is presented as that to which the "shadow" of the sacrifices pointed. Thus the continual OT sacrifices by human priests are to be abolished, since what they pointed to has come, which is "better" (Heb. 7:19) and "greater" (Heb. 9:11).[22]

It is possible that "body" refers to Christ's fleshly body, in light of Col. 1:22 and 2:11, where "body" does refer to this (and 2:9 uses the adverb "bodily" in the same way). Alternatively, some think that the phrase "body of Christ" (σῶμα τοῦ Χριστοῦ, *sōma tou Christou*) refers to the church, since the church is called Christ's "body" (σῶμα, *sōma*) in Col. 1:18, 24 (?); 2:19; and 3:15 (the latter by implication).[23] Accordingly, the most straightforward translation of these first two options would be something like "but [and] the body is of Christ." While these are possible, it is more likely that "body" here refers to the person of Christ as the "substance" of fulfillment.[24] The rendering could be "the substance [or body] is Christ" (an appositional genitive) or "the substance [body] belongs to Christ" (NASB, NRSV, ESV, cf. ASV; genitive of possession). The NLT puts it nicely: "Christ himself is that reality" (likewise NIV, NJB, NET). "Substance" is a better counterpoint to "shadows" than is Christ's flesh or the church as Christ's body.

The idea is that the things mentioned in Col. 2:16 are typological foreshadowings of Christ, and these foreshadowings have found the substance to which they point in Christ. Since typology entails that the antitype is seen more clearly retrospectively,[25] it appears that the literal notion of a "substantive body" or "reality" casting a shadow is in mind here (see BDAG 984, s.v. σῶμα; a "shadow" always follows a "body"; Philo, *Decal.* 82; *Virt.* 118, 181).

22. Hebrews 8:5 also speaks of the tabernacle as a "shadow" of the heavenly tabernacle, so that this might be called vertical typology (cf. Heb. 8:1–4). The full substance of the "shadow" of the heavenly reality came in Christ. On this concept of vertical typology and its relationship to the NT, see Vos 1956: 55–58.

23. E.g., see Sumney 2008: 152–53. The word occurs in this corporate sense also nine times in 1 Cor. 12; likewise Rom. 12:4–5; 1 Cor. 10:16–17.

24. Some think both ideas of the corporate "body" of Christ and the individual Christ as the "substance" could be in mind (e.g., Wilson 2005: 220; Pao 2012: 186–87; cf. similarly N. Wright 1986: 120–21), but this overstrains the meaning (cf. also Gupta 2013a: 100, who sees three layers of meaning: substance, human body of Christ, and communal body of Christ).

25. Typology may be defined as the study of analogical correspondences between persons, events, and institutions, within the historical framework of Scripture, which from a retrospective view are of a prophetic nature and are escalated in their meaning. Typology is retrospective in the sense that the type is seen more clearly from the NT vantage point. Typology involves escalation in that the NT correspondence (the antitype) to the OT type is heightened (e.g., Jesus as a lamb in John 19:36 is greater than the Passover lamb that was slain in Exod. 12:46; cf. also Num. 9:12; Ps. 34:20). See Ribbens (2011) for an overview of different definitions of typology, not all of which include a forward-pointing aspect.

It is true that the shadows in the OT point forward to Christ, but they do so only because Christ has now come, and it is clear that he himself is the "body" casting those shadows (likewise Hendriksen 1964: 124).[26] Accordingly, among possible metaphorical associations of the ancient "body-shadow" picture relevant here is that the person of Christ casts his shadow back onto the OT, so that he "overshadows" the OT institutions, showing himself to be more dominant and important than the inferior institutions that pointed to him (e.g., cf. Ezek. 31:6; Dan. 4:9, 12). Fittingly, the phrase σκιὰ τῶν μελλόντων would be a subjective genitive ("shadows cast by what things [Christ] were about to come"). The two other renderings of σῶμα (sōma) as Christ's flesh or the church as Christ's body could still fit within such a typological framework, but not as nicely as "substantive body."

In this epistle we have already seen OT types fulfilled in Christ and his people: Israel's exodus from Egypt pointed to a greater exodus of God's people led by Christ (1:13–14a); the promised land pointed to a greater inheritance for Christ's followers (1:12); the Torah, as the epitome of wisdom, pointed to and was fulfilled by Christ as the greater wisdom (2:3); circumcision pointed to Christ's death and the spiritual circumcision of his followers (2:11, 13); the OT temple pointed to Christ and was fulfilled in him (1:19; 2:9) and his people as part of the temple (1:9–10; 2:10). And we shall see more types in Col. 3. Beetham (2008: 251) says that the dietary regulations and the sacred holidays found their typological "reality . . . in Christ of the new age." But precisely how do the clean and unclean laws and the prescribed holidays find their typological fulfillment in Christ? More specifically, the function of the dietary laws to make people clean for temple worship finds its reality in Christ's sacrificial cleansing of people through his death in the new temple (see Rom. 3:25; see also Beale 2011: 486–96) to make them pure for worship in that temple. Christ's spiritual circumcision of his people has also qualified them to be clean to enter the spiritual temple and worship there (see on Col. 2:13).

But how do the sacred holidays point to Christ? We concluded (above) that the tripartite formula of "festival, new moon, and Sabbaths" is inextricably linked to temple sacrifices or temple worship. The regulations (e.g., fasting, various bodily disciplines) connected with keeping these holidays were typically part of the preparation for temple worship. These holiday regulations are no longer needed, since the old temple has superseded, and Christ is the new temple and the ultimate temple sacrifice, and only by faith—not through OT rituals—are believers in union with him as the temple. As a consequence, the observance of these holy days is not obligatory in the new-covenant age. Some conclude from this that the "Sabbaths" mentioned in Col. 2:16 mean that the Christian Sunday is not a continuation of the OT Sabbath-day observance (e.g., see D. Moo 2008: 223). This is a possible view, though we think not the best. Yet this is a thorny biblical-theological issue that cannot be fully addressed here (see the additional notes).

26. I am indebted to my research assistant, Todd Scacewater, for alerting me to this notion based on BDAG.

Thus the dietary laws and holidays pointed to Christ as the temple, in whom people are now pure. Consequently, they are able to worship in him as the temple. Paul's contrast of the former OT epoch of shadows with the new age in Christ, the substance, shows that believers are not obligated to follow the shadowy laws but only Christ. The OT-NT contrast also further reveals the OT root of the laws mentioned in verse 16.

2:18 This verse is one of the most debated texts in Colossians and perhaps in the entire NT. The verb καταβραβεύω (*katabrabeuō*) is likely a synonym of "judge" (κρίνω, *krinō*) in verse 16 (indeed, NET translates the verb in verse 18 as "let no one . . . pass judgment on you"; likewise NLT). The word has a judicial sense of "condemn" or "rule against" in its extrabiblical Classical Greek and Hellenistic uses (Beetham 2008: 202–3). The command, as with the negative command of verse 16, further enforces the warning of verse 8 "not to be captivated" by the false teachers (D. Moo 2008: 229). Some versions translate the verb as "Let no one disqualify you" (NRSV, ESV, HCSB), while others have something like "Let no one rob you of your prize" (ASV, likewise KJV). These are two sides of one coin: whoever is disqualified in a race does not get the prize at the end. The NIV 1984 puts both notions together: "Do not let anyone . . . disqualify you for the prize" (likewise NJB). The notion of judging one's actions (as does an umpire)[27] is common to both renderings. The false teachers are contending that if one does not follow their "self-made religious" rules, then one is disqualified from and robbed of the prize of fully experiencing Christ's presence. They would be declared to be second-class Christians at best. In reality, as Paul will get to later, the Colossians need to be assured that only "the peace of Christ should judge"* or "act as arbiter" (or rule, βραβευέτω, *brabeuetō*) over them (Col. 3:15).

Accordingly, Col. 2:18 is probably parallel to verse 16 in offering more regulations by which Christians are being judged. And verse 18, like verse 16, is based on the main point of 2:6–15. That is, Christian living focused squarely on Christ (vv. 6–15) is the basis for Paul saying, "Let no one disqualify you . . ." by anything other than the standard of Christ himself.

The false teachers are wrongly disqualifying people by means of at least two criteria, which are not based on a Christ-centered faith: "by taking pleasure[28] in self-abasement and worship of angels."* The word ταπεινοφροσύνη (*tapeinophrosynē*) can be rendered "self-abasement" (NRSV, NASB), "voluntary humility" (ASV, KJV), "false humility" (NIV, NET), or merely "humility" (ISV). The context of false teaching shows that this is not true, godly humility, so the NIV may express the idea well, though the ESV's "asceticism" is best

27. See BDAG 515, s.v. καταβραβεύω. Foster (2016: 286–87) prefers the renderings of "condemn" (in a forensic context) or "injure, mistreat, victimize," since he does not see that any judging with athletic imagery carries over into the use in verse 18.

28. So BDAG 448, s.v. θέλω 3. Some translate "by delighting in," viewing the use of θέλων ἐν (*thelōn en*) here to be a Septuagintalism (so seven times in the LXX, where the Greek phrase translates the Hebrew חפץ [*ḥpṣ*] + prefixed preposition ב [*b*]).

(likewise HCSB, "ascetic practices"). The mention of dietary laws in verses 16 and 21 points to such a meaning, as does verse 23, which explains the same word ταπεινοφροσύνη by "severe treatment of the body." Furthermore, the verbal form of ταπεινόω (*tapeinoō*) inextricably links "humility" with "fasting."[29] The noun form ταπεινός (*tapeinos*) is used in the same way (1 Clem. 55.6).

Why would the readers be urged toward such asceticism?[30] The next clause answers this question: to prepare for "the worship of angels." The NJB paraphrases it well: one "who chooses to grovel [ταπεινοφροσύνη] to angels and worship them." It is beyond coincidence that becoming "humble" in terms of "fasting" in OT and early Christian literature was a preparation toward seeing heavenly visions (Dan. 10:1–12; Herm. 18.6–10 [= *Vis.* 3.10], which includes "injuring your flesh"; 56.5–7 [= *Sim.* 5.3]; cf. also 6.1; 9.1–2 [= *Vis.* 2.2; 3.1]). Also, Jos. Asen. 10–13 portrays Aseneth's "humiliation" (11.1, ταπείνωσις, *tapeinōsis*)[31] as preparing her for a visitation of an angel, who announces that God accepts her. In addition to Joseph and Aseneth, fasting was likewise preparatory for heavenly temple visions in other Jewish texts.[32]

There is debate about whether θρησκείᾳ τῶν ἀγγέλων (*thrēskeia tōn angelōn*) refers to actually "worshiping angels" (an objective genitive)[33] or to "worship by the angels" (a subjective genitive).[34] According to the latter view, the misguided teachers were not merely taking pleasure in beholding angels worshiping but presumably wanted to worship along with them. The preposition ἐν (*en*) before ταπεινοφροσύνῃ (*tapeinophrosynē*) and its absence before θρησκείᾳ suggest a close conceptual link between the asceticism and worship (e.g., see Harris 2010: 107). This could mean either that the asceticism is directed toward a view for preparation to worship angels (according to the objective genitive option) or that this refers to the humility of the angels themselves and worship by angels (the subjective genitive alternative).[35] Accordingly, under either view, this placement of the preposition would also suggest that

29. So Ezra 8:21; Ps. 34:13 (35:13 Eng.; including wearing "sackcloth"); Isa. 58:3, 5 (including wearing "sackcloth" and harsh treatment of the body); Dan. 10:1–12 (including "mourning" and fasting: no "tasty food," no "meat or wine," no "ointment," and "mourning" for three weeks).

30. "Asceticism" may be defined as a life of self-denial, including such things as fasting and rigorous bodily discipline, and a general avoiding of any bodily pleasure, which could be construed as "neglecting the body" (see on 2:23; cf. "ascetic," *Merriam-Webster.com*, http://www.merriam-webster.com/dictionary/asceticism).

31. Her "humiliation" included weeping (10.2), beating the chest (11.1), fasting (10.2, 17), taking off all ornamentation (10.9–11), wearing sackcloth (10.14), lying down in ashes (10.16; 11.1), giving her dinner to dogs (10.13), and pulling her hair from her head (11.1; following Beetham 2008: 209).

32. E.g., Apoc. Ab. 9.7 and Mart. Ascen. Isa. 2.7–11, cited by Francis 1975b: 169; see further in the additional note on 2:18.

33. The majority of commentators have supported this view here; e.g., Arnold 1995: 92–95.

34. So Francis 1975b: 176–80. Following Francis are, e.g., Lincoln 1981: 111–12; Barth and Blanke 1994: 345–46; Dunn 1996: 179–82; O'Brien 1982: 142–43; Rowland 1983; Sappington 1991: 158–61. This view has had increasing popularity in recent years.

35. This construction with ἐν (*en*) could be a hendiadys: "false human humility expressed in angel worship" (Harris 2010: 107, expressing the objective genitive view) or "humility expressed

the genitive τῶν ἀγγέλων would modify both θρησκείᾳ and ταπεινοφροσύνῃ (so Lenski 1961: 130; Sumney 2008: 154).

The immediate context must ultimately decide the issue about whether this is an objective or subjective genitive. The context could allow either of these options. Nevertheless, the first option appears to be preferable, since elsewhere typically "the being who is worshiped is given the objective genitive" after θρησκεία (BDAG 459, s.v. θρησκεία; see further in the additional note on 2:18). There is some evidence of actually worshiping angels elsewhere in Asia Minor (BDAG 459, s.v. θρησκεία) and in Judaism (LAB 13.6; 1QSb 4.28, "You will glorify His name and his Holy Ones"; t. Hul. 2.18).[36]

Therefore, actually "worshiping angels" is likely correct, which expresses an idea of idolatry. The immediate context of 2:18 repeatedly refers to idolatrous ideas, so that it is more probable that "worshiping angels" is in mind in 2:18. For example, "the tradition of men" in 2:8 and "commandments and teachings of men" in 2:22 are allusions to Isa. 29:13 LXX, which is about idolatry (see on 2:22). Furthermore, the "philosophy" of Col. 2:8 is said "not to be based on Christ,"* and similarly the false teaching in verse 19 is said to be "not holding fast to the head [Christ]." This means that the errant philosophy is focused, even if subtly so, on an object of worship other than Christ, which is idolatry. In addition, "self-made religion" in 2:23 appears to be idolatrous, since it does not come from God (Walsh and Keesmaat 2004: 142–44, with further discussion of the idolatry context of Col. 2). In addition, the unique threefold combination of θέλω (*thelō*), ταπεινοφροσύνη, and θρησκεία in 2:18 shows that the parallel combination of ἐθελοθρησκία (*ethelothrēskia*) and ταπεινοφροσύνη (*tapeinophrosynē*) in 2:23 is developing in 2:18. This points further to an objective genitive in the latter text. That is, in 2:23 the "self-made worship" ἐθελοθρησκία is clearly conducted by humans and not angels, so it is probable that the worship (θρησκεία) in 2:18 is conducted by humans with angels as the object of the veneration (so Arnold 1995: e.g., 93–95).[37]

---

in worship by angels" or "the angels' lowliness with which they bring their worship to God" (reflecting the subjective genitive option; the latter rendering is preferred by Lenski 1961: 130).

36. See further, e.g., Dunn (1996: 179–80) and Arnold (1995: 32–60), esp. in Judaism, and the additional note on 2:18.

37. In particular, Arnold (1995: 11–102) cites evidence in Asia Minor and the environs of Colossae that angels were invoked through magical practices for help and protection from evil powers, thus becoming the object of veneration by personal petitioners, and such angelic veneration became tantamount to worshiping the angels. This was the case in Jewish, Christian, and pagan contexts (Arnold 1995: 88). However, see Witherington (2007: 162) for reasonable caution in accepting Arnold's conclusions, including that the majority of Arnold's evidence from the magical papyri comes from the third and fourth centuries AD and that requesting angels to placate hostile powers may not be the same as worshiping angels. However, Arnold (1995: 102) qualifies his view by saying that there is no evidence that angels are worshiped in a cultic context; it appears that, to the neglect of Christ, the Colossians were either calling on angels for protection or were putting angels on the same level as Christ. See also Stuckenbruck (1995) for evidence of varying degrees of angel veneration in Judaism. See on Col. 2:23 below for a response to this view and for alternative translations of this word ἐθελοθρησκία (*ethelothrēskia*).

Even trusted Christian leaders elsewhere were guilty of such idolatry. For example, Rev. 19:10 says that John "fell at his feet to worship" an angel; so also Rev. 22:8. Similarly, Mart. Ascen. Isa. 7.21, in a context where Isaiah ascends into the temple,[38] has Isaiah saying, "I fell on my face to worship him, and the angel who led me would not let me" (see likewise Mart. Ascen. Isa. 9.36). In an apparently unguarded moment, Justin Martyr (*1 Apol.* 6) says that Christians "worship and adore" the Father "and the Son . . . and the host of angels who follow and are made like to Him."[39] Thus it is easy to see how false teachers could worship angels and propagate such a teaching. A major concern of Colossians has been to highlight the superiority of Christ over all spiritual beings (1:16, 20; 2:10, 15). For Paul to minimize the importance of angels at this point would be suitable, if, in fact, the false teachers are worshiping them (D. Moo 2008: 227). Perhaps the errant teachers are so obsessed with speculations about angels (e.g., how they might provide protection) that they are either neglecting Christ or putting Christ and angels on the same level, thus having an angel-centered faith instead of a Christ-centered one (Arnold 1995: 102; cf. also N. Wright 1986: 122). This is idolatry.

But even if a subjective genitive is preferable, which is plausible, the main focus is on practicing asceticism in order to experience a revelatory vision of angels, as the immediately following phrase shows: "whom [angels] he has seen."

Now we come to the most controverted word in the whole epistle. What does the participle ἐμβατεύων (*embateuōn*) mean, and how does it relate syntactically to ἃ ἑόρακεν (*ha heoraken*)? There are at least four main ways to understand the meaning of this word.

1. "Taking his stand [or setting foot] on visions he has seen" (NASB; similarly ASV, NRSV; so also Caird 1976: 199). The phrase ἃ ἑόρακεν is the object of ἐμβατεύων, which is translated as "taking his stand."
2. A second meaning is "investigating" or "entering into detail" about visions that have been seen (NIV, ESV, NET) or about the errant "philosophy" (cf. 2:8). This is the least likely option, since its meaning is possibly attested in only one place (2 Macc. 2:30)[40] throughout uses in the LXX, Hellenistic Judaism, Classical Greek, and other Hellenistic sources.[41]

38. Cf. Mart. Ascen. Isa. 8.17; 9.28–33; with a temple setting in 7.17, 27; 9.27, 37; 10.6; and 11.32.

39. Cited by Houlden (1977: 165), followed by Garland 1998: 194.

40. Even here the standard translations do not have "investigate" or "enter into detail." KJV has "to stand upon every point," and RSV and NETS have "to occupy the ground."

41. Wall 1993: 124; likewise Barth and Blanke 1994: 348; D. Moo (2008: 229) also prefers this view, contending that most of the English translations follow this kind of rendering, but this is not apparent to me. Some cite Philo (*Plant.* 80) as a supporting use, but the word here in the LCL edition, though perhaps related, is ἐμβαθύνω (*embathynō*), "make deep, hollow out, go deep into, sink deep in" (LSJ 538), which LCL translates as "go deeper." Lohse (1971: 119) recognizes ἐμβαθύνοντες (*embathynontes*) as the LCL reading but also cites a variant reading of ἐμβατεύοντες (*embateuontes*), which he translates as "research." Though the LCL text

3. "Entering into possession of [something]." Some see this as entering into "a visionary realm of heaven" to fully possess salvation (cf. HCSB),[42] while others see this as "entering to possess the full inheritance," the latter of which is supported by uses of ἐμβατεύω in the LXX to refer to the Israelites possessing the inheritance of the land promises (Josh. 19:49, 51).[43] Joshua 19:49 also uses the word "inheritance" (κλῆρος, *klēros*) of Israel's possession of the land, after their exodus from Egypt. This could be significant, since the Colossians context mentions that believers have an "inheritance" (1:12, κλῆρος; 3:24, κληρονομία, *klēronomia*), and this is also in connection with allusions to Israel's exodus (see above on Col. 1:12–14). Beetham (2008: 206–8) contends that this LXX exodus-inheritance background is the best way to understand ἐμβατεύω in Col. 2:18, especially since this notion is enforced by other classical and Hellenistic uses of ἐμβατεύω referring to "entry into possession of an inheritance." He says this would make sense of 1:12, where Paul stresses that believers have been "qualified to share in the saints' inheritance in the light" (Pao [2012: 190] follows Beetham). This would counter the false teachers' insinuation that Christians are unworthy of a heavenly inheritance if they have not experienced and "entered into" the heavenly visions mentioned in 2:18. This is certainly a viable option.
4. A fourth meaning is that of "entering into the innermost sanctuary."[44] This is the view Dibelius put forth in 1917 (see 1975: esp. 85–90), though he

lists no textual variants, the critical text of Philo by Cohn and Wendland (1897: 149) lists three MSS (M, U, F) attesting ἐμβαθύνοντες, one MS (G) with the similar form of ἐμβαθοῦντες (*embathountes*), and only one MS (H) attesting ἐμβατεύοντες, while preferring as the original reading ἐμβαθύνοντες. Apparently Lohse was aware of the Cohn and Wendland apparatus, but he omits mentioning that, in addition to LCL, they also prefer the ἐμβαθύνοντες reading. It is not clear if Lohse sees ἐμβατεύοντες as the preferred reading, but he leaves that implication open, and at least cites the Philo text as a use of this word in the sense of "research, investigate." Others who cite Philo in support of using ἐμβατεύοντες as "research" or "investigate" do not mention the textual problem or that LCL and Cohn and Wendland do not see it as the original reading (e.g., see H. Preisker, *TDNT* 2:535–36).

42. Some focus only on "entering into" a visionary realm of heaven, where heavenly worship occurs and the vision itself is vain; e.g., N. Wright 1986: 123; MacDonald 2000: 113; Witherington 2007: 162; Sumney 2008: 149, 146.

43. The following sources also use the word with the sense to "enter into" (possession of) an inheritance: Demosthenes, *Leoch.* 16 and 19; Euripides, *Herc.* 876; Isaeus, *Astyph.* 3 (74); and Pausanias, *Lexicon*, "ἐξούλης δίκη" (three times; see full trans. of Pausanias in Beetham 2008: 206). See likewise MM (205, ἐμβατεύω), who observe this usage in the papyri (cf. similarly P.Tor.Choach. 8 [127 BC], where someone "enters into possession" illegally of a house, which a son should have inherited). Other uses of this word in the LXX refer to someone "invading" ("entering into") another country (1 Macc. 12:25; 13:20; 14:31; 15:40) or to a male dog sexually "possessing" or "entering" a female dog (Palaephatus, *Unbeliev.* 39; cf. Stern 1996: 71); straightforwardly the line reads, "Put under him [the male dog] a female dog *to enter* [or to *possess*]."

44. BDAG 321, s.v. ἐμβατεύω, lists these four options, though with the last it also gives the alternative meaning of "enter the oracular chamber for consultation," or "what he saw when he was initiated [into the mysteries]," or "*taking his stand on what he has seen* in the mysteries," the latter of which overlaps with category 1 in BDAG.

was anticipated a few years earlier by Ramsay (1914: 287–90). Dibelius's view about ἐμβατεύω dominated the interpretation of Col. 2:18 during the last half of the twentieth century (Francis 1975b: 166) and has become "the dominant interpretation" (O'Brien 1982: 144).[45]

All four of these meanings are possible,[46] especially the first, third, and fourth. The third is attractive because of its affinity with the inheritance theme in the broader context of Colossians. Some commentators merely acknowledge some of these options without choosing one and arguing for it.[47] However, the fourth view is preferable, as we will argue (though we will see that it has some overlap with the third option). More recently Arnold (1995) has argued for this fourth option most persuasively, and some of the following is a summary of his view, with qualifications here and there.

According to the fourth view, there are two main ways to understand how ἐμβατεύω functions syntactically. First, the participle is adverbial, modifying ἑόρακεν (the later view of Dibelius 1953: 34–36; also Francis 1975b: 167; Sappington 1991: 156–58):[48] "Let no one disqualify you by taking pleasure in asceticism and worship of angels, whom[49] he has seen when he enters [into the heavenly sanctuary]."[50] The formal parallelism of verse 18 with verses 17 and 22 supports this view. In verses 17 and 22, the neuter plural accusative relative pronoun ἅ (*ha*) sums up a list of preceding members, which in verse 16 are feminine and neuter[51] (so also in 3:6, likewise referring to preceding feminine and neuter nouns, though introduced with διά, *dia*). However, the parallel might break down a bit, since the ἅ in 2:18 could refer back only to "angels" and not also to "asceticism."[52] Furthermore, there is no parallel employment

45. So also Foster 2016: 291–92. Likewise, Wilson (2005: 223–24), who leans toward this view and says that Dibelius's view is perhaps "the most widely accepted meaning." So also Schweizer (1982: 160–62), who says, "Most likely, then the idea here is of a visionary experience . . . in which the Colossians did indeed experience entry into the heavenly sanctuary." Likewise Lohse 1971: 119–21; Bruce 1984: 12–122; Ernst 1974: 210; Schweizer 1982: 161–62. Lona (1984: 210–11) sees this view as a possibility but thinks it must be understood as an entering into the temple where there is "Engel-verehrung" (angel worship). See Arnold (1995: 106) for a long list of commentators following this view. Gnilka (1980: 151) combines the mystery-cult context proposed by Dibelius and others with the translation of "was er eintretend (= bei der Weihe) geschaut hat" (what while entering [= at the consecration] he has beheld).

46. A fifth meaning is based on a textual variant that adds μή (*mē*) after ἅ (*ha*); see the additional note.

47. E.g., Garland 1998: 180–81; likewise Moule 1957: 104–6.

48. Francis (1975b: 167) and Sappington (1991: 156–58) at this point mention only the notion of "entering heaven" and not specifically "entering into the temple."

49. Here the neuter accusative plural relative pronoun can easily be rendered as "whom," as it is likewise in Matt. 11:16; Luke 7:32; Heb. 2:13; Rev. 1:4; 3:4. Or it could be rendered "which," referring both to the "asceticism" and "the worship of angels" (see further below).

50. This is my own rendering of this view.

51. And in 2:21 the reference is to verbs that assume objects of touch and taste.

52. Moule (1959: 130) says, "Sometimes a neuter relative is used where strictly a masculine or feminine might have been expected—presumably with reference to the 'whole idea' of the preceding clause rather than to the single word which is the immediate antecedent of the relative." If

of ἐστίν (*estin*) to introduce a judgment about the items that precede, as occurs in 2:17, 22 and 3:5, though a different verb than ἐστίν appears in 3:5 (as argued by Arnold 1995: 122).

On the other hand, Arnold (1995: 122–23, following another view of Dibelius 1975: 88) contends that the causal adverbial participle ἐμβατεύων (*embateuōn*) modifies the verb for "Let no one disqualify you" and should be rendered "because he 'entered the things he has seen.'" This adverbial understanding of the participle forms a nice parallelism with the preceding adverbial participle, θέλων (*thelōn*), which also modifies "Let no one disqualify you." In addition to the weaknesses just noted above about the first view, Arnold (1995: 122) says that this first view becomes especially improbable because "asceticism" (or "humility") must be viewed as the object of the vision together with the angels; and it would make no sense for "asceticism" to be understood as something that is "seen" (D. Moo [2008: 228–29] makes the same objection as Arnold). However, this is not a necessary entailment, since, as noted above, the object of the vision could be narrowly focused only on the directly preceding "angels" and not include "asceticism" ("humility").

But even if the neuter relative ἅ includes reference both to "self-abasement" (or "humility") together with "angels," it is possible that it refers to the "humility" of the angels, as well as "worship of the angels" (the subjective genitive view), both of which were seen in vision (understanding τῶν ἀγγέλων, *tōn angelōn*, to modify both "self-abasement" and "worship").[53] As noted earlier, the viability of this is pointed to by the observation that ἐν (*en*) before ταπεινοφροσύνῃ (*tapeinophrosynē*, self-abasement) is not repeated before θρησκείᾳ (*thrēskeia*, worship), so that the two should be taken together with τῶν ἀγγέλων, modifying both. Such a double duty of ἐν is common in the syntax of contemporary Hellenistic Greek (Francis 1975b: 180). Francis also argues in favor of this alternative but takes τῶν ἀγγέλων as a subjective genitive and renders the two clauses as "humility and worship by angels."[54]

---

that is the case here, then the relative pronoun would refer to both "asceticism" and "worship of angels." But this rule is the case only "sometimes," so that it is still possible to limit the antecedent only to the preceding "angels." In this respect, the ἅ (*ha*) could be a *constructio ad sensum*, "a construction according to sense," whereby the relative pronoun is neuter because, though ἄγγελος (*angelos*) is masculine in Greek grammatical gender, "angels" are neuter as actual beings. See BDAG (726, s.v. ὅς 1.c.ג.β) and Wallace (1996: 337–38) for such a construction having a change in gender with respect to relative pronouns. Wallace (1996: 337) notes that the *constructio ad sensum* in general for relative pronouns is not infrequent. Interestingly, BDAG (726) cites Col. 2:19 as one of its examples for this kind of specific construction, where Christ as "head" (κεφαλή, *kephalē*) is feminine and the following relative pronoun "whom" (ὅς, *hos*) is masculine because Christ in natural gender is masculine.

53. So, e.g., Sappington 1991: 158–61; and also Foster 2016: 290. Or alternatively, again the neuter relative ἅ (*ha*) could refer to both clauses, and the first clause would be understood in the sense of "acts of asceticism to foster visions of angels" followed by "worshiping angels" (the NJB similarly paraphrases by "to grovel to angels and worship them"), which would view the genitive as objective.

54. Francis 1975b: 180. Among others, Sappington (1991: 160) takes the same position as Francis. If this were the case, it would radically soften Arnold's criticism.

Arnold (1995: 123) proposes the following translation of his view:

"Let no one condemn you
by insisting[55] on
ascetic practices and
invoking angels
because he 'entered the things he has seen' (i.e., he based his knowledge/authority on visionary experiences he received during the final stage of his mystery initiation)."

He simplifies the meaning of the verse thus: "Let no one condemn you . . . because he has been initiated [and you have not]" (1995: 123). He proposes that Paul quotes ἃ ἑόρακεν ἐμβατεύων (*ha heoraken embateuōn*) as "a formula from a local mystery cult that summarizes the visionary experience of the one initiated" (1995: 125; so also Ramsay 1914: 286–87; Dibelius 1975: 88). Arnold's view includes taking "what things he has seen" as the object of "entering" (as does Dibelius 1975: 87). Accordingly, the inner sanctuary would be the main object of entry, but the neuter relative pronoun would take into view the entire experience of the visionary, which here would include seeing angels (Arnold 1995: 123). This is an alternative and very plausible way to understand the neuter relative pronoun.

In the Asia Minor mystery cults, there were two stages of initiation: (1) an initial entrance into an oracular grotto, followed by (2) a climactic entrance into the inner sanctuary, where the presence of the god resided. Three inscriptions were discovered in the Apollo temple at Claros, the earliest dated at AD 132 and the others to sometime later, likely in the mid-second century (Arnold 1995: 110–11). Strikingly, the second, climactic part of the initiation there is designated by ἐμβατεύω (*embateuō*), which describes the "entering" of the initiate into the innermost sanctuary of the god. In this respect, there are a total of four relevant inscriptions employing ἐμβατεύω.[56]

1. The earliest inscription describes men who came to the oracle for consultation and concludes by saying, "These men were initiated and then they entered [ἐμβατεύσαν, *embateusan*]."
2. Another inscription at Claros speaks of a man named Androcos, who "received the mysteries [the first stage of the initiation] and then he entered [ἐνεβάτευσεν, *enebateusen*]."
3. The third inscription describes two men, who "after they were initiated and they entered [ἐνβατεύσαντες, *enbateusantes*], they consulted the oracle."

55. Though this could be a causal adverbial participle ("because of insisting"), which would make the parallelism with the following adverbial participle even closer.

56. See Arnold (1995: 110–13) for a convenient presentation of the full Greek and English translations of the first four inscriptions.

4. Yet a fourth inscription was found in Laodicea, which also refers to some men who "were initiated and then they entered [ἐμβατεύσαντες]. Following this they consulted the oracle." Likewise, five other inscriptions associated with the Apollo temple from Claros were found, which also described an implied two-step process of initiation. Each refers to the initiates as *theopropoi*,[57] as do the Claros inscriptions, but instead of using ἐμβατεύω (*embateuō*), these inscriptions use the phrase ἐπετέλεσε καὶ τὰ μυστήρια (*epetelese kai ta mystēria*): "He completed also the mysteries." This phrase summarizes the two-stage initiation into the mysteries as a whole (Arnold 1995: 114). Arnold (1995: 114–18) cites numerous scholars who agree that the ἐμβατεύω (*embateuō*) inscriptions at Claros and Laodicea indicate a second, climactic stage of initiation, in which the initiate "entered" into the inner sanctuary in the very presence of the god (Ramsay 1914: 288–93; Dibelius 1975: 86–87; H. W. Parke 1985: 146, 219–24).[58] Also, Arnold (1995: 118) notes that the standard lexical sources affirm this meaning as one of its accepted usages (see the second additional note on 2:18).

More broadly speaking, it is significant that ἐμβατεύω in Classical and Hellenistic Greek refers to a god who habitually enters or dwells in a sacred space or temple. Josephus uses the verb to describe entry into Mount Sinai, which he views as a divine mountain sanctuary (see the second additional note on 2:18). In addition to the Claros and Laodicea inscriptions, though these uses are not part of a mystery initiation context, they further associate ἐμβατεύω (*embateuō*) with a sacred space or temple.[59]

Arnold (1995: 136–41) bolsters his position about ἐμβατεύω by arguing that the Isis mystery initiation recorded in Apuleius's *Metamorphoses* (AD 170) is representative of earlier mystery rites, including those of Claros and Laodicea, and has unique parallels with Col. 2 (though it does not contain the word ἐμβατεύω since it is written in Latin): (1) "entering" into a sanctuary (cf. Col. 2:18) (2) in conjunction with a *visionary* experience (cf. 2:18); (3) the vision of passing through the *elements* (*stoicheia*) provides a backdrop against which to understand the "elements" in Colossians (cf. 2:8, 20); (4) *fasting and other prohibitions* of discipline are to make the initiate pure and prepare for experiencing the god in the inner sanctuary (cf. 2:16, 18, 23); (5) the mystery cult ritual is made known to the initiate by means of a secret *tradition* (cf. 2:8); (6) one of the motives for going through the mystery initiation is to gain authority and protection against evil powers (cf.

57. One "sent to inquire of an oracle" (LSJ 791) or "questioners of the god" (Ramsay 1914: 288).

58. See Arnold (1995: 114–16) for others supporting this position.

59. Arnold (1995: 105n6) mentions only some of the classical texts in passing, not mentioning that they could enhance the notion in Col. 2:18 of "entering" into a temple; Arnold makes no mention of the relevant Josephus or Septuagintal texts.

Col. 2:10, 15).[60] However, one could object to Arnold using a late second-century text to inform a first-century text like Colossians, written over a hundred years earlier.

In contrast to Arnold, Dibelius, and others, Francis (1975a: 202–3) contends that "'entering' at Claros had no particular technical meaning to distinguish it from other verbs of 'entering' in the contemporary oracle literature." He sees the initiation into the mysteries to refer only to consulting an oracle and not to a formal, second step of entering into the god's sanctuary. To support this nontechnical use of ἐμβατεύω, Francis (1975a) appeals throughout his essay to other Classical, Hellenistic, and papyrological uses, many of which revolve around acquiring or taking possession of (or entering into) land rights, though other various uses are also found. He concludes that the upshot of these various uses for Col. 2:18 is that "the Colossians sought to enter heaven in order to possess themselves of salvation, a portion in the Lord" (1975a: 199; this is similar to the conclusion of Beetham noted earlier).

While Francis is likely right that this is not a technical use of the mystery rites language (so also O'Brien 1982: 145), it is more likely that ἐμβατεύω (*embateuō*), even if not formally considered a technical term here from the mystery cult, still carried general connotations of "entering into a sanctuary," a conclusion that Francis agrees is a viable alternative (1975b: 176 [with minor qualifications in 1975a: 203–4], on which see below).

Thus, in favor of this conclusion about ἐμβατεύω being focused on "entering" the temple is that it is uniquely used with that sense in the Claros and Laodicea inscriptional evidence (all relatively near Colossae in Asia Minor) that is closer in time and geography with Colossians than any other extant uses of this verb in Classical, Hellenistic, and LXX literature. The even more contemporary text of Josephus gives corroboration to the inscriptional usage of "entering into a sanctuary," as do other significant uses in association with "entering a temple" or "sacred space" in extrabiblical Classical and Hellenistic literature (see the second additional note on 2:18).

H. Preisker (*TDNT* 2:535–36) acknowledges that the mystery background at Claros by which the "ἐμβατεύειν takes place in a sanctuary" may be the lens through which to understand better ἐμβατεύω in Col. 2:18. But he sees this as the second-best interpretation, preferring to view the verb to express "entering by painful investigation into what has been seen in ecstasy." But we have already seen that this is the most weakly attested of the four possible meanings for ἐμβατεύω. Preisker does not prefer the mystery-sanctuary background for two reasons: (1) he sees ἐμβατεύω in the Claros and Laodicea inscriptions as "a technical term for the true mystery" and "the entering of the inner sanctuary," after receiving the mysteries. Thus the inscriptions use ἐμβατεύω not by itself but together with other directly preceding verbs (i.e., "they were initiated and entered" or "he received and entered"). He does not,

60. One of Arnold's parallels about "freely chosen worship" has been omitted, since it is weakly attested in the *Metamorphoses*.

however, see the word as a technical term in Col. 2:18, since it does not use the additional verbs or refer to a two-step process.[61] However, one does not need a full photographic reproduction of the inscriptional formulas for them *to be alluded to* in Colossians. Preisker's point, however, is an excellent basis for concluding that in Col. 2:18 ἐμβατεύω is not part of a *technical formula* or a technical term from Claros but is an allusion to the concept of entering the sanctuary there. Nevertheless, Ramsay's point (1914: 299) that ἐμβατεύω in Col. 2:18 is awkward in syntax and in meaning ("which everyone feels") may point to its technical use, though this could just as well point to an allusion to "entering" from the Claros cult without it being part of a technical formula.[62]

Then (2) Preisker's second objection is that the inscriptions have the "entering" occurring in a sanctuary, but he says a sanctuary is not mentioned anywhere in 2:18 (or, apparently, its immediate context). However, this commentary has been at pains to detect probable OT allusions to a temple idea at a number of significant points in chapters 1 and 2, both with respect to Christ as the temple (1:19; 2:9) and believers as the temple (1:9, as temple builders; 2:10a; so also echoes of the temple in 1:22, 23; 2:7, 11). Especially important are the temple allusions in 1:19/2:9 and 1:9/2:10a, applied respectively to Christ and then to believers. In particular, 1:19 and 2:9–10 are usually seen as key verses in the epistle, particularly with respect to presenting Christ as the only source of true "filling" in contrast to the errant visionaries' view of filling, though most commentators do not relate these verses to a temple notion.[63] It should not be forgotten that the clear temple allusion in 1:9 also mentions believers being "filled" by the Spirit in order to complete the building of the temple of believers.[64] Particularly relevant is 2:9–10a, where Christ as the temple and

61. See Nock (1933: 132–33), Sappington (1991: 155), and Pao (2012: 190) for the same assessment. In addition, Luz (in Becker and Luz 1998: 217) contends that the special meaning from the mystery cult is not in mind, since the uses in the inscriptions are in the aorist tense, referring to an initiation into a mystery cult that is "usually a onetime thing," whereas the present tense is used in Col. 2:18.

62. Sometimes biblical authors signpost an allusion to the OT by intentionally carrying over the syntactical form of an OT phrase and not transforming it to fit smoothly in the new NT context in which it is placed (see Beale 1998: 318–55).

63. E.g., above all, Lohse (1971: 127–31) says that the divine fullness of Christ in Col. 2:9–10 is Paul's polemical response to the false teachers' empty claim in 2:16–23 that their ascetic rules and worship are the way to obtain divine "fullness," though he does not mention that the "fullness" relates to the temple in 2:9–10; so similarly, see Bornkamm (1975: 133–34, 142–43) and Ernst (1974: 214, 218–19), who say that 1:19 and 2:9–10 are polemical responses to the preceding mention of the false philosophy in 2:8 (see further Bornkamm 1975: 125, 127–28), on which 2:16–23 expands (so also Lähnemann 1971: 150–51, though not highlighting 2:8 as much). Also see other commentators citing either Col. 1:19 or 2:9/10: R. Martin 1991: 119; Garland 1998: 144–45; Lincoln 2000: 632–33; Thompson 2005: 62, 65, 68; D. Moo 2008: 218; Pao 2012: 190–91. So likewise J. Kim 2004: 153–54.

64. Garland (1998: 145) also sees Col. 1:9 as part of this polemic. Recall that the Exod. 31 and 35 allusion to Bezalel as the builder of the tabernacle in 1:9 is understood by Philo (*Plant.* 26) as including the notion that Bezalel himself, like Moses, was "summoned up" to Sinai to see the vision of the tabernacle, since he was to make the "sacred furniture" of the tabernacle.

believers in him as the temple are set in direct contrast to the false "philosophy and empty deception" of 2:8, which is expanded upon in 2:16–23; recall the temple language of 2:7, believers being "rooted, built up, confirmed in faith," in direct contrast to the bondage of the false teaching (2:8). In 2:16 Paul shifts the perspective back to the errant teaching and to false temple worship, especially in relation to fasting (2:16a and 23), holidays (v. 16b), self-abasement (v. 18, 23), and bodily discipline (v. 23), which had as their main OT purpose a preparatory function to make one pure for temple worship.

Such a number of allusions, with both positive and negative ideas of the temple in the preceding close context of Col. 2:18, warrant understanding that the "entering" is an "entering" into a heavenly temple through a visionary experience. On the basis of references in apocalyptic Judaism and the Claros and Laodicea inscriptions, Lincoln (1981: 113) and Dunn (1996: 183–84) have independently agreed that Col. 2:18 is about a visionary journey of entering the heavenly temple[65] but have not offered any supporting contextual evidence of temple references in the context of Colossians itself (see further in the second additional note on 2:18), which could have strengthened their case.

In this regard, Carr (1973: 499) briefly suggests that the preceding word θρησκεία (*thrēskeia*) in verse 18 further points to the "worship of angels" *in a temple*. But Carr provides no supporting evidence for this. In fact, a survey of the usage of θρησκεία (*thrēskeia*) in Classical and Hellenistic pagan and Jewish sources makes viable Carr's passing suggestion. Although the word can often be used of worship settings outside of a formal temple context, it is very common for the word to be employed with reference to worship in a temple setting, whether Jewish or pagan (see the second additional note on 2:18). For example, Josephus uses the word θρησκεία at least thirty-five times to refer to "worship" in Israel's temple.[66] The word likewise occurs elsewhere in Judaism (Philo, *Emb*. 298, 232; Sib. Or. 8.380, the latter referring to a pagan temple) and later Christianity (Clem. Hom. 10.22, referring to worship at an idol's temple). Likewise the word is used in Classical and extrabiblical Hellenistic writings to allude to worship in or in association with a pagan temple.[67]

And when biblical literature portrays angels in heaven, they are typically seen around God's throne in the heavenly temple.[68] This is also often the case in Judaism (see the second additional note on 2:18), thus suggesting that the

65. Yet here both Lincoln and Dunn acknowledge a viable possibility that Col. 2:18 may merely be about entering into a visionary experience of heaven.

66. These are the most explicit uses in Josephus; there are several additional uses that likely have to do with association of worship within a temple context.

67. See, e.g, Dionysius of Halicarnassus, *Rom. Ant*. 2.63 (1st cent. BC); Dio Cassius, *Hist*. 26.87; 49.22 (2nd–3rd cent. AD); Sextus Empiricus, *Pyr*. 3.24 (3.220; 2nd–3rd cent. AD); Herodian, *Hist*. 5.3.6; Chaeremon (1st cent. AD), frag. 10 (three times), in Porphyry, *Abst*. 4.6–8; see several other examples in *TLNT* 2:201–2.

68. Gen. 28:12; 2 Sam. 6:2; Pss. 80:1; 99:1; Isa. 6:2, 6; 37:16; Ezek. 1:5, 13–15, 19–22; 3:13; 9:3; 10:1–9, 14–20; 11:22; 28:14; John 1:51; Acts 7:35, 38; Rev. 4:6, 8–9; 5:6, 8, 11; 8:2–5; 14:15, 17–18; 15:6; cf. Matt. 18:10; Rev. 7:11; 19:4. Often when angels appear on earth, they are in a sacred space or temple: Exod. 3:2; Zech. 1:11.

"angels," who are part of "what is seen" in 2:18, appear in a heavenly temple setting.

What we then have in 2:18 is a warning against a false view of the temple, an antitemple detour, which the false teachers are contending people need to experience in order not to be disqualified from first-class Christian status. Paul has repeatedly been making allusion to the temple of Christ and the temple of believers identified with Christ to insist that Christians already have all the temple experience needed for Christian existence. Therefore no one can "disqualify" them by claiming that they have not had a vision of angels and the heavenly temple. Paul has been building up to 2:18 with positive temple references in order to anticipate and contrast the false temple experience with the true. The false teachers in Colossae themselves may have gone through a mystery initiation before professing Christ; they may have heard about the Asia Minor Claros and Laodicea initiations;[69] or they may have been acquainted with the association of ἐμβατεύω (*embateuō*) with "entering a sacred place or temple" from these mystery rites as well as broadly from elsewhere, as attested in Classical and Hellenistic literature. And they may be trying to integrate this dramatic, charismatic experience into their new Christian faith. Accordingly, the misguided teachers "may have understood humility followed by visions seen upon entering 'the heavenly temple' to be analogous to initiation followed by reception of oracles upon entering the Apollos sanctuary" (Francis 1975b: 176).[70] They appear to have found further justification for this in the OT dietary and holiday laws, which are preparatory for participation in temple worship.[71] They wrongly believe these laws are still valid, and they

69. This appears likely, since the Claros inscriptions mention delegates from several cities in Asia Minor, including Laodicea (so Francis 1975b: 176). Arnold (1995: 117, 129) notes that 75 percent of the inscriptions extant from the Apollo temple at Claros show that delegations from various Anatolian cities were sent to seek the services of Claros.

70. Subsequent to writing the above essay, after doing a word study on Classical, Hellenistic, and papyrological evidence of ἐμβατεύω (*embateuō*), Francis (1975a: 203–4) concludes with almost exactly the same statement, except that at the end he adds: "Even this may be saying too much: . . . entrance into heaven is saving." Yet none of the evidence in his word study warrants an association with "entering into heaven"; but some of it, such as in Claros, does warrant a reference to "entering a temple." In fact, Francis (1975a: 198–99) sees the inheritance context of Josh. 19:49, 51 (with Josh. 22:22–24; on which see above) and to some significant degree the Claros inscriptional uses (1975a: 199–204) to be the most relevant uses of ἐμβατεύω for comparison with Col. 2:18 (together with the same concept in T. Levi 2, 4, 5, and 8). Both the Joshua text and Testament of Levi have to do with the goal of entering God's temple (or tabernacle) to worship (see the second additional note on 2:18).

71. Dibelius (1975: 114n2), however, argues that the "feast or new moon or Sabbaths" has its background in the mystery cults and not in the OT. As we have argued, this is an overstatement, since we have seen that a Jewish background is in view to a significant extent. But, in addition to Dibelius's statement, there *is* evidence that pagan temple rites involved dietary laws for purification, and new moons and feasts were part of purification rites. For the cults of Eleusis in Greece and of Cybele and Attis in Phrygia, see Sumney 2008: 150; and Chaeremon, frag. 10, in Porphyry, *Abst.* 4.7; Diogenes Laertius, *Notes* 8.33.

Similarly, as seen earlier, sometimes the celebration of feasts and new moons together with fasting was part of cultic rituals performed in conjunction with mystery religions (so Plutarch,

combine them with the pagan mystery background. What may also have played into this syncretism from the Jewish side is that certain traditions in Judaism focus on various ways in which humans could ascend into the temple throne-room of God (see the second additional note on 2:18). To whatever degree the pagan mystery cults are in view, Paul probably uses God's "revelation of the mystery" in this epistle as a polemic against the pagan cult's revelation of its mystery. That is, the true mystery is now fully revealed in Christ in contrast to the pseudomystery.[72] Thus the false teaching is based on a combination of distorted Hellenistic and Jewish ideas. Such syncretism is not new, since false teaching in the OT arises from combining pagan idolatry with the worship of Yahweh.

The last clause of Col. 2:18 starts with an adverbial participle of means (φυσιούμενος, *physioumenos*) modifying καταβραβευέτω (*katabrabeuetō*; Wheeler 1990): "Let no one disqualify you . . . by means of being puffed up in vain[73] by his fleshly mind."* "Flesh" (σάρξ, *sarx*), as an adjectival genitive here, has to do with the world's way of thinking in contrast to God's revelatory word (e.g., see Rom. 8:4–9, 12–13; 1 Cor. 1:26; 2 Cor. 1:17; 5:16; 7:1; 10:2–3 [cf. 10:4–5]; 11:18). Such a person is "puffed up" or arrogant without reason because of having wrong views of asceticism (claiming to be more godly than others because of self-discipline) and claiming a privileged experience of worshiping (or seeing the worship by angels) and entering into the heavenly temple, where the angels surround God. Because of arrogant overconfidence about their visionary experiences and views, the false teachers condemn others who do not have such experiences or abide by such views.[74]

In 2 Cor. 12:1–9 Paul shows only too well that such visionary experiences have the potential to cause pride unless God quickly humbles a person to prevent it (among others, see Sumney 2008: 157; Bruce 1984: 122; Yates 1993: 59; cf. O'Brien 1982: 145).

This verse is a continuation of verse 18 in that κρατῶν (*kratōn*, holding fast) **2:19**
is a fourth adverbial participle modifying καταβραβεύω (*katabrabeuō*) at the beginning of verse 18. This means that verse 19, like verses 16 and 18, is based on the main point of 2:6–15: Christian living is to be founded only on Christ

Def. Orac. 13–14; and regarding Egyptian religion, Plutarch, *Is. Os.* 42–43). It may well be that in Colossae there was a syncretistic combination of both Jewish and Hellenistic backgrounds, with the former being dominant. Philo (*Contempl.* 2, 22) describes the Therapeutae, showing how a Jewish group could combine Hellenistic elements of dieting and fasting into its practices, including perhaps philosophical elements (cf. DeMaris 1994: 112–14).

72. On this kind of contrast between Paul's general use of "mystery" and the pagan mystery cults, see Beale and Gladd 2014: 305–19.

73. See Ps.-Clement, *Ep Virg.* 1.11, which takes εἰκῇ (*eikē*) to modify ἐμβατεύων (*embateuōn*) instead of φυσιούμενος (*physioumenos*): "entering in vain" (though any of the above-proposed translations of ἐμβατεύω could fit here). It is possible to take εἰκῇ φυσιούμενος directly with the preceding ἅ (*ha*) as an accusative of respect: "inflated in vain *about what* he saw when he was entering" (as suggested by Zerwick and Grosvenor 1981: 608; so similarly BDF §154).

74. In agreement with D. Moo (2008: 225), who also notes that "puff up" renders a verb used elsewhere in the NT only in 1 Corinthians, in every case referring to arrogance.

(vv. 6–15). As we have seen, this is the basis for Paul saying in verse 18, "Let no one disqualify you" by criteria that are not Christ-centered. This fourth adverbial participle offers another reason why no one should "disqualify you" (v. 18a): because such people who are attempting to disqualify Christians are "not holding fast to the head," which is Christ. Thus this point complements the main point of 2:6–15, that the Christian walk should be grounded only on Christ. The phrase "not holding fast to the head" highlights the false basis of the misguided teaching, since Paul has already said that the false "philosophy" is "not based on Christ"* (2:8; so D. Moo 2008: 229–30).

These may have been unbelieving Jews of whom Paul is speaking, or they may have been professing Christians who did not understand the true essence of the Christian faith. If the latter is the case, which is probable, these people were likely not genuine Christians, since they were "not holding to the head" of the body, which is Christ. Thus they are outside of the "body of Christ" (Campbell 2013: 43–44). Ironically, instead of true Christians being disqualified from being part of God's authentic people, Paul is now saying that these very accusers are to be judged as not being vitally connected to Christ (N. Wright 1986: 124).

Before the phrase "from whom the whole body," the implied statement "but you hold to the head" should be inserted. Paul is now shifting positively to why the readers should hold to the head (Christ) and not allow themselves to be "judged" and disqualified by the standards of the false teaching. Verse 19 is verbally parallel with Eph. 4:15–16:

Ephesians 4:15b–16	Colossians 2:19
Let us grow up in all things into him, who is the head, even Christ, from whom the whole body, being fitted together and held together by every joint of the supply, according to the measure of each part, makes the body grow unto the building up of itself in love.*	[Such a visionary is] not holding fast to the head, from whom[a] the entire body, being supplied and held together by the joints and ligaments, grows with a growth which is from God.

Note: Underlining shows common Greek words or word groups.
[a]A "construction according to sense" is observable here, since Christ as "head" (κεφαλή, *kephalē*) is feminine and the following relative pronoun "whom" (ὅς, *hos*), which grammatically should be feminine, is masculine because Christ in natural gender is masculine.

This is one of the clearest verbal parallels between Ephesians and Colossians. In Ephesians this passage further develops the Eph. 2:21 description of the temple:

Ephesians 2:21	Ephesians 4:16
[In Christ] the whole [πᾶσα, *pasa*] building [οἰκοδομή, *oikodomē*], being fitted together [συναρμολογουμένη, *synarmologoumenē*], grows [αὔξει, *auxei*] into a holy temple in the Lord.*	[In Christ] the whole [πᾶν, *pan*] body, being fitted together [συναρμολογούμενον, *synarmologoumenon*] and held together by every ligament of support, according to the measure of each part, makes the body grow [αὔξησιν, *auxēsin*] unto the building up [οἰκοδομήν, *oikodomēn*] of itself in love.*

It is probable, in light of the common wording, that Eph. 4:16 is developing the organic concept of the temple in terms of the church as the organic body of Christ. However, it is difficult to know whether the parallel wording of Eph. 4:16 is dependent upon and developing Col. 2:19 or vice versa, since there is broad consensus that Colossians and Ephesians were written around the same time. If the latter view is correct, then the Colossians passage could also be developing the ideas of the temple and body present in Eph. 4:16. If the former, one might argue that it would be hard to find a temple idea present in Col. 2:19 but that Paul uses the wording of the Colossians text in Eph. 4:16 to develop the temple notion from Eph. 2:21. However, even if this is the case, Col. 2:19 arises in the midst of Paul's polemic against a pseudo-temple teaching, which he has earlier contrasted with the true temple experience of being in Christ (e.g., 1:19; 2:9–11). Thus 2:19 may itself be a development of the earlier temple ideas in terms of the body of Christ. This may be why Paul would develop the temple picture of Eph. 2:21 through the body image of 4:16. Consequently, whatever the direction of dependence, it is plausible that Col. 2:19 was associated in Paul's mind with the organic idea of the temple, however implicit that association was. If so, it makes the contrast with the pseudo-temple experience of 2:18 even stronger ("not holding fast to the head, from whom . . .").

The organic growth of the temple nourished by Christ[75] is virtually identical to believers "being filled in [or by] him" in 2:10, which we have seen, together with 2:9, is one of the key texts in Colossians referring to Christ filling believers as his temple. With respect to 2:19, D. Moo (2008: 232) says, "How individual believers find spiritual 'fullness' . . . is one of the precipitating issues in the letter," affirming that the organic "growth" of the body here is to be understood in terms of the "fullness" (likewise Wolter 1993: 150), though he does not relate this to the temple. I agree with his point, but if this fullness is that of Christ filling the temple of believers, then this further enhances our line of argument that verse 19 continues to be associated with the temple theme.

Christ's exaltation has placed him in the position of being "head of the corner" (or "head corner stone") of the temple, which is a repeated quotation of Ps. 118:22 (κεφαλὴν γωνίας, *kephalēn gōnias*) in the NT (Ps. 117:22 LXX; Matt. 21:42//Mark 12:10//Luke 20:17; Acts 4:11; 1 Pet. 2:7; cf. Eph. 2:20). On 2:10 we noted (see additional notes) Macaskill's (2013: 149–54, 163–71) novel idea that the use of this passage in the NT with reference to the temple may be the origin of Paul's view of Christ as the "head" (κεφαλή, *kephalē*) of the church, which is his "body." Christ is an actual organic part, the chief part of the temple, which includes his corporate people. If Macaskill is correct, then

75. The concluding phrase τοῦ θεοῦ (*tou theou*) may be a genitive of source ("from God") or an adjectival genitive ("divine growth"). If the former, then the growth comes both from Christ (2:19a) and from God (2:19b; a subjective genitive would be similar: "growth by God"); if the latter, then the growth coming from Christ is a divine growth, perhaps pointing to Christ as the divine grower or to the notion that the growth will reach end-time perfection (on this latter idea, see O'Brien 1982: 148).

the use of "head" in Col. 2:19 would have not only an idea of authority but may implicitly convey organic temple associations and further strengthen our above analysis that 2:19 is about the organic temple in Christ.

2:20 Verses 16 and 18–19, as we saw, were deductions based on the main point of 2:6–15: Christian living is to be grounded only on Christ (vv. 6–15), and therefore two things can be concluded from this: believers (1) are not to be "judged" (v. 16) (2) nor "disqualified" (v. 18) from being first-class Christian citizens because of the non-Christ-centered standards of the false teaching. Verse 20 now draws a result from these two deductions: that the hearers "died with Christ to the elements of the world"* (see the additional note on the οὖν variant). However, this result is introduced by the conditional particle εἰ (*ei*). This is a first-class condition, in which the first clause (the "if" clause in the indicative mood) is assumed to be true for the sake of the argument. But this is not some merely hypothetical or theoretical statement. That Paul assumes the reality of the first clause, "You have died with Christ," is apparent from the context (though Paul likely has in mind not everyone but the majority of the readers; see further on 1:23).[76] In Col. 3:3 Paul says, "For you have died and your life is hidden with Christ in God" (likewise Col. 2:12, "having been buried with Him"). And he repeats the same thing in Romans (Rom. 6:2, 8–10).

On the basis that the Colossians have "died with Christ to the elements of the world," Paul asks, "Why, as if you were living in the world, do <u>you submit yourself to decrees</u>?"[77] This conditional sentence can be rephrased as "If you have died with Christ to the old world [which has happened], then you do not live in the old world anymore and must not submit yourself to decrees of the old world." Those who do not heed Paul's implied prohibition about not submitting to the old world's decrees should have no assurance that they, indeed, "have died with Christ," and should conclude that they are still part of the old world. The "if" indicates that Paul is not merely asserting that Christians have died with Christ; he is also inviting them to reflect on whether they have in fact died with Christ and to contemplate the implications for their lives (so D. Moo 2008: 233). Suppose the translation "Why submit?" is preferred instead of "Why do you submit?" Then the last clause would be part of the rhetorical warning and not an accusation of an already adopted practice (an alternative recognized by Dunn 1996: 188).

Some versions translate the phrase τῶν στοιχείων τοῦ κόσμου (*tōn stoicheiōn tou kosmou*) "the elementary [basic] principles of the world" (so NIV 1984, likewise NJB), while other translations render it "the elementary spirits of the universe [world]" (NRSV, ESV, NET, similarly HCSB and NLT), and still others have "the elements [rudiments] of the world (Vulgate, Douay-Rheims, KJV, ASV). These three different renderings represent three major different

76. Pao (2012: 193) observes that a first-class conditional phrase followed by a question serves to highlight "that the condition is a claimed fact."

77. The form δογματίζεσθε (*dogmatizesthe*) is likely a direct middle. MHT 3:57 takes the verb to have an intransitive active idea: "submit to rules."

interpretations of the phrase, all of which are possible.[78] Under any interpretation, the genitive τοῦ κόσμου (*tou kosmou*) most likely is a genitive of source ("elements from or arising from the world").[79]

The first view is that the plural στοιχεῖα (*stoicheia*) refers to basic or first principles. Sometimes the word could be used to refer to the ABC's. This notion is applied to the beginning of knowledge, on which further advanced knowledge is built.[80] Accordingly, some see that the word in this context refers to the earlier OT laws as basic principles to abide by, but now they should be jettisoned because of the advanced knowledge with Christ's coming. The mistake of the false teachers is that they are going backward to the OT shadows instead of forward to the progressive revelation in Christ. Appeal is made to Gal. 4:3 in support of this view: Israel "was held in bondage under the elementary principles of the world."* Here the phrase "under the elementary principles of the world" is parallel with "under the Law" in Gal. 4:4, which is superseded by the coming of Christ. Also, στοιχεῖα appears again in Gal. 4:9–10 in direct connection to the keeping of OT holidays ("You observe days and months and seasons and years"). Some see the "elements" here applying to the basic principles or teachings of Gentile and Jewish religion (cf. O'Brien 1982: 130). Some apply this to the teachings of food laws and of the calendar in Col. 2:16 and 21 (cf. Caird 1976: 190), which most see as having a Jewish background, though some see a Gentile background, and others a mix of the two.

The second view, held by the majority of commentators, is that the plural στοιχεῖα here refers to evil spiritual powers that exercise control over people.[81] Again appeal is made to Gal. 4:3, especially in the light of 4:8–9, where the Galatians are said to have been "slaves to those which by nature are no gods," and then asks, "How is it that you turn back again to the weak and worthless elemental things [viewed as spirit powers], to which you desire to be enslaved all over again?" Further appeal for this meaning comes from the use of στοιχεῖον (*stoicheion*) or its plural in T. Sol. 8.2; 18.1, 2 (cf. similar uses in T. Sol. 15.5) and from second-century evidence, which also uses στοιχεῖα to refer to malevolent spirit forces. In addition, the sun, moon, and stars were worshiped and sometimes referred to as spirit powers that controlled human destiny. This view could fit well with Colossians, especially with respect to the notion that placating such spiritual beings could come by asceticism in order to obtain heavenly visions, participate in the liturgy of angels, and thus gain

78. See Sappingon (1991: 164–68) for a survey of generally representative commentators holding each of the three respective views.

79. So Campbell 2013: 43, though it could be a genitive of reference: "the elements with respect to the world" (cf. Harris 2010: 85).

80. E.g., Heb. 5:12, "For though by this time you ought to be teachers, you have need again for someone to teach you the [beginning <u>elements</u>] of the oracles of God, and you have come to need milk and not solid food."

81. E.g., Lohse 1974: 96–99; Caird 1976: 190–91; N. Wright 1986: 101–2; more recently Garland 1998: 143–44.

protection from evil powers and spiritual fullness in God's presence (cf. Col. 2:18; so O'Brien 1982: 132).[82]

A third view is preferable. It is based on the repeated usage of the full phrase τὰ στοιχεῖα τοῦ κόσμου (*ta stoicheia tou kosmou*) in contemporary Hellenistic writings. This precise phrase is used often, repeatedly, and exclusively to refer to the elements that ancient peoples believed composed the world: air, earth, fire, and water.[83] These uses include those even within Hellenistic Judaism, bringing them even closer to Paul's framework of thought.[84] It is probable that Paul would use this phrase substantially in the same way that it is always used in early Hellenistic Greek literature: a reference to the entire earthly creation.[85] However, in the context of the epistle and his other writings, he integrates the expression into his own redemptive-historical worldview. Paul likely applies the expression to the entirety of the old, fallen, and sinful world, which is destined for corruption (Col. 2:22) and destruction (2 Pet. 3:10, "the elements [στοιχεῖα] will be destroyed with intense heat, and the earth and its works will be burned up"). Believers' death with Christ has "separated" them "from" (ἀπό, *apo*, Col. 2:20; cf. BDAG 105, s.v. ἀπό 1) their part in the old, fallen world, the στοιχεῖα, which no longer have control over them.[86] Paul would consider the constituent components of the old world not merely to be material elements but spiritual elements as well: the devil (in the light of 1:13), demonic spirit beings (in the light of 2:10, 15 and Gal. 4:8–9),[87] sinful

82. Cf. the critique of this view by Barth and Blanke 1994: 374.

83. Two significant articles substantiate this usage in literature outside the NT: Blinzler (1963) and Rusam (1992) together adduce twenty uses of the phrase τὰ στοιχεῖα τοῦ κόσμου, all of which refer to the four (sometimes five) basic elements that compose the cosmos. So also Schweizer (1988: 455–56) mainly studies uses of "elements" and does not focus on the phrase τὰ στοιχεῖα τοῦ κόσμου, contending that there was widespread fear that the harmony of the elements might become disharmonious and that the answer to this was the Christ-centered hymn of Col. 1:15–20.

84. Philo, *Heir* 140, "the four elements of the world"; *Etern.* 109, "the elements of the world," in context meaning the four elements; note the phrase "all the elements of the world" in referring to the destruction of the world (composed of more than four elements) in Sib. Or. 2.206; 3.80–81; 8.337. These formulaic uses with the same meaning occur also in early Christianity (Irenaeus, *Her.* 1.4.2, 3; 1.5).

85. D. Moo (2008: 187–93) and Barth and Blanke (1994: 373–78) are generally correct to argue that Paul uses the phrase to accuse humanity of venerating the creation rather than the Creator, which is in line with the references to idolatry that we have already seen in 2:18–22.

86. Caird (1976: 200) renders (ἀπό, *apo*) with the sense of "out of the control of." Likewise, Rom. 7:4–6 says that believers "have been released from the Law, having died ["through the body of Christ," so v. 4] to that by which we were bound, so that we serve in newness of the Spirit and not in oldness of the letter" (following Lohse 1971: 123).

87. So also D. Moo 2008: 190–92. This inclusion of the spiritual along with material was likely facilitated by the observation that the sun, moon, and stars were associated or identified with false gods and demonic realities; e.g. see Philo, *Decal.* 53–56, which begins with Philo asserting that "some nations have made divinities of the four elements, earth and water, and air and fire." See D. Moo (2008: 191) for further similar primary references from Philo, Wisdom, and early Christian writers, as well as a listing of commentators who affirm that "the elements of the world" refer to spiritual powers. See likewise Dunn (1996: 149–51), who also cites primary

humans (whom Paul says elsewhere live in the "flesh"), and, as we will see, the application of outmoded aspects of the OT law. The main effect of these spiritually sinful elements is that of division of humans from God and from one another. We might say that a chief spiritual building block of the old world was divisiveness, beginning with Satan's separation from God and Adam's separation from God and Eve, at the instigation of the serpent (Adam became known in rabbinic Judaism as "the man of separation"; see, e.g., Exod. Rab. 30.13). The OT's nationalistic laws were introduced further to enhance the division among humans, distinguishing Israelites from all other people groups. Galatians 4:3–10 supports the notion that *both* the spiritual powers and the OT law were divisive elements of the old world. And, of course, human sin in breaking the law was a major constituent of the old world's composition.

Thus, this third view—that "elements of the world" refer to the fourfold material makeup of the world, including the spiritual dimensions of the old world—incorporates as part of it the first two alternative views of "elementary principles" and spiritual powers (following D. Moo 2008: 192).[88] Each of the first two views (taken individually) is weak in substantially neglecting the observation that in Hellenism the often-occurring phrase τὰ στοιχεῖα τοῦ κόσμου is used only to mean the four cosmic elements. It is unlikely that Paul would use this phrase without carrying over the substance of this meaning.

Consequently, when Paul says, "You have died with Christ from the elements of the world,"* he means, "Your identification with Christ's death has caused you to die to the *old world and to be separated from that world*."[89] Since Christ's place with respect to his old-world body has been removed from the old world, and believers' spiritual place has been removed from the old cosmos, a significant piece of that world has been removed, providing partial evidence that this old world has begun to fall apart. Although believers have been removed only spiritually from the old world, the sure consummation of this process will result in their full physical resurrection and complete removal from the old creation at the final coming of Christ. Christ's defeat of the cosmic evil powers (Col. 2:10, 15) has further guaranteed the demise of the old world, which will consummately occur through destruction even of its material elements. The defeat of such powers means that this demonic part of the old world has lost its spiritual power over those now identified with Christ's death and resurrection (cf. Dunn 1996: 189).

At the same time, a new cosmos has been launched in Christ's resurrection as the "new creation," of which those identified with him have begun to become a part (2 Cor. 5:14–17 NIV). This is why, in the nearby following context of Col. 2:20, Paul tells the Colossians, "You have been raised up with Christ"

---

source references alluding to angels controlling the basic elements of the world and for equating angels with stars.

88. Yet D. Moo (2008: 192n29) does not prefer that "the elements of the world" refer to Paul's redemptive-historical perspective of the old fallen world or creation from which Christians have been spiritually removed.

89. Harris (2012: 60–61) thinks the preposition ἀπό (*apo*) indicates "separation or severance."

(3:1), and a little later, "You . . . have clothed yourselves with the new man, which is being renewed" (3:10). They have spiritually died with him to the old world and have been spiritually raised with him into a new world, which will inevitably be completed in final, physical resurrection.

Now the only "element" or fundamental building block of the new creation is Christ. And since there is only one Christ, of which the new creation consists and on which it is built, there can be no divisions but only one new created people subsisting in that renovated creation. The elements of divisiveness (the law, evil powers, etc.) that sustained the sinful structure of the old world have been decisively decimated by Christ, and he has replaced them by himself as the only foundational pillar or element of the new world. As discussed earlier concerning the dietary laws, one of the purposes of OT law was to divide Jew from Gentile in the old creation.[90] Such laws, which compose part of "the elements of the world," are no longer valid, so that Jew and Gentile may now become one in Christ. This is one of the reasons why Paul has said that the dietary laws (Col. 2:16a, 20b–23) and holiday laws (2:16b) have been abolished for Christians (Gal. 4:9–10 also identifies "the elements" with "observ[ing] days and months and seasons and years"). This is also why Col. 3:10–11 says that "clothing yourselves with the new man, who is being renewed,"* is a sphere of renewal "in which there is no distinction between Greek and Jew, circumcised and uncircumcised, barbarian, Scythian, slave and freeman, but Christ is all, and in all."

This new creation in Christ—where Jew and Gentile are no longer separated by Israel's nationalistic laws or by demonic powers or by sin, but are one in Christ—is not new in Colossians. We see in 1:26–27 that "the glory of this mystery among the Gentiles . . . is Christ in you [Gentiles + a remnant of Jewish Christians]." This entails Gentiles and Jews, "every man" becoming "complete in Christ" (1:28). Christ's coming has abolished Israel's nationalistic laws that separated Jews from Gentiles (Col. 2:16, 20–23), which pointed all along to Christ. This abolishment in Christ has brought Jews and Gentiles together in him as a new creation.

We can picture Christ as a hermeneutical filter through which the law must pass in order to get to the new creation. The parts of the law that are more nationalistic in nature or are overt nationalistic tags distinguishing Israelites ethnically from other people groups are too large or ill-shapen to be able to pass through the filter. The parts of the law more moral and less ethnic in nature are able to pass through the filter. This appears to be the significance of 1 Cor. 7:19: "Circumcision is nothing, and uncircumcision is nothing, but <u>what matters is</u> the keeping of the [moral] commandments of God." This is parallel with Gal. 6:15 and 5:6, both of which begin with the same negative

90. Bandstra (1964) contends that the "elements of the earth" are the "law" and the "flesh," which are at work in the world of humanity before Christ's coming and outside of him (e.g., see his summary, 1964: 171–89). While this is true, there is more that composes the "elements of the world." For a summary of Bandstra's view, see Weiss 1972: 299–303.

statement about circumcision, and then respectively add in the contrastive clause: "[There] is . . . a new creation" and "In Christ Jesus . . . faith working through love [means everything]." The "commandments" to be kept in Christ, in the "new creation," are summed up in the statement "Love your neighbor" (cf. Gal. 5:6 with 5:14). These moral laws are in contrast to what distinguishes people ethnically, which must therefore exclude those parts of the law distinguishing Israelites as a unique ethnic group.[91]

Therefore, because of the OT prophecy of new creation that has begun fulfillment in Christ, there can no longer be any nationalistic distinctions between Jew and Gentile: the only distinguishing element is Christ. Those nationalistic distinctions entailed in the law are no longer valid. This is why Paul quotes only from the moral law when he applies OT law to believers, or when he quotes other facets of the OT law (such as the civil rules), he uses it in a typological or nontheocratic manner in employing it within the covenant community of the church (e.g., see Paul's use of Deut. 17:7 in 1 Cor. 5:13). Thus the purely moral aspects of the law, in contrast to those that nationalistically divide, continue to be valid for Christians, since they do not separate believing Jew from believing Gentile.

Therefore, because of having died with Christ and risen with him into a new world (Col. 3:1), the Colossians are "not to submit to decrees"* (δογματίζω, *dogmatizō*) from the OT that divide. What further confirms this is that δόγμα (*dogma*) in Eph. 2:15, the nominal form of the verb δογματίζω, refers to "the law of [OT] commandments in decrees," which Christ "abolished in order to create in himself one new man, thus making peace."* We have found that δόγμα in Col. 2:14 has the same meaning of OT commandments (see discussion at 2:14).

The contents of the decrees that are uppermost in mind at the end of Col. 2:20 **2:21**
are now listed in this verse: "Do not handle, do not taste, do not touch!"[92] This is another way of referring to the OT dietary prohibitions of "food and drink" in 2:16. In addition to one of the law's purposes of dividing Jew from Gentile, we saw that the main purpose of the dietary laws was to cleanse people so that they could worship in the temple (see on 2:16).[93] In the LXX the word ἅπτω (*haptō*) refers to "handling" or "touching" something that would make one unclean.[94] In 2:16 we concluded that the phrase "food and drink and touch" (ἁφή, *haphē*; Let. Aris. 142, 162) refers to what is unclean for Israelites. Here is the full statement: "To prevent our being polluted by contact with others or by mixing with bad influences, [God] fenced us in on all sides with purity

91. The parallelism between 1 Cor. 7:19; Gal. 5:6; and 6:15 has been pointed out by Fuller 1992: 348–49.

92. Verse 21 is likely a virtual quotation of the false teachers; cf. MHT 1:124.

93. Indeed, we saw that even the ultimate purpose in the law dividing Jew from Gentile was to enable Jews to be clean to worship God in the tabernacle/temple and to keep the temple pure.

94. Lev. 5:2 and likewise nineteen other times in Leviticus; so also Num. 19:11, 16, 21–22; 31:19; Deut. 14:8; Hag. 2:13.

observances connected with food and drink and touch and hearing and sight, after the manner of the Law" (Let. Aris. 142).

The prohibition not to "taste" translates the Greek verb γεύομαι (*geuomai*), which 2 Macc. 6:18–20 uses to describe a Jewish martyr who would not eat swine's flesh because "such things are not lawful to be tasted."[95] Similarly, Exod. 19:12 uses θιγγάνω (*thinganō*) synonymously with ἅπτω (*haptō*) to prohibit unclean Israel from touching holy Mount Sinai; the word, used rarely, refers to not touching forbidden objects for those "involved in purification rites" (Let. Aris. 106; also cited by Beetham 2008: 211–12).

In the light of this, probably the "handling" and "touching" in Col. 2:21 pertains to "food and drink" but extends to other unclean things as well. But that "food and drink" (from 2:16) is the focus is apparent from verse 22, which says these are "things destined to perish with use." Such uncleanness makes one impure for temple worship. The touching of unclean things is sometimes explicitly related to the temple. For example, "Anyone who touches a corpse . . . and does not purify himself, defiles the tabernacle of the Lord"; hence such a person is prohibited from entering into the tabernacle (Num. 19:13). Elsewhere in the OT and Judaism it is repeatedly mentioned that uncleanness cannot be tolerated within the temple precincts (see the additional note on 2:21).

In this light, as concluded in 2:16, the false teachers are exhorting believers to be meticulous about not contaminating themselves with unclean food or drink, according to OT law, in order to foster a visionary experience of angels and of the heavenly temple, though this was a false cultic experience.[96]

2:22 These decrees about clean and unclean foods[97] were appropriate in the OT epoch, but in the new age they have only one purpose: they "are all destined to corruption with the using."* Rather than enhancing a visionary experience and purifying one for participation in a heavenly temple, they are useless and only result in "corruption" (φθορά, *phthora*). Such outmoded laws must eventuate in corruption because they are now part of the old creation, all of which will be finally destroyed. In contrast, the new creation and the temple in Christ are incorruptible and will never break down, decay, or decompose like the old world and its old institutions.[98] For example, Israel's old temple was destroyed, and likewise all the laws pertaining to it, including the dietary laws,

95. Cited by Beetham (2008: 211), who also notes that the word was used in early Judaism in relation to voluntary fasting and that the related word ἀπογεύω (*apogeuō*) is used in Philo and 4 Maccabees with respect to forcing other Jews to eat swine's flesh.

96. Some Gentile customs included laws about not touching unclean animals (e.g., see Lohse 1971: 123), but since Col. 2:21 is clearly discussing the Jewish laws of purity listed in 2:16, that is still likely the focus here.

97. Most translations acknowledge that verse 22 is about the laws of verse 21 but focus on what the laws primarily "refer" to—food and drink (e.g., NRSV: "All these regulations refer to things that perish with the use"; so also NASB, ESV, HCSB; cf. also NLT, NJB).

98. On believers being resurrected and set free from the "corruption" (φθορά) of their old-world bodies, see Rom. 8:18–23; 1 Cor. 15:42; believers have begun to "escape the corruption [φθορά]"* through their regeneration (2 Pet. 1:4); unbelievers "are slaves of corruption [φθορά]" (2 Pet. 2:19; cf. likewise Gal. 6:8; 2 Pet. 2:12).

are no longer useful for drawing near to God.[99] When such laws are made a requirement for Christians, then a corrupt religion is created, which in fact is idolatrous. It is idolatrous because the focus is on "self-made religion" and not on Christ; it is idolatrous because it focuses on outmoded laws that pointed to Christ and not on Christ as the fulfillment of those laws.

The idolatrous nature of these laws is expressed in the next clause of verse 22: the "decrees" are "in conformity with" and "based on"* (κατά, *kata*)[100] "the commandments and teachings of men" (τὰ[101] ἐντάλματα καὶ διδασκαλίας τῶν ἀνθρώπων, *ta entalmata kai didaskalias tōn anthrōpōn*). This is an allusion to Isa. 29:13 LXX: "This people draws near with their lips [and] they honor me, but they remove their heart far from me, and they worship me vainly by teaching the commandments and teachings of men [ἐντάλματα ἀνθρώπων καὶ διδασκαλίας, *entalmata anthrōpōn kai didaskalias*]."*[102] The Colossians context likely links such "commandments and teachings" to "empty deception" based on "the tradition of men" instead of "on Christ" (2:8). Paul's expansion of the earlier "tradition of men" by Isaiah's "commandments and teachings of men" associates the false teaching with idolatry, since that is the contextual sense in the Isaiah passage itself, where the wording concerns the sin of idol worship (see the additional notes).[103]

Paul says that the OT "shadows" (v. 17 NLT), particularly the food laws (about unclean "food and drink" and the commandments "Do not handle, do not taste, do not touch!"), are called "the commandments and teachings of men." In the inaugurated age of fulfillment, it is idolatry to substitute the "shadows" for Christ, who is their eschatological substance (see further on 2:17). Furthermore, among the seven times that the tripartite formula "feasts, new moons, and Sabbath days" occurs in the OT, two refer to them as having become idolatrous.[104] Thus there is already a precedent for the transforming

99. Of course, the temple had not yet been destroyed in Paul's time; yet because Christ had come as the true fulfillment of all that the temple pointed to, the temple and its laws had already become outmoded, and it was seen as destined for destruction.

100. See again BDAG (512, s.v. κατά B.5.δ), who state that sometimes both the notions of "in conformity with" and "basis" are in mind. Here κατά (*kata*) modifies not the directly preceding phrase of verse 22 but the triple imperative "Do not touch, do not taste, do not handle!" of verse 21, which explains the "decrees" at the end of verse 20. Many translations also view κατά to be modifying verse 21 (Geneva, NASB, NRSV, ASV, TNIV, ESV, HCSB).

101. The article does double duty despite the fact that the first noun is neuter and the second feminine, which is a rare usage, though here probably due to the unity of the concepts of the nouns; see Buttmann 1873: 100–101; cf. similarly BDF §276.1.

102. The validity of this allusion is accepted by many commentators; see Beale (2007: 860) for an extensive list of commentators, though Foster (2016: 300), without much argumentation, does not see "any direct literary link." The following material on the use of Isa. 29:13 is based on Beale 2007: 860–62.

103. Pao (2012: 196) agrees that the allusion to Isa. 29:13 LXX is a reference to idolatry and is applied in that manner here.

104. See Isa. 1:13–14 and the direct association with βδέλυγμα (*bdelygma*), "abomination," a common reference to idolatry in Isaiah and elsewhere in the OT; cf. Hosea 2:11 in the context of 2:6–13.

of OT festivals into idolatrous activities. In Gal. 4:8–10 virtually the identical phrase ("You observe days and months and seasons and years"), together with the word "elements" (cf. Col. 2:20), is directly linked to objects of idolatry. That Col. 2:16–23 describes idolatrous traditions may also be suggested by 3:3–7, where at least part of the saints' former unbelieving life is summarized as "idolatry."[105]

In Paul's time this sin manifested itself by Israel worshiping not stone or wooden idols, but rather the idol of human tradition, which was a distortion of the law. The same reference in Mark 7:7//Matt. 15:9 carries with it in context the same idolatrous notion. Mark 7:8 sums up the Isa. 29:13 quotation by referring to it with the phrase "the tradition of men." Since Paul uses that same phrase in Col. 2:8 to refer to the false philosophy, it appears that he alludes to Isa. 29:13 there and also here in 2:22, under the influence of Jesus's earlier usage.[106] Thus the Isa. 29:13 allusion expands on the earlier reference in 2:8. The context of the Isaiah reference in Mark 7 also reflects that Isa. 29:13 was understood in terms of idolatry[107] (and all this in a context dealing with Jewish laws prohibiting eating with impure hands; Mark 7:1–5).[108] An idol, in essence, is anything that is worshiped in place of the true God. For example, in Eph. 5 and Col. 3 Paul says that idol worship can be expressed in other ways than merely bowing down to a literal statue; he says in the latter text that "greed . . . [is] idolatry," though the preceding sins of "immorality, uncleanness, passion, evil desire"* are also likely associated with this idolatry (Col. 3:5).[109] Paul is saying in Col. 2:22 that to trust in the shadowy dietary laws of the OT more than in Christ (or on the same level as Christ) is to worship an idol. Colossians 2:17–19 also counters idolatry, since it says that trusting in the "old shadows" also involves substituting "the worship of the angels" for worship of Christ (which is "not holding fast to the head").[110] The reference to Isa. 29:13 in Titus 1:14 is used similarly, since "commandments of men" is parallel to "Jewish myths," both of which result in "turning away from the

105. In this respect, note the verbal and conceptual similarity of "You have died" and "Put to death the members [of your body] upon the earth"* in 3:3, 5 to "You have died . . . to the elements of the world"* in 2:20, the latter closely linked to the Isa. 29:13 allusion in 2:22 and to the "worship of angels" in 2:18.

106. See Dunn (1996: 193), D. Moo (2008: 238), Lightfoot (1875: 204–5), and Pokorný (1991: 153–54), though these commentators see allusion to Isa. 29 only in 2:22 but not in 2:8; cf. Wilson 2005: 229; and Sumney 2008: 163–64. In confirmation of this, Dunn (1996: 193) notes that the phrase "these are all destined to perish with use" in Col. 2:22 also echoes Mark 7:19//Matt. 15:17: unclean food should not any longer be a concern, since it goes through the stomach only to go into the latrine.

107. "Neglecting the commandment of God, you hold to the tradition of men. . . . You are experts at setting aside the commandment of God in order to keep your tradition, . . . invalidating the word of God by your tradition" (Mark 7:8–9, 13).

108. Following Dunn 1996: 194; D. Moo 2008: 237–38.

109. See my comments on Col. 3:5 for the focus on "greed" as "idolatry," but secondarily the preceding sins being also associated with this idolatry.

110. That the genitival phrase "worship of the angels" likely refers not to "worshiping with the angels" but to "worshiping angels" and to angelic idolatry, see our comments on 2:18 above.

truth." Elsewhere Paul also understands that Jews who trust only in the law and not in Christ are idolaters.[111]

Paul probably uses Isa. 29:13 analogically: just as Israel was idolatrous in its past, so again professing Jewish believers (i.e., Jewish Christians) are propagating trust in idolatrous objects.[112]

Paul continues to elaborate on the meaning of the decrees. The sentence is **2:23**
syntactically difficult. Though there are several ways of solving this problem, we prefer the following translation: "Such things are matters having, to be sure, the appearance[113] [or reputation][114] of wisdom in self-made worship and self-abasement in neglect of the body, but they are of no value with respect to satisfying the flesh."*[115]

Such commandments "have the appearance of wisdom," but it is a hollow wisdom. This wisdom does not derive from God but arises from idol worship. Rather, "all the [true] treasures of wisdom and knowledge" have their unique origin in Christ (D. Moo 2008: 240).

The very first mention of "wisdom" in Colossians comes in 1:9. There we saw that 1:9 was part of an explicit allusion to Exod. 31:3 (cf. likewise 35:31), where Israelites were "filled . . . with a divine Spirit of wisdom and understanding and knowledge in every good work."* The point is that believers are "filled" with such wisdom to do their part in contributing to the building of the spiritual temple (see on 1:9). If the "wisdom" of 1:9 is in mind, then this first mention of divine "wisdom" related to the true temple is a contrast here with false wisdom about visions of angels in the pseudo-temple. In addition, recall that commentators generally acknowledge that Christ is presented as "wisdom" in Col. 1:15–18 (see my comments on these verses), and we saw that Christ was portrayed in 1:19 as the end-time temple of God's presence from Ps. 67:17–18 LXX (68:16–17 Eng.). The link between Col. 1:15–18 and 1:19 may reflect early Judaism, which viewed "wisdom" as having its "headquarters" in the temple (see the additional note on 1:19). To whatever degree this may be in mind, the contrast would include Christ as the temple and the source of true wisdom[116] versus false wisdom about the temple.

This apparent wisdom is expressed in "self-made religion and self-abasement and neglect of the body." The word ἐθελοθρησκία (*ethelothrēskia*) can be

111. Rom. 2:22; cf. Gal. 4:8–10, where "elements" are equated with false "gods"; note "the elements of the world" used similarly in Col. 2:20.

112. If Col. 2:22 is closely identified with the use of Isa. 29:13 in Mark 7:7//Matt. 15:9, then it has a typological notion, since that is its likely use in the Gospel passages, as both Mark 7:6 and Matt. 15:7 introduce the Isa. 29:13 quotation by "rightly did Isaiah prophesy concerning you."

113. The rendering of BDAG 599, s.v. λόγος.

114. See LSJ 1057.I.4, s.v. λόγος; Barth and Blanke 1994: 358; likewise Abbott 1897: 275.

115. See the second additional note on 2:23 for discussion of the syntactical problem and the various options for translating the verse.

116. Says 2 Bar. 54.13, "You [God] have prepared under your throne the treasures of wisdom," which is likely a reference to God's throne in his heavenly temple, borne out by 51.11, where is seen "the majesty of the living beings under the throne"; this is a reference to Ezek. 1 and 10, where the "living beings" are pictured as under the divine throne in the temple. Cf. again Col. 2:3.

rendered in the following ways: (1) "self-made religion," (2) "do-it-yourself religion," (3) "idiosyncratic religion" (BDAG 276, s.v. ἐθελοθρησκία), (4) "self-made worship," (5) "will-worship" (ASV, KJV), (6) "self-imposed worship" (NIV, NET), (7) "self-chosen worship" (MacDonald 2000: 117), (8) or "freely chosen worship" (D. Moo 2008: 240). Any of these translations are viable. This "wisdom" then is a "self-manufactured religion" (Thompson 2005: 65), which has its source in the human will in contrast to wisdom rooted in God's or Christ's will (1:9, "You [should] be filled with the knowledge of His will in all spiritual wisdom and understanding"; cf. likewise 1:27–28; 3:16).

This notion of "self-made religion" is another way of expressing idol worship, that is, worshiping something of one's own making and not worshiping the unmade Creator. This is an elaboration of 2:18a, where also is found the unique combination of pleasure-taking or self-desiring (θέλων, *thelōn*) that is expressed in legalistic "self-abasement" (ταπεινοφροσύνη, *tapeinophrosynē*) and idolatrous "worship" (θρησκεία, *thrēskeia*; i.e., actually "worshiping angels"). In the light of the parallel with verse 18, the idea of "self-made worship" should be expanded to "self-made worship *of angels*."[117] The "self-made religion" specifically in mind is that of "self-abasement and neglect of the body," which apparently was thought to foster a spiritual experience of seeing and then venerating angels. This passage justifies our earlier rendering of ταπεινοφροσύνη in verse 18 as "asceticism," since here the word is further explained by "neglect of the body" (ἀφειδίᾳ σώματος, *apheidia sōmatos*), which is characteristic of asceticism (so also D. Moo 2008: 241). Some MSS omit the "and" in this phrase, thus reading "self-abasement in [or by] neglect of the body" (see the first additional note on 2:23). Either way, "neglect of the body" likely further explains "self-abasement" (or "asceticism"). Uppermost in mind here is the avoiding of "food and drink" (2:16; so also 2:21). We have already observed that the verbal form of ταπεινοφροσύνη was closely connected to fasting, wearing sackcloth, and mourning (see further on 2:18).

Such ascetic practices have "no value in checking self-indulgence" (NRSV, followed by BDAG 830, s.v. πλησμονή). The false teaching aimed at neglecting basic bodily needs apparently in order to sharpen one's spiritual senses to prepare for a visionary experience[118] of angels in the heavenly temple (as argued at 2:18a above). But on the contrary, such harsh practices, Paul says,

117. However, Francis (1975b: 182) does not see this as nullifying the preference for a subjective genitive ("worship by angels") in 2:18, arguing that the sense could merely be "the Colossians chose for themselves the worship performed by angels" (followed by Barth and Blanke 1994: 346–47). But even if "chose for themselves" is the preferred rendering, Calvin (1972: 343) is likely correct that it "denotes a voluntary worship which men choose of their own will, without a command from God."

118. Philo (*Sobr.* 2) says, "Sobriety is confessed to be a most advantageous thing, not only for souls but also for bodies, for it drives away the diseases which arise from immoderate *repletion* [πλησμονή, *plēsmonē*], and it sharpens the outward senses to an exceeding degree of acuteness." In *Emb.* 2, Philo says, "We obscure the vision of our reason, though it is far more acute than those bodily powers of sight . . . , some of us confusing it by indulgence in wine and *satiety* [πλησμονή]" (trans. Yonge 1993: 757). So likewise Philo, *Mos.* 2.24; *Contempl.* 37. It is

do not make one's spiritual senses keener. Rather, these external ascetic practices have their origin in the "flesh" (σάρξ, *sarx*, v. 18) and therefore cannot prevent fulfilling inner sinful desires of the flesh or "checking self-indulgence" (πλησμονὴν τῆς σαρκός, *plēsmonēn tēs sarkos*).[119]

This last phrase of verse 23 could be rendered "but are of no value for the purpose of[120] filling of the flesh" (so Geneva, Douay-Rheims; "flesh" refers to the person of the old world in parallel with the "mind of the flesh" in v. 18). Often πλησμονή has the idea of "filling" in the LXX, and that may be the notion here,[121] so that a preferable translation might be "for the full satisfaction of the flesh" (Abbott 1897: 278), especially with respect to being *filled* with spiritual *satisfaction*.[122] If so, the "filling" in verse 23 would be a polemical and sarcastic reference to the opponents' attempt to be filled with God's presence through asceticism and fasting and to dispose themselves to ascend into the heavenly temple to worship angels and then to receive God's fullness.[123] This would be more in line with the notion in Col. 2:18 of "self-abasement and neglect of the body" fostering a spiritual experience of seeing and then venerating angels in a heavenly sanctuary. Paul opposes this false experience with the earlier reference to Christ being the one in whom "all the fullness"

easy to see how the false teachers would have integrated such an apparently widely circulating idea into their philosophy.

119. Sometimes πλησμονή was viewed as obtaining "complete satisfaction," particularly through food and drink (BDAG 830, s.v. πλησμονή, a notion to which Philo repeatedly attests: *Agr.* 38; *Sobr.* 2; *Dreams* 1.122; *Mos.* 2.24, 156; *Spec.* 4.129; *Virt.* 163; *Contempl.* 37; *Emb.* 2). The word could also refer to "excess" or "satiety" that leads to sin and apostasy; O'Brien (1982: 155) shows positive and negative uses of the word in the LXX. See O'Brien (1982: 154–55) for an overview of alternative interpretations of this last clause in 2:23.

120. This translation also lines up with a more typical view of πρός (*pros*) in contrast to the above contrasting option, which translates the last phrases as "are of no value in checking [against] the indulgence of the flesh."

121. The NETS translation of the LXX renders this word by "fullness" of food or drink (several times), "plentitude" of food, "plenty" of food, "plenteous" bread, "full" as a figure for God's anger or blessings or wisdom, "abundance" of food (several times) or of rain or of dishonor, "satiety" with food (several times), "surfeit" of food, "repletion" of bread, "satisfaction" in completing a task or in lacking spiritual satisfaction, "satisfy" as lacking spiritual satisfaction or some other satisfaction, and "excess" of bread. For this word LSJ 1421 gives three definitions: "a being filled, satiety, abundance." The word can generally refer to "the condition of fullness and also the act of filling or process of filling," and sometimes a distinction between the two cannot be made (G. Delling, *TDNT* 6:131, s.v. πίμπλημι κτλ). Beetham (2008: 214–15) also sees an LXX background, and comments that under πλησμονώδης (the related adjectival form) in LSJ one of the two definitions is "filling." Hollenbach (1979: 254) renders the last clause of Col. 2:23 as "fulfillment of the flesh."

122. Beetham (2008: 214) notes that the use in Isa. 56:11 offers a nice parallel for "spiritual satisfaction" and that both this and the idea of "fullness" may be in mind in Col. 2:23. Likewise Sir. 1:16 says, "To fear the Lord is fullness of wisdom" (NRSV).

123. Though Col. 2:23 does not mention the temple, I have found agreement on this point with Lohse (1971: 126–27) and Bornkamm (1975: 125–28, 133–34, 142–43); e.g., Bornkamm says the false teachers are affirming that fullness comes through worship of the "elements," which represent spirit beings related to God. So also Ernst 1974: 214; Lähnemann 1971: 149; cf. similarly Gnilka 1980: 162; Hay 2000: 110–12.

of God's temple presence "dwells" (1:19; 2:9), with the result that believers in Christ "have been filled" with that presence (2:10a).[124] Accordingly, it is possible to translate ἐθελοθρησκία (*ethelothrēskia*) as "would-be worship," Paul's way of casting doubt on the opponents' claim about their visionary experience of the temple, which purportedly has "filled" them.[125] Since they have cut themselves off from "Christ the head" (2:19), they cannot experience the true temple and the divine presence therein.[126] They can never be filled with God's special presence because they exist in the "flesh" of the old world.

Additional Notes

2:17. Philo uses σκιά (*skia*) together with σῶμα (*sōma*) to refer to the words of Scripture as "shadows" and the deeper meaning to be the "substance" or "reality." In *Post.* 112 the name of Zillah, one of Lamech's wives (Gen. 4:19), is "interpreted" to mean "'shadow,' a symbol of the equalities of the *body* and of the external good things, which, in their real essence, are in no way better than a shadow" (trans. Yonge 1993: 143). In *Conf.* 190, Philo says, "The mere words of the scriptures are, as it were, but *shadows of bodies*, and . . . the meanings . . . apparent to investigation beneath them, are the real things to be pondered" (trans. Yonge 1993: 251, emphasis added); see likewise *Heir* 72, where Philo says that it is "impossible" to "use shadows to point to *substances* [*bodies*], words to point me to facts" (similarly *Migr.* 12). In a literal sense, a "shadow" always follows a "body" (Philo, *Decal.* 82; *Virt.* 118, 181). Josephus (*J.W.* 2.28) says Archelaus "desires the *shadow* of that royal authority, whose *substance* [*body*] he had already seized to himself." Common to all these uses is the notion of something that is a shadow pointing to the substance of something, whether that be words to true, deeper meanings or literal shadows pointing to a physical human body. Paul is the only one who uses σκιά and σῶμα in a redemptive-historical context to refer to OT institutions that point to later realities (substances) in the NT era that are of a prophetic fulfillment nature (though Heb. 10:1 uses σκιά in this manner). The uses in Judaism above show that the rendering of "substance" for σῶμα (*sōma*) in verse 17 is viable; yet in light of the idea of "a body casting a shadow," a better rendering might be "substantial body" (in line with the discussion in the commentary above).

2:17. Some affirm that the Christian Sunday is not a continuation of the OT Sabbath day since v. 17 identifies the "Sabbaths" of v. 16 to be part of the "shadows" of the OT dietary laws and other religious holidays that have passed away because the substance, Christ, to which they pointed has come.

I have argued elsewhere that Gen. 2:2–3 expresses a creational mandate to rest, in which there is a creational pattern of one day in seven that is "blessed and set apart" from the other days (Beale 2011: 776–81). The goal of this creational pattern predates Israel's Sabbath (and all of its added detailed requirements for observance), was partially expressed through the nation's

124. As noted earlier on verse 18 above, Lohse (1971: 128–31) also links Col. 2:9–10 with 2:16–23 as Paul's polemical response to the false teachers' empty claim that their ascetic rules and worship are the way to obtain divine "fullness," though he does not mention that the "fullness" relates to the temple in 2:9–10. See likewise Bornkamm (1975: 133–34, 142–43) and Ernst (1974: 214, 218–19), who affirm that 1:19 and 2:9–10 are polemical responses to the directly preceding mention of the false philosophy in 2:8 (Bornkamm 1975: 125, 127–28), on which 2:16–23 expands; cf. similarly Hay 2000: 111–12. G. Delling (*TDNT* 6:134, s.v. πίμπλημι κτλ) disagrees, without much explanation, and says that 2:23 is not an antithetical reference to the "filling" of the adversaries in the light of 1:9 and 2:10.

125. So Francis 1975b: 181. Thompson (2005: 65) similarly renders with "would-be religion."

126. Here cf. Beetham (2008: 214–15), though without reference to the temple.

Sabbath, and continues on after Israel's institutions find their completion in and are abolished in Christ. In this regard, Calvin affirms,

> Therefore when we hear that the Sabbath was abrogated by the coming of Christ, we must distinguish between what belongs to the perpetual government of human life [the creational mandate], and what properly belongs to ancient figures [i.e., what was unique to Israel], the use of which was abolished when the truth was fulfilled [when Christ came].[127]

That Israel's Sabbath observance was partly based on a creational mandate and partly on the nation's unique observance is clear from the two versions of the Sabbath law, respectively in Exod. 20:8–11 and Deut. 5:12–15. The first gives God's rest after creation as the basis of Israel's Sabbath, and the second appeals to God's deliverance of the nation from Egypt as the basis, when God delivered Israel from laborious bondage to the rest of freedom. The Sabbath commemoration of the exodus redemption also points forward to the greater end-time exodus redemption through Christ, which has been fulfilled in his death and resurrection as the Passover Lamb (e.g., see John 19:34–37; 1 Cor. 5:7–8). Thus in various ways the Sabbath pointed to and was fulfilled in Christ, but the aspect of Israel's Sabbath that is based on and reflects the creational mandate of Gen. 2 continues on into the church age. "Creation and redemption are both motives for its [Israel's Sabbath] observance, the one for all men [including Israel], the other especially for Israel" (W. Stott, *NIDNTT* 3:406). Vos sums up well the relationship of the creational mandate to Israel's Sabbath and to the church's Sabbath:

> The Sabbath . . . has passed through the various phases of development of redemption, remaining the same in essence but modified as to its form, as the new state of affairs at each point [epoch] might require. . . . From all this [the various laws related to Israel's Sabbath and typological sabbatical celebrations] we have been released by the work of Christ, but not from the Sabbath as instituted at Creation. (Vos 1948: 139–40, 142–43)

Thus the unique nationalistic aspects of Israel's laws, including the way the Sabbath was practiced and on what day it was observed, do not continue. There is still a one-day special observance on Sunday for the church, the purpose of which is to look forward to the consummation of end-time rest in the new heavens and earth. This Sunday observance is focused around worship of God and Christ in church (and likely not complete rest throughout the day, as was the case with the intense form of the Jewish Sabbath) and is a continuation of the creational Sabbath ordinance of Gen. 2:3, whose purpose was to look forward to consummate eschatological spiritual and physical rest. The pre-Israelite observance of every seventh day was probably not a day of complete physical rest but was to recall God's seventh day of resting, and the worshipful observance of every seventh day was apparently to remind humanity of a final eternal Sabbath rest without "evening and morning," which would no longer need to be repeated.

Consequently Col. 2:16 appears to be referring to Israel's system of sabbatical holidays (not merely the weekly Sabbath) and not to the creation mandate in Gen. 2:2–3 (for an expansion of this discussion on the Sabbath, see the comments on 2:16, esp. the note on "Sabbaths," and Beale 2011: 775–801).

2:18. A textual variant adds μή (*mē*) after ἅ (*ha*), which is preferred, e.g., by the KJV: "intruding into those things which he hath *not* seen" (likewise Geneva, Douay-Rheims). The idea would be that the false teachers' claim to have seen visions is a false claim. Though the majority of MSS support including the negative, the earliest and best MSS support the omission of μή (*mē*), which is likely the original reading.

2:18. Josephus uses ἐμβατεύω (*embateuō*) in narrating Moses's ascent to Sinai by observing that no shepherd hitherto was "daring to enter into it" (τολμώντων ἐμβατεύειν εἰς αὐτό, *tolmōntōn embateuein eis auto*) because of "the opinion people had that God dwelt there" (*Ant.* 2.265). Thus Moses was "daring to approach a spot unto which no man had arrived before because it was divine [θεῖον, *theion*]" (2.267). Moses entered into Sinai and to him "were delivered divine

127. Calvin 1984: 106–7, bracketed wording supplied.

oracles from the fire" (2.269). At Sinai, Moses was "granted speech from Him and vision of Him," and when Moses was later to be "sacrificing" at Sinai, he was to "invoke him [God] by name to be present at the sacred rites" (2.275). Sinai was known as the place of "God's sojourning," making it "terrible and unapproachable" (3.76).

In this light, Josephus likely viewed Sinai to be a mountain sanctuary, which is suggested further by his saying that God "desired that a tabernacle should be made for Him . . . so that when we [Israel] move elsewhere we may . . . have no more need to ascend to Sinai, but that He himself, frequenting the tabernacle, may be present at our prayers" (*Ant.* 3.100–101, likewise 212, 222). Thus God's sanctuary at Sinai was transferred to the tabernacle.

Philo likewise refers to Sinai as a "most sacred [ἱερώτατον, *hierōtaton*] mountain" (*Mos.* 2.70), to which Moses had "been called up" (so almost identically "most sacred [ἱερώτατον, *hierōtaton*] of mountains" in *Spec.* 3.125). Part of the meaning that "the glory of God came down upon Mount Sinai" is that it was "the divine place" (Philo, *QE* 2.45, trans. Marcus 1953); Sinai was "a holy and divine place" (*QE* 2.39, trans. Marcus 1953) and was "the unchanging habitation of the divine place" (*QE* 2.40, trans. Marcus 1953). Moses (perhaps including the seventy elders and Aaron) is also said "to enter a dark cloud [on Sinai] and to dwell in the forecourt of the palace/temple[128] of the Father" (*QE* 2.28). Similarly, while Moses "was remaining above [on the mountain], he was initiated [ἐμυσταγωγεῖτο, *emystagōgeito*][129] by being taught according to all the prominent matters of the priesthood" (*Mos.* 2.71). Indeed, Moses himself was a "high priest" on Sinai who performed "the rites belonging to his sacred office" (*Mos.* 2.75; Colson 1935).

Therefore we have in Josephus the notion of Moses "ascending" into the mountain sanctuary of Sinai,[130] a place where no one else had formerly "entered" (ἐμβατεύω), to experience the theophanic presence of God,[131] which Philo terms his being "initiated" or "instructed in the mysteries" on the "most sacred mountain." Perhaps not coincidentally, Josephus also notes that the Israelites were "practicing purity" and abstaining from sexual relations with their wives while Moses was on the mountain to promote God's "converse with Moses" (*Ant.* 3.78). And Moses himself fasted during the entire forty-day experience (3.99), presumably to prepare himself for continually encountering the very presence of God at Sinai. Philo (*Mos.* 2.68–70) says that in "having gone up" to Sinai (where he, along with others, was "desiring the vision of God,"[132] "it

128. Marcus (1953: 69) has only "palace"; for the rendering "palace/temple," see Borgen 1996: 151. Marcus also proposes that the Greek equivalent for the Armenian "forecourt" is αὐλή (*aulē*), which occurs only twelve times in Philo, nine of which refer to the court of Israel's tabernacle or temple, and six of these referring to the court of the tabernacle that was shown to Moses on Sinai (*Mos.* 2.80, 82, 90, 91a, 91b, 93); see further Borgen, Fuglseth, and Skarsten 2000: 55. In particular, in *Prelim.* 116–17 Philo says that "God's dwelling-place, the tabernacle" is symbolic of "wisdom," which "is the court [αὐλή, *aulē*] and palace of the All-ruler." This is quite similar to *QE* 2.28 and points further to the latter being a reference to God's heavenly temple-palace. Also of note is the observation that αὐλή (*aulē*) occurs thirty-five times in the LXX of the Pentateuch, Philo's frame of reference in *QE*, exclusively with the meaning of a "court" in the tabernacle. Sometimes the word can refer only to a court in a king's palace (e.g., see uses in Esther and Jeremiah), but the majority of the references throughout the OT are the same as in the Pentateuch.

129. Yonge (1993: 497) renders this verb as "initiated," and Colson (1935) translates it as "He was being instructed in all the mysteries," combining this verb with the directly following participle "being taught."

130. That Sinai was a sanctuary is further evident from the description in Exodus; see Beale 2005: 100–102, citing OT scholars who support the same idea.

131. Exodus 24:18 LXX refers to Moses, who "entered into [εἰσέρχομαι, *eiserchomai*] the midst of the cloud, and went up to the mountain" of Sinai, which is parallel to him "entering into [εἰσέρχομαι] the tabernacle" when "the pillar of cloud descended" (33:9).

132. Which Philo also associates with a "voluntary vision" (*QE* 2.27); Moses's vision on Sinai occurred during his "ethereal and heavenly journey" (*QE* 2.44).

was necessary that he [Moses] purify" himself partly by having no "food and drink" in order that he should not be "defiled."

In addition to the Claros and Laodicea inscriptions, and not recognized previously, this reference in Josephus is another significant instance of ἐμβατεύω referring to "entering" into the very presence of God in his sanctuary.

Francis (1975a: 198–99) says that ἐμβατεύω in Josh. 19:49, 51 LXX refers to "entering" into the promised land to possess an inheritance, defined as "a portion in the LORD" in light of Josh. 22:24–27. He says it is possible that Col. 2:18 has drawn from a tradition related to Joshua, so that the idea is to "enter heaven to possess themselves of salvation, a portion in the LORD." But the "portion in the LORD" is more fully unpacked in these very Joshua passages as Israel being able to worship at the tabernacle. First, Eleazar the priest "divided by lot" a portion of land each of the tribes was to possess. This division took place "at the door of the tabernacle of witness" (Josh. 19:51 LXX). In Josh. 22:24–27 the sons of Reuben say that they have built an altar on the border of the land only as a memorial to assure that no one could say they "had no portion in the LORD," and this is explained as "not being able to worship the LORD"* (22:25). Thus the sons of Reuben did not build the altar "for burnt-offerings, nor for meat-offerings"* (22:26). This is further explained as their desire "to do service to the LORD before him, with our burnt-offerings and our meat-offerings"* (22:27). To be able to worship in this way means that no one can say they "have no portion in the LORD" (22:27). The place where they want to "do service to the LORD" and to give these offerings is then said to be at "the altar of the LORD which is before His tabernacle" (22:29). Thus Reuben's ability to worship at the tabernacle in the land is virtually equated with having "a portion in the LORD" or is evidence of having such a portion. The two notions are inextricably linked, so that if there were some connection to Col. 2:18, "entering" would still have to do with having "a portion in the LORD" in direct connection with temple worship. Schweizer (1982: 161–62) suggests the possibility that the mystery cults' idea of entry into the sanctuary, combined with the LXX notion of entering into the promised land, is applied to the Colossians' entry into heaven.

There are other uses of ἐμβατεύω where it refers to a god habitually walking or entering into a sacred space or temple (in the following references, the translations of ἐμβατεύω are in italics):

1. Sophocles (*Oed. Col.* 679–80) speaks of "Dionysus," in a sacred garden space of "the god's inviolate foliage," who "always *treads* [*enters*] with the nursing nymphs [goddesses] who constantly attend him" (5th cent. BC; partly trans. Jebb 1989).
2. Euripides (*Rhesus* 225, in LCL) portrays Apollo, the "King Thymbraean, O Delian Lord," who habitually "*treads* [*enters*] the temple of Lycia" (5th cent. BC).
3. Dionysius of Halicarnassus (*Rom. Ant.* 1.77.1–2) says a young woman was raped by a god in a sacred "grove consecrated to Mars," in a "sacred precinct . . . consecrated" to the "divinity" who "*treads* [*enters*] into the place"* (1st cent. BC).
4. Euripides (*Telephus* frag. 696, in Page 1941: 17.3) refers to the god "Pan, who *haunts* [*habitually treads or enters*] Arcadia's stormy massif," apparently the sacred space where Pan dwells (5th cent. BC); see Dionysius of Halicarnassus, *Lit. Comp.* 26 (this Dionysius text is actually a quotation of the Euripides fragment); cf. similarly Cratinus, *Test. Frag. P.* 359 (5th cent. BC).
5. Aeschylus (*Pers.* 447–49, in LCL) says: "There is an island in front of Salamis . . . whose seashore is a *haunt* of Pan [lit., Pan *trod* on the seashore]," who helped the Greeks defeat the Persians there (6th–5th cent. BC). This again refers to a sacred space where the god Pan dwells.

The next references pertain to humans stepping into sacred spaces:

6. Sophocles (*Oed. King* 820–30, in LCL) has Oedipus say, "Am I not altogether unholy, if I must leave my country, and in my exile never see my dear ones, nor *enter* [*set foot upon*] my native land?" He asks whether this exile is coming upon him "by the action of a cruel deity" and concludes, "Never, never, O sacred majesty of the gods, may I see that day."

The native land of Oedipus is not just his homeland but is a kind of sacred space for him, entrance to which is determined by the gods and requires him to be "holy."

7. Almost identical to the reference to sacred space under control of the gods in Sophocles, *Oedipus King*, is Euripides (*El.* 585–95, in LCL), who refers to the "exile" of Orestes and has the choir say, "You have arrived. . . . Some god, some god is bringing us victory, dear friend. . . . Utter prayer to the gods that with good luck . . . your brother may *enter* [*tread*] the city."

I have provided more context for the references in points 1, 2, and 5 above as well as to points 6 and 7 in an attempt to confirm the same conclusion drawn by Carr (1973: 498) about ἐμβατεύω referring to either a god or a human entering or treading in either a sacred space or a temple.[133] I have adduced additional Classical Greek and Hellenistic examples to further strengthen his conclusion. In the light of these references, he then concludes that ἐμβατεύω in Col. 2:18 refers to "treading upon a sacred place," i.e., entering the heavenly sanctuary or "haunting the courts of heaven" (Carr 1973: 499). While his conclusion is correct as far as it goes, his citations, plus the above references to the Claros and Laodicea inscriptions, together with uses in Josephus and Joshua, form a conceptual association of entering the temple as a background for understanding the verb in Col. 2:18.

In the LXX the concept of "entering" into the temple is common, expressed often through the verbs εἰσπορεύομαι (*eisporeuomai*) and εἰσέρχομαι (*eiserchomai*), as well as εἴσειμι (*eiseimi*). For example, εἰσέρχομαι is used for "entering into" the "tabernacle" (σκηνή, *skēnē*, about thirteen times) or the "temple" (ναός, *naos*, or ἱερόν, *hieron*, about twelve times) or "holy place" (ἅγιος, *hagios*, about eight times) or "sanctuary" (ἁγιαστήριον, *hagiastērion*, twice). In Rev. 15:8, "No one was able to enter [εἰσέρχομαι] the temple" in heaven "until the seven plagues of the angels were finished" (likewise Rev. 21:27). In 1 En. 14.9–14, Enoch "enters into" (εἰσέρχομαι) various outer parts of the heavenly temple until he "enters into (εἰσέρχομαι) the house," which is the equivalent of the heavenly temple's "holy place," and there he peers into the holy of holies "and sees a vision" (cf. further 1 En. 14.15–23); finally God asks him to "come near" (14.24).

The standard lexical sources affirm that one of the options for ἐμβατεύω is a meaning derived from the mysteries and associated with "entering into the inner sanctuary," as the climax of initiation, which most of these sources prefer for the meaning in Col. 2:18: LSJ 539: "to be initiated into the mysteries," which LSJ applies to Col. 2:18; another meaning offered by LSJ is "enter into a sacred cave"; BAA, citing the Claros inscriptions, sees the word to be a technical term of the mystery language, which concerns one who steps into *the temple* (*das Heiligtum*) that he has seen in the ecstatic experience; likewise BDAG (321, s.v. ἐμβατεύω) offers this meaning as a viable option. About ἐμβατεύω MM 206 (following Ramsay 1914) say, "More significant, however, than any of the above citations [of papyri usage] for the meaning of the verb in its only occurrence in the NT (Col. 2:18) is its use in the mystery religions to denote the climax of initiation, when the *mystēs* 'sets foot on' the entrance to [the sanctuary and] the new life which he is now to share with the god." L&N 1:533–34 write: "ἐμβατεύω in Col. 2.18 is a technical term derived from the mystery religions"; while acknowledging the other possible renderings, they offer three translations of ἐμβατεύω (*embateuō*) that they consider most likely: (1) "who enters the sanctuary which he saw in ecstasy"; (2) "taking his stand on what he has seen in the mysteries"; (3) "by what he saw when he was initiated."[134]

In addition to the possible relevance of the passage about Sinai from Josephus (above), other aspects of Judaism may also have been combined with this pagan focus on "entering the sanctuary" in the mysteries. Certain Jewish traditions focus on saints practicing purification rites in order to ascend in mystical visions into the heavenly temple and throne room of God (Davila 2000a: 261–62; 2000b: 103, cf. 112–13, 138; these refer only to people who mystically ascend

133. H. Preisker (*TDNT* 2:535) concludes that the uses in Sophocles (*Oed. Col.* 680) and Euripides (*Rhesus* 225) refer to gods "coming to a holy place when invoked."

134. Arnold (1995: 118) has cited and briefly discussed the lexical references in this paragraph, which I have independently checked and summarized.

into the heavenly temple without explicit mention of purification rites). Some argue that in their earthly liturgy the Qumran sectarians self-identified with the heavenly temple worship and with the angels who participated in that worship (esp. in the Songs of the Sabbath Sacrifice; see Davila 2000b: 89–90; and Newsom 1990: 115–18, with some qualifications). One could call this a vicarious ascent to heaven. The Testament of Levi pictures Levi "entering" (though not the word ἐμβατεύω) through various stages of heaven (2.7–8) and being commissioned to "tell forth his mysteries," which he sees there (2.10). In the "holy of holies" God dwells with "archangels," who worship and offer sacrifices (3.3–6). An angel opens for Levi "the gates of heaven," and he sees "the Holy Most High sitting on the throne" (5.1). Levi is then commissioned as a priest while he is in heaven (8.1–18). In T. Isaac 4.45–47 we read of the righteous who ascend to heaven, when "they will be engaged in holy, angelic service by reason of purity. They will be presented before the Lord and his angels because of their pure offerings and their angelic service, . . . and the angels will be their friends" (trans. W. F. Stinespring, *OTP* 1:908; cited by Francis 1975b: 178).

In addition to Qumran's Songs of the Sabbath Sacrifice and the Testament of Isaac, other Jewish texts cited by Francis (1975b: 176–79), Sappington (1991: 91–94), and Dunn (1996: 180–81) argue in favor of a subjective genitive by appealing to the following texts, where they contend that humans worship *with* angels: T. Job 48–50; 1 En. 71.5–12; 3 En. 1.9–12; Apoc. Zeph. 8.2–4 (praying with angels); Apoc. Ab. 17.1–7 (temple in 18.3–13); Mart. Ascen. Isa. 8.17; 9.28–33; 1QH 11.20–22 (*olim* 3.20–22); 1QSb 4.25–26. D. Moo (2008: 227), however, claims that some of these texts do not precisely portray humans worshiping God with angels; he contends that T. Job 48–50 refers to humans employing the speech of angels in praising God, 1 En. 71.11–12 refers to humans only being in the presence of angels before God, Apocalypse of Zephaniah alludes to someone praying with angels, and 1QH 11.20–22 (*olim* 3.20–22) is only about humans being in the midst of angels. But even these texts are close to the idea of humans worshiping with angels: e.g., praying with angels in Apocalypse of Zephaniah should be considered participating in a heavenly liturgy with angels; 1 Enoch says Enoch was "blessing, glorifying, and extolling" God in the presence of angels; and 1QH pictures the hymnist not only in the company of angels but also "entering into communion" with them and "praising" God's "name in joyful concord" with the angels (see Dupont-Sommer 1962: 209; 1QH 11.23 [*olim* 3.23]). All of these above texts may lend some support to the subjective genitive option, but our interest in these texts is also that most of them—likely not coincidentally, as in Qumran's Songs of the Sabbath Sacrifice—portray people entering not merely heaven but into the heavenly temple[135] (so 1 En. 71.5–12 [and cf. its development of the temple scene in 1 En. 14.9–20]; 3 En. 1.9–12 [and cf. 1.5–7, 10, 12; 2.1–2]; see Apoc. Ab. 17.1–7 [and cf. 18.3–13]; 1QSb 4.25–26, 28; Mart. Ascen. Isa. 8.17; 9.28–33 [and cf. a temple concept expressed in 7.17, 27; 9.27, 37]; 10.6; 11.32). Note also b. Hag. 14b: R. Jose the priest and Rab Johanan b. Zakkai were seen in a dream "reclining on Mount Sinai, when a voice said, 'Ascend hither, ascend hither! [Here are] great banqueting chambers . . . for you and your disciples'" (which is in the context of explanations about chariot visions regarding the heavenly temple). Although none of these references contain the word ἐμβατεύω, they still lend further conceptual support to the apocalyptic visions "which you have seen" in Col. 2:18 being a vision of entering into the heavenly temple. Dunn (1996: 183–84) also argues the same thing on the basis of the above apocalyptic evidence. Stuhlmacher (2018: 441–42) sees the Qumran Songs of the Sabbath Sacrifice as the background for the "entering" in Col. 2:18, since these songs refer not only to angels worshiping in the heavenly sanctuary but also to people "raising" themselves to join the angelic worship in the heavenly temple.

As noted earlier, it is possible that θρησκείᾳ τῶν ἀγγέλων (*thrēskeia tōn angelōn*) could be an objective genitive (humans' "worship of angels") or a subjective genitive ("worship by angels"). As noted above, to argue for a subjective genitive, appeal is sometimes made to Qumran's

135. See Baumgarten (1988: 201), who observes that in these Songs of the Sabbath Sacrifice human worshipers are brought progressively through parts of the heavenly temple and finally to a vision of the throne itself. See also Dunn (1996: 183) for the focus in the Songs of the Sabbath Sacrifice on the heavenly temple as the place of angelic worship (citing 4Q405 frags. 14–15 1.3–4; frag. 23 1.8–10).

Songs of the Sabbath Sacrifice, where repeatedly there is description of angels worshiping in the heavenly temple (and some contend that the Qumranites believed they were identified with the angels in their heavenly temple worship [see Davila 2000b: 89–90]). Francis has argued this, appealing to other Qumran texts and Jewish apocalyptic literature that depicts angelic liturgies (see Francis 1975b: 177–79). In this respect, if it is true that Col. 2:18 is referring to angels surrounding God in his temple, this may support a subjective genitive.

We have argued earlier, however, that the immediate context of Col. 2:18 points to the probability of an objective genitive. An objective genitive is further pointed to by observing that θρησκεία followed by a genitive in the LXX and early Judaism is *usually* an objective genitive (Wis. 14:27, "worship of idols"; Philo, *Spec.* 1.315, "worship of gods"); the following all involve θρησκεία followed or preceded by a modifying objective genitive where "God" or the personal pronoun for God is the object of worship: Josephus, *Ant.* 1.222; 4.306; 7.341; 8.225, 251, 256, 270, 395; 9.133; 10.53; 12.271; cf. similarly 12.253; 13.199; 17.214. See also 1 Clem. 45.7 ("worship of the Most High"). In addition to these Jewish Greek sources, other Hellenistic sources support θρησκεία being modified by an objective genitive.[136] Significant in this respect is Origen, *Cels.* 5.6, which portrays Celsus as accusing Jews of "worshiping [σέβουσι, *sebousi*] the heaven and the angels who dwell therein" and "*treating with great respect*" [θρησκύνειν, *thrēskynein*] "demonic-like beings" who appear in visions or dreams (see *ANF* 4:545). Significant also is the Pre. Pet. frag. 4a, quoted by Clement of Alexandria (*Misc.* 5), saying that the Jews "worshiped angels and archangels, the month and the moon," in conjunction with not holding faithfully to the holidays of the "Sabbath, . . . new moon, . . . nor the feast" (cf. here Col. 2:18 with 2:16).[137] Even more relevant is an early Christian section of Sib. Or. 8.380–94 (probably early 2nd cent., no later than 300 AD), where people treat idols as "divine . . . [and] sing their praises over dumb idols . . . with supplications and unholy *worship* [θρησκεία]"; they offer "the smell of sacrifice filling the feast; . . . they . . . burn offering on altars" and "offer libations"; they sacrifice "unto dead demons, as *to heavenly beings* [οὐρανίοισιν, *ouranioisin*], performing godless and destructive *worship* [θρησκεία]." Here we have idol worship in the context of a temple (or "altar") together with cultic rituals, and this worship is offered "as to heavenly beings [angels]." In response, God says, "As if they for my honors deemed these things all useful" (Sib. Or. 8.383), but "I have no need of your burnt offerings, nor your libations, or polluted smoke" (8.390–91, trans. Evans 2009).

Less frequent is θρησκεία modified by a subjective genitive, occurring primarily in Josephus (*Ant.* 8.229, "worship by their forefathers"; 12.253, "worship by the Jews"; 16.115, "the worship by the whole nation"; *J.W.* 2.198, "worship by men"); yet also 4 Macc. 5:7 ("worship [religion] by the Jews"). Arnold (1995: 91) also cites Chariton, *Chaer.* 7.6.6 ("worship by the Barbarians"). While acknowledging objective genitive uses, Francis (1975b: 180) appeals to Josephus (*Ant.* 12.253) and 4 Macc. 5:7 for the viability of a subjective genitive and thus contends that only the context of Col. 2:18 can determine which is the case.

2:20. In verse 20 some scribes ($\aleph^{(*),2}$, 0278^{c}, 6, 326, 365, 614, 629, 630, 1505, ar, m, vg^{mss}, sy^{h}; Ambr, Spec) inserted a "therefore" (οὖν, *oun*) before "you died," expressing explicitly the scribes' view that verse 20 is drawing a conclusion based on verses 16 and 18.

2:21. Anything or anyone unclean could not enter into the temple complex. It was the priests' task to keep whatever was unclean out of the temple (2 Chron. 29:5, 15–19). To do this the priests themselves were to "touch [ἅπτω, *haptō*] nothing unclean" but "purify themselves" (Isa. 52:11; the first part is quoted in 2 Cor. 6:17). Qumran repeatedly affirms that no unclean

136. BDAG 459, s.v. θρησκεία. See Arnold (1995: 92), who cites additional Jewish and Hellenistic examples, including worship of pagan gods or idols and concludes that "a survey of θρησκεία fails to turn up one example of a divine being, or a typical object of worship, . . . related to θρησκεία in the genitive case that should be taken as a subjective genitive."

137. While caution must be exercised when outsiders evaluate Jews or Christians, there is probably some basis, however small, in historical reality for these descriptions (following Arnold 1995: 58–59).

person or thing is to enter the temple: 11QT^a 45.7–18, esp. line 10, "They are not to enter My temple while unclean, for that would defile it"; 46.1–3, 9–12; 47.3–7, "My name and temp[le] there must be holy and pure from anything that is in any way unclean by which one might be defiled. Everything inside it must be pure: wine, oil, edibles, . . . all must be pure"; 47.13–18; 1Q20 12.4, "They are not to enter My temple while unclean, for that would defile it"; CD 5.6–7, "They also defile the sanctuary, for they do not separate clean from unclean according to the Law";[138] Jub. 3.13. The Mishnah records fastidious rules for keeping the temple pure from any uncleanness. For example, one of the main ways to bring about "the purification of the Temple court" is to continually keep the utensils cleansed with water and to have clean duplicates and triplicates to replace the "unclean" ones (Hag. 3.8). Sacrifices offered "on the new months," on "the festivals," and on "the Day of Atonement" "effected atonement for a clean person who has eaten something unclean," and all such sacrifices "are offered up to effect atonement for imparting uncleanness to the sanctuary and its Holy Things" (Shevu. 1.4–5); "awareness of uncleanness" was inextricably linked to awareness of being in the sanctuary or "holy things" that were part of it (Shevu. 2.1, 3). Among the transgressions subject to extirpation in the Torah is "coming to the sanctuary when unclean" (Ker. 1.1); eating "unclean foods" or drinking "unclean liquids" and "entering the sanctuary" requires certain measures to become clean (Ker. 3.3); he who is unclean "is forbidden to enter the sanctuary" (Parah 11.4).[139] For other Mishnaic texts pertaining to rules for keeping the temple pure from uncleanness, see Eruv. 10.15; Sotah 3.4A–C; Mak. 3.2A; Ker. 1.1H; 2.4E; Kelim 1.8. For the notion in Philo that the temple is to be kept from uncleanness, see *Cher.* 1.96; *Mos.* 2.90, 138, 152, 231; *Spec.* 1.100, 118–19, 270; 3.130. Likewise in Josephus, see *Ant.* 3.278; 12.145, 318; 19.332; *Ag. Ap.* 2.102, 104, 110.[140]

2:22. That Isa. 29:13 LXX ("the commandments and teachings of men") concerns the sin of idol worship is apparent from several observations. Isaiah 29:13 is part of a pericope that begins with an allusion to Isa. 6:9–10 (29:9–10, "Blind yourselves and be blind; . . . the Lord . . . has shut your eyes"), which is a literary taunt against Israel, mocking them because they were becoming like the idols that they worshiped (just as the idols had eyes and ears but could not see or hear, so the Israelites had eyes and ears but could not spiritually see or hear; on which, see Beale 1991; see also Ps. 135:15–18). Isaiah 29:9–13 views Isa. 6 to be commencing fulfillment. Israel's "removing their heart far from" God and "worship" of God "by teaching the commandments and teachings of men" (29:13 LXX) was, thus, part of their idolatry. When Israel is described as "far" from God elsewhere in the OT, they are "far" in the sense that they are "worshiping" idols and not God (Jer. 2:5; Ezek. 44:10); when they are said to worship in "vain" (Isa. 29:13 LXX), sometimes it is when they are worshiping idols (Isa. 41:29). Isaiah 30:1–5 explains that part of Israel's sin was to trust in Egypt's help against another nation that was about to invade Israel. In particular, Isa. 30:1 MT says the Israelites "pour out a drink offering" (NASB marg.), but not to God (rather, implicitly, to an idol to seal a political pact); Isa. 30:3 also says that Israel sought "refuge in the safety of Pharaoh."* This involved some degree of compromise with idol worship, since Pharaoh claimed to be God, the incarnation of the sun-god; the divine kingship of Pharaoh was a cornerstone of Egyptian religious beliefs. Also, Isa. 30:22 explicitly refers to Israel's "graven images" and "molten images," which Israel worshiped apparently in some connection with its alliance with Egypt; so also Isa. 31:7, "Every man will cast away his silver idols and his gold idols, which your sinful hands have made for you as a sin"; cf. with 31:1–6 in relation to Egypt. Thus Isa. 29:13, to which Paul alludes, is about idolatry,[141] and he employs these words to characterize the false teaching as idol worship.

Comparable to Col. 2, Paul says in Phil. 3:2: "Beware of the dogs, beware of the evil workers, beware of the false circumcision." And then in 3:18–19 he calls them "enemies of the cross of

138. The preceding quotations of Qumran documents are from Wise, Abegg, and Cook 2005.
139. All Mishnah quotations are from Neusner 1988.
140. I am indebted to my research student Peter Moore for the last five references to the Mishnah and for the references to Philo and Josephus that follow.
141. On which, see also Beetham 2008: 194–95.

Christ, whose end is destruction, whose god is their belly, and whose glory is in their shame, who set their minds on earthly things." Paul's statement that the unbelieving Jews have their "belly" as their "god" is most probably a reference to their preoccupation with human traditions concerning all kinds of cleansings associated with eating. Commitment to such traditions, versus trust in Christ, is idolatry.

2:23. The "and" (καί, *kai*) is omitted by some very good and early MSS (𝔓[46], B), as well as MS 1739. The inclusion of "and" is supported also by some early and good quality MSS (א, A), as well as many good though later MSS (e.g., C, D, F, G, H, K, L, P, Ψ). The more difficult reading is the omission, since it results in a bit more awkward translation, though not impossibly so. Thus the omitted reading is slightly preferable (see further the note in the NET Bible).

2:23. The syntactical difficulty of this verse is notorious. There are three major views.

1. The ἐστίν (*estin*) could go with "having" (ἔχοντα, *echonta*),[142] as we have preferred in the commentary discussion: "Such things are having, to be sure, a reputation [or appearance] of wisdom in self-made worship and self-abasement in neglect of the body, but are of no value with respect to satisfying the flesh"* (so likewise, e.g., NASB, TNIV).[143] The problem with this view is that μέν (*men*) is usually placed as the second word at the beginning of the sentence, and it is also unusual to place it between the finite verb and participle.
2. Or, the ἐστίν could go with the final prepositional phrase of the verse, as, e.g., the NET renders it: "even though they have the appearance of wisdom with their self-imposed worship and [false] humility achieved by an unsparing treatment of the body—a wisdom with no true value—they in reality result in fleshly indulgence." The phrase "a wisdom with no true value" modifies the directly preceding subordinate concessive clause (beginning with "even though"), and the main clause (ἅτινά ἐστιν, *hatina estin*, lit., which things are, rendered by the NET as "they in reality") resumes with the prepositional clause concluding the sentence, "result in fleshly indulgence" (the NET's rendering of πρὸς πλησμονὴν τῆς σαρκός, *pros plēsmonēn tēs sarkos*); Hollenbach (1979) argues for this view in the most depth. This rendering presents a problem: it is awkward to have two subordinate clauses intervening between a main verb and its complement. The awkwardness is compounded by having the second subordinate clause subordinate to the first one (for these critiques of the first two translation options, see Pao 2012: 197).
3. A variant of this second view connects the main clause (ἅτινά ἐστιν, they are) to the very end of the verse, which begins with "of no value against gratification of the flesh," preceded by a concessive clause: "While they have a semblance of wisdom in rigor of devotion and self-abasement [and] severity to the body, they are of no value against gratification of the flesh" (NABRE; argued for in some detail by Pao 2012: 197). The difficulty with this option is similar to that of the preceding view: it is difficult to have a long subordinate clause interrupting the flow of the main verb with its complement. Thus the distance between ἐστίν and either οὐκ (*ouk*) etc. or πρός (*pros*) etc. renders the second two options weaker (Harris: 2010: 115).

Any of these options are viable, but the first has fewer problems, reads more straightforwardly, and lines up with the majority of commentators and English translations.

142. As a periphrastic present participle; so Robertson 1934: 880–81; and BDF §353.4.
143. D. Moo (2008: 239) discusses a variant of this view as represented by the church fathers.

D. Believers Should Seek Heavenly Things and Not Old Earthly Things (3:1–4)

Here is a fuller statement of the main idea of this unit: *Believers should seek heavenly things and not old earthly things because they have died to the old world and have been raised with Christ as a new creation in a new heavenly world.*

Believers have died with Christ (cf. 2:11–12, 14) to the old world (2:20a). Because saints have died to the old world, they should not be subject to outmoded OT commandments (cultic and civil laws)[1] of that old world in order to obtain a closer relationship with God. Faith in and identification with Christ is all they need to be close to God (2:19), since Christ represents the full presence of God in the end-time heavenly temple. They also should not be subject to outdated statutes because these decrees are part of the corrupt world that is fading away and have their origin in human tradition, which is rooted in self-made religion (2:21–23). Therefore, as we have seen, the main point of 2:16–23 is that true believers *should not be required to submit to the false teachers' outmoded and distorted laws in order to experience the tabernacling fullness of God's presence, since only faith in Christ is necessary for that.*

The "therefore" in 3:1 should be paraphrased as "on the basis that you have died with Christ to the old world, so that you must not submit to old-world laws, you have also been 'raised up with Christ.'" Real identification with Christ's death necessarily leads to identification with his resurrection, just as Christ's own death necessarily led to his own resurrection. Identification with Christ's death released believers from the old world and resulted in believers not needing to submit to the old-world's laws (2:20–23). Likewise, identification with Christ's resurrection (3:1a) results in God's people being able to "seek the things above, where Christ is"* (3:1b). Then 3:2 reiterates this: "Think on the things above, not on the things on earth."* The "things on earth" include, in context, the old "commandments of the world" in 2:16–23. They are not to think on "the things of the [old] earth" because they "have died" (3:3a). The remainder of verses 3b–4 continues to elaborate on the effects of this death as the basis for "not thinking on the things of the [old] earth." This death has led to a new "life hidden with Christ in God" (3:3b). Consequently, "when Christ will be manifested, who is your life, then, you also with him will be manifested in glory"* (3:4).

1. Comments above on 2:16–23 identify particular OT laws that Paul thinks are outmoded.

Thus the exhortation "to seek the things above" (3:1) and its expansion in verses 2–4 and later in verses 5–10 is a polemic against those who falsely claim to experience heavenly temple visions and exalt themselves in superiority over the rest of the Colossian Christians (see Pao 2012: 204–5, though not specifying a notion of the temple). In this light, it is not surprising to continue to see echoes of a focus on the true heavenly temple in 3:1–11.

The main point highlighted in verses 1–4 is to "think on the things above." Everything else in verses 1–4 in one way or another supports that point. This first paragraph of Col. 3 continues the Christ-centered theme begun in 1:14–23, reiterated in 1:24–2:5, and intensified in 2:6–15 (see D. Moo 2008: 243, on 3:1–2 picking up especially the imperative to focus on Christ in 2:6 and the implied imperatives in 2:7).

Exegesis and Exposition

[1]Therefore if you have been raised up with Christ, keep seeking the things above, where Christ is, seated at the right hand of God. [2]Set your mind on the things above, not on the things that are on earth. [3]For you have died and your life is hidden with Christ in God. [4]When Christ, who is our life, is revealed, then you also will be revealed with Him in glory.

3:1 The "therefore" (οὖν, *oun*) at the beginning of the verse refers back to the main point of 2:16–23: that Christians should not be required to submit to the false teachers' outmoded and distorted laws from the old world because they have died with Christ to that old world. This main point of the preceding segment is the basis for the rest of 3:1. As the conditional particle εἰ (*ei*) introduces "You have died with Christ" in 2:20, so likewise the same particle introduces "You have been raised up with Christ" in 3:1. As in 2:20, the particle εἰ introduces a first-class condition, where the first clause is assumed to be true for the sake of the argument. This is not, however, a hypothetical or theoretical assertion. Indeed, Paul assumes the reality of the first clause, "You have been raised up with Christ," so that "seeking the things above" is a necessary result (however, Paul thinks not of all in the church but of the majority; see further on 1:23). This assumption that the Colossians have really been "raised up with Christ" in the past is apparent from the context, where 3:3 says, "For you have died and your life is hidden with Christ in God" (likewise Col. 2:12–13, "Having been buried with Him, . . . you were also raised up with Him. . . . [God] made you alive together with Him"). And Paul writes the same thing in Romans (6:4–5, 8–10, 13).

Like the "if" in 2:20 (see my comments there), the "if" here shows that Paul is not only stating that the Colossians have "been raised with Christ," but he is also bidding them to consider whether they have truly been raised with Christ (by faith) and to reflect on the consequences for their existence (see my comments on 2:20).

Some commentators think that the notion of already having been "raised with Christ" is an overrealized eschatology and reveals that Paul is not the author of Colossians, since in the so-called authentic letters Paul purportedly always sees the believers' resurrection to be future. We have discussed this problem at 2:12 (see my comments there). There we saw that Paul does, indeed, express the concept that believers have already been raised with Christ in this age. Then 3:1–4 shows that their resurrection has begun spiritually in this age and will be consummated physically at Christ's final coming[2] (esp. cf. v. 4; so likewise D. Moo 2008: 245–46). So there is an "already and not yet" in Colossians, as elsewhere in Paul.

The first statement, "You have been raised up with Christ," should result in believers "seeking the things above." The second part of the conditional clause (the apodosis) is a present imperative. This is a classic indicative-imperative pattern: because the Colossians have come into union with Christ's resurrection, they now have resurrection power to obey God's commands ("keep seeking the things above"). "Resurrection" and "death" (in v. 3) are not figurative metaphors for spiritual realities but refer to a real holistic death and resurrection in Christ.[3] In this respect, believers' spiritual death has occurred and will be followed by physical death: a real redemptive-historical spiritual resurrection has been inaugurated and will be completed at the eschaton in physical resurrection. Thus they are not merely *like* beings resurrected from the dead; they really *are* such beings.

Thus Paul commands them to "seek the things above."[4] "Above" (ἄνω, *anō*) is often used with "heaven" (οὐρανός, *ouranos*) in the LXX (so ten times, as in Exod. 20:4 and Deut. 4:39, usually rendered "the heaven above") and occasionally in the NT (Acts 2:19). In this light and in view of the immediate context, the word here designates "heaven." They are to "seek the things above" in heaven because their "hope [is] laid up . . . in heaven" (1:5), Christ's reconciliation of them has affected even "heaven" (1:20), and their "Lord," Christ, has his dwelling "in heaven"* (4:1).[5]

The heaven above is "where Christ is, seated[6] at the right hand of God," and his followers, who are united with Christ and have been "raised up with Christ," have also been "seated with him in the heavenlies"* (Eph. 2:6). For this reason, they should "seek the things above," where their true and ultimate

2. Colossians 3:4 does not explicitly say that their future "manifestation with Christ in glory"* will be physical resurrection, but it is implied in the light of Paul's other letters (e.g., see Rom. 8:18–25; Phil. 3:20–21).

3. Contra Callow (2002: 95, 109, 115), who argues for a metaphorical approach.

4. Adverbs of place preceded by the neuter plural article can function like substantives (following Harris 2010: 120, citing among others BDAG 688, s.v. ὁ, ἡ, τό). Here ἄνω (*anō*) preceded by τά (*ta*) becomes part of the object of "seek."

5. That "Lord" refers to Christ in 4:1 is apparent from 3:17 and 3:24, where "Lord" is clearly identified respectively with "Jesus" and "Christ."

6. A comma could be placed between "is" and "seated," separating them syntactically, but it may be better to see ἐστιν . . . καθήμενος (*estin . . . kathēmenos*) as a periphrastic present participle (so Robertson 1934: 880–81), though Porter (1994: 46) thinks it difficult to decide (so also Porter 1989: 456).

home is, that is, where their "mother" is (Gal. 4:26, "the Jerusalem above [ἄνω, *anō*] is free," which "is our mother") and their true country (Phil. 3:20, "our citizenship is in heaven, from . . . which we eagerly await . . . Christ").[7]

The reference to Christ "seated at the right hand of God" is an allusion to Ps. 110:1: "Sit at my right hand."[8] This allusion often occurs elsewhere in the NT, where it refers to the exalted position of Christ in heaven, as a result of the resurrection.[9] In fact, Ps. 110:1 is referred to more in the NT than any other OT passage (the passage is referred to twenty-three times; see Hay 1973: 163–64). Psalm 110:1 says, "The Lord says to my Lord: 'Sit at my right hand, until I make Your enemies a footstool for Your feet.'" The first phrase, "The Lord says to my Lord," appears to indicate that the king being addressed is a divine king. At the very least, David refers to a coming king who is greater than him, since he calls this king "my Lord" (Adonai, not Yahweh or Elohim). This points strongly to the original messianic nature of the psalm, and Jesus interprets it this way (Mark 12:35–37, where Jesus also assumes that the psalm is written/spoken by David, not just about David).

Later Judaism applied the text to pious individuals or the Messiah (for use in Judaism, see Hay 1973: 21–33). Psalm 110:1 can be read to mean that the Messiah will be given a place of honor beside God's throne, as some rabbis understood it; but the uses elsewhere in the NT and here in Colossians are better understood to mean that Jesus "participates in the unique divine sovereignty over all things" (Bauckham 2008: 21–22). Thus it is likely that "my Lord" is on the same divine functional level as "the Lord" (God) at the beginning of Ps. 110:1.

Psalm 110 later refers to "my Lord" in verse 1 as "a priest forever" (110:4) also in reiteration of verse 1, "the Lord is at Your right hand" in 110:5. Hebrews 1:3; 8:1; and 10:11–13, following this link in Ps. 110:1, 4–5, connect Jesus as a "priest" (only implied in Heb. 1:3) with "sitting at the right hand" of God (Heb. 8:1–2 places this in the heavenly "sanctuary and in the true tabernacle").[10] In

7. Note that "heaven" here in Phil. 3:20 is in parallel with "above" (ἄνω, *anō*) in Phil. 3:14: "the upward call of God in Christ Jesus." See D. Moo (2008: 246) for the similar significance of the Gal. 4 and Phil. 3 passages.

8. See Beetham (2008: 219–20) for the validity of the allusion and a list of many commentators who see the allusion in contrast, e.g., to the negative assessment of Hay (2000: 116–17) and Foster (2016: 310–11), the latter of whom sees neither an allusion nor echo because the phrase was "embedded . . . in early Christian thought to such an extent that here it can be used without intentional reference to the original context." That the phrase is embedded in early Christian tradition is likely, but it is unlikely that recognition of the Ps. 110 allusion completely faded; at least such needs to be proved and not assumed.

9. On which, see explicit citations in Matt. 22:44 parr.; Acts 2:34–35; Heb. 1:13; cf. allusions in Matt. 26:64 parr.; Rom. 8:34; 1 Cor. 15:25; Eph. 1:20; Heb. 1:3, 13; 8:1; 10:12–13; 12:2; 1 Pet. 3:22; see Hay 1973.

10. The only probable use of Ps. 110:1 in Second Temple Judaism is T. Job 33.3 from the first century BC to first century AD (so Bauckham 2008: 22): "My [Job's] throne is in the upper world, and its splendor and majesty come from the right hand of the Father" (here notice "upper world" in comparison to "above" in Col. 3:1). Significantly, this portrayal is set in a broader context that reflects a temple atmosphere: cf. 32.5, "a throne of precious stones"; 32.8, "the

this connection Hebrews quotes Ps. 110:4 seven times and applies it to Jesus as the everlasting priest (5:6, 10; 6:20; 7:3, 11, 17, 21). Romans 8:34 also portrays Jesus "at the right hand of God" (cf. Ps. 110:1) as an "interceding" priestly figure. In addition, the phrase "in holy array" (בְּהַדְרֵי־קֹדֶשׁ, *bəhadrê-qōdeš*) in Ps. 110:3 MT, which describes the clothing of the king's people who serve him, refers elsewhere in the OT to those bringing praise or offerings in the temple.[11] In the light of previous references to the temple and heaven in the epistle, could the psalm's priestly links, especially with "the one seated at God's right hand," be in the peripheral vision of Paul at this point in Colossians? A positive answer to this question is pointed to by recalling that God's heavenly throne (clearly implied in Ps. 110:1[12] and Col. 3:1) is in the heavenly temple (e.g., among numerous references, see Ps. 11:4; Isa. 6:1; Ezek. 1:26; 10:1; Rev. 7:15; 8:3; 16:17; 1 En. 14.18–19; 3 En. 1.12).

Psalm 110:1 is also used elsewhere in the NT to underscore the exalted position of Christ or believers or to highlight the subjection of all powers (including evil ones) to Christ.[13] The idea of the Messiah defeating enemies may also be included in Paul's reference to the psalm, since such an idea is found in the second part of Ps. 110:1 itself and in verse 2, as well as in verses 5–7. The psalm's application to Christ's exalted position over all angels (Eph. 1:20–22; Heb. 1:3–6, 13–14; Pol. *Phil.* 2.1),[14] including evil ones, is particularly pertinent here. Accordingly, the false teachers are guilty of worshiping angels (2:18), and such worship likely includes a deceptive practice of revering evil angelic powers, since such powers are mentioned as having been defeated and subjected to Christ (Col. 2:10, 15; cf. also Eph. 6:10–12). The false teachers are saying that believers need a heavenly experience of seeing or worshiping (with?) angels in the temple, but Paul counters this by saying they already have all the heavenly experience they need through their union with the exalted Christ in heaven. Furthermore, why should they worship heavenly powers that are evil and have been defeated by Christ?

Beetham (2008: 224) summarizes the main thrust of the Psalm as follows: "Psalm 110 portrays a Davidic priest-king through whom YHWH will extend from Zion his dominion over all nations." The point of Ps. 110:1 is not merely the prophesied achievement of a sovereign position of rule ("Sit at my right hand"); the future focus is on the beginning fulfillment in achieving

---

censers"; 32.9, "golden lamps on silver stands"; and 33.9, associating the heavenly kingdom with "the chariots of the Father" (trans. R. P. Spittler, *OTP* 1:854–56).

11. See the same phrase in this respect in Ps. 29:2 (in light of the concluding 29:9); 96:8–9 (cf. v. 6); 1 Chron. 16:29; 2 Chron. 20:21; following Beetham 2008: 221–22. The Chronicles passages depict this attire as priestly clothing, and the psalm texts apply the clothing to all who would worship in the temple.

12. As apparent, e.g., from the use of Ps. 110:1 in Heb. 8:1 and 12:2.

13. Psalm 110:1 is also used to support specific titles of Jesus. See Hay (1973: 52–155) for these four uses of the psalm in the NT.

14. See Bauckham (2008: 198) for other texts in early Christianity that use Ps. 110:1 to indicate Christ's exalted position over all angels. In addition, Col. 1:16 presents Christ as the creator of all things, including all angels.

that rule ("until I make Your enemies a footstool for Your feet"). Psalm 110:2 expands further on this inaugurated rule: "The Lord will stretch forth Your strong scepter from Zion, saying, 'Rule in the midst of Your enemies.'" This fits perfectly into the broad NT notion that Christ commenced his messianic rule during his ministry, death, resurrection, and exaltation. Colossians 3:1 depicts Christ as the beginning fulfillment of Ps. 110:1.

The notion of an inaugurated rule is also appropriate within the immediate context of Colossians. In 2:10 Paul says that Christ "is the head over all rule and authority"; similarly in 2:15, "When He [Christ] had disarmed the rulers and authorities, He made a public display of them, having triumphed over them through it [the cross]" (NASB marg.). The Ps. 110:1 allusion underscores Christ's exalted position that has been given to him as a result of winning the decisive victory over evil angelic powers, which is also how the psalm verse is applied in 1 Cor. 15:25; Eph. 1:20; 1 Pet. 3:22; and possibly Rev. 3:21 (cf. 1 Clem. 36.5; Pol. *Phil.* 2.1; see O'Brien 1982: 162). Although the crucial battle has been won at Christ's cross and resurrection, the enemy is not yet completely defeated. In Col. 1:20 Paul says that God has designed "to reconcile all things [whether things on earth or things in heaven] to Himself, as a result of having made peace through the blood of His [Christ's] cross." This complete reconciliation has not yet been accomplished by the time Paul writes Colossians, which is clear from observing that he needs to warn the readers against the detrimental influence of false teachers (2:8, 18–23), who are part of the "authority of darkness" (1:13 NASB marg.) and through whom the unseen demonic "rulers and authorities" (2:15) still work, even though they have been decisively defeated.

The Colossians are to focus on Christ's exalted position ("Keep seeking the things above") and to want to be identified with their exalted Lord in order continually to be related to their "head," Christ (2:19). The "seeking" is a desire to have one's thinking and lifestyle continually oriented around Christ's kingship over all things (similarly, see the use of ζητέω, *zēteō*, in Matt. 6:33; John 5:44; 7:18; Rom. 2:7; cf. Phil. 2:21; 1 Thess. 2:4–6; cf. Phil. 3:19–20).[15]

Commentators sometimes speak conceptually of a vertical (or spatial) and horizontal (or temporal) eschatology in Col. 3:1 (cf. O'Brien 1982: 161, 168; Sumney 2008: 182; Harris 2010: 119). That believers have been "raised with Christ" in the heavenly realm "above," where Christ is seated and ruling, indicates a horizontal inaugurated eschatology: the end-time kingdom and resurrection have penetrated back into history at the cross and resurrection. But this also entails a vertical eschatology. The end-time kingdom has not come in its new-creational and material fullness but penetrated back into the old creation and exists in the invisible dimension of "heaven" or the sphere "above."[16] This is not old-earth topography but indicates merely an invisible realm, which will become visible at the consummation.

15. See further Beale (2007: 863–65) on Ps. 110:1 in Col. 3:1.

16. See Lincoln (1981: 131–34) for good discussion of the spatial and horizontal aspects of eschatology.

The command to seek "the things above," the main point of verse 1, is now specifically explained as "think on the things above, [but do not set your mind] on the things on earth."[17] For Paul, "thinking" is inextricably linked to the way one lives life (O'Brien 1982: 163). To seek and set the mind on "the things above" is to seek and focus on not "submitting yourself to decrees" of the false teachers (2:16–18, 21) that are "of the [old] world" (2:19–20); consequently, such decrees are "destined for corruption"* (2:22) and thus cannot satisfy the desire for ultimate fulfillment because they have their origin in human-made religion (2:23).[18] **3:2**

As contended earlier, Paul wants to assert that the readers have all they need of the "fullness" of Christ's presence in the heavenly sanctuary. They have this "fullness" since they already participate in heaven by being "in Christ" (1:2), who resides in heaven (see on 2:18). The false teachers are contending that their approach to get to the heavenly temple is something that can be added to their faith in order to enhance the fullness of God's presence. But Paul says that if you are in Christ, you have already ascended to heaven's temple in him, since one cannot be in the true heavenly sanctuary without being in Christ. Lincoln (2000: 638) well observes that the false philosophy starts from an earthly viewpoint, from which by their own efforts (e.g., asceticism) they attempt to transcend their own bodily existence and rise into the heavenly dimension (2:18). Paul starts from the reverse direction: from the resurrected Christ in heaven and his fullness (2:9–10; 3:1–2), which "works itself out in earthly life" (Lincoln 2000: 638; see 3:5–17).

Verses 3–4 state that the reason (γάρ, *gar*) saints should seek and focus on heavenly and not old-earthly things is because they "have died" to the old world. This repeats 2:20: "You have died with Christ to the elements of the [old] world." The result of "having died" is that they have also been raised with Christ" (3:1), so that their true life ("your life") is in union with Christ's resurrection life. Resurrection life with Christ, as in verse 1, is now offered again here in verse 3b as a reason why they should seek heavenly things and also as a basis for not seeking earthly things (v. 2). Their "life has been hidden with Christ's" new life and hidden "in God." Specifically, we saw that applying the Ps. 110:1 prophecy to Christ means that being at God's right hand (on his throne) shows Christ participating in the unique rule of God over everything. Therefore, those whose "life is hidden with Christ," who is divine, are also included within the sphere of God's presence (ἐν τῷ θεῷ, *en tō theō*, being a dative of sphere, as in 1 Thess. 1:1; 2 Thess. 1:1; 1 John 4:15–16; and Jude 1). **3:3**

17. As in 3:1, here again the adverb "above" (ἄνω, *anō)* is transformed into a noun by the prefixing of the article (Wallace 1996: 233).

18. As in Col. 3:2b, elsewhere the verb φρονέω (*phroneō*) indicates "setting the mind on the things of men"* (Matt. 16:23) or "on the things of the flesh" (Rom. 8:5) or "on earthly things" (Phil. 3:19), all of which are old-world realities. And especially like Col. 2:2, in Phil. 3:19–20 the old world is set in contrast to the believers' "citizenship . . . in heaven, from which also we eagerly wait for a Savior, the Lord Jesus Christ."

Some think the "hiddenness" refers to protection of believers during the time before their final manifestation in Christ.[19] While there is no mention of persecution in the letter, there is certainly danger from false teaching. So perhaps the idea may be spiritual protection from deviant doctrine. But the only words for "hiddenness" elsewhere in the epistle refer to an apocalyptic concealment followed by revelation (1:26; 2:3). Furthermore, this is the typical meaning of κρύπτω (*kryptō*) and κρυπτός (*kryptos*) elsewhere in the NT.[20] In this light, it is more likely that the same notion with the same term is to be found in Col. 3:3. That this is the idea in 3:3–4 is especially confirmed by noticing that the same combination of a form of κρύπτω (ἀποκρύπτω, *apokryptō*) and φανερόω (*phaneroō*, in v. 4) occurs in 1:26, expressing God's revelation of something previously hidden (see a similar idea in 1 Cor. 2:7–10 and Eph. 3:3–5, 9).

It is possible that the believers' "life hidden with Christ in God" is an echo of Ps. 26:4–5 LXX (27:4–5 MT, Eng.), where David says that he "will earnestly seek" to "dwell in the house of the LORD" throughout his "life."[21] The goal of wanting to be in the temple is "that I should see the beauty of the LORD." He will seek this "because . . . God has hidden him in his tabernacle" and because God has "exalted"* him. This is the only place among many uses of κρύπτω (*kryptō*) and κρυπτός (*kryptos*) in the LXX where a believer's "life" is said to be "hidden with God"[22] in an invisible sacred space while the believer is still living amid earthly vicissitudes. And, just as in Col. 3:1–3, this hiddenness is given as the reason for why the saint "seeks"[23] God in the temple. Also, as in Col. 3:1, the saint has been "exalted . . . over his enemies" in the spiritual tabernacle (Ps. 26:5b–6 LXX [27:5b–6 MT, Eng.]; note here the full context of the Ps. 110:1 allusion in Col. 3:1).[24] And finally, just as Col. 3:4 concludes with an eschatological hope of future "life," so does Ps. 26:13–14 LXX (27:13–14 MT, Eng.): "I believe that I shall behold the good things of the LORD in the land of the living."*[25]

19. So, e.g., D. Moo 2008: 250–51; Pao 2012: 213–14. The word κρύπτω (*kryptō*) especially has the meaning of protection in the LXX (D. Moo 2008: 250). However, it rarely means that in the NT.

20. This meaning represents about half of the uses of the verb and almost half of the noun uses. The idea of "protection" occurs only three times among the verbal uses and once among noun uses.

21. Allusion is made to Ps. 26:6 LXX (27:6 MT) in Eph. 6:19; see Bauckham 2008: 220.

22. That David is "hidden" with God is clear from Ps. 26:8 LXX (27:8 MT, Eng.), "I have sought your face," and 26:10 LXX (27:10 MT, Eng.), "The LORD has taken me to himself."*

23. Note the repeated use of "seek" (ἐκζητέω, *ekzēteō*, in Ps. 26:4 LXX; ζητέω, *zēteō*, in 26:8a, 8b LXX) similar to "seek" (ζητέω, *zēteō*) in Col. 3:1 and the following synonymous "Set your mind on" in 3:2.

24. See verses 1–3 of Ps. 26 (27) and observe also that the phrase "He exalted [lifted up] my head" (ὕψωσεν τὴν κεφαλήν, *hypsōsen tēn kephalēn*) in Ps. 26:6 is found elsewhere in the LXX only in Ps. 109:7 (110:7 Eng.; ὑψώσει κεφαλήν, *hypsōsei kephalēn*), with reference to the conquering king, so that there may be some relationship between the two passages.

25. The targum clarifies "land of the living" of Ps. 26:13 LXX (27:13 MT, Eng.) with "land of eternal life."

The related verb κατακρύπτω (*katakryptō*) is also used only once out of a number of occurrences with reference to the very same notion found in Ps. 26:5 LXX (27:5 MT, Eng.) of saints "hidden" with God in the invisible "hidden"[26] space of the "tabernacle," while still living in the physical presence of those who cause "trouble" and who speak in "contradictory tongues":[27] Ps. 30:21 LXX (31:21 MT; 31:20 Eng.) says, "You will hide them in the hidden place of your presence from the trouble of men; you will shelter them in the tabernacle from the contradiction of tongues."[28]

In addition to Paul alluding to the notion of an apocalyptic hiddenness in the heavenly temple from the LXX of Pss. 26 (27) and 30 (31), the notion of protection is included, since that is also a major idea in both psalms.

Accordingly, the major point in Col. 3:3 is that believers must not live by sight but rather by faith in their resurrected identity with Christ in the heavenly temple. They must continue to trust that their "hope has been laid up . . . in heaven" (1:5), where their "inheritance" is (1:12–13), even though they cannot see it or feel it in the present. Such trust will protect them from false teaching. This is in contrast to the false teachers, who live by sight, the "visions . . . of angels" (2:18) and the concomitant emotions inextricably linked to such visions. The mention of Christ four times (in addition to the pronoun "Him") in 3:1–4 has been observed by several commentators (e.g., Sumney 2008: 183). But why is this repetition significant? The repetition likely shows that Paul wants to emphasize the centrality of Christ as the heavenly focus in contrast to the false teachers' focus on angelic powers.

This verse continues to elaborate on the "hidden" resurrection "life" of believers **3:4**
with Christ, which continues to explain why they should seek heaven and not the old earth. Believers are "hidden with Christ" (v. 3) because he himself is hidden, since he is in the unseen heavenly dimension (v. 1). Nevertheless, "he will be manifested"* in the future. Just as the prophesied but "hidden mystery" of Christ was manifested in an inaugurated manner at his first coming (Eph. 3:8–11; Col. 1:26), so who Christ is in his present hiddenness will be revealed at his final coming. At this time, it will be even more clearly revealed that Christ is the repository of "all the treasures of wisdom and knowledge" (2:3), which had formerly been "hidden" during the interadvent age in him (except for those with believing eyes).

Also, at this final manifestation of Christ, believers "will be manifested with him in glory."* Is this the glory of God, of Christ, or of believers? (cf. Harris 2010: 123). Since the believers' life ("your life") is completely bound up with Christ's life in the hidden heavenly sphere, "glory" likely refers to Christ's

26. "Hidden" in Ps. 26:5 LXX (27:5 MT, Eng.) is a rendering of ἀπόκρυφος (*apokryphos*); cf. the same word in Col. 2:3.

27. See 2 Chron. 22:12, which says that the young king heir apparent, Joash, was "hidden . . . in the house of God."

28. See Arnold (2002: 95–96), who argues that Col. 3:3 uses the language of Pss. 27:5; 31:20; and Isa. 49:2. (cf. similarly D. Moo 2008: 250).

glory, in the sphere of which believers find themselves at the eschaton. This is a further explanation of Christ being "the hope of glory" (1:27; so likewise Rom. 5:2: "exult in hope of the glory of God"). Since believers have died with Christ, have been raised with Christ, and will be revealed with Christ, their life can be described wholly as "Christ" being "your life." They have no life apart from their identification with him, a point Paul makes elsewhere: "To live is Christ" (Phil. 1:21; so also Gal. 2:20; following O'Brien 1982: 167).

Christ being the believers' "life" may be repeated twice in verses 3–4 to anticipate Christ being "all things and in all [every believer]" in verse 11, which underscores that in Christ there no longer are Jew or Gentile distinctions, but Christ is equally present in every believer regardless of ethnicity. This declaration further associates 3:3–4 with the "hidden mystery" of 1:26–27, where the "mystery among the Gentiles" was "Christ in you, the hope of glory." In 1:26–27 we saw that the "hidden mystery" entails Christ being equally present with Gentile saints as with Jewish Christians. In this way in 3:3–4, 11 the focus is also on Christians becoming part of the "hidden mystery" first expressed in Christ in 1:26–27,[29] and it will be even more fully revealed at the eschaton how thoroughly Jews and Gentiles are on the same footing in Christ, the true Israel and last Adam.

Verse 4 is probably a reference to the final glorious resurrection of Christians on analogy with Phil. 3:19–21, where Christ will "transform the body" of those who have their "citizenship in heaven" (in contrast with those "who set their minds on earthly things") and transform it "into conformity with the body of his glory" on the last day. This is the focus of "the hope laid up . . . in heaven" (Col. 1:5) and of the "inheritance of the saints" (Col. 1:12). That saints "will be manifested in glory with him [Christ]" probably refers to Christ's glory in the midst of which they will be and which they will reflect (on analogy with the Phil. 3:19–21 parallel and 1 Cor. 15:43 in relation to 15:44–49). In this sense, "in glory" is a possession of Christ's followers, since they share in it.[30] Colossians 3:4 focuses on the "not yet" of eschatology, while verses 1–3 are centered on the "already" or beginning of eschatology (likewise O'Brien 1982: 170).

29. So likewise N. Wright (1986: 132–33), though he argues this on other grounds than presented here.

30. For "glory" as an eschatological possession of Christians, see also Rom. 8:18, 21; 1 Cor. 2:7; 2 Cor. 4:17.

E. Believers Must Lay Aside the Sinful Lifestyle of the Old World (3:5–11)

Here is a fuller statement of the main idea of this unit: *Because saints must seek heavenly things as a result of having died to the old world and having been raised with Christ into a new heavenly world, they must lay aside the sinful lifestyle of the old world.*

Because believers have died with Christ (cf. 2:11–12, 14) to the old world (2:20a; 3:3) and have risen with him into a new world (3:1, 3–4), they must focus on this new heavenly world (vv. 1b–2a). On the basis of such a focus, they are to consider themselves dead to participation in the sinful lifestyle of the old world (3:5). It is on account of such sinful living that the wrath of God will come on people who persist in such a life (3:6). The Colossian Christians themselves stood under the threat of that final wrath when they were unbelievers living in such sins (3:7). "But now," since they have died and risen with Christ and are focused on his new world, they are to "lay aside" the lifestyle characteristics of those who live as part of the old, corrupt world (3:8–9a). This command "to lay aside" the sinful lifestyle of the old creation is the main point of all of verses 5–11. The reason why they must lay aside the old-world lifestyle is that they "have stripped off the old man with his practices and have clothed themselves with the new man"* (3:9b–10a). This new man is in the process of "being renewed . . . according to the image of the one who created him" (3:10b). The new creation, in which the new man dwells, has no room for nationalistic distinctions (e.g., "Greek and Jew") or class distinctions ("slave and free") but is completely filled only with Christ (3:10), in whom all people in the new creation exist.

Exegesis and Exposition

5Therefore consider the members of your earthly body as dead to immorality, impurity, passion, evil desire, and greed, which amounts to idolatry. 6For it is [on account] of these things that the wrath of God will come ⌜. . .⌝, 7and in them you also once walked, when you were living in them. 8But now you also, put them all aside: anger, wrath, malice, slander, and abusive speech from your mouth. 9Do not lie to one another, since you have [stripped off] the old [man] with its evil practices, 10and have [clothed yourself with] the new [man] who is being renewed to a true knowledge according to the image of the One who created him—11a renewal in which there is no distinction between Greek and Jew, circumcised and uncircumcised, barbarian, Scythian, slave and freeman, but Christ is all, and in all.

3:5 Similar to 3:1, the "therefore" (οὖν, *oun*) gives the basis for the command "put to death what is earthly in you" (RSV, ESV; cf. NLT): believers have died with Christ to the old world (2:20; 3:3a) and been raised with him into a new world (3:1, 3b–4). The vast majority of translations have "put to death [or mortify/kill]." However, the NASB's rendering, which seems better, has "consider the members of your earthly body as dead to . . ."[1] The difference is that whereas most versions see an active putting to death of sins,[2] the NASB presumably understands that in the light of 3:3 ("You have died") and verse 9 ("You have laid aside the old man"), that believers have truly "died" to the old world. Therefore, they must "consider" the fact that they have *already* died (so likewise Moule 1957: 114–15; Bruce 1984: 140). The translation "put to death" appears to be like saying, "You have died" (v. 3), and you need to die again, which would be confusingly redundant. This appears to be a conceptual parallel with Rom. 6:11: "Consider yourselves to be dead [λογίζεσθε ἑαυτοὺς εἶναι νεκρούς, *logizesthe heautous einai nekrous*] to sin, but alive to God in Christ Jesus."[3] Accordingly, as they reflect on the fact of their dead condition with respect to the old creation, they are to act on the basis of that fact and not to act like spiritually dead people who commit sexual sins. They are now a new creation in Christ and are to act in confidence that God will supply the new-creational ability to fulfill the commands with which they are addressed.

Whichever rendering is best (and it is difficult to decide), Paul knows they have the power to obey this command, since they truly are newly created people through resurrection. "The members which are upon the earth [τὰ ἐπὶ τῆς γῆς, *ta epi tēs gēs*]" refers to the believer's old-world body,[4] within which their resurrected spirit of the new world dwells. This identification is clear from 3:2 which says they are to "think on the things above, not the things on the earth" (τὰ ἐπὶ τῆς γῆς, *ta epi tēs gēs*), the identical phrase found in 3:5. Just as 3:1–2 says that Christians have been resurrected and are to think on the things of the new world and not those of the old world, so now 3:5 explains how this is worked out in the life of God's people (see likewise Rom. 6:19). Though they still have a body that is affected by the conditions of the old world

1. The phrase "the ones [members] upon the earth" (τὰ ἐπὶ τῆς γῆς, *ta epi tēs gēs*) is either in apposition to explicit reference to "the members" or both could be double accusatives (cf. Lightfoot 1875: 211).

2. Likely stressing sexual sins performed by the members of the body (esp. in the light of the following wording, "immorality, impurity, passion, evil desire").

3. So also Rom. 4:19 uses this verb in almost the same sense: Abraham "considered his own body, now as good as dead since he was about a hundred years old"*; Heb. 11:12, in the same context about Abraham's sexual fecundity, says he was "as good as dead." Hendriksen (1964: 144) says that "consider dead" is not viable in Col. 3:5, since the verb is active in voice (unlike in Rom. 4:19; Heb. 11:12).

4. Μέλος (*melos*) refers to the entire body (cf. 1 Cor. 12:13–27, where the word refers to the entire anatomical body as an analogy for the entire body of Christ). However, the focus here especially is on the sexual parts of the body, though "evil desire and greed" go beyond mere sexual references.

(but is not in itself sinful),[5] they are not to let those conditions lead them to use their bodies for acts of sin. They are to "consider their old bodies dead to"[6] "immorality [illegitimate sexual intercourse, BDAG 854, s.v. πορνεία], impurity, passion, evil desire, and greed, which is idolatry."*[7] Similarly, Gal. 5:24 affirms, "Now those who belong to Christ Jesus have crucified the flesh with its passions and desires."

Some commentators and translations render 3:5a as "put to death what is earthly in you" (NRSV, ESV, NJB, cf. NLT) or "what belongs to your worldly nature" (HCSB, NET; NIV has "earthly nature").[8] But this could imply that the body itself is bad.[9] The more straightforward translation of "consider the members of your earthly body as dead" (NASB; likewise Geneva, KJV, ASV, Douay-Rheims) better avoids this possible implication. Accordingly, the body ("the members") itself is not sinful but it can participate in "unrighteousness" or in "righteousness" (Rom. 6:13; so also Rom. 6:19; see Lohse 1971: 137 on the relevance of the Romans texts). "Put to death [or mortify] the members of your body on earth" (Geneva, KJV, ASV) and the similar translations directly above represented by the NRSV and NIV also could seem to play into the false teachers' hands, who affirm "self-abasement" (2:18) or "harsh treatment of the body" (2:23; cf. Wall 1993: 137).

However, the best and simplest solution to the exact translation of verse 5a is to see "put to death" (or "consider dead") being in exact parallelism with "lay aside" in verse 8, since the imperatives in both verses are directly followed by a fivefold list of sins. Thus "put to death your earthly members on earth" is figurative for "lay aside sins." In this light, those who have died to their part in the old world (vv. 3, 9) and have become part of the new

5. So also D. Moo 2008: 256. However, O'Brien (1982: 178) goes too far in saying that the idea here is that of the entire personality organized toward and geared for opposition to God. Rather, "the members on earth" do not have to do sinful acts if presented faithfully to God.

6. On 3:8–9 below see further discussion of the preference for "consider oneself to be dead." See also N. Wright (1986: 130) for parallel NT passages containing a similar list of sins, which "reflect standard early Christian teaching."

7. See O'Brien (1982: 181–84) for descriptions of each of these five sins.

8. In line with these ideas is Gundry (1976: 42), who sees "the members" in verse 5 as "a figurative expression for sins which constitute the earthly 'old man' (v. 9)" and not as a synonym for σῶμα (*sōma*). Part of the problem with Gundry's view is that it apparently misunderstands "the old man" to be part of the inner identity of the Christian that still needs to be "put off" (1976: 136), whereas 3:9–10 views the believer to have definitively "disrobed the old man" and "clothed himself with the new man" (see further on vv. 9–10). But the notion in itself that "the members" in verse 5 is figurative for sins is viable.

9. This translation may be supported by the apparent parallel of Rom. 8:13, "If by the Spirit you are putting to death the deeds of the body, you will live." But the Romans passage speaks of "putting to death the deeds of the body," not of "putting to death your worldly nature." "Worldly nature" is too ambiguous. If Col. 3:5 is understood in line with Rom. 8:13, then it would mean "to put to death the sinful deeds of the body," which is not inconsistent with our approach: believers have died to their part in the old world in Christ, and therefore they need increasingly to show that they are dead to sexual sin by not committing it but bearing the fruit of righteousness.

world (vv. 1–4) will increasingly lay aside the sins so characteristic of that old world.[10]

"Greed" or "covetousness" is singled out as being "idolatry"[11] (note the singular feminine ἥτις, *hētis*, referring to the directly preceding feminine singular "greed," πλεονεξία, *pleonexia*). Nevertheless, commitment to the other sins (three of which are feminine nouns and one neuter) that are sexual likely also is idol worship.[12] Singling out "greed" is also apparent from observing that the first four nouns have no article, but πλεονεξία does (cf. O'Brien 1982: 174). Likewise "greed" (or "covetousness") is singled out as idolatry in Eph. 5:5, but again it concludes a list of sexual sins ("immorality/uncleanness"). If "greed" ("covetousness") is linked to the list of preceding sexual sins, then it suggests that people's ever-increasing desire for more and more sexual pleasures is nothing other than idolatry (D. Moo 2008: 258).[13] That "covetousness" likely includes "sexual greed" is apparent from the exhortation against sexual immorality in 1 Thess. 4:3–7, where the combination of the same Greek words for "immorality," "uncleanness," "passion," and "desire" all occur and are equated with sexual "greed" (or "covetousness": πλεονεκτέω, *pleonekteō*, the verbal form of πλεονεξία).[14] Thus "covetousness" may be the source for these preceding four sins (Barth and Blanke 1994: 404). "Covetousness" may be singled out as more dangerous than the others because it "may assume so many respectable forms" (Bruce 1984: 144). Since the tenth commandment (Exod. 20:17) condemns "covetousness" with respect to both possessions and sex ("You shall not covet your neighbor's wife"), it is natural that both are in mind here (so Sumney 2008: 190). In this connection, Grant (1947: 6) may be on the right track in suggesting that "immorality, impurity, passion" sums up

10. This is parallel with Rom. 13:12, "Let us, therefore, lay aside the works of darkness" (cf. NRSV); and Heb. 12:1, "Let us also lay aside every encumbrance, and the sin which so easily entangles us." Our discussion here follows that of Foster 2016: 326–27. See also Bullinger (1968: 677), who likewise sees "put to death the members which are upon the earth" as figurative.

11. As similarly is the case in Eph. 5:5: a "greedy man, who is an idolater."* So also T. Jud. 19.1.

12. Note that the virtual verbatim parallel of Eph. 5:5 refers to an "immoral or impure or greedy person" (just as in Col. 3:5) and then adds the phrase "who is an idolater" (HCSB). In Eph. 5:5, the Greek relative pronoun "who" is neuter (ὅ, *ho*) and not the expected masculine (as the direct antecedent of the relative), which is used to express the "whole idea of the preceding clause," so that all three preceding nouns are collectively considered to be idolatry (Moule 1959: 130). Though the relative pronoun is the expected feminine in Col. 3:5, the Ephesians parallel suggests that all the preceding nouns in Col. 3:5 may be considered to be under the umbrella of idolatry. This is also pointed to by observing that the relative pronoun (ὅ/ὅστις, *ho*/*hostis*) typically "conforms in Gender to the Substantive of its own clause, instead of the preceding clause to which it strictly refers" (Buttmann 1873: 281, capitalization original). This leaves open the possibility that the relative in Col. 3:5 could refer to all three preceding nouns (though Buttmann believes that the relative in this particular case refers back only to πλεονεξία).

13. See Rosner (2007: 103–29), who contends that "Greed is idolatry" refers not to sexual sins but only to "those who have a strong desire to acquire and keep for themselves more and more money and material things." See also his historical survey of interpreting the expression (2007: 7–47).

14. Cf. R. Martin (1991: 122) on the relevance of the use of this verb in 1 Thessalonians for Col. 3:5.

the sixth commandment on adultery, and "evil desire and greed" sums up the tenth commandment on coveting, both commandments of which are inextricably related to the first table of the law, which prohibits idolatry. Judaism understood the sin of "covetousness" (ἐπιθυμία, *epithymia*) in the garden as "the origin of every sin" (LAE [Apoc.] 19.3), just as Rom. 7:7–12 designates it the primal sin in the garden.[15]

"On account of" the sins listed in verse 5, "the wrath of God comes[16] [upon 3:6
the sons of disobedience]."[17] Those who have violated God's moral laws and have not turned to Christ in repentance will be held to account and accordingly judged on the last day. This judgment will be an expression of God's holy and just anger for breaking his holy moral laws (so O'Brien 1982: 184–85).

Paul's readers themselves had not formerly been immune from the threat 3:7
of this judgment, since they "too" (καί, *kai*; so ESV)[18] had lived the same sinful disobedient lifestyle. The ἐν οἷς (*en hois*) could be translated "among whom" (i.e., among the "sons of disobedience" they had lived) on analogy with Eph. 2:2b–3a. Based, however, on the plausibility that the omission in verse 6 is the original reading (see the additional note on 3:6), it may be better rendered "in which" (i.e., "in which" sins you walked), referring to the sins listed in verse 5 (on analogy with Eph. 2:1b–2a) and summarized by ἅ (*ha*) in verse 6.

Even though (δέ, *de*) they have lived in the iniquities of the old, corrupt world, 3:8–9a
"now" (νυνί, *nyni*) that they have died to the old world and been raised into the new world, they must "indeed,[19] lay aside" their old manner of existence.[20] Just as they "also" had "once walked in" the sins of the old world, now they are "also to put them aside." They are able to fulfill this command to "lay aside" because they have the real power of the new creation to do so (Augustine reflects this in his prayer: "Give me the grace to do as you command, and command me to do what you will!" *Conf.* 10.29). Those whose hearts have not been created anew are unable to respond to commands intended for those who have become part of the new creation.

15. Though in LAE and Rom. 7:7–8 the word rendered "covetousness" is ἐπιθυμία.

16. Ἔρχεται (*erchetai*) may be a futuristic present (so Porter 1989: 232) or similarly may express imminence, or it may merely be a progressive present, focusing on the notion that the wrath has been set in motion and will reach its object ("the wrath of God is coming"). The latter would fit well into an "already and not yet" framework in which God's wrath has begun to be revealed in the present age (so Rom. 1:18, "The wrath of God is revealed from heaven against all ungodliness"), and it will be consummated in the future (cf. Campbell 2013: 52). Cf. 1 Thess. 1:10 NABRE, "Jesus, who delivers us from the coming wrath."

17. See the additional notes for a discussion of the textual variant here.

18. The vast majority of other English translations have the synonymous "also."

19. Καί (*kai*) is emphatic here; so Dana and Mantey 1957: 251.

20. Some translations (NIV, TNIV) translate ἀπόθεσθε (*apothesthe*) with a middle sense ("rid yourselves"). However, the verb in its other eight uses in the NT is always to be rendered actively ("lay aside"), so it likely is a deponent verb (formally middle but active in meaning). Thus it is active here (following D. Moo 2008: 262–63).

"Now" indicates an eschatological turning point for Paul's audience. While there are varying uses of "now" in the NT (e.g., a logical use, "now at this point in my argument"; or a reference merely to present time), the eschatological use of "now" to demarcate the beginning of an age in contrast to a former old age occurs elsewhere in Paul and the NT. The combination of "now" (νυνί or its alternate form νῦν, *nyn*) with "time" (καιρός, *kairos*) appears in Paul six times, most of them clearly in connection to latter-day contexts.[21] The use of "now" by itself can often have the same temporal association.[22] Thus Paul's use of an eschatological "now" in Col. 3:8 fits naturally into his other such uses and underscores an inaugurated eschatological context for the verse.

Romans 13:11–12 similarly uses νῦν (*nyn*) in an eschatologically charged context: "Do this, knowing the time, that it is already the hour for you to awaken from sleep; for <u>now</u> salvation is nearer to us than when we believed. The night is almost gone, and the day is near." This turn of the ages reference is the basis there for the imperatives: "Lay aside the works of darkness and put on the armor of light." Romans 13:14 follows up with "Clothe yourselves with the Lord Jesus Christ [= put on the armor of light], and make no provision for the flesh with a view to its <u>lusts</u> [ἐπιθυμία, *epithymia*]."* This teaching corresponds to Col. 3:10a, "You have clothed yourself with the new man,"* both using sartorial metaphors.

The sins to be discarded in addition to ("also," καί, *kai*) the list of mainly sexual sins in verse 5 are "all" (τὰ πάντα, *ta panta*) other sins (so also Barth and Blanke 1994: 406). Commentators have recognized the clear parallel between verses 5 and 8 (respectively "consider dead" and "lay aside" followed by a five-term list of sins). Verse 8 is a formal further specification of the list of sins in verse 5, by noting that "all" sins are in mind, and then again giving a more specific example of another fivefold iniquity list, which focuses on nonsexual sins detrimental to personal relationships: put aside "anger, wrath,

21. See Rom. 3:26; 8:18; 11:5; 13:11; 2 Cor. 6:2; 8:14. The use of νυνί in Rom. 3:21 is likely to be included in this category of inaugurated eschatology. Note likewise the following uses of νῦν in Paul: the use in Rom. 8:18 is part of the time period when resurrection existence for God's people is beginning (8:10–11), as is their experience of the end-time Spirit (8:5–17, 22–23); Rom. 13:11–12a is fairly straightforward in this respect (see below). Also, 2 Cor. 6:2 refers to the present time, when the latter-day Isaiah prophecy about God helping his servant is beginning realization (Isa. 49:8), which continues the earlier reference to the "now" of the inaugurated resurrection life and new creation, when proper evaluative judgments about Christ will be made (2 Cor. 5:14–18). The uses in Rom. 11:5 and 2 Cor. 8:14 are not explicitly eschatological but are susceptible of such a meaning.

22. The more obvious examples of this single use of "now" (*nyn*) are Rom. 16:25–26; Eph. 3:5, 10; Col. 1:26; and outside of Paul, see John 4:23; 5:25; 12:31; 1 John 2:18; 4:3; with respect to the alternate form of "now" (*nyni*), see Rom. 3:21; 7:6; 1 Cor. 15:20; Eph. 2:13; Col. 1:22. The single use of "now" in 2 Thess. 2:6 refers to the same time when "the mystery of lawlessness is already at work" (2:7), which is a beginning fulfillment of the end-time opponent prophecy of Dan. 11:36. Outside of Paul see Heb. 9:26: "Otherwise, He would have needed to suffer often since the foundation of the world; but now once at the consummation of the ages He has been manifested to put away sin by the sacrifice of Himself."

evil, slander, and filthy speech from your mouth.[23] Do not lie to one another." While the personal sexual sins listed in verse 5 result in dividing people from one another, here the focus is on social sins that especially cause separations in broader relationships, especially in the church community (on the community emphasis, see Sumney 2008: 196–98). This list of alienating sins is not here haphazard but is anticipating the need for unity in the body of Christ, where there should be unity, as highlighted by verse 11.

The command "Do not lie" may include reference to the false teachers' attempt to "deceive" (2:4, 8), especially in light of the directly following negative and positive Adamic allusions to Gen. 1–3 in Col. 3:9b–10 (on which see below).[24]

3:9b–10

Now the basis for not living in the previously listed sins is given. This passage opens with an adverbial participle ἀπεκδυσάμενοι (*apekdysamenoi*) that modifies "do not lie." As most commentators agree, the participle in verse 9b likely gives the reason they are not to lie: "because you have stripped off the clothes of the old man with his practices."* And another following participle (ἐνδυσάμενοι, *endysamenoi*) in verse 10, parallel to the preceding one, gives a second ground for not lying:[25] "because you have clothed yourselves with the new man." These two participles, while formally modifying "do not lie" in verse 8, implicitly also give the ground for "putting off . . . all" sins of the corrupt old world and the sins listed in the remainder of verse 8 (of which the sins of v. 5 are included). This implication is evident from the reference to "stripping off the clothes of the old man with its evil practices." "Evil practices" refer not merely to the singular sin of lying in verse 9b and not merely to the sins listed in verses 8 and 5 but also to "all" sins, as prefixed to the list of vices in verse 8. "Having stripped off the old man . . . and put on the clothes of the new [man]" is a reiteration of having "died" to the old world (3:3) and having "been raised with Christ" (3:1).

That believers have "stripped off the clothes [ἀπεκδύομαι, *apekdyomai*] of the old [sinful] man" and "clothed themselves [ἐνδύω, *endyō*] with the new

23. "From your mouth" likely modifies only "filthy speech," though some see it as modifying also "slander" and still others think it modifies all the sins listed in verse 8.

24. Could this also contain faint echoes of the deception in Eden? See Gen. 3:13 and Rom. 7:11, both of which use the same Greek word group for "deception" as in Col. 2:8; see also LAE (Apoc.) 23.5 on the Serpent "deceiving" Eve.

25. Some, however, view the participles as having imperatival sense (so Lightfoot 1875: 214–15; Lohse 1971: 141, citing the parallel of Rom. 13:14 in support; Pokorný 1991: 168–69, who cites commentators in agreement and disagreement). O'Brien (1982: 188–89) sees the imperatival view as possible but unlikely, being one of many who interpret the participles as adverbial of cause. That the participles are adverbial of cause is apparent from (1) understanding the unclothing of the old man and the clothing with the new as something already actually accomplished: thus the basis for not lying is natural and the ground for the following imperative "Clothe yourself" with godly attributes in verse 12; (2) the parallel passage of Eph. 4:25 is clearly based on the prior "putting off of the old man" and "clothing with the new man" in verses 22–24 (following Harris 2010: 131; Lightfoot 1875: 215 wrongly construes the infinitives in Eph. 2:22–24 as having imperatival sense).

man" indicates their inaugurated new-creation relationship with God.[26] Thus the "stripping off of the old man" and the "clothing with the new man" has occurred definitively in the past as the reason for no longer being characterized by sin. The imagery is not precisely "laying aside" and "putting on," the usual rendering of the English translations, but is explicit sartorial language, as our above translation indicates. The references to clothing in 3:9–10 may be an allusion to Gen. 3 (Pao 2012: 225–26, following my conclusion here). In Gen. 3:7 we are told that Adam and Eve tried to cover their sinful nakedness by their own autonomous efforts, directly after their sin: "They sewed fig leaves together and made themselves loin coverings." On the other hand, in an apparent expression of their beginning restoration to life with God after the fall (esp. in light of Gen. 3:20),[27] Gen. 3:21 says, "the LORD God made garments of skin for Adam and his wife, and clothed [ἐνδύω, *endyō*] them." The clear implication is that their first self-made suit of clothes was removed and replaced by divinely handmade clothing, indicating that the handmade clothing was associated with their alienated condition and sinful shame (Gen. 3:7–11) and was an insufficient covering for those who have begun to be reconciled to God. That Adam's and Eve's "loin coverings" were not proper attire to wear in God's holy presence is clear from the fact that, while wearing them, they "hid themselves from the presence of the LORD God" and still considered themselves "naked" (Gen. 3:8–10).[28]

The Colossian believers have laid aside the clothes of the first Adam (the "old man"), in which neither Adam nor they could come into God's presence, and have "clothed themselves" with the last Adam ("the new" man), in whom they are in the process of being "renewed." By donning their new clothing they have begun to be restored to life with God and will do so consummately in the future. Paul appears to be using the Gen. 3 clothing language analogically and perhaps typologically: the new clothes with which Adam himself was clothed to indicate his inaugurated restored relationship with God are analogical to and proleptic of Christians being clothed with the new clothes of the last Adam.

Hence, one is either in the position of the old, fallen Adam, the corporate "embodiment of unregenerate humanity," or in the new resurrected last Adam, the corporate "embodiment of the new humanity."[29] The new life of

26. The NRSV and NLT also have apparel metaphors: "you have stripped off . . . and have clothed yourselves"; cf. similarly NJB and NET; see Eph. 4:22–24 for closely parallel wording; similarly Barn. 6.11–12, which also quotes Gen. 1:26, 28.

27. Adam was created with "life" from God (Gen. 2:7), which likely included spiritual as well as physical life. The fall brought immediate spiritual death and eventual physical death, but the clothing in Gen. 3:21 brought a beginning restoration of life with God (see J. Kim 2004: 13–17).

28. This view of the stripping of clothing and creation of new clothing in Gen. 3:7–11, 21 is also taken by Sib. Or. 1.47–49; and Jub. 3.21–22, 26–27, 30–31.

29. O'Brien 1982: 190–91; so likewise, among others, see Calvin 1972: 211; N. Wright 1986: 138; Bruce 1984: 148; Moule 1957: 119–20; R. Martin 1974: 107; the latter side of the identification is made clear by Rom. 6:5–11; 13:14; and Gal. 3:27. J. Kim (2004: 164–67) likewise sees

believers exists in union with Christ (Campbell 2012: 317). The old man has been abolished, and the new man has taken his place (see Lenski 1961: 163).

As observed earlier, the participles often translated "putting off" and "putting on" in verses 9–10 are likely not commands but are understood better as describing the reality of what has happened in the past: "because you have stripped off the old man, . . . and because you have clothed yourselves with the new man."* On this basis, Paul exhorts them to stop being identified with the traits of the former life in the "old Adam" but to be characterized by those of the new life in the last Adam. The reason Paul commands his readers to lay aside sinful traits (3:8) is because they have already and decisively laid aside their old unregenerate man and put on the new re-created man, which gives them the power to obey the commands. The point is that once "the old man has been stripped off," the sins that characterize the old man also begin to be laid aside. On the basis that the believers are a "new man," thus breaking the determinative power of sin from the old world, they are given commands. The "indicative" of the new creation must precede the "imperative" to act as a new creation. Without the power of the new creation, there is no ability to obey God and please him. The believer's "ethical conduct flows out of the indicative reality of their new identity, and thus Paul exhorts the Colossians to act in accord with the new man that they have donned as a garment" (Beetham 2008: 241).

It is also significant that the lexical combination of ἐκδύω (*ekdyō*) and ἐνδύω (*endyō*) occurs seven times in the canonical books of the LXX (within a twenty-five-word range), five and possibly six of which refer to high priests' "clothing" themselves with clean garments to serve in the holy of holies and then "taking off" the clean garments and putting on less-clean garments to serve elsewhere in the temple courts, where such a high level of holiness is not required (so Lev. 6:3–4 [6:10–11 Eng.]; 16:23–24; Num. 20:26–28;[30] Ezek. 44:19; see also 1 Macc. 10:62).[31] Of course, this assumes the reverse: that the

an old Adam–new Adam identification and roots it partly in the prefall disrobing and postfall clothing in Gen. 1–3, especially as seen by Judaism.

30. Actually Num. 20:26–28 depicts "taking off garments" from Aaron and "clothing" his son with the same garments, so that the removal of garments here is not negative but shows a passing on of the office of priesthood. Also relevant is Zech. 3:4–10, where the high priest, Joshua, has his filthy garments "taken away" (ἀφαιρέω, *aphaireō*) and he is "clothed" (ἐνδύω) with clean "garments" in order to do faithful priestly duty in the temple, which will represent other faithful Israelites, resulting in their "iniquity being removed" (so more clearly in the MT). J. Kim (2004: 166, 174–75) sees Zech. 3 as corresponding closely to the idea of the clothing in Col. 3:9–10.

31. In addition to the canonical texts, we have included 1 Macc. 10:62, since it seems to refer to priestly garments. Here, according to 1 Macc. 10:20–21, Jonathan is to take off garments and "put on purple vestments," supplied by the king, indicating that he is "the high priest . . . and . . . the king's friend." Accordingly, Jonathan follows the command and "put[s] on the holy robe" to perform his duties as "high priest."

If Isa. 52:1–2 also has priestly connotations, then six of the seven canonical uses refer to priestly clothing, the only exception being Song 5:3. The priestly notion of Isa. 52:1–2 is expressed more clearly by Pss. Sol. 11.7 (see the additional notes on 3:9–10). There are also three LXX apocryphal references to this lexical combination and several significant references in early

high priest would also "take off" the unclean garments and "clothe" himself with the clean garments to serve in the holy of holies.

Could such a priestly background be in mind here? That washing with water is closely linked to the priestly disrobing and robing in Lev. 16:23–24 (likewise in Exod. 29:4–9) points to its influence in Col. 3:9–10, since it is possible that the background of baptism may be in mind (see J. Kim 2004: 158). A background of priestly clothing is also suggested since believers have already been identified as temple builders (1:9–10)[32] and identified with the temple (in Christ; 1:19 and 2:9–10).[33] Furthermore, we have seen that Paul conducts a polemic against a false view of the temple in 2:18. The clear identification of believers with the "new man" (Christ, the last Adam) in contrast with the "old man" (the old Adam) may be linked to a priestly notion. Adam was identified as a priest in Eden, and early Judaism understood that certain of his descendants down to Aaron were regarded as priests. The OT high priest's clothing symbolically represented the temple, the creation (Beale 2004: 29–60; both in the OT and Judaism; see the additional note on 3:9–10), the twelve tribes of Israel (Exod. 28:9–21; 39:6–14), and God's glory and image (Exod. 28:2, 40). This has unique parallel with the portrayal of Christ in Colossians, who represents the end-time temple (Col. 1:19; 2:9), the new creation through his resurrection (see on 1:18), the church as the eschatological Israel (see on 1:26–27 and the parallel in Eph. 3:3–6),[34] and the perfect image of God (Col. 1:15).

That priestly clothing may be in mind is apparent from the allusion to Adam's change of clothes in Gen. 3 (argued above), which elsewhere in the OT and Judaism is associated with Adam's priestly clothing and with Adam being in God's image (for elaboration of this point, see the additional notes on 3:9–10), to which Paul directly refers in 3:10 in the wording directly following

---

Judaism to clothing together with unclothing with respect to priests (for these and other uses in Judaism, see additional notes on 3:9–10).

32. Recall also the possibly relevant context of the Ps. 110:1 allusion in Col. 3:1, where the phrase "in holy array" in Ps. 110:3 describes the clothing of the end-time king's people who serve him, and this clothing refers elsewhere in the OT to those (often priests) bringing praise or offerings in the temple.

33. See J. Kim (2004: 158, 166, 169), who holds that the Exodus and Leviticus priestly clothing texts are part of the background in Col. 3:9–10, which initially attracted me to this view. Pao 2012: 225 follows J. Kim here.

34. See further Beale 2011: 653–56. Note also that "firstborn" refers to Israel in the OT, and it is applied to Christ in 1:18 (see my comments there) in direct connection to him being "the head of the church." Christ is "circumcised" as an eschatological Israelite, in whom his people are also circumcised (see on 2:11c).

For the OT and Jewish background to the association of Adam with priesthood and the significance of the priestly clothing, see the additional notes on 3:9–10. MHT 2:309–10 suggests that ἐκδύω (in distinction from ἀπεκδύομαι, used in Col. 3:9) might suggest a partial stripping and ἀπεκδύομαι a complete stripping, but context must determine such a meaning, and the LXX's uses of ἐκδύω and ἐνδύω with respect, e.g., to priestly clothing, show that a complete removal of clothing (outer garments and linen underwear) is in view (e.g., see Lev. 6:9–11; 16:23–28; see also C. Van Dam, *DOTP* 643–45). As far as we know, ἀπεκδύομαι is used first by Paul and then often by church fathers in the following centuries.

the phrase "clothed yourself with the new man" (on the "image" see further below). In Gen. 1–3 it is evident that Adam was created as a king-priest in the image of God.[35] If a priestly background is in mind in Col. 3:9b–10, then it might point to believers as having been created as eschatological Adamic priests who minister in the last Adam's temple.

Many translations render παλαιὸν ἄνθρωπον (*palaion anthrōpon*) and νέον ἄνθρωπον (*neon anthrōpon*)[36] as "old self" and "new self."[37] Some commentators follow this translation (e.g., Sumney 2008: 198–202). But the more straightforward rendering is "old man" and "new man" (so Geneva, KJV, ASV, Douay-Rheims, NET). This translation is preferable, since, as we saw above, in mind are two men: the old sinful Adam, the corporate embodiment of unrenewed humanity; and the new and resurrected last Adam, the corporate expression of renewed humanity. The translation of "self" is not completely incorrect inasmuch as it refers to individual old and new people, but it eviscerates the redemptive-historical reference to the representative, corporate old man (the first Adam) and the representative new man (the last Adam).[38] Furthermore, the translation of "self" could lead to a misunderstanding of Paul's anthropology. It leaves open the possibility that there are two "selves" within Christians, which are at constant war within them. For some who take the participles imperatively, the Christian life is one of continuing to "put off the old self and putting on the new self."[39] Accordingly, Christians must "put to death" the old self (a misconstrual of 3:5) and put on the new self (Eph. 4:20–24 and Rom. 7:14–25 are sometimes combined with this approach). Accordingly, there is a constant battle between the "old self" and "new self" within each believer. In contrast, Paul's view is that believers' position in the old Adam has been spiritually destroyed and replaced by the last Adam, so that one is now only in the last Adam, which progressively gives one strength to be renewed and overcome ongoing indwelling sin in this old world and fallen body (similarly see Melick 1991: 296).

The spiritual identification with the old Adam has been destroyed, though believers still live in an old-world body. While a genuine saint grows as an inaugurated new-creational being in Christ, one increasingly sheds the sinful

35. On which, e.g., see Beale (2004: 81–93) and Middleton (2005: 110–11, 117–19), the latter especially showing that in the ancient Near East, king-priests were understood to be in the image of their gods.

36. Though ἄνθρωπον (*anthrōpon*) after "new" is only assumed and not explicitly stated in verse 10.

37. RSV, NIV, TNIV, NJB, NASB (marg. has "man"), ESV (marg. has "man" only for "old self"; so also HCSB). The NLT reads respectively "old sinful nature" and "new nature," and the NEB reads virtually identically.

38. While Barth and Blanke (1994: 409–14) and Wall (1993: 142–43) prefer the translation of "old and new self," they put it into the context of the representative first Adam and last Adam. So also Melick (1991: 295–96), who sees the "old self" as the unregenerate person and the "new" as the regenerate person.

39. As seen above, some commentators wrongly take the participles as imperatives, which would especially be compatible with the view described and rejected here.

lifestyle traits that have characterized the former existence of the "old man." At the consummation even the physical identification with the old world will be destroyed through physical resurrection (as Col. 3:4 suggests).

Nevertheless, it must be kept in mind that the reference to "man" is not only corporate but individual, as pointed out not only by context but also by 2 Cor. 4:16: "Though our outer man is decaying, yet our inner man [ἔσω (ἄνθρωπος), *esō* (*anthrōpos*)] is being renewed day by day" (so also Eph. 3:16; following O'Brien 1982: 190).

Likewise, the same "indicative-imperative" pattern occurs in Eph. 4:22–25. The saints have "laid aside the old man"* (4:22), which they were taught is what happened when they first believed (4:20–21). Then on the basis that they "laid aside the old man"* in the past (the indicative), in 4:25 Paul commands them to "speak truth to one another by laying aside the falsehood"* (the imperative). The "new man" in Eph. 4 is then said to be that "which in the likeness of God has been created in righteousness and holiness of the truth" (4:24 NASB).[40] And Col. 3:10 also directly relates the "new man" to having been created "according to the image of the One [God] who created him."

In this respect, the concluding phrase of verse 10 goes into more detail about the "new man": he is presently "being renewed" (present tense), which clearly shows the inaugurated end-time notion of believers being part of a new creation that is not yet consummated but is in process of growing in them.[41] They are "being renewed resulting in [εἰς, *eis*][42] a knowledge <u>according to the image of the one who created him</u> [κατ' εἰκόνα τοῦ κτίσαντος αὐτόν, *kat' eikona tou ktisantos auton*]," which is an allusion to Gen. 1:26–27: "Then God said, 'Let Us make man in Our image.' . . . God created man <u>in His own image, in the image of God He created him</u> [τὸν ἄνθρωπον, κατ' εἰκόνα θεοῦ ἐποίησεν αὐτόν, *ton anthrōpon kat' eikona theou epoiēsen auton*]." Whereas Paul uses κτίζω (*ktizō*) for "create" in 3:10, Gen. 1:26–27 LXX uses ποιέω (*poieoō*), though Aquila, Symmachus, and Theodotion use κτίζω (*ktizō*) in 1:27.[43] This allusion develops the earlier one to Gen. 1:26–27 in 1:15 (Christ as "the image of the invisible God"), as well as to the repetition of the allusion to Gen. 1:28 in 1:6, 10 (e.g., 1:6, "in all the world . . . it is constantly bearing fruit and increasing"). Thus Gen. 1:26–28 forms an important thread running throughout this epistle. Genesis 1:26–28 is a reference to Adam and Eve as the

40. For fuller analysis and clarification of Eph. 4:20–25, see Beale 2011: 838–41.

41. In line with Rom. 12:2, "Be transformed by the renewing of your mind," and 2 Cor. 4:16, "Though our outer man is decaying, yet our inner man is being renewed day by day" (see likewise D. Moo 2008: 269); without using the exact phrase, both verses refer to "the image of God" being renewed, as in Col. 3:10 (on the relevance of "image" in Romans, see 8:29; 12:2; and Beale 2008: 202–22; likewise in 2 Corinthians, see 3:18; 4:4, 6).

42. So Moule (1959: 70), who also suggests "with a view to." Thus the preposition here expresses either purpose or intended result. Porter (1994: 153) prefers "purpose."

43. Seeing an allusion to the same Genesis passage in Col. 3:10 are Lohse 1971: 142; Gnilka 1980: 188; NA[27]; Lightfoot 1875: 215–16; Robertson 1931: 503; Bruce 1984: 147; Hugedé 1968: 175–77; Caird 1976: 205, who calls it a "quotation"; Patzia 1990: 76; Lincoln 1990: 644; MacDonald 2000: 138, 146.

crown of creation, created in God's image to function as God's vice-regents over the world and to multiply their progeny as bearers of the divine image.

Paul's point in 3:10 is that believers, who have begun to be identified with Christ's resurrection (i.e., they "have clothed themselves with the new man,"* the resurrected Christ), are those who have begun to be identified with the new creation in Christ. The original purpose of creation in God's image (i.e., ruling and subduing, and being fruitful and multiplying; Gen. 1:26–28) is now first applicable to Christ and then also to his people, since he has finished his Adamic work and believers have entered into the sphere of the new creation through Christ and have begun to do in him what Adam failed to do. Here the emphasis is on new creation in the divine image, but ruling is not far away (cf. 3:1), nor is the notion of multiplying (1:6, 10, which allude to Gen. 1:28). It may be important to recall that part of "ruling and subduing" in Gen. 1:26–28 was to "be fruitful and multiply and fill" the earth not only with literal, but also, after the fall, with spiritual children who would join Adam in reflecting God's image and join him in his kingly dominion over the earth (for this notion in Gen. 1–3, see Beale 2004: 81–86). This idea fits quite well with the believers' identification with Christ's resurrection and sovereign kingship in 3:1, which is part of the basis for the paraenetic section beginning in 3:5 and continuing with 3:10. Paul uses the allusion to Gen. 1:28 typologically (see likewise Beetham 2008: 244): the image of God in humanity, marred by Adam, foreshadowed a last Adam (and his people) who would be faithful and truly reflect the divine image. The gap of disobedience in faithfully reflecting God's image had to be filled in at some future point, and that point has come with Christ and his people.

The "image" into which they "are being renewed," then, is Christ's image, especially in the light of the link back to 1:15[44] and in light of our conclusion that the "new man" in 3:10 is the new resurrected last Adam, Christ, the corporate embodiment of the humans in the new creation.

Accordingly, "the One who created" them in this image is God (following Hugedé 1968: 177; Hay 2000: 126; Furter 1987: 173), although it is possible that the "creator" here could be Christ, especially in light of 1:16. That God is the "One who created them in his image" is apparent also from the Gen. 1:26–27 allusion,[45] where "God" is the one creating "Adam" in his image, and now in Colossians God is creating new humanity in his image. This is further evident from the above-cited parallel of Eph. 4:24, where "the new man according to God has been created"* (following O'Brien 1982: 191).

44. See on 1:15 for discussion of Christ as the prototypical image of which the first Adam (imperfectly) and last Adam (perfectly) were ectypal copies.

45. See also Beetham (2008: 232), who cites many commentators in agreement. But Foster (2016: 57–58, 336) doubts the likelihood of a direct allusion to Gen. 1:26 because of widespread circulation of the Gen. 1 story and its well-known nature. But why must we assume that the Gen. 1:26–27 allusion has faded in the widespread circulation of the creation story? Furthermore, Paul alludes to Gen. 1:26–27 in Rom. 8:29 and 1 Cor. 11:7 (see, e.g., NA[28]). Foster (2016: 336) likewise sees no reference to a first Adam–new Adam theology.

Thus, while saints are accountable for striving to lay aside sin, it is God, not their own independent efforts, who has unclothed them, stripping off their "old man," and has made them a new man who is being "renewed" (note the passive voice) by God (likewise Caird 1976: 206). This is in line with the first creation: Adam and Eve did not create themselves but were created by God, who made them in God's image (Gen. 1:26–27; 2:7, 22).

Even the reference to being "renewed unto a true knowledge [ἐπίγνωσις, *epignōsis*]" in 3:10 may echo the Genesis context, where "knowledge" was at the heart of the fall (cf. Gen. 2:17, "From the tree of the knowledge of good and evil you shall not eat"; following Dunn 1996: 221–22). Humanity's "failure to act according to their knowledge of God by not acknowledging him in worship was the central element in Paul's earlier analysis of the human plight" in Rom. 1 (see Rom. 1:21; Dunn 1996: 222; followed by MacDonald 2000: 138). Thus "knowledge" in 3:10 is not merely intellectual but especially moral, which entails one's actions.

Related to this is the observation that the second allusion to Gen. 1:28 in Col. 1 (cf. 1:10, "bearing fruit and increasing") is directly appended by "in the knowledge [ἐπίγνωσις, *epignōsis*] of God" (which develops "the knowledge of his will" in 1:9). This further connects being in God's image with knowing him and his will, since Gen. 1:28 is part of the functional manner in which humanity was to reflect the divine image. Adam and his wife's "knowledge" of God also included remembering God's word addressed to Adam in Gen. 2:16–17, which his wife failed to recall in Gen. 3:2–3. In this respect, it is likely not coincidental that "the word of truth, the gospel" (1:5) "is bearing fruit and increasing" (1:6), which is the first allusion to Gen. 1:28 (so note the importance of the "word" also in Col. 1:25, "word of God"; 3:16, "word of Christ").

Being "renewed unto a knowledge of the image" of God will be the remedy for the Colossian believers against being "deluded with persuasive arguments" (πιθανολογία, *pithanologia*, 2:4) and not being "taken captive through . . . empty deception" (2:8) in the way Adam and Eve had been through the serpent's deceptive speech (the last time "knowledge" was used in the epistle was, not coincidentally, in the context of false teaching, 2:2–3 [ἐπίγνωσις, *epignōsis*, followed by γνῶσις, *gnōsis*], which is the antidote to the errant doctrine in 2:4, 8).

Since the "knowledge of God" in 1:10 and 2:2 is a desired goal, it is likely that it is a goal of the "renewal" in 3:10 (thus εἰς, *eis*, in 2:2 and 3:10 expresses purpose: "unto," "with a view to"). This is confirmed further from recalling that the true "knowledge" of God was not achieved by Adam and Eve and now is the aim of those who have begun to be irreversibly changed into the image of the last Adam.

3:11 The sphere of the corporate "new man who is being renewed" is now described. This description continues 3:9b–10 as the basis for not living in the sins listed in verses 8–9a. In that location of the "new man" there is "no . . . Greek and Jew, circumcised and uncircumcised, barbarian, Scythian, slave and freeman."

One of the themes of Colossians early on was that in Christ there is no longer a distinction between Jew and Gentile; the nationalistic distinctions of Israel's law no longer separated Jews from Gentiles (see on 1:26–27 for discussion). Of course, Christians still retain an ethnic identity, but their ultimate identity is in Christ, the true Israel and new Adam, where such distinctions do not finally define who a person is. That is highlighted here: "no Greek and Jew" nor "circumcised and uncircumcised." Though each of these polarities occurs elsewhere alone,[46] Col. 3:11 is the only place in the NT where the pairing of these two Jew-Gentile polarities occurs, enhancing the emphasis on that polarity here and in Colossians. The following references to "barbarian, Scythian" further elaborates on the preceding mention of "Gentile" and "uncircumcised." The lack of a conjunction before "barbarian" and "Scythian" may indicate that both further explain "Greek" and "uncircumcised" (cf. Barth and Blanke 1994: 415–16). Some Jews referred to "Greeks and barbarians" as a reference to a major portion of the Gentile world outside of Judaism.[47] "Barbarians" were considered to be the uncouth peoples who did not speak Greek and lived outside the Hellenic regions, and Scythians appear to have been similarly conceived and perhaps seen as even worse culturally (see, e.g., Dunn 1996: 227). Jews considered "barbarians" to be enemies (Midr. Pss. 25.14; cf. Exod. Rab. 20.14), and they despised "Scythians" (Josephus, *Ag. Ap.* 2.269; 2 Macc. 4:47; 3 Macc. 7:5; 4 Macc. 10:7).

Thus "barbarians" is a further elaboration of the Gentile part of the world first mentioned as "Greek" and "uncircumcised." It is apparent that sometimes "Scythians" referred to peoples living in the far north of the world and "barbarians" living in the far south of the earth. If the two still have this idea, then we would have another polarity (so Sumney 2008: 206, 208–9), though even then it would still further amplify the "Greek" and "uncircumcised" in the general sense of non-Jews or Gentiles. If "barbarians" and "Scythians" are considered as inferior non-Greeks, then even this social-cultural distinction has been abolished in Christ (Lohse 1971: 144).

These nationalistic polarities are concluded with an economic polarity: "slave or free," which was relevant both within Judaism and outside (note the later concern about "slaves" and "masters" in 3:22–4:1). This last pairing is likely included because problems between slaves and masters may have existed in Colossae and surely more broadly throughout Asia Minor and the Greco-Roman world. We also know that problems existed between Christian masters and slaves, to which Philemon bears testimony. This may be pointed

46. See elsewhere "Jew" and "Gentile" in Rom. 3:29; 9:24; 1 Cor. 1:23–24; Gal. 2:14–15; see elsewhere in Paul "Jew" and "Greek" ten times. The pairing of "circumcision" with "uncircumcision" occurs thirteen times in Paul apart from Col. 3:11.

47. Philo so uses "Greek and Barbarian" ("Greece and Barbarian") about nineteen times and uses combinations of the two words in very close proximity (e.g., "Greek or Barbarian") about sixteen times. Josephus also uses "Greek and Barbarian" five times and a similar combination seven times. For similar references from Classical and Hellenistic pagan writers, see Thompson 2005: 79.

to by the four-verse conclusion of the household instructions in this epistle that focus on slave and master relationships (Col. 3:23–4:1). It may also be an echo continuing the reference to Gentile peoples, since slavery was the opposite of the Greek conception of true freedom. Thus again, "slave" would accordingly refer to lower-class Gentiles, as perhaps with "Scythians," and "free" to a higher class of Gentiles (cf. Dunn 1996: 226).

Especially comparable to Col. 3:11 is Gal. 3:28: "There is neither Jew nor Greek, there is neither slave nor free man, . . . for you are all one in Christ Jesus."[48] The parallelism of these two passages further highlights the Jewish flavor of the false teaching, since the Galatians context is also dominated with a false teaching concerning a "Jew-Gentile" issue.[49] The "mystery" in 1:26–27 was that the two groups now compose true end-time humanity, because the nationalistic distinctions of the law have been dissolved in Christ, and believing Jews and Gentiles are now incorporated into Christ as the true Israel and last Adam. The mantle of Adam had been passed on to Israel in the OT (see Beale 2011: 46–58), so that Israel was conceived to be a corporate or national Adam. Christ came to fulfill all that Adam and the corporate Adam, Israel, was to be. Thus Christ as true Israel and Christ as last Adam are two ways of saying virtually the same thing. And to be incorporated into Christ as true Israel and last Adam is to be true humanity. In the new creation there are no nationalistic or racial distinctions that determine a person's ultimate identity. The only determiner of that identity in that new sphere is "Christ."

That "Christ is all things" means that he exhausts all there is in the new creation in its inaugurated phase. In fact, the only person in the new creation, "the renewed new man," is Christ; others are there only as they have been incorporated into him. Therefore, if one wants to be in that new creation, that person must be in Christ. That "Christ is in all" means that those who are in the new creation have Christ dwelling in each one. This is an application to the new creation from Col. 1:17–18 (cf. Barth and Blanke 1994: 417), where respectively "all things hold together in Him" and "He should come to have first place in all things." At least part of what this means is that believers are not to "seek and think on" interests dominated by the distinctions of the old world (cf. vv. 1–2), but "*Christ is the sum total of all desires and strivings, and that in all individuals*" (Meyer 1885: 356, emphasis original).

48. D. Moo (2008: 271–72) observes that Col. 3:11; 1 Cor. 12:13; and Gal. 3:28 have in common the following: (1) reference to water baptism, (2) two or more of the same pairs of polarities, (3) and affirming the inclusiveness of God's new people. However, Colossians does not explicitly mention baptism, and the reference to baptism focuses on Spirit baptism in the other two passages, though, of course, there is debate about the nature of this baptism.

49. The "slave and free" distinction is one also that in a Jewish context was directly related to disparagement of Gentiles: rabbinic tradition says that among God's blessings to an Israelite is that God did not make him a "heathen" (i.e., Gentile) and a "brutish man" or a "slave." See b. Menah. 43b; a variant of the tradition is cited in t. Ber. 6.18, where "Gentile" is mentioned, immediately followed by "boor," which in the following context is referred to as a "slave."

Additional Notes

3:5. *The possible relation of the list of sins in 3:5 to idolatry.* In addition to the commentary discussion on 3:5, the notion that "immorality, uncleanness, passion, [and] evil desire" are implicitly included as "idolatry" is further attractive by observing that in T. Reu. 4.6, "The sin of immorality [πορνεία, *porneia*] is the pitfall of life, separating man from God and leading on toward idolatry." Wisdom 14:12 affirms that "the devising of idols was the beginning of spiritual immorality [πορνεία]."* The same word is also directly linked to "idolatry" in Acts 15:20 and Rev. 2:20–21 (following Dunn 1996: 214). Likewise, "idolatry" (εἰδωλολατρία, *eidōlolatria*) is directly associated with "immorality" (πορνεία) in 3 Bar. 8.5 and T. Benj. 10.10 (for other OT and Jewish references relating idol worship to immorality, see Sumney 2008: 191). In Rom. 1:21–32 "evil" (κακός, *kakos*, v. 30) together with "greed" (πλεονεξία, *pleonexia*, v. 29) are identified as an effect of idolatry.[50] See also Eph. 4:19, where "the practice of every kind of impurity [uncleanness, ἀκαθαρσία, *akatharsia*]" is inextricably linked with "greediness" (πλεονεξία). Judaism equates other sins with "idolatry" (e.g., lack of charity of lending to the poor in b. B. Bat. 10a; "despising festivals" in b. Pesah. 118a, and likewise b. Mak. 23a and b. Sukkah 45b; "deceiving" in b. Sanh. 92a).

"Evil desire" (ἐπιθυμίαν κακήν, *epithymian kakēn*), even if limited to sexual sin here, is synonymous with "covetousness" (πλεονεξία). The latter is named "idolatry" because it was the first sin in the garden of Eden (Gen. 3:6), which is prohibited in the tenth commandment.[51] For this reason, Judaism viewed the sin of "covetousness" (ἐπιθυμία, *epithymia*) in the garden as "the origin of every sin" (LAE 19.3 [Apoc.]), just as Rom. 7:7–12 denominates it the primal sin in the garden (using both ἐπιθυμία and ἐπιθυμέω, *epithymeō*, vv. 7–8). Likewise in James 1:15, "When desire has conceived, it gives birth to sin" (NKJV; Dunn 1996: 215). Also in Col. 3:5 ἐπιθυμία is used for "desire," and the verbal form (ἐπιθυμέω) occurs in the tenth commandment's prohibition "You shall not covet" (Exod. 20:17). Thus in Col. 3:5 ἐπιθυμία is inextricably linked to the directly following πλεονεξία. In light of the clear allusions we have found (and will find below) to the "unclothing and clothing" from Gen. 3 in Col. 3:9–10a and from Gen. 1:26–27 concerning the "image" of God in 3:10b, the "covetousness" in 3:5 may best be understood by its use in the Eden narrative of Gen. 3.

The possible relation of the list of sins in 3:5 to defilement of temple worship. Some of the sins mentioned in this list resonate with associations of temple worship. For example, "uncleanness" (ἀκαθαρσία) occurs repeatedly in the LXX to refer to those who must be pure and not "unclean" in order to enter into God's presence in the temple.[52] On this basis, Paul appears to be combining purity laws with sexual ethics[53] in order to portray the church as a place of sacred space set apart from the world, where God's special presence is in the midst of his people (so Sumney 2008: 189–90).

This notion of the close link of sexual uncleanness with temple pollution and purity laws needs a bit more filling out, but the constraints of the commentary do not allow for much elaboration. Note briefly Lev. 15:31: "Cause the children of Israel to beware of their uncleanness [ἀκαθαρσία], so they shall not die for their uncleanness [ἀκαθαρσία], in polluting my tabernacle that is among them."*[54] "Uncleanness" as explicit sexual sin (its connotation in Col. 3:5) also was similarly

50. Similarly, Wis. 14:27 affirms, "For the worship of idols . . . is the beginning and cause and end of every evil [κακός, *kakos*]" (NRSV).

51. Note the *niphal* perfect use of the verb חָמַד (*ḥāmad*, to desire), which also is used twice in Exod. 20:17 imperatively in the *qal* imperfect, "You shall not covet [or desire]."

52. Sumney (2008: 189) is the only commentator I know of who has made this observation.

53. Likewise see b. Sotah 4b, "One who eats without washing the hands is as though he had intercourse with a harlot."

54. So also explicitly with reference to the sanctuary see uses of ἀκαθαρσία in Lev. 16:16; 22:4; Num. 19:13; 2 Chron. 29:5, 16; Jer. 39:24; 1 Esd. 1:49; 1 Macc. 13:48; Pss. Sol. 8.12, 22. Numerous other uses in Leviticus are set within a broad context of the clean and unclean laws, the ultimate purpose of which is to qualify people to be clean to worship in the temple courts

linked with polluting temple worshipers, as apparent from Lev. 17–18, the latter chapter of which lists various kinds of immoral sins of illicit sexual intercourse that would pollute one's worship of God at the tabernacle (where also there is an occurrence of ἀκαθαρσία; cf. the introductory setting of tabernacle worship in Lev. 17:1–10). Indeed, T. Levi 15.1 prophesies that "the sanctuary . . . shall become desolate through the uncleanness [ἀκαθαρσία]" of the Levitical priests (so similarly T. Levi 16.1). This "uncleanness" is due to three things: the priests "having intercourse *with whores*" (pl. of πόρνη, *pornē*), "inflated with pride [φυσιόω, *physioō*] over their priesthood" and "inflated with pride [φυσιόω], they deride [or deceive about] the sanctuary."[55] An earlier parallel to T. Levi 15.1 is T. Levi 9.9 (in a context of being clean to "enter the sanctuary" [9.11–14]), but it replaces ἀκαθαρσία with πορνεία (*porneia*): "Be on guard against the spirit of *immorality*, for . . . through your descendants it is about to defile the sanctuary."[56] Likewise Ezek. 43:7, 9 LXX says that Israel will no longer commit "immorality" (πορνεία) to profane the end-time sanctuary.

3:5–10. A concept similar to Col. 3:5–10 is expressed in Rom. 7:5–6: "For while we were in the flesh, the sinful passions, which were aroused by the Law, were at work in the members of our body to bear fruit for death. But now we have been released from the Law, having died to that by which we were bound, so that we serve in newness of the Spirit and not in oldness of the letter." The notion of having "died to the Law" is relevant in Col. 3 here, since 2:16–23 has focused on believers not being under the demands of the law, which the false teachers are trying to impose upon them. Indeed, that they have "died with Christ to the elements of the world"* (i.e., to the old creation) in 2:20 means in context that they have especially died to the legal demands of the old world (cf. 2:20b–21 and 2:16).

3:6. The wording ἐπὶ τοὺς υἱοὺς τῆς ἀπειθείας (*epi tous huious tēs apeitheias*) is omitted by 𝔓[46], B, b, sa, though the wording occurs in such early and valued MSS as ℵ, A, C, and other quality witnesses. It is hard to know which is original, as indicated by the placement of the wording in brackets by the editors of NA[28] and UBS[5], reflecting their uncertainty. Perhaps the edge should be given to the omission, since 𝔓[46] is so early (ca. AD 200) and B is from the AD 300s. The very same phrase occurs in Eph. 5:6 (also preceded by "the wrath of God comes"), where there are no textual variants (so almost identically in Eph. 2:2). This may have influenced a later scribe to insert the phrase in Col. 3:6.

3:9–10. Though it is possible that the portrayal of stripping off old clothing and donning new clothing in 3:9–10 may reflect a background of changing clothes in relation to the rite of baptism (so many commentators, e.g., R. Martin 1974: 106), this is uncertain.[57] Also, the portrayal of putting on and putting off garments, though widespread in antiquity, is likely not the background here; even the parallels of initiation into the Isis mysteries and of gnosticism are post-first century, belong to a different realm of ideas, and have no literal verbal parallels with Paul's language portraying a person as clothing that is put on or taken off (on which, see O'Brien 1982: 189).

Christ was "stripped" (ἀπέκδυσις, *apekdysis*) in his death, but since he was a corporate representative for believers, they were "stripped" "in him" (Col. 2:11). For saints this begins with a definitive inaugurated spiritual stripping followed by a consummative spiritual and bodily unclothing at the end of the age. Thus the "flesh" for both Christ and his people represents the old-world condition, from which people must be unclothed. This is comparable to our conclusion

---

or for the priests to perform their service (see further the above discussion at Col. 2:16 on the laws of uncleanness).

55. In Col. 2:18 φυσιόω is used in a temple context of false teaching about the temple.

56. CD 4.17–19, apparently dependent partly on T. Levi 9.9 and 15.1, mentions three major sins of "fornication; the second, wealth; the third, defiling the sanctuary. Who escapes from one is caught in the next; and whoever escapes from that is caught in the other."

57. The custom of changing clothes as a part of the baptismal rite is not attested until after the middle of the second century AD (on which, see Lincoln 1990: 643), though Lev. 16:23–24 could have influenced this later practice. See Dunn (1996: 221), who concludes that baptism "may be in mind," but the word "clothe" itself "does not refer to baptism."

above in 3:9–10 that believers have been "stripped" (verbal form of ἀπέκδυσις) of their old-world identification and "clothed" with the resurrected last Adam, who is the corporate embodiment of God's new creation people.

The relevant OT and Jewish background of the change in Adamic clothing in Genesis 1–3. There are some early Jewish and Christian writings that enrich the Gen. 3 background of "undressing" and "clothing oneself" that we saw in the commentary discussion of Col. 3:9–10. This literature noted below expresses the belief that Adam and Eve were clothed in glorious garments before the fall, lost that glory in the fall, and then tried in the wrong way to cover their inglorious shame with fig leaves. Some also held that the new set of clothes given to Adam and Eve in Gen. 3:21 actually possessed some degree of glory (so Gen. Rab. 20.12; Num. Rab. 4.8; Tg. Ps.-J. on Gen. 3:21; Tg. Onq. on Gen. 3:21; Tg. Neof. 1 on Gen. 3:21; Pirqe R. El. 20) or designated Adam as the *first high priest* (see below) or pointed to a greater inheritance[58] of the final glorious clothing of immortality, all of which to varying degrees may lie behind the clothing picture of Col. 3:10. On Gen. 3:21, according to Tg. Ps.-J., "The Lord God made garments of glory for Adam and for his wife, . . . to be worn on the skin of their flesh instead of their (garments of) fingernails[59] of which they had been stripped, and he clothed them." Similarly Pirqe R. El. 14 says that Adam was in a "dress" of "a skin of nail and a cloud of glory," the former of which was "stripped off him, and the cloud of glory departed from him." The Life of Adam and Eve, a Jewish work (ca. AD 100–200), expresses the belief that after Adam had lost "the glory" and "the righteousness" with which he had been "clothed" (ἐνδύω, *endyō*), he made for himself "skirts" (περίζωμα, *perizōma*) from a fig tree to "cover" his nakedness and shame (LAE [Apoc.] 20.1–5, where Eve is the focus); and at his death he was clothed with divinely given garments (LAE [Apoc.] 40.1–4), indicating his beginning restoration to life and glory with God. See likewise LAE (Vita) 47–48; cf. LAE (Apoc.) 43.1–4; Armenian LAE (Vita) 48.2–3, 5b–6 (= LAE [Apoc.] 40.2–3, 5b–6), regarding Adam and Abel being clothed at death; and LAE (Vita) 44.1–2 (= LAE [Apoc.] 20.1–21.2), regarding Adam and Eve clothed with glory, losing it, and clothing themselves with fig leaves; so likewise Apoc. Adam 1.1–7, regarding Adam and Eve clothed with glory, losing it, and being in darkness; cf. 4Q504 8.4–5: Adam was "fashioned in the image of your glory" (Wise, Abegg, and Cook 2005); 2 Bar. 4, a building taken away from Adam; 3 Bar. 4.16, "Adam . . . was stripped of the glory of God"; at death Adam was "adorned in such glory" (T. Ab. [rec. A] 11.8–10); and the end-time believers will inherit eternally "all the glory of Adam" (1QH 4.14–15; 1QS 4.21–25; CD 3.19–20; cf. 4Q171 3.1.1–2). Adam's new garments were likely to be associated with his possession of God's image (as Pirqe R. El. 11 contends).

In line with the above Jewish traditions, Num. Rab. 4.8 says that Adam was the firstborn of all humanity and "donned high-priestly garments," worn by subsequent priests directly after him and by Aaron, who became the first formal high priest in Israel's tabernacle. Similarly, Pirqe R. El. 24 says that Noah, Ham, Nimrod, and Esau inherited the coats of Adam and Eve. Adam was associated with the temple from the very beginning of his creation (Tg. Ps.-J. on Gen. 2:7): part of the "dust" with which Adam was created was "from the site of the sanctuary." According to CD 3.20–4.4, the Qumran saints who persevere will inherit "eternal life and all the glory of Adam": it supports this affirmation by appealing to Ezek. 44:15, which refers to faithful priests serving in the temple and which the CD text applies to all faithful Israelites at Qumran. Thus at Qumran a priestly context, which deals with "unclothing and clothing" (Ezek. 44:17–19), is directly linked to receiving "all the glory of Adam."

Significantly, Ezek. 28:12–13 pictures Adam in Eden wearing the high priest's jewels from Exod. 28:17–21.[60] The clothing of the high priest symbolized holiness (pure "linen"), and "glory and

58. See Gen. Rab. 63.13 and 97.6, viewing this clothing of Adam to be symbolic of his coming inheritance, which was possessed temporarily by Esau.

59. "Fingernails" may be figurative for some kind of precious stone like onyx (e.g., see Maher 1992: 26). See Gen. Rab. 20.12: the garments with which Adam was clothed in Gen. 3:21 "were as smooth as a fingernail and as beautiful as a jewel."

60. For debate about whether this being in Ezek. 28 is an angel or Adam, see Beale (2008: 137–38), where I argue in favor of the latter.

beauty" (Exod. 28:2, 40; see further Beale 2004: 39–45), the latter of which forms an interpreting *inclusio* around the description of the high priest's garments in Exod. 28—that is, the main purpose of the clothing is to reflect God's "glory and beauty" (so Fletcher-Louis 2004b: 81), which refers to God's image. Elsewhere in the OT, NT, and Judaism "glory" is interchangeable with the "image" of God (see, e.g., the equivalence of "glory" and "image"/"likeness" in Ps. 106:19; Ezek. 1:28; Rom. 1:23; 1 Cor. 11:7; 2 Cor. 3:18; 4:4). In the light of this clear connection between Exod. 28 and Ezek. 28, could this beautiful description of the high priest's clothing be related to that of Adam's in Ezek. 28? Exodus 28 sartorially portrays Israel's high priest as a divine image set in the tabernacle, thus corresponding to Adam as God's image in priestly clothing set in the first Edenic sanctuary.[61] In fact, Sir. 49:16–50:11 makes a direct connection between "the beauty of Adam" and "the beauty" of Israel's high priest, Simeon, using the same Hebrew word for "beauty" in both cases[62] (significantly Simeon's clothing is described with "beauty and glory" in Sir. 45:8, in allusion to Exod. 28:2, 40, which explains why he can be described with "beauty" in Sir. 50:1; see Fletcher-Louis 1999: 126–27). Ezekiel 28:12, 17 also refers repeatedly to the "beauty" of Adam's star-studded garment, though using a different Hebrew word.

Generally Judaism considered Adam to be a priest: Jub. 3.27, He "offered a sweet-smelling sacrifice"; T. Adam 3.6 mentions "the offerings Adam had taken out of Paradise." So likewise LAE (Apoc.) 29.1–29, "Let me take fragrances from Paradise, so that . . . I might bring an offering to God." In Judaism there are also significant references to varieties of clothing (often together with unclothing) and clothing with respect to priests without mention of Eden or Adam:[63]

1. In 2 En. (MS J) 22.7–9, Enoch is "to stand in front of my face forever. . . . Extract Enoch from [his] earthly clothing, . . . anoint him with my delightful oil, and put him into the clothes of my glory. . . . Michael . . . anointed me and clothed me. . . . Its ointment is like sweet dew, and its fragrance myrrh" (for this scene as a "priestly investiture," see J. Kim 2004: 36).
2. Similarly in 3 En. 12, Enoch is "clothed" in "a majestic robe" like a priest's robe.
3. See "anointing" and "unclothing and clothing" of the high priest in Lev. 6; 16.
4. In 2 En. 69.8, the elders "attired Methusalam in the designated garments," which in context are priestly attire.
5. Also, 2 En. 70.4 says, with respect to Lamech's second-born son, "Invest him in the garments of your consecration"; in context, this is a priestly consecration. In 2 En. 70.13 Methusalam "invested him [son of Lamech] with the vestments of priesthood."
6. In 2 En. 71 Melchizedek was born to Nir to be a priest, "and they dressed him in the garments of priesthood" (71.21).
7. Josephus, *Ant.* 20.216–17: the Sanhedrin "might lay aside their former garments, and wear such a linen one [like that of priests] as they desired."
8. Philo, *Dreams* 1.225: "Let us put off this flowery robe, and put on that sacred one" (1.216 shows this as the high priest's robe).
9. In 1QM 7.9–11, priests wear "garments of war," which they must take off before going back into the "sanctuary."
10. In T. Levi 8.1–10, Levi is commanded, "Arise, put on the vestments of the priesthood. . . . From now on be a priest, you and all your posterity" (8.2, 4).
11. According to Sir. 45:6–8, Moses "gave [Aaron] the priesthood. . . . He beautified him with comely ornaments, and clothed him with a robe of glory" (likewise Sir. 50:11).
12. Also Pss. Sol. 11.7 alludes to Isa. 52:1 LXX, which says, "Clothe yourself with strength, O Zion, and clothe yourself with your glory, Jerusalem the holy city; the uncircumcised and

61. Importantly, on this see Fletcher-Louis 2004b; and 2004a: 96, where he presents a convincing case.

62. Following Fletcher-Louis 2004b; 2004a: 96. Also Let. Aris. 96 refers to the high priest's "glorious clothing," and 3 En. 39.2 mentions angelic priests "robed with royalty, covered with glory, girded with beauty."

63. Translations are from the OT Pseudepigrapha (*OTP*); Josephus (Whiston 1987); Philo (Yonge 1993).

unclean shall no longer pass through you." The Psalms of Solomon text has "Jerusalem, put on the clothes of your glory, prepare the robe of your holiness, for God has spoken well of Israel forevermore." This interprets Isa. 52:1 by combining it with Exod. 28:2–3: "Make a holy robe for Aaron, . . . for honor and glory; . . . make a holy robe for Aaron."[64] Thus Psalms of Solomon here portrays Jerusalem in a priestly manner and may express the more subtle idea of the Hebrew text of Isa. 52:1–2, which also in the LXX uses the combination of ἐκδύω (*ekdyō*) and ἐνδύω (*endyō*), verbs we have earlier seen as usually describing priestly clothing in the LXX.[65] Indeed, Isa. 52:1–2 may anticipate Isa. 56:1–8 (describing eunuchs and Gentiles as priests) and 61:6 (portraying end-time Israel as a nation of priests). Baruch 5:1 ("Disrobe, O Jerusalem, the robe of your mourning, . . . and clothe yourself with beauty of the glory that comes from God for ever"*) may also allude to priestly ideas in Isa. 52:1–2 (where also, as in the Isaiah text, the above lexical combination occurs), especially in light of Bar. 5:2 ("Set a diadem on your head of the glory of the Everlasting"*), likely referring to the high priest's plate of gold with "holy to the Lord" written on it; this plate was placed on a "turban" or "headgear," which was set on his forehead "for honor and glory" [Exod. 28:36–40 MT]).

13. The priests "undress" or "strip" themselves and "put on" clean garments (m. Yoma 3.4; 7.2).

In the mystery religions, initiates were known to wear a linen garment at the climax of the ritual, at which point the initiate, led by a priest, entered into the innermost part of the god's temple (see J. Kim 2004: 81–88, discussing Apuleius, *Metamorphoses*).

Early Christian background for redemptive significance in the change of clothing. Early Christian tradition also understands *removing old clothing and putting on new clothing* to represent a new condition in a latter-day Eden or in a newly created converted condition, both with respect to Adam and others: Odes Sol. 11.10–14; Mart. Ascen. Isa. 9.6–18; likewise Apoc. El. (C) 5.6; Hist. Rech. 12.3: Christians have "a stole of glory [similar to that] which clothed Adam." In T. Levi 18 the end-time messianic priest "shall open the gates of paradise, . . . and he will grant the saints to eat of the tree of life, . . . and all the saints shall be clothed in righteousness" (18.10–14); in 2 Esd. (4 Ezra) 2:33–48 saved saints "have put off mortal clothing and put on the immortal; Gos. Truth 20.28–34 says Christ was "clothed in eternal life, having put off the corrupt rags, he put on incorruptibility"; cf. from the Nag Hammadi texts, Three Forms 48.6–18 repeatedly refers to "stripping" off inferior corrupt clothes from saints and "putting" on garments of light.

Most of the above uses refer not only to a new spiritual status but also one that entails an inheritance, whether this is the inheritance of eternal life with God and of rule in a new creation (the focus of the texts associated with Gen. 1–3) or more general eschatological blessings. Even in the ancient Near East or in the OT, to receive a robe from a parent or to be disrobed by a parent indicated respectively the rights of inheritance or disinheritance (Hugenberger 1994: 198–99).

Paul himself elsewhere expresses virtually the same sartorial contrast in relation to Adam and Christ with regard to the consummation (most clearly in 1 Cor. 15:51–54). Virtually the same clothing metaphor occurs in Gal. 3:27 and is even more closely linked to gaining an "inheritance" (Gal. 3:29).[66]

64. Likewise Sir. 45:7–8 and 50:11, in describing the high priest's clothing, makes allusion to Exod. 28:2–3, the latter of which is very close in Greek to Pss. Sol. 11.7: "He took up the robe of glory; . . . he glorified the garment of holiness."

65. Note also that Pss. Sol. 11.7 uses "clothes" (ἱμάτιον, *himation*) and "robe" (στολή, *stolē*), which often refer to priestly garments; ἱμάτιον occurs in Num. 20:28; Exod. 28:36–40; and 1 Macc. 10:62; στολή appears in Lev. 6:3–4 LXX (6:10–11 Eng.); 16:23–24; and Ezek. 44:19, texts that combine ἐκδύω (*ekdyō*) and ἐνδύω (*endyō*) in describing priestly garments, as we have seen. Also cf. στολή in Exod. 28:2–4 with respect to priestly clothing.

66. I am indebted to my research students Ben Gladd and especially Keith Williams for their survey and listing of references to clothing in Judaism, which have alerted me to study the various contextual uses of several of these references and their relationship to Col. 3. Just as I

Other uses of stripping off and putting on clothing. See in general other uses of "undressing and dressing" without mention of Eden or priestly clothing, yet representing various kinds of new spiritual identities.

1. For example, Israel or saints strip off former clothing and put on clothing of mourning to represent a change from blessing to judgment: Hist. Rech. 8.2; Bar. 4:20; with almost the same wording as Bar. 4:20 is Pss. Sol. 2.19–21 about Israel; and also with respect to Esther, Additions to Esther 14:2 uses similar language when she hears about the edict against the Jews; the same thing is said about Rome in Sib. Or. 8.73–74; and 1 Macc. 2:14 gives a similar response after Antiochus Epiphanes's desolation of the temple. Baruch 5:1 gives the reverse response: "Put off, O Jerusalem, the garment of mourning and affliction, and put on the comeliness of the glory that cometh from God for ever" (KJV).
2. In Mart. Ascen. Isa. 3.25, "exchanging the glory of the robes of the saints for the robes of those who love money" represents a change from identity as a confessing true believer to that of an unbeliever.
3. In Jos. Asen. 10.8–11; 13.2–5; and 14.12–14, Aseneth "strips off" her clothing that symbolizes unbelieving paganism and "clothes" herself with new clothes, which symbolize her conversion to becoming a newly created true Israelite (e.g., 15.4, 7).
4. Joshua changed into Moses's "garments" and "became another man," a prophetic second Moses figure (LAB 20.1–2).
5. After defeating the Amorites, Kenaz "took off his clothes and threw himself into the river and washed himself. And he came up again, changed his clothes, and returned to his servants" (LAB 27.12).
6. In T. Ab. (A) 17.12–14, "Death put off all the bloom of youth and beauty and all the glory and sunlike form which he had worn, . . . put on (his) robe of tyranny," and revealed himself to be demonic.
7. The poet in Odes Sol. 15.8 says, "I have put on incorruption through his name, and stripped off corruption by his grace"; 25.8, "And I was covered with the covering of your spirit, and I removed from me my garments of skin."
8. In Mart. Ascen. Isa. 9.9, "There I saw Enoch and all who (were) with him, stripped of (their) robes of the flesh; and I saw them in their robes of above, and they were like the angels who stand there in great glory."
9. According to Jub. 31.1, "On the first of the month, Jacob spoke to all of the men of his house, saying, 'Purify and change your clothes, and having arisen, let us go up to Bethel, where on the day when I fled from the face of Esau, my brother, I made a vow to him who has been with me and has returned me unto this land in peace. Remove the strange gods that are among you.'"
10. In Jub. 41.9, "She [Tamar] put off the clothes of her widowhood. And she put on a veil. And she made herself beautiful and sat by the gates which are toward the Timnah road."

For apparent nonspiritual uses see: Song 5:3; T. Zeb. 4.10; 2 En. 71.22; Sib. Or. 8.73–74; Jdt. 10:3; 16:7–8.

completed my research on the Gen. 1–3 background of Col. 3:9–10 for Beale 2007, I discovered the relevant monograph by J. Kim (2004), who has made all the same essential points that I make about the "clothing" background of Col. 3:9–10 on the basis of most of the same biblical, Jewish, and Christian texts.

F. Believers Should Live a New-Creational Lifestyle with a Christocentric Focus (3:12–17)

Here is a fuller statement of the main idea of this unit: *Since believers must seek heavenly things because they have become a new creation in Christ (3:1–11), they should live according to a new-creational*[1] *lifestyle that is instilled with a Christocentric focus.*

The main point of 3:1–4 is that believers must seek heavenly realities, as a consequence of having died to the old world and having been raised with Christ into a new heavenly world. Then 3:5–11 builds on this preceding section. That is, because Christians must seek heavenly things as a result of having died to the old world and having been raised with Christ into a new world, they must lay aside the old-world manner of living. The corollary to 3:5–11 is 3:12–17: because Christians must seek heavenly things as a result of having died to the old world and having been raised with Christ into a new world, they must clothe themselves with the traits of that new world. Thus, if they are a "new man," they must act like a "new man," not like unregenerate descendants of the Adamic first man.

The first traits God's people are to be characterized by ("clothed with") are "compassion, kindness, humility, gentleness and patience" (v. 12). The manner in which this "clothing" activity is to be expressed is in "forgiving each another" (v. 13a). The basis of forgiveness among believers is Christ's prior forgiveness of them (v. 13b). The Colossians are to put "over" the clothing of these preceding virtues the larger clothing of "love." This means that love is to instill all the other virtues just listed (v. 14a). Such love is the overgarment binding all these virtues into a harmonious unity (v. 14b). This bond of love leads to Christ's peace ruling in peoples' hearts, which is the goal of their calling (v. 15a). This goal is achieved in the sphere of "one body" (v. 15b). Thankfulness must flow from the achievement of this goal (v. 15c). All these virtues instilled by love and leading to peace, unity, and thanksgiving lead further to letting Christ's word dwell within (v. 16). The godly traits and activities of verses 12–16 are summarized in verse 17: all that one does or says should be done in the name of the Lord Jesus with thanksgiving. Verse 17 is the main point of the passage, since all the preceding verses build toward it, and it summarizes the preceding verses.

1. "New-creational" here and throughout the commentary refers to the inaugurated end-time new creation.

Exegesis and Exposition

[12]So, as those who have been chosen of God, holy and beloved, put on a heart of compassion, kindness, humility, gentleness and patience; [13]bearing with one another, and forgiving each other, whoever has a complaint against anyone; just as the ⌜Lord⌝ forgave you, so also should you. [14]Beyond all these things put on love, which is the perfect bond of unity. [15]Let the peace of Christ rule in your hearts, to which indeed you were called in one body; and be thankful. [16]Let the word of ⌜Christ⌝ richly dwell within you, with all wisdom teaching and admonishing one another with psalms and hymns and spiritual songs, singing with thankfulness in your hearts to God. [17]Whatever you do in word or deed, do all in the name of the Lord Jesus, giving thanks through Him to God the Father.

3:12 Part of the focus of the previous paragraph was about "putting off" the vices of the old-world manner of living, but now in verse 12 Paul commences an exhortation to believers to clothe themselves with the positive attributes characteristic of the new creation (likewise O'Brien 1982: 197). The contrast is strengthened by noticing that in 3:5 and 3:8 are two sets of five vices, each set introduced by an aorist imperative to negate them; then five positive attributes in 3:12, also introduced by an aorist imperative, now reinforced by "therefore" (οὖν, *oun*; among others, see O'Brien 1982: 195–96). This exhortation extends through to verse 17. Christians have been commanded to seek heavenly things, as a result of having died to the old creation and having been raised with Christ into the new heavenly world (3:1–11). On this basis (οὖν, *oun*), they are now commanded in verse 12 to "clothe themselves" with the lifestyle characteristics of the new creation in Christ. They have "clothed themselves [ἐνδυσάμενοι, *endysamenoi*] with the new man" (v. 10), which is their identification with Christ in the new creation. Now, consequently, they are to "clothe themselves" (ἐνδύσασθε, *endysasthe*) with the attributes of the new man, which means to reflect the new man's character. Such ethical clothing is necessary also because it must befit the condition of those who are "elect ones of God, holy ones and beloved ones."[2] All three of these terms are descriptions of Israel in the OT (see the additional note on 3:12).[3] This is highlighted by Deut. 7:6–8: "You are a <u>holy</u> people. . . . God has chosen you. . . . The Lord did . . . choose [<u>elect</u>] you. . . . The Lord <u>loved</u> you."[4] This OT text appears to be echoed here (see also Dunn 1996: 228, who sees Deut. 7:6–7 as an echo). The phrase "elect ones of God"* (Col. 3:12a) is a subjective genitive meaning "elected by God" (esp. in light of the OT use of "elect ones," on which see

2. See BDAG (1105, s.v. ὡς) for the possible use of the relative adverb ὡς (*hōs*) with a causal sense, which seems best here: "Clothe yourselves <u>because</u> [ὡς, *hōs*]" you are "elect ones of God, holy and beloved."

3. Paul similarly combines "beloved" (ἠγαπημένοι, *ēgapēmenoi*; identical to Col. 3:12), with "election" (ἐκλογή, *eklogē*) in 1 Thess. 1:4, with similar implications for the church's identification as eschatological Israel; see Beale 2011: 669–70.

4. Following Lincoln (2000: 647), D. Moo (2008: 276), and Thompson (2005: 81). The three words marked above are part of the same word group that occurs in Col. 3:12.

below; e.g., Isa. 44:1–2; 2 Macc. 1:25). Thus the implication is that the church is the continuation of true Israel.[5]

The reason this triad of names is a ground for their ethical "clothing" is most clearly expressed by the OT use of "holy ones," though implied by the other two names. God repeatedly tells Israel, "You shall be holy because I, the Lord your God, am holy" (Lev. 11:44; so likewise 11:45; 19:2; 20:7, 26; 21:6). The Colossians should be "holy" because God the Father and Jesus are holy. That the demand upon their ethical lives is based on Jesus's own life is clear in verse 13: "Just as the Lord forgave you, so also should you" (note the implication of this in 3:24–25 and 4:1). "Beloved" also evokes a family relationship, where family members resemble each other (as seen clearly in Eph. 5:1: "Be[come] imitators of God, as <u>beloved</u> children"). As we will soon see, this means that saints are to reflect Christ's "image" into which they are being "renewed" (Col. 3:10). They are "beloved" because of their identification with Christ, who is God's "beloved Son" (see on 1:13).

The expected lifestyle that comes first in focus is "a heart of compassion, kindness, humility, gentleness and patience." While "kindness" (χρηστότης, *chrēstotēs*) and "humility" (ταπεινοφροσύνη, *tapeinophrosynē*) are relatively self-evident, "compassion" (οἰκτιρμός, *oiktirmos*) refers to concern about someone else's bad circumstances (BDAG 700, s.v. οἰκτιρμός), "gentleness" (πραΰτης, *prautēs*) expresses the humble quality of consideration for people and not thinking that one is more important than others (cf. BDAG 861, s.v. πραΰτης), and "patience" (μακροθυμία, *makrothymia*) alludes to being forbearing in the face of provocation (BDAG 612, s.v. μακροθυμία). These qualities, especially the latter two, are especially to be understood in the light of verse 13's focus on extending forbearance and forgiveness to those who have offended. Humility (ταπεινοφροσύνη) refers to true humility in Christ, in contrast to the use of the same word in 2:18 and 23, indicating "self-abasement" or "asceticism," which referred to the "false humility" of the false teachers (so NIV; cf. MacDonald 2000: 140).

All of these qualities (and the particular Greek words translated here) are attributed either to God or Christ in the NT,[6] showing further that the good behavior of the Colossians is necessary because it is to mirror the behavior of

5. Among others, see also Lightfoot 1875: 221, followed by Moule 1957: 122; see also Caird 1976: 207; E. Martin 1993: 156; N. Wright 1986: 141; Davids 2008a: 289; Garland 1998: 210.

6. One or more of these characteristics is attributed to God or Christ in Matt. 11:29; Luke 1:78; Rom. 2:4; 9:22; 11:22; 12:1; 2 Cor. 1:3; 10:1; Eph. 2:7; 4:2; Phil. 1:8; 2:8; 1 Tim. 1:16; 2 Pet. 3:15. "Compassion" (οἰκτιρμός) is the only quality not found attributed to God or Christ, though in Phil. 2:1 it is found with σπλάγχνα (*splanchna*), and both are implicitly said to be "in Christ" and are related to Christ's own lifestyle in Phil. 2:5. See also Lohse (1971: 147), who makes the same observation about these attributes (followed by MacDonald 2000: 140; Patzia 1990: 78–79; and a number of other commentators). Barth and Blanke (1994: 418–22) also observe that in the LXX most of the attributes in Col. 3:12–13 are attributed at times to God. The phrase "heart of compassion" here is a qualitative genitive ("compassionate heart"; so several commentators).

God and their Lord Jesus, in whose image they have been created.[7] This notion is implicit from the wider context of Colossians, which says that believers are "strengthened with all power, according to his glorious might" (1:11). Earlier we saw that the phrase "according to his glorious might" explains that the origin or basis of the saints' strength is God's (or Christ's) own "glorious might." "Glory" here refers to the sum of God's attributes, which are imparted to his people. The purpose of this "strengthening . . . according to his glorious might" in 1:11 is the "attaining of all steadfastness and patience" (μακροθυμία), the latter word appearing also in 3:12. Again we find that Christians are to image God's character. Just as God or Christ is compassionate, kind, humble, gentle, and patient toward believers, so are the believers to be toward one another (for an expansion of this notion, see further Pao 2012: 241–42). That imaging is in mind in verse 12 is apparent from verse 13b, where believers are to imitate Christ's forgiveness.

3:13 The manner of putting on the clothes of verse 12 is expressed by two adverbial participles: "bearing with one another and forgiving each other."[8] Forgiveness probably specifies what it means to "bear with one another." Forgiveness itself is explained by the phrase "whoever has a complaint against anyone, just as [καθώς, *kathōs*][9] also the Lord forgave you, in this manner [οὕτως, *houtōs*] so also should you."* Those who are truly related to Jesus will forgive in reflection of Jesus's forgiveness of them. Ephesians 4:32 likewise says, "Become unto one another kind, tenderhearted [cf. Col. 3:12],[10] forgiving each other, just as God in Christ also has forgiven you."* Likewise Eph. 5:2, 25 affirm that believers should love one another "as Christ also loved [believers] and gave himself for" them (following O'Brien 1982: 202; similarly see Matt. 6:12, 14–15; 18:23–35, cited by Harris 2010: 141). This is directly followed by "Therefore be imitators of God, as beloved children" (Eph. 5:1). The Ephesians parallel expresses explicitly that being "kind, tenderhearted," and

7. So also Hay (2000: 136), MacDonald (2000: 140), Patzia (1990: 78–79), and Barth and Blanke (1994: 418–22), among several other commentators; contra Lohse (1971: 147n100), who sees no notion of imitating God or Christ. Hendriksen (1964: 158) sees the attributes to refer elsewhere to Christ's attributes, which one imitates because one has "put on" Christ (so 3:10) or (better) come into union with Christ by being incorporated into him, who is the corporate "embodiment of the new humanity" (O'Brien 1982: 190–91).

8. Along with designating the manner of the "clothing" (3:12), these participles likely convey an imperatival notion, since they modify an imperative verb ("clothe yourself"; Harris 2010: 140), thus deriving their mood from the verb they modify (as can sometimes occur; D. Moo 2008: 278; likewise Lightfoot 1875: 224), while the verbal action is nuanced by the adverbial function of the participle; i.e., they are to "clothe themselves in the manner of bearing with one another." Though Harris thinks an imperatival nuance is mutually exclusive of manner, it does not have to be. See Wallace (1996: 652), who questions whether there can be an imperative use of the participles here in 3:13.

9. Though καθώς (*kathōs*) can indicate various notions (e.g., comparison, degree, manner, cause, time), here it clearly refers only to manner, since the following οὕτως (*houtōs*) further explains the adverb and typically in the NT connotes comparison or manner (and never cause or time), the latter of which is primary here, specifying the generality of the comparison.

10. Where virtually the same Greek words for "kind" and "tenderhearted" occur.

"forgiving" is to imitate God's image, which shows that imitation of God is also in mind in Col. 3:12–13. That Christ "the Lord" is the one forgiving here underscores his deity, since in the Ephesians parallel it is "God in Christ" who forgives (cf. Foster 2016: 351). "Bearing with one another and forgiving" is the atmosphere that saturates the five virtues of verse 12. These virtues are all linked to "bearing with" and "forgiving." The fact that believers' sins have been "forgiven" through Christ's vicarious death (1:14; 2:13–14) demands that they must show forgiveness to one another (cf. Sumney 2008: 217). It is not fitting for one who has experienced the release and joy in benefiting from Christ's forgiveness not to extend that joy and release to others; likewise, it is unbelieving arrogance not to forgive those whom Christ himself has already forgiven (N. Wright 1986: 142).

All the virtues (v. 12) and the manner by which they are to be carried out (v. 13) dovetail to prevent the friction of the divisive vices in verses 8–9 (following Wilson 2005: 256, 271) and to enhance unity among believers, as verses 14–15 will highlight.

The precise connection between verses 12–13 and verse 14 is debated. How **3:14**
should the preposition ἐπί (*epi*) with the dative be understood? One translation renders it as "beyond all these things" (NASB), while most prefer "above all" (NRSV, NLT, HCSB).[11] Such renderings suggest that love is the greatest among the preceding list of virtues. Other translations view it as a marker of addition: "to all these virtues add love" (e.g., NET),[12] so that love is seen as merely one more virtue to be added to the prior virtues mentioned. It is also possible to translate it as "in all these things." In this respect, love would be that which instills all the other qualities just mentioned. The preferable understanding is expressed by the NJB: "Over all these clothes, put on love."[13] This is in keeping with the clothing metaphor of verse 12, which continues the clothing picture of 3:9–10 and has been in mind up through verse 13.[14]

Accordingly, Paul views love as an overgarment, perhaps like slacks or a dress along with a shirt or blouse, or better, as an overcoat, which is put over the undergarments of the other virtues and completes the proper attire of a person. The undergarments are not complete or rightly ordered or bound together well without the outer covering garment of love. The overgarment

11. Almost identically Geneva, KJV, ASV have "above all these things," and RSV and ESV have "above all these."

12. So also BDAG (365, s.v. ἐπί), who take it as "a marker of addition."

13. Similarly the NIV has "over all these virtues put on love."

14. N. Wright (1986: 142–43) and Lincoln (2000: 648) express uncertainty about whether the clothing image continues in verse 14. Dunn (1996: 232) does not see the clothing picture continued in verse 14. Pao (2012: 244) also sees no continuation of the clothing image because there is no other syntactical parallel in the NT or Biblical Greek of ἐνδύω (*endyō*) followed by the preposition ἐπί (*epi*) with the meaning of "clothe" or "put on top of." But D. Moo (2008: 281) is right in contending that the immediate context is key and warrants seeing a continuation of the clothing notion (so also Lightfoot 1875: 222; Lindemann 1983: 60; Dübbers 2005: 301, all of whom see love as an overgarment holding the underlying clothes in place; cf. also Luz 1998: 231).

of love is to keep the other traits in their proper place or perspective.[15] And this is just what the last clause of verse 14 asserts: love "which is the bond of [completeness]." The NEB's paraphrase is to the point: love is "to bind all ["everything," REB] together and complete the whole" (so also Caird 1976: 207; Heil 2010: 155–56). The word σύνδεσμος (*syndesmos*) supports the notion of the overgarment of love as the key bonding agent that binds the other virtues together.[16] Ephesians 4:15–16 also sees "love" as a key agent of bodily growth: "from whom [Christ] the whole body, being fitted and [unified] together by what every joint supplies, according to the proper working of each individual part, causes the growth of the body <u>for the building up of itself in love</u>" (likewise Eph. 4:2). Earlier, in Col. 2:19, the word σύνδεσμος is translated as "ligament," which together with the word "joints" and the verb "held together" or "unite" (συμβιβάζω, *symbibazō*)[17] focuses on binding the body together as a working unity:[18] the "body, being supplied and held together by the joints and ligaments, grows." Love plays that binding and unifying role here in 3:14, especially with respect to holding the virtues together to work most effectively.[19] Even earlier, in 2:2, Paul speaks of "the hearts" of the Colos-

15. The image of inner and outer clothing is also in keeping with the priestly clothing, which we saw to be in mind in 3:9–10, since the high priest wore "a linen tunic" over "linen undergarments . . . next to his body," and then was "girded with a linen sash and attired with the linen turban," all summarized by the clause "These are holy garments" (Lev. 16:4; cf. also Exod. 28:4; 29:5). This full array of clothing correctly worn was necessary for the priests "to carry on their priesthood" (Exod. 31:10). And so the thought may be that believers cannot carry on their priestly calling without their full array of clothing, bound together in the right loving way.

16. So also Harris 2010: 151; D. Moo 2008: 280–81; Thompson 2005: 84; Abbott 1897: 288. Or the image could be that of the σύνδεσμος as a fastener, clasp, or belt that keeps the clothes together or keeps them on (LSJ 1701; cf. Thompson 2005: 84; Sumney 2008: 218d). For example, the word can refer to a "crown" (or headband) or a hairpiece on a woman's head that functions as a clasp to hold together her hair (Euripides, *Med.* 1193; Euripides, *Bacch.* 697). Moule (1957: 123–24) does not see the clothing image from verses 12–13 continuing into verse 14 because he believes that there is no evidence that σύνδεσμος can refer to an article of attire like a belt or girdle; likewise Barth and Blanke 1994: 423. However, the above-mentioned crown and hair clasp is likely to be considered an article of clothing, which comes close to the idea of a belt or girdle around clothing. Meyer (1885: 360) agrees that "love" is to be viewed as an overgarment holding the undergarments together, but he believes this is mutually exclusive, with "love" also being a kind of girdle (σύνδεσμος) binding the undergarments together. But this is an unnecessary deduction, since the point appears to be that of the overgarment of "love" functioning *like* a girdle or other kind of clothes' fastener, keeping the underclothes together. Foster (2016: 351–53) sees no clothing imagery carried over from verses 12–13, whether with respect to "putting on love" or "the perfect bond of unity."

17. BDAG (956, s.v. συμβιβάζω) renders this verb in Col. 2:19 as "bring together into a unit."

18. BDAG (966, s.v. σύνδεσμος) gives the basic definition as "that which binds together" and specifies well that the use in Col. 3:14 refers to "<u>the bond that unites all the virtues</u> (which otherwise have no unity) <u>in perfect harmony or the bond of perfect unity</u>."

19. Similarly in Rom. 13:8–10, "Love is the fulfillment of the law," and the "law" is said to be "summed up" (or "headed up") in the statement "You shall love your neighbor as yourself" (likewise Gal. 5:6, 14). Also see 1 Cor. 16:14, "Let all that you do be done in love"; and cf. 1 Cor. 13:13. See Dunn (1996: 232) for extrabiblical parallels of various virtues as a "bond" holding something together.

sians "having been knit together [συμβιβάζω] in love," a love that they have begun to demonstrate (Col. 1:4, 8).[20] Now they are exhorted to let this "love" continue to bind together the virtues of their heart for the goal of unity. This "body" picture will continue on into 3:15, "You were called in one body." Thus "the bond of completeness" (σύνδεσμος τῆς τελειότητος, *syndesmos tēs teleiotētos*) is a genitive of destination or purpose ("bond that leads to completeness"; so also Pokorný 1991: 172), or better, a genitive of product ("bond that produces completeness").[21]

In light of this, verse 14 indicates that love is what achieves the goal of uniting all the virtues (in vv. 12–13) into a working unity. These virtues "attain their full power only when they are unified by and empowered by love" (D. Moo 2008: 282). And when all the virtues are bound together by love, there will be a unity of all the believing members of the body of Christ.[22]

The unity that love brings about (v. 14) leads to the next command to "let the **3:15**
peace of Christ rule in your hearts."[23] The harmonious unity of verse 14 is the indicative reality, which provides the fuel for the Christians to be able to fulfill this command to let peace reign in their relationships; N. Wright (1986: 143) makes a similar point. The inextricable link between "the bond producing completeness" in verse 14 and "peace" here is observable from Eph. 4:3: "striving to keep the unity of the Spirit in [by/through] the bond of peace [ἐν τῷ συνδέσμῳ τῆς εἰρήνης, *en tō syndesmō tēs eirēnēs*]" (cf. NABRE). Likewise Eph. 2:14 even equates Christ with "our peace." The phrase "peace of Christ" (Col. 3:15) could be a genitive of source ("peace from Christ") or product ("peace produced by Christ") or a subjective genitive ("peace given by Christ"; cf. Harris 2010: 143), all of which are very similar. If one has not come into a relationship of vertical peace with God, accomplished through Christ's blood (Col. 1:20), then one cannot have true horizontal peace with others in Christ's body; such also is the case with love in 1 John 4:10–11, God "loved us and sent His Son to be the propitiation for our sins. Beloved, if God so loved us, we also ought to love one another." The word βραβεύω (*brabeuō*) carries the notion of "rule" and "arbitrate" (for the latter, see on 2:18),[24] which indicates that the "hearts" of believers should be governed by Christ's peace

20. Sumney (2008: 219) sees 3:14 picking up the thread of these earlier uses of "love" in the epistle.

21. MHT 3:212 and BDF §163 give virtually the same translation but classify it as an objective genitive (likewise Porter 1994: 94).

22. Pao (2012: 245) affirms only the latter point about unity of believers, which he unnecessarily views as mutually incompatible with the sartorial binding of virtues by love. Schweizer (1982: 208) sees love as binding together the community members and not the virtues.

23. The preposition ἐν (*en*) may be spheric in an individual sense ("in") or "among" (= "in all"), but here it is difficult to determine which is intended (Moule 1959: 75).

24. Here the cognate verb καταβραβεύω (*katabrabeuō*) has the sense of "judge" or "arbitrate." Some commentators prefer the meaning of "rule" and others "arbitrate" or "acts as umpire," since both are attested in ancient Greek (see O'Brien 1982: 204). Some commentators see no nuance of "arbitrate," but both "rule" and "arbitrate" may be in mind (D. Moo 2008: 283). Rule through arbitrating is the notion. Not only does the use in 2:18 point to this, but so

or that they need to let "the peace of Christ arbitrate" or "be the umpire" among them. Such "ruling" or "arbitrating" would then be the goal in all their dealings that should overcome their "complaints against anyone" (3:13). This dominating peace is a sign of the inbreaking eschatological new creation (see on 1:20; cf. also Pao 2012: 245–46).

That Christ's peace is to "rule in your hearts" refers to the prevailing penetration of such peace to the true inner being and thought not merely of a person but of the corporate members (note the pl. "hearts") of the new man in Christ.[25] Similarly, the prayer "that Christ may dwell in your hearts through faith" in Eph. 3:17 refers to the increasing presence of Christ "in the inner man" (see 3:16b), the ultimate goal of which is that believers would "be filled up to all the fullness of God" (Eph. 3:19). Likewise, Paul prays that the predominating "peace of God . . . will guard your hearts and your minds in Christ Jesus" (Phil. 4:7). In contrast to the false teachers who wrongly pass judgment on true Christians about their not keeping external cultic rituals (see on Col. 2:16–18), Christ's peace is to be that which arbitrates internally, in their hearts by faith (Pao 2012: 246).

The reality of unity (3:14b) in which the believers exist is restated in the next phrase of verse 15: "[un]to which indeed you were called in one body." This is better translated as "You were called in one body unto the goal[26] of peace" (so similarly see 1 Cor. 7:15 NASB marg., "God has called you to peace"). Some translations and commentators view the preposition ἐν (*en*) to indicate the unified manner of the calling: "as members of one body" (e.g., Col. 3:15 NIV, NLT, likewise NET). Preferable, however, is "in [ἐν] one body," designating the unified sphere of the calling, which includes the condition in which they were called.[27] In the repetition of the relationship between "unity" in verse 14 and "peace" in verse 15a, believers are said again to be able to fulfill the imperative to peace, *because* from the beginning of their spiritual existence they have been incorporated into "one body." That is, the basis for such peace is their calling in one body (so likewise Melick 1991: 302). The notion of a unified body being the cause of peace is expressed in several translations: thus the NIV has "Let the peace of Christ rule in your hearts, since as members of one body you were called to peace" (so likewise NLT, NJB, and NET).

Why were they called in one body? It was for the goal of peace. Their existence as part of this "one body" enables them to fulfill the mandate of

---

does the immediate context in 3:13 about letting forgiveness override complaints that people have against one another.

25. "Heart" in the OT, NT, and here refers to the psychical unity combining the volitional, intellectual, and emotional aspects of a person; as such it represents the inner spiritual center of one's relationship to God (see further on 2:2).

26. The εἰς (*eis*) here indicates goal or intended result; see also Moule 1959: 70.

27. Likewise Rom. 12:4–6: "Just as we have many members in one body [ἐν ἑνὶ σώματι, *en heni sōmati*], . . . so we, who are many, are one body [ἓν σῶμα, *hen soma*] in Christ, . . . according to the grace given to us"; for "in the/one body," see also 1 Cor. 12:18, 20, 25: "God has placed the members . . . in the body, . . . one body, . . . so that there may be no division in the body."

peace. Apart from their existence in "one body," they have no ability to be at peace with others. This idea of unity is a development of 3:10–11, where Jew and Gentile exist together as one "new man" (Pao 2012: 236), where also there are no ethnic or social distinctions to cause distraction and division (Sumney 2008: 221). This causal link between being "in one body" (ἐν ἑνὶ σώματι, *en heni sōmati*) as providing energy to be peaceable occurs also in Eph. 2:14–16: Christ "made both groups into one . . . so that in Himself He . . . might reconcile them both [Jew and Gentile] in one body [ἐν ἑνὶ σώματι] to God," consequently destroying "the enmity," which is the other side of the coin of peace. Christ's purpose is that "in Himself He might make [or create] the two [Jew and Gentile] into one new man [ἕνα καινὸν ἄνθρωπον, *hena kainon anthrōpon*], thus [making] peace" (2:15 marg.). Similarly Eph. 2:17–18 refers to Christ's preaching of "peace," which is based on (and thus in essence a result of) both [Jew and Gentile] being "in one Spirit [ἐν ἑνὶ πνεύματι, *en heni pneumati*] [before] the Father." Already Col. 1:20, 22 have inextricably linked "reconciliation," a Pauline synonym of "peace," with "making peace through the blood of the cross" and the fleshly "body" of Christ on the cross: "He reconciled you in the body of His flesh."* Thus believers have benefited from the end-time inaugurated "peace" and "reconciliation" achieved through Christ's cross and should exude peace and reconciliation to fellow saints. This is a mark of the eschatological new creation (see on 1:20). The more particular OT background of "the peace of the Messiah ruling" in Col. 3:15 would appear to be Isa. 9:6, where the coming divine Messiah's "rule" is to bring "peace" (likewise 52:7, where God's "reign" is to bring "peace," on which cf. Gnilka 1980: 198–99; see also 11:1–9).

The focus of the "one body" is the corporate unity of believers as members of one another; yet, as Eph. 2:15–18 shows, believers are part of one body because they have been placed into Christ and into his Spirit and are members of his body.

That they have been "called" to peace "in one body" underscores the idea that God has placed them into this unified condition apart from their own efforts, as highlighted also by the above "one body" references in Rom. 12:6, "according to the grace given to us"; and 1 Cor. 12:18, "God has placed the members." Accordingly, the verb "call" (καλέω, *kaleō*) in Paul can be almost synonymous with "elect" or "predestine" (Rom. 8:30; 9:7, 11),[28] the former focusing on God's carrying out his decree through effectually calling people to himself in space-time history. This gives assurance to the Colossians that they have real ability to heed this command to be peaceful if they have truly believed (cf. Col. 2:20; 3:1) and first experienced peace with God, achieved through the cross (1:20, 22). Elsewhere God "calls" (καλέω) people not merely to be his people but also to live in a certain godly manner.[29] This

28. Similarly see Gal. 1:15: God is the one "who . . . called [Paul] through His grace."

29. "God has called us to peace" (1 Cor. 7:15), "to freedom" (Gal. 5:13), to "hope" (Eph. 4:4), to holiness (1 Thess. 4:7), "with a holy calling" (2 Tim. 1:9).

shows that the calling to salvific faith in Christ is inextricably linked to the direction of an entire lifestyle as a necessary outcome of such faith (so see D. Moo 2008: 284).

The result of peace ruling over the one body of Christ is that those in the body ought to "become thankful ones."* This further develops the initial mention of thanksgiving in 1:3 and 1:12. It is assumed the thanks are for a gift. Thus the peace to which they have been called in one body has not come about through their own efforts but is completely given by God's grace.

3:16 Paul progresses onto another command: "Let the word of Christ dwell in you richly" through "teaching and admonishing" in worship centered around OT psalms. This may be the instrumentation by which the "peace of Christ reigns" over the church (v. 15). "The word of Christ" could be a subjective genitive ("word spoken by Christ" in his earthly ministry) or an objective genitive ("word about Christ" = the gospel). A subjective genitive could be supported by 1 Thess. 4:15 (words spoken by Jesus in the Gospel traditions), and an objective genitive may be pointed to by 1 Thess. 1:8 and 2 Thess. 3:1 ("word about the Lord").[30] "Word of God" in Col. 1:25 refers to the word revealed by God (subjective genitive, which vv. 26–27 bear out).[31] On the other hand, "God opening up a door for the word" in Col. 4:3 is likely referring to the "word" as that which is about Christ (in the light of 4:3b, "so that we may speak forth the mystery of [about] Christ." Likewise, "the word" in 1:5 is interpreted to mean "the truth of the gospel," again referring to the "word" about Christ. Thus, on balance, "word of Christ" in 3:16 could be either a subjective or objective genitive, and it may be best not to try to specify one over the other here (as held by Dunn 1996: 236). Both the subjective and objective genitives may be packed into the genitive construction, conveying an intentional ambiguity.[32] But Col. 2:3 ("in [Christ] are hidden all the treasures of wisdom") tips the scales to a focus on a subjective genitive (or genitive of source). Perhaps also in mind are Christ's revelatory words spoken by believers through Christ's Spirit in early church worship gatherings (see 1 Cor. 14:1–33; e.g., cf. Sumney 2008: 223) and Paul's own words, especially expressed in his letters, which were equated with God's word or Scripture or were viewed as from the Spirit (see, e.g., 1 Cor. 7:12, 40; 1 Thess. 4:8; 2 Thess. 2:13; 2 Pet. 3:15–16; cf. 1 Cor. 3:10; cf. Hay 2000: 134). And, as we will see below, Christ's word is especially expressed through OT psalms that are read among believers and mediated upon.

30. In 1 Tim. 6:3 "words . . . of our Lord Jesus Christ" could go either way as subjective or objective genitive. In all these passages, "Lord" likely refers to Jesus, though "Christ" is the preferred reading in Col. 3:16 (see the first additional note on 3:16).

31. For this meaning, especially with respect to God revealing his promised word from the OT that begins fulfillment in the NT epoch, see the additional notes to 1:25 (where also is discussion of "word of the Lord" in the Gospels and Acts). Likewise "word of God" is apparently a subjective genitive ("the word spoken by God") elsewhere in Paul: Rom. 9:6; 1 Cor. 14:36; 2 Cor. 2:17; 4:2; 1 Thess. 2:13; 1 Tim. 4:5; 2 Tim. 2:9; Titus 2:5.

32. Wallace (1996: 119–21) refers to this as a "plenary genitive."

The phrase "in all wisdom" (ἐν πάσῃ σοφίᾳ, *en pasē sophia*) directly preceded by "richly" (πλουσίως, *plousiōs*) likely develops Col. 2:3, where in Christ "are hidden all the treasures of wisdom and knowledge." Thus, Christ's own word of wisdom is in mind in contrast to the pseudo-wisdom of the false teachers who dilute the centrality of Christ (see on 2:23).[33]

We have just seen in 3:15 the parallel of "Christ dwell[ing] in your hearts through faith" in Eph. 3:17, which refers to the prevailing presence of Christ "in the inner man" (see Eph. 3:16b). The same parallel suggests that Christ's indwelling[34] word in Col. 3:16 should be the prevailing influence in the believers ("in you," pl.), which is then further specified as "singing" what amounts to Christ's word "in your hearts."[35] And just as "the peace of Christ" is to be an ongoing predominant influence in believers, so it is the case with the indwelling of "the word of Christ."

The "teaching and admonishing" are adverbial participles that explain the manner (or possibly the instrumentation) of how "the word of Christ dwells within" them. As we saw with these two participles in 1:28, so also here the "admonishing" (νουθετέω, *noutheteō*) specifies that the teaching focuses on counsel about avoiding a wrong course of action inspired by the false teaching (see on 1:28). This meaning is important in light of the preceding cautions about false teaching in 2:4 and 2:8 and implied elsewhere in the epistle.

Paul has prayed that the readers would be "filled with the knowledge of His [God's] will in all wisdom [ἐν πάσῃ σοφίᾳ, *en pasē sophia*]" (1:9), and he sees his efforts of "admonishing" and "teaching . . . in all wisdom [ἐν πάσῃ σοφίᾳ]" in 1:28 as one of the ways that his prayer will be answered. The same verbatim expression from 1:28 is used again here, presumably because Paul thinks his prayer of 1:9 will *also* be answered if the believers "let the word of Christ richly dwell within you, . . . in all wisdom teaching and admonishing one another [ἐν πάσῃ σοφίᾳ διδάσκοντες καὶ νουθετοῦντες ἑαυτούς, *en pasē sophia didaskontes kai nouthetountes heautous*]" (3:16 NASB marg.).[36]

The content (or possibly manner) of the "teaching and admonishing" here is "in [ἐν] all wisdom" and "in [ἐν] psalms and hymns and spiritual songs,"[37]

33. See MacDonald (2000: 143) on this contrast with 2:23; so also Wall 1993: 149–50; Sumney 2008: 223.

34. In Col. 3:16 the verb is ἐνοικέω (*enoikeō*); Eph. 3:17 has κατοικέω (*katoikeō*), a cognate.

35. Similar to Luke 24:32, where the Emmaus road travelers said, "Were not our hearts burning within us while [Christ] was speaking to us on the road, while He was opening the Scriptures to us?" (NASB marg.).

36. The preposition-plus-dative phrase ἐν πάσῃ σοφίᾳ modifies the following two adverbial participles, as is the case in the verbatim parallel of 1:28, though there "in all wisdom" follows the two participles (as further support, in 4:5 "in wisdom" modifies the directly following "walk"; so Schweitzer 1982: 210). The punctuation of NA[28] also favors this. It is possible that the dative clause modifies the verb "dwell" (3:16a) on analogy with 1:9 and Eph. 1:8–9, but 1:28 is the closer parallel.

37. See on 1:9 and 1:28 for this meaning of the dative clause beginning with ἐν (*en*); likewise the same idea of content (or manner) is conveyed by the dative clause beginning with "psalms"

the latter of which all refer to OT psalms or are based on such psalms, a part of the Bible of the early church.

The close syntactical combination of "psalm" (ψαλμός, *psalmos*), "hymn" (ὕμνος, *hymnos*), and "song" (ᾠδή, *ōdē*) within the space of one verse occurs only two times in the psalter, in the LXX of Pss. 66:1 and 75:1 (where they are part of the superscriptions; cf. superscriptions of Pss. 67 and 76 Eng.). In both psalms, the three words are placed directly next to one another[38] without a conjunctive καί (*kai*) and without an article before any of the words, as in Col. 3:16. However, "song" is placed first in order and two of the words are in different case forms, and these same two words are in the singular instead of the plurals found in Colossians: thus Ps. 66:1: ὕμνοις ψαλμὸς ᾠδῆς (*hymnois psalmos ōdēs*). The syntax of the wording of these two psalms could be different than in Colossians, since it is possible to punctuate Ps. 66:1 LXX in the following way: "Among hymns. A Psalm. Of an Ode" (so NETS). However, NETS gives a marginal reading closer in line with that of Colossians: "*a psalm* (instrumental music) *accompanied by a song of praise* (vocal music)" (emphasis original; "praise" is a rendering of ᾠδή, *ōdē*). The most formally equivalent reading would be "among hymns, a psalm of a song." NETS renders Ps. 75:1 LXX as "Among hymns. A Psalm. Pertaining to Asaph. An Ode." The three words in Colossians may be plural since the allusion is to both psalms as representing the whole corpus of psalms. Strikingly, both psalms also mention eschatological salvation of Gentiles (a theme not far away in Colossians; e.g., 3:11). Psalm 66 LXX highlights this in six of its eight verses (e.g., v. 3 NETS [67:2 Eng.], "that we may know your way upon the earth, among all nations your salvation"), and Ps. 75 mentions it in verse 10 NETS (76:9 Eng.; "to save all the meek of the earth").[39] Consequently, the threefold wording of the two psalms appears to be reflected in Col. 3:16 not only because the combination occurs *only* in the OT in those two psalms,[40] but also partly because of the connection to Gentile salvation, a theme not far away in Colossians (e.g., 3:11). In this respect, saved Gentiles are certainly included among the ones who are to follow the instruction of 3:16.

Furthermore, it is likely not coincidental that the threefold lexical combination referring to psalms in the superscription of Ps. 66:1 LXX (67 Eng.) is

---

(ψαλμοῖς, *psalmois*) as expressing content or possibly manner or means (for the latter cf. Harris 2010: 146). Moule (1959: 45) takes the threefold dative clause to be a dative of accompaniment.

38. Yet Ps. 75:1 LXX has "pertaining to Asaph" (NETS) intervening between ψαλμός and ᾠδή.

39. The added phrase "for the Assyrian" is appended as a variant reading at the end of the superscription (75:1 LXX), which is not preferred in NETS but is in the Rahlfs LXX edition; see Rahlfs 1931: 208 for significant MSS supporting this reading (e.g., MS B) as well as the omission of it (e.g., א, following the Hebrew text). The addition would add to a Gentile flavor of the psalm and even indicate that the psalm was also intended for a Gentile audience. See also Ps. 79:1 LXX, where also "for the Assyrian" occurs, with mixed MS support.

40. The threefold combination of the same words occurs in Josephus (*Ant.* 6.214), referring to David singing before King Saul: "singing out in psalm and hymns" ("singing out" is a verbal form [with a prefixed preposition] of "song" [ᾠδή; the end of Col. 3:16 also has a cognate verbal form]). The twofold combination of "psalm" (ψαλμός) and "song" (ᾠδή) appears about fourteen times in the psalter and three times in the Psalms of Solomon, referring to psalms.

directly followed by an allusion to the Aaronic blessing from the tabernacle in Num. 6:24–26, "May the Lord bless you, and . . . may the Lord make his face shine upon you and show mercy to you"*; thus Ps. 66:2 LXX (67:1 Eng.) has "May God have compassion on us and bless us and make his face shine upon us." Similarly, after the same superscription containing the threefold psalm reference in Ps. 75:1 LXX, verse 3 (76:2 Eng.) also refers to the temple: "His [God's] place was in peace, and his dwelling place was in Sion."*[41]

Thus both superscriptions introduce psalms that begin with reference to God being in his temple.[42] Accordingly, when Col. 3:16 concludes its reference to "psalms and hymns and spiritual songs" with "singing with thankfulness in your hearts to God," the reference may be to worship directed to God in his heavenly temple (note the mention of "God" and Christ being in heaven in 3:1 and Christ residing in "heaven" in 4:1). This would certainly fit with the earlier references to the temple in the epistle that we have observed (e.g., 1:9–10; 1:19; 2:9–10, 18). In the light of these preceding references to the temple, especially in 2:18, part of the point here would be that believers in their worship[43] have no need of special visions of angels nor "worship of angels" to enrich the wisdom that they already possess in Jesus (e.g., see 2:3; cf. 1:28; so Garland 1998: 212; Lincoln 2000: 648), in whom their temple worship consists. In this respect, the notion of "the word of Christ dwelling in" believers may convey the notion of Christ's word dwelling in the church community as his temple in development of 1:19 and 2:9, since ἐνοικέω (*enoikeō*) is part of the same word group and semantic domain as κατοικέω (*katoikeō*), which has been used with a clear temple reference in 1:19 and 2:9.[44] The idea would be that Christ's presence dwells in his earthly temple community through his word. This is in line with the OT temple being the typical place of God's revelatory word.[45]

All of this points to the three terms in Col. 3:16 referring to actual OT psalms or songs/hymns composed on the basis of such psalms, which would now be related to the new revelation of Christ. Since all three words refer to OT

41. "Place" (τόπος, *topos*) is typically a reference to the temple in the LXX and the NT (e.g., see Beale 1999a: 648–49), and over half of the LXX uses of "dwelling place" (κατοικητήριον, *katoikētērion*) refer to God's temple. One of only two NT uses of the latter word refers to "dwelling [place] of God in the Spirit" (Eph. 2:22), of which believers are a part and of which Christ is the "cornerstone" (2:19–22). Notice also that Ps. 75:3 LXX (76:2 Eng.) mentions God's cultic "place" being "in *peace*" and "his *dwelling place*" being "*in Zion*," which is similar to the parallelism of Col. 3:15, "Let the peace of Christ rule in your hearts"; and 3:16, "Let the word of Christ richly dwell within you."

42. In Ps. 66 LXX (67 Eng.) this is implied through the allusion to Num. 6:25–26.

43. Most commentators acknowledge that the worship of the Christian community is the central focus in Col. 3:16. For the suitablility of singing hymns in the temple, see Josephus (*Ant.* 8.102; 20.216–18) and Philo (*Spec.* 1.193; *Plant.* 126, where the world is viewed as a temple).

44. Pokorný (1991: 173–74) also sees "indwelling" in 3:16 applied to Christians in development of the "dwelling" of 1:19 that is applied to Christ; though he sees no reference to the temple in 3:16, he sees OT temple texts such as Ps. 68:17 (67:18 LXX) as significant parallels to 1:19.

45. See additional notes for 3:16 as a development of 1:19 and 2:9, as well as for the notion that the temple was the usual place where God's word of revelation came.

psalms, there is no need to try to find distinct meaning among them.[46] Indeed, as we saw above, Paul says "letting the word of Christ dwell within you" takes place by means of or, better, in the manner of "teaching and admonishing" in OT psalms. The OT psalms are now viewed to be the very word of Christ![47] The psalms should now be understood fully through the lens of Christ.

The "wisdom" of 1:28 likewise originates from the same sources, though we have seen that Christ is the zenith point of the OT revelation of God's wisdom (2:3), so that this older revelation must be seen through a Christ-centered lens. And this is just why Col. 3:16 says that the "word of Christ" is expressed in the OT "psalms, hymns, and spiritual songs." He is the full source of wisdom (2:3), so that "in all wisdom" in 3:16 refers to Christ's wisdom and conveys the Christocentrically wise manner of the "teaching and admonishing." He is the full divine revelation to which the OT pointed, since it was incomplete without his coming (so see on Col. 2:17).

The revelatory nature of these "songs" is expressed with the adjective "spiritual" (πνευματικός, *pneumatikos*). We saw in 1:9 that in the phrase "all spiritual wisdom and understanding," the adjective "spiritual" (πνευματικός) refers to God's Spirit, who imparts the "wisdom" and "understanding" (see on 1:9). The same is probably the case here with "spiritual songs" (and by implication "psalms" and "hymns"). God's or Christ's Spirit inspires such OT "songs," which are now sung by the new-covenant community.

And just as verse 15 concluded with thanksgiving, so does verse 16: "singing with thankfulness in your hearts to God." The word translated "thankfulness" (χάρις, *charis*) often means "grace, favor, gratitude, or gift" (cf. BDAG 1079–81, s.v. χάρις). This is not εὐχάριστος (*eucharistos*), as at the end of verse 15. Perhaps the reason for the slight change is to underscore the same thing that was concluded about "thanksgiving" in verse 15: it is assumed that for which thanks and "gratitude" are being given is a gift of God's grace (here in v. 16 it is Christ's word). The adverbial participial phrase is most likely syntactically parallel with "teaching and admonishing" ("with psalms, hymns, spiritual songs"), which likewise modifies "indwell" at the beginning of the verse.[48] And like the other two participles, it also indicates the manner (or

46. This is in contrast to the majority of commentators who try to make some distinction of meaning among these three words, though others admit it is difficult to do so (see Lohse 1971: 151n148; Barth and Blanke 1994: 427; likewise MacDonald 2000: 143).

47. Commentators typically see the word "psalms" to refer to the OT psalms and often see the following two words, "hymns" and "songs," to be Christian compositions sung to God or Christ (e.g., see Lightfoot 1875: 225; Beekman 2002: 134; Witherington 2007: 181; Pao 2012: 249; cf. N. Wright 1986: 145; Bruce 1984: 160–61).

48. Among those seeing the phrase "with psalms, hymns, songs" modifying the participles "teaching and admonishing" are O'Brien 1982: 208–9, who gives convincing syntactical reasons for this alternative, which should be preferred (so also Pao 2012: 248–49 and KJV, NASB, TNIV). Thus the first double participial phrase and the last participial phrase both begin with the preposition ἐν (*en*) plus the dative; this symmetry of the two participial clauses is also supported by the parallel of Eph. 5:18–19. Others do not see the threefold hymnic phrase modifying the first two participles but modifying the last adverbial participle "singing" (ᾄδοντες, *adontes*;

possibly means or result) in which Christ's word is to dwell in the saints (cf. also Harris 2010: 138). As in the case of the participles in verse 13 also carrying an imperatival sense because they modify an imperative verb, so it is the case with these participles.[49]

The worship of verse 16 begins with the phrase "the word of Christ" and ends with "to God." Thus Paul's prescription for Christian worship is bounded by references to Christ and God. This indicates the Christ-centered and God-centered focus of this worship.

Verse 16 places squarely on the shoulders of each Christian the responsibility to "teach and admonish one another" through psalm-based material and to sing psalm-like hymns to God. This does not mean that there was not a hierarchy of elder-teachers in the Colossian church[50] (as in the Pastoral Epistles) but only that there is a place for each believer in teaching and admonishing other believers through Christ's word. By so doing, the Colossian believers will prevent one another from being "lured into the false teaching that may be captivating some of the group," especially a teaching focusing on mystical experiences instead of Christ-centered instruction (Foster 2016: 360–61).

Now the thought proceeds a step further: "Whatever you do in word or deed, **3:17**
do all in the name of the Lord Jesus." The verse appears to be an interpretive summary of all of verses 12–16. This is pointed to by observing that Christ's own lifestyle of forgiveness was the basis for the lifestyle instructions in verses 12–13, the "peace of Christ" was central to Christian living in verse 15, and "the word of Christ" was the focus of worship in verse 16. And even the thanksgiving is to be given "through" Christ "to God the Father." As elsewhere in Colossians (e.g., see 2:9–15), we have another Christ-centered paragraph.

In the OT the "name" of God represented his character, especially his sovereign presence,[51] and was interchangeable with his person (Eichrodt 1967: 41–43). The precise phrase "in the name of the Lord" (ἐν ὀνόματι κυρίου, *en onomati kyriou*) occurs eighteen times in the Greek OT,[52] referring to saints either saying or doing something in that name. The formula expresses God's

so also RSV, NIV, NJB, NRSV, NLT, ESV, HCSB, NET). This syntactical difference does not significantly affect the meaning, since all of the three participles modify and unpack the verb "dwell." There are other smaller syntactical issues in verse 16, but they do not affect the overall meaning (see Harris 2010: 145, 147–48).

49. An imperative sense is not mutually exclusive with an adverbial participle of manner, means, or result, as Harris (2010: 146) and Barth and Blanke (1996: 427) seem to imply. The participle may take on the imperative mood of the verb it modifies and, at the same time, modify the verb in some adverbial way. So BDF §468.2 views the participles in verses 16–17 as imperatival; Porter (1989: 376) suggests the possibility that each of the participles in verses 16–17 "serves in place of an Imperative." In contrast, Wallace (1996: 652) doubts whether there can be an imperative use of the participles here in verse 16. Robertson (1934: 946) says the participle is without mood, so context must decide what mood it carries.

50. As held, e.g., by Sumney (2008: 224–25), who argues that there was no such hierarchy because Colossians is silent about it. Arguments from silence can be tenuous, as in this case.

51. E.g., see H. Bietenhard, *TDNT* 5:255–57, 260; Eichrodt 1967: 41–45; Jacob 1958: 82–85.

52. Sumney (2008: 228) has independently observed the same statistic of the formula's usage.

sovereign presence, to which appeal is made when one is about to speak or act. The ἐν (*en*) plus the dative ὀνόματι indicates that the divine sovereign presence is both the *reference point* that OT saints are zealous to keep in mind (when acting and speaking) and *the basis* for their actions or speech[53] (e.g., Mic. 4:5, "We will walk in the name of the LORD our God forever").[54]

The same ideas are present with the same precise formula in Col. 3:17, which is unique in all of Paul. "Name" mainly expresses Christ's sovereign presence. This notion is illustrated by 1 Cor. 5:4. There almost the identical formula, adding an article before "name" (ἐν τῷ ὀνόματι κυρίου, *en tō onomati kyriou*), gives the interpretive parallel of "with the power of our Lord Jesus." Thus Christians must consider how their actions are to be influenced by Christ's sovereign presence and character, and they should realize how, as the basis for their behavior, it should affect how they act.[55] This is consistent with the context. We have just seen how consideration of the person of Christ is positively to affect one's thinking and behavior in Col. 3:13, 15, and 16, and we will see this again in 3:18, 20, 22–24; and 4:1. Perhaps the most striking parallel is 3:23, "whatever you do, do your work heartily, as for the Lord rather than for men." And why should there be such conscious reverence for Christ in all that one does? It is because he is none less than the God of Christians. Indeed, the OT formula "in the name of the Lord" is adapted by Paul here to apply it to Christ: "in the name of the Lord Jesus." Jesus is now identified with Yahweh of the OT,[56] and believers are to revere him in all they do as OT believers revered God in what they did. What may heighten Jesus's identification with deity is that a number of the eighteen Septuagintal formulas have "in the name of the Lord your [or our or my or the] God."[57] Jesus replaces "God" in the formula!

The exhortation to "do all things, in word or deed, in the name of the Lord Jesus"* specifies the general command in 2:6 to "walk in" Christ. Furthermore, in imperatival form 3:17 reiterates the earlier purpose that Paul had formulated for Christians in 1:10: "Walk . . . worthy of the Lord, to please Him in all respects, bearing fruit in every good work."[58]

And just as "thanksgiving" was the proper result for letting Christ's peace reign at the conclusion of verse 15 and was the conclusion at the end of verse

53. This preposition, with the dative sometimes to indicate "reference to" and in other cases "cause," occurs in both the LXX (Muraoka 2009: 232) and the NT (Wallace 1996: 144–46, 167–68). The preposition has "thick" meaning here, so that both ideas appear to be included.

54. So also see, e.g., 1 Sam. 17:45; 20:42; 2 Sam. 6:18; 1 Kings 8:44; 22:16; Ps. 123:8 (124:8 Eng.); Sir. 47:18. See the additional note on 3:17 for other similar formulas in the LXX explicitly or implicitly employing God's name.

55. Some commentators want to see the idea that acting "in the name of the Lord Jesus" refers to being a "representative" of Jesus (e.g., MacDonald 2000: 144), which may be included but is not the focus.

56. So also Pao 2012: 251. Eichrodt (1967: 45) says generally that "it is in the person of Jesus that the function of the Name of Yahweh as a form of the divine self-manifestation finds its fulfillment."

57. See Josh. 9:9; 1 Sam. 17:45; 1 Kings 18:24; Ps. 19:8 (20:7 Eng.); Sir. 47:18; Mic. 4:5.

58. See Pao (2012: 250), who sees 3:17 developing both 1:10 and 2:6.

16, so "giving thanks" is again the expected result at the close of verse 17, this time the result of doing all in Christ's name.[59] And, as also in verses 15–16, the "giving of thanks" presupposes that what they have (in this verse it is the sovereign presence of Christ over their lives) has not come about through their own efforts but is completely given by God's grace. One aspect of Christ's sovereign presence among them is that even their thanks to God are given "through" Christ. Consequently, though all of verses 12–17 is Christ-centered, the interpretive summary of verses 12–16 in verse 17 ends with its main point being thanksgiving to "God the Father," which is what all of verses 12–17a have been working toward.

Additional Notes

3:12. "Elect ones" (ἐκλεκτοί, *eklektoi*) is a common OT name for Israel (e.g., Pss. 78:31; 105:6, 43; 106:5 [LXX: 77:31; 104:6, 43; 105:5]; Isa. 42:1; 43:20; 45:4; 65:9, 15), and it is found likewise in the Pseudepigrapha (e.g., Sib. Or. 3.69; T. Job 1.5). The phrase "elect one of God" is used of such figures as Moses (Liv. Pro. 2.11 [14]), Jeremiah (4 Bar. 7.9, 16), Ezra (Gk. Apoc. Ezra 1.8), and the Messiah (T. Benj. 11.4). "Holy ones" is also a typical OT name for Israel (ἅγιοι, *hagioi*: e.g., Lev. 11:44–45; 19:2; 20:7, 26; 21:6; Num. 15:40–41; Isa. 4:3), which is also found in the Pseudepigrapha (Sib. Or. 5.161; Gk. Apoc. Ezra 6.25–26; T. Sim. 6.2). The perfect passive plural participle "beloved" (ἠγαπημένοι, *ēgapēmenoi*) is less common but is found in the singular perfect passive participle as a reference to God's love shown to Israel (Deut. 32:15; 33:12; Isa. 44:2; Jer. 11:15; 12:7) and a virtual semantic and verbal nominative equivalent also referring to Israel is ἀγαπητοί (*agapētoi*, in Pss. 60:5; 108:6 [LXX: 59:7; 107:7]). The noun is used likewise in T. Levi 18.13 and the participle in 4 Bar. 4.7 and 3 Macc. 6:11 (cf. similarly Jub. 31.15, 20). Especially noteworthy are the same (or virtually the same) Greek combinations in Tob. 8:15 ("your holy ones . . . and your elect"); Wis. 4:15 ("Mercy is with his elect ones and providence with his holy ones [τοῖς ὁσίοις, *tois hosiois*]"); Isa. 44:2 ("beloved Israel whom I have elected"); Mart. Ascen. Isa. 3.4 (Jerusalem is "this beloved and elect city").

3:12–15. Ephesians 4:1–4 is parallel with Col. 3:12–15, which both have in common significant mention of "love" (Eph. 4:2)[60] and work toward the goal of harmonious unity.

3.13. Instead of "Lord," some MSS have "Christ" or "God in Christ" or "God." The earliest and best MSS support "Lord" (which NA[28] also prefers), though א* supports "God." For further elaboration, see Metzger 1994: 557–58.

3:14. The relative pronoun ὅ (*ho*) likely has its antecedent in the preceding "love" (ἀγάπη, *agapē*), though its gender could be related to the following predicate substantive "bond" (σύνδεσμος, *syndesmos*). However, ἀγάπη is feminine and σύνδεσμος is masculine, but the relative pronoun is neuter, which is problematic since relatives should agree with their antecedents or following predicate adjectives in gender. For the various solutions to the problem, see Harris (2010: 143),

59. Thus εὐχαριστοῦντες (*eucharistountes*) is an adverbial participle indicating "giving thanks," which is the result of the implied imperative "do," though it possibly could show the manner or means by which the verb is to be carried out. For the possibility of an imperatival sense of the participle together with its adverbial function, see discussion of the participles in verses 13 and 16.

60. Both sections also have in common the following phrases: "you were called," "humility," "gentleness," "patience," "bearing with one another," "bond," "peace," and "one body," all of which are translations of the same Greek words in the two passages.

the most likely of which is that the phrase ὅ ἐστιν (*ho estin*) is a fixed idiomatic expression that "is used without much regard to the gender . . . of antecedent or predicate" (Robertson 1934: 411), or alternatively, the neuter relative here refers "to the general notion of 'thing'" (Robertson 1934: 713), i.e., a neuter idea of love.

3:16. Though "Christ" is the preferred reading in Col. 3:16, the substitution of "Lord" is supported by some good MSS (א*, 1175), as is the substitution of "God" (A, C*, 33, 104).

3:16. The combination of all three words "psalm" (ψαλμός, *psalmos*), "hymn" (ὕμνος, *hymnos*), and "song" (ᾠδή, *ōdē*) occurs in the NT not only in Col. 3:16 but also in Eph. 5:19, the latter of which reads, "speaking to one another in psalms and hymns and spiritual songs, singing and making melody with your heart to the Lord." This indicates either the means or, more likely, the result of being "filled with the Spirit" in Eph. 5:18.[61] As we have seen, the "filling" (πλήρωμα/πληρόω, *plērōma/plēroō*) in Colossians has typically been used with respect to the divine presence in the temple (1:19; 2:9–10) or in being able to build the temple (1:9).[62] Likewise the word in Ephesians can have the latter association (see esp. Eph. 3:19 and the discussion on Col. 2:10a). The Eph. 3 and 5 parallels may further enhance Col. 3:16's link with the temple.

The idea of "the word of Christ dwelling in" believers may express the concept of Christ's word dwelling in the church community as his temple, since ἐνοικέω (*enoikeō*) is part of the same word group and semantic domain as κατοικέω (*katoikeō*),[63] which is used with a clear temple reference in 1:19 and 2:9. Accordingly, it may develop the concept of the temple from these two earlier verses. The term ἐνοικέω is used only four times in the NT outside Col. 3:16, one of which refers to God "dwelling" in his people, who are "the temple of the living God" (2 Cor. 6:16). The verb there is used as the equivalent to σκηνή (*skēnē*) in Lev. 26:11 (though some LXX MSS omit this word) and κατασκήνωσις (*kataskēnōsis*) in Ezek. 37:27, both of which are combined in the temple quotation in 2 Cor. 6:16. Likewise, ἐνοικέω in Col. 3:16 may be the same kind of equivalent with κατοικέω in 1:19 and 2:9. Similarly, 1 Cor. 3:16 says that believers are "a temple of God" because "the Spirit of God dwells [οἰκέω, *oikeō*] in you," the Greek word for "dwell" here also being part of the same word group and semantic domain as ἐνοικέω and κατοικέω.

In addition, Lohse (1971: 150) has adduced Sir. 24 as a significant parallel to Col. 3:16: Wisdom made her "dwelling" (σκηνή, *skēnē*) in Jacob, "dwelt [κατασκηνόω, *kataskēnoō*] in Jacob," and "ministered in a holy tent [σκηνή]," referring to Wisdom dwelling in Israel's temple (Sir. 24:8, 10). This parallel of Sir. 24 is significant, since Col. 3:16 also combines the notion of "dwelling" with "wisdom." This is enhanced by recalling how Philo says that "God's dwelling place, the tabernacle," is symbolic of "wisdom," which "is the court and palace of the All-ruler" (*Prelim.* 116–17). In a context about the "holy tabernacle," Philo (*Dreams* 1.208) says, "[Knowledge's] most holy [cultic] image will be enshrined in all the house of Wisdom both in heaven and on earth" (LCL). Similarly, Philo (*Migr.* 4–6) says that the "word" is God's "abode" and equates this abode with "the House of God." This is significant, since Philo sometimes either equates the "word" (λόγος, *logos*) with "wisdom" (σοφία, *sophia*; e.g., *Alleg.* 1.65; *Prelim.* 174; *Dreams* 2.245) or closely associates the two (*Flight* 97, 137; *Dreams* 1.165–66; 2.242), as in Col. 3:16. Philo (*Heir* 112–13) refers to "the sacred tabernacle" that was "made after the model and in imitation of wisdom. For he says that he has erected his oracle [λόγιον, *logion*] as a tabernacle in the midst of our impurity, in order that . . . we may be purified" (trans. Yonge 1993: 285). Wisdom 9:1–17 portrays "wisdom," which is equated with God's "word" (9:1–2), as being in his holy temple and being the source of God's law and "commandments" for humans. Colossians 3:16 is also uniquely similar to John 1:14: The "Word [= Christ] . . . dwelt among us" (ὁ λόγος . . . ἐσκήνωσεν ἐν ἡμῖν, *ho logos . . . eskēnōsen en hēmin*).

61. "Speaking, . . . singing and making melody" are adverbial participles of result.

62. Though the two uses in Col. 1:25 and 4:17 have no such link.

63. See L&N 731, and note that ἐνοικέω (*enoikeō*) and κατοικέω (*katoikeō*) in the LXX both translate three of the same Hebrew words, as well as translating respectively מִשְׁכָּן (*miškān*, tabernacle, dwelling) and שָׁכַן (*šākan*, to tabernacle, dwell).

The OT temple was the usual location where God's revelatory word came. Representative examples of this are: the Eden sanctuary, where God's word came to Adam and Eve (Beale 2004: 66–87); the Sinai mountain sanctuary, where God spoke to Moses and Israel (Beale 2004: 105–6); the tabernacle, where God spoke to Moses (Exod. 33:7–11); the temple as the place where God spoke to Isaiah (Isa. 6:1–13), Ezekiel (Ezek. 1–2), and other prophets (see further Beale 2004: passim). The Urim and Thummim were likely stones kept in the high priest's pouch, which he would cast in the temple, and the way they landed revealed a yes or no answer to the priest's question. In early Judaism this revelatory answer through the stones was even referred to as "tongues of fire" (Beale 2004: 207).

Thus our contention that Col. 3:16 is about God's revelatory word in the temple community is in line with God's revelation in the OT temple (the above Sir. 24 and Philo references enhance this conclusion). This is further pointed to from Col. 1; Eph. 4; and 1 Cor. 3. We observed earlier that Col. 1:9–10 is one of the clearest references to the temple in the epistle (see on 1:9–10). This clear allusion to Christians building the temple is directly followed by "bearing fruit and increasing," referring to the believers' works, but the very same phrase is directly linked in 1:5–6 to "the word of the truth of the gospel," which was "bearing fruit and growing," and which is in mind to some degree in the same phrase in 1:9–10. Thus, building of the temple in 1:9–10 takes place through the believers' "good works" and their spreading of "the word of the truth of the gospel" (1:5–6).[64]

Likewise, we have observed that Eph. 4:16 is another reference to an organic growing temple, developing the earlier temple discussion of Eph. 2:21 (see on Col. 2:19). In Eph. 4:15–16 "speaking the truth in love" is the way believers "grow" in Christ, who is the "head" of the "body," the organic temple of Christ. Paul and Apollos spoke the word of the gospel "causing the growth" and laying the "foundation" of the temple in Christ; and this "foundation" must continue to be built by pastoral leaders faithfully proclaiming God's word (see 1 Cor. 3:5–17).[65]

"Psalm" (ψαλμός, *psalmos*) occurs five times by itself in the NT outside Col. 3:16 and Eph. 5:19, referring to OT psalms, except possibly once, where it refers to believers offering a "psalm" in the church gathering (1 Cor. 14:26). "Hymn" (ᾠδή, *ōdē*) occurs elsewhere outside the Ephesians and Colossians passages only in Revelation, where it alludes to the "song of Moses" (Exod. 14:31–15:1) at the exodus (Rev. 15:3), which is viewed as pointing to the messianic Lamb (note "song of the Lamb" that follows in Rev. 15:3); in Rev. 5:9 and 14:3 "song" also alludes to Pss. 40:3; 96:1; 98:1; 144:9; 149:1; Isa. 42:10 (though in the OT these passages employ different synonyms for "song" in Greek; Isa. 42:10 likely alludes to the psalms usage). "Song" (ὕμνος, *hymnos*) occurs in the NT only in Eph. 5:19 and Col. 3:16. All of this points further to Col. 3:16 as referring to actual OT psalms or songs/hymns based on such psalms (possibly together with other OT texts), both of which are now related to the new revelation of Christ and viewed as Christ's word.

3:17. The only other NT uses of the very same Greek formula "in the name of the Lord" (ἐν ὀνόματι κυρίου, *en onomati kyriou*) are references to Jesus as the ultimate fulfillment of Ps. 118:26a (117:26a LXX): "Blessed is he who comes <u>in the name of the Lord!</u>" (NKJV; Matt. 21:9; 23:39; Mark 11:9; Luke 13:35; 19:38; John 12:13). This psalm is about an anonymous faithful Israelite leader (probably a king) whom God delivers from his enemies and who is blessed "from the house of the Lord" (Ps. 118:26b) and on whose behalf sacrifice is made in the temple (118:27). This person is, in fact, the temple "stone which the builders rejected" and who "has become the chief corner stone" (Ps. 118:22). In the psalm this likely refers to the person's crucial importance for the temple, and it is applied to Jesus as the cornerstone of the new temple (so Matt. 21:42; Mark 12:10; Luke 20:17; Acts 4:11). The observation that this verbally precise Greek

64. At Col. 1:6, 10 we also saw that the phrase "bearing fruit and multiplying" is an allusion to Gen. 1:28, which is inextricably linked to Adam's commission of spreading God's revelatory tabernacling presence from Eden throughout the earth.

65. Likewise 1 Pet. 2:2 sees the "word" causing "growth," which is then directly connected to believers being "built up" in Christ as a temple (1 Pet. 2:4–5). See Beale and Kim (2014: 104–9) for further discussion of Col. 1:5–6; Eph. 4:16; 1 Cor. 3:5–17; and 1 Pet. 2.

formula is associated elsewhere in the NT only with the Ps. 118 temple text[66] may suggest a similar association here in Col. 3:17.

Similar LXX formulas to that of Col. 3:17's "in the name of the Lord" (ἐν ὀνόματι κυρίου) and referring explicitly or implicitly to God's name with a similar notion are found, all of which employ the dative singular ὀνόματι in phrases such as "in the name of his glory," "in my name," "in your name," "in the name of God," and "in his name." Particularly of note in the LXX is ἐπὶ τῷ ὀνόματι κυρίου (*epi tō onomati kyriou*), which appears to be used in the same way as the ἐν plus dative ὀνόματι construction (e.g., see Isa. 50:10; Jer. 11:21; 33:16). None of these LXX alternative dative constructions occur in the NT except for a few references to "in your [Jesus's] name" in the Gospels and Acts.

66. The formula in Eph. 5:19–20 (which is a larger verbatim parallel with Col. 3:17) and 2 Thess. 3:6 is very close to Col. 3:17, but they add an article τοῦ (*tou*) before "Lord," which is lacking in Colossians. Acts 9:28; 1 Cor. 5:4; 6:11; and James 5:14 also have the formula but add the dative article before "name" as well as the article before "Lord." James 5:10 merely adds the article before "name" in the formula. It is not clear whether Jesus is the referent in the James texts, though 5:8 makes it plausible that he may be in mind. Certainly all these variant formulas have the same meaning, but the precise verbatim identification of Col. 3:17 with the Ps. 118 quotations in the Gospels may show a specific stylistic connection with an echo of these uses. The NT also contains other references to the "name" of Jesus in different syntactical configurations apart from the ἐν (*en*) plus the dative construction, a number of which may express the same general idea.

G. Believers Should Live Out the New-Creational Lifestyle in the Family and Workplace (3:18–4:1)

Here is a fuller statement of the main idea of this unit: *The new-creational lifestyle of love, unity, peace, and Christocentric focus (3:12–17) must especially be lived out in the family and workplace.*

The new creation that was inaugurated by Christ's death and resurrection (see on 1:15–20) is participated in by those who believe in him and are identified with his new-creational death and resurrection (2:20; 3:1–4, 9–10). Because they have died to the old world and been placed into the new world, they now have power to overcome the sin of the old world (3:5–9a) and to live according to the pattern of the resurrected Christ in the new creation (3:12–14).

The new-creational life portrayed in 3:12–16 (love, unity, peace, adherence to Christ's word) and summarized in verse 17 (doing everything in Christ's name) is now particularized by showing how it is to be lived out in everyday life, in the family and workplace (3:18–4:1). The tripartite family structure (marriage, parent-children, and master-slave) to a large extent covered the relationships in which Christians then found themselves. The instructions for the family in this section are a depiction of how the family is to be transformed in its new-creational sphere.

In particular, we have seen that Christ's reconciliation and peacemaking "on earth" and "in heaven" (1:20, 22) are one of the main expressions of Christ's inauguration of the new creation (see on 1:18–22). Those who have been reconciled and affected by Christ's peace have "clothed themselves with the new man who is being renewed unto the knowledge according to the image of the one who created him"* as a new creation (3:10). Such people are now one body in Christ (3:11, 15). People who have experienced the new-creational reconciliation and peace will show reconciliation and peace to one another (3:12–15). For example, they forgive as Christ forgave them (3:13), and they let Christ's "peace" rule among them (3:15). The family, the main social unit of society, is the place where Paul believes such new-creational reconciliation and peace should be exhibited by those who have become part of this new creation.

In the history of the interpretation of this passage, some have viewed the household instructions of 3:18–4:1 as an attempt to focus on this-worldly living instead of eschatological expectations, which were purportedly waning.[1] However, the focus on the family household here actually illustrates how Christians live transformed lives in the sphere of the inaugurated latter-day new creation until the future consummation takes place (e.g., see on 3:1–4 in relation to 3:5–17). There is general acknowledgment that Paul has been influenced by a Greco-Roman household code,[2] which apparently first had some of its roots in Aristotle's formulation of it (*Pol.* 1.2.1–4) and was adapted by the Greco-Roman world (e.g., Seneca, *Ep.* 94.1; Dionysius of Halicarnassus, *Rom. Antiq.* 2.24–27) and Hellenistic Judaism (Ps.-Phoc. 175–227; Philo, *Hypoth.* 7.1–14; *Decal.* 165–67; Josephus, *Ag. Ap.* 2.190–218).[3] This household code prescribes behaviors for husbands-wives, parents-children, and masters-slaves. It has been transformed in light of Christ's lordship, so that every member of the household, including its male head, is to live under Christ's lordship above all else (e.g., see Pao 2012: 263–66). In this respect, the word "Lord" occurs eight times in this section (Garland 1998: 258), and the charge to regard Jesus as Lord in what one does occurs explicitly six times (3:18, 20, 22, 23, 24 ["you serve the Lord Christ"]; 4:1b). Though there are some exceptional similarities to Paul's household code in Hellenism,[4] none have the Christocentric transformative element. This transformative aspect is especially evident from observing that half of the references to Christ as "Lord" in Colossians occur in this household code (eight out of fourteen uses; so Hay 2000: 142). As a corollary to this, none of the pagan household codes give wives, children, or slaves reasons to disobey the

1. See O'Brien (1982: 218–19) for discussion of this aspect of the interpretive history of the passage, as well as for other proposed backgrounds for the origin of the household structure given in Col. 3:18–4:1.

2. Among others see, e.g., Lohse (1971: 15), Wolter (1993: 193–94), Dunn (1996: 243–44), Wilson (2005: 272–74), and Sumney (2008: 230–34) for a good thumbnail sketch of the primary and secondary sources explaining this household code; among the best of these is Balch (1988), who provides a survey of the most relevant literature and the various positions taken on the household code; likewise Barth and Blanke (1994: 462–75), esp. focusing on a history of debate about the code's origin and how it came to be used in Colossians; see also the bibliography on the household codes in relation to Paul in Patzia (1990: 87) and recent bibliography in particular in relation to Colossians in Heil 2010: 166.

3. As cited by several commentators.

4. Ps.-Plutarch (*Ed. Child.* 10 [*Mor.* 7E]) describes "how a man must . . . honour one's parents, . . . respect one's elders, . . . be chaste with women, . . . be affectionate with children, and not . . . be overbearing with slaves" (cf. Schweizer 1982: 224). Plutarch also speaks of parents' "honourable practices by means of encouragement and reasoning" with children (*Ed. Child.* 12 [*Mor.* 8F]), as well as husbands "controlling" wives "as the soul controls the body, by entering into her feelings and being knit to her through good will, . . . so it is possible to govern a wife, and at the same time to delight and gratify her" (*Advice* 33 [*Mor.* 142E]; both cited by Barth and Blanke 1992: 444, 437). See Talbert (2007: 232–33) for other Hellenistic sources affirming that husbands should love wives, fathers should treat sons sensitively and not harshly, and masters should be kind to slaves. See Seneca (*Ep.* 47, passim) for his view that masters should view slaves as equal human beings like themselves (e.g., *Ep.* 47.1); in this respect Seneca offers a master's pagan "golden rule" by which to abide: "Treat your inferiors as you would be treated by your betters" (*Ep.* 47.12).

commands of the household head, but, as we will see, Paul's instructions here do allow for this, since all believers "must obey God rather than human beings!" (Acts 5:29 NIV) when earthly commands conflict with God's or Christ's instruction (Hendriksen 1964: 177). Another dissimilarity is that Hellenistic and Jewish household codes address only the ones in authority, whereas in Paul's code here the powerless are addressed first and then those in authority. Could this suggest Paul's conviction that all are spiritual equals in Christ (cf. Foster 2016: 372)?

Some conclude that the household instructions do not offer timelessly valid commands (e.g., Lohse 1971: 157). To attempt to refute this conclusion would take us too far afield, since other Pauline passages would need to be consulted. Here we can offer only the barest outline of why the commands in this passage are timelessly binding. First, the husband-wife relationship is grounded in the order of creation (1 Cor. 11:8; 1 Tim. 2:13) and in the redemptive-historical reflection of Christ and the church throughout the interadvent age (e.g., in Eph. 5:22–33, the husband is to reflect the unconditional authoritative love of Christ in relation to the wife, and the wife is to reflect the church's submissive respect for Christ in relation to her husband). Likewise, the parent-child relationship is rooted in creation (Gen. 1:28) and in the moral law (Deut. 5:16), which is reiterated in Eph. 6:2–3. "Submission" in some relationships is just as timeless as Christ's submission to the Father during the interadvent age, which, of course, does not entail any ontological inferiority. Likewise "submission" of wives to husbands or children to parents does not entail any inferiority. The issue of slavery is more complicated: we will wait to discuss it until the comments on 4:1, where also there will be further brief discussion of the husband-wife[5] and parent-child relationships.

The section continues the explicit Christ-centered emphasis of 1:15–20; 2:8–23 (the Christ-centered critique of the false teachers); 3:1–4; and 3:12–17; yet even 3:5–11 refers to putting off sin and the old man and putting on the new man, based on Christ's death and resurrection (see Pao 2012: 257–58; cf. O'Brien 1982: 233).

Exegesis and Exposition

18Wives, be subject to your husbands, as is fitting in the Lord. 19Husbands, love
your wives and do not be embittered against them. 20Children, be obedient to your
parents in all things, for this is well-pleasing to the Lord. 21Fathers, do not ⌜exasperate⌝
your children, that they may not lose heart. 22Slaves, in all things obey those who are
your masters on earth, not with external service, as those who merely please men,
but with sincerity of heart, fearing the Lord. 23Whatever you do, do your work heartily,
as for the Lord rather than for men, 24knowing that from the Lord ⌜you will receive⌝

5. On the timeless authority structure of the husband-wife relationship, see Hurley 1981.

the reward of the inheritance. ⌜ ⌝ It is the Lord Christ whom you serve. [25]For he who does wrong will receive the consequences of the wrong which he has done, and that without partiality. [4:1]Masters, grant to your slaves justice and fairness, knowing that you too have a Master in heaven.

3:18 Paul now applies the principles of the new-creational lifestyle to the family household (or the "household table," as some refer to it). He begins by addressing the role of wives in relation to their husbands. Wives are to be subject to their husbands. The word ὑποτάσσω (*hypotassō*) refers to the wives' subjection or submission to husbands. The word is best translated as either "subjection" or "submission" each place it occurs in the NT.

The middle voice of ὑποτάσσω ("subject yourselves") *could* indicate that it is the wives' responsibility to be *voluntarily* subject to husbands.[6] This suggests that it is not the husbands' role to demand such subjection (O'Brien 1999: 419). This may be pointed to further by the absence of any husband's command to a wife "to be subject."[7] However, we will see below that the middle voice of the verb with a reflexive sense does not necessarily express specific notions of accountability and voluntary submission (see the additional notes on 3:20). But even if an active voice were used and not the middle, would not the wives' responsibility and voluntary obedience still be expressed in the light of the context? Perhaps the middle enforces the aspect of accountability apparent in the context.

What does it mean for wives to do that which "is fitting in the Lord"? Some have been perplexed by the imperfect tense form ἀνῆκεν (*anēken*), offering various speculative views for why the imperfect is used (see Harris 2010: 154).[8] However, the focus should only be upon its imperfective aspect and not on a time reference of the imperfect. What should be underscored here is the *ongoing* state[9] of being "fitting in the Lord" with respect to all who properly subject themselves.

This verb could be understood to mean why the wife's submission is necessary, or it could indicate a limitation of the scope of the submission.[10] Most translations have "It is fitting," which could be taken either way. But the verb

6. On which cf. O'Brien 1982: 222, 224; Barth and Blanke 1994: 434–35; Garland 1998: 244; Pao 2012: 262; likewise Schweizer 1982: 221.

7. Note the absence also of commands in Eph. 5:22–33 and in the master-slave relationship, though we will see that it is different with the parent-child relationship.

8. E.g., one such view listed by Harris (2010: 154) is that the imperfect refers to a past period between a person's conversion and the present time (i.e., the rendering would be "ever since your conversion" or perhaps "what was fitting"). See similarly Foster (2016: 374), who sees the verb as being idiomatic and connoting "behavior that needs to be practiced in the present, though inaugurated in the past."

9. On this aspect of the imperfect, see Wallace 1996: 548. Cf. the similar use of the imperfect of the same verb in Eph. 5:4.

10. See, e.g., O'Brien (1982: 222) and D. Moo (2008: 302), who favor the first alternative; Pao (2012: 267) and Dunn (1996: 248) see both as possible; as support for some limitation of scope of the submission, Dunn cites 1 Cor. 7:15, where Paul says that spouses are "not under bondage" to a spouse who "leaves" them.

can also have the sense of "relate to," "belong to," "be proper to," or "be harmonious with," which also could have either sense of what is necessary or a limitation of scope. Accordingly, here the rendering could be "as is proper in the Lord" or "as is harmonious with the Lord." The use of the word in Philem. 8 could favor the idea of necessity or duty over limitation of the scope of an action: "to order you to do what is proper."

The introductory ὡς (*hōs*) preceding ἀνῆκεν (*anēken*) could be taken to indicate the reason why ("because") wives must be submissive to the Lord, a use sometimes expressed by ὡς (*hōs*).[11] But the predominant use expresses "the manner in which something proceeds."[12] And that is likely the use here: "Wives, be subject to husbands <u>in a manner that is proper</u> in the Lord," with behavior that is appropriate to her relationship to the Lord and especially "in the sphere [or realm] of the Lord" (Campbell 2012: 164 prefers "realm"). The use of the verb in Eph. 5:4 appears to favor or at least include a notion of limiting the scope of behavior: "And there must be no filthiness and silly talk, or coarse jesting, <u>which are not fitting</u>, but rather giving of thanks."[13] The Geneva Bible may catch the sense: "as it is comely in the Lord."

The parallel with Eph. 5:22 favors the notion of limiting the scope of the submission rather than focusing on it as a necessary duty. According to 5:24, "Wives ought to be [subject] to their husbands <u>in everything</u>," but 5:22 has already qualified this by saying, "Wives be subject to your own husbands, <u>as to the Lord</u>" (i.e., "in the [same] manner that you submit to the Lord"). Likewise Col. 3:18 qualifies this subjection "in everything" (as in Eph. 5:24) by what "is fitting in the Lord," which is parallel with "as to the Lord" in Ephesians.

Thus in Col. 3:18, in light of the above, the idea of duty is likely included in ἀνῆκεν, but the focus seems to be more on a limitation of the scope of submission. This means the wife's submission is not a "blind obedience" but is an obedience to those things only that are consistent with living faithfully in relation to her Lord Jesus (cf. Barth and Blanke 1994: 434–35), as is the case with children and slaves (see on 3:20–24). It is obvious that believing wives are addressed here, since the following verses are addressed to believing husbands, parents, fathers, slaves, and masters. Equally obvious is that in each of these relationships there also often were unbelieving spouses, children, parents, slaves, and masters. Christians did not need to obey when unbelievers in authority in the household ordered them to do something that would obviously violate their conscience as Christians.[14]

11. So D. Moo (2008: 302), who cites BDAG (1105, s.v. ὡς) generally in support of this view.

12. BDAG (1103–4, s.v. ὡς) actually places Col. 3:18 into this category of "manner," as does Pao 2012: 267.

13. Though again here the comparable καθώς (*kathōs*), like ὡς (*hōs*), can express the manner of behavior or the reason for the behavior, and both are possible here; see Beale, Brendsel, and Ross 2014: 56.

14. Here, e.g., Barth and Blanke (1994: 434–35) point out that wives are not bound to obey unbelieving husbands who demand that their wives venerate their pagan gods.

"In the Lord" (ἐν κυρίῳ, *en kyriō*) occurs many times in Paul. Consequently, each context in which the phrase appears must shape its meaning. Recall that 3:18–4:1 is Paul's explanation of how the new-creational lifestyle of 3:12–16 is lived out in the family and workplace, and verse 17 is the summary of the preceding section. In this light, the meaning of the phrase "in the name of the Lord Jesus" in verse 17 likely informs "in the Lord" in verses 18 and 20. We have concluded, in light of the formula's OT use, that in verse 17 it refers to Christ's sovereign, authoritative presence (see on v. 17). Accordingly, as in verse 17, here it refers to wives considering how their behavior is to be based on and influenced by Christ's divine sovereign and authoritative presence (and character) in the sphere where they dwell.[15]

In particular, the manner of their submission to their husbands is to be influenced by conforming their lives to the humble and sacrificial lifestyle of Christ (as in 3:12–13) together with striving for love, unity, and peace in Christ (vv. 14–15), as well as living in subjection to Christ's word in Scripture (v. 16). This is what it means in the light of the immediately preceding context to do what "is fitting in the Lord." Likely included is the notion that the wife does not "submit" in a way that is *not* "fitting in the Lord." For example, her subjection would not include anything her husband asked that is against God's precepts. Therefore her subjection is not unqualified with respect to anything a husband might ask of her. The reason for this is that what determines her subjection is what is according to the Lord's preceptive will. While the husband is "the head of the wife" (Eph. 5:23a), Christ is the "head" of not only the husband and the wife but "of the church" in general (5:23b).

What further favors that "fitting in the Lord" limits the scope of submission is recollecting that Paul is using the ubiquitous household code and reformulating it by underscoring that Christ is the ultimate Lord whom believers serve, and their behavior in the household must be reformulated always with Christ's lordship in mind (Schweizer 1982: 223). The following expressions also express some significant degree of limiting the scope of the child's and slave's submission: "well-pleasing to the Lord" (3:20), "fearing the Lord" (3:22), "as for the Lord" (3:23), and "it is the Lord Christ whom you serve" (3:24).

3:19 The husbands' responsibility to wives focuses on loving them. There is no suggestion that they are to demand subjection from them. This command stands out against the Greco-Roman background of familial expectations. Commentators generally acknowledge that in this background husbands are never commanded to love their wives (e.g., see Lohse 1971: 158); yet some Hellenistic sources encourage husbands to love their wives (Talbert 2007: 232).[16]

15. Harris (2012: 129) sees ἐν κυρίῳ here as designating a personal relationship ("as is appropriate for those belonging to the Lord"), which is not incompatible with the idea proposed above.

16. See Ps.-Plutarch, *Education of Children* (*Mor.* 12); and Plutarch, *Advice to Bride and Groom* (*Mor.* 33), quoted in a note in the introduction to this section (cf. Barth and Blanke 1992: 444, 437).

The husband is commanded to exhibit the new-creation trait of love, the supreme virtue rooted in Col. 3:14. Such constant love will increasingly seal the "bond of completeness" (cf. v. 14b) between them and enhance their unity as husband and wife. Notice how the Ephesians parallel says this happens: husbands "love" wives as "their own bodies," indicating the unity of the two in reflection of Christ's unity with believers as a part of his own body (so Eph. 5:28–30). And just as believers are to forgive one another in imitation of Christ's forgiveness of them (so Col. 3:13b), so husbands are to "love wives, just as Christ also loved the church and gave Himself up for her" (Eph. 5:25). In Col. 3:19 husbands are told, "Love your wives," no doubt in imitation of Christ's forgiving love for the church, as in Eph. 5:25. Ironically, just as Christ did, so also the husband expresses his authority through sacrificially giving himself for his wife, especially by considering her needs before his own (5:25–30). The husband's love in imitation of Christ and especially love for his wife as his own body means that the husband will consider the interests of his wife to be his own interests. He will care for her as he cares for himself, since they are, indeed, one unified flesh. The husband's love for his wife "involves his unceasing care and loving service for her entire well-being" (O'Brien 1982: 223). If a husband would not mistreat his own body, so neither must he mistreat his own wife, who is part of his body.

Husbands are also commanded not to "be[come] embittered against" their wives (Col. 3:19b).[17] The cognate word group of πικραίνω (*pikrainō*) occurs in Hellenistic Greek sometimes to refer to exercising authority in some oppressive manner (e.g., Jer. 44:15 LXX [37:15 MT, Eng.]; 3 Macc. 5:18; Josephus, *Ant.* 17.148; *J.W.* 1.494; Philo, *Mos.* 1.172; *Good Pers.* 90; *Emb.* 89).[18] Paul may be saying that husbands should not exercise their authority in the way the world does but should express that authority through first considering the needs of their wives.

Paul now addresses the third category of household members, "children." **3:20**
They are to "be obedient to their parents in all things." The reason for such obedience is "because this is well-pleasing to the Lord." This means that such obedience is not obedience to anything without exception but only to that which "is pleasing in the sphere of [one's relationship with] the Lord."[19] Again, "in

17. The noun cognate with the verb "embitter" is πικρία (*pikria*), carrying nuances of not only emotional "bitterness" but also of being emotively "harsh" or "angry" or expressing "animosity" (BDAG 813, s.v. πικρία), which may be included in the verbal idea here.

18. Here D. Moo (2008: 303) cites an especially relevant passage from Plutarch, *Anger* 8 (*Mor.* 6.457A): "Angry persons declare their littleness and weakness, not only when they rend little children and rage bitterly against women. . . ."

19. Campbell (2012: 164) prefers "in the domain of the Lord." See Pao (2012: 270–71) for possible alternative interpretations of this last clause of verse 20. The word εὐάρεστος (*euarestos*) in the LXX and NT means "pleasing" or "acceptable" to God, except possibly in Titus 2:9 (i.e., that which is pleasing is acceptable, but to whom?) and in Eph. 5:10 ("what is pleasing to the Lord [Jesus]"). The two notions are probably overlapping and are relevant for the usage in Col. 3:20. Sometimes the word takes a following dative, but here it takes the preposition ἐν (*en*), though some MSS replace ἐν (*en*) with the dative τῷ (*tō*), and some commentators and translations prefer

the Lord" (3:20 NASB marg.) is to be understood (as in v. 18) in the light of "doing all things in the name of the Lord Jesus"* in verse 17. This means that children are to act toward their parents in a way that is based on and influenced by Christ's sovereign and authoritative presence in the midst of which they dwell. Thus what "is pleasing in the Lord" focuses more on living (making choices) influenced by one's relationship with the Lord than doing that which is one's duty in the Lord, though there is a fine line between the two, and the latter is likely included.[20] And as with the wife in verse 18, the manner of the children's obedience is to be colored by the traits of the new-creational lifestyle laid out in Col. 3:12–16. The parallel with Eph. 6:2–4 also sheds light on the scope of the "everything" in which children are to obey, since there explicitly the scope of the fathers' authority over children is limited by "the instruction and admonition of the Lord."*[21] In the light of the quotation from Deut. 5:16 (honoring parents and its attendant promise) in Eph. 6:1–2,[22] the father's "instruction and admonition" likely has its OT background in the duties of parents to "teach" the law to their children (Deut. 4:9; 6:7; cf. Pao 2012: 269).

That the children are younger is apparent from the parallel in Eph. 6:4, which instructs fathers to "raise" or "bring up" their children. Furthermore, the younger age of the children is also apparent from observing that they are addressed as those who are still part of the authoritative structure of the family household (and this is true in application to modern households, though the family structures of the first century and of today are not identical). Presumably when children leave the structure of their household to establish a new family structure, they are not under the authority of the former household (cf. Gen. 2:24). Nevertheless, such older children continue to "honor" their parents (cf. Eph. 6:2–3; for similar discussion, see D. Moo 2008: 304).

As in the case of husbands loving wives, so another departure from the ancient household code occurs here with children being responsible parties in choosing to "obey" parents (O'Brien 1982: 224).

3:21 Just as Paul gave the husbands' obligation following that of the wives, so now he gives the fathers' duty after addressing the proper role of children. Some

the rendering "this is pleasing to the Lord" (e.g., Harris 2010: 156; likewise cf. RSV and ESV: "This pleases the Lord"). Dunn (1996: 250) may be correct in rendering 3:20 as "well-pleasing (to God) in the Lord (Jesus Christ)," since we saw that every use of εὐάρεστος in the LXX and NT (with two exceptions) refers to "pleasing God"; MacDonald (2000: 154–55) also prefers this translation. Our following explanation still maintains the basic meaning of "pleasingness."

20. O'Brien (1982: 225) and D. Moo (2008: 305) appear to highlight the latter; e.g., D. Moo says, "The obedience of children is appropriate behavior within the community that acknowledges Christ as their Lord."

21. Philo (*Spec.* 2.234–36) suggests that children should obey only those commands by parents that are "just and beneficial" (see Hay 2000: 145).

22. Dunn (1996: 251) cites Philo, *Names* 40: "If you honor your parents, . . . you are also pleasing [εὐαρεστήσεις, *euarestēseis*] in the sight of God," which also likely has its background in the Deut. 5 passage. Likewise Philo in *Virt.* 208: Jacob was "obedient to both his parents, and was also in the same manner pleasing [εὐάρεστος, *euarestos*], so that he obtained the praises even of God"; also on sons "pleasing" God, see the verbal form in Philo, *Rewards* 24, 167.

view "fathers" here to be representative of "parents" (as in Heb. 11:23; e.g., see BDAG 786, s.v. πατήρ), but probably only "fathers" are in mind, since "parents" have just been mentioned in verse 20, and the change to "fathers" here is likely intentional; in the Greco-Roman and Jewish world, furthermore, fathers were the ultimate authority over the household (as many commentators acknowledge) and are also addressed as the authority in verses 18, 22, and 4:1.

Fathers are not to "embitter" or "provoke" their children. The idea is not "to stir up" a child to be "angry" or to be "contentious," "quarrelsome," or "violent" and thus disobedient.[23] The notion of "provoke to anger" resulting in disobedience may be the focus since the parallel in Eph. 6:4 has παροργίζετε (*parorgizete*, provoke to anger). In fact, παροργίζετε may even be the original reading here, since good and early manuscripts have this reading (see additional notes).

Deuteronomy 21:18–20 LXX may be the background against which to understand Col. 3:21: "If anyone has a disobedient and <u>contentious</u> [ἐρεθιστής, *erethistēs*] son not <u>obeying</u> [ὑπακούων, *hypakouōn*] the voice of his father and . . . mother, and they discipline him and he does not listen to them, . . . they shall say to the elders . . . , 'This son of ours is disobedient and contentious [ἐρεθίζει, *erethizei*], he does not obey [ὑπακούει, *hypakouei*] our voice.'"*[24] Deuteronomy 21:18–20 is the only LXX use of ὑπακούω (*hypakouō*) with ἐρεθίζω (*erethizō*) in the context of the parent-child relationship, and the verbal combination occurs uniquely in Col. 3:20–21. In Deut. 21 the son has already become disobedient and contentious, whereas Paul exhorts children to be "obedient" and fathers not to act in such a way that would "arouse contentiousness" in a child, such as has occurred with the errant child of Deut. 21. The purpose of such a fatherly posture is to prevent the child from "becoming disheartened to the extent of losing motivation"[25] to do that which is "pleasing in the Lord" (Col. 3:20b).

Though not mentioned in Colossians, the fathers here are likely to do what Paul commands fathers to do in Eph. 6:4: "to nourish them in the instruction and admonition of the Lord."* The word "nourish" (ἐκτρέφω, *ektrephō*) in Eph. 6:4 is sometimes used in the LXX of parents or guardians raising their children by "nourishing" them and sustaining them with the necessities of growing up successfully (e.g., see [ἐκ]τρέφω in Esther 4:8; Tob. 14:10; 1 Macc.

23. All these meanings can be found in Hellenistic Greek (either in the NT, LXX, or Josephus); e.g., see BDAG 391, s.v. ἐρεθίζω; Muraoka 2009: 290; Rengstorf 1973–83: 2.203.

24. Philo (*Drunk.* 14, 17) also quotes Deut. 21:18–20 and surmises that "mother and father" in this passage refers to "parents" (γονεύς, *goneus*; so also in Col. 3:20). Philo also says that "to be contentious [ἐρεθίζειν, *erethizein*] and obstinate is a quality which comprehends every extravagance of evil" (*Drunk.* 16).

25. For this definition of ἀθυμέω (*athymeō*), see BDAG 25, s.v. ἀθυμέω. In addition to "disheartened," ranges of meanings of ἀθυμέω (*athymeō*) in the NT are "discouraged, dispirited" (see BDAG 25), "despondent" (in LXX; see Muraoka 2009: 13), and "dejected" (Rengstorf 1973–83: 1.31). Hannah's despondency is a good illustration of being so depressed that motivation to do good or love ceases. Being barren is a "tribulation" for her, which results in her being "disheartened" (ἀθυμέω, *athymeō*): "She wept and would not eat" (1 Sam. 1:6–7).

3:33; 11:39). God "nourishes" his children in the same way (e.g., Gen. 48:15; Deut. 32:18). Fathers are to imitate God by "instructing and admonishing" their children with Christ's word in application of Col. 3:16.[26]

One can see how all the virtues of the new creation listed in 3:12–17 are expressed in the obedience of wives and children, the love of the husband, and the fathers' sensitive upbringing of their children. The actions of verses 18–21 all lead to enhancing a lack of conflict (cf. vv. 12–14, 16), which is fueled by love (v. 15) and continued adherence to Christ's word (v. 17).

3:22 Paul now addresses slaves. Just as the wives and children are to be subject or obedient[27] respectively to husbands and to fathers, so slaves are to be so to their masters. Precisely the same verbal command and the extent of the command to children is given to slaves: "Be obedient in all things" (ὑπακούετε κατὰ πάντα, *hypakouete kata panta*). The slaves' obedience is to be directed toward their earthly masters. The manner of their obedience is not to be merely out of external, legalistic, and begrudging duty: "not in eyeservice as men-pleasers" (cf. ASV). The expressions probably include working hard while the master is looking but slacking off when the master is not present (among others, see Wilson 2005: 283). In contrast, their obedience is to be "with sincerity of heart, fearing the Lord." The phrase "but in wholeness of heart"* is in contrast to the preceding clauses. This means that serving with "eyeservice as men-pleasers" expresses *insincere* service, which is hypocritical (appearing one way on the outside with actions but thinking in another way on the inside). "With sincerity" and "by fearing" express the internal disposition of their obedience.

"Fear" (φοβέω, *phobeō*) expresses having "a great reverence for" due to a "fear of offending" God (BDAG 1061, s.v. φοβέω). Thus both "reverence" and "fear" are combined to one degree or another. This idea is expressed in many uses in the Greek OT.[28] This notion is also evident from Paul's use (Rom. 11:20; 13:3). Especially clear is Eph. 5:33 (NASB marg.), where the wife is commanded to "fear" her husband. Certainly this does not mean to "be afraid of" her husband but to "revere with great respect." Likewise, slaves are to "revere" the Lord, and out of such reverential respect arises their sincere motivation to obey their masters. Accordingly, the adverbial participle "<u>revering</u> the Lord"* connotes not only the inner manner of their obedience but also the cause of it (D. Moo [2008: 311] acknowledges both options). The slave should look beyond the earthly master as the motivation for obedience and look to God for it, as Eph. 6:5 makes explicit: "Obey . . . in reverence and trembling, in sincerity of your heart, <u>as to Christ</u>."* Obeying "as to Christ" should likewise be added or

26. Note in Eph. 6:4 that "instruction and admonishment" are noun forms that are virtually synonymous with the same two verbal forms in Col. 3:16, one of which ("instruction") is cognate with "admonishing" in Col. 3:16.

27. See on 3:20 for the synonymity of ὑποτάσσω (*hypotassō*) and ὑπακούω (*hypakouō*).

28. E.g., Pss. 34:7, 9; 61:5; 67:7; 85:9; 103:13; 111:5; 115:11; 118:4; 128:1; 147:11 (LXX: 33:8, 10; 60:6; 66:8; 84:10; 85:11; 102:13; 110:5; 113:19; 117:4; 127:1; 146:11); Prov. 14:2; 24:21; Eccles. 3:14; 5:7 (5:6 LXX); 7:18; 8:13; 12:13.

is implied in Col. 3:23. However, there is one circumstance in which the slave is to pay careful attention to the earthly master. Slaves are to serve Christian masters with special zest, since they are "brothers" and because those who "benefit by their service are believers and beloved" (1 Tim. 6:2 RSV).

This expression "fearing the Lord" (with φοβέω + κύριος, *phobeō* + *kyrios*) echoes the oft-repeated OT formula "fear the LORD" (so over twenty times in the LXX; e.g., Deut. 6:2, 24; Josh. 24:14; 2 Kings 17:28; Pss. 15:4; 118:4 [LXX: 14:4; 117:4]; Jer. 5:24; Mal. 3:16). In particular, the wording "with sincerity of heart, fearing the Lord" may specifically reflect 1 Sam. 12:24: "fear the LORD . . . with your whole heart"* (so likewise Deut. 10:12). The point of the OT echo is to identify Jesus with Yahweh, "the LORD," of the OT (so Bauckham 2008: 188; following in this paragraph, Pao 2012: 273), an identification that we have seen earlier in Colossians (see, e.g., on 3:17). A very striking verbal parallel occurs in T. Reu. 4.1 (ca. 150 BC; cited by Dunn 1996: 254): "But walk in sincerity of heart, fearing the Lord" (ἀλλὰ πορεύεσθε ἐν ἁπλότητι καρδίας φοβούμενοι τὸν κύριον, *alla poreuesthe en haplotēti kardias phoboumenoi ton kyrion*; cf. Col. 3:22b: ἀλλ' ἐν ἁπλότητι καρδίας φοβούμενοι τὸν κύριον, *all' en haplotēti kardias phoboumenoi ton kyrion*). The preceding wording in T. Reu. 4.1 is an exhortation to "pay no attention . . . to the [outward] beauty of women," much as in Col. 3:22 slaves are not to be ultimately motivated by outwardly pleasing masters. Paul may have been influenced by this passage, though Paul and the writer of the Testaments may merely share the same association of thought based on the repeated "fear of the LORD" texts from the OT.[29] The Testament of Reuben parallel enforces the notion in Col. 3:22 that "in sincerity of heart, fearing the Lord" is part of an exhortation not to live merely by sight but basically by faith in God.

Now Paul clarifies verse 22 by interpreting it for the slaves: "Whatever you do, **3:23**
work from the soul as to the Lord."* "As to the Lord" refers to the manner in which (ὡς, *hōs*; Beale, Brendsel, and Ross 2014: 93–94) they work: in all they do as slaves, they are obeying and working for the Lord and not ultimately for human masters. This is a particular application of 3:17: "Whatever you do in word or deed [work, ἔργον, *ergon*, noun cognate of the verb "to work" in v. 23], do all in the name of the Lord Jesus."

The reason the slaves are to "work for the Lord" even more than for earthly **3:24**
masters is conveyed by the adverbial participle "knowing": "because you know that from the Lord you will receive the reward of the inheritance."* The motivation for "obeying" masters (κυρίοις, *kyriois*, v. 22) is that slaves have a greater "Lord" (κύριος, *kyrios*), and whatever reward they may receive from their masters (whether food, lodging, kind treatment, or any kind of remuneration) pales in comparison to the "repayment" or "recompense" (ἀνταπόδοσις, *antapodosis*) "from the Lord" (see BDAG 87, s.v. ἀνταπόδοσις). "Reward of

29. Or could the Testament of Reuben passage be a later Christian interpolation influenced by Col. 3:22?

the inheritance" is an appositional genitive (so also, e.g., Hugedé 1968: 198), "reward which is the inheritance."

This is not a recompense in response to believers' autonomous efforts, for which they truly deserve payment, since we have already seen in 1:12 that it is God himself who has "qualified" saints "for a share of the inheritance [κλῆρος, *klēros*]." The "inheritance" in 1:12 is an allusion to the "inheritance" of the promised land that Israel was to receive (cf. uses in Numbers, Joshua, and Deuteronomy; see on 1:12). This background of Israel's promised inheritance is enhanced here by an echo in 3:24 to the same thing: the clause "You will receive the reward of the inheritance" (ἀπολήμψεσθε τὴν ἀνταπόδοσιν τῆς κληρονομίας, *apolēmpsesthe tēn antapodosin tēs klēronomias*)[30] is found in canonical OT writings only in Josh. 18:7, where some of Israel's tribes "received their inheritance" as a part of God's promise of the land (ἐλάβοσαν τὴν κληρονομίαν, *elabosan tēn klēronomian*).[31] Likewise, Heb. 11:8 refers to Abraham going to the land "he was to receive for an inheritance" (λαμβάνειν εἰς κληρονομίαν, *lambanein eis klēronomian*), which typologically was expected to come to fruition in the new "city" and the "heavenly" new creation (Heb. 11:10, 16). Likewise, Heb. 9:15 refers to saints "who . . . may receive the promise of the eternal inheritance [τὴν ἐπαγγελίαν λάβωσιν . . . τῆς αἰωνίου κληρονομίας, *tēn epangelian labōsin . . . tēs aiōniou klēronomias*]," referring to the coming inheritance of the new creation. And this eternal inheritance is that to which Col. 3:24 refers. Regardless of whether this is an actual OT echo, it is the language of the OT land inheritance, which was promised to Israel. The household code in Eph. 5–6 also refers to the land inheritance promised to Israel. Ephesians 6:2–3 quotes Exod. 20:12, which is directed also to children: "'Honor your father and mother'—this is the first commandment with a promise: 'so that it may be well with you and you may live long on the earth [land].'" Here living long in the promised land, as in the Exodus passage, is taken as a typological foreshadowing of living long on the eternal new earth.

Thus the OT's promised land inheritance is typologically applied to Christians,[32] as we also saw was the case in Col. 1:12 (see my comments there). Colossians 1:5 affirms that this hoped-for inheritance has been inaugurated in the believers' participation in Christ's resurrection. The promised land in the OT is a foreshadowing of the new creation that has begun in Christ's

30. The future form of the verb λαμβάνω (*lambanō*), without the prepositional prefix, occurs in some very good uncials and some good minuscules (see the first additional note on 3:24).

31. The main difference in wording is that Colossians uses the prefixed form of the verb ἀπολαμβάνω (*apolambanō*) in the future tense (though in the first additional note on 3:24 I explain that the unprefixed form could be original), while Joshua uses the unprefixed form in the aorist tense. In the Apocrypha, the same word combination of the unprefixed verbal form plus "inheritance" occurs with reference to "receiving an inheritance" in the promised land (1 Macc. 2:56; but in Tob. 6:13 the same combination occurs without reference to the promised land). Cf. similar but looser wording in Josephus (*Ant.* 16.66), also not referring to inheritance of the promised land.

32. Several commentators connect the "inheritance" here generally with the promised land (e.g., Moule 1957: 130–31).

resurrection. Colossians 3:24 is referring to the consummation of this inaugurated inheritance, probably referring to believers' full salvation in the form of bodily resurrection in a renewed earth.[33] That the inheritance here refers to the new creation is apparent from observing that there are eight references to "Christ" and nine to Jesus as "Lord" in 3:1–4:1. None of these refer to the earthly Jesus but all to the post-resurrection/ascended Jesus. Colossians 3:1 refers to Christ as "raised" and at God's "right hand" in heaven "above." At that heavenly location, believers' lives are "hidden with Christ in God" (v. 3). Christ presently "is [the] life" of saints; especially their identification with him means they share in his resurrection "life" (3:4a). These passages refer to Christ's present status and believers who are identified with him in the present age. Colossians 3:4, however, points to Christ's final "manifestation," when believers will be "manifested with him in glory." We concluded that this consummative "manifestation" of saints refers to their glorious resurrection (see on 3:4). All the remaining occurrences of "Christ" and "Lord" in Col. 3 refer to his present resurrected status, and Christians are in union with him and thus share his resurrected status.[34] As we will see, 4:1 refers to an "already / not yet" idea of the "Lord in heaven," though the focus is on the "not yet," the time when God will deal out judgments and rewards.

The upshot is that Christians have begun to receive "the inheritance" of resurrection life through the new creation in Christ (so 1:5, 12 and the above-cited verses in 3:1–4:1). This initial stage of resurrection existence will be consummated for eternity at the final coming of Christ. It is this future completed inheritance of resurrection to which Col. 3:24 refers.[35]

Typically slaves did not receive inheritances (a fact that Paul observes and applies to redemptive-historical realities in Rom. 8:15–17 and Gal. 4:7).[36] That Christian slaves are promised the eschatological "inheritance" is yet another indication of how Paul is transforming the traditional Hellenistic household idea; they are truly members of God's eternal household (following Pao 2012: 274–75).

The last sentence, "It is the Lord Christ whom you serve," gives a second reason (in addition to "receiving the inheritance") why slaves should "work for the Lord" even more than for their earthly masters (v. 23). That is, they should submit to masters because Christ is their ultimate Lord, who commands them to submit to human lords (so vv. 22–23). Some scribes also saw

33. See Beale (2011: 750–72) for the idea of Israel's promised land being understood as a typological foreshadowing of the inaugurated and consummated resurrection of Christ and of the final full new creation.

34. Thus their lives are "hidden with Christ" (3:3); they are to conduct their lives "in the Lord" (3:18–19) and live their lives in service to the resurrected "Lord" (3:23–24).

35. Psalms of Solomon 14.3, 10 view the saints to be those who "inherit" and "shall live forever." Cf. 1 En. 40.9, referring to "the hope of those who would inherit eternal life" (following Schweizer 1982: 226).

36. In both texts believers are said to have been spiritual "slaves" but now are spiritual "heirs," which includes the coming physical inheritance of resurrection life.

the causal sense of the phrase and so insert a causal γάρ (*gar*) as an introduction to this last clause (e.g., the majority of MSS but not the earliest and best). "Serving[37] Christ" here is virtually repeating "fearing the Lord" (v. 22), which also functions to give a reason for obeying earthly masters. Both there and here the reason slaves should be motivated to serve their master is that they ultimately serve Christ.

3:25 Slaves have been given two reasons as motivations for "working from the soul, as for the Lord" (v. 23a NASB marg.): "You will receive the reward of the inheritance" (v. 24a) and "It is the Lord Christ whom you serve" (v. 24b). Now in verse 25 yet a third reason is given for slaves to be "working heartily, as for the Lord": "the one doing wrong <u>will receive the consequences of the wrong</u>,[38] and there will be no respect of persons."* This threat of judgment is the antithesis of the promise of the redemptive "inheritance" in verse 24 (Pokorný 1991: 183). If slaves "do wrong," they will be judged for it. And God's judgment is unbiased. God is no respecter of persons (e.g., concerning their earthly positions, their bribes) in the way he carries out his judicial decisions. Slaves who do shoddy work while at the same time trying to put on a good show before the boss will not be exempt from divine punishment (N. Wright 1986: 150). On the other hand, it is implicit throughout admonitions to slaves here that they are not to obey when asked by a master to do something contradictory to their faith (like believing in the pagan god of the unbelieving master). In the immediate context, 3:5 warns believers to consider themselves "dead to immorality" and other similar vices. Certainly this would include Christian slaves, so that they do not need to obey pagan masters who demand sexual favors from them, as sometimes happened in the ancient master-slave relationship (cf. Bird 2009: 117). First Peter 2:18–21 makes this explicit, affirming that even if a slave will "do what is right and suffer for it [and] patiently endure it, this finds favor with God" (following Hendriksen 1964: 177).

There may be a link with Philem. 18, where Paul tells Philemon that if Onesimus "has wronged [ἠδίκησεν, *ēdikēsen*] you in any way, or owes you anything, charge that to my account." Here Paul may want to make clear that, despite his mercy shown to Onesimus, other slaves should not deduce that past or future wrongs against masters will go unpunished or be treated as light

37. In contrast to most translations, several commentators take "serve" here to be an imperative rather than an indicative verb, which is possible; see the second additional note on 3:24.

38. For this rendering of κομίσεται ὃ ἠδίκησεν (*komisetai ho ēdikēsen*), cf. BDAG (20, s.v. ἀδικέω), though this precise translation here follows the NASB. The ὅ (*ho*) functions as a direct object: the wrongdoer "will get back <u>that which</u> he did wrong" (Harris 2010: 161, who cites this option as one possible alternative). This more straightforward translation may point to the notion of lex talionis by which the wrongdoer receives the punishment equal to the gravity of the crime, sometimes actually being punished by the very same means used to commit the crime/sin: e.g., Prov. 26:27, "He who digs a pit will fall into it, and he who rolls a stone, it will come back on him." So similarly several commentators: e.g., O'Brien 1982: 230; Dunn 1996: 258, who cites 2 Pet. 2:13 as a very close parallel: sinners "suffering wrong as the wages of doing wrong" (ἀδικούμενοι μισθὸν ἀδικίας, *adikoumenoi misthon adikias*).

matters.[39] That Onesimus may be in mind could be pointed to by mention of him as one of Paul's coworkers in Col. 4:9.

Thus, a third reason why slaves should be motivated to "work for the Lord" (3:23) is in order to avoid God's final judgment. This is not likely a reference to judgment by earthly masters but by Jesus, since Jesus has been mentioned as the one for whom slaves are ultimately to work (3:22b, 23a, 24b) and from whom they are to receive their end-time inheritance. Furthermore, this is pointed to also by 4:1, where the masters' accountability is to the "Lord in heaven,"* which likely refers to being called to account at an end-time judgment rather than a judgment by earthly authorities.

Some think 3:25 applies only to masters, and some believe both slaves and masters are included. The reason for seeing a reference to both slaves and masters is because of the apparent generalized nature of the verse, which could express a general principle applicable to many people: "the one doing wrong will receive the consequences of the wrong" (so Pao 2012: 276–77). The reason for seeing a reference to masters is that the verb ἀδικέω (*adikeō*), "to do harm," is thought to be more appropriate as a reference to masters wrongfully doing harm to slaves. Accordingly, the thought would be that slaves are being encouraged to persevere in serving Christ in order to "receive the inheritance" (v. 24) because of their knowledge that their unjust masters will be punished at God's final judgment. But slaves just as well are capable of "doing wrong," and the above-proposed apparent link with Philem. 18 points to this. Furthermore, Col. 3:25 is still under the heading of the address to "slaves," and the formal address to "masters" does not begin until 4:1 (generally following O'Brien 1982: 230–31). So, slaves are likely the primary focus in 3:25.[40] However, that an address to masters may be implicitly included could be apparent through the parallel in Eph. 6:9, which applies the expression "there is no partiality with Him" to masters (cf. Hay 2000: 147; and more explicitly Patzia 1990: 95).[41] This may then serve as a natural transition to the address to masters in the next verse.

Colossians 3:22–25 transforms the typical Hellenistic household conceptions: now the male head of the family is not the ultimate head of slaves, but Christ is the ultimate authority over the slave (Pao 2012: 271–72). Indeed, "Lord," referring to Jesus, occurs four times in this brief section, all referring to the slave as directly related to Jesus as their primary "Lord."

Next, masters of slaves are addressed. They are to "grant to [their] slaves jus- **4:1**
tice and fairness." Just as God deals with slaves without partiality, so masters
are to treat their slaves. They are to be "just and fair" toward them. Implicit

39. Among others, see esp. Garland (1998: 250–51), followed by D. Moo (2008: 314–15); others also see a link to Philemon and Onesimus. Lohse 1971: 159 sees no such link.

40. See Barth and Blanke (1994: 449) for a listing of commentators supporting only slaves as being addressed in 3:25, those supporting only masters as being addressed, and those claiming that both are in mind.

41. Appearing to make a similar point is Eph. 6:8: "Whatever good thing each one does, this he will receive back from the Lord, whether slave or free" (following Hendriksen 1964: 175).

is the notion that they are to imitate God in their dealings with their slaves. The notion of being "just" (δίκαιος, *dikaios*) is explained by the following word ἰσότης (*isotēs*), which refers not to absolute social "equality," suggesting emancipation (Harris 2010: 162), but absolutely "equal treatment" of all slaves according to a just standard. Thus being "just" suggests an "even-handed, impartial treatment" and qualifies the "equality" in mind (Lightfoot 1875: 230). No slave should be given preferential treatment over other slaves. This is *equal* treatment within the context of slavery.[42] Equal treatment of free people would, of course, be different, at least to the extent that they would be subject to different laws than slaves. Thus "equality" (within the context of slavery) is a better translation than "fairness" (see the additional note on 4:1).

Sumney (2008: 253) challenges this view by arguing that ἰσότης (*isotēs*) does mean absolute equality and that masters are called to treat slaves as equals in every way, thus "subverting the system that previous verses seem to support." He bases this on two uses of ἰσότης by Philo (*Good Pers.* 79; *Spec.* 2.68), clearly supporting the notion that both the Essenes and Philo himself affirmed an idea of "equality" such that slavery should not exist. But it is unlikely that Paul would contradict himself in the space of a few short verses, supporting subordination of slaves in 3:22 and denying it in 4:1. Since ancient Greek uses of ἰσότης support both the notion of "equity" (or "fairness") within a framework of a subordinate relationship and also an absolute notion of "equality" among human slaves and free people, then it appears that, if Paul is not contradicting himself, he uses the Greek word with the former sense.

This "justice and fairness" extends to all aspects of the master-slave relationship: not mistreating slaves, compensating them justly in some way for their labor (likely such things as money, clothing, or housing). Part of this "justice and fairness" also includes masters recognizing that slaves and masters have equal status before God in Christ and in the church (esp. cf. Col. 3:11; see Sumney 2008: 254).

Paul's demand that masters grant "justice" (δίκαιος) to slaves shows a further departure from the typical household perspective in which with respect to "justice [δίκαιος] between a master and slave, . . . there is no such thing as injustice [ἀδικία, *adikia*] in the absolute sense toward what is one's own and [is] a chattel" (Aristotle, *Nic. Eth.* 5.1134b).[43]

Masters are to treat slaves justly and fairly because they know that they themselves have a Master in heaven who will judge them on the final day. "Lord" here refers to Jesus, as it does throughout chapter 3. Thus the "Master"

42. For this understanding of ἰσότης, see Plato, *Laws* 757, 776–88 (using ἴσος, *isos*, "equal"); cf. Aristotle (*Pol.* 3.1282b), who says that "justice" (δίκαιος) includes "some sort of equality" (ἰσότης) in different contexts. See Dunn (1996: 260), citing in further support other Classical and Hellenistic uses of "justice" (δίκαιος) and "fairness" (ἰσότης; or cognates of the two words); see also Lohse (1971: 162) for further uses of these combined cognates, though it is questionable whether "fairness" alone is the best translation (see the additional note on 4:1).

43. Following Witherington 2007: 195. In this passage Aristotle also applies this concept to children.

(or "Lord") is Jesus who presently "sits at God's right hand" in heaven (3:1), from where he will come on the last day and judge all evil (cf. Pao 2012: 278). That Jesus is "Master" ("Lord") of human masters means that they are also slaves of Christ, which further suggests their equal status to human slaves "in Christ" and in the church (Sumney 2008: 254).

Why is so much material (five verses) dedicated here to slaves and masters? Probably part of the reason for this is that Paul will later mention the slave "Onesimus, our faithful and beloved brother" (4:9), whom Paul is sending with Tychicus, the letter carrier (4:7–9).[44]

Additional Notes

3:18. The word ὑποτάσσω (*hypotassō*) is best translated as "be subject to" or "submit to" everywhere it occurs in the NT, whether of children being subject to parents (Luke 2:51), of demons to Jesus's followers (Luke 10:17–20; 1 Pet. 3:22), of creation to futility (Rom. 8:20), of people to governing authorities (Rom. 13:1, 5; Titus 3:1; 1 Pet. 2:13), of the spirits of prophets to prophets (1 Cor. 14:32), of women to church authorities (or to husbands? 1 Cor. 14:34), of all things to Christ (four times: 1 Cor. 15:27, 28a; Eph. 1:22; Heb. 2:8), of the Son to the Father (1 Cor. 15:28b), of Christians to leading ministers (1 Cor. 16:16), of all Christians to some hierarchal order (Eph. 5:21), of the church to Christ (Eph. 5:24), of wives to husbands (Eph. 5:22; Col. 3:18; Titus 2:5; 1 Pet. 3:1–5), of slaves to masters (Titus 2:9; 1 Pet. 2:18), of Christians to God (Heb. 12:9; James 4:7), and of younger men to elders (1 Pet. 5:5). Except for the above uses referring to forcible subjection (of demons to Jesus's followers, of creation to futility, and of all things to Christ), the majority of these uses refer to voluntary subjection to some degree.

3:19. In light of the Eph. 5:25 parallel, some think that "submitting to one another" (ὑποτασσόμενοι ἀλλήλοις, *hypotassomenoi allēlois*) in 5:21, followed by the particular command for husbands to "love your wives" (Eph. 5:25), means that husbands "will often 'submit' to their needs, desires and wishes (Eph. 5:21)."[45] This view is based on understanding the instruction "Be subject to one another" in Eph. 5:21 in an unqualified way: every Christian is to be submissive to every other Christian. The various relationships that follow in Eph. 5:22–6:9 (husband-wife, parents-children, slaves-masters) are all relationships in which each person is to be submissive to the other. For example, husbands are to be submissive to wives, just as wives are to be subject to their husbands.

The problem with this view is that the combination of ὑποτάσσω (*hypotassō*) plus ἀλλήλων (*allēlōn*) in some contexts can be unqualified or qualified. Unqualified (or fully reciprocal) uses of ἀλλήλων occur in several texts, such as Eph. 4:25: "We are members of one another" (so also John 13:34, 35; 15:12, 17; Rom. 1:12). Qualified uses (not fully reciprocal) also occur, such as Rev. 6:4: "that men would slay one another" does not refer to each person slaying the other at precisely the same time (so also see 1 Cor. 11:33; Gal. 6:2; cf. Luke 2:15; 12:1; 24:32). Therefore, the directly following context of Eph. 5:22–6:9 determines how the reciprocal pronoun is used (following O'Brien 1999: 403–5). It is best to see that the pronoun is not fully reciprocal. That is, wives are to submit to husbands but not husbands to wives; children are to obey parents and not parents also obeying children; slaves are to obey masters but not also masters obeying slaves.

44. So several commentators, among whom is D. Moo 2008: 309.

45. D. Moo (2008: 301), though he slightly qualifies this later by saying with respect to Col. 3:19 that "to love one's wife therefore will often mean to put her interests ahead of the husband's—thus approaching (though not quite the same as) the 'mutual submission' required by Ephesians 5:21." See also Harris (2010: 154), but with no qualification.

The same qualified reciprocal submission is to be seen in Col. 3:18 (though in this passage the reciprocal pronoun is not used as in Eph. 5:21). Wives are to be subject to the authority of husbands but not husbands to wives' authority. However, the husbands have another responsibility to wives, but it is not to be subject to them.

Another reason wives are to be subject to husbands and not also husbands to wives is because of the basic meaning of ὑποτάσσω, which is often used in Hellenistic Greek in the sense of "arranging oneself under." In fact, no uses of ὑποτάσσω in the ancient Greek world have been found that do not convey the notion of being subject to some authority (so Grudem 2006: 117–19). In particular, it often meant submitting to someone in a higher position of authority, such as soldiers to an officer of higher rank. It is a word that, as far as discernible, is never used of someone submitting to an authority and then of the authority submitting to the subordinate (see Grudem 2006: 117–19 and the sources cited there).

Finally, some understand that the command for husbands to love their wives "just as Christ also loved the church" (Eph. 5:25) indicates that they also "submit" to wives. The husbands' submission is based on the purported notion that Christ in loving the church through his sacrifice was submitting himself to the church. However, this is incorrect. It is true that Christ "[took] the form of a bond-servant [slave] . . . and . . . humbled Himself by becoming obedient to the point of death" (Phil. 2:7–8; so also Mark 10:42–45; Rom. 15:8–9). Christ, however, never gave up his authority by sacrificing himself for and serving the church: even in his sacrificial service, he was expressing his divine authority. One might say that such authority was ironically expressed: Christ's defeat in death was in reality his ironic victory over Satan and sin. Christ's death is surely included in Eph. 5:23, "Christ . . . is the head of the church, . . . being the <u>Savior</u> of the body."[46]

Some affirm that the wife's submission is of a different kind from that of the child's and slave's, since ὑποτάσσω, especially in the middle voice, is used for the wife's submission and ὑπακούω (*hypakouō*) is used for the children's and slaves' obedience. Accordingly, the conclusion is sometimes made that the wife is in a less authoritarian relationship with the husband (e.g., D. Moo 2008: 300–301; cf. Pao 2012: 269). However, as we have seen, 1 Peter uses both words for the wife's responsibility (including ὑποτάσσω in the middle) and for the children's and slaves' responsibility. It is unlikely that Paul's view of the wife's obligation is different from Peter's (so also Harris 2010: 155; Talbert 2007: 232).[47] Indeed, Paul himself uses ὑποτάσσω in the middle voice with respect to both wives' "submission" to husbands (Titus 2:5) and slaves "submission" to masters (Titus 2:9). Recall that the wife's submission is voluntary and qualified by "as is fitting in the Lord" (Col. 3:18). Thus, the wife should disobey the husband when the husband expects behavior that is unchristian. But the same qualification is made with respect to children (see Col. 3:20; Eph. 6:1) and slaves (Eph. 6:5–7; Col. 3:22–24), who also yield voluntary obedience in line with what is consistent with Christian behavior.

It is likely that the nature of submission is colored by different dynamics in each of the three relationships, but these dynamics do not operate outside of an authority-submission framework.[48] For example, Eph. 5:25–33 indicates that the husband and wife are unified ("one flesh") in a way that is not the case in the parent-child and master-slave relationship (Eph. 5:28–31). This

46. Sumney (2008: 242–43) sees that the concept of being one in Christ necessitates mutual submission between husband and wife (e.g., in Col. 3:11; see also Gal. 3:28). However, this does not likely abolish the authoritative office of elder, and so it should not abolish the authority of husbands. Also, there are still slaves who must submit to masters (Col. 3:22–23; though Sumney [2008: 253–54] asserts that the "equality" in Col. 4:1 subverts the slavery system, while later qualifying this statement). Furthermore, the notion of "one in Christ" focuses on the equal access to entering the covenant community of salvation only on the basis of faith and not to regulating relationships within the community (see further Hurley [1981: 125–28] with respect to Gal. 3:28).

47. Similarly, Sumney (2008: 241, 244) sees little difference between ὑποτάσσω and ὑπακούω in Col. 3:18 and 3:22.

48. Sumney well reports even various Greco-Roman writers recognizing that household heads should express authority differently with subordinates of different kinds (wives, children, and slaves; e.g., see Aristotle, *Pol.* 1.1–9; and *Nic. Eth.* 5.6).

results in some kind of special caring relationship between husband and wife that is not the case with the other relationships.[49] On the other hand, all three relationships are shaped more broadly by the fact that all Christians are part of the unified body of Christ.[50] And, indeed, that submission does not imply ontological inferiority is apparent from the fact that the husband is to "honor [the wife] as a fellow heir of the grace of life" (1 Pet. 3:7), just as masters are to "grant . . . justice and fairness" to their slaves (Col. 4:1).

3:20. While the wife's submission is expressed by ὑποτάσσω (*hypotassō*) in the middle voice, the children's submission is expressed by ὑπακούω (*hypakouō*) in the active voice. The different lexical choice is likely not significant, since the two verbs share the same semantic domain. This synonymity is apparent from 1 Pet. 3, where ὑποτάσσω is applied to the wife (3:1, 5) and is in direct parallel with "Sarah" who "obeyed" (ὑπακούω, Gen. 18:12 LXX) her husband (1 Pet. 3:6).[51] Likewise the difference in middle and active voice between the command to wives and children is not significant since Paul appears to have a predilection for using the middle voice with ὑποτάσσω when referring to one human's subjection to another,[52] such as wives to husbands (Titus 2:5) and slaves to masters (2:9), and he always uses ὑπακούω in the active voice when referring to the same human relationships (which is also observable, e.g., in the use of the two words in 1 Pet. 3:1–6). This may mean that the middle of ὑποτάσσω functions actively just as the active of ὑπακούω or that the lexeme ὑποτάσσω is merely often more naturally expressed by the second person in the middle voice but still is nearly synonymous[53] with the active of ὑπακούω.[54]

3:20. The neuter-singular demonstrative pronoun τοῦτο (*touto*) that introduces the last phrase of verse 20 does not have its grammatical antecedent in any one word of the preceding phrase but is a "construction from sense," referring to the sense of the whole preceding phrase (cf. Wallace 1996: 334).

3:21. "Provoke to anger" could be the original reading in 3:21, since very good MSS in Col. 3:21 have παροργίζετε (*parorgizete*) instead of ἐρεθίζετε (*erethizete*); so ℵ, A, C, D*, F, G, L, and several good minuscules support this reading, while B and a couple of other good uncials together with several good minuscules support ἐρεθίζετε, and 𝔓[46] apparently also has this reading, though this is not certain. Internal considerations point to ἐρεθίζετε, since it is more likely that a scribe would have harmonized the text with Eph. 6:4 and changed the text to παροργίζετε. There would have been no motivation to change an original παροργίζετε to ἐρεθίζετε. Thus ἐρεθίζετε is likely the original reading.

3:24. The future form of the verb λαμβάνω (*lambanō*), without the prepositional prefix ἀπο-, occurs in some very good uncials (𝔓[46], ℵ[2], A, C[2], K, L, Ψ, 075, 0278) and some good minuscules (81, 104, 365, 630, 1505, 1739, 1881, 2464), whereas the prefixed form is found in several good

49. According to D. Moo (2008: 301), this dynamic suggests that husbands are also to submit to wives.

50. See D. Moo (2008: 301), who appears to think that the "oneness" of all Christians in Christ applies only to husbands and wives and sets "a trajectory that leads to a more equal sharing of all dimensions of the marriage relationship" and that this "oneness" apparently does not apply in the same way to the other two sets of relationships.

51. Interestingly, Gen. 16:2 LXX says Abraham "listened [ὑπήκουσεν, *hypēkousen*, obeyed] to the voice of Sara" to have sexual relations with Hagar, but this was a sinful thing for him to do.

52. This construction also appears in the Gospels: Jesus submitting to his parents, Luke 2:51; demons submitting to the disciples, Luke 10:17, 20.

53. Even here if the middle "expresses more direct participation, specific involvement or some form of benefit of the subject doing the action" (so Porter 1994: 67), this does not differentiate it significantly from the active ὑπακούω.

54. It would be difficult or awkward to have a middle sense of ὑπακούω, which typically has the sense of "obey, follow, hear, listen," or similar senses, though BDAG (1028–29, s.v. ὑπακούω) does give "be subject to" as an alternative sense.

uncials (א*, B, C*vid, D, F, G) and a couple of good minuscules (33, 117). On purely external grounds the unprefixed verb appears to be preferable. On internal grounds, it is hard to know which is the more difficult reading and thus preferable, though the prefixed form might have seemed more difficult in contrast to the simpler verb form. It is difficult to know which is the original.

3:24. As observed earlier, several commentators take "serve" here to be an imperative and not an indicative verb in contrast to most translations, which is possible (Pao 2012: 275–76 elaborates in some depth in favor of this option). But if the end of verse 24 is a ground or cause of the first clause of verse 24 (as many later scribes took it; see below) or preferably a second ground for verse 23, then an imperative would not fit into such a ground clause. Nowhere else in Colossians or Ephesians does a causal clause contain an imperative (e.g., sixteen times outside Col. 3:24 where γάρ [*gar*] occurs, it never introduces a clause with a verb in the imperative mood; see the additional note on 3:24b). Accordingly, if the verb were in the mood of command, the implied causal clause would read awkwardly: "do your work heartily [v. 23a] . . . because [I am commanding] you [to] serve the Lord Christ." On the other hand, if one takes "serve the Lord Christ" as a new train of thought and thus as a command, not directly related to verse 23a or verse 24a as a ground, then the following γάρ clause in verse 25 would give the reason for the command rather than offering a third reason for "working from the soul as for the Lord" in verse 23a. The combination of δουλεύω (*douleuō*) with τῷ κυρίῳ (*tō kyriō*) occurs elsewhere in Paul; e.g., the close parallel in Eph. 6:7 ("with goodwill serving, as to the Lord"*) supports an imperatival use, as does Rom. 12:11, since both are in an imperatival context. On the other hand, the same combination in Acts 20:19 (describing Paul in Ephesus) and in Rom. 16:18 are clearly indicative uses. See Harris (2010: 160–61), who presents arguments for both sides of the debate. Campbell (2013: 66) slightly prefers the indicative reading in Col. 3:24b "due to the emphasis in the context on the fact that slaves are servants of Christ rather than men." Whether the verb is indicative or imperative, the main point remains essentially the same: slaves work ultimately for Christ rather than merely for their earthly masters (cf. likewise Sumney 2008: 251).

3:24b. Several scribes add γάρ (*gar*) in verse 24b to make explicit that the clause is a ground clause, which means that these scribes likely understood the verb to be an indicative.

4:1. In the comments I argue that "equality" (within the context of the relationship of slaves to one another) is the best translation of ἰσότης (*isotēs*). Vassar (2017) supports the "equality" translation, but he understands the context of this translation differently. He convincingly argues that the usual texts appealed to for a meaning of "fairness" in the extant Greek literature are better understood as referring to "equality," so that a translation of these texts as "fairness" is not best. He appeals to Seneca's *Epistle* 47, where Seneca argues that slaves should be treated by all as true equals yet without suggesting the abolition of slavery (as inconsistent as a modern reader might think this is). Vassar argues that Paul is doing the same thing in Col. 4:1.

H. The New-Creational Lifestyle Should Lead to Prayer for the Effective Spread of the Gospel (4:2–6)

Here is a fuller statement of the main idea of this unit: *The new-creational lifestyle of love, unity, peace, and Christocentric focus (3:12–17), which especially is to be lived out in the family and workplace (3:18–4:1), is to lead to prayer for the effective spread of the gospel and to witness about Christ to unbelievers.*

As we have seen, the new-creational life portrayed in 3:12–16 (love, unity, peace, adherence to Christ's word) and summarized in verse 17 (doing everything in Christ's name) is particularized by showing how it is to be lived out in everyday life, in particular, in the family and workplace (3:18–4:1).

The family, the main social unit of society, is the place where Paul believes new-creational reconciliation and peace should be exhibited by those who have become part of this new creation. Colossians 4:2–6 now shows how such an exhibition of new-creational living and reconciliation "in word or deed" (3:17) outside of the household and church family will serve as a witness to the unbelieving world; as we will see, there is likewise a link between "thanksgiving" in 3:17 and 4:2 (so also D. Moo 2008: 318; O'Brien 1982: 234). Most commentators agree that the paragraph represents the formal end of the body of the letter.

The paragraph breaks down into two segments, the first about devotion to prayer (vv. 2–4) and the second about walking wisely toward outsiders (vv. 5–6). Some commentators sum up the two segments as "speaking to God about people" and "speaking to people about God" (R. Lucas 1980: 171; E. Martin 1993: 196–97). These two segments are further discerned by (1) observing that imperatives introduce both ("Devote yourselves to prayer," v. 2a; and "Walk wisely,"* v. 5a; following Garland: 1998: 271); (2) the first segment is dominated by the subject of Paul's evangelism and the second by the Colossian believers' evangelism; (3) at the end of each section (v. 4 and v. 6) is a declaration composed of the phrase "how it is necessary for"; (4) in both sections the "word" (λόγος, *logos*) plays a significant part.[1] Verse 2 is an exhortation to pray in general. Verses 2–3 begin to specify some of the things the Colossian believers are to pray about. In particular, they are to pray that Paul will have an effective gospel witness toward unbelievers. The logical climax of verses 2–4 is on the final clause of verse 4 ("that I should make it manifest how it is necessary for me to speak"*). Verses 5–6 switch

1. These last two observations have been made by Barth and Blanke 1994: 451.

from prayer to exhortation and change the focus of evangelism from Paul to the Colossian saints. The main logical emphasis shifts from verses 2–4 to verses 5–6, since the latter elaborates further on the subject of evangelism introduced in verses 3–4.

They are to make the most of every opportunity for witness when out in the pagan world (v. 5). They are to do this through being sensitive to each encounter they have with a view to effectively communicating the gospel (v. 6). Thus verse 6 supports verse 5 as the main point of this second section and of all of verses 2–6.

Exegesis and Exposition

[2]Devote yourselves to prayer, keeping alert in it with an attitude of thanksgiving; [3]praying at the same time for us as well, that God may open up to us a door for the word, so that we may speak forth the mystery of Christ, for which I have also been imprisoned; [4][in order] that I may make it clear in the way I ought to speak. [5]Conduct yourselves with wisdom toward outsiders, making the most of the opportunity. [6]Let your speech always be with grace, seasoned, as [it were], with salt, so that you [may] know how you should respond to each person.

4:2 Paul begins the conclusion of the letter's body as he began the introductory thanksgiving. In 1:3 he "gives thanks to God, . . . praying always for you." There Paul is praying at the time of his thanksgiving, and the thanksgiving is actually also a part of his prayer. As in Paul's other epistolary openings (Phil. 1:3–4; 1 Thess. 1:2; Philem. 4), his continual thanksgiving emerges because he is remembering in prayer how the believers have experienced the grace of God (Col. 1:6, "You understood the grace of God in truth"). And in 1:9 Paul elaborates on the content of his constant prayer, "We do not cease praying on your behalf and requesting . . ."*

Likewise, in 4:2 Paul commands the audience to "devote yourselves to prayer, [while being] alert[2] in it with an attitude of thanksgiving." To "devote to" ("persevering in," NJB; "continue steadfastly," ESV) has to do with continually praying, since it corresponds to "<u>always</u> praying for you,"* which opens the introductory thanksgiving in 1:3. The correspondence between the expressions of prayer in 1:3, 9 at the beginning of the letter and 4:2–3 toward the end emphasizes the importance of unceasing prayer in relation to people being converted to Christ. The first prayer focuses on the Colossians coming to faith (1:4–7) through Paul's coworker, Epaphras (1:7), and the last prayer focuses on the Colossians being exhorted to petition that others come to faith through Paul's preaching.

2. Γρηγοροῦντες (*grēgorountes*) is an adverbial participle of time, though manner and means are possible; an imperatival sense carries over because the participle modifies a verb in the imperative mood, but it is not a truly independent imperative (contra Lohse 1971: 164; Furter 1987: 197), since such participial imperatives are unusual and have no verb in the context that they could modify, so they stand independently (cf. Wallace 1996: 650, 759).

The "alertness" likely does not refer to being watchful in expectation of Jesus's final coming, as many commentators contend.[3] Even though twelve of twenty-two occurrences of γρηγορέω (*grēgoreō*) refer to "watchfulness" for Christ's last coming, only two of these are in Paul (1 Thess. 5:6, 10). Rather, the combination of "watching and praying" recalls Jesus's exhortation to his disciples in the garden of Gethsemane (Matt. 26:41//Mark 14:38; so Caird 1976: 210; Garland 1998: 271). This is supported by observing that the combination of γρηγορέω and προσεύχομαι (*proseuchomai*) in all of the LXX and NT occurs only here in Colossians and in Matt. 26:41 and Mark 14:38. In fact, even the Matthew-Mark order of "watching" and "praying" is followed in Col. 4:2–3a. The exhortations in the two Gospel narratives are to prevent the "temptation" of "falling away" and "denying" Jesus (Matt. 26:31–45). In this light, the exhortations in Colossians may be to encourage the listeners not to fall to the temptations of the pseudo-attractive teaching of the false teachers, who have their own version of what the "mystery" is. This connotation of "watch" is found also in Acts 20:31 as an exhortation to be on guard against false teachers (cf. 20:29–30; likewise the word occurs in 1 Pet. 5:8, referring to the devil's wiles; so Barth and Blanke 1994: 452).

The parallel of Eph. 6:18 is in line with this: "With all prayer and petition pray at all times in the Spirit, and with this in view, be on the alert with all perseverance and petition [concerning] all the saints." The "alertness" in the Ephesians passage (a different Greek word than in Col. 4:2, yet a synonym) is not focused on the Lord's final return but on the issues "concerning all the saints." So in Col. 4:2, the believers are to be "alert" about what issues for which their Christian brothers and sisters need prayer. Verse 3 confirms this: there Paul says the Colossians are to be "praying at the same time [concerning] us," which implies that they are to pray for themselves in verse 3. As in 1:3, "thanksgiving" will arise continually as the readers reflect on aspects of their prayer, which has begun to be answered.

The conclusion on the lifestyle of new-creational living in 3:17 ("Whatever you do in word or deed, do all in the name of the Lord Jesus, giving thanks"), which has launched the household code of 3:18–4:1, is picked up again here with repetition of "thanksgiving." This points further to the close link between 3:5–4:1 and 4:2–6.

Following the above pattern in 1:3 and 1:9, here 4:3 again elaborates further **4:3**
about the details of the prayer that Paul has in mind for the Colossians. The prayer in verse 2, which has focused on the Colossian believers' own lives, now shifts to concentrate on Paul and his companions: "praying[4] at

3. Contra, e.g., O'Brien 1982: 237–38; Dunn 1996: 262; D. Moo 2008: 320–21; Pao 2012: 291.

4. The adverbial participle προσευχόμενοι (*proseuchomenoi*) is probably pleonastic (on which cf. Wallace 1996: 649–50, 759), reiterating the same meaning as "persevere in prayer"* in verse 2; yet, as with the adverbial participle in verse 2, an imperatival sense carries over because the participle modifies a verb in the imperative mood; but again, it is not a truly independent imperative, since such participial imperatives are unusual and have no verb in the context that they can modify (cf. Wallace 1996: 650, 759). The participle is broadly and temporally contemporaneous

the same time concerning us." The content of the prayer is "that [ἵνα, *hina*][5] God may open to us a door for the word to speak the mystery of Christ." "That God should open to us a door for the word" refers to God giving Paul not merely an opportunity but also success in evangelism, as supported by the meaning of the open-door image applied to Paul's ministry in Acts 14:27, as well as 1 Cor. 16:9; 2 Cor. 2:12. Likewise Rev. 3:8–9 uses the same picture to indicate the identical notion: "Behold, I have put before you an open door which no one can shut . . . Behold, I will cause those of the synagogue of Satan . . . [to] come and bow down at your feet, and make them know that I have loved you."[6] All of these passages refer to God making effective in the hearts of people the message of the gospel that is preached. Acts 14:27 makes especially clear what the other passages have in mind: "they began to report all things that God had done with them [Paul and his colleagues] and how He had opened a door of faith to the Gentiles." For God to "open a door for the word" is to pave the way for the word to have effect, so that one may have faith in that word (cf. likewise N. Wright 1986: 152). This entails that the opening of a door for Paul is for him to have opportunities *effectively* to communicate the word[7] (cf. Thompson 2005: 99), as the parallel in Eph. 6:18–20 shows.[8] This active role of God's word (the word portrayed as going through an open door) in relation to evangelism develops further 1:5–6, "the word of truth, . . . which has come to you, just as in all the world also it is constantly bearing fruit and increasing."[9] As a significant parallel to Col. 4:3, the active role of God's word is also highlighted in 2 Tim. 2:8–9: Paul speaks of "my gospel, for which I suffer hardship even to imprisonment as a criminal; but the word of God is not imprisoned" (cf. Garland 1998: 272–73).

The specific "word" that Paul wanted an open door for was "to speak forth the mystery of Christ." The infinitive λαλῆσαι (*lalēsai*) is an infinitive giving the purpose or desired result of the "opening of the door" (Brooks and Winbery 1979: 129): "praying . . . that God will open . . . so that we may speak forth the mystery of Christ."[10] This develops 1:25–26 (as many commentators contend), where both "word," representing Paul's apostolic message, and "mystery" occur together: "that I might fully carry out the preaching of the

with the main verb of verse 2, which is made clear by the directly following syntagmatic link with "at the same time."

5. In support of this being a ἵνα of content, see Pao (2012: 292), who notes the parallel with 1:9, where ἵνα also functions to introduce the content of the prayer there and not the purpose; contra Campbell (2013: 68), who takes the ἵνα in Col. 4:3 to indicate purpose.

6. See Beale (1999a: 285–89) for the idea that this refers to evangelism leading to belief.

7. See the first additional note on 4:3 for discussion of the genitive "a door of the word."

8. "Pray on my behalf, that utterance may be given to me in the opening of my mouth, to make known with boldness the mystery of the gospel" (Eph. 6:19).

9. Pao (2012: 292) mentions the same active role of the word growing and spreading in Acts 6:7; 12:24; 19:20; also D. Moo 2008: 322. O'Brien (1982: 239) compares Col. 3:3 to 2 Thess. 3:1, where Paul says, "Pray for us that the word of the Lord may run and be honored"* (cf. NASB marg.).

10. If this is an infinitive of result, it would be "intended result" (Dana and Mantey 1957: 215).

word of God, that is the mystery which has been hidden from the past ages and generations, but has now been manifested to His saints." The "now" in 1:26 is an eschatological "now," underscoring that the "mystery" has been revealed in the latter days. The "revelation of the mystery" in Dan. 2 also focused on end-time events. The "mystery" in Col. 1:26 is then defined as the "mystery among the Gentiles, which is Christ in you, the hope of glory" (1:27). We saw that "Christ in you" underscores that the mystery of Christ has included the Gentiles, whereas they had been excluded from Israel where God's promissory revelation was experienced in the OT epoch. Though during this earlier period they were "separate from Christ" and "having no hope" (Eph. 2:12), now Christ "is in" them and they possess "the hope of glory, . . . which is Christ" (Col. 1:27). This revealed "mystery" among the Gentiles means that they can now become members of authentic end-time Israel without holding to the nationalistic badges of old Israel. Christ has become the only badge for membership that they need (for fuller explanation, see on 1:25–27 and Beale and Gladd 2014: 159–74). The "mystery among the Gentiles, which is Christ in you" (1:27) and "God's mystery, which is Christ" (2:2) are shortened in 4:3 to "the mystery of Christ."[11] The genitive "mystery of Christ" could be a genitive of reference ("the mystery with respect to Christ") or more probably is an appositional genitive ("mystery, which is Christ").[12] The appositional genitive is likely, since we have already had "God's mystery of Christ" in 2:2, where "of Christ" is also an appositional genitive ("God's mystery, which is Christ"), and 1:27 is conceptually the same: "the glory of this mystery among the Gentiles, which is Christ in you, the hope of glory." "Christ is the center of Christian commitment" (MacDonald 2000: 171). Christ is the centerpiece of the mystery, since he is the key to Gentiles and Jews becoming one people in himself.

Thus, in 4:3 Paul also has in mind this Gentile notion of the "mystery," which is further apparent through observing that both in 4:4 (the continuation of v. 3) and in 1:26–27 the verb "make manifest" (φανερόω, *phaneroō*) occurs, its use in 1:26–27 about revealing the "mystery" (among others, see Lincoln 2000: 662; Pao 2012: 294). Accordingly, Paul is asking the Colossians to pray that God would open up more doors to speak forth and reveal this "mystery" to more Gentiles in order that they may believe in Christ, become identified with Christ, and become part of true eschatological Israel. By inviting them to pray in this manner, Paul is urging them to participate with him in the spread of the end-time mission of declaring the eschatological mystery (Pao 2012: 292).

The apostle adds that "speaking forth the mystery of Christ" is that for which "I have been bound" (δέδεμαι, *dedemai*). This could refer to Paul's apostolic call to the Gentiles, which he must obey in carrying out. However, the

11. See on 1:26–27 and 2:3–4 for elaboration of the above discussion of the "mystery."

12. Following Robertson 1931: 509; so also Gupta (2013a: 187) recognizes the possibility of a genitive of reference.

only use of δέω (*deō*) in this sense is in Acts 20:22, where the verb δεδεμένος (*dedemenos*, "bound in the Spirit") is in parallel with "bonds [δεσμός, *desmos*] and afflictions await me [Paul]" in 20:23. The expression here refers to Paul being imprisoned because of preaching the gospel, since this use of the word occurs sometimes in the Gospels, is the typical meaning in Acts, and can be found elsewhere in Paul.[13] That Paul's imprisonment because of speaking forth the gospel is in mind in Col. 4:3 becomes clearer in 4:18, where Paul says, "Remember my imprisonment" (or "bonds," pl. of δεσμός, *desmos*). This also becomes clear from the parallel with Eph. 6:18–20:

> With all prayer and petition pray at all times in the Spirit, and with this in view, be on the alert with all perseverance and petition for all the saints [cf. Col. 4:2], and pray on my behalf, that utterance may be given to me in the opening of my mouth, to make known with boldness the mystery of the gospel, for which I am an ambassador in chains; that in proclaiming it I may speak boldly, as I ought to speak [cf. Col. 4:4].[14]

It is *possible* that being "bound in the Spirit" is implied, as in Acts 20:22, but neither in Eph. 6:18–20 nor in the Colossians context is the Spirit mentioned in this respect. However, Eph. 6:20 does refer to Paul as "an ambassador in chains," which may allude to his apostolic calling to the Gentiles, though the Colossians parallel omits the word "ambassador."

This reference to being "imprisoned" is probably linked to the initial statement about Paul's suffering in 1:24, since it introduces the first references to mystery (1:25–27). Paul's imprisonment for preaching the mystery is an instance of suffering mentioned in 1:24 (Pao 2012: 293).

It is possible to take the phrase "for [or because of] which I have also been imprisoned" in 4:3 not as parenthetical but as introducing 4:4: "because of which [the mystery] I have been imprisoned in order that I may make it manifest how it is necessary for me to speak." Thus verse 4 would follow directly from the last phrase of verse 3 and not from "to speak the mystery of Christ." Since Paul has mentioned his suffering in direct connection to his commission to preach the mystery in 1:24–27, it makes sense that he would do the same here. Accordingly, Paul's imprisonment is not a hindrance to the gospel but part of the instrumentation by which Paul is able to spread the gospel in fulfilling his

13. So nine times in Acts and once in 2 Tim. 2:9 (three times in Paul it refers to a wife or husband bound to their mate). Many translations of Col. 4:3b render the verb δέδεμαι (*dedemai*) as "I have been imprisoned" or "I am in chains" or other similar renderings.

14. Cf. also Phil. 1:7, 13, 14, 17; 2 Tim. 2:9, where Paul also uses the δέω/δεσμός word group for his imprisonment; though these references may refer to several imprisonments, they could mean the same imprisonment as that mentioned in Colossians. Nevertheless, Paul says he experienced a number of "imprisonments" (2 Cor. 11:23). See also δέσμιος (*desmios*) in Paul referring to himself as a "prisoner of [in] the Lord" (Eph. 4:1; Philem. 1, 9; likewise 2 Tim. 1:8); it is unclear whether these are references to Paul's actual imprisonment or to his being a "prisoner of the Lord" in the sense of being "bound to the Lord," just as he says elsewhere that believers are "slaves of Christ" (Eph. 6:6).

apostolic commission.[15] Philippians 1:12–20 is a good example of this (e.g., "my circumstances [imprisonment] have turned out for the greater progress of the gospel"; cf. Bruce 1984: 173).[16]

Paul has asked the Colossians to "pray for <u>us</u> in order that God would open to <u>us</u> a door for the word," but at the end of verse 3 he has made personal mention of himself, and the continued request for prayer in verse 4 narrows its focus to Paul. This does not mean that the "us" in verse 3a is merely figurative for Paul as an epistolary plural. Rather, Paul goes from considering himself together with those in his apostolic circle (e.g., those coworkers mentioned in 1:1 and 4:7–15, 17) to only himself.[17]

This verse could give further explanation of the purpose of the Colossians' prayer that "God opening a door" for Paul and his colleagues is "to speak forth the mystery of Christ" (v. 3c; so Campbell 2013: 68). If so, it should be rendered, "<u>in order that</u> I may make it clear in the way I ought to speak [about the mystery of Christ]" (v. 4). A purpose clause would be supported by the preceding phrase "for which I have been bound" (v. 3d), if it is not parenthetical but actually introductory to verse 4 (as we saw above in the discussion of v. 3): "for which I have been bound in order to make manifest how it is necessary that I should speak" (vv. 3d–4). The ἵνα (*hina*), however, more likely indicates not the purpose but another part of the content ("that") of the prayer (so Pao 2012: 294). This is apparent because it is in parallel with the ἵνα of content in verse 3 (Pao 2012: 294). Such a construal is also supported by the same parallelism in Eph. 6:19–20: "Pray on my behalf, <u>that</u> [ἵνα] a word may be given to me in the opening of my mouth, to make known with boldness the mystery of the gospel [cf. Col. 4:3], for which I am an ambassador in chains; that in proclaiming [the mystery] that [ἵνα] <u>I may speak boldly, as I ought to speak</u> [cf. Col. 4:4]."* Since the newly revealed "mystery" about Christ was, indeed, a "mystery" in the OT, Paul wants to make sure that he is clear in explaining what was formerly not clear. Nothing is more important for Paul than to be clear about the new revelation of the gospel in order that people can come to faith in Christ. **4:4**

The ὡς (*hōs*) could indicate the manner or the reason for "making manifest" the mystery. Most translations take it as indicating the manner in which Paul is

15. Bockmuehl 1988; Barth and Blanke 1994: 454; MacDonald 2000: 170; Wilson 2005: 292; cf. Peake (1970: 544), who sees this as a possibility. Bockmuehl (1988), in particular, argues that δι' ὅ (*di' ho*) in 4:3 should be read as διό (*dio*), to be seen as introducing a new sentence, then completed in verse 4. He paraphrases verses 3–4 thus: "And pray that God may open for us an opportunity for proclamation, so that we may speak forth the mystery of Christ. For it is to this end that I have been imprisoned, in order that I might manifest it, as indeed I am obliged to do."

16. Likewise Bockmuehl (1988: 492) adduces Eph. 3:1, "I, Paul, the prisoner of Christ Jesus for the sake of you Gentiles"; Philem. 9 and 13, "a prisoner of Christ Jesus, . . . in my imprisonment for the gospel"; Acts 28:20, "I am wearing this chain for the sake of the hope of Israel"; and 2 Tim. 2:9, "for which [my gospel] I suffer hardship, . . . but the word of God is not imprisoned."

17. So O'Brien (1982: 328) and D. Moo (2008: 321–22), who notes that elsewhere Paul requests prayers on behalf of "us," which includes Paul and at least one of Paul's associates (cf. 1 Thess. 5:25 with 1:1, and 2 Thess. 3:1 with 1:1).

to speak: "that I may make it clear in the way I ought to speak" (NASB). The idea of manner is supported by the possible following parallel in verse 6: "so that you may know how you should [πῶς δεῖ ὑμᾶς, *pōs dei hymas*] respond to each person." It is perhaps preferable, however, that ὡς gives the reason for his speaking, which the following discussion may support ("that I may make it known publically since I am obliged to declare it").[18]

The use of δεῖ could indicate here an apocalyptic or prophetic "predestined destiny and unavoidable compulsion" (as Dunn [1996: 264] contends and as found abundantly elsewhere in the NT). We have already seen that the "mystery" in 4:3 is the same as that mentioned in 1:26–27. In 1:25–26 Paul positions himself as having a significant role in that "mystery": "I became a servant according to the administration of God, which was given to me for you, to fulfill [carry out] the [prophesied] word of God, the mystery hidden from the past ages and generations but now has been manifested."* The apostle views himself as a special agent serving God's act of "manifesting" his "mystery."[19] Indeed, the phrase "how [because] I ought to speak" appears to be a recasting of the earlier expression, "according to the administration from God given to me to fulfill the word of God"* (1:25). Paul continues to make clear the mystery, which has been initially revealed.[20]

On the other hand, some see that the prophetically "necessary" nuance is not the focus; rather, it was an ethical "necessity" (δεῖ) that Paul make clear the message: "how [or because] it is necessary for me to speak" (or "how it is right for me to speak"; cf. O'Brien 1982: 240; Garland 1998: 273). The ethically obligatory sense of δεῖ is apparent from observing that δεῖ again occurs in 4:6, where it appears to be applied to the Colossian believers' correct manner of speech: "that you may know how it is necessary for you to respond to each person."*

Paul elsewhere uses δεῖ with the sense of something necessitated by God's predestined plan (three times)[21] and something that refers to the "oughtness" of ethical behavior (at least sixteen times).[22] As apparent, Paul uses δεῖ much more with an ethically imperatival sense compared with the predestined-plan nuance. But he uses the latter enough that one must determine each of his uses on a case-by-case contextual basis. While the uses in Col. 4:4 and its parallel in Eph. 6:20 are not clear, either of the two senses is viable in the Colossians and Ephesians passages. The contextual connection with the mystery and Paul's commission to announce the foreordained mystery in Col. 1 tips the scales toward Paul continuing that thought in Col. 4:3–4.

18. Callow 2002: 153, emphasis added; yet he acknowledges the viability of the ὡς (*hōs*) as indicating manner.

19. Titus 1:3 expresses the same view of Paul's role.

20. See Pao (2012: 294–95) for this discussion of the prophetically "necessary" sense of δεῖ (*dei*) in Col. 4:4 and the links with 1:25–26 in relation to Paul's apostolic commission.

21. As in 1 Cor. 11:19; 15:53; 2 Cor. 5:10.

22. Rom. 8:26; 12:3; 1 Cor. 8:2; 2 Cor. 2:3; 11:30; 12:1; Col. 4:6 (?); 1 Thess. 4:1; 2 Thess. 3:7; 1 Tim. 3:2, 7, 15; 5:13; 2 Tim. 2:6, 24; Titus 1:7, 11; cf. Rom. 1:27.

Thus Paul sees himself as a necessary instrument in spreading the revelation of that ordained mystery. But could the ethical notion of δεῖ still be entailed with this meaning? Since Paul sees himself as part of the fulfillment of God's plan to reveal the mystery (which is explicit in 1:25: "to fulfill the word of God"*), he likely also sees that he *must be obedient* to his apostolic call, which is part of that plan (so likewise Moule 1957: 133). Paul expresses the tension elsewhere between being prophetically called and then accountable to follow the call in 1 Cor. 9:16: "For if I preach the gospel, I have nothing to boast of, for I am under compulsion; for woe is me if I do not preach the gospel" (see further 1 Cor. 9:16–27; likewise Acts 9:15–16; Rom. 1:14–15).[23] The conclusion of the parallel in Eph. 6:19–20 supports this same tension: "Pray on my behalf, that utterance may be given to me in the opening of my mouth, to make known with boldness the mystery of the gospel, for which I am an ambassador in chains; that in proclaiming I may speak boldly, as [it is necessary (δεῖ) for me] to speak."

Thus Paul's *prophetic call* entails upon him an *ethical responsibility*, both of which are the basis for his proclaiming the mystery.

Now Paul continues the same topic of Christian witness by going into more detail about it. However, he takes the focus off his evangelistic responsibil- **4:5**
ity and addresses the Colossians about their own responsibility to witness to unbelievers. The content of this witness is likely aligned with Paul's: to "speak forth the mystery of Christ" (4:3). In view of this eschatological mission of witness, the hearers "are to walk about in wisdom toward outsiders."* "Outsiders" (τοὺς ἔξω, *tous exō*) probably does not refer to the false teachers, who were considered to be part of the church community (though likely pseudo-Christians) and had influence within the community, but to the general unbelieving populace outside the church community in Colossae.[24] The word "wisdom" (σοφία, *sophia*) has been used five times earlier in Colossians, four of which are positive and one negative.

The lone negative use of "wisdom" is in 2:23, which focuses on the false teachers' twisted and superficial "wisdom." This is a narrow and parochial "wisdom," teaching that all believers, including Gentiles, must be subject to the OT laws, especially the nationalistic expressions of those laws. It is false wisdom because Paul has declared that Christ has fulfilled those laws (2:17), so they are no longer valid.

The first positive use of "wisdom" refers mainly to Gentile Christians being "filled with the knowledge of His [God's] will in all spiritual wisdom" (1:9). A second time it refers to Paul "teaching every man with all wisdom," where the phrase "every man" is repeated three times, underscoring that Gentiles are

23. In Rom. 1:14–15 Paul expresses the tension that, on one hand, he is "under obligation both to Greeks and to barbarians" as a divine necessity (esp. in light of 1:5), and on the other hand, he is ethically motivated and "eager to preach the gospel to [those] also who are in Rome."

24. Paul uses the very same Greek phrase for "outsiders" elsewhere always to refer to unbelievers outside the covenant community: 1 Cor. 5:12, 13; 1 Thess. 4:12; following D. Moo 2008: 326.

being addressed (1:28), which develops the "mystery" in 1:26–27 that "Christ is in Gentiles." The word is used in 2:3 to refer to a possession of Christ: in Christ "are hidden all the treasures of <u>wisdom</u> and knowledge." The phrase in Col. 2:3 is a further elaboration of the directly preceding wording in 2:2, "God's mystery, that is, Christ Himself." "Mystery" in 2:2 is a further development of the Christ-Gentile-focused "mystery" in 1:26–27. Both 1:28 and 2:2–3 refer to the revelation of God's "mystery," which manifests God's and Christ's wisdom. A fourth positive occurrence of "wisdom" appears in 3:16b, which repeats part of 1:28: "Let the word of Christ richly dwell within you, with all <u>wisdom</u> teaching and admonishing one another." The references to "all wisdom" in 1:28 and 2:3 directly associate the two phrases with the revelation of God's mystery in Christ's salvation of Gentiles as demonstrating divine "wisdom." The same references to "all wisdom" in 1:9 and 3:16 are indirectly linked to 1:28 and 2:3 and thus also are probably linked to the same idea of the revealed mystery.

Thus the fifth positive use of "wisdom" in 4:5, though lacking the adjective "all," likely also is to be associated with this Christ-Gentile-oriented use of "wisdom," especially because of the links to the mystery in 4:3–4. The "wisdom" of 4:5 is to be expressed through the act of witnessing to the gospel. To "walk in a wise manner" is to "conduct" oneself in such a way as to be conducive to sharing the gospel. The coming of Christ has broken through the former boundary markers of old Israel, and now God's revelation in Christ has shone out into the Gentile world. Paul has this specifically in mind with the "wisdom" in 4:5. It should be recalled that the use of "wisdom" in 1:9–10 is likely related to the thought here, since there the hearers being "filled with . . . all wisdom and spiritual understanding" has its goal in them "walking worthy of the Lord . . . <u>in every good work</u>, . . . <u>bearing fruit</u> . . . <u>and increasing</u> in the knowledge of God." The same phrase "bearing fruit and increasing" in 1:6 is an allusion to Gen. 1:28 (as it is in v. 10), where it refers to the spread of the gospel "in all the world, just as also among you"* (1:6). Such an evangelistic-growth notion is probably not out of mind in 1:10, where the focus is on "bearing fruit . . . and increasing in the knowledge of God," though this is directly related to "walking . . . in every good work," which, in light of the rest of the epistle, must include good works of witness.[25] Thus the "wisdom" of 1:9–10 is associated partly with the task of witness, which is also the point of 4:5.[26]

The notion of this revealed "wisdom" going to Gentiles through witnessing is expressed in the phrase "walk in wisdom toward the ones outside." The phrase "the ones outside" refers to those who are not members of the covenant community, who are predominantly Gentile, though a small group of unbelieving Jews would not be excluded.

The concluding phrase "buying up the time" (cf. NASB marg.) expresses the manner of how the believers are to "walk about in wisdom toward the

25. Indeed, it is very possible that "bearing fruit" syntactically completes the preceding clause, so that it would read "in every good work bearing fruit" (as NA^{28} so punctuates).

26. D. Moo (2008: 327) sees the "wisdom" of 4:5 picking up the concern of "wisdom" in 1:9.

ones outside" (ἐξαγοραζόμενοι, *exagorazomenoi*, an adverbial ptcp. of manner, though means is possible).[27] The etymological meaning of the verb could be translated as "buy [or redeem] out of," and it is used in this way in Gal. 3:13 and 4:4–5: Christ's death bought believers out from the captivity to sin. Some have tried to apply this meaning to Col. 4:5 and Eph. 5:16: believers are to buy time out from under its captivity to Satan and sin. But this is unlikely, since the immediate contexts do not suggest such a meaning. Rather, the prepositional prefix ἐκ- (*ek-*) is probably to be understood intensively ("buy up eagerly"), as is the meaning in the parallel use of the phrase in Dan. 2:8 LXX (for the discussion and this conclusion, see D. Moo 2008: 327–28).[28] "Buy up the time" is a metaphor that can express the idea of "making the most of the opportunity." They are to make the most of every opportunity that they have for witness (the same phrase in Eph. 5:16 similarly should be rendered as "making the most of your time"). The partial verbal parallel in Eph. 5:15–16 is significant. There the phrase is "be careful how you walk, not as unwise men but as wise, buying up the time." This parallel confirms that Col. 4:5 is about witness, since Eph. 5:15–16 is clearly set in a context of witness: "Now you are Light in the Lord; walk as children of Light" (Eph. 5:8). "Expose . . . the unfruitful deeds of darkness" (5:11). "All things become visible when they are exposed by the light" (5:13).

Many commentators see this as "making the most of the *eschatological* time," since the immediately preceding context (4:4–5) is about the preaching of the end-time mystery (Pao 2012: 296), and the end is drawing near. The Eph. 5:16 parallel also supports the end-time nuance of the phrase, since the preceding context is about the believers being new-creation light in the midst of an old-world darkness (Eph. 5:8–13), which climaxes as Paul identifies them with fulfilling the resurrection prophecy of Isa. 26:19 and the new-creational light prophecy of Isa. 60:1 (Eph. 5:14), which leads right into and is the basis for Eph. 5:15–16. In addition, the reason given for "making the most of the time" in Eph. 5:16 is "because the days are evil," which refers to the inaugurated end-time tribulation (see the additional note on Col. 4:5). Many commentators note that the word "time" here has an eschatological flavor. The observation that Paul uses "time" (καιρός, *kairos*, as in 5:16) for the most part to refer to the beginning of the end time[29] enhances the notion that "time" here also has an "already / not yet" eschatological tone.

27. It may also be a participle of time ("while buying up the time"), purpose ("in order to buy up the time"), or result ("resulting in buying up the time"), as suggested by Foster 2016: 406.

28. The intensive use in Colossians is observed by several commentators; e.g., on this word, see F. Büchsel (*TDNT* 1:128): "a buying which exhausts the possibilities available"; Rienecker 1980: 238. The middle voice is likely an indirect middle and expresses the subjects acting in relation to themselves, probably for their own interest (cf. Wallace 1996: 419–21), the sense of which Robertson (1934: 810) renders as "buying the opportunity for yourselves out of the open market."

29. Rom. 3:26; 5:6; 8:18; 11:5; 13:11; 1 Cor. 7:29 (cf. 7:29–31); 2 Cor. 6:2; Eph. 1:10; 5:16; 1 Tim. 4:1; 2 Tim. 3:1; 4:3; Titus 1:3. Also, 1 Cor. 4:5 and 1 Thess. 5:1 refer to the time of the consummate judgment, Gal. 6:9 to the consummate period of final reward.

The phrase "buying up the time" (τὸν καιρὸν ἐξαγοραζόμενοι, *ton kairon exagorazomenoi*) in Col. 4:5 is not merely a parallel to Dan. 2:8 but also an allusion: "You buy up the time" (καιρὸν ὑμεῖς ἐξαγοράζετε, *kairon hymeis exagorazete*). In all of the LXX and NT, this Greek expression occurs only three times; Dan. 2:8 and Col. 4:5 are two of those occurrences. The other is in Eph. 5:16, which is also an allusion to Dan. 2:8 (e.g., see the margin of NA^{28}).[30] One might well doubt that Dan. 2 and its use of ἐξαγοράζω (*exagorazō*) is in mind in Colossians, since the contexts seem different.[31] In Colossians the phrase refers to believers making the most of every opportunity in order to witness effectively to others. On the other hand, Dan. 2:8 is about the Babylonian king's demand that his magicians tell him his dream and its interpretation, with the threat of death if they cannot do so. They know they cannot reveal the king's dream and its true interpretation, so they try to delay their fate for as long as they can. The king then accuses the magicians of trying to "buy up time" to prevent their assured death. They are making the most of every opportunity in order to avoid execution.

Though the uses in Daniel and Colossians have differences, there are several overlapping notions: (1) There is the common expression "buying up the time." (2) Both also deal in context with the obligation to reveal truth to someone else. The magicians are trying to avoid letting the king know that they are unqualified to reveal the truth and are unethically trying to conceal this, and the Colossians are qualified and have an ethical obligation to reveal the truth. Thus the common element in both uses of the expression "buying up the time" is about "making the most of the opportunity." (3) The subject in the context of the expression in Dan. 2, as in Colossians, is the revelation of eschatological truth (OG: Dan. 2:28–29; 2:45) to a Gentile concerning salvation and judgment (Dan. 2:44–45), which further suggests the eschatological notion of the Colossians expression. (4) Such revelation requires "wisdom" to make known the truth, which is repeatedly called a "mystery." Daniel is the opposite of the magicians: he goes to the king and requests "that he would give him time, in order that he might declare the interpretation to the king" (Dan. 2:16). And indeed, Daniel is given "wisdom" from God and is able to reveal the "mystery" of the dream to him. All of this is familiar, since we have seen already that the use of a revealed "mystery" together with "wisdom" in 1:26–27 and 2:2–3 (see above) is traceable to Dan. 2:19–22, 28–30. In this light, Paul uses the phrase "buying up the time" from Dan. 2:8 with the positive example of Daniel the prophet in mind, who asks for time to discover the king's dream so that he can reveal the truth to him. The Colossians are not to buy time the way the magicians did but in the way the prophet Daniel did in order to witness effectively to the surrounding Gentile culture. They are to

30. The verb can be translated "buy out of" (i.e., "redeem") in Gal. 3:13 and 4:4–5, but the verb can just as well be rendered "buy up," as the contexts of Ephesians, Colossians, and Daniel show is best.

31. As Moule (1957: 133) and F. Büchsel (*TDNT* 1:128), among others, contend.

"allow no opportunity to slip through their hands, but buy up every passing moment" (Lightfoot 1875: 230).

Paul gives further details about the manner in which the Colossians are to **4:6**
conduct their witness toward unbelievers. Alternatively, verse 6 could be the means by which they are to "buy up the time" (v. 5). The most straightforward rendering of the beginning of verse 6 is "Your word always with grace," where there is no verb but some implied verb must be supplied. The beginning of verse 6 appears to be parallel with verse 5, which starts with the imperative "walk." If so, the best implied verb to insert at the beginning of verse 6 is the third-person singular imperative of the verb "to be" (εἰμί, *eimi*; so Buttmann 1873: 137): "<u>Let</u> your word always <u>be</u> with grace."[32] "Word" here likely refers to the general conversation ("speech," NASB) of believers with unbelievers and not specifically the gospel message, the latter of which is its meaning in 1:5 and in 4:3, though it would not exclude speaking about the gospel. The "word" in verse 6 probably develops 3:17: "Whatever you do in <u>word</u> or in deed, do all in the name of the Lord Jesus." Part of the audience to whom these Christians are to express their "word" are those living outside the church community, and this "word" is to be communicated to these unbelievers "in the name of the Lord Jesus."

The manner in which the Colossians' word is to be communicated "with graciousness," referring to the attractiveness of their speech,[33] or the translation could be "with grace" (so NASB, KJV) or "full of grace" (NIV), referring to God's grace being conveyed through their conversation (see Wallace 1996: 161–62, on the use of ἐν, *en*, with the dative as indicating manner). Such a manner of speaking must be a continual trait ("always"). The notion of "with grace" rather than with attractiveness of speech may be best, since Paul never uses χάρις (*charis*) to mean "graciousness" of speech but only to refer to God's grace. If so, Paul is directing that there always be a beneficent, grace-giving intention in all of their conversations with unbelievers (see BDAG 1079–80, s.v. χάρις 2–3).[34]

On the other hand, the word can mean "graciousness, attractiveness, charm, [or] winsomeness" in the contemporary Greek world, including Hellenistic Judaism (BDAG 1079, s.v. χάρις 1). That the gracious manner of the Christians' speech is in mind is suggested by the syntagmatic combination of λόγος (*logos*), χάρις (*charis*), and ἅλας (*halas*, salt) in Hellenistic Greek to refer to some aspect of human speech (usually only two of the three words occur in combination; see the additional note on 4:6).

The remaining two clauses of verse 6 point to the idea that the graciousness of human speech is, indeed, in mind.

32. This is also supported from noticing the analogy with 3:16: "<u>Let</u> the word of Christ richly <u>dwell</u> within you," where the third-person singular imperative of "dwell" appears with the "word of Christ" as the subject.

33. Accordingly, many translations have "gracious": e.g., NRSV, ESV, NET, HCSB, NLT.

34. This nuance is mostly used when God is the subject intending to dispense grace, though sometimes humans work together with God as agents in this (on which, e.g., see 2 Cor. 6:1). However, humans, such as emperors, could be said to dispense grace.

The phrase "seasoned as it were with salt" is an adverbial participial clause modifying the implied verb "let be," further explaining the manner in which the word is to go forth. Foods were "seasoned with salt" in the ancient world in order to preserve them or often to improve their taste. Jesus applied the image of seasoning with salt to the disciples' witness to the world (cf. Matt. 5:13 with 5:14–16; cf. also Mark 9:50; Luke 14:34). Paul uses the image in the same way here. Just as food seasoned with salt has a good tasteful effect, so should the Colossians' word of witness be attractive to unbelievers' spiritual appetites. Since "seasoned with salt" is in direct syntactical relation to ἐν χάριτι (*en chariti*), it likely further explains what ἐν χάριτι (*en chariti*) means. This points to ἐν χάριτι to be referring to the graciousness or attractiveness of the Colossians' speech and not God's grace (many commentators reach this conclusion).

Paul gives a similar exhortation to believers in relation to one another in Eph. 4:29: "Let no rotten word proceed from your mouth, but only such a word as is good for edification according to the need of the moment, so that it [may] give grace to those who hear" (NASB marg.). The Ephesians parallel can support the idea that God's grace is in mind in Col. 4:6, since most versions translate the crucial phrase ἵνα δῷ χάριν τοῖς ἀκούουσιν (*hina dō charin tois akouousin*) in Eph. 4:29 as "that it may/will give grace to those who hear" (NASB, ESV, NET; almost identically, HCSB, RSV; likewise KJV, NRSV). Some translations, however, render the phrase as referring to something other than God's grace: NIV, "that it may benefit those who listen"; NLT, "so that your words will be an encouragement to those who hear them"; NJB, "Do good to your listeners." We lean toward this latter translational option of χάρις (*charis*) in Eph. 4:29, referring to the idea of a "benefit" for believers. The Ephesians parallel may indicate that Paul here in Col. 4:6 may also have in mind the metaphorical notion of salt being a preservative against corruption of food: words seasoned with salt will not corrupt or rot but will build up and benefit others (see Hendriksen 1964: 183).

The goal of speaking with grace and attractiveness is "in order that" the Christians "should know how to respond to each person." The verb usually means "answer," though here "respond" is best, since the context is that of witnessing in which there would be a back-and-forth dialogue (cf. BDAG 113, s.v. ἀποκρίνομαι).[35] This is quite similar to 1 Pet. 3:15: "Sanctify Christ as Lord in your hearts, always being ready to make a defense to everyone who asks you to give an account for the hope that is in you, yet with gentleness and reverence [respect]." Verse 6 is parallel to Paul's prayer that he may know "how it is necessary for me to speak"* forth the gospel to people (v. 4). Implicitly, Paul would see his exhortation to the Colossians in verses 5–6 to be also applicable

35. A good example of this is Stephen's speech, where the persecuting Jews "were unable to withstand the wisdom and the Spirit with which he was speaking" (Acts 6:10), in apparent fulfillment of Luke 21:15: "I [Jesus] will give you a mouth and wisdom which none of your opponents will be able to resist or refute" (NASB marg.); see Bruce 1984: 174–75. A striking parallel is found in m. Avot 2.14: "R. Eleazar says, 'Be constant in learning of Torah and know what to reply to an Epicurean [an unbeliever]'" (cited by Dunn 1996: 267).

to himself, so that these two verses amplify the details of the subject of witness introduced in verses 3–4 and thus form the main logical climax of this paragraph. The use of δεῖ (*dei*) again carries over from 4:4 the foreordained sense that, like Paul, the Colossians participate in proclaiming the prophesied mystery that has begun fulfillment. But here the ethical sense appears to be prominent in the light of the concluding purpose of verse 6: "in order that you should know how [πῶς, *pōs*] it is necessary for you to respond to each person."* Thus the ethical manner of the speech rather than its prophetic nature may receive greater emphasis.

Verses 5–6 find parallel with 1 Cor. 10:31–33: "Whatever you eat, then, or drink, and whatever else you do, do it all for the glory of God [cf. Col. 3:17]. Never be a cause of offence, either to Jews or to Greeks or to the church of God, just as I try to accommodate everybody in everything, not looking for my own advantage, but for the advantage of everybody else, so that they may be saved."*[36] The Colossians were to be "a church not on the defensive against powerful forces organized against it, but expected to hold its own in the social setting of market place, baths, and meal table and to win attention by the attractiveness of its life and speech" (Dunn 1996: 267). Through commencing the paragraph with exhortations to pray (vv. 2–4), Paul may be suggesting that conversation with God should come before and guide speaking with those outside the church community (vv. 5–6; Hay 2000: 154).

Additional Notes

4:3. Here the genitive θύραν τοῦ λόγου (*thyran tou logou*) is best taken as a genitive of direction or destination: "that God should open to us a door <u>where the word enters</u>" (BDF §166); even the dative "to us" here is probably a dative of destination (to paraphrase, "a door we can enter and the word through us can enter"). This genitive of destination fits well with the other use of the "opening door" image in Acts 14:27 (God "opened a door <u>where faith entered</u> to the Gentiles"*)[37] and works conceptually for the other "opened door" uses even though they do not contain a genitive (1 Cor. 16:9, "For a wide door has opened <u>to me</u> [dative of destination = where I could enter] for effective service"; 2 Cor. 2:12, "A door opened <u>to me</u> [dative of destination = where I could enter] in the sphere of the Lord's sovereignty."* Possibly Col. 4:3 and Acts 14:27 are a genitive of advantage, indicating that the door is opened for Paul's benefit ("a door for the word"; Brooks and Winbery 1979: 17). Could the genitive in 4:3 indicate both destination and advantage? Also in Col. 4:3 and the other relevant passages, the dative "to me [us]" can easily be seen as a dative of advantage. Campbell (2013: 68) views the genitive to be a genitive of reference ("a door/opportunity with respect to the word/message"), though this is probably too general.

4:5. The parallel of Eph. 5:16 to "making the most of [the] time" is further seen to have eschatological tones because of the reason for the imperative: "because the days are evil," which refers to the beginning end-time tribulation of apostasy and false teaching that was expected in the OT,

36. Similarly see 1 Thess. 4:11, 12; 1 Tim. 6:1; Titus 2:8, following in part O'Brien (1982: 241), though he applies this only to Col. 4:5. Likewise see 1 Pet. 2:1–2 (cited by Talbert 2007: 235).

37. MHT 3:212 also favors these translations of the genitive in Col. 4:3 and Acts 14:27 but refers to them either as genitives of destination or as subjective genitives (i.e., with respect to the latter, the "word" and "faith" respectively are doing the action of "entering").

early Judaism, and early Christianity: cf. Dan. 7–12; Matt. 24:4, 22, 29, 37; Mark 13:5, 9, 19–20, 23–24, 33; Luke 21:20, 22; Gal. 1:4–9; 1 Tim. 4:1–3; 2 Tim. 3:1–9; 1 John 2:18; 4:1–3. For the similar Jewish notion, see, e.g., T. Iss. 6.1; T. Zeb. 9.5; T. Jud. 18.1; T. Dan 5.4; 2 Esd. (4 Ezra) 4:51–5:13; 7:72–73; Sib. Or. 2.161–70; 2 Bar. 41.1–5; note references in 1QpHab in Qumran on false teachers in Jerusalem (note also the Apostolic Fathers, including, e.g., Barn. 2.1; 4.9; 8.6). Note further mention of false teachers in Eph. 4:14 and 5:6, as well as 6:10–13, where "evil day" is used in connection with 4:14 (cf. "schemes of the devil" of 6:11) and in the context of 6:10–17, which alludes to OT prophecies about the final conflict with ungodly powers and the divine victory over them. All of this enhances the eschatological tones for the phrase "make the most of the time" in Col. 4:5.

4:6. The ancient world (as does the modern world) regarded as one of salt's benefits its use as a seasoning to make food more tasteful. Commentators cite some of the most important of these parallels with Col. 4:5, but there is little discussion of these uses even when some of the references are quoted (e.g., see Abbott 1897: 298; Lightfoot 1875: 232; O'Brien 1982: 243; Lohse 1971: 168; Wolter 1993: 212). Plutarch in *Table Talk* (*Mor.* 669) says, "Nor is salt a seasoning only for food; it also seasons drinks. . . . Moderately salty foods, on account of their pleasant taste, bring out the sweetness and smoothness of any kind of wine, and also make any water agreeable and tonic. . . . Salt [ἅλας, *halas*] contributes at once the savour [χάρις, *charis*] of a relish" (LCL). Again, Plutarch in *Table Talk* (*Mor.* 685) says, "Salt . . . is delicious as a seasoning and condiment to other seasoning; some even call it joys [*charites*], because it makes needful food enjoyable" (LCL). These two texts are significant for Col. 4:6, since in the first Plutarch says "salt" (ἅλας) leads directly to the attractive taste (savor, χάρις) of food, and in the second passage he equates "salt" (ἅλας) with "joys [*charites*, pl. of χάρις]." Both texts closely associate "salt" and "attractive taste" (χάρις), which, especially in the last Plutarch text, supports the idea that "seasoned with salt" is appositional to χάρις in Col. 4:6.[38] Thus Paul was applying metaphorically to Christian speech what appears to be a common view of salt as a seasoning in order to underscore that such speech is to be attractive to the hearer.

In *Training for Public Speaking* (*Or.* 18.13) Dio Chrysostom explicitly applies the food metaphor to the attractive taste of speech: "I shall now turn to the Socratics, writers who, I affirm, are quite indispensable to every man who aspires to become a man of words [λόγος, *logos*]. For just as no meat without salt [ἅλας] will be gratifying to the taste, so no branch of literature, as it seems to me, could possibly be pleasing to the ear if it lacked the Socratic grace [χάρις]."[39]

Plutarch himself applies the same metaphor as Paul. In *Platonic Questions* (*Mor.* 1010.3), he says that the "elegant" use of verbs and attractive use of nouns (1010.2) "make a contribution to it [speech] just as salt does to a dish of food" (LCL). Similarly, in *Talk.* 23 (*Mor.* 514F): "When men talk, it is either for their own sake, because they need something, or to benefit their hearers, or they seek to *ingratiate* [χάρις] themselves with each other *by seasoning with the salt* [ἅλας] *of conversation* [*words*, pl. of λόγος] the pastime or business in which they happen to be engaged" (LCL, emphasis added). Here in Dio Chrysostom and Plutarch we have the combination of the same three Greek words found in Col. 4:6: λόγος, χάρις, and ἅλας. The last phrase in the Plutarch reference beginning with "by seasoning with salt" is a little ambiguous, but the expression appears to refer to the use of conversation ("words") as a seasoning to make their occupations more enjoyable.

Finally, Cicero (*Orat.* 159) says similarly about the nature of oratory that "we have to cull, from all the forms of pleasantry, a certain charm of humour, with which to give a sprinkle of salt, as it were, to all of our discourse" (LCL).

38. Job 6:6 LXX similarly says, "Shall bread be eaten without salt? And is there taste in empty words?" (NETS). Symmachus renders the first phrase as "Neither shall unseasoned food be eaten without having salt." Here cf. Eccles. 10:12a LXX, "The words of a wise man's mouth are gracious" (λόγοι στόματος σοφοῦ χάρις, *logoi stomatos sophou charis*), with Col. 4:5–6, where the same Greek terms for "word," "wise," and "gracious" occur (cf. similarly Ps. 45:2 [44:3 LXX]; Sir. 21:16; on these references, see Lightfoot 1875: 232).

39. As far as I know, Wolter (1993: 212) is the only commentator who mentions this Dio Chrysostom reference.

IV. Letter Closing: Paul Emphasizes His Pastoral Concern for the Colossians (4:7–18)

Here is a fuller statement of the main idea of this unit: *Paul emphasizes his sincere pastoral concern for the Colossians by reminding them that not only he but also his coworkers have pastoral concern for them and they should show the same concern to others.*

Paul progresses on to the formal conclusion of his epistle. He gives information about and greetings from his coworkers to the Colossian church (4:7–14). He asks the Colossians to give greetings to believers in Laodicea (v. 15), tells the Colossians to have his letters read in the Laodicean and Colossian churches (v. 16), instructs Archippus through the Colossians to persevere in the ministry (v. 17), and gives his own final greetings to the Colossian church (v. 18).

Though it is difficult to know precisely the way the conclusion should be divided up, it appears that four broad sections are discernible: (1) Paul's sending of Tychicus and Onesimus to inform the Colossians of Paul's situation in imprisonment (vv. 7–9); (2) greetings from Paul's other coworkers (vv. 10–14); (3) the Colossians' greetings and responsibility (vv. 15–17); (4) Paul's personal greeting to the Colossians and appeal that they remember his imprisonment (v. 18).[1] Paul's care for the hearers is especially evident by observing that he begins the epistolary conclusion by informing them about the circumstances of his imprisonment (vv. 7–9; cf. v. 10) and at the very end asking them to "remember [his] imprisonment" (v. 18). Calling to their mind his circumstances of suffering reveals that, despite his imprisonment and suffering, his concern for them remains ever constant. Paul's book-ending this section with calls to be aware of his imprisonment shows that the entire section expresses in one way or another his concern for the Colossians, regardless of his own circumstances. In the section, he shows his concern by sending people to encourage them (vv. 7–10), sending greetings from people they know (vv. 10–14), asking them to greet others (v. 15), telling them to exchange Paul's letters with Laodicea and to read the Laodicean letter (v. 16), encouraging them to exhort Archippus to persevere in his ministry (v. 17), greeting them himself,[2] reminding them of the authority of

1. NA[28] divides the segment up into these four divisions, apparently based especially on the personal greeting introducing each of the last three sections. Pao (2012: 305), O'Brien (1982: 246), and N. Wright (1986: 154), among others, recognize the same fourfold division.

2. The greetings they are to give and the exhortation to Archippus show Paul's confidence in their own loving care for others, encouraging them and showing Paul's concern that they themselves develop in their Christian character.

his letter and of the situation of his imprisonment, and commending them to God's grace (v. 18). This pastoral concern is to have the ultimate goal of "encouraging their hearts" (cf. v. 8),[3] which is supported by everything in verses 7–18 and thus is the main point of the entire section (see below at 4:8 on how his imprisonment encourages them, since it is on "behalf" of them that he suffers; see 1:24).

Thus the conclusion shows Paul's great pastoral concern for the Colossian believers (vv. 7–9, 16, 18), even by employing his coworkers for their benefit. And the apostle wants them to know that his fellow workers also have much concern for them (vv. 10–14). Accordingly, the rhetorical role of the epistolary conclusion is to ingratiate Paul to the listeners and assure them that he has their best interests at heart. Earlier in the letter, he has done this in part (cf. 1:3–12, 24, 29; 2:1–2), but now he wants to highlight his sincere pastoral concern for them. The rhetorical purpose of emphasizing it is to motivate the readers so that they want to listen sympathetically to what Paul has said throughout the letter and to move toward the beliefs and actions about which he has exhorted them.

As discussed in the introduction, some scholars regard Colossians as a pseudepigraphical epistle. If this is the case, then one must understand the personal instructions and comments by Paul in verses 7–18 to be fictional, unless Paul wrote the section earlier, before his death, and it was inserted here. But even then, this conclusion would have been intended to make it look as though Paul had written the entire letter, which would still result in a fiction. Together with these personal details in verses 7–17,[4] in the final verse Paul signs the letter with his own unique signature (v. 18), which enhances the Pauline authenticity of this letter. But if all of this were a literary technique to give the pseudepigraphical author an aura of Pauline authority, would not the readers have known this, which would nullify such an intent? (D. Moo 2008: 333). Or if they did not know that the letter was pseudepigraphical, then one cannot avoid the conclusion that the pseudepigraphical writer (whether a disciple of Paul or not) intended to deceive the readers, even if the deception was designed as a means to achieve a good pastoral and theological end.[5] MacDonald (2000: 184) has argued that verses 7–18 function to enhance the authority of some anonymous pseudepigraphical writer. But how could a pseudonymous epistle strengthen the authority of an unknown figure?[6]

3. I have subsequently found that Hay (2000: 157) comes very close to this conclusion, but he does not say precisely what is to encourage them about Paul's imprisonment, which we think is his pastoral concern for them despite his being in prison.

4. A good example of such details is Paul's personal and urgent request that the Colossians are to convey to Archippus in verse 17; following Witherington 2007: 2001.

5. Cf. similarly D. Moo 2008: 332–34. See further the introduction for the arguments for and against Colossians being a pseudepigraphical epistle.

6. So see Witherington (2007: 201–2) for this critique of MacDonald and other arguments against the idea that Col. 4:7–18 has marks of inauthenticity.

Exegesis and Exposition

[7]As to all my affairs, Tychicus, our beloved brother and faithful servant and fellow bond-servant in the Lord, will bring you information. [8]For I have sent him to you for this very purpose, that ⸢you may know about our circumstances⸣ and that he may encourage your hearts; [9]and with him Onesimus, our faithful and beloved brother, who is one of your number. They will inform you about the whole situation here. [10]Aristarchus, my fellow prisoner, sends you his greetings; and also Barnabas's cousin Mark (about whom you received instructions: if he comes to you, welcome him); [11]and also Jesus who is called Justus; these are the only fellow workers for the kingdom of God who are from the circumcision; and they have proved to be an encouragement to me. [12]Epaphras, who is one of your number, a bondslave of ⸢Jesus Christ⸣, sends you his greetings, always laboring earnestly for you in his prayers, that you may stand perfect and ⸢fully assured⸣ in all the will of God. [13]For I testify for him [bear him witness] that he has a deep concern for you and for those who are in Laodicea and Hierapolis. [14]Luke, the beloved physician, sends you his greetings, and also Demas. [15]Greet the brethren who are in Laodicea and also ⸢Nympha⸣ and the church that is in ⸢her⸣ house. [16][And] when this letter is read among you, have it also read in the church of the Laodiceans; and you, for your part read my letter that is coming from Laodicea. [17]And say to Archippus, "Take heed to the ministry which you have received in the Lord, that you may fulfill it."

[18]I, Paul, write this greeting with my own hand. Remember my imprisonment. Grace be with ⸢you⸣.

A. Paul Wants the Colossians to Know about His Imprisonment, Which Is for Their Benefit and the Progress of the Gospel, in Order to Encourage Them (4:7–9)

In this first section Paul begins the formal conclusion of the epistle by highlight- 4:7
ing that he expresses his pastoral concern for them through his coworkers (vv. 7–9). He first tells them that "Tychicus will make known to you all the things with respect to me."*[7] Paul's circumstances that were to be made known had to do with his situation of imprisonment, as apparent from 4:3, 10, and 18. Tychicus was Paul's "beloved and faithful servant and bond-servant," who traveled with him at various points (Acts 20:4; Eph. 6:21; 2 Tim. 4:12; Titus 3:12). They were bound together because of their work "in the Lord," a phrase expressing that Tychicus (and Paul and his colleagues) are genuine believers (an expression used in the same way elsewhere by Paul).[8] "Fellow bondservant" can also be rendered "fellow slave," which the hearers can identify in some way with the extended section on slavery (3:22–4:1), and the same is true with Paul

7. The phrase κατ' ἐμέ (*kat' eme*) is best rendered "with respect to me" (see BDAG 514, s.v. κατά 6) or "the things concerning me" (cf. MHT 2:15).

8. See Rom. 16:8, 11; 1 Cor. 4:17; 7:39; Eph. 6:21; Phil. 1:14; Philem. 16; see Campbell 2012: 174–75, 371.

calling Epaphras a "bondslave of Christ" (cf. 1:7; 4:12). Perhaps the point of the link is that Tychicus and Epaphras, together with Paul, are slaves of Christ in the same way that slaves are obedient to their masters (so Pao 2012: 312). Could it not also show that, while there is "no distinction between . . . slave and free" in Christ (3:11), all Christians (represented by the leaders in 4:7, 12) are slaves of Christ? That Paul's imprisonment is in mind is apparent from the unique parallel with Eph. 6:21, where Paul's imprisonment is mentioned and where the phrase τὰ κατ' ἐμέ . . . πάντα γνωρίσει (*ta kat' eme . . . panta gnōrisei*) is exactly parallel with the wording of Col. 4:7: τὰ κατ' ἐμὲ πάντα γνωρίσει.

The "circumstances" referred to in Eph. 6:21 refer back to 6:20, where Paul has just said, "I am an ambassador in chains."[9] Virtually the same parallel wording is found in Phil. 1:12 (though omitting "all" and substituting another word for "know"), where also Paul's imprisonment is clearly in mind: "Now I want you to know [γινώσκειν, *ginōskein*] brothers, that my circumstances [τὰ κατ' ἐμέ] have turned out for the greater purpose of the gospel" (cf. Phil. 1:13–17 for the clear references to imprisonment).[10]

4:8 In verse 7, Paul has said that he sent[11] Tychicus "to make known" his circumstances. Now he repeats this for emphasis by saying he "sent" Tychicus "for this very purpose in order that you should know our circumstances."[*12] The "our" likely includes Timothy (1:1) and possibly Epaphras (1:7; 4:12), as well as Tychicus, who represents the ministry team (Pao 2012: 310). Such knowledge about Paul will "encourage your hearts." Why will it encourage their hearts to know about the circumstances of Paul's imprisonment? To answer this we must rehearse some earlier thoughts in the epistle. In 1:24 Paul speaks of his own "sufferings for the sake of" the Colossians in particular and more broadly "for the sake of Christ's body, which is the church." These sufferings are then clarified in 4:3, where Paul says that his "speaking forth the mystery of Christ" is the reason why "he has been imprisoned."

Recall that it is viable to translate the end of verse 3 not as parenthetical but as introducing verse 4: "because of which [the mystery] I have been imprisoned in order that I may make it manifest how it is necessary for me to speak"; or "for it is to this end that I have been imprisoned, in order that I might manifest it, as indeed I am obliged to do." Either way, the imprisonment

9. The verbal parallel is further strengthened through observing that Eph. 6:22 is exactly parallel in wording with Col. 4:8.

10. Lohse (1971: 170) observes that the phrase τὰ κατ' ἐμέ and its close variants is a typical expression in the Greco-Roman and Jewish world to refer to a person's circumstances (citing also close verbal parallels in Acts 24:22; 25:14).

11. Commentators generally recognize this as a classic example of an epistolary aorist, where words for "write" or "send" in the aorist are used by the author in self-consciously describing a letter from the temporal standpoint of the audience (Wallace 1996: 562–63). The translation "I am sending" in verse 8 is preferable to "I have sent," since it better represents the time perspective of the audience (so D. Moo 2008: 335; likewise Dana and Mantey 1957: 198; Brooks and Winbery 1979: 102).

12. Thus the phrase "this very purpose" refers backward and forward.

is seen, not only as a part of his suffering on behalf of the Colossians (cf. 1:24), but also as a means through which Paul furthers his preaching of the gospel. If this is the correct way to understand verses 3b–4, then it highlights even more clearly than the alternative translation that Paul's imprisonment, far from being a detriment to the spread of the gospel, is a springboard for it. In fact, it appears that his suffering on behalf of the Colossians (cf. 1:24) includes sufferings in imprisonment, which ironically has furthered the progress of the gospel among the Colossians themselves. And we saw that there were other parallels in Paul where the same idea is expressed (see Phil. 1:12–20; cf. Eph. 3:1; 2 Tim. 2:9; Philem. 9, 13; Acts 28:20). He has asked the Colossians to pray that his imprisonment will be a step in the spread of the gospel (see 4:2–4). In doing so, they themselves participate in Paul's apostolic ministry, from which they have initially benefited at their conversion.

In this light, Paul's desire to update the hearers about his imprisonment serves to remind them of two things: his ongoing suffering for their sake (and for the church universal) and his request for them to keep praying for the continued furtherance of the gospel through his imprisonment (4:3). Both these reminders show his ongoing concern for them and will "encourage their hearts." The only other use of παρακαλέω (*parakaleō*) in the epistle is at 2:1–2: "For I want you to know how great a struggle I have on your behalf, and for those who are at Laodicea, and for all those who have not personally seen my face, that their hearts <u>may be encouraged</u>." In the light of the directly preceding discussion, it is likely that Paul's "struggle . . . on your behalf and of those who are at Laodicea" includes his imprisonment.[13] And the purpose of that struggle in imprisonment is "in order that your hearts may be encouraged," the same purpose of Paul's imprisonment that we have just seen above.

The Greek text starts abruptly: "with Onesimus, my faithful and beloved brother." That is, Paul has "sent" Onesimus "with" Tychicus to "make known" Paul's situation and to "encourage" the Colossians (v. 8), the mission of which is reiterated in abbreviated form in verse 9. Although from the earthly perspective Onesimus is a slave (cf. the Epistle to Philemon), from the new-creational perspective he is Paul's "faithful and beloved brother" in Christ. Both slave and free are equal in the inaugurated new creation (cf. Col. 3:11). Onesimus is also "from among" the Colossians (cf. Philem. 10). From the brief description of Onesimus, it is hard to know if Philemon has yet responded to Paul's appeal, in the Letter to Philemon, to release the slave or whether Colossians precedes the writing of Philemon and Onesimus is still in his same slave status. **4:9**

The last clause of verse 9 reiterates verses 8–9b: "They [Tychicus and Onesimus] will make known to you all things here."* This section begins with "making all things known" to the Colossians (v. 7a), it ends with "making all things known" (v. 9b), and it is marked in the middle (v. 8a) with "knowing

13. Note that Paul uses ἀγών (*agōn*) to refer to his "struggle" in imprisonment in Philippi (Phil. 1:30; cf. 1 Thess. 2:2, which includes sufferings in imprisonment).

the things concerning" Paul. This is a classic chiasm by which the repeated patterns highlight Paul's desire that the Colossians know about his imprisonment for their sake and also for the spread of the gospel (as noted above). Thus the middle of the chiasm that repeats "knowing the things" about Paul is close to the main point but more precisely supports the main point, also in the middle of the chiasm, which is the purpose of the "making known" about Paul's circumstances: to "encourage your hearts."[14]

Apparently, since Paul repeats that Tychicus's mission is "to make known" the things about Paul, many commentators think that he was also the letter carrier, which is likely correct (if so, Onesimus should be included as carrying the letter). Among the functions of Jewish and Hellenistic letter carriers was communicating further information about the letter sender and his situation, just as is reiterated about Tychicus (as well as Onesimus) in verses 7–9 (see Thompson 2005: 104). Another function of letter carriers was to make clear parts of the letter and provide fuller information about what was only partly revealed in the letter (see further in the additional note on 4:7–9). Thus Tychicus (and possibly Onesimus) also plausibly functioned in this way as an interpreter of the letter to the Colossians. Indeed, he (and possibly Onesimus) has Paul's imprimatur as an authoritative interpreter, to whom the hearers should submit as they do to Paul. Likely Tychicus would have noted and explained some of the OT allusions that occur earlier in the letter.

B. In Addition to Himself, Paul Wants the Colossians to Know That His Coworkers Are Pastorally Concerned for Them (4:10–14)

This section is marked out by the introductory and repeated "greetings" from various colleagues of Paul. The section can be divided into two subsections: Paul's three Jewish-Christian coworkers (vv. 10–11) and his three Gentile coworkers (vv. 12–14).

4:10 Aristarchus and Mark are mentioned first as sending their greetings. Aristarchus is named as a traveling companion with Paul on some of his journeys (cf. Acts 19:29; 20:4; 27:2). He was from Thessalonica (Acts 20:4; 27:2). The reference to Aristarchus as "my fellow prisoner" (lit., "fellow captive") is the second clue in the letter that Paul is in prison (see earlier 4:3b). Some commentators, however, think the word is used metaphorically to refer to Aristarchus as a spiritual "fellow captive" of the Lord,[15] since the word is used metaphorically in Luke 4:18, and the verb form is likewise used in 2 Tim. 3:6 (αἰχμαλωτίζω, *aichmalōtizō*).[16] Some think a metaphorical use is also pointed to by arguing that "fellow captive" would be a strange way for Paul to refer to literal imprisonment, since it would have connotations of being a prisoner of war (e.g.,

14. I have subsequently found that Wall (1993: 170–71) also sees a chiasm, though defining the borders a little differently but with the same main point.

15. Moule 1957: 137; Caird 1976: 211; Harris 2010: 177; Pao 2012: 312.

16. See D. Moo (2008: 338), who observes the 2 Timothy and Luke uses yet holds a literal view.

Moule 1957: 136). However, other observations point to Aristarchus being an actual fellow prisoner with Paul.

First, the immediate context, as argued above in the introduction to this unit, is dominated with the notion of Paul's own actual imprisonment. Paul commences verses 7–18 by desiring to inform the Colossians about the situation of his actual imprisonment (vv. 7–9; cf. v. 10) and asking them at the conclusion to "remember his imprisonment" (v. 18). Second, reference to real imprisonment in Col. 4 is borne out by the parallel of Philemon. There Paul refers to himself as "a prisoner [δέσμιος, *desmios*] of Christ Jesus" (Philem. 1, 9), "my bonds [chains]" (vv. 10, 13), and then toward the end of the letter he refers to Epaphras as "my fellow prisoner [συναιχμάλωτος, *synaichmalōtos*] in Christ Jesus" (v. 23; as in Col. 4:10). Since actual imprisonment is clearly in mind in Philem. 10 and 13, it is probable that the references in Philem. 1 and 9 and "fellow prisoner" in verse 23 should be understood likewise. Third, the word αἰχμάλωτος, which occurs only twice elsewhere in the NT (Luke 4:18; Philem. 23, with prefixed συν, *syn*), appears in the LXX, where it often refers to Israel (or sometimes other nations) nonfiguratively, as actually being taken captive by another nation.[17] Fourth, while Paul refers to Tychicus as a "fellow slave in the Lord"* (4:7) and to Epaphras as a "bondslave of Christ" (4:12), here in 4:10 "fellow prisoner [captive]" has no qualifying clause (like "of Christ"), so it is natural to take it literally (so, e.g., Lohse 1971: 172; Callow 2002: 162). Finally, since Paul also elsewhere refers to his coworkers as "fellow soldiers" (Phil. 2:25; cf. also 2 Tim. 2:3), it is natural for him to refer to Aristarchus and others (Rom. 16:7; Philem. 23), along with himself, as "fellow prisoners" of war (see Bruce 1984: 178–79).[18] That Aristarchus is an actual prisoner together with Paul is likely implied by Acts 27:1–2, which refers to "Paul and some other prisoners" being delivered over to a centurion and then adds that Paul was "accompanied by Aristarchus" (Dunn 1996: 275). Furthermore, Acts 19:29 earlier reports that Aristarchus, one of Paul's traveling companions, is "dragged" into the civic assembly of Ephesus, which possibly leads to his facing criminal charges (Acts 19:38–39; see MacDonald 2000: 180). Another possibility is that Aristarchus "shared the apostle's captivity by living with him" (Lightfoot 1875: 236, who does not see this as probable).[19]

Mark, the cousin of Barnabas, appears as a traveling coworker with Paul and Barnabas during some of their missionary ministries. His mother hosted meetings of Christians in her house in Jerusalem (Acts 12:12). On his second missionary journey, when Paul wants to revisit some of the cities where people have become believers, Barnabas wants to take Mark along (15:36–37).

17. Roughly half of the twenty-four uses refer to actual captivity by another nation, as in Isa. 46:2; 52:2, the latter reading, "Loose yourself from the chains around your neck, O captive daughter of Zion." Though not all Israelites were "chained," those led into captivity with literal chains represent the whole nation in actual captivity.

18. On the other hand, since "fellow soldier" is used metaphorically in Phil. 2:25 (as is "soldier" in 2 Tim. 2:3), it could well argue for a metaphorical use of "fellow captive" here.

19. See Foster (2016: 420–21) for further arguments in favor of a literal meaning of αἰχμάλωτος.

However, Paul does not want to do so because Mark earlier "had deserted them in Pamphylia and had not gone with them to the work" (15:38) but had "returned to Jerusalem" (Acts 13:13). As a result of the disagreement, Paul chose Silas to go with him on his travels, and Barnabas chose Mark. We do not know what "instructions [commandments]" about Mark that Paul (or possibly others) have given the Colossians, but apparently the rift has been healed, since Paul tells the church to "welcome" Mark, "if he comes."[20] This is testified to by 2 Tim. 4:11, where Paul instructs Timothy to "pick up Mark and bring him with you, for he is useful to me for service." Later Mark apparently is a coworker with Peter in the church at Rome (1 Pet. 5:13). Many think this is the same Mark who wrote what we know as the Gospel according to Mark, which is likely. These instructions about Mark amount to a commendation of him: the Colossians are encouraged to accept his authority if he comes to them.

Both Aristarchus and Mark are mentioned as Paul's "fellow workers" in Philem. 24.

4:11 In addition to Aristarchus and Mark, "Jesus who is called Justus" also sends greetings (the verb "greet" is carried over from the beginning of v. 10). The three together, Paul says, are his only fellow workers presently with him who are ethnic Jewish believers in Christ (lit., "who are from the circumcision").[21] The remark implies that only a remnant of ethnic Jews have been converted to Christ, as the book of Acts testifies. Justus, together with Aristarchus and Mark, is part of the "true circumcision" (Phil. 3:3).

The phrase οἱ ὄντες ἐκ περιτομῆς, οὗτοι μόνοι συνεργοί (*hoi ontes ek peritomēs, houtoi monoi synergoi*) could be rendered in one of three viable ways: (1) "these are the only Jews among my coworkers"; (2) "these alone of the circumcision are my coworkers"; or (3) "the ones from the circumcision, these alone are coworkers." The first is the most paraphrastic interpretive translation of the three and highlights a contrast of the three with the other coworkers who are Gentiles, which requires turning συνεργοί (*synergoi*) into a dative or adding a Greek word that could be translated "among" before "fellow workers." The second and third renderings would both focus on the three people being contrasted with unbelieving Jews. Various translations

20. Most translations see this remark about Mark to be parenthetical but some do not (see NRSV, NLT). Wallace (1996: 697–99) lists the phrase in this verse "if he should come to you, then welcome him" as a third-class condition, which in different contexts can mean the following: (1) a logical link in the present, not indicating anything with respect to fulfillment of the protasis; (2) merely a hypothetical condition or a condition that will not be fulfilled; (3) a more probable future event. Here it likely means something that is going to probably happen, since otherwise why would Paul give "commandments" about Mark, if he were not likely coming to the Colossians? Pao (2012: 313) leans toward this conclusion. Possibly the apodosis of the third condition indicates what Paul wishes to happen if the protasis ever occurs (so Brooks and Winbery 1979: 184).

21. Acts 20:4 says that Aristarchus was "of the Thessalonians," on which basis Dunn (1996: 278) says he may be Gentile; if so, then the reference to the "ones being from the circumcision"* (Col. 4:11) includes only Mark and Justus. But Aristarchus could well be a converted Jew from Thessalonica.

support all three alternatives, and it is very difficult to know which is best (see the fuller discussion of D. Moo 2008: 340–42). The third carries the same sense as the second but is a bit awkward, especially since the οὗτοι (*houtoi*) is not directly related to the preceding clause but starts a new clause, and some might reject it for that reason (e.g., cf. D. Moo 2008: 341).[22] Nevertheless, it is the most straightforward rendering (preferred by Geneva, KJV, ASV, NJB, NET). Thus the second is a dynamic equivalent to the third. The third should perhaps be given the edge, since it is the most straightforward, and as such the abruptness of the second clause, beginning with "these alone" (οὗτοι μόνοι, *houtoi monoi*), is intended for strong emphasis: Aristarchus, Mark, and Justus are ones "who are of the circumcision—these alone are fellow workers," the only ethnic Jews who "have remained with me, other ethnic Jews have not" (so Lohse 1971: 173; likewise Abbott 1897: 301). References to people being of the "circumcision" elsewhere in the NT can refer to Jewish Christians (Rom. 4:12; 15:8; Gal. 2:12; Titus 1:10 [?])[23] or to unbelieving Jews (Eph. 2:11; Phil. 3:2) or to ethnically Gentile and Jewish Christians (Phil. 3:3). Here the reference is to Christians who are the only ethnic Jews presently with Paul as "fellow workers." It is possible that "those of the circumcision" refers to a group of legalistic Jewish Christians, who were often opposed to the Pauline Gentile mission (Gal. 2:12; Titus 1:10).[24] If so, then Paul's three coworkers are the only ones from this group who have remained with him and supported him in his mission (MacDonald 2000: 181).

That these three people apparently were the only Jews among Paul's coworkers does not mean that other Jews were not coworkers with him but only that they were the only Jewish Christians among the group *presently* residing with Paul (note other Jews as coworkers at other times, in Rom. 16:3, 21; 2 Cor. 1:24; following Dunn 1996: 279). Furthermore, this does not mean that there were no other Jewish Christians in the general area where Paul was (probably Rome) but that these three are the only ones *gifted* as coworkers with Paul, who are ethnic Jews (cf. the implications of Calvin 1972: 360).

Paul identifies his gospel as having to do with the "kingdom of God." The "kingdom of God" is also an essential aspect of Paul's gospel preaching in Acts (19:8; 20:25; 28:23, 31; cf. 14:22). Elsewhere Paul refers to the inaugurated aspect of the "kingdom" (Rom. 14:17; 1 Cor. 4:20; 1 Thess. 2:12 [?]), as well as to the yet-future and to-be-consummated aspect (1 Cor. 6:9–10; 15:24, 50; Gal. 5:21; Eph. 5:5; 2 Tim. 4:1, 18; 2 Thess. 1:5). Here in Col. 4:11 the "kingdom of God" is likely an extended reference to "the kingdom of His [God's] beloved Son" (1:13), which clearly focuses on the end-time kingdom being present, so that a consummate reference would not primarily be in view in 1:13. Here in

22. Pao (2012: 314) thinks that this most straightforward translation is not preferable, since it would mean that Aristarchus, Mark, and Justus were Paul's only fellow workers and the passage goes on to indicate that Epaphras, Luke, and Demas are also listed as Paul's coworkers (vv. 12–14).

23. Though Gal. 2:12 and Titus 1:10 refer to a legalistic sect of Jewish Christians.

24. Cf. Pao (2012: 314), who sees a variant of this view as a possibility.

4:11 it is likely an "already / not yet" reference. The Son's preincarnate and incarnate kingship has been initially introduced in 1:15–18.

These three coworkers have been an "encouragement" to Paul.

4:12 Greetings are also sent from "Epaphras, who is from among you [Colossians]."* In 1:7 we discovered that the Colossians had first learned and accepted the gospel through Epaphras, who is not only a "servant of Christ" but also a "beloved fellow bond-servant, who is a faithful [minister] of Christ." Elsewhere the phrase "a servant [or slave] of Christ" (δοῦλος Χριστοῦ, *doulos Christou*) is used by Paul to refer only to himself (Rom. 1:1; 2 Cor. 4:5; Gal. 1:10; Titus 1:1) and Timothy (Phil. 1:1; cf. 2 Tim. 2:24). In light of these uses, the application of this phrase to Epaphras in 4:12 probably emphasizes his authority and importance in the Colossian church community (D. Moo 2008: 343). Epaphras was not only a servant "on behalf of" Paul and his coworkers (1:7), but as 4:12 adds, he was also "laboring earnestly for you [Colossians] in his prayers, that you may stand perfect [as complete ones] and fully assured in all the will of God." By praying in this manner, Epaphras desires to be an agent participating with Paul in fulfilling Paul's goal of "presenting every man complete [τέλειος, *teleios*] in Christ" (1:28; "stand perfect [complete, τέλειος]" in 4:12), a goal toward which both Paul and Epaphras are "striving" (see the use of the middle participle ἀγωνιζόμενος [*agōnizomenos*] in both 1:29 and 4:12). That Epaphras is "always laboring earnestly on behalf of you" (Colossians) also reflects Paul's prayer for the Colossians, as in 1:3, "always praying in behalf of you" (so Hübner 1997a: 120).

Indeed, Epaphras's prayer that the Colossians "be fully assured" even mirrors Paul's prayer that the readers be "filled with the will of God" (on this point see D. Moo 2008: 344). Some manuscripts even change the verb in 4:12 to the same verb "filled" (though a different ptcp., πεπληρωμένοι, *peplērōmenoi*) as in 1:9, no doubt trying to conform the verse to 1:9 (see the additional note on 4:12). In fact, the verb πληροφορέω (*plērophoreō*) can not only mean "fully assured" but also "filled," so that the verb may merely be a synonym with πληρόω (*plēroō*),[25] still bringing it close in line with 1:9.[26] However, the meaning could be "fully assured" here, since this would line up with another parallel with Paul's ministry in 2:2, where Paul uses the noun cognate of πληροφορέω in expressing the desire that his encouragement would lead the Colossians "unto all the richness of <u>assured</u> [πληροφορία, *plērophoria*] understanding."*[27] In addition to the parallel with 2:2, what also may favor the meaning of "fully assured" is that the entire purpose of the epistle is

25. See BDAG (827, s.v. πληροφορέω 1), acknowledging both possible meanings in Col. 4:12 but inclining toward "filled"; it places uses of this verb in 2 Tim. 4:5, 17 under the categorical heading "fill (completely), fulfill."

26. I have subsequently found that Hübner (1997a: 120) also sees this parallel with 1:9 and takes πληρόω (*plēroō*) as a synonym of πληροφορέω (*plērophoreō*).

27. This is the preference of D. Moo (2008: 345), though it is possible that the noun here could mean merely "full" (e.g., see BDAG 827, s.v. πληροφορία, though usually the meaning of the word is "full assurance"). In addition to "filled" and "fully convinced," according to Harris (2010:

aimed at safeguarding or guaranteeing the gospel, so that the assurance of the Colossians about this gospel is "rooted in the insight in all the will of God" (Gnilka 1980: 240). However, on balance the verbal parallel is stronger with 1:9, and the use of the synonym πληρόω in 2:10 and the noun form in 1:19 and 2:9, all occurring at critical theological and polemical junctures of the letter (see my comments on these verses), points to the meaning of "filled" in 4:12.[28] Indeed, the verbal parallels to 1:28–2:2 (set in contrast to the false teaching in 2:4) indicate echoes of "standing" against the false teaching here in 4:12 (Dunn 1996: 280). Perhaps the difference between the meanings of "fully assured" and "filled" is not great, since both would be closely related to standing against the false teaching.

The reason (γάρ, *gar*) why Epaphras is so consumed with this prayer on be- **4:13**
half of the Colossians is that "he has a deep concern for" them, as well as for the nearby churches of "Laodicea and Hierapolis." Hierapolis was located about twelve miles northwest of Colossae and six miles north of Laodicea (O'Brien 1982: 255). This phrase ἔχει πολὺν πόνον (*echei polyn ponon*) could be translated as "he has deep concern" or "he has worked painstakingly" for the Colossians.[29] This verse continues the portrayal of Epaphras as joining Paul's efforts in his apostolic task, since Paul has said earlier "how great a struggle" (ἡλίκον ἀγῶνα, *hēlikon agōna*) he had "on behalf" of the Colossians and Laodiceans (2:1).[30] Epaphras's prayer thus arises from his great concern for them. The modeling of Epaphras's ministry on that of Paul's and his efforts on behalf of the Colossians, as well as the Laodiceans and saints in Hierapolis, should motivate the hearers and other Christians in the region to listen to Epaphras and submit to his authority (Sumney 2008: 276), knowing that he has their best interests at heart.

The final greeting of this section comes from "Luke, the beloved physician,"[31] **4:14**
and Demas. Though "Luke" is mentioned only in Paul's Letters, there is external evidence that identifies him as the author of Acts.[32] The "we" passages

180) there is a third alternative: τέλειοι καὶ πεπληροφορημένοι (*teleioi kai peplērophorēmenoi*), which could be a hendiadys, "ripe in conviction" or "fully mature."

28. In line with the conclusion of O'Brien (1982: 254), who has reminded me of the relevance of the crucial uses in 1:19; 2:9–10; see also Hübner (1997a: 120), who views πληρόω (*plēroō*) as a parallel to both 1:9 and 2:10 as central theological sayings in Colossians.

29. See the additional note on 4:13 for the range of meaning of πόνος (*ponos*) and the preference of "deep concern." If the idea is "worked hard or painstakingly," then this may refer to working hard in prayer (Harris 2010: 180), and the γάρ (*gar*) would be a further explanation of verse 12 instead of a ground.

30. I have found that Pao (2012: 316–17) has also observed the above parallels to Col. 1–2 in 4:12–13, concluding explicitly in 4:12 that Paul views Epaphras as extending his own pastoral ministry; likewise Deterding 2003: 187; Wilson 2005: 302–3; Thompson 2005: 106; and Heil 2010: 194–95. Furter (1987: 207) and Callow (2002: 164) observe several of these parallels. However, Hübner (1997a: 120) is apparently the only one who has seen the parallel with 1:3.

31. See 2 Tim. 4:11 for Luke as a faithful companion to Paul.

32. See 𝔓[75], which identifies Luke as the author of the Gospel of Luke in the attached title, as pointed to by the Muratorian Canon, dated around the same time as 𝔓[75] (following Pao 2012:

in Acts likely identify him as Paul's traveling companion on the second and third missionary journeys (Acts 16:10–17; 20:5–15; 21:1–18; 27:1–28:16), which conclude with their trip to Rome, possibly the place where Paul is writing from prison. In this light, it makes sense that Luke is with Paul in Rome and that Paul sends greetings from Luke here in verse 14 (following Pao 2012: 317–18). Since Paul has said in verses 10–11 that Aristarchus, Mark, and Justus "alone of the circumcision are my coworkers" (HCSB), it is likely that Luke, as well as Epaphras and Demas, are of Gentile origin.

Luke and Demas are called "fellow workers" of Paul in Philem. 24. Here Demas is portrayed implicitly also as a faithful servant (as in Philem. 24), but in 2 Tim. 4:10 an opposite description is given: "for Demas, having loved this present world, has deserted me."

C. The Responsibility of the Colossians in the Ministry (4:15–17)

4:15 The Colossians, to whom the pastoral concern has been directed in verses 7–14, are to show that kind of concern to others. They are to "greet the brethren who are in Laodicea and also Nympha and the church that is in her house." The καί (*kai*) following "Laodicea" is likely not a coordinating conjunction ("and"), nor is it epexegetical ("that is"), but it is likely focusing on those to whom Paul wants "especially" to send greetings (following Pao 2012: 319).[33] According to some, this function of καί (*kai*) suggests that there was more than one house church in Laodicea: "the brothers at Laodicea" forming at least one church, and another church in Nympha's house (see Thompson 2005: 107). It is difficult to know whether this is the case. Some also think that the second-person plural command "greet" is just Paul's way of sending greetings to the Laodiceans and could be paraphrased as "greet for me." This is especially based on the series of greeting imperatives in Rom. 16:3–16 (D. Moo 2008: 15). But why would Paul ask the Colossians to greet the Laodiceans since he likely did so in his letter to Laodicea, mentioned in 4:16? The likelihood is that Paul wants the Colossians to join with him in the greeting in order to express their affection and concern to the Laodiceans (following for the most part D. Moo 2008: 348–49). These are not merely amoral or nonspiritual greetings but greetings in the Lord, showing care for them.

Many commentators note the textual uncertainty over whether Νυμφαν (*Nymphan*) should be rendered "Nympha" as a female name or "Nymphas" as a male name (see the additional note on 4:15). However, the most likely reading of the accompanying pronoun is "her" (αὐτῆς), indicating that Νυμφαν is female. Commentators reading Νυμφαν as female think that she may have been a wealthy widow who hosted a small church in her house. Some think that Nympha is being acknowledged here as a leader of the church in Laodicea (e.g., Sumney 2008: 278; Foster 2016: 439; cf. Hay 2000: 162), but nothing more

318). Eusebius (*Eccl. Hist.* 3.4.1–7) also attests to Luke as the author of Acts (cf. Dunn 1996: 283) and of the third Gospel (3.24.14–15; 5.8.3; and 6.25.6).

33. The NASB renders the καί as "and also"; cf. Harris 2010: 183.

than hosting the church in her house is being expressed. House churches were typical during the early Christian movement (see Acts 16:15, 40; Rom. 16:5, 23; 1 Cor. 16:19; Philem. 2; see O'Brien 1982: 256–57).

Paul tells the Colossians to read his letter, then to send it along to Laodicea and **4:16**
read the letter the Laodiceans received from Paul. He wants them to read both letters because they convey God's authoritative word. The very fact that Paul wants his letters distributed to multiple churches suggests their authoritative nature. This is expressed more explicitly in 1 Thess. 5:27: "I adjure you by the Lord to have this letter read to all the [brothers]." Most probably 1 Thess. 5:27 refers to one person who reads the letter to the rest of those in the church (or house churches in Thessalonica), as Rev. 1:3 makes explicit: "Blessed is the one reading and the ones hearing the words of the prophecy and keeping the things having been written in it."* We know this refers to *at least* seven lectors reading to the seven historical churches addressed in Revelation.[34] That the Colossians were *commanded* by Paul to read the letter from the Laodiceans and vice versa suggests that Paul believed his letters, rather than having only passing significance, had wider authority and relevance than merely for the church directly addressed (Dunn 1996: 286; Sumney 2008: 280).[35] The exchange of letters also suggests that the false teaching had influence not only in Colossae but also in Laodicea, so that both churches would benefit from reading each other's letters (Schweizer 1982: 242).

Indeed, Paul's letter arises from the fact that, as he says, "I was made a minister according to the stewardship from God bestowed on me for your benefit" (Col. 1:25). That is, his letter is divinely authoritative for the Colossians. The authoritative nature of the letter also arises from recalling that Jews read Scripture aloud in their synagogue worship (cf. Luke 4:16–22; Acts 15:21; 2 Cor. 3:15; Pao 2012: 320).

Some have tried to postulate that the "letter from Laodicea" was from the Laodiceans themselves or that it is to be identified with the Letter to Philemon or with a lost letter to Laodicea or with the circular Letter of Ephesians.[36] The latter two options are reasonable, especially the last, since Ephesians was a

34. Or it refers to the letter carrier who reads the letter to each of the churches as he delivers it. Likewise Paul sends his Letter to the Galatians specifically "to the churches of Galatia" (Gal. 1:2), also implying the authoritative nature of his letters.

35. The imperative ποιήσατε (*poiēsate*) also gives an imperatival sense to the following ἵνα (*hina*) plus the aorist subjunctive: "have it also read" (so most English translations), though KJV and Geneva have "cause that it be read also" (perhaps in line with a Semitic idiom involving the Hebrew causative *hiphil*; see MHT 4:90), or alternatively it could be rendered "see that it is read" (so MHT 3:95; Zerwick and Grosvenor 1981: 612): the latter two translations are able explicitly to render the ἵνα as "that"; the aorist active subjunctive in the last clause of verse 16 should be taken in an imperatival sense, "that you also read."

36. See O'Brien (1982: 257–58), Bruce (1984: 184–85), and Barth and Blanke (1994: 487–88) for speculative theories about the identification of the "letter from Laodicea." For an overview of all the various options in table form, see Lightfoot (1875: 274), and likewise see Hendriksen (1964: 194–97), who leans toward the letter being identified either with Paul's letter to the Laodiceans (now lost) or to Ephesians.

circular letter and was written around the same time as Colossians (e.g., see Abbott 1897: vii–ix, 306). Nevertheless, all we know for certain is that this letter was by Paul, since it is in parallelism with "this letter" of Colossians by Paul in verse 16a, which was sent by Paul to Colossae and was to be exchanged ("in turn, read," NET) for the Laodicean letter. Buttmann (1873: 378) paraphrases accordingly: "my letter which is *now* in Laodicea and to reach you *from thence*."[37]

4:17 Now the pastoral concern of the Colossians is most explicitly expressed. They are to exhort Archippus to "take heed to the ministry which you have received in the Lord, <u>that</u>[38] you may fulfill it." Rather than translating ἐν κυρίῳ (*en kyriō*) as "in the Lord" or "because of the Lord," a better rendering is "from the Lord," since this makes the most sense of the preceding verb "received" (Campbell 2012: 154). Archippus is listed as one of the recipients of the Letter to Philemon, along with Philemon and Apphia (Philem. 2). There he is called a "fellow soldier." This suggests that the exhortation to him is about the "ministry" in which Paul himself is engaged, which is about spreading the gospel and building up saints who have believed.[39]

As with Epaphras, Paul's description of Archippus's task with the words "fulfill" and "ministry" echoes Paul's portrayal of his own ministry: "I was made a minister [διάκονος, *diakonos*] according to the stewardship from God . . . that I might fulfill [πληρόω, *plēroō*] the word of God"* (1:25; Pao 2012: 322). And, as in the case of Epaphras, the point of the echo is to indicate that Archippus is an arm of Paul's own work of ministry. Therefore, like Epaphras, Archippus is also being commended to the Colossians as an authoritative servant (Sumney 2008: 281). And likewise Paul uses Epaphras and Archippus as models for other Christians to follow, just as they were imitating Paul (Pao 2012: 324).

D. Paul Reaffirms His Pastoral Concern Expressed in Verses 7–9 by "Greeting" the Colossians (4:18)

4:18 That Paul[40] "writes this greeting with" his "own hand" is a way of expressing the epistle's Pauline authenticity and thus its apostolic authority. It also assumes that the majority of the letter has been dictated to a secretary (O'Brien

37. Here the preposition ἐκ (*ek*) is used with the sense of ἐν (*en*), with the resulting idea of "the letter that is *at* Laodicea" not "from Laodicea" (following BDF §437).

38. The ἵνα (*hina*) is best taken as indicating goal or purpose of "taking heed to the ministry" rather than as introducing an object clause of an implied repeated "see" or "take heed"; Harris (2010: 184) renders this latter possible option as "see that you fulfill it."

39. Paul often uses διακονία (*diakonia*) to refer to various facets of Christian "service" ("varieties of service," 1 Cor. 12:5 ESV, NRSV) related to the spread of the gospel (e.g., Rom. 11:13; 2 Cor. 3:9; 1 Tim. 1:12; 2 Tim. 4:5) and building up believers (Eph. 4:12) who have believed in the gospel, including the "service" of giving financial support to needy saints (2 Cor. 8:4; 9:1, 12, 13).

40. Παύλου (*Paulou*) is best understood as a subjective genitive modifying "greeting" ("the greeting by Paul in my own hand" = "I, Paul, write this greeting in/with my own hand," so NASB, RSV, NRSV, NIV, ESV, NET), though a possessive genitive is possible ("Paul's greeting,

1982: 259). Use of secretaries was typical practice in the ancient Greco-Roman world, and often secretaries were not referred to or named.[41] So it is the case here. This significance of writing in "his own hand" is expressed more clearly in 2 Thess. 3:17: "I, Paul, write this greeting with my own hand, and this is a distinguishing mark in every letter: this is the way I write." Such a signature protected against false teachers writing in Paul's name (as warned against in 2 Thess. 2:2). This authoritative apostolic signature reminds the hearers of Paul's authority in all he says in the epistle, especially his warnings about and objections to the false teachers. His signature together with a note in his own hand in 1 Cor. 16:21 and in Gal. 6:11 probably has the same significance. Even the signature in Philem. 19 affirms Paul's authoritative promise that he will pay Philemon for the cost of the runaway slave Onesimus. It is commonly known that such added signatures at the ends of letters were a feature in Greco-Roman letters as well.[42]

That Paul asks the hearers to "remember my imprisonment"[43] shows further that Paul's circumstances (τὰ κατ᾽ ἐμὲ πάντα), which Tychicus is to make known, concern his situation of imprisonment (4:7). This is also an implicit reminder that his suffering in prison is ultimately a means to benefit them in their ongoing faith and a springboard for the continued spread of the gospel (as discussed in 4:7–9; cf. 1:24 with 4:3–4 and see my comments on these verses). The hearers should be motivated to submit to Paul's instructions in the letter not only because of his apostolic authority but also because he loves them so much that he suffers on their behalf (Sumney 2008: 282). While they are continually to recall that Paul is in prison, the use of the verb μνημονεύω (*mnēmoneuō*) suggests that they are to "remember Paul's imprisonment" by praying for him. The verb can connote prayer in the Greek OT (Ps. 62:7 [63:6 Eng.]), and the noun form (μνεία, *mneia*) preceded by the verb "make" or "have" ("make or have remembrance") is an expression of prayer elsewhere in Paul (Rom. 1:9; Eph. 1:16; 1 Thess. 1:2; 2 Tim. 1:3; Philem. 4; likewise Phil. 1:3 without a verb).[44]

The concluding note of "grace be with you" replaces the typical "farewell" in contemporary Hellenistic epistles. The entire letter is bounded by Paul's opening greeting of "grace" (1:2) and the final benediction of "grace" here in 4:18. This inclusion is significant: all that Paul says to the Colossians and all that he exhorts and commands them can be believed and obeyed only by God's grace (building on O'Brien 1982: 260).

---

with my own hand"). See Harris (2010: 184–85) for various other options for interpreting the genitive Παύλου (*Paulou*).

41. Pao (2012: 322 and sources cited there) also notes that at the end of Romans, Paul does not supply an autograph, yet Tertius makes explicit that "I, Tertius" am Paul's secretary (16:22).

42. See references in Dunn (1996: 289) and in Bruce (1984: 186), who also notes that such signatures were appended when a secretary wrote the letter.

43. Most translations render the plural of δεσμός (*desmos*) straightforwardly as "bonds, fetters, or chains," but the NASB and the HCSB have "imprisonment," taking "chains" as a metonymy (the substitution of one thing for a closely associated thing; see Harris 2010: 185).

44. Following O'Brien (1982: 260) on the significance of "remember" here.

Additional Notes

4:7–9. We saw in 4:7–9 that one function of letter carriers was clarifying parts of the letter and supplying more information that was only partially revealed in the epistle. On this function of letter carriers in early Hellenism, early Judaism, and early Christianity, P. M. Head has written several articles. Head (2009a) says, e.g., that in some Jewish epistolary literature, letter carriers had the role of "reinforcing and supplementing the message of the written letter and thus facilitating the communication process envisaged by the author and sender of the letter" (2009a: 219). Likewise Head (2009b) asserts that when a letter carrier in Greek epistles (i.e., the Oxyrhynchus papyri) was identified and named within a letter, "the letter carrier frequently supplements the written communication with some oral" addition (2009b: 279). This helps us understand the role of Paul's letter carriers, including Tychicus in Col. 4:7–9 (cf. 2009b: 280–81, and passim). Similarly, Head (2015) affirms that the letter carrier of 1 Clement, among other functions, serves to make clear the content of the epistle, "reinforcing and even personally embodying the appeal of the letter" (2015: 492–93).

4:8. Some MSS, including 𝔓[46] and C along with several other good quality MSS, have "He should know the things concerning you" (γνῷ τὰ περὶ ὑμῶν, *gnō ta peri hymōn*). The reading preferred by NA[28], "You should know the things concerning us" (γνῶτε τὰ περὶ ἡμῶν, *gnōte ta peri hēmōn*) is supported by a grouping of excellent MSS (A, B, D*, and ℵ*, though the latter MS concludes with "you" instead of "us"). This is also the reading that may best explain how the other variants came into being (see further Metzger 1994: 559; Lightfoot 1875: 235). Bruce (1984: 176), on the other hand, thinks the external MS evidence is "evenly balanced" and wonders whether this is a case where the harder reading, "He should know the things concerning you," is preferable. This reading is harder because it conflicts with 4:7b and 9b, where Tychicus is to explain to the Colossians Paul's own situation.

4:12. Some good MSS have πεπληρωμένοι (*peplērōmenoi*; e.g., cf. 𝔓[46]) instead of πεπληροφορημένοι (*peplērophorēmenoi*). Better MSS support the latter reading (ℵ, A, B, C, D*,c, F, G), and it is probable that a scribe mistook πεπληροφορημένοι for πεπληρωμένοι because it is so similar in spelling and sound. Also, πεπληρωμένοι has already occurred at an earlier critical theological juncture of the letter (2:10, "in him you are *filled*"*) and in part of the initial prayer that has wording similar to the prayer here (1:9, "that you may be filled with the knowledge of His will"), though there the aorist passive subjunctive of the verb appears instead of a perfect passive participle. Hence it is natural that a scribe would have expected to see πεπληρωμένοι, especially as part of a prayer, instead of πεπληροφορημένοι, which does not appear anywhere else in the epistle.

4:13. The word πόνος (*ponos*) occurs elsewhere in the NT only in Revelation, where it always means "pain" (Rev. 16:10, 11; 21:4). In the LXX, the word can mean "labor, toil" (e.g., Deut. 28:33; Pss. 77:46; 104:36 [Eng.: 78:46; 105:36]; Prov. 3:9; Isa. 65:22), "trouble" or "distress" (e.g., 1 Kings 8:37; 2 Chron. 6:28; Pss. 7:15, 17; 89:10 [Eng.: 7:14, 16; 90:10]), "sorrow" (e.g., Num. 23:21; Job 3:10; Isa. 53:11; 65:14; Hab. 1:3; Sir. 3:27), or "pain" (e.g., Gen. 34:25; 1 Sam. 15:23; Isa. 66:7; 2 Macc. 7:36; 9:18).[45] Most English versions translate the word in Col. 4:13 as "work" (NRSV, RSV, NIV, NJB, ESV, HCSB, NET). While "labor" or "work" is possible here, the NASB alone has "deep concern" for πολὺν πόνον (*polyn ponon*), which comes close to a nuance of "pain."[46] Both "much labor" and "deep concern" are viable in the light of the parallel with ἡλίκον ἀγῶνα (*hēlikon agōna*, how great a struggle) in 2:1. Perhaps best is the paraphrase "He has worked painstakingly for you"

45. In 2 and 4 Maccabees "pain" is often the best translation. Muraoka (2009: 576) adds the following ranges of LXX meanings: "suffering, hardship," "physical pain, ache," and "product of toil."

46. The marginal reading of the NASB has "much toil" or "great pain," "physical pain, ache," and "product of toil."

(cf. BDAG 852, s.v. πόνος 1). The KJV has "great zeal," which is more in line with the NASB. The rendering of "sorrow" is possible, which also comes close to a notion of "pain" or "concern" but does not appear as relevant to the context. Likewise, "trouble" or "distress" would be possible if Epaphras were suffering on behalf of the readers due to conflict with the false teachers, which is not at all inconceivable—which D. Moo (2008: 346) says is behind the Greek expression in 4:13.

4:15. There is textual uncertainty about whether Νυμφαν (*Nymphan*) should be rendered "Nympha" as a female name or "Nymphas" as a male name. If the original is Νύμφαν (as in NA[28]) with an acute accent over the upsilon, then it refers to a female; if the original is Νυμφᾶν with a circumflex over the alpha, it refers to a male. The earlier manuscripts did not have accents, so the name could have been pronounced either as a male or female. Thus the following pronoun is the only evidence for whether the name referred to a woman or a man (see Yates 1993: 89–90). But even this manuscript evidence is mixed. Some scribes understand a woman to be the reference, which is indicated by the following reference to "her [αὐτῆς, *autēs*] church" (B, 0278, 6, 1739, 1881, sy[h], sa). Others understand it to be a male name, as indicated by the reading of "his [αὐτοῦ, *autou*] church" (D, F, G, K, L, Ψ, 365, 630, 1241[s], 1505, 𝔐, sy[p.hmg]). Still other MSS have "their [αὐτῶν, *autōn*] church," which likely arose due to a scribe thinking the church of the "brothers" together with either a male Nymphas or female Nympha was the reference in the original[47] (א, A, C, P, 075, 33, 81, 104, 326, 1175, 2464, bo); or "their" was written because it was unclear how Νυμφαν should be accented (see the note in NET). The female name Nympha would be the harder reading apparently because scribes would have thought that the name Nympha directly following male "brothers" would most naturally be taken as a male (i.e., one among the "brothers"). But just as naturally, Nympha as a female could be singled out from the preceding male brothers. However, many scholars believe the female Nympha is preferable as the difficult reading because of the likelihood that a scribe would have thought a male would be the head of a house in which a church was meeting and would have been tempted to change an original female name to the male (this may explain why the reading not only of "his" but also of "their" arose, as Hay 2000: 162 argues). Together with this, the weight of better MSS support the reading of "her" (αὐτῆς), thus meaning a female Nympha and making it the most likely original reading (so Metzger 1994: 560).

4:18. Some later and lesser quality MSS have "Amen" at the end of 4:18, while it is absent from earlier and better MSS. It is likely that a scribe added "Amen" at a later point because Paul ends some of his epistles with "Amen" (Rom. 16:27; Gal. 6:18), as do some other NT writers (2 Pet. 3:18; Jude 25; Rev. 22:21).

47. Campbell (2013: 76) also sees this as a possible reason for the presence of this variant.

Introduction to Philemon

Commentators agree that Philemon is Paul's most unique letter, both because of its brevity and because it was written mainly to one person (though the church in Philemon's house, as well as Apphia and Archippus, are secondarily also addressed). Thus the letter has both private and public aspects, with an emphasis on the former, while Paul's other letters are addressed only to churches (except for the Pastoral Epistles). In addition, the epistle is consumed with only one problem, and a personal problem at that (though entailing possible legal ramifications): the problematic relationship of the slave, Onesimus, to his master, Philemon.

Authorship

With very few exceptions (e.g., see discussion in D. Guthrie 1970: 638–39), scholars have agreed that Paul is the author of Philemon.

Place and Date of Writing

The two most viable candidates for the place from where Paul wrote are Rome and Ephesus. Most commentators prefer that Paul wrote from Rome. Those who prefer Ephesus do so because of Paul's statement in verse 22 that a lodging be prepared for him because of his "hope that through [their] prayers" he would be able to visit them imminently. Ephesus is much closer to Colossae than is Rome, making a possible trip to Colossae much easier.[1] This position is enhanced by the greater likelihood that Onesimus would have fled to the closer region around Ephesus than the much more distant Rome. Nevertheless, it is still possible that Paul could well have conceived of making the trip from Rome.

Thus Paul wrote while he was in prison either in Ephesus (more probably; AD 55 or 56)[2] or Rome (AD 60–62; cf. Acts 28:14–21).[3] The problem with the

1. For the location of Colossae and who the Colossians were, see the introduction to the commentary on Colossians.

2. So see N. Wright (2013: 7–8), who cites others following the same view.

3. Some propose that Paul wrote from his imprisonment in Caesarea (ca. AD 57–59; cf. Acts 23:23–26:32), though most commentators have not preferred this provenance. For the substance

former view is that there is no mention of Paul's imprisonment in Ephesus anywhere in the NT. The problem with the Rome view is that it seems to be a journey that is too far away for either Onesimus to make or for Paul to return from (as he may imply in Philem. 22). History, however, is filled with unique and strange occurrences, so it is likely best not to be confident about either an Ephesian or Roman provenance.

Paul probably wrote the letter around the same time as he wrote Colossians, since the introductions and conclusions of both letters are so similar: (1) both have Timothy as the cosender or letter carrier (Col. 1:1; Philem. 1); (2) both refer to Epaphras as a coworker with Paul (Col. 1:7; 4:12–13; Philem. 23); (3) as is the case also with Aristarchus, Mark, Demas, and Luke (Col. 4:10, 14; Philem. 24). (4) Likewise, Onesimus is a "beloved brother" (Col. 4:9; Philem. 16). Since Onesimus is a member of the church in Colossae (Col. 4:9), it is probable that the Letter to Philemon was also sent to the church in Colossae.

Occasion and Purpose

Byron (2008: 116–37) has given a broad overview of the main lines of interpretation for this epistle, which are generally related to its occasion: (1) the traditional view that the letter does not condemn slavery and is about an errant slave needing to be returned to his master; (2) various challenges to the traditional view, especially disputing the notion that Onesimus was an illegal fugitive slave; and (3) sociorhetorical views, focusing not on Onesimus's legal status but on how Paul brings pressure to bear on Philemon to induce him to acquiesce to Paul's requests.

Several proposals have been offered for the letter's specific occasion. (1) Some hold that Onesimus has fled from his master and stolen from him in the process (the latter based on vv. 18–19). (2) Others contend that the slave has fled to Paul for asylum, since this was a typical thing for runaway slaves to do. (3) Still others believe that Philemon has sent Onesimus to help Paul in prison. All three of these proposals lack evidence in the epistle itself.

It seems more likely that (4) Paul writes this letter primarily to Philemon because Philemon's slave, Onesimus, has wrongly left Philemon's service in order to seek out Paul to mediate between him and his master.[4] Though this view also involves speculation,[5] it appears that the most likely reason why Onesimus has come to be with Paul is that he wants to be reconciled to Philemon. Onesimus has presumably heard about Paul from Philemon while in service to his master and thus thinks Paul is a good person to mediate for him. The difference between this view and the traditional view (view 1) is not too great, though the latter technically views Onesimus as leaving temporarily with

of this paragraph, cf. Carson and Moo (2005: 592), though they prefer a Roman provenance instead of an Ephesian one (citing commentators on both sides of the issue).

4. Llewelyn (1992: 55–59, 101–3) gives examples in the papyri about runaway slaves.

5. Pao (2012: 343–46) discusses these four views and the specific circumstances prompting Paul to write the letter.

the apparent intent to return, after Paul has mediated on behalf of the slave.[6] This latter view is, nevertheless, distinct and preferable in that harboring a renegade, runaway slave was against the law in the Greco-Roman world, so it is unlikely that Paul would have done such a thing, and if he had, it would have been difficult to win Philemon's favor concerning his appeal (so Garland 1998: 299). On the other hand, since Paul is in prison, he can hardly be viewed as harboring Onesimus, even if Onesimus is ministering to his needs.

Other proposals about how Onesimus came to be with Paul do not answer this question as adequately as this fourth view. The traditional position (view 1) is the next-best position, though it does not explain as well how Onesimus came to be with Paul; yet the slave, having second thoughts about running away, may still have gone to Paul for mediation because he has heard of him while residing in his master's household (cf. Barclay 1997: 101). Pao favors view 3 (that Philemon sent Onesimus to help Paul in prison), but the biggest and insurmountable problem with this view is Paul's comment that Onesimus was formerly "useless" to Philemon but now (apparently since leaving Philemon's service) is "useful," as a result of his conversion (cf. v. 11). This view also does not seem to account specifically enough for how problems have arisen between Onesimus and Philemon after Onesimus began serving Paul (see vv. 18–19); nor does it account well for the divine passive in verse 15 ("He was separated [parted] from you for a while") or for Paul's desire to obtain Philemon's consent to keep Onesimus with him (vv. 13–14; on this point, see Garland 1998: 296).

The consensus among scholars is that Onesimus is away without Philemon's permission (Barclay 1997: 98–99). Paul writes and appeals to Philemon to release the slave with a view to Onesimus coming back to minister to Paul in prison. Paul does not make his appeal based on any expression of remorse or repentance on Onesimus's part, as sometimes was the case by mediators of runaway slaves in the ancient world (Barclay 1997: 104, 108–9). Instead, Paul bases his appeal on both his authoritative apostleship and especially on his brotherly love of Philemon, with whom he has a common faith in Christ. In particular, he so identifies Onesimus with himself that Philemon must reckon that how he treats his slave is the same as how he would treat Paul (v. 17); Paul can present Onesimus as himself because not only has the slave's moral character changed since he left his master, but he now has a changed identity, a Christian identity, which both he and Paul have in common because of their faith-union with Christ (cf. vv. 16, 20; 1 Cor. 7:22b; Barclay 1997: 109). Paul soars to the heights of rhetoric in making this appeal, hoping that Philemon will willingly acquiesce to Paul's request.

6. See N. Wright 2013: 8–9; Dunn (1996: 304–6) leans heavily in this direction, noting that it was common for a slave who had wronged a master in some way to seek for a third party to mediate between the slave and master, with the intent of ultimately returning to the master; accordingly, legal opinion did not regard such a slave technically as a *fugitivus*. On the other hand, the popular conception was that a slave who was gone overnight without permission was a fugitive (Barclay 1997: 102).

Paul writes also to the whole house church in Colossae, especially singling out Apphia and Archippus among those in the congregation (Philem. 2). The apparent purpose for writing also to them is to make known to them the appeal he is making to Philemon, perhaps implying that he is trying to get the house church involved in Paul's appeal. Likely the rest of the congregation is addressed so that they can hold Philemon accountable to Paul's request. At the very least, some kind of pressure is put on Philemon by knowing that the congregation meeting in his house is overhearing what Paul says to him. Though some doubt that the mention of the "church in your house" is intended to put pressure on Philemon, the fact that this is the only letter in the NT (except for the Pastoral Epistles) where one person is mainly addressed throughout the letter suggests that Philemon will feel some degree of accountability before the "church in [his] house."

The Issue of Slavery

It is difficult to find a hard-and-fast universal definition of slavery in the first century, except to say that slaves were considered property of the master and that at some point in their life they would be emancipated, except for those put into slavery due to criminality or as prisoners of war.[7] Around the environs of Rome, slaves were typically emancipated at a young age (around 30 years old). In other parts of the Roman Empire, slaves were emancipated at various ages. Often people voluntarily entered into slavery to learn a trade or to better their lives in some way.

There is much debate about whether Paul is asking Philemon to emancipate Onesimus or to accept him back graciously as a Christian "brother" (v. 16, though still a slave) and then allow him to return to minister to Paul. Barclay (1997: 116–17) concludes that Paul was rhetorically subtle and ambiguous about whether Philemon should free Onesimus from slavery or should merely welcome him back as a Christian "brother" with continued slave status. According to Barclay, the reason for this ambiguity is that Paul simply did not know what to recommend. Some observe that when slaves were emancipated, the economic and personal well-being of the slave worsened.[8]

Hence, if Philemon were to emancipate his slave, the slave's own living condition might well become worse than it was before leaving Philemon's service. Is it likely that Paul would want such a thing to happen to Onesimus? Yet one may respond: Paul has personal knowledge that such a bad thing would not happen to Onesimus if he were emancipated. This appears to be likely, since Paul has vouched financially for Onesimus's debts and will likely see to it that,

7. For a brief bibliography of slavery in the Greco-Roman world, see Collange 1987: 16, 29; Dunn 1996: 302; Barclay 1997: 126; and Pao 2012: 349–51. Wiedemann (1981: 1–275) offers a wide-ranging collection of primary source texts about slavery from the Classical and Hellenistic periods.

8. Sometimes, after emancipation, slaves still had certain social and economic obligations to their former masters, so that, in reality, there was a continuum between the two poles of slavery and absolute freedom; see Pao 2012: 351.

if the slave is emancipated, his basic needs will be taken care of. Thus it would not be radical for Paul to ask Philemon to emancipate his slave, since this was something commonly done anyway and often at a younger age. Garland (1998: 305) contends that Paul in Col. 4:7–9 puts Onesimus on the same level as Tychicus, not only as a "beloved brother" (so explicitly in Philem. 16) but also as a "faithful minister and fellow [bondslave] in the Lord." He concludes that on this basis, "to become one of Paul's coworkers he needs complete emancipation, not simply his manumission to serve Philemon as his freedman. . . . It was impossible to be a slave and a Christian missionary, who must speak boldly and move freely." This is a possible conclusion, but could not Onesimus have remained a slave and yet been given a lot of flexibility to serve as a Christian in the local church as well as elsewhere as a missionary? It seems likely that Paul is not attempting to overturn the institution of slavery in this epistle, since elsewhere he says "Each . . . must remain in that condition in which he was called," including a "slave" (1 Cor. 7:20–21); in addition, the "household codes" of Paul's other letters "assume that slaves remain slaves" (Thompson 2005: 198–99). But in tension with this is his statement in the same context (1 Cor. 7) that if a slave is "able . . . to become free, rather do that" (7:21).

But even if Paul is asking Philemon to emancipate his slave, it says nothing about Paul's general attitude toward slavery, nor does it mean that what he is asking Philemon to do should become a model for all slave owners, even Christian slaveholders. The reason for this, as noted briefly above, is that most slaves were emancipated anyway at some point in their life, often at a relatively young age (around 30 years old or younger; S. S. Bartchy, *ABD* 6:70–71). In fact, manumission occurred so often in the Mediterranean world of the first century that they "were entirely normal events of urban daily life and were expected by both owners and slaves" (S. S. Bartchy, *ABD* 6:71). Therefore Paul's request would fit and not contradict the institution of slavery as it was practiced in the Greco-Roman world. According to Bartchy, "Roman practice suggests that Paul was pleading with Philemon at the least not to delay Onesimus's anticipated manumission because of the wrongs he had done" (*ABD* 6:70–71; cf. Philem. 16, 18).

However, would Paul have regarded slaves as property, which was the general view of slaves in the ancient world? Paul does not directly address this issue! There is a fine line between the conception of owning a slave as property and owning a slave's work (i.e., considering a slave to be an indentured servant, as Hebrew slaves and some foreign slaves in the OT were regarded).[9] Either way, a slave was legally bound to serve the master for a certain period of time, so to some extent the distinction between legally owning a slave as property and legally owning the slave's labor is subtle and academic.

9. Even in the OT when one "buys a slave as his property with his money" (Lev. 22:11), the word "property" could be translated "possession," so that what is "possessed" could be the work of the slave and not the body of the slave himself. Significant in this verse also is that a Jewish or foreign slave is not specified, so it may include both.

Some brief biblical-theological reflections must suffice at this point, since there is not space adequately to address this issue. Nevertheless, the following shows the direction in which an argument can be further developed. Since Paul believes all are in the image of God (and Christians are in the renewed image of Christ), he believes that God "owns" all his creation, including humans, slave and free. In the case of Christians, they do not own themselves ("You are not your own") but have been "bought with a price" by God, so they are ultimately his slaves, whom he owns (1 Cor. 6:19–20).[10] Adam was not the owner of Eve or of the animals or any part of the creation but a caretaker of God's creation, so it is likely that Paul views humans as only "caretakers" and not "owners" of whatever part of God's creation comes into their care, including slaves.[11] The Epistle to Philemon certainly shows that Paul does not regard the Christian convert Onesimus as Philemon's property but as a "beloved brother, . . . both in the flesh [as a slave] and in the Lord" (v. 16; so also Col. 4:9, "Onesimus, our faithful and beloved brother").

It is important to contrast first-century Greco-Roman slavery with "old South nineteenth-century slavery." Among the differences are the following features of Greco-Roman slavery (based on S. S. Bartchy, *ABD* 6:66–71): (1) slavery was much, much more common among a vaster span of the population; (2) culture and economy came to depend on slavery (though the latter was also true in the "old South"); (3) slavery was not limited to one ethnic race; (4) most slaves (except those enslaved due to criminality) were typically emancipated at a relatively young age, and this became a motivation for faithful slave work, since such work was eventually rewarded with emancipation; (5) conditions of a person in slavery were often better than conditions of those emancipated from slavery; (6) similarly, large numbers of people would often willingly enter into slavery to better their economic and social welfare (which sometimes included payment for their debts); (7) education was encouraged, and slaves carried out important social and political functions; (8) slaves could own property (and even own other slaves); (9) the public assembly of slaves was not prohibited by law.

The last two hundred years have seen at least four approaches to slavery in scholarship. (1) Some scholars argued that Paul was a social conservative and thus one who supported the institution of slavery (e.g., Charles Hodge in the 19th cent.). (2) Others contended that Paul viewed slavery within a philosophical framework of Stoicism and was more concerned with inner freedom than with external slavery (1 Cor. 7:20–24 was often understood in this way; see, e.g., Adolf von Harnack). (3) Still others held that ancient slavery was more benign than the nineteenth-century slavery institution (e.g., S. S. Bartchy, *ABD* 6:65–73). (4) Some regarded first-century slavery as institutionalized

10. Note Exod. 34:9, where Moses asks God, "Take us [Israel] as Your own possession."

11. That Gen. 1–3 (including references to Adam) was generally influential on Paul's thought is apparent from a quick look at the list of quotations and allusions to that section of Genesis in NA[28] (836).

violence and inherently evil. These four views have not always been clear-cut categories: some aspects have overlapped with others (Orlando Patterson). The last two approaches are the most recent, especially the last as a reaction to the third. Our approach in the commentary perhaps fits best within the third category.[12]

Overshadowing the issue of slavery in the letter is how the gospel transforms human relationships despite class or race distinctions.[13]

The Outline and Argument of Philemon

I. Letter opening: Paul the apostle and Timothy desire that Philemon and the Colossian church have *grace and peace from God* (vv. 1–3).[14]
   Transition: To what does the notion of grace and peace from God lead? Probably the entire letter is an explanation of this grace and peace, which may be pointed to by observing that the letter ends with "Grace . . . be with you" (v. 25).

II. Introductory thanksgiving and prayer: *Paul thanks God for Philemon* because he recognizes in him genuine love and faithfulness, *and he prays* that his faith will continue to grow effectively (vv. 4–7).

III. Letter body: On the basis of Philemon's love and faith and Paul's prayer that he will increase in such qualities (vv. 4–7), Paul appeals to Philemon to release his slave to minister to Paul, *so that Philemon will have his slave back forever as a Christian brother and so that Paul's heart will be refreshed* (vv. 8–21).
   A. On the basis of Philemon's love and faith, Paul appeals to Philemon's inner heart to release Onesimus *to allow him to return to minister to Paul in prison* (vv. 8–14).
      Transition to verses 15–21, which give the results of Philemon's willingness to do his "good deed" of releasing his slave (v. 14). Two results are to occur: (1) Philemon will have his slave back as a Christian brother forever (vv. 15–16), and (2) Philemon's releasing his slave will "benefit" Paul by "refreshing his heart."
   B. Paul confidently appeals to Philemon to accept his slave as he would Paul *because this will refresh Paul's heart in Christ* (vv. 15–21).

IV. Letter closing: Paul asks Philemon to show pastoral concern for him, and Paul shows his sincere pastoral concern for the church in

12. This fourfold approach is based on Byron (2008: 1–37, 140–43), who favors the last approach. Likewise Byron (2008: 138–40) gives an overview of historical sources from the ancient world used to inform scholars' views of slavery, such as Roman law, as in the Digest of Justinian; philosophical and literary works; ancient novels and satirical works. Yet all of these have limitations and do not provide a full picture of slavery. Byron also lists scholars holding the various views.

13. Among several commentators who hold this view, see Felder 2000: 885.

14. The italics in the exegetical summary of each section of Philemon represent where the logical prominence is in each statement.

Philemon's house by reminding them that not only he but also his coworkers have pastoral concern for them (vv. 22–25).

Is it possible to highlight what is most logically and thematically prominent in Philemon? The main point toward which the body of the letter has been driving appears to be in verse 20, where Paul says that Philemon's release of the slave to help Paul in prison will "refresh my heart in Christ." The broad goals of the letter are that God will give Philemon and the church grace and peace, so that Philemon can carry out Paul's requests about Onesimus. The essence of Paul's request is not that Onesimus be emancipated but that Philemon treat the slave as a Christian brother, both in his capacity as a slave and as a fellow church member. This does not mean that Paul did not consider emancipation, about which we cannot be sure, but the greater issue at hand is that faith in Christ, which Philemon and Onesimus now share in common, will transform the way they relate as master and slave and as fellow members in the church (cf. likewise D. Moo 2008: 372–73).

Though some think the central theme of Philemon is the fellowship that Philemon and Onesimus have in common through their faith in Christ (so, e.g., D. Moo 2008: 378; N. Wright 1986: 170, 183–87), this is not the main point toward which Paul's logic is moving in the body of the letter. We have seen above that the main goal of his thought development is how Philemon's accepting his slave as he would Paul *will refresh Paul's heart in Christ*. The refreshment of Paul's heart is the main logical point of the epistle. The important theme of the shared fellowship between the master and the slave is the key instrumentation by which Philemon is to accept back his slave, which will result in refreshing Paul. It may seem strange to see refreshing Paul's heart as the main logical point of the letter, but this point highlights that the refreshment occurs because of the hoped-for reconciliation between Philemon and Onesimus. So the main focus of the logical development in the body is that of (1) common fellowship in Christ leading (2) to reconciliation and unity,[15] which results in (3) Paul's spiritual refreshment or "his heart being set at rest" from the anxiety that the two are presently unreconciled and might continue in that condition. The notion of reconciliation is struck explicitly in verses 15–16 and verse 17. It is this that overshadows the entire letter, which leads to Paul's "heart being set at rest" because he takes pleasure in the unity and reconciliation of God's people. Even if emancipation were implied in the letter (e.g., in v. 21), it would not be the main issue, since reconciliation and unity leading to Paul's refreshment is the overriding concern for Paul.[16]

15. See N. Wright (1986: 166–68, 170, 183–87), who acknowledges that reconciliation is the main aim of the shared fellowship in Christ; so also N. Wright (2013: 13–15, 68), where he repeats that reconciliation is the "central" appeal and point of the letter.

16. Several commentators hold this view (though not mentioning the important goal of "refreshment"), such as N. Wright 2013: 11–12, 15, 68; and D. Moo 2008: 369–78.

I. Letter Opening: Paul and Timothy Desire Grace and Peace for Philemon and the Colossian Church (1–3)

As noted on Col. 1:1–2, Hellenistic letters typically have four parts: an opening address, often an introductory wish, a body that contains the main part of the epistle, and a concluding farewell. Paul in Philemon adapts this variant fourfold Hellenistic letter style, particularly inserting Christian theology into it. For instance, the initial identification of "Paul" in Philemon is expanded to "a prisoner of Christ Jesus," an expression unique among Paul's letter openings. This is an adaptation of the Hellenistic letter, in which the letter is a substitute for the writer's presence. As we will see in the case of Paul, however, the letter represents not merely Paul's presence but also his apostolic authority over the recipients, though he does not explicitly identify himself as an apostle in this epistle. As we saw in Colossians (see on Col. 1:1), which is also true in Paul's other introductions, apostolic authority actually entails that the letter carries with it the authority of God and Christ, whom Paul represents in each letter, including the letter sent to Philemon. The second part of the ancient letter is a greeting, which Paul replaces with the theologically charged "grace and peace," typically followed in Paul's epistles by "from God our Father and the Lord Jesus Christ," which expresses further that behind Paul's letter writing stand God and Christ. Philemon follows this pattern.

As we saw with Colossians, Paul does not structure the parts of his epistles according to merely stylistic formulas; instead, he fills his letters with theological substance. He cares intensely about the people to whom he writes, and there is much emotion expressed in his letters, including his introductory greetings, which are not mere perfunctory addresses. This is no less true of his letter to Philemon.[1] The main point of verses 1–3 appears to be in verse 3, which states the general goal of the letter: that God and Christ will bestow "grace and peace" on the recipients, especially on Philemon (see further below on v. 3). The remainder of the letter will explain in what way Philemon needs such "grace," which will bring about "peace."

Exegesis and Exposition

1Paul, a prisoner of Christ Jesus, and Timothy our brother, to Philemon our beloved brother and fellow worker, 2and to Apphia our sister, and to Archippus our fellow

1. For expansion of this introduction, see relevant comments in the introduction to Col. 1:1–2.

soldier, and to the church in your house: [3]Grace to you and peace from God our Father and the Lord Jesus Christ.

1 Paul's greeting first focuses upon him being "a prisoner [δέσμιος, *desmios*] of Christ Jesus," which Paul repeats in verse 9 (also found in parallel though variant form in Eph. 3:1 and 4:1). Is this metaphorical, or was Paul really a "prisoner"? In light of verses 10 and 13, Paul is identifying himself as actually being in prison (v. 10, "whom [Onesimus] I have begotten in <u>chains</u> [δέσμιος, *desmios*]"*; v. 13, "that he might minister to me in my chains [δέσμιος, *desmios*] because of the gospel"*). Literal imprisonment is also suggested by the parallel with real imprisonment in Col. 4:10, 18 (the former referring to Aristarchus as a "fellow prisoner"). Likewise real imprisonment is in mind in 2 Tim. 1:8 ("Do not be ashamed of . . . me His prisoner, but join with me in suffering"). Similarly, references to Paul being in actual "chains" (or actual "prison") in Phil. 1:7, 13, 14, 17 point even further to the same here in Philem. 1. That physical and not spiritual imprisonment is in mind is in line with the use of the "prisoner" (δέσμιος, *desmios*) / "chain" (δεσμός, *desmos*) word group in Acts, where it always denotes actual imprisonment when referring to Paul.[2] Last, Philem. 9's allusion to "Paul, . . . a prisoner of Christ Jesus," is strikingly parallel to "Paul, a <u>prisoner</u> [δέσμιος, *desmios*]" in verse 1, which refers to real imprisonment. We have concluded that Ephesus was the place of Paul's imprisonment while he was writing Colossians, though it is quite possible that Rome is the location. Since Philemon was written around the same time as Colossians and Ephesians, the place of imprisonment is plausibly the same (see the introduction).

Since the phrase in verse 13 is a genitive of cause ("chains because of [or in the cause of] the gospel"), so likewise is the genitive in verse 1 ("a prisoner because of [or in the cause of] Christ Jesus"). It is because of Paul's witness to Christ that he has come to be in prison. However, the expression could be a genitive of relationship or a possessive genitive, the latter stressing that Paul may be possessed in chains by the Romans but he is really possessed by Christ Jesus. Such a point might be suggested in the letter by the three other mentions of Paul as a "prisoner" (v. 9) or "in chains" (vv. 10, 13). He is only there because Christ possesses him and nothing happens to him apart from Christ's will.[3]

Paul's reference to himself as a "prisoner" already hints at the anticipatory role that verses 1–7 play: to appeal to Philemon to give up his rights of slave ownership for the cause of Christ, just as Paul has given up his personal rights to become a "prisoner of Christ" (so Garland 1998: 316). Or the point may be that Paul is highlighting his vulnerability as a prisoner and thus his

2. For δέσμιος, see 16:25, 27; 23:18; 25:14, 27; 28:17; for δεσμός, see 16:26; 20:23; 23:29; 26:29, 31. However, Acts is more of a historical genre than Paul's epistolary genre, so one might expect more literal uses of "prison" and "prisoner" than metaphorical uses.

3. Banker (1999: 18–19) also understands the genitive to express that Paul is "serving Christ" or "because he serves Christ." He bases this primarily on 2 Tim. 1:8, 11–12a; and 2:9.

solidarity with Onesimus as a slave, since runaway slaves could be disciplined by being put into chains when caught. Accordingly, Paul's identification with Onesimus's possible chains will elicit sympathy from Philemon and make him reluctant to punish his runaway slave (see Thompson 2005: 206). Either of these rhetorical forces (and both may be in mind) is highlighted by observing that elsewhere Paul usually identifies himself as an "apostle" in the beginning of his epistles (O'Brien 1982: 271). This is the only letter opening in which Paul refers to himself as "a prisoner of Christ Jesus" (Pao 2012: 363).[4]

This does not mean that Paul does not appeal to his apostolic authority in the letter (contra O'Brien 1982: 272). Reference to Paul's "boldness in Christ to order"* Philemon to do what is right (v. 8) suggests that he has not given up some degree of appeal to his apostolic authority;[5] likewise, reference to Philemon's doing something out of "compulsion" (v. 14) and his expected "obedience" imply apostolic authority.[6]

But verses 1–7, especially the description of Paul as "a prisoner," anticipate Paul's later specific request that Philemon release his slave to return to minister to Paul in prison, as he has been doing. This may be hinted at in verse 21: "I write to you, since I know that you will do even more than what I say." "What I say" alludes to the explicit request to release Onesimus, and "do even more than what I say" seems to refer to releasing the slave to return to Paul and aid him in prison. It is also implicit in verse 13, where Paul says that he "wished to keep" Onesimus with him "that on your behalf he might minister to me in my [chains] for the gospel."[7]

As we noted on Col. 1:1, here Paul's mention of "Christ [Messiah] Jesus" is not a merely perfunctory use of the name, carrying little theological significance. The name conjures up the OT expectation of a Messiah, who is now identified with Christ Jesus.[8] This point is possibly enhanced by the placement first of "Christ," thus meaning "Messiah Jesus."

The greeting of verse 1 is not only from Paul but also from Timothy[9] (so also in the greeting sections of 2 Cor. 1:1; Phil. 1:1; 1 Thess. 1:1; 2 Thess. 1:1). The mention of Timothy here and in the other introductions indicates that he is one of Paul's "fellow workers" (Rom. 16:21; 1 Thess. 3:2; cf. 1 Cor. 16:10), but it may also suggest that he is Paul's secretary (it is less likely that this implies multiple authorship). Paul and other NT writers used secretaries in other letters (Peter used Silvanus as a secretary: 1 Pet. 5:12; and Paul dictated

4. Though Paul elsewhere does refer to himself as "slave" (Rom. 1:1, together with "apostle"; Phil. 1:1, using the plural for Paul and Timothy; Titus 1:1, together with "apostle"), which would have had a similar rhetorical force in Philem. 1 if Paul had used it.

5. Elsewhere Paul uses "boldness" (παρρησία, *parrhēsia*) to express his apostolic confidence in expressing the message of the gospel (2 Cor. 3:12; Eph. 6:19; Phil. 1:20).

6. Following Weima (2016: 206–7) on Paul's continued-though-implicit reference to his apostolic authority.

7. Following Weima (2016: 208–9) on the significance of the mention of "prisoner" in verse 1.

8. See on Col. 1:1 for fuller discussion, including commentators in support and a survey of the OT background of the messianic idea.

9. Some of the remainder of this discussion of verse 1 is based on our analysis of Col. 1:1.

Romans to Tertius: Rom. 16:22). Besides being a "fellow worker," Timothy has accompanied Paul in his travels (Acts 16:1–20:4; Phil. 2:19; 1 Thess. 3:6), preached alongside him (2 Cor. 1:19), and represented Paul's teachings to others (1 Cor. 4:17). Therefore it is understandable that Paul refers to him as a "brother,"[10] and, accordingly, it is appropriate that Timothy would be one of Paul's secretaries.

Use of a secretary is also suggested by how Paul brings attention to his unique signature at the end of several of his epistles.[11] This is underscored in Col. 4:18: "The greeting [is] by my hand, Paul."* In Philemon the same is underscored by the declaration "I, Paul, am writing this with my own hand" (v. 19). It also shows that Paul is the real author, even if dictating to a secretary.

In addition to Timothy being the apostle's secretary and fellow worker, mention of Timothy in verse 1 may also be Paul's way of endorsing him as the letter carrier (so cf. Doty 1973: 30). Perhaps the three ideas of Timothy being a secretary,[12] a coworker, and a letter carrier are all intended in his reference to Timothy.

The end of verse 1 identifies Philemon as among the recipients of the epistle. Philemon is mentioned nowhere else in the NT. This letter reveals that he is the slave owner of Onesimus and that Paul is appealing to him for Onesimus's release. Paul calls Philemon "beloved" and a "coworker." Often Paul calls believers in Christ "beloved" (e.g., see Rom. 1:7; 16:5, 8–9, 12). The term conveys a family relationship.[13] Onesimus himself is a "beloved brother" (Col. 4:9; Philem. 16) and "child" who is "begotten by" Paul (v. 10), and Timothy is a "beloved son" (2 Tim. 1:2). Already Paul is laying the groundwork for his appeal to Philemon to free Onesimus, since they both are *equally* "beloved" members of Christ's family. That Philemon is also Paul's "coworker" might derive from his being "beloved," since the close family relationship with Paul would naturally entail that they work closely together in that family. Indeed, "coworker" is found inextricably linked with family terms elsewhere in Paul (cf. "brother" and "coworker" in Phil. 2:25; 1 Thess. 3:2). God as "Father" is the authoritative head of the family (v. 3).[14]

2 Paul is also addressing this letter to "Apphia our sister," which underscores further the family relationship that believers have with one another. Paul refers to other female believers as "sister" elsewhere (Rom. 16:1; 1 Cor. 7:15; 9:5 NASB marg.; 1 Tim. 5:2). Many commentators think this could be Philemon's

10. Though we will see in verse 2 that "brother" includes the notion of fellow believers being part of a family.

11. With expressions like "I, Paul, write this greeting in my own hand, and this is a distinguishing mark in every letter. This is the way I write" (2 Thess. 3:17); likewise in 1 Cor. 16:21; Gal. 6:11.

12. See on Col. 1:1 for further background on secretaries, how they take dictation, and how this relates to Timothy as a secretary although Paul is the ultimate author.

13. E.g., Paul sometimes refers to Christians as "beloved children" (1 Cor. 4:14; Eph. 5:1; cf. 1 Cor. 4:17) and "beloved brothers" (1 Cor. 15:58; Eph. 6:21; Phil. 4:1; Col. 4:7).

14. Pao (2012: 375) has observed that Onesimus as a "child" fits into the family portrait here, as does God as "Father" (v. 3).

wife or actual sister (e.g., Dunn 1996: 312), but this is speculation. We just do not know who she is.

In addition, another addressee of the epistle is Archippus. Paul urges the Colossians to tell Archippus, "Take heed to the ministry which you have received in the Lord, that you may fulfill it" (Col. 4:17). This may be why Paul calls him here a "fellow soldier," since he is working for the same cause of the ministry as Paul (Epaphroditus is also a "fellow soldier" in Phil. 2:25). Archippus is probably exhorted by Paul (through the Colossians) to persevere in the ministry (Col. 4:17) because it involves hardship, a condition that soldiers also need to face, as in 2 Tim. 2:3: "Suffer hardship with me, as a good soldier of Christ Jesus." Presumably for this reason Paul calls Archippus a "fellow soldier."

A fourth recipient of the letter is "the church in your house." This may refer to the church that meets in the house of Archippus, though we will see below that it more likely refers to "the church" in Philemon's "house," whether to one of the house churches in Colossae or to the entire church there, since Col. 4:17 (see above) appears to place Archippus in Colossae. "Church" refers to the assembly of believers in Colossae who meet regularly for worship. The word has an OT background, where it refers to the assembly of Israel. The term now is applied to the Christian congregation because they are the continuation of the true Israel, the true people of God.[15]

Paul wishes these believers "grace" and "peace."[16] This greeting is addressed 3
to "you" (ὑμῖν, *hymin*), the second-person plural pronoun, thus still having in view all four of the recipients of the letter listed in verses 1–2. Though Paul also addresses his letter to Apphia, Archippus, and the church in Colossae, Philemon is the addressee of focus, as the remainder of the letter in verses 5–21 reveals. Yet in verses 22–25 Paul returns to the second-person plural pronoun "you," including all of the recipients again. Why does Paul begin with naming multiple addressees and conclude in the same way, but focus only on the individual Philemon in the body of the letter? It is clear that Paul wants Apphia, Archippus, and the church body in Colossae to be aware of his appeal to Philemon, since the whole congregation will hear the letter read. Therefore, even the body of the letter, while focusing on Philemon, is secondarily addressed to the entire church. Since they are all part of the same family, the whole family ("brothers," "sisters," and "beloved" ones) needs to be addressed (D. Moo 2008: 384–85).

Perhaps Paul includes them all as recipients so that they will encourage Philemon to heed Paul's appeal to him. Or perhaps Onesimus's illegally running away from Philemon has fractured the entire church community, so that not merely Philemon but also the whole church needs to forgive Onesimus and receive him back as a Christian brother (Garland 1998: 318). Both notions are probably in mind. The problem involving Onesimus and Philemon is a

15. For fuller discussion of ἐκκλησία (*ekklēsia*), see comments and additional notes on Col. 1:18.

16. Discussion of verse 3 is based on our analysis of Col. 1:2; see my comments there.

significant moral and spiritual issue that can impact the entire church, since the church is an extended family (brothers, sisters, beloved ones, children). Therefore the entire church needs to be addressed about this issue (Garland 1998: 323–24). In addition, Philemon is accountable to the church,[17] though implicitly all in the church are also accountable to one another for the decisions they make with respect to Philemon.

Some think Archippus is the main recipient of the letter. But Philemon is likely the primary recipient, since the first addressee mentioned in Greco-Roman letters is usually the main addressee.[18] The second-person singular pronoun in the phrase in verse 2, "the church in <u>your</u> house," may refer either to Philemon, Apphia, or Archippus. Perhaps since the latter is the closest antecedent, then the church may be seen as meeting in Archippus's house, and this would suggest, together with other considerations, that Archippus is the one mainly being addressed in the letter as the owner of Onesimus.[19] On the other hand, since Philemon is the main recipient of this letter, it seems more probable that the phrase refers to the church in Philemon's house.

As we saw in Col. 1:2, the typical introductory "greeting" (χαίρειν, *chairein*) of the Hellenistic letter is replaced by the similar sounding "grace" (χάρις, *charis*), as a theological play on words (on Col. 1:2, e.g., see O'Brien 1982: 4). Paul inserts a theology of grace into what was the typical way of saying "hello" in the ancient Greek letter. After the greeting in Hellenistic letters, there is usually a wish about the letter's recipients (or comment about the author's health). Paul replaces this with an invocation of "peace" upon his readers (following Sumney 2008: 29, on Col. 1:2).[20] Paul issues a formulaic introductory "Grace to you and peace from God our Father" nine times in the openings of his epistles (cf. likewise 1 Tim. 1:2; 2 Tim. 1:2; Titus 1:4). Some may think that such a standard formula might be just a default stylistic greeting without exegetical or theological significance, much as the contemporary "*Dear* so-and-so." But since Paul uses "grace" and "peace" often throughout the body of his letters with theological significance, it is likely that it also has significance in the letter openings. The context of each letter explains what is meant by the twofold greeting. Is the "grace and peace" greeting a prayer, a statement of fact, or a wish? In the case of Colossians, we decided that it is best not to make these distinctions, since, as is clear in the context of Colossians, Paul thinks that the Colossians now benefit in different ways from God's grace,

17. Wilson (2005: 335) sees this as a possibility.

18. So D. Moo 2008: 382; likewise Harris 2010: 211. For an example of such a Greco-Roman letter, see Lohse 1971: 190–91.

19. Knox (1959: 56–70) argues this in some depth by adducing a number of considerations that he believes strongly point to this conclusion. For example, he contends that Paul's exhortation in Col. 4:17 to Archippus ("Take heed to the ministry which you received in the Lord, that you may fulfill it") is the main message of Philemon, where Paul is exhorting Archippus to let his slave Onesimus return to Paul to "minister" to him in his imprisonment (Philem. 13).

20. For the typical pattern of "greeting" followed by comments about health in Hellenistic letters, see Hunt and Edgar 1932: 269–395.

and he also prays that God will continue to extend his grace to them in the future.[21] Though there is not much context in Philemon, the observation that Paul begins with "grace" and concludes the letter with "grace" highlights how, from beginning to end, Paul sees grace as necessary for Philemon to respond positively to Paul's requests.[22] Furthermore, that Paul thanks God for Philemon's faith and prays that "the fellowship of your faith may become effective" (vv. 4–6) indicates that what Philemon presently has as a Christian is by God's grace (otherwise why thank God for it?) and that what he will have spiritually is by God's grace.

Real "peace" also comes only "from God our Father and the Lord Jesus Christ." While Paul employs these words "grace" and "peace" in each of his epistolary introductions, they are not superficial polite terms but seem to be the goal of verses 1–2, though this may also be said of Paul's other epistles, where the "grace and peace"[23] introduction occurs as the conclusion of the letter opening. The only way one can ever have grace and peace is if one is "in Christ Jesus" (v. 16, 20).

"God our Father" is followed in verse 3 by "the Lord Jesus Christ," as in most of Paul's other epistles. Placing "Christ Jesus"[24] in conjunction here with "God our Father" implies his divine identity. The introductory "Lord" further confirms Christ's divine status, since it has its background in the "Lord" of the Greek OT, which is a translation of "Yahweh."[25] This is thus a reference to Jesus's deity.

21. For the former, e.g., see Col. 1:6, 12–14; cf. 2:12–13; and for the latter, see Col. 1:9–11; cf. 1:28; 3:4.

22. An observation I have subsequently found made by other commentators; e.g., Pao 2012: 366.

23. The introductory "grace" and "peace" may have its broader background in the OT and early Judaism, though there not "grace" (χάρις, *charis*) but "mercy" (ἔλεος, *eleos*) and "peace" are found (see the additional note on Col. 1:2). However, Paul and other NT writers see "mercy" to be generally synonymous with "grace" (see 1 Tim. 1:2; 2 Tim. 1:2; 2 John 3; cf. Jude 2). Note also Paul's conclusion of "peace and mercy" in Gal. 6:16, which refers to God's fulfilling the promise of end-time restoration to Israel (see Beale 1999a: 204–23).

24. See on verse 1 for the OT background of "Christ."

25. See further on Col. 1:3 for this OT background of "Lord."

II. Introductory Thanksgiving and Prayer: Paul Thanks God for Philemon and Prays for Him (4–7)

Here is a fuller statement of the main idea of this unit: *Paul thanks God for Philemon because he recognizes in him genuine love and faithfulness, and he prays that Philemon's faith will continue to grow effectively*.

"Giving thanks" (v. 4) and "praying" (v. 6) are the two major points of the paragraph; everything else in the paragraph (vv. 4b–7) forms part of the logical basis to support these main points. Paul gives thanks because he discerns in Philemon the traits of genuine Christian living, and he prays that those traits will increase (esp. his faithfulness).

Likewise, in Philem. 4–7 Paul prayerfully remembers God's grace, which has been imparted to Philemon. Paul gives thanks, therefore, "because" of what he prayerfully recalls about Philemon (v. 4), particularly "because he has heard of his love and faith" (cf. v. 5). In verse 6 Paul explains further what was uppermost in his prayers mentioned in verse 4: "that the fellowship of [Philemon's] faith may become [increasingly] effective" in his life, which develops also the "faith" mentioned in verse 5. Verse 7 then shows the effects of Philemon's "love" (mentioned in v. 5) on Paul, who found "much joy and comfort" in that love.

The reason Paul thanks God for these things is to assure Philemon of the truth of his Christian faith by causing him to reflect on the evidence of love and faith working within him. It has probably been about three years since Paul has seen Philemon, so instead of moving directly to the body from the letter opening to make the explicit request about Onesimus, the thanksgiving is first inserted to reestablish his relationship with the slave owner and show gratitude for his love and faith. The thanksgiving also functions to exhort Philemon to persevere even more in the love and faith that he has already exhibited. Likewise, the initial mention of prayer in the thanksgiving shows that Philemon is always in Paul's prayers.[1]

Much powerful Pauline theology can be found packed into Paul's opening thanksgivings throughout his letters, and that is certainly the case here.

Exegesis and Exposition

4I thank my God always, making mention of you in my prayers, 5because I hear of your ⌜love, and of the faith⌝ which you have toward the Lord Jesus, and toward all

1. See Weima (2016: 214–15) for this role of reestablishing the relationship through the thanksgiving and its exhortative role before moving to the body of the letter.

the saints; [6]and I pray that the fellowship of your faith may become effective through the knowledge of every good ⌜thing⌝ which is in ⌜you⌝ for Christ's sake. [7]For I have come to have much joy and comfort in your love, because the hearts of the saints have been refreshed through you, brother.

Now Paul launches out on how "grace and peace" (v. 3), the ultimate goal 4
of the letter, may begin to be achieved: through "giving thanks." Part of participating in divine grace is to recognize it, and this can begin through thanksgiving. Furthermore, thanking God for Philemon is Paul's beginning move to initiate "peace" with Philemon, to which the remainder of the letter will contribute. "Giving thanks" is based on a prayerful consideration of the effect of God's grace in the readers' lives.[2] "Give thanks" is modified by the phrase "making mention" (μνείαν . . . ποιούμενος, *mneian . . . poioumenos*), here an adverbial participle of manner ("in the manner of praying") or time ("on the occasion when we make mention"). The "making mention" by Paul occurs at the time that he prays (ἐπὶ τῶν προσευχῶν μου, *epi tōn proseuchōn mou*; cf. Harris 2010: 215). Paul is praying specifically for Philemon (note the singular "you"), which implies that his daily prayer list must have been extensive (Dunn 1996: 316). As is typical elsewhere in his epistles, his introductory thanks grow out of a previous attitude and activity of prayer. In this light, while the adverbial participle can be viewed as manner or temporal, the occasion of prayer probably is the ultimate ground from which his thanksgiving arises. In his other letters, the prayers placed directly after the opening thanksgivings almost always include some remembrance of God's gracious work among the Christian readers, followed by expressions of concern that aspects of their faith become increasingly established (Rom. 1:8–11; Eph. 1:15–17; Phil. 1:3–6; Col. 1:3–11; cf. 2 Cor. 1:11). From this pattern one can observe that in these other introductory thanksgivings, Paul initially meditates prayerfully on the divine grace that has begun to affect the lives of believers; then, together with this, he gives an explicit cause for his thanksgiving. Paul's reflection on how God's grace has impacted his readers leads him to give thanks to God for it. When there is no prayerful contemplation of divine blessings, there can be no attitude of thanksgiving. Certainly such prayerful remembrance includes making requests to God for his people, in whom he has begun to work.

Paul suggests that prayerful reflection on these divine blessings should occur "always."[3] Otherwise one's thankful perspective will be intermittent and inconsistent. Whoever does not continually reflect on such blessings will

2. Discussion of this verse is based to a significant extent on Beale 2003: 45–46.

3. "Always" is an adverb that could well modify "I give thanks," but it more likely modifies "making mention," since it is closer to the latter and is parallel with Col. 1:3, where "always" could also modify "giving thanks" and/or "praying" but more probably modifies "praying" (for the reasoning, see on Col. 1:3). D. Moo (2008: 386) concludes the opposite but rightly says that it does not make a lot of difference in the meaning of the verse, since giving thanks and praying are so closely related here.

not be continually aware of them, thankful for them, or desiring to be thankful. Continual reflection on the Giver of good gifts to us causes us to be more conscious of and thankful for those gifts. The causal link between persevering prayerful reflection and thanksgiving may also be implied in 1 Thess. 5:18: "Pray continually; give thanks in all circumstances."* The statement that Paul's praying occurs "always" is not to be taken woodenly but is figurative of a habitual or continual attitude or activity. This letter reveals that Paul is in a family relationship with Philemon, Onesimus, and others in Colossae (vv. 1, 2, 10, 16, 20), and just as close family members in physical families are not far from the thoughts of one another, so Paul is continually mindful of his spiritual brothers, sisters, and children.[4]

Thankfulness arises, at least in part, from the following aspects of continual prayer, consistent with the broad sweep of Paul's theology (cf. Eph. 5:20; Phil. 4:6): (1) from reflection on how God has answered prayers in the past (whether with "no" or "yes"); (2) from adoration of God's person, faithfulness, and providential provisions in spiritual and material ways; (3) from the times when we acknowledge our sin and recall that Christ paid the penalty for sin and overcame that penalty by his resurrection (cf. 1 Cor. 1:4–6). Christians impoverish themselves when they do not prayerfully consider how they have experienced God's grace, and this theological impoverishment results in an unthankful attitude. To the extent that one has a prayerful attitude, to that extent one will have an attitude of thanksgiving.

Part of what is packed into Paul's prayer in verse 4 is explicitly elaborated on in verse 6.

5 Paul now adds another adverbial participial modifier of "giving thanks." This second participle is best translated "because I hear [ἀκούων, *akouōn*]," which in addition to prayer (v. 4) gives another ultimate ground for why Paul is thanking God in verse 4. According to verse 5, Paul recognizes that his thanksgiving arises out of recognizing in Philemon the true marks of Christian existence: "love" and "faith." "Love" and "faith" are combined closely together as essential Christian traits throughout Paul's writings (so twenty times). Thus he is also thanking God because he has heard of Philemon's "love [ἀγάπη, *agapē*] and of the faith [πίστις, *pistis*] which [he has] toward the Lord Jesus and toward all the saints." Paul commences the verse by saying that Philemon has "love," which implicitly is love for Christ and other believers. The horizontal relation of love with fellow Christians is inextricably linked to the vertical relationship with Christ (the attitude of love toward Christ).[5] The former always gives rise to the latter. "Giving thanks" of verse 4a continues to be the main point in verses 4b–5a, since the attitudes of "love" and "faith" are the supporting cause of the thanksgiving, as was the occasion of prayer in verse 4.

4. See Gaventa (1998: 13–14), who makes the same point about Paul's thanksgiving in 1 Thess. 1:2, which I have applied here.

5. Dunn (1996: 56) makes the similar point about Col. 1:4, which I have applied here.

It may be that both the "love" and "faith" are directed "toward the Lord Jesus and for all the saints" (so ESV, HCSB, NJB; cf. RSV;[6] Barth and Blanke 2000: 271–72, 278; Dunn 1996: 315, 317). However, since the relative feminine pronoun is singular, it seems that only "faith," the closest preceding antecedent to the relative, is directed toward the Lord and the saints (typically relative pronouns must agree in number and gender with their antecedents).[7] Furthermore, if both are modified by the two following clauses, then the relative pronoun would more likely be neuter, which could then include both "love" and "faith" as plural concepts within the relative pronoun. But even if both "love and the faith" are directly related to the Lord and the saints, there is ambiguity about the exact meaning of "the faith, which you have toward the Lord Jesus and [unto] all the saints." Having faith "toward the Lord Jesus" (πρὸς τὸν κύριον Ἰησοῦν, *pros ton kyrion Iēsoun*) is fairly clear in that it refers to Jesus as the object of Philemon's faith. But what does "faith . . . unto [εἰς, *eis*][8] the saints" mean? This expression is unique in all of Paul and, indeed, all of the NT, LXX, Josephus, and Philo. Believers certainly do not trust in one another as they do Jesus. Some manuscripts change the order of the wording to "because I have heard of the faith and the love, which you have toward the Lord Jesus and unto all the saints." This makes perfect sense and seems to fit perfectly with Col. 1:4 ("because we have heard about your faith in Christ Jesus and the love which you have for all the saints") and Eph. 1:15.[9] And on

6. That these translations favor this view is apparent from observing that they have no punctuation at all in the verse, thus not separating "love" from "faith," so that both appear to be viewed as being "toward the Lord Jesus and for all the saints."

7. Wallace (1996: 336) also gives exceptions to this rule, none of which appear to apply to the phraseology of Philem. 5 (Wallace 1996: 337–42). Likewise Meyer (1885: 399–400), who argues that the phrase "to the Lord and unto all the saints" "is attached as one whole to τὴν πίστιν" and is not directly related to "your love."

8. Some commentators attempt to see significance in the different prepositions πρός (*pros*) and εἰς (*eis*), especially with respect to "faith" going with "to the Lord Jesus" and "love" going with "unto all the saints" (e.g., see Lenski 1961: 955–56). However, εἰς can "stand for ἐπί (*epi*) and πρός. Except for mere stylistic variation there is no point in the change" of prepositions in Philem. 5 (MHT 3:256). Indeed, in verse 5 some MSS (A, C, D*, and some minuscules) replace πρός with εἰς, perhaps trying to bring it into conformity with the following εἰς, but showing the possible synonymity of the two prepositions. Nevertheless, and with more sophistication, Lightfoot (1875: 335) argues that, while the two prepositions can be used interchangeably, "where a distinction is necessary," the former can mean "*direction* . . . 'towards'; the latter . . . *arrival* and so *contact* 'in-to,' 'unto,'" so that "there is a propriety in using πρός of the faith which aspires *towards* Christ, and εἰς of the love which is exerted *upon* men." Harris (2012: 83) appears to agree with Lightfoot on the distinction in Philem. 5. Moule (1959: 67–68) agrees with Lightfoot on the distinction in meaning when the two prepositions are not synonymous, but in Philem. 5 he concludes that the use of the two different prepositions "looks like a purely stylistic variation." While Lightfoot's view is reasonable, MHT's and Moule's conclusion appears more cautious until there is more forthcoming argumentation otherwise.

9. Ephesians 1:15, which most likely reads "faith in the Lord Jesus and the love which is unto all the saints," has a textual variant that omits "love," resulting in "faith in the Lord Jesus and which [faith] is unto all the saints." Very good MSS support this shorter reading (e.g., 𝔓[46], ℵ*, A, B), but it seems probable that "love" was omitted by accidental homeoarcton (skipping from

this basis, commentators (e.g., D. Moo 2008: 388–89) and some translations (e.g., NRSV) change the order of the wording to fit Paul's usual usage: "your love for all his people and your faith in the Lord Jesus." This no doubt is also fueled by the fact that when Paul refers to "faith" and "love," "faith" typically comes first, though there are times when "faith" and "love" are combined in which "love" precedes "faith" (see the second additional note on v. 5).

On the other hand, I have found no one who acknowledges that πίστις (*pistis*) followed by the preposition πρός is very rare (occurring only elsewhere in 1 Thess. 1:8, and the verb form is never followed by this preposition; so Moule 1959: 54). Thus the clause construction is not parallel with Col. 1:4 or Eph. 1:15.

There is no clear basis for changing the word order, though it is surprising that the majority of commentators propose a chiastic arrangement to support the change. However, such a chiasm cannot be clearly discerned (see the additional note on vv. 5–7 for an explanation of why this is so).

So we need to let Paul be Paul, even when he speaks exceptionally. What could Paul have possibly meant by this expression? Perhaps the solution lies in not translating πίστις by "faith" but by "faithfulness," which is a common way to render this Greek word. The specific notion of "faithfulness" may be that of "fidelity toward," "devotion toward," "loyalty to," or "commitment toward," maybe even "confidence toward" (for these ranges of meanings, see BDAG 818–20, s.v. πίστις).[10] These renderings make sense of how such "faithfulness" or "loyal commitment" could be directed toward Christ, as well as toward fellow believers. Christians express faithful loyalty to Christ above all (through belief and resulting evidence of works), yet they also show faithful loyalty, commitment to or confidence in one another as fellow saints in Christ. "Faithfulness" is not the typical sense of πίστις in Paul, but it is attested elsewhere in his writings, as are the other senses of "fidelity toward," "devotion toward," "commitment toward," and "confidence in."[11]

What especially favors these related senses of πίστις is that Paul is setting up his appeal to Philemon to release Onesimus, and he is thanking God for Philemon's Christian quality of "commitment" or "devotion" to the best interests of his brothers and sisters in Christ. Indeed, his love *toward the saints* (which is implied) in the beginning of the verse is not far out of mind

---

the first τήν [*tēn*] to the second τήν [*tēn*]; so Metzger 1994: 533). Thus this variant's shorter reading, which has unique correspondence with Philem. 5, is not valid because it is not in the original Greek.

10. Interestingly, BDAG categorizes πίστις (*pistis*) in Philem. 5 as "faith . . . toward the Lord Jesus" (BDAG 819) and classifies the second implied occurrence as "faith" or "firm commitment," which is directed to the saints, "as a Christian virtue" (BDAG 819–20).

11. See BDAG 818–20, s.v. πίστις; and see D. Moo (2008: 388), citing Rom. 3:3; Gal. 5:22; and 1 Tim. 2:7, though he does not prefer that meaning here. Meyer (1885: 399–400), Houlden (1977: 229), and Bruce (1984: 208) are the only commentators that I have found who agree that πίστις here refers to faithfulness or loyalty; Meyer prefers this over the chiasm proposal (see the additional note on vv. 5–7). See Barth and Blanke (2000: 273) and Meyer (1885: 399) for a list of commentators who also favor the notion of "faithfulness," especially older scholars.

and has likely shaped the kind of faithful commitment that he has toward his fellow believers. Paul believes that his imminent appeal to Philemon to release Onesimus will fall on a fertile heart because of Philemon's general spiritual condition of commitment and devotion to others in the community of faith. Paul is reminding Philemon about this general commitment that he has. This understanding of "faithfulness unto the saints" will be borne out by Paul's expansion of what it means in verse 6. Indeed, this anticipated appeal is enhanced by recalling that Paul has just recognized Philemon's trait of "love," and he will acknowledge it again in verse 7, which also becomes part of the grounds for his imminent appeal to accept Onesimus as a "beloved brother" (v. 16). In this light, Paul's reference to Philemon as "beloved" to him (v. 1) also can be viewed as part of the basis for this anticipated entreaty (esp. as expressed in v. 16).

Believers are called "saints" (pl. of ἅγιος, *hagios*). This refers to the same notion of "saints" discussed in Col. 1:2 (see my comments there): the people (i.e., Christians) of the new-covenant age who are inheriting the end-time promises made to Israel.

Now Paul picks up his prayer description begun in verse 4 and specifies what 6
he has been praying about in that prior mention of prayer. The initial ὅπως (*hopōs*) should be translated as "that," introducing the focus of his prayer from verse 4. At the beginning of the verse, almost all translations insert the phrase "I pray that," which they are carrying over from verse 4. This is plausible, but perhaps more precisely the actual phrase from verse 4 should be resupplied in the following way: "*making mention of you in my prayers* that . . ."[12] This would be an implied repetition of μνείαν . . . ποιούμενος + ἐπὶ τῶν προσευχῶν μου (*mneian . . . poioumenos + epi tōn proseuchōn mou*) from verse 4; again the implied participle would be adverbial of manner ("in the manner of making mention") or time ("on the occasion when we make mention").

The content of the prayer expands on and interprets what he has meant by "faithfulness . . . unto the saints" in verse 5. The prayer is that "the fellowship of your faith should become effective in the knowledge of every good thing in you[13] toward [with respect to or with reference to] Christ." Among other issues in this verse, there are at least two major problems to solve: (1) the meaning of κοινωνία (*koinōnia*) and (2) the meaning of πίστις.

First, the most basic ranges of meaning for κοινωνία are "fellowship," "communion," "participation," and "sharing."[14] Each of these definitions has the common notion of a close relationship due to partaking of the same

12. Most translations and commentators supply some expression of prayer at the beginning of verse 6, since it does not make much sense to see verse 6 as introducing the purpose or content of verse 5; if such were the case, it would read, "your love and faith [v. 5] . . . in order that the participation in your faith should become effective"; e.g., see Pao 2012: 369.

13. Some MSS have ἡμῖν (*hēmin*, us) here instead of ὑμῖν (*hymin*, pl. you); see the third additional note on verse 6.

14. See BDAG (552–53, s.v. κοινωνία), though for Philem. 6 BDAG prefers "participation, sharing."

reality, which in this case is being in union with Christ by faith. Thus these meanings overlap, and all are plausible here.[15] Perhaps the idea can best be summarized as "mutual participation" (so N. Wright 1986: 176). In what is Philemon participating or sharing? There are at least three ways of understanding the expression ἡ κοινωνία τῆς πίστεώς σου (*hē koinōnia tēs pisteōs sou*). (1) Probably the best is as "mutual participation [sharing] in your faith" or "your mutual participation in the faith," viewing ἡ κοινωνία τῆς πίστεώς σου as a genitive designating the sphere in which Philemon is participating. (2) It is possible that it could be an objective genitive, where the genitive is the object of the verbal idea of "fellowship": "sharing your faith." (3) Finally, it could be rendered "mutual participation [sharing] arising from [or produced by] your faith" (a genitive of source or a subjective genitive).[16]

Second, the "faith" in which Philemon is participating is the faith that he holds in common with other believers, faith in Christ: that this "faith" is directed toward Christ is apparent from the end of the verse, "unto Christ" (also see on v. 5 above). This "faith" refers to the condition of Philemon's belief "based on the reliability of the one [Christ] trusted" (BDAG 818, s.v. πίστις). It is likely that "faith" here refers not to "a body of faith" (as some take it) but to an object in which faith is placed,[17] since it would be odd to try to understand an objective body of faith "becoming effective" but more natural to see one's active faith increasing and thus "becoming effective." The concept here is similar to 1 Cor. 3:21, 23, where Paul is trying to unify divided believers: "All things belong to you, . . . and you belong to Christ" (Thompson 2005: 215). Likewise, Philemon participates in a faith that he has in common with other Christians, which then becomes "effective."

The expression "<u>making mention of you in my prayers</u> . . . that participation in your faith [held in common with other saints] <u>should become effective with the knowledge of every good thing</u>"* (Philem. 4, 6) is parallel with Col. 1:9–10, "<u>praying</u> and requesting that you <u>should be filled</u>[18] with the <u>knowledge</u> . . . in <u>every good</u> work."*[19] The point of being "filled with knowledge . . . in every good work" is equivalent to saying that their knowledge should become effective "in every good work." That the prayer in Col. 1:9–10 continues with mention that the Colossian saints would be "strengthened in power [by God] . . . with a view to all endurance" highlights the idea of perseverance (1:11). The idea of an *effective faith* (*implicitly based on God's power*) *that perseveres* appears also to be in mind in Philem. 6,

15. Wilson (2005: 340) rightly says that "the term κοινωνία . . . covers a whole complex of ideas and associations which cannot easily be brought under a single English equivalent."

16. See the first additional note on verse 6 for support of the spheric or objective genitive view of the construction and discussion of alternative options.

17. For the category, see BDAG 820, s.v. πίστις.

18. Here underlining "should be filled" represents a conceptual but not verbal parallel, while the other underlined phrases represent verbal parallels.

19. On the variant ἔργου (*ergou*, work) found in Philem. 6 in some MSS, see the second additional note on verse 6.

as paraphrased here: "may be effective in deepening your understanding of every good thing" (TNIV; likewise NET).

"Good work" (ἔργον + ἀγαθόν, *ergon* + *agathon*) is a favorite phrase of Paul's,[20] and sometimes it occurs in the form of "every good work" (πᾶς + ἔργον ἀγαθόν, *pas* + *ergon agathon*).[21] The uses of both phrases "good work" and "every good work" are typically very general but do refer to some kind of righteous acts performed or done rather than to something as an object of knowledge or something possessed (Moule 1957: 143). For example, a gift of financial support is specified in the context of 2 Cor. 9:8. But as just noted, the closest parallel is Col. 1:10, where "every good work" is general and refers to righteous acts. "Knowledge of every good thing" is an objective genitive ("knowing every good thing"), but the idea is that this knowledge is inextricably linked to the actual doing of good: it is a knowledge that leads to good actions. "Every good work" is initially general also in Philem. 6, but the following context shows that, among "all the good works" Paul has in mind, the particular work to which Philemon is to accede is Paul's request to release Philemon. The preposition ἐν (*en*) before "knowledge" could signify the "sphere" in which their partnership would be "effective" (Pao 2012: 371); or better, the means by which it would become effective; or best, the manner ("in," "with," or "by way of") in which the partnership would become effective. Thus Paul is praying that Philemon will demonstrate the proof of his faith by that faith "becoming effective" through producing "every good thing [work]." This is obviously an anticipation of Paul's asking Philemon to do a good work of releasing Onesimus (vv. 8–21). One translation (NLT) even asserts that this request is already being made: "I am praying that you will put into action the generosity [κοινωνία] that comes from your faith as you understand and experience all the good things we have in Christ." Some commentators support the same idea.[22] Indeed, the standard NT lexicon gives "generosity, altruism" as a possible definition of κοινωνία.[23] Nevertheless, "generosity" is probably not the best specific choice of meaning here. The "every good thing" (παντὸς ἀγαθοῦ, *pantos agathou*) only anticipates Paul's appeal specifically to Philemon's "goodness" (τὸ ἀγαθόν, *to agathon*, v. 14).[24] It likewise anticipates in verse 8 "what is fitting" (or "what is proper" or "the

20. As in Rom. 2:7; 13:3; Eph. 2:10; Phil. 1:6; 1 Tim. 2:10.

21. As in 2 Cor. 9:8; Col. 1:10; 2 Thess. 2:17; 1 Tim. 5:10; 2 Tim. 2:21; 3:17; Titus 1:16; 3:1.

22. Harris (2010: 217) summarizes versions and commentators holding this position. See O'Brien (1982: 275, 280) and Lightfoot (1875: 335), who like the rendering "your kindly deeds of charity." Most recently, see Weima 2016: 220. The use of κοινωνία in Phil. 1:5, in light of Phil. 4:14–18, likely includes but does not exhaust the notion of "sharing" financial aid with Paul for his needs.

23. See BDAG (553, s.v. κοινωνία), citing 2 Cor. 9:13 and Heb. 13:16 for the meaning of "generosity" and Rom. 15:26 for the rendering of "gift, contribution."

24. So D. Moo 2008: 385. Weima (2016: 220) argues that *only* Paul's request of Philemon is in mind here, but it is more likely that, while the request is the "good" that is anticipated, other good works are secondarily included.

right thing"; cf. BDAG 79, s.v. ἀνήκω) for Philemon to do, which is to release Onesimus.

The clause "faith may become effective for every good"* work is indirectly related to other believers (note "the faith" they "share" and "every good thing which is in us") and related to Christ (end of v. 6), which forms a nice parallel with the similar phrase in verse 5 ("faith . . . toward the Lord Jesus and unto all the saints"). Verse 6 shows a development of the idea from verse 5.

That verse 6 anticipates Paul's imminent request of Philemon is apparent from recalling that κοινωνία (fellowship, communion, participation, and sharing) occurs in verse 6 and κοινωνός (*koinōnos*, sharer, partner), a word closely related in meaning and part of the same word group, appears in verse 17: "If you [Philemon] have me as a partner, then receive him [Onesimus] as [you would] me."* Thus Paul's reference to Philemon as *sharing in the common faith* of all the saints in verse 6 is a basis later for Paul's appeal to accept Onesimus into brotherly Christian fellowship in the same way as he would accept Paul. Since Philemon shares a common faith with all true believers,[25] including Paul and Onesimus, he should accept back Onesimus on the same basis as he would accept Paul as a brother believer.

Another problem in verse 6 is determining what the prepositional phrase εἰς Χριστόν (*eis Christon*, to/toward Christ) modifies. It could modify (1) "the fellowship of your faith should become effective" or (2) "in knowledge" or (3) "every good thing which [is] in us." The first option is favored by observing that since prepositional phrases usually modify verbs, "become" is the only explicit verb in the verse. This could also be favored by recalling that already in the preceding verse Paul has mentioned "faith toward the Lord Jesus." If "faith may become effective" is directly related to "unto [or toward] Christ," then it forms a nice parallel with the similar phrase in verse 5. On the other hand, "every good thing which [is] in us" is closer to the preposition, and it does have an implicit verb "is." Furthermore, the Col. 1:10 parallel supports the close connection of "every good work" in relation to the Lord: "to please Him [the Lord] in [every respect], bearing fruit in every good work." Both are plausible in Philem. 6, but it may be best to focus on the εἰς Χριστόν clause as broadly modifying the whole phrase: "a faith that acts by way of the knowledge of the good which God has imparted to us—should be for Christ" (paraphrasing Lohse 1971: 194–95), in the sense of pleasing Christ (in line with Col. 1:10).

Thus the preposition εἰς here is best expressed as "unto, toward," and possibly "for." Paul prays that Philemon's participation in the faith he shares with the saints should become effective in every good work, and the aim is to do such good works "for Christ" (as in NRSV, NJB)[26] or "with a view toward Christ," with the goal of pleasing Christ or of the end-time goal of leading

25. Note BDAG (553, s.v. κοινωνός), placing Philem. 17 under the semantic category of "one who takes part in something with someone."

26. D. Moo (2008: 394) follows the NASB, TNIV, and ESV, which have "for the sake of Christ," a rendering for εἰς by itself that is possible but only if understood in the sense of means to an end (as D. Moo does) and not a causal notion.

them to Christ as their final salvific destination (on the latter cf. Fitzmyer 2000: 99).[27] In addition εἰς expressing sphere, "in Christ," is also viable (KJV, RSV, NIV, NLT, NET). The latter rendering would highlight the believers' union with Christ and the "good" they share with one another because of that union. According to this view, Philemon's "good" works would be done because he, together with all Christians, shares in Christ, in whom is found all good. But the parallel with "toward the Lord Jesus" (πρὸς τὸν κύριον Ἰησοῦν, *pros ton kyrion Iēsoun*) in verse 5 tips the scales to εἰς Χριστόν referring to the goal ("unto, toward, for") of Philemon's "good" work.[28] In the light of the Col. 1:10 parallel, pleasing Christ is likely the goal in mind.

Thus, in Philem. 4–7, Paul does not thank Philemon, nor does he thank both Philemon and God; instead, he thanks only God for Philemon's love and faithfulness. This indicates that it is not Philemon's independent, autonomous efforts, even to some small degree, that earned God's grace in his life, but it shows that everything about his Christian life is a result of God's unconditional "grace," as evidenced from verses 3 and 25: "grace [χάρις, *charis*] . . . from . . . the Lord Jesus Christ."[29] Human significance does not reside in self-determination apart from divine influence. Rather, Paul sees that human self-worth has its foundation in the grace of God alone (see 1 Cor. 4:7). There is difference of opinion among commentators about whether salvation is based to a significant degree in human actions apart from God's working or in God's absolute unconditional work. This commentary affirms that the context of Philemon (esp. vv. 3 and 25), as well as the evidence of Colossians and the rest of Paul's writings, reflects the latter perspective.

Paul's prayer that Philemon's faith may become effectively expressed in real **7**
actions (v. 6) is based on (γάρ, *gar*, for) his "great joy and comfort" that Paul has already found in Philemon's "love," which itself is based on the fact that "the hearts of the saints have been refreshed through" Philemon.[30] Thus, since Philemon has already expressed his faith through loving works toward other saints, Paul in verse 6 prays that Philemon's faith would express itself in even more loving works, that is, in releasing Onesimus from slavery, as he will explicitly say in verses 8–21. The words describing Philemon, "love" and "brother," are intentionally used to help Philemon recall that all believers,

27. This latter option could also be understood in the sense of "bringing believers into closer relationship to Christ" (Moule 1957: 142), which can be understood as an "already and not yet" process that culminates at Christ's final coming.

28. See Beale, Brendsel, and Ross (2014: 39, 85) for the overlapping notions of the meanings of πρός (*pros*) and εἰς (*eis*) as designating purpose or aim.

29. Philemon 3 has additional wording between "grace" and "from the Lord Jesus Christ."

30. The γάρ (*gar*) could be explanatory, "in that" or "in particular," but this does not make as much sense as the causal use. The γάρ could be directly related to the giving of thanks in verse 4, so that verse 7 gives another reason for thanksgiving (so Lightfoot 1875: 336), which yields good sense: Paul's thanksgiving arises from the joy and comfort he has received in Philemon's love. While this is possible, it appears more likely that verse 7 gives the specific ground for verse 6, since verse 7 is directly related to verse 6, and verse 7 is further away from verse 4.

including Onesimus, are in a family relationship with one another and are thus equal family members in the eyes of God and one another. This should further support Paul's appeal to Philemon about Onesimus. In further support of the imminent appeal to Philemon is Paul's recognition that generally "the hearts of the saints have been refreshed [ἀναπαύω, *anapauō*] through" him. This lays the basis for Paul's verse 20 appeal to Philemon that he specifically will express his "refreshment" in particular to Paul's "heart"[31] (using the very same verb and noun as in v. 7) by releasing Onesimus from being his slave. The word for "heart" in both verses 7 and 20 is the plural σπλάγχνα (*splanchna*),[32] and it occurs again in verse 12: "I have sent him [Onesimus] back to you in person, that is, sending my very heart." The use in verse 12 may strengthen the rhetorical punch: if Philemon refreshes the saints' hearts (including Paul's heart, v. 7), and if Onesimus is the heart of Paul (v. 12), then if Paul's heart is to be refreshed, Philemon can do that by releasing Onesimus (v. 20; so Church 1978: 24). Paul refers much more to "heart" (καρδία, *kardia*, fifty-two times outside Philemon) in his writings, while "inward parts" (σπλάγχνα) occurs much less (only eight times in Paul, three of which are in Philemon). This suggests that Paul intentionally chose this word over "heart." "Inward parts" carries much more emotional freight than "heart." The point highlights Paul's deep, intense feelings of love for Onesimus (v. 12), and the emotional bonds between the saints and Philemon are equally strong (so v. 7). Philemon should increasingly recall and recognize these close bonds of emotion as he reads the letter, and this should endear him all the more to Paul and motivate his listening to Paul's imminent request, being assured of Paul's own love for him (as in v. 1 Philemon is "beloved" to Paul).[33]

Additional Notes

5. Possibly the participle "hearing" describes an activity also occurring during the "time" of the thanksgiving (as esp. does the first participle in v. 4). The most preferable option, however, is that, while contemporaneous time is not out of mind, the participle "hearing" focuses on the "reason" or "cause" for the thanksgiving. A causal use is evident from observing that the verb "to give thanks" in Paul's other introductory thanksgivings is always linked to a causal expression, which usually follows but sometimes precedes (often with the word "because" or the phrase "for this reason"): cf. Rom. 1:8; 1 Cor. 1:4; 2 Cor. 1:11–12; Eph. 1:15–16; Phil. 1:3–6; Col. 1:3–4; Philem. 4–5. This pattern is confirmed also elsewhere, as in the Thessalonian correspondence (1 Thess. 2:13; 5:18; 2 Thess. 1:3; 2:13). The first participial phrase (making mention) probably indicates the occasion when Paul has given thanks, though at the same

31. D. Moo (2008: 385) has brought to my attention that "hearts of the saints" in verse 7 anticipates mention of Paul's "heart" in particular in verse 20.

32. The word can mean "inward parts," "entrails," "emotions," or "heart" (cf. v. 7 NASB marg.). Many of the terms found in verses 1–7 and mentioned thus far in our analysis as occurring and being developed in verses 8–25, as I have later discovered, have also been observed by a number of commentators (e.g., among several, see Thompson 2005: 214).

33. Following for the most part Weima (2016: 218–19) on the significance of Paul's use of σπλάγχνα.

time it also implies that what is prayerfully considered gives the grounds from which the thankful attitude arises.

5. Some MSS have "faith and love unto the saints," which makes excellent sense, but only one very early and good MS supports that reading and the variant itself is not clear in the MS ($\mathfrak{P}^{61vid}$). This variant probably arose from a scribe under the influence of the original reading of Eph. 1:15 ("faith in the Lord Jesus and the love which is unto all the saints"). Thus, because the variant clarifies the more difficult reading and because it is not supported by early and good MSS, "faith . . . unto all the saints" should be maintained as the original reading. It is possible, however, that conceptually this reading is so impossibly difficult that it could not have been original, recalling also that this expression occurs nowhere else in biblical or biblically related material.

5–7. Many observe two chiasms in verses 5–7. The first is seen in verse 5:[34]

A Love
  B faith
  B′ in the Lord Jesus
A′ for all the saints

This chiasm is proposed to justify that "faith" goes with "in the Lord Jesus" and "love" goes with "for all the saints," resulting in the translation of "your faith toward the Lord Jesus and your love unto all the saints." It is proposed to solve the above-discussed problem in verse 5 of how Paul could assert that there is a "faith unto all the saints." But the chiasm is not clear. In fact, the phrases have to be readjusted to justify the chiasm. The text as it reads straightforwardly does not reveal obvious chiastic parallels. Chiasms are notoriously subjective and need substantial and clear verbatim parallels in each pair to be convincing, which is not the case here. It is surprising that seeing a chiasm is so prevalent among commentators, since it is not a straightforward reading, especially in the attempt to connect the very last phrase, "for all the saints," to "love," which is separated by ten words! Nevertheless, commentators have preferred the chiasm because of the parallels in Eph. 1:15, "having heard about the faith in the Lord Jesus among you and [your] love unto all the saints"*; and Col. 1:4, "your faith in Christ Jesus and the love which you have unto all the saints."*

The second proposed chiasm is observed in verses 5–7[35] (partly paraphrased):

A I hear of your love (v. 5a)
  B faith toward Jesus and all saints (v. 5b)
  B′ faith in common with saints and for Jesus (v. 6)
A′ I have comfort in your love (v. 7)

In this case, the parallels do have the very same words, so it is more plausible. Most who propose chiasms believe that the main emphasis is with the middle element(s). If so, here Paul would be highlighting the importance of the faith that Philemon has in common with other saints. This then would be a springboard to launch Paul's rhetorical appeal to Philemon to release Onesimus, since he shares with both Paul and Onesimus the same faith in Christ, a faith in which there is neither "Greek and Jew, . . . slave and free" (Col. 3:11). On the other hand, although the chiasm may be intended, the interpretive significance of it may not be so clear, since the main points of chiasms may lie in the bookends as much as in the middle of the structure. Some think that the outer bounds of the purported chiasm in verse 5 emphasize "love" (cf. Lohse 1971: 193), which is said to be supported by observing that when Paul refers to "love" coming from "faith," the latter always is placed first, but here the reverse is the case. However, when "faith" and "love"

34. Among commentators discerning a chiasm, see the list in Lohse (1971: 193) and Dunn (1996: 317); more recently, see Garland 1998: 319; D. Moo 2008: 388–89; Pao 2012: 368–79; and most recently Weima 2016: 216. Among those being skeptical of a chiasm are Dunn 1996: 315, 317; and Heil 2001: 182.

35. So, e.g., see, among others, Heil 2001: 182.

occur closely together, while the former usually precedes the latter (over fifteen times),[36] there are places where "faith" and "love" are combined and "love" precedes "faith" (Eph. 6:23; 1 Tim. 4:12; cf. Gal. 5:22). It is possible that the word order in verse 5 may merely be due to stylistic variation and is not an intended chiasm.

6. The rendering of the genitive ἡ κοινωνία τῆς πίστεως (*hē koinōnia tēs pisteōs*) as "participation in the faith"[37] that the saints hold in common is supported by observing that whenever κοινωνία is directly followed by a genitive in Paul, the translation of the genitive is best construed or at times can easily be understood as being introduced by "in," as in 1 Cor. 10:16a and 16b, "a sharing in the blood of Christ, . . . a sharing in the body of Christ"; Phil. 3:10, "sharing in sufferings"; see likewise 1 Cor. 1:9, "fellowship in His Son"; 2 Cor. 8:4, "sharing in the ministry"; 13:14, "sharing in the Holy Spirit"; Phil. 2:1, "sharing in the Spirit"; see for Philem. 6 accordingly the NJB, HCSB, TNIV, which have "participation [or fellowship or partnership] in the faith" (so also BDAG 553, s.v. κοινωνία); likewise more ambiguously NEB, CEB, NASB, NRSV, KJV have "fellowship [or sharing or communication] of your faith" (this ambiguous rendering with "of" is also plausible for the other seven uses of κοινωνία + a genitive in Paul). All of these renderings of κοινωνία + a genitive, as in Philem. 6, could be classified as genitives of place or sphere (for the category, see Wallace 1996: 124–25), and Philem. 6 appears to fit best into this category. The phrase viably could be an objective genitive, "sharing your faith" (Harris 2010: 216–17; likewise Campbell 2013: 81; NIV;[38] this view can fit with the other seven constructions in Paul by deleting "in" or "of" and turning κοινωνία into a verb like "sharing").

Alternatively, the construction in Philem. 6 could be a genitive of source (e.g., Lightfoot 1875: 335) or, closely related, a subjective genitive, "fellowship arising from [or by] your [common] faith" (e.g., Wallace 1996: 116; D. Moo 2008: 391–92), which also can fit elsewhere with some of the uses of κοινωνία followed by a genitive in Paul (1 Cor. 1:9; 2 Cor. 13:14; Phil. 2:1, the latter two possibly being rendered as "fellowship" [or sharing] arising from the . . . Spirit").[39] However, when κοινωνία in Paul is followed by an impersonal genitival noun (as "faith" is in Philem. 6), it is not a genitive of source or a subjective genitive but always refers to an active "participation" or "sharing" either in the sphere of something or "sharing" something (as the object): so 1 Cor. 10:16a, "sharing [in] the blood"; 1 Cor. 10:16b, "sharing [in] the body"; Phil. 3:10, "sharing [in] the sufferings"; 2 Cor. 8:4, "sharing [in] the ministry."[40] Thus the best translation in Philem. 6 is "participation [sharing] in your faith" (or "your participation [sharing] in the faith"), which is held in common with other saints.[41]

6. Some scribes (e.g., MSS F, G) recognized that Paul's wording here is similar to Col. 1:10 and inserted ἔργου (*ergou*, work) so that it would read "every good work," conforming the entire phrase more closely to Col. 1:9–10. It is not the original reading, however.

36. See 1 Cor. 13:2, 13; Gal. 5:6, 22; Eph. 1:15; 3:17; Col. 1:4; 1 Thess. 1:3; 3:6; 5:8; 1 Tim. 1:14; 2:15; 6:11; 2 Tim. 1:13; 2:22; 3:10; Titus 2:2.

37. A translation, e.g., preferred by Campbell 2013: 81.

38. The 1984 NIV's rendering "that you may be active in sharing your faith" appears to see the expression as referring to the modern notion of evangelism, but the main notion of "sharing" (κοινωνία) in Paul (and here in Philemon) is what one already has in common with other Christians or with Christ, not some kind of relationship with unbelievers. Likewise, while the word can well mean "fellowship" here, the word should not be understood in the sense of Christians "sharing oral communication with one another," such as at a "church fellowship dinner" or at some such occasion.

39. The same construction may express a genitive of association, "sharing with your faith," which you have in common with the saints (suitable for 1 Cor. 1:9; 2 Cor. 13:14; Phil. 2:1; cf. also Eph. 5:7, fellow sharers with them), but this does not make good sense in Philem. 6.

40. Garland (1998: 320), though not citing 1 Cor. 10:16a or 16b.

41. Barth and Blanke (2000: 283) propose what amounts to an adjectival genitive, "your faith communion," but this never occurs elsewhere with Paul's use of κοινωνία + a genitive.

6. Some MSS have ἡμῖν (*hēmin*, us) instead of ὑμῖν (*hymin*, pl. you). If the plural "you" is original, then Philemon is specifically in mind; if "us" is original, then the corporate body of believers as a whole is in mind, including Philemon. Thus the variants do not significantly affect the overall meaning of the verse. Nevertheless, commentators generally regard the MS evidence slightly to favor plural "you," though nevertheless inclining toward "us" on the basis of internal considerations: a scribe would more likely have altered an original "us" to "you" because of the immediately surrounding cluster of second-person singular and plural pronouns ("you") in verses 3, 5, 6a, 7, 8, 10, 12, and enforced by the remainder of the letter (e.g., see Metzger 1994: 588; Omanson 2006: 449–50), though the NET dissents and favors "you," arguing that external evidence slightly favors it. The English translations are mixed between "us" and "you."

III. Letter Body: Paul's Appeal (8–21)

On the basis of Philemon's love and faith, Paul appeals to Philemon's inner heart to release Onesimus and allow him to return to minister to Paul in prison (vv. 8–14).

In verses 4–7, Paul has thanked God for Philemon because he recognizes in him true love and faithfulness, and he prays that his faith will continue to grow. "Giving thanks" for Philemon (v. 4) and praying for him (v. 6) are the major points of the paragraph, and everything else in the paragraph (vv. 4b–7) forms part of the logical basis to support these two main points. Now in verses 8–14 Paul makes explicit what thanksgiving and prayer in verses 4–7 have implicitly anticipated: the request that Philemon release Onesimus in order that he return to minister to Paul in prison, resulting in "refreshing" Paul's heart (v. 20). This is the major point of the *body* of the letter ("grace and peace" [v. 3] being the goal of the *whole* letter).

The majority of commentators agree that verse 8 begins the formal body of the epistle (see D. Moo 2008: 397). Most also agree that the body ends at verse 20 (e.g., see the division of the paragraphs in NA[28]). This may be supported by observing that "brother" and "refresh the heart" occur at the beginning (v. 7) and toward the end of the letter (v. 20), thus perhaps forming an *inclusio* (so D. Moo 2008: 398). The letter body may end at verse 20, yet verse 21 appears to be a formal summarizing conclusion of the whole body, where Paul repeats his request to Philemon to release his slave. Verse 20 is the final admonition or statement in the letter, and verse 21 summarizes and emphasizes what has been said in the body of verses 8–20 (following Pao 2012: 379–80). The body of verses 8–21 may also be discernible from recognizing the possible marking of an *inclusio* with a beginning "in Christ" (v. 8) and a concluding "in Christ" (v. 20), making up two of the three occurrences of the phrase "in Christ" in the entire epistle (see v. 23). Twenty-one second-person pronouns appear in the letter, all referring to Philemon, while 20 first person singular pronouns occur, all referring to Paul. This repetition indicates that Paul has Philemon in mind throughout the letter, and that others (including those listed in v. 2) are listening in (following Jeal 2015: 59–60).

Though commentators differ about how the body of the letter should be divided and where precisely the closing begins (at v. 19 or at v. 21 or at v. 22), we propose that the first section of the body is verses 8–14, and the last section of the body consists of verses 15–21. Then verses 22–25 form the letter's closing. Many commentators have proposed a chiastic structure to Philemon, the most cogent perhaps being that of Heil (2001), and most recently that of D. Moo (2008: 400). However, while such chiastic proposals are possible, they tend to be too subjective unless there is a substantial number of tight verbal parallels between specific verses, which is lacking in this case.[1]

Verses 8–14 as a paragraph may *possibly* be discerned by a unique conceptual *inclusio*: Paul wants Philemon to act not because of his apostolic authority but out of love (vv. 8–9a); Paul wants Philemon to act not under compulsion but from his own voluntary motives (v. 14).[2] In addition the unit is recognizable by the introductory "therefore" in verse 8 and the introductory "for . . . for this reason" in verse 15, which introduces the following literary unit.[3]

1. In the case of Heil's proposal, some linguistic parallels scattered throughout whole paragraphs are proposed and not in single verses, which makes the proposal more difficult to validate. In addition, conceptual parallels in paragraphs are offered, but this entails more subjectivity than verbal parallels. The search for chiasms throughout Scripture is too often a case of parallelomania.

2. I have subsequently found that D. Moo (2008: 416), along with numerous other commentators, has made the same point.

3. Lohse (1971: 196–97) supplies some of Pliny the Younger's *Epistles* that reflect the same situation and pattern of Philemon. Thus *Ep*. 9.21 reveals a respected person (Pliny the Younger) writing to a slave owner about a runaway slave who has come to him and begged him to intercede with his owner to receive him back amicably, without anger and punishment. Pliny does not want to "compel" but wants to "request" that the slave owner "forgive him." Then *Ep*. 9.24 shows that the slave owner has acceded to the intercession and request and forgiven the delinquent slave. How much more would Philemon be motivated to forgive Onesimus, since he is in Christ (cf. Philem. 5–6), who has forgiven him? If caught, runaway slaves could be subjected to imprisonment, whipping, crucifixion, being thrown to wild beasts in the arena, or sold to others to work on farms, in mines, or in galleys (see Garland 1998: 327).

A. Paul Appeals to Philemon's Inner Heart (8–14)

Here is a fuller statement of the main idea of this unit: *On the basis of Philemon's love and faith, Paul appeals to Philemon's inner heart to release Onesimus and allow him to return to minister to Paul in prison.*

Exegesis and Exposition

[8]Therefore, though I have enough confidence in Christ to order you to do what is proper, [9]yet for love's sake I rather appeal to you—since I am such a person as Paul, the aged, and now also a prisoner of Christ Jesus—[10]I appeal to you for my child Onesimus, whom I have begotten in my imprisonment, [11]who formerly was useless to you, but now is useful both to you and to me. [12]I have sent him back ⌜to you in person, that is, sending my very heart⌝, [13]whom I wished to keep with me, so that on your behalf he might minister to me in my imprisonment for the gospel; [14]but without your consent I did not want to do anything, so that your goodness would not be, [as it were], by compulsion but of your own free will.

8 This verse commences the formal body of the letter (vv. 8–21), which will continue to show how the goal of "grace and peace" (v. 3) can be achieved through Paul and Philemon. The verse commences with "therefore" (διό, *dio*), which refers back to the main points of verses 4–7. That is, on the basis of Paul's thanksgiving for Philemon's love and faithfulness and his prayer that he increase in those qualities, Paul begins to make his request about Onesimus in verse 8 and completes it in verse 9 (παρακαλέω, *parakaleō*, I appeal), though the request is not yet even completed there. Paul is confident that the request he is about to make of Philemon will be responded to positively *because* of the "love" and "faith" Philemon has already demonstrated (vv. 6–7, 9). Likewise, Paul is confident that his prayer for Philemon to increase in effective good works resulting from his faith will be answered positively (v. 6). The adverbial participle ἔχων (*echōn*) in verse 8 modifies "command" in a concessive way:[1] "<u>even though I have</u> much boldness in Christ <u>to command</u> you to do that which is proper."* Paul has apostolic "boldness in Christ to command" Philemon to "do what is proper." Sometimes Paul uses the word παρρησία (*parrhēsia*, confidence) with respect to his apostolic office and ministry,[2] and the same sense

1. Among those holding a concessive view of the participle, see MHT 3:157.
2. See 2 Cor. 3:12; Eph. 6:19–20 (verb form in v. 20); Phil. 1:20; 1 Thess. 2:2 (verb form).

occurs here in Philem. 8.[3] This is not merely a "freedom" to speak in general (see LSJ 1344) but "'a freedom to speak' authoritatively" (Moule 1957: 144) as an apostle[4] "because" he has been commissioned by Christ as an apostle (thus ἐν Χριστῷ [*en Christō*, in Christ] is a dative of cause).[5] And "because of Christ" he can exercise his apostolic authority freely in the context of the church (see "church" in v. 2; also Witherington 2007: 66) and with Philemon, a fellow believer, because both certainly acknowledge and respect Paul's apostolic office. The word "command" (ἐπιτάσσω, *epitassō*) that follows further reflects a reference to Paul's apostolic authority, since the word typically refers to a person in authority decreeing to an underling what should be done.[6]

The word ἀνήκω (*anēkō*) refers to that which is "proper" or "fitting." The verb can also have the meaning of "belong to" or possibly "be harmonious with" (BDAG 78–79). These meanings overlap. All of these nuances are suitable here, but the rarer notion of "that which is harmonious" perhaps best fits the immediate context, since the major concern of this short epistle is reconciliation between Philemon and Onesimus, as well as between Paul and Philemon (cf. the goal of "peace" in v. 3). So BDAG (79, s.v. ἀνήκω) translates the phrase as "order you to do the *right thing*" but then explains parenthetically that this means "an appeal for reciprocity," which is virtually synonymous with "that which is harmonious."[7] In 2 Cor. 5:18–20 Paul uses "reconciling" language five times to underscore that his apostolic office is especially that of *reconciling* people to God, which in the context includes reconciliation of the Corinthians with himself as an apostle (e.g., see 2 Cor. 6:11–13; 7:2). In 2 Corinthians, for one to be reconciled to Christ is to be reconciled to Paul the apostle, through whom "Christ speaks" (2 Cor. 13:3; on which see further Beale 1989: 565–66,

3. The word also is associated with an apostolic role or ministry in Acts 2:29; 4:13, 29, 31; 28:31 (the last with respect to Paul).

4. O'Brien (1982: 287–88) thinks that both the ideas of speaking openly and intimately with affection and speaking with responsibility as an apostle are in mind, but the latter is clearly the focus, as the following word "command" indicates. I have found agreement here with Wall 1993: 203–4.

5. So Campbell 2013: 84. A causal use is pointed to because the "in Christ" phrase in verse 8 is directly contrasted with the antithetically parallel causal expression "rather on account of love I appeal" (v. 9; relying partly on Campbell's [2012: 110–11] rationale for such a use). Harris (2012: 223) also, in addition to a causal use, lists the following possibilities: "in the name of Christ," "in Christ's service," "as a Christian," "as your brother in Christ," or "with Christ's authority." The first and last options mentioned by Harris come close to the causal use.

6. So Mark 1:27; 6:27, 39; 9:25; Luke 4:36; 8:25, 31; 14:22; Acts 23:2 (most of which refer to Jesus's authority); likewise often in the LXX.

7. Various English dictionaries give ranges of meaning for "reciprocal" or "reciprocation" that conceptually express the notion of "that which is harmonious"; e.g., one range of meaning for "reciprocation" listed by the *OED* is "the state of being in a reciprocal or harmonious relation; correspondence." Note that 1 Clem. 35.5 translates ἀνήκω (*anēkō*) as "*things that are in harmony* with his [God's] faultless will." BDAG (79, s.v. ἀνήκω) translates the same passage as "*what is in harmony* with God's will." The "reciprocal harmony" in mind is that Philemon should receive his slave back just as he would receive Paul, since all have the same "shared faith" in Christ (v. 17); likewise, Paul asks Philemon to forgive his slave's debts, just as he himself is in debt to Paul for his very salvation, which Paul is not demanding that he pay back (vv. 18–19).

568). Later we will see in Philem. 18–19 that Paul is modeling Christ's reconciling role in reconciling Philemon to Onesimus and to himself. In this light, Philemon should do what is "fitting" to his common share in the faith in doing what will bring about harmony in his relationship with Paul and Onesimus.

9 As mentioned above, the adverbial participle ἔχων in verse 8 modifies "command" in a concessive way. The completion of the concessive statement is in verse 9: "even though I have much boldness in Christ to command you to do what is harmonious (v. 8), because of love I appeal to you." But as noted above (see on v. 8), the διό at the beginning of verse 8 shows that Paul's appeal is also based on his thanksgiving for Philemon's love and faithfulness and his prayer that he may increase in those qualities (mentioned in vv. 6–7). The commas placed after "therefore" at the beginning of verse 8 and at the end of verse 8[8] show a decision to highlight that the appeal in verse 9 is based on the "therefore" of verse 8, which itself points to verses 5–7 as the basis for the following appeal in verse 9: "Therefore . . . I appeal to you" (following Pao 2012: 383). The material of verse 8 within the commas highlights the contrast between what Paul could do with his authority and what he would rather see Philemon do out of love.

Paul does not want to force Philemon to do this by appeal to his apostolic authority (as in v. 14 he does not want Philemon to release Onesimus "as it were by compulsion, but willingly").[9] The content of the appeal begins in verse 10, which is the request about Onesimus, the slave. But before Paul gets to the appeal, he further describes himself. The adverbial participle ὤν (*ōn*), from the verb "to be" and modifying the preceding verb "I appeal," is concessive and makes a contrast with the preceding verb: "I appeal on account of love" (v. 9a), "even though I am[10] such a person as Paul, the elder [or aged], but now [I am] also a prisoner of Christ Jesus."* Moule (1957: 144) paraphrases the first part of verse 9 as "yet I prefer to appeal to Christian love rather than to exercise my right to demand." Paul goes back and forth: he acknowledges his own apostolic authority (v. 8), then says he would rather appeal to Philemon not out of that authority but out of love (v. 9a), and in verse 9b he reverts back to acknowledging his apostolic authority, and as we will see, he abruptly in verse 9c contrastively appeals again to something other

8. As in Geneva, ASV, KJV, NASB, NEB, RSV, NRSV, NIV, NJB, TNIV, ESV, HCSB, NET, and RSV; following Pao (2012: 383) on the significance of the punctuation of the English translations.

9. Likewise in 1 Thess. 2:6–8, 11, Paul appeals on the basis not of his apostolic authority but of his parental love in order to get the Thessalonians to perceive his sincere motives in ministering to them.

10. Following Moule 1957: 144. Yet in his later *Idiom Book* (1959: 102) he says the participle is ambiguous, so that besides concessive it could be causal. While likewise acknowledging a concessive use, Fitzmyer (2000: 105) also suggests an adverbial participle of cause, which could be rendered as "on account of love I entreat *because I am* such a one as Paul"; but this likewise does not fit the contrast demanded by the clause "I appeal to you on account of love" and the mention of Paul as "the aged" (in the sense of an apostolic ambassador; see below).

than his apostolic position: he is a helpless prisoner.[11] Such back-and-forth appeals reinforce for Philemon that Paul is making his appeal on the basis of love and lowliness rather than on the basis of his apostolic status, to which he could appeal, if he wanted to do so. His references to his authority are "very thinly masked by his rhetoric," as is the case elsewhere in the letter (Petersen 1985: 188).

The reference to "aged" (πρεσβύτης, *presbytēs*) is not a mere allusion to his actual old age. By referring to himself as "aged" or "old" Paul reiterates his authoritative status as an apostle, which he has just mentioned implicitly in verse 8. This word πρεσβύτης often refers to someone who is merely old in age in the NT, in Hellenistic Judaism, and elsewhere in Hellenistic Greek. But there are significant uses also in Hellenistic Judaism and early Christian literature where the word connotes an older person possessing authority,[12] honor,[13] or respect.[14]

Some commentators agree but do so by positing the conjectural emendation to πρεσβευτής, which means "ambassador" and could well be understood with apostolic associations (e.g., Paul is an apostle commissioned and sent as an ambassador to Gentiles).[15] But it is best not to speculate about such conjectural emendations, since there are absolutely no textual variants in this passage that support it. There are other uses of πρεσβύτης with the meaning of "ambassador" in 1 and 2 Maccabees (1 Macc. 13:21; 14:22; 2 Macc. 11:34), but they are textual variants in place of πρεσβευτής and are likely not original. Furthermore, the uses of πρεσβύτης with the sense of "authority, honor, and respect" (as noted above) point to the same conclusion of an implicit notion of "authoritative ambassador"[16] or apostolic association, without speculating about a variant that has no attestation.

Nevertheless, Hock (1995: 74–81) observes that in contemporary pagan Hellenistic sources, references to old age in contexts where children occur

11. Hendriksen (1964: 217) is unconvinced about this back-and-forth positioning, holding that after Paul has "appealed on account of love" (v. 9a) in contrast to "appealing" to his apostolic authority (v. 8), it makes no sense that he would revert again to alluding to his authority in the reference to "old man."

12. Lam. 5:14 LXX; Josephus, *Ant.* 12.87; Philo, *Agr.* 56; *Flacc.* 74; Irenaeus, *Her.* 1.15.6, where the elder has divine authority; Gos. Nic. (Christ's Descent into Hell) 9 (25), where the "old men" are the prophets Enoch and Elijah.

13. Philo, *Hypoth.* 11.13; Isa. 9:15 LXX; Hist. Rech. 6.3; 4 Macc. 7:10.

14. Philo, *Emb.* 142; cf. Mart. Pol. 7.3. For the full text of these references here and in the preceding two notes, see the additional note on verse 9. As would be expected, in Classical Greek πρεσβύτης (*presbytēs*) has the sense of old age (e.g., LSJ 1462; *NIDNTT* 4:128) and likely sometimes includes the sense of weakness or helplessness, but it can also have the nuance of "seniority" (LSJ 1462) or "often connotes a certain rank" (*NIDNTT* 4:128).

15. See BDAG (863, s.v. πρεσβύτης) for commentators in favor of and against this view that "ambassador" is the meaning in Philem. 9. See D. Moo (2008: 404–6) for more reasons to reject the view that verse 9 reads πρεσβευτής (*presbeutēs*), "ambassador."

16. Lenski (1961: 960–62) views the word to mean only "old man," with connotations of someone deserving respect, but is unconvinced that there is any association with the idea of an authoritative ambassador.

allude to children helping their parents who have become helpless. In this light, Hock argues that Paul casts himself "in the role of an old father who is in need of his child's support—an accepted convention of children toward their aged parents" (1995: 81). Hock's argument is conceptually viable, but there are several problems: (1) the word πρεσβύτης does not occur in any of the Hellenistic texts that he adduces;[17] (2) the uses of πρεσβύτης in Hellenistic Judaism, Paul's closer conceptual world, rarely attest to "old" being associated with helplessness (see below). D. Moo (2008: 405–6), following Hock (1995), likewise believes the reference to "old man" underscores Paul's own helplessness and enforces his helpless position as a prisoner (so likewise Witherington 2007: 67). Accordingly, he translates νυνὶ δὲ καί (*nyni de kai*) as "and now also," instead of contrastively, "but now also." D. Moo's rendering is possible. However, though νυνὶ δὲ καί does not occur much in the NT (only three times total), when it does occur elsewhere it is contrastive, especially in the nearby text of Philem. 11: Onesimus "who formerly was useless to you, <u>but now also</u> is useful to you and to me." The other clearly contrastive use is in 2 Cor. 8:10–11: You, "who were the first to begin a year ago not only to do this, but also to desire to do it [give financial support to Jerusalem saints], <u>but now also</u> [νυνὶ δὲ καί] finish doing it"* (i.e., don't just start giving and desire to do it, <u>but now also</u> finish it). And so it is probably contrastive here, which supports Paul's use of πρεσβύτης as having positive authoritative or apostolic associations. In addition, the shorter phrase νυνὶ δέ (*nyni de*) occurs fifteen times elsewhere in Paul, and except one time (Rom. 7:17), it signals a contrast with something that precedes.[18]

Furthermore, the notion that πρεσβύτης carries the idea of "helpless" is clearly attested only a few times in the NT, LXX, Hellenistic Judaism, and early Christian writings.[19] In contrast, interestingly, "old" can refer to a young man who is greatly respected because he possesses the wisdom of an old man (Philo, *Emb.* 142).

Thus it is likely Paul uses πρεσβύτης to refer to his honorific role as an apostle, especially because (1) the uses of πρεσβύτης in Hellenistic Judaism, Paul's closer conceptual world, rarely attest to "old" being associated with helplessness; (2) the word often is associated with honor or respect in Hellenistic

17. The word does occur in Plutarch, *T. Talk* (*Mor.* 631B; Clement and Hoffleit 1969: 116–19); and πρεσβυτικός (*presbytikos*) appears in Dio Chrysostom, *Hunt.* (*Or.* 7.1; Cohoon 1932: 286–87); both are cited by Hock (1995), but neither of these have to do with the helplessness of old men, nor do they appear in contexts of old men and children. The main references cited by Hock that conceptually deal with the old as helpless (as "an invalid") are Philostratus (*Lives Soph.* 541) and Ps.-Menander, *One* 39–40, 830 (Jaekel 1964: 35, 81). Ps.-Menander uses γεραιός (*geraios* = old), which is a conceptual synonym for πρεσβύτης (*presbytēs*). See further Hock's (1995) reference to Longus (Jaekel 1964: 79).

18. Rom. 3:21; 6:22; 7:6; 15:23, 25; 1 Cor. 12:18; 13:13; 15:20; 2 Cor. 8:22; Eph. 2:13; Col. 1:22; 3:8.

19. So see LXX of 1 Sam. 4:18 and 1 Kings 1:15; also Josephus, *Ant.* 8.236; Philo, *Cher.* 68; *Post.* 71. And one could make the ubiquitous human observation that extremely old people tend to become increasingly helpless.

Judaism; and (3) νυνὶ δὲ καί most probably indicates a stark contrast between "old man" and "a prisoner."[20]

So what is Paul's point in alluding so quickly again to his apostolic position? It is to highlight his present lowly position of being a prisoner. Paul is "such a person . . . as the aged" (or the honored and authoritative apostle), "but now also a prisoner of Christ Jesus." The main point of verse 9 is that, even though Paul is an honored apostle, he nevertheless is a person of low status, a "prisoner."[21]

As we have noted earlier, Paul's point in underscoring his position as a prisoner is to persuade Philemon to empathize with his lowly status and then to empathize with Onesimus's lowly status as a runaway slave, who deserves to be chained up for his outlaw status. As we noted on verse 1, Paul may be appealing to Philemon not to exercise his rights of slave ownership for the same reason that Paul has given up his rights and become a "prisoner" for the cause of Christ. Together with this, Paul appears to be alluding to his vulnerability in prison. By so doing he seems to be identifying with Onesimus as a slave, since part of the punishment of runaway slaves when caught was to be put into chains. Thus Paul's highlighting his lowly status as prisoner would presumably cause Philemon not only to feel sympathy for Paul but also for his slave.[22] Thus Paul parenthetically interrupts his appeal by alluding to his apostolic status ("Paul, the aged," to highlight that he could command Philemon to release Onesimus) and simultaneously to highlight his imprisoned helplessness. The parenthetical interruption is obvious from noticing the repetition of the same first-person singular verb "I appeal" in verse 10, which picks up from the first "I appeal," in verse 9.[23]

N. Wright (1986: 181) is probably correct to conclude here that Paul is writing as an apostolic ambassador for Christ (continuing the allusion to his apostolic authority in v. 8) and is setting aside his apostolic rights (presenting himself as a helpless prisoner) in appealing to Philemon, thus modeling Christ himself, who gave up his rights as God in order to become a "slave" and die to bring salvation to others (Phil. 2:1–11). We will see that this giving up of rights continues in verses 12–14, where Paul gives up his right to have Onesimus minister to him in prison and sends him back to Philemon (and in vv. 18–19 Paul gives up his financial rights). Paul, like Christ at the cross,

20. Among those seeing such a stark contrast, see Petersen (1985: 125–27), who shows that the context of Philem. 8–16 is composed of a series of nine contrasts, within which this contrast in verse 9 naturally fits: e.g., "bold enough to command" versus "I prefer for love's sake to appeal" (vv. 8–9a); "whom I sent to you" versus "whom I wanted to keep with me" (vv. 12–13); "formerly useless" versus "now useful" (v. 11); "not by necessity" versus "by free will" (v. 14); "not as a slave" versus "as a beloved brother" (v. 16a); "especially to me" versus "so much more to you" (v. 16b); "in the flesh" versus "in the Lord" (v. 16c).

21. Cf. Houlden (1977: 230), who asserts that Paul's status as a prisoner goes with his being an "ambassador": Paul's imprisonment has not caused him to cease his activities as an ambassador.

22. See on verse 1 for these two rhetorical purposes of Paul's reference to being a "prisoner" and commentators supporting these views.

23. D. Moo (2008: 403–4) also notes other ways to punctuate verse 9; likewise Harris 2010: 225.

exercises his strength in the midst of weakness and, like Christ, is the key to reconciling Philemon with his slave (N. Wright 1986: 179–81).

However, Paul will issue this "appeal" not because of his apostolic authority but "because of love." Likely Paul is referring to Philemon's love rather than his own love, since he has just spoken of Philemon's love in verse 5 and has just mentioned that he has "come to have much joy and comfort in your [Philemon's] love" (v. 7). The article before "love" here then appears to be an article of previous reference (an anaphoric article),[24] referring back to the double mention of "love" in verses 5 and 7. Accordingly, Paul is "appealing" to Philemon's already demonstrated quality of love to inspire him to demonstrate it further by acquiescing to Paul's request to release Onesimus and let him return to minister to Paul in prison as before.[25]

10 Now Paul gives the explicit subject of his appeal to Philemon: it is about his "child, which I have borne in my imprisonment, Onesimus."* The word παρακαλέω (*parakaleō*) here and in verse 9 is translated as "appeal" by most modern translations. Older translations have "beseech" (e.g., Geneva, ASV, KJV, Douay-Rheims). "To urge strongly" or "request, implore, entreat" seems to be the idea (so BDAG 765, s.v. παρακαλέω, preferring the latter ideas for vv. 9–10). It is not a general "appeal in behalf of" Onesimus nor merely an appeal "about" or "with regard to" Onesimus but an "appeal for Onesimus." This rendering is supported by unique syntactical parallels in Hellenistic Greek. Paul is asking for Onesimus himself to be returned to him in prison (see Knox 1959: 22–25; see further the additional note on v. 10).

But before making his actual request about Onesimus, Paul wants to tell Philemon how much Onesimus means to him. The slave is like a child to him. Thus, before Paul gives the content of his "appeal" to Philemon (vv. 8–9), Paul wants to change Philemon's view of his runaway slave in order to induce him to be more open to his appeal. Instead of Philemon having ill will toward Onesimus as a runaway, Paul wants Philemon to think of Onesimus positively as a true Christian believer, a "child" of God "borne" through Paul's preaching (following Lohse 1971: 199–200). Outside of Philem. 10, the word τέκνον (*teknon*) occurs often in Paul, referring to believers being spiritual "children" of God.[26] Likewise the word τέκνον can also refer to believers being children of Paul (so ten times).[27] Two of these latter uses refer to the plural "children" of Paul and indicate a nourishing spiritual parent-child relationship between Paul

24. So Harris 2010: 223. Banker (1999: 33) sees this as a viable option; D. Moo (2008: 403) mentions this use of the article as a possibility.

25. It is possible that "love" here refers to a general love "which governs the Christians' dealings and association with one another," which is to inspire Philemon to respond to Paul's request (Lohse 1971: 198–99). Likewise Lightfoot (1875: 337) views the "love" as alluding generally to the principle of love. For various dimensions of the meaning of "love" here, see Barth and Blanke 2000: 315–16.

26. See, e.g., Rom. 8:16, 17, 21; 9:8; Gal. 4:27, 28, 31; Eph. 5:1, 8; Phil. 2:15.

27. See 1 Cor. 4:14; Gal. 4:19; Phil. 2:22; 1 Thess. 2:7, 11; 1 Tim. 1:2, 18; 2 Tim. 1:2; 2:1; Titus 1:4.

and the believers in the church (1 Thess. 2:7, 11), which may include the idea that their initial spiritual birth has occurred through Paul. Almost identically, when the above category of uses about children of Paul employs the singular (a "child" of Paul), it refers to someone (usually Timothy) who is a spiritual child of Paul's in the sense that Paul has a parent-child relationship with that person, though the notion that the person was born spiritually through Paul's ministry seems also to be in mind. That this is clearly the idea here is apparent from the phrase in verse 10 "my child, <u>whom I have begotten</u>." Thus Onesimus has become an actual spiritual child of Paul's, since it was through Paul's ministry that Onesimus became a born-again Christian.[28] Onesimus was born through Paul's message during Paul's "imprisonment." This is further confirmed by the unique employment of "children" (pl. of τέκνον) with γεννάω (*gennaō* = become the parent of) in 1 Cor. 4:14–17. This passage reveals that elsewhere not only "child" by itself likely includes a nourishing parent-child relationship but also the notion of someone being born spiritually through Paul:[29] "I admonish you as my beloved children, . . . for in Christ Jesus I begot you through the gospel. . . . Timothy . . . is . . . my beloved child."* The similar unique use of "children" (pl. of τέκνον) with a synonym of γεννάω in Gal. 4:19, 23, 29 confirms further that Onesimus was born spiritually through Paul's ministry.[30] Regardless of whether the birth language is that of the begetting by a father or by a mother, the point is Onesimus's spiritual birth through Paul.[31]

Accordingly, Paul's appeal is not for the Onesimus who belonged to the old fallen world but for the newborn Onesimus, who has become a part of the new creation (D. Moo 2008: 408), "in which there is no distinction between Greek and Jew, . . . slave and freeman, but Christ is all, and in all" (Col. 3:11). This

28. For γεννάω (*gennaō*) in the sense of spiritual birth elsewhere in Paul, see 1 Cor. 4:15; Gal. 4:23, 29; outside of Paul, see likewise John 1:13; 3:3–8; 1 John 2:29; 3:9; 4:7; 5:1, 4, 18. Most translations render this with a gloss like "I fathered" (HCSB; likewise RSV, NRSV, NLT, NJB, ESV, NET, NEB); others render it as "begotten" (Geneva, KJV, ASV, Douay-Rheims, NASB).

29. Dunn (1996: 328) affirms that Paul's use of "child" in his writings generally refers to "those converted through his ministry."

30. In Gal. 4:19 Paul applies a female birth metaphor to himself, saying that the Galatians are "my <u>children</u>, with whom <u>I am again in labor</u> until Christ <u>is formed in you</u>," suggesting oxymoronically an earlier salvific birth of the Galatians through Paul and another birth-like experience through him. The reason for the reapplication may be that persevering in the faith (after appearing to lapse from it) that started with the Galatians' spiritual birth is a continuation of growth that organically stems from that birth. Paul continues to "labor" so that their inaugurated birth will be consummated at the end of time (e.g., see a birth metaphor for the consummated redemption of the "children of God" in Rom. 8:17–22). In Gal. 4:19 both "children" (τέκνον, *teknon*) and a synonym of γεννάω are used, which makes this uniquely parallel to Philem. 10.

31. Paul may be portraying himself as a mother giving birth, since that is the image in Gal. 4:19, and he depicts himself as a nursing mother in 1 Thess. 2:7 (see Bird 2009: 138–39). On the other hand, Paul applies γεννάω to himself in 1 Cor. 4:15 as he converts people through his ministry, which clearly refers to him becoming a "father" of the Corinthians. See Barth and Blanke (2000: 329–36) for several alternative meanings of the birth image. Thus b. Yevam. 48b: "One who has become a proselyte is like a child newly born"; Boring, Berger, and Colpe (1995: 508) alerted me to this reference.

should prompt Philemon all the more to be favorable toward accepting Paul's appeal for Onesimus the slave, since they are now spiritual equals.

The purpose of Paul telling this to Philemon before making his explicit appeal is to reveal to the slave owner how much the slave means to Paul: he is Paul's very child in the faith and loves him dearly as a child. This lays a further rhetorical basis for persuading Philemon to want to listen to and grant Paul's entreaty.

11 The article τόν (*ton*) functions as a relative pronoun ("whom"), referring to Onesimus and further describing him. Though Paul feels as a father toward Onesimus, he acknowledges that the slave has been "useless" (ἄχρηστος, *achrēstos*; see the alpha privative) to Philemon, likely since he has run away from the service he should have been giving to the slave owner. Paul uses the term "useful" (εὔχρηστος, *euchrēstos*; the εὐ- prefix = good/well) elsewhere of "a vessel for honor, sanctified, <u>useful</u> to the Master, prepared for every good work" (2 Tim. 2:21); likewise he refers to "Mark" as "useful to me for service" (2 Tim. 4:11).[32] Onesimus has become useless as a slave in service to Philemon presumably because he has illegally escaped that service, as well as having caused his master financial damage in some way, loss of labor or stealing from him (suggested by vv. 18–19; see my comments there).[33]

"But now also he is useful to you and to me."* Why is Onesimus "now useful" (εὔχρηστος) to Philemon and Paul? It is because the slave has become a true believer "now" (spiritually "begotten" through Paul) and a fellow believer in Christ, who can minister as a Christian brother to both of them. The combination of "formerly . . . but now" (ποτέ . . . νυνὶ δέ, *pote . . . nyni de*) likely reflects not only conversion but also a contrast of the old age with the new eschatological age, and thus a new-creational birth and new "usefulness." The same threefold word combination appears in Eph. 2:13, "<u>But now</u> in Christ Jesus you who <u>formerly</u> were far off have been brought near by the blood of Christ," which is inextricably linked to Jew and Gentile becoming "one <u>new</u> man" (2:15). Likewise in Col. 1:21–22 the same combined wording indicates end-time conversion in a context of new cosmic peacefulness (1:20), which results in a new change of character (to "holy and blameless"), similar to Onesimus's new change in character.[34] In Col. 3:7–8 Paul also employs the same threefold wording (ποτέ . . . νυνὶ δέ) to contrast the past age of bad conduct (sins "in which you walked <u>formerly</u>"), followed by the imperatival phrase, "<u>but now</u> you lay aside"* such sins. And this is directly linked to "putting off the old man" and "putting on the new man," both of which refer to the eschatological transition in going from the old cosmic Adam to the new Adam, Christ,

32. The word in Josephus also refers to oxen (*Ant.* 4.281), an oversized "table of showbread" (*Ant.* 12.61), and a fortification being either useful or not useful (*Ant.* 15.293). Cf. similarly Philo, *Prelim.* 141; LXX: Prov. 31:13; Wis. 13:13.

33. See Fitzmyer (2000: 108) for the suggestion of Onesimus doing Philemon some financial harm.

34. And Col. 1:21–22 is closely linked to the eschatological "mystery . . . hidden from <u>past ages</u> [= a synonym of ποτέ] . . . <u>but now</u> manifested"* in the new, eschatological age (Col. 1:26).

in whose "image" they are being "renewed" (Col. 3:9–10*).[35] Again, cosmic end-time language is used in describing new behavior in contrast to old, bad behavior, as in Philem. 11. Thus Philem. 11 carries overtones of old creation and new creation in connection with conversion and new conduct, much like that of 2 Cor. 5:17: "If anyone is in Christ, there is a new creation; old things have passed away; behold, new things have come about."*[36]

This new word "usefulness" may be with respect to Onesimus's service within Philemon's household or within the church or as a helper to Paul in prison (see Harris 2010: 226). Probably all of these are included, though the latter two are likely the focus. The reference to Onesimus's usefulness both to Philemon and Paul continues to establish more of a rhetorical foundation intended to sway Philemon to be favorable to and yield to Paul's impending request. Adding to the rhetorical force is the observation that ἄχρηστον and εὔχρηστον is a wordplay (observed by many commentators), which can be conveyed in English as "useless" and "useful." That this construction in verse 11 comes just after Paul introduces the name "Onesimus" in verse 10 reinforces the idea of the wordplay, since "Onesimus" means "useful" (e.g., see BDAG 711, s.v. Ὀνήσιμος).[37] Paul is saying that Onesimus, since his conversion, now is truly living up to the meaning of his given name. The pun highlights the contrast between a previously unbelieving Onesimus and a spiritually renewed Onesimus.[38] Paul says in Col. 4:9 that Onesimus is now "our faithful and beloved brother" (Pao 2012: 389), which likely refers to his new postconversion usefulness.

The rhetorical punch of the pun is intended to soften Philemon's heart in acquiescing to Paul's request "to forgive his slave and welcome him back as a 'beloved brother'" (Weima 2016: 225). Furthermore, the point is that Philemon is not losing anything by sending back Onesimus to Paul, since the slave has now become "useful" and spiritually and materially profitable in that he can serve Paul on behalf of Philemon (cf. v. 13; following Weima 2016: 225).

Like verse 11, this verse uses a relative pronoun (ὅν, *hon*) to introduce an ad- **12**
ditional description of Onesimus. Verse 12 further explains Paul's evaluation

35. See comments on Col. 1:22–23 and 3:7–10 for support of these ideas. I have subsequently found that Patzia (1984: 112) comes close to making this observation with respect to the "once . . . now" language in Eph. 2:11, 13; and Col. 3:7–8.

36. This discussion confirms Barth's and Blanke's (2000: 347–50) view that Philem. 11 entails a cosmic eschatological transformation of Onesimus.

37. Commentators have generally recognized the meaning of the name "Onesimus" ("useful") as an enhancement of the following wordplay in verse 11 (e.g., Pao 2012: 388). The name "Onesimus" is a well-documented name for slaves in ancient Greek literature and rarely attested for those of freeborn status (see Roth 2014: 108n27). On the other hand, Connolly (1987: 179–81) lists sixty examples from inscriptions dating from the fourth century BC up to the fourth century AD in which the name "Onesimus" appears. The majority of these refer to slaves or freedmen, but a significant number refer to those who were born free and possessed high social status.

38. On the possibility that an additional pun is included here, see the additional note on verse 11.

of Onesimus as a Christian. Paul "has sent" the slave back to Philemon.[39] It is possible that Paul is also sending Onesimus as the letter carrier. If so, this provides the possibility that Onesimus himself will explain part of the letter to the church and to Philemon. However, it is not clear that Onesimus is carrying the letter. On verse 1 we argue that Timothy may well be the letter carrier.

Paul makes redundant reference to the slave: "whom I have sent to you, him [αὐτόν, *auton*]." The redundancy is to emphasize the person of the slave: accordingly some translations have "I have sent him back to you in person" (= αὐτόν; e.g., NASB, likewise ASV).[40] This emphasis on the *person* of Onesimus is intended to be inextricably linked to Paul's following statement that this *person* is Paul's own "heart" ("inward parts," σπλάγχνα, *splanchna*).

Even the phrase "that is" (τοῦτ' ἔστιν, *tout' estin*) stresses that the *person* of Onesimus is to be understood to represent (i.e., to be interpreted as) Paul's own "heart" or "inward parts." "Inward parts" connotes more emotion than "heart" (καρδία, *kardia*). As we saw in verse 7, the word σπλάγχνα in place of "heart" highlights Paul's, together with other saints', strong tender affection, which has been greatly affected by Philemon's love and compassion. Paul is sending Onesimus, who represents to Philemon his very heart and who has been the source of compassion for Paul in prison (cf. Wall 1993: 209).[41] This notion of Onesimus representing Paul's very self is reiterated in verse 17b ("Receive him as you would me"*). And if Philemon is going to obey the apostle's command to "refresh my heart [inward parts] in Christ," then he must do it by releasing Onesimus, who is the apostle's "very heart" (accordingly, see further the use of σπλάγχνα in v. 20; Weima 2016: 219). This should especially endear Paul to Philemon and motivate him to pay close attention to his coming explicit request, being convinced also of the apostle's affection for him (Philemon is "beloved" to Paul, v. 1). Paul thus tells Philemon that he has the same tender affection for Onesimus, which should help Philemon understand how very dear the slave is to Paul. This likewise should motivate Philemon to grant Paul's request.

Paul's continued delay in explicitly making his request of Philemon is designed to lay even further rhetorical footing for motivating Philemon to acquiesce and grant Paul's forthcoming appeal.

13 For the third time in sequence (cf. vv. 11, 12) another relative pronoun refers to Onesimus, introducing yet more information about the slave. In further describing the slave, Paul begins to come close to making his actual request of Philemon. Though Paul had sent Onesimus back to Philemon (v. 12), he "wished [ἐβουλόμην, *eboulomēn*][42] to keep" the slave "for himself."* The

39. Commentators generally recognize that "I have sent back" is an epistolary aorist, which can be rendered "I am sending back" (e.g., Dunn 1996: 322; Wallace 1996: 563).

40. See Barth and Blanke (2000: 355–60) on the different interpretations of the phrase "I have sent back to you."

41. Wall (1993) thinks only the latter idea of the slave being a source of compassion is in mind.

42. The imperfect has a "conative or desiderative" sense "of incomplete or interrupted action, which" here rhetorically "softens the harshness of the remark" by Paul (so MHT 3:65; likewise

preposition πρός (*pros*) plus the accusative ἐμαυτόν (*emauton*) carries the sense of purpose:[43] "for my purpose." Paul's purpose is expanded upon in the directly following clause: "in order that on your behalf he should serve me in [my] chains for the gospel."* This shows that Paul is not merely requesting Onesimus's release but specifically that he wants him released in order to return to Paul and serve him in his imprisonment. With the phrase "in order that he should serve me on behalf of [ὑπέρ, *hyper*] you," Paul informs Philemon that already, even without him knowing it, he has been serving Paul through his estranged slave.[44] The preposition ὑπέρ conveys the notion of substitution: "to minister to me *in your stead*" (Zerwick 1963: 30, italics added) or "*in your place* he might serve" (italics added).[45] Onesimus is a substitute for Philemon, so his actions toward Paul represent the very actions of Philemon himself. Such an idea would likely have begun to sway Philemon toward regarding his slave in a favorable manner.

In verse 1 we concluded that Paul's imprisonment is actual and not figurative. Furthermore, in verse 1 we saw that the phrase "a prisoner of Christ Jesus" is a genitive of cause: "a prisoner because of [or in the cause of] Christ Jesus."[46] Likewise the clause "chains of the gospel"* (v. 13) is also a genitive of cause ("chains because of [or in the cause of] the gospel").[47] Consequently, Paul wants Onesimus to care for the apostle's own personal needs, which will ultimately further the cause of the gospel while he is in prison. That personal needs are in mind appears logical from the phrase "serve me <u>in the chains</u> of the gospel" and the parallel with Phil. 2: "Epaphroditus, . . . is . . . [a] minister to my need" (2:25), "risking his life to complete what was deficient in your service to me" (2:30).[48] Some commentators take Onesimus's "ministering"

Brooks and Winbery 1979: 94). Robertson (1934: 919) calls this the "courteous or polite use of the imperfect indicative." See Barth and Blanke (2000: 364–66) for various views of the sense of the imperfect; they note that if Paul's wish be viewed as constant and firm, Paul is nevertheless expressing himself "in a reticent, shy, and humble way" in light of the immediate context: e.g., the fulfillment of Paul's wish is conditioned on the free decision of Philemon (v. 14); whatever Philemon may decide and Paul may intend, it is God's guidance and providence that determines the outcome of the slave's destiny (Barth and Blanke 2000: 365); cf. similarly Dana and Mantey 1957: 190. Moule (1959: 9), among others, also sees the imperfect tense here possibly to have an epistolary sense (likely rendered, "I am wishing").

43. See BDAG (874–75, s.v. πρός 3.c) for this function of the preposition.

44. Among others holding this view, see Garland (1998: 330), who generally follows E. Scott 1930: 108.

45. So Porter 1994: 177; likewise others such as Robertson 1934: 630–31; Moule 1959: 64; and Harris 2012: 228.

46. Though we also suggested that the phrase could be a genitive of possession or relationship, the former highlighting that, while Paul was possessed by Roman chains, he was ultimately possessed by Christ, and it was by Christ's will that he was imprisoned, which verse 13 shows was for the cause of the gospel.

47. Harris (2010: 228) notes that the genitive could be subjective, "(in the chains) that the gospel has brought me," or, among other options, could be a genitive of reference, which he renders as "because of" and "in the interests of" the gospel, the latter of which is close to my own preference.

48. Following Bruce 1984: 215; D. Moo 2008: 414–15.

as equivalent to calling him "a minister of the gospel," since the verb and noun form of διακονέω (*diakoneō*) are "always used in a religious/theological context" (so Pao 2012: 391). While this is true, it is a very broad statement. It does not mean that the word cannot refer to meeting someone's personal needs within the context of the church, which in one way or another promotes the gospel.[49] Commentators often observe that Paul calls Onesimus "our faithful and beloved brother" in Col. 4:9, but this is too general to know whether it means "faithfulness" with respect to gospel ministry or personal help to Paul.

14 In stark contrast (note v. 14's contrastive δέ, *de*, "but") to the statement in verse 13 "I wished to keep him with me," Paul says that he did not want to keep Onesimus with him without his master's agreement: "but without your consent I did not want to do anything." The HCSB highlights the sharp contrast between verses 13a and 14a: "I wanted to keep him with me, . . . but I didn't want to do anything without your consent" (see D. Moo 2008: 413). This suggests that Paul's request is not merely for the slave's release in general but that, in particular, he would be released to return to Paul and minister to him (which v. 21 also implies). On the other hand, two rhetorical points can be observed (following Pao 2012: 400): (1) Paul is willing to give up Onesimus as one who gives him crucial aid (vv. 13–14), which suggests that Philemon should be willing to give up his own claim on his slave's service to him. (2) Likewise, Paul restrains his own will in not demanding that Philemon obey him (v. 14), which implies that Philemon should do the same with Onesimus.

Paul refers to "the good" that Philemon is to do willingly, which recalls "every good thing" from verse 6. There we saw that the phrase "every good" or "every good work" is used to refer to righteous acts in general. Elsewhere Paul uses the phrase "every good work" (πᾶν ἔργον ἀγαθόν, *pan ergon agathon*) to refer to the specific work of a financial gift given to someone else to relieve their financial burden (2 Cor. 9:8). And we have argued that, while the phrase refers to good works in general in Philem. 6, it nevertheless anticipates the more specific good work in verse 14 (see on v. 6). The phrase τὸ ἀγαθόν σου (*to agathon sou*) in verse 14 can be translated as "<u>the</u> good thing <u>by you</u>" or "the good thing <u>from you</u>." First, the article precedes "good," which English translations do not express. Inserting the article (omitted from the Greek phrase in v. 6) highlights that a specific good deed is now in mind.[50] Second, the

49. The verb διακονέω can refer to meeting more menial needs among the Christian community (for the verb with this nuance, see Rom. 15:25–26; 2 Cor. 8:19–20; 1 Tim. 3:10, 13; see likewise the noun form in Rom. 15:31; 1 Cor. 16:15–19; 2 Cor. 8:4; 9:1, 12, 13; 11:8). And, as in Philem. 13, such more mundane service promotes the ultimate glory of God (e.g., 2 Cor. 8:19; 9:13) and no doubt the spread of the gospel.

50. As I have subsequently found, BDF §263.1 understands that the article with "the neuter sing." adjective employed as a substantive is used "in an individual sense of a particular definite thing or act," thus rendering τὸ ἀγαθόν σου as "your good deed" (so also Douay-Rheims, NRSV, HCSB, NET); likewise Harris (2010: 229), who sees the construction referring to a "specific and concrete" good work. Some translations render the phrase as "your goodness" (NASB, ESV, ASV), "any favor you do" (NIV), or "your benefit" (Geneva, KJV, Webster).

rendering of the genitive σοῦ as "the good thing from [or by] you" interprets the genitive as source or subjective, which underscores that "the good thing" is something not merely to be "possessed" by Philemon but something that is to be done by him (or arises from him).[51] While the rendering "the good by you" is more awkward than "your good deed" or "your good thing" or some such smoother translation, it brings to the fore the particular emphasis that Paul wants to highlight at this point in the letter.

The purpose (ἵνα, *hina*) in Paul not wanting to decide on his own authority anything about the slave's release was that he wanted Philemon's "goodness" in releasing his slave not to "be, as it were, by compulsion, but of your own free will."* The word "compulsion" (ἀνάγκη, *anankē*) has the notion of something that is "necessary." Paul can use this word in referring to the "necessity of being in subjection" to ruling authorities (cf. Rom. 13:5) and referring to himself not merely "preaching the gospel . . . under compulsion" but doing it also "voluntarily" (1 Cor. 9:16–17). Likewise, with respect to giving, Paul wants people not to give "grudgingly or under compulsion" but as each "has purposed in his heart" (2 Cor. 9:7; cf. similarly 1 Cor. 7:37). In line with these other uses of ἀνάγκη, Paul does not want to "compel" Philemon by using his apostolic authority to insist that Philemon free the slave, but he wants Philemon to do it willingly or voluntarily.[52] The use of the phrase κατὰ ἑκούσιον (*kata hekousion*) with γνώμη (*gnōmē*) occurs several times in Philo and is typically to be translated as "according to one's own voluntary purpose [or inclination]" (see the additional note on v. 14). Even though the uses in Philo have γνώμη directly following κατὰ ἑκούσιον and here it precedes and is separated by two clauses, γνώμη is still likely implied after the κατὰ ἑκούσιον phrase. So the last clause of verse 14 should read "but it should be according to your own voluntary intention [or willingly,[53] be voluntary[54]]." The point is that Philemon should be motivated to release Onesimus, not because of outside pressure from Paul or anyone else but from his own heart's desire to do so. As noted in the introduction to this section, verse 14 reiterates the point of verses 8–9, where Paul tells Philemon that he does not want to "command him to do that which is proper" but to make a decision out of love.

Paul could have chosen to act on the precedent of Deuteronomic law to receive Onesimus and have him stay with him.[55] On the other hand, Roman

51. I have subsequently found Harris (2010: 229) proposing that the genitive may be possessive ("your") or subjective (interpreting the latter as "done by you").

52. The word ἀνάγκη also can refer to the "pressure" of "distress" or "tribulation" (e.g., 2 Cor. 12:10; 1 Thess. 3:7; so D. Moo 2008: 416), so that perhaps there is a nuance of Paul not wanting to put extreme pressure on Philemon about his decision.

53. Geneva, KJV; NET has "from your own willingness." The rendering of "according to [your own] willingness" is also possible.

54. So NRSV, TNIV.

55. Deut. 23:15–16: "You shall not hand over to his master a slave who has escaped from his master to you. He shall live with you in your midst, in the place which he shall choose in one of your towns where it pleases him; you shall not mistreat him." N. Wright (1986: 182) notes that this law was part of the Mosaic covenant and related to the civil laws in Israel's land, but such laws no

law forbade harboring a fugitive slave. But Paul appeals neither to OT nor to Roman law but to Onesimus's new status[56] and the kindness of Philemon's own voluntary will (see further in the additional note on v. 14).

Additional Notes

9. See the following early Jewish Hellenistic and early Christian texts for the meaning of "authority, honor, and respect" for πρεσβύτης (*presbytēs*), the translations of which are in italics below:

Josephus, *Ant.* 12.87: "He then made haste to meet *the elders* that came from Jerusalem for the interpretation."

Philo, *Agr.* 56: "It is customary for *old men* to be appointed to offices of irresponsible authority."

Philo, *Flacc.* 74: "For he arrested thirty-eight members of our council of elders [*gerousias*], which our savior and benefactor, Augustus, elected to manage the affairs of the Jewish nation after the death of the king of our own nation. . . . He arrested them, . . . a body of *old men* prisoners" (*old men* in parallel with "elders").

Philo, *Emb.* 142: "Moreover, he, even while he was still a young man, was called the *old man* as a mark of respect because of his exceeding wisdom."

Philo, *Hypoth.* 11.13: "Accordingly the *old men*, even if they happen to be childless, as if they were not only the fathers of many children but were even also particularly happy in an affectionate offspring, are accustomed to end their lives in a most happy and prosperous and carefully attended old age, being looked upon by such a number of people as worthy of so much honour and provident regard that they think themselves bound to care for them even more from inclination than from any tie of natural affection."

Isa. 9:14 LXX (9:15 Eng.): "The *old man* and them that respect persons, this is the head; and the prophet teaching unlawful things, he is the tail."

Lam. 5:14 (NASB marg.): "*Elders* have ceased from the gate."

Hist. Rech. 6.3: "There were in that crowd *old men* like sons of God, and young men were standing by the elders."

4 Macc. 7:10: "O aged man, mightier than torture; revered *elder* more vigorous than the flame; great king, ruler of the passions, Eleazar!"

Mart. Pol. 7.3: "When they consented, he stood and prayed, so full of the grace of God that for two hours he was unable to stop speaking; those who heard him were amazed, and many regretted that they had come after such a godly *old man*."

Irenaeus, *Her.* 1.15.6: "With good reason, therefore, and very fittingly, in reference to your rash attempt, has that divine *elder* and preacher of the truth burst forth in verse against you as follows: 'Marcus, you former of idols, inspector of portents, skilled in consulting the stars, and deep in the black arts of magic, ever by tricks such as these confirming the doctrines of error, furnishing signs to those involved by you in deception, wonders of power that is utterly severed from God and apostate, which Satan, your true father, enables you still to accomplish, by means of Azazel, that fallen and yet mighty angel,—thus making you the precursor of his own

---

longer apply in the new-covenant age (likewise Witherington 2007: 75). But could the moral principles behind slavery in Deut. 23 and 15:12–15 possibly be carried over into the new epoch? Witherington (2007: 76) points out that sending Onesimus back to Philemon violates the Deuteronomic law, which supports Wright's view. On the other hand, Jeal (2015: 144) says that Paul knew of Deut. 23:15–16 and would have respected the law, so this might suggest that Onesimus was not to be categorized officially as a runaway slave (a *fugitivus*). If so, Paul would not be violating the Deut. 23 law.

56. Dunn 1996: 329; followed by Garland 1998: 332.

impious actions.' Such are the words of the divinely-favored *elder*. And I shall endeavour to state the remainder of their mystical system, which runs out to great length, in brief compass, and to bring to the light what has for a long time been concealed. For in this way such things will become easily susceptible of exposure by all."

Gos. Nic. (Christ's Descent into Hell) 9 (25): "And setting out to paradise, he took hold of our forefather Adam by the hand, and delivered him, and all the just, to the archangel Michael. And as they were going into the door of paradise, there met them two *old men*, to whom the holy fathers said: 'Who are you, who have not seen death, and have not come down into Hades, but who dwell in paradise in your bodies and your souls?' One of them answered, and said: 'I am Enoch, who was well-pleasing to God, and who was translated hither by Him; and this is Elijah the Tishbite; and we are also to live until the end of the world; and then we are to be sent by God to withstand Antichrist, and to be slain by him, and after three days to rise again, and to be snatched up in clouds to meet the Lord.'"

It is significant to note, along with numerous commentators, that there are several uses of πρεσβύτης with the meaning of "ambassador": 2 Chron. 32:31, "the ambassadors of the princes of Babylon" (Codex B); 1 Macc. 13:21, "sending envoys to Trypho"; 14:21, "the ambassadors that were sent"; 14:22, "ambassadors of the Judeans" (e.g., Codex ℵ); 15:17, "the ambassadors of the Jews" (e.g., Codex ℵ); 2 Macc. 11:34, "ambassadors of the Romans." However, in every one of these cases πρεσβύτης is a textual variant (supported by a variety of witnesses; see Metzger 1994: 588), in which the original reading is likely πρεσβευτής (*presbeutēs*).[57] The variant of πρεσβύτης likely arose from accidental scribal transmission (by confused sound or mistaken copying).[58] Nevertheless, despite its lack of originality, it must be acknowledged that these instances of πρεσβύτης with the sense of "ambassador" are found in the Septuagint textual tradition, so that these LXX texts would have been received by some readers who would have understood the word with this notion, since that is its meaning in the immediate contexts of these textual variants.[59] The parallel of "I am an ambassador [πρεσβεύω, *presbeuō*] in chains" in Eph. 6:20 may also point in Philem. 9 to the order of "old" as an apostolic ambassadorial reference followed by a reference to suffering ("in the chains of Christ Jesus").[60] Some also see that the use of the verb form of πρεσβευτής in 2 Cor. 5:20 is a parallel that likewise points to "ambassador" in Philem. 9.[61]

57. In 1 and 2 Maccabees of the Göttingen edition of the LXX, πρεσβευτής (*presbeutēs*) is preferred as the original text. The Rahlfs-Hanhart edition of the LXX in 2 Chron. 32:31 likewise prefers the plural of πρεσβευτής as the original and not the plural of πρεσβύτης (*presbytēs*).

58. Pao (2012: 385) notes the uses in 1 Maccabees but does not appear to acknowledge that the uses are textual variants and unlikely to be from the original hand. So likewise Metzger (1994: 588), who includes the 2 Chronicles reference.

59. Some readers may well have glossed over πρεσβύτης (*presbytēs*) and read it as πρεσβευτής (*presbeutēs*), while others would have read πρεσβύτης as "elder" with an ambassadorial sense because of the immediate context and because they would have been familiar with the word as carrying the sense of an honorable or authoritative person. Those hearing these LXX texts read probably would have heard πρεσβύτης as πρεσβευτής, since the former is a rare replacement for the latter (it occurs only in the six above LXX texts, which also explains why some readers would have glossed over πρεσβύτης; likewise it is rare in Greco-Roman literature for πρεσβευτής to be confused with πρεσβύτης (on which, e.g., see Hock 1995: 73).

60. So, e.g., cf. Moule (1957: 144), Lightfoot (1875: 338–39), and Bruce (1984: 212), though the latter two see the expression "in chains" not as a reference inducing sympathy. Barth and Blanke (2000: 321–23) see that the sense of apostolic "ambassador" is in mind. See O'Brien (1982: 290) for a list of numerous commentators who understand πρεσβύτης (*presbytēs*) with the sense of πρεσβευτής (*presbeutēs*); cf. Metzger (1994: 588), who also summarizes arguments for and against reading "ambassador" in Philem. 9. Birdsall (1993: 625–30) believes it to be highly improbable that Philem. 9 originally read πρεσβευτής.

61. E.g., Petersen (1985: 125–26) sees a parallel to Philem. 9 in 2 Cor. 5:20 of πρεσβεύω (*presbeuō*) and καταλλάσσω (*katallassō*) in the clause "Therefore, we are ambassadors for Christ, as though God were appealing through us."*

Therefore, Paul uses πρεσβύτης as a reference to his honored or respected status, which is an implied way of referring to his apostolic office, reverting back again to his reference to his office in verse 8. In that this carries an apostolic notion, the idea of ambassadorship would be entailed to some degree, since ἀπόστολος (*apostolos*) itself carries that nuance.[62]

10. Knox (1959: 22–25) contends that Paul is not "appealing on behalf of Onesimus" but "appealing for Onesimus" in the sense of asking for Onesimus himself to be returned to Paul in prison. This appears to be supported by the following context, where Paul says that Onesimus is his own spiritual child (i.e., "whom I have begotten," v. 10b), who is "useful" to Paul (v. 11), who represents Paul's "very heart" (v. 12), and who might return to "minister" to Paul in prison (v. 13). Knox adduces a couple of parallel syntactical uses of παρακαλέω (*parakaleō*) followed by περί (*peri*) + genitive in Hellenistic Greek where it represents the content or object of the request (e.g., "I beseech [παρακαλέω] the great god Serapis for [περί] your life," Appian, *Rom. Hist.: Punic Wars* 136).[63] Knox's view is quite viable, especially since it fits the context so well.

Περί plus a genitive with the sense of "on behalf of" is very rare in the NT, though it is possible in this context.[64] Knox's view is more viable, since it also has syntactical support in Hellenistic Greek. It is also possible that περί is to be taken more generally in the sense of "about, concerning, in regard to, or with reference to" (cf. BDAG 797, s.v. περί).

11. Most commentators acknowledge that there is a wordplay on *achrēston* and *euchrēston*, which can be carried over into English as "useless" and "useful." But some think another wordplay is included, which is based mainly on the Roman historian Suetonius's (*Claud.* 25.4) wrong rendering of *Christos* as *Chrestos*, so that perhaps the wordplay in Philem. 11 is *achrestos* and *euchrestos*, "without Christ" and "good Christian." First, such an additional pun would fit the context of the contrast between a previously unbelieving Onesimus and a spiritually renewed Onesimus, but is it necessary? It would seem odd to have a double pun; even single puns are somewhat hard to detect. Second, this additional pun is based on a misspelling of *Christos* as *Chrestos*. It is possible but not really probable that Paul would have utilized the same misspelling to make a second pun work, since there is apparently only one extant case of this misspelling in ancient literature and that by a Roman historian, who was not a Christian. Third, Paul always spells "Christ" as *Christos*, and it is unlikely that he would change the spelling in this instance to produce the pun.[65] He could have produced the pun with the right spelling (*a-christos* and *eu-christos*).[66] Fourth, to have two puns in one phrase seems to be a rare phenomenon. Fifth,

62. Weima (2016: 223) accepts the idea that πρεσβύτης refers to Paul in a way that was to "induce respect and obedience" but objects to the notion that it refers to his apostolic, ambassadorial office, since Paul, if he meant that, could have used more explicit words like "apostle" or "ambassador" (πρεσβευτής). But this objection is answered by recalling that Paul is going back and forth in referring to his authority and his helpless situation, and when referring to his authority can do so obliquely. Furthermore, we have indeed seen that πρεσβύτης (*presbytēs*) can carry the idea of "ambassador" in the reception history of the LXX textual tradition, especially for subsequent readers.

63. I have been unable to confirm this reference to Appian by Knox. Knox also adduces a similar parallel in P.Oxy. 1070. To these two references may be added 4 Bar. 9.4, where three times this construction occurs with the sense of περί (*peri*) introducing the object for that which is being appealed.

64. See BDAG (797–98, s.v. περί), where it is noted that sometimes περί (*peri*) can take the place of ὑπέρ (*hyper*).

65. However, some commentators contend that *achrestos* and *achristos* would have been pronounced the same way, perhaps making plausible the double pun. On this see N. Wright (1986: 182) and Garland (1998: 329–30), who holds this view among other reasons for affirming the double pun; likewise Wall 1993: 206; Thompson 2005: 217–19; and Bird 2009: 139.

66. Though Fitzmyer (2000: 109) is probably right that if such a pun were intended, the first word would be *a-christianos* ("non-Christian") and the second, contrasting word would be

in addition, the semantic "rule of maximal redundancy" may be applicable here. That is, the interpreter should opt for the meaning that "contributes the least new information to the total context" (so Titrud 1992: 248, likewise 255).[67] Such a second purported pun seems to add unnecessary new information to the context and message of Paul. That is, Paul has gone to great pains to refer to himself, Onesimus, and Philemon as cautiously, circumspectly, and implicitly as possible. A pun describing Onesimus in such blunt "non-Christian" and "Christian" terms seems to go against this overly cautious strain. As D. Moo (2008: 409–10) says, though not appealing to this rule, "all the contextual data are fully accounted for on the single interpretation of the *achrēstos/euchrēstos* contrast."

12. For the textual problem, see Metzger (1994: 589), who prefers the shorter reading of NA[28] over the longer, added reading of προσλαβοῦ (*proslabou*, receive) found in the later and the majority of MSS. The KJV, for example, follows this later reading, which it renders as "whom I have sent again: thou therefore receive him, that is, mine own bowels." Metzger views the added variant to be a scribal attempt to smooth out the awkward syntax of the original and to have been added under the influence of verse 17, where the very same word appears.

14. The rendering of the word combination κατὰ ἑκούσιον (*kata hekousion*) with γνώμη (*gnōmē*) is typically to be translated as "according to one's own voluntary purpose [or inclination]." See Philo, *Alleg.* 3.144 (with reference to the wise man as a spiritual priest), "'He washes his belly and his feet with water,' without any command, *according to his own voluntary inclination*"; *Cher.* 96, humans "have contracted all this pollution and mutilation *according to their own voluntary will*"; *Heir* 68, "not that reasoning which remains in the prison of the body *according to its own voluntary intentions*"; *Mos.* 1.273, Balaam "had not sinned *according to voluntary* [or *deliberate*] *purpose*"; *Decal.* 177, God gave the Ten Commandments so that people might choose what is right "from wise consideration and *according to his own voluntary* [*deliberate*] *purpose*"; *Spec.* 1.259, "the imperfections and stains which you have imprinted on your whole life, partly in consequence of unexpected events, and partly *according to voluntary* [*deliberate*] *purpose*"; *Virt.* 202, a person whom people were "mocking and reviling . . . because he committed an error not *according to his own voluntary intention*." Especially significant is Philo, *Contempl.* 68, virgins who are pure "not from *necessity* [ἀνάγκη, *ananke*], as some of the priestesses among the Greeks . . . who have been compelled to preserve their chastity more than they would have done *according to their own voluntary intention*." Cf. also *Spec.* 3.15, sinful "actions committed according to ignorance and not *by voluntary will*." In Num. 15:3 καθ' ἑκούσιον *refers to someone offering "according to a voluntary offering"* (or *"according to voluntariness"*). Accordingly, Paul wants Philemon to release his slave "according to his own voluntary purpose [or inclination]" and not from any outside pressure.

It seems more than coincidental that Philo, in discussing the Deuteronomic law of releasing native-born slaves after six years (Deut. 15:12–15), says that masters who set free such slaves "without hesitation" are enabling slaves to experience "freedom" as "a good" (ἀγαθόν, *agathon*), the very same neuter nominative singular word used of "the good" that Philemon is to do in releasing Onesimus (*Spec.* 2.84). Garland (1998: 332) brought my attention to this connection, but D. Moo (2008: 418) sees no link to Philo's use here, since ἀγαθός (*agathos*) is used hundreds of times in Philo and in Biblical Greek. However, the link with this word and with the Deuteronomic context of releasing slaves for freedom is unusual, and it may represent a broader idea in Hellenistic Judaism of which Paul may have had some awareness, especially

synchristos ("with-Christ"), which would have been suitable, instead of *euchristos* (lit., "good Christ"), which would be awkward. There is no evidence that *achristos* or *euchristos* ever meant respectively "non-Christian" and "good Christian" (see Barth and Blanke 2000: 345).

67. See further Ray (1994) for application of this rule to Gal. 6:16; for general discussion of this rule, see Silva 1983: 151–56.

since forms of the word do occur elsewhere with respect to slaves' freedom.[68] However, as we have seen, Paul's main concern is not that Onesimus be emancipated but that he be released to return to Paul so that he can minister to the apostle.

Could it be that Paul has in mind this particular Deuteronomic law about how to treat fellow Israelite slaves, since Onesimus has become a true spiritual Israelite (cf. Gal. 3:16; 6:15–16)?[69] Jeal (2015: 144) contends that the notion of freeing Israelite slaves (Deut. 15) and providing security for runaway slaves (Deut. 23) was part of Paul's Jewish-Christian worldview and becomes "a feature of his rhetoric in the Letter to Philemon." In this connection, perhaps it is not too much of a reach to suggest, as above, that Onesimus can be viewed as a "true Israelite," deserving freedom because he is a genuine member of the true Israel (in line with Deut. 15:12–15), a member of the ἐκκλησία (*ekklēsia*), the word for membership in Israel that is used five times in Deut. 23:2–9, only six verses from the Deut. 23:15–16 passage on providing security for runaway slaves. Indeed, Targum Pseudo-Jonathan on Deut. 23:16 says the runaway slave should not be returned to his owner "because . . . he has fled from the worship of his idol" and has come to be "a refugee among you to [be] put under the protection of my Shekinah" and thus a convert to Israel (likewise Midr. Pss. 54.2; Sifre Deut., Piska 259).[70]

68. In this respect, Philo uses forms of "good" (ἀγαθός, *agathos*) elsewhere (which I have put in italics) to indicate the advantageous condition of freedom from slavery, especially focusing on slaves in Israel. In a context discussing slavery in Deut. 5:14 and Exod. 20:10, Philo says masters should let slaves "have relaxation every six days as a kind of spark and kindling of freedom," thus teaching them "not to despair of *better* hopes" and "to look forward to a complete relaxation hereafter" (*Spec.* 2.67). In a context of discussing the laws of Exod. 21:16 and Deut. 24:7 together with classical Greek and Platonic notions (see *Spec.* 4.13–14), Philo says that masters who emancipate slaves do a "praiseworthy deed" since they are imparting to the slave "*the most excellent* of all possessions, freedom" (*Spec.* 4.15). See also *Mos.* 1.86: God "promised them [Israel] freedom [from Egyptian slavery] and a departure from there to a *better* country." Though not focusing on slavery within Israel, see also *Good Pers.* 64, where "the overflowing abundance of all other *good things*" includes "peace" and "freedom" from "slavery"; *Good Pers.* 131 (in discussing slavery), "The freedom of the wise" is included among "all other human *good gifts*"; *Good Pers.* 139 (again regarding slavery), "Let us not reject the most beautiful of *good things* among men, freedom"; *Alleg.* 3.86, "Freedom" is identified as a "*good thing*."

69. Various commentators suggest that Deut. 23:15–16 pertains to foreign slaves (e.g., see McConville 2002: 350–51; Merrill 1994: 312). They conclude this because the slave law in Deut. 15:12–18 explicitly points out that a native "kinsman" and "Hebrew" person is in mind, and no such explicitness is found in 23:15–16, though C. Wright (1996: 249) thinks native Hebrews are also included. Furthermore, the verb used for "oppress" at the end of Deut. 23:16 appears elsewhere to refer to the merciful treatment of a foreigner (Exod. 22:21; following Merrill 1994: 312). Some segments of later Jewish tradition affirmed that Deut. 15:12 included reference to "a runaway Hebrew slave who returns (to his master; Sifre Deut., Piska 118). However, other segments of later Judaism believed that the Deut. 15:12–15 law did not apply to "runaway" slaves (e.g., see b. Qidd. 16b). Under certain conditions a female foreign slave is to be set free (Deut. 21:10–14), as also a female Hebrew slave (Exod. 21:7–11); likewise, masters are to free Hebrew and foreign slaves if they mistreat them (Exod. 21:26–27). On these last three OT texts, see further discussion in Barth and Blanke 2000: 74.

70. Some believed that Deut. 23:15 (23:16 MT) refers to a slave bought "on the condition that he would set him free" (b. Yevam. 93b; b. Git. 45a; b. Qidd. 63a). Others affirmed that Deut. 23:16 MT refers to a slave who has escaped from some country outside of Israel to within the borders of Israel (b. Git. 45a). In one of the minor tracts of the Talmud, b. Gerim 61a identifies the slave of Deut. 23:16 (23:17 MT) as a proselyte, and Sifre Deut., Piska 259, sees that Deut. 23:15 (23:16 MT) includes "a resident alien" along with a slave. The first above reference directly and the second and third indirectly indicate that Jewish tradition associated Deut. 23:15–16 (23:16–17 MT) with not merely providing refuge for slaves but ultimately setting slaves free. If Paul was familiar with such a tradition and agreed with it, then sending Onesimus back to

If Paul was aware of such an interpretive tradition, then he may have thought the law only prohibited returning slaves to unbelieving masters. Paul actually alludes to these uses of ἐκκλησία in Deut. 23:2–9 (esp. 23:3) together with Neh. 13:1 repeatedly when referring to the ἐκκλησία τοῦ θεοῦ (*ekklēsia tou theou*, the church of God) in his letters (so eight times in the singular and three more times in the plural, "churches"; also once in Acts 20:28, in part of a speech by Paul; see further in the additional note on Col. 1:18). The observation that Onesimus will be a full-fledged member of "the church" (ἐκκλησία) in Colossae, in Philemon's "house" (stated as a fact in Col. 4:9), thus may not be coincidental in relation to the relevance of the Deuteronomic texts.

Philemon and asking for his freedom (if this is what Paul is requesting) does not contradict the Deuteronomy injunction against sending a slave back to a nonbelieving master but allowing it for a believing master.

B. Paul Confidently Appeals to Philemon to Accept His Slave (15–21)

Here is a fuller statement of the main idea of this unit: *Paul confidently appeals to Philemon to accept his slave as he would receive Paul because this will refresh Paul's heart in Christ.*

We have seen that the overall thrust of the body of the letter is the request that Philemon release Onesimus from slavery in order that he may return to minister to Paul in prison, so that Paul's heart may be "refreshed." Though it is debated, we have also observed that verses 8–14 appear to be a distinct literary unit through two observations: (1) a conceptual *inclusio*: Paul wants Philemon to act not because of his apostolic authority but out of love (vv. 8–9a); Paul wants Philemon to act not under compulsion but from his own voluntary motives (v. 14). (2) Such a unit is also recognizable by the introductory "therefore" in verse 8 and the introductory "for . . . for this reason" in verse 15, which introduces the following literary unit. The phrase διὰ τοῦτο (*dia touto*) occurs twenty-two times in Paul; NA^{28} recognizes διὰ τοῦτο (*dia touto*) as marking the beginning of a new literary unit six of those times, including Philem. 15, though others disagree.

But the meaning of "for, for this reason" (γὰρ διὰ τοῦτο, *gar dia touto*) is not clear, leaving its logical relationship to verse 14 ambiguous. The following are five possible options for how to understand this complicated construction.

1. The διὰ τοῦτο could be redundant with γάρ, both referring back to and providing the ground for verse 14 (Philemon's willingness to release Onesimus). That is, Philemon's willingness for releasing his slave (v. 14) is based on and inspired by the slave having been parted from his master "in order that [ἵνα, *hina*][1] he [Philemon] would have him back forever."* Accordingly, this redundant emphatic construction of γὰρ διὰ τοῦτο, though awkward, can be paraphrased as merely "for this reason!" or "because!" or "for . . . it was for this reason."[2]
2. "Because" (γάρ), the reason why Philemon should willingly release Onesimus (v. 14), is "for the reason" (διὰ τοῦτο) that Philemon should

1. The ἵνα would accordingly designate the purpose of the διὰ τοῦτο clause.

2. So the HCSB and NET, which also render the following ἵνα as "so that," giving the purpose of the clause "he was separated from you for a while," so that the ἵνα does not explain the content of the διὰ τοῦτο phrase, which appears to show that these translations view the latter phrase as not pointing forward but backward to verse 14.

realize his slave was "parted from" him "that [ἵνα][3] he could have him back forever." Here the γάρ again refers back to verse 14 (giving the ground and inspiration for it), and the διὰ τοῦτο refers forward to "was parted . . . that," which gives the content of the ground (γάρ) for verse 14.[4]

3. The γάρ is a marker of clarification or continuation ("for," "moreover," "indeed," "furthermore") of verses 8–14, further expanding on Paul's appeal to Philemon, and the διὰ τοῦτο . . . ἵνα launches that further explanation ("for this reason . . . that"), which continues on through verse 21 (so NIV and TNIV, which do not explicitly translate the γάρ).[5] Here the διὰ τοῦτο refers forward to "that[6] you should have him back forever" as the reason why "he was parted from you."[7]
4. "For" (γάρ) refers back to the preceding verses and is inferential, indicating that Philemon's willing release of his slave (vv. 13–14) would result in his having him back forever (v. 15b). Accordingly, the "for this reason" (διὰ τοῦτο) clause refers forward and introduces the content of this intended result or purpose: that Philemon should realize his slave was "parted from" him "that [ἵνα][8] he could have him back forever."[9]
5. The γάρ is a marker of clarification or continuation ("for," "moreover," "indeed," "furthermore") of verses 8–14, further expanding on Paul's appeal to Philemon, and the διὰ τοῦτο is inferential, referring back to verse 14 as the ground for the remainder of verse 15.[10] The translation would be "furthermore [moreover, for], . . . therefore" (so Geneva,[11] KJV, Webster, ASV, Bishop's Bible, Douay-Rheims).

3. The ἵνα would accordingly designate the content of the διὰ τοῦτο clause.

4. So Pao 2012: 393. D. Moo (2008: 418) comes close to this option, seeing the γάρ (*gar*) as giving a further reason for Paul's decision to return Onesimus in verse 12. Outside of Philem. 15, when ἵνα follows διὰ τοῦτο, apparently only once does the ἵνα give the content of the διὰ τοῦτο clause (2 Cor. 13:10), while otherwise διὰ τοῦτο refers backward to preceding material as the basis for what follows the διὰ τοῦτο (Rom. 4:16; Eph. 6:13; 1 Tim. 1:16; 2 Tim. 2:10).

5. The NLT and NJB do not translate γὰρ διὰ τοῦτο at all but clearly take it in the way that the NIV and TNIV do.

6. Here the ἵνα does not indicate the goal of "he was parted from you" but introduces the content of the διὰ τοῦτο. Bruce (1984: 217), Wallace (1996: 333), and D. Moo (2008: 418–19) think this is a clear case of διὰ τοῦτο pointing forward.

7. I have found that D. Moo (2008: 418) sees the possibility that γάρ functions to introduce the following material in verses 15–16 as an elaboration or explanation of the preceding in verses 8–14.

8. Again, the ἵνα would accordingly designate the content of the διὰ τοῦτο clause.

9. In addition to preferring a version of option 2 (see above), D. Moo (2008: 418) also prefers a version of this option, seeing verses 15–16 as giving the outcome of Philemon's "good deed" in verse 14. How Moo would explain the logical compatibility of holding views 2 and 4 is unclear.

10. Knox (1959: 26) takes this position on the γάρ and διὰ τοῦτο. According to this view, the following ἵνα would designate the goal of "He was parted from you."

11. Which does not translate the γάρ.

Any of these five options is viable.[12] What makes the construction difficult is that γάρ, together with διὰ τοῦτο, occurs only one other time in the NT: Rom. 13:6. Commentators do not agree about how the phrase is to be construed in the Romans passage, especially with respect to whether it points backward or forward.[13] It seems that the best options are that the phrase points backward, either to all of verses 1–5 ("be in subjection to governing authorities") or to only verse 5 ("being in subjection . . . for conscience sake") as the basis for verse 6a ("You also pay taxes"). Some English translations of Rom. 13:6 explicitly render the γάρ as "*for*, because of this" (NASB, ESV, likewise Geneva), while others merely have "for this cause" (KJV, ASV, likewise NET).[14]

But the lone use of the clause in the Romans passage cannot be determinative for Philem. 15. Only immediate context can help, and that context is not clear in the Philemon text. The first two options would have verses 15–21 supporting verse 14 (Philemon's willingness to release his slave) as the main point of verses 8–21. The third option sees verses 15–21 as a further elaboration of verses 8–14, so that the logical weight tilts toward the end of verses 15–21. The fourth and fifth options view verses 8–14 to support verses 15–21, so that the logical emphasis again would be on that latter section. Among the five options of understanding γὰρ διὰ τοῦτο, the last three options edge out the others as appearing to be best, pointing to the logical climax of all of verses 8–21 being in verses 15–21, especially verse 20. This flow of the argument seems natural, especially according to options 4 and 5, since verses 15–21 show two major results or purposes of Paul's appeal to Philemon to release Onesimus out of his own gracious will: (1) Philemon would have his slave back as a Christian brother forever (vv. 15–16), and (2) Philemon's releasing Onesimus would "benefit" Paul by "refreshing his heart" (v. 20). Verse 20 ("Refresh my heart") is the main point of the entire paragraph, since everything in verses 15–19 supports the verse, as does verse 21. These last three options for γὰρ διὰ τοῦτο are also preferable, since their translation is perhaps smoother and less awkward than the first two options.

Exegesis and Exposition

15[Furthermore] perhaps he was for this reason [parted] from you for a while, that you [should] have him back forever, 16no longer as a slave, but more than a slave, a

12. Theoretically, there are still more options, but we think they are less viable. A number of the other English translations not mentioned above in options 1–5 are ambiguous with respect to which option they fit into (e.g., NASB, RSV, NRSV, ESV).

13. See Schreiner (1998: 685–86) for the various options held by commentators.

14. In Rom. 13:6 some render διὰ τοῦτο γάρ as "for the same reason" (NRSV, likewise NLT); others render the phrase "this is why" (NIV, TNIV). HCSB has "and for this reason"; Douay-Rheims has "for therefore."

beloved brother, especially to me, but how much more to you, both in the flesh and in the Lord. [17]If then you regard me a partner, accept him as you would me. [18]But if he has wronged you in any way, or owes you anything, charge that to my account; [19]I, Paul, am writing this with my own hand, I will repay it ([lest I should] mention to you that you owe to me even your own self as well). [20]Yes, brother, let me benefit from you in the Lord; refresh my heart in Christ. [21]Having confidence in your obedience, I write to you, since I know that you will do even more than what I say.

We have concluded above that the introductory γὰρ διὰ τοῦτο indicates that **15**
verses 15–21 give the results of Philemon's willingness to do his "good deed" of releasing Onesimus (v. 14). The remainder of this verse gives the first result. Paul's first word of the verse, "perhaps," indicates that he does not yet want to assume Philemon's positive response and so wants to leave the result of that response as tentative. Or more likely, the "perhaps" may reveal that Paul is making a tentative proposal about God's providence in the slave's departure, since Paul does not have absolute certainty that this is God's plan (D. Moo 2008: 420).

An intended result or purpose of the master's willing good deed is that "he was parted [from you] for a while in order that you might have him back forever."* In the letter this is the first explicit mention of Onesimus's leaving his service to Philemon (D. Moo 2008: 419). The verb "he was parted" (ἐχωρίσθη, *echōristhē*) may be a "divine passive," whereby the implied subject is God (the clear divine passive in verse 22 points further to the same here).[15] If so, then it is God's providence that Onesimus left his master. The divinely orchestrated departure was for the purpose that the slave be converted and give his master opportunity to exercise his Christian quality of love and forgiveness in receiving him back as a beloved brother, with whom as such he would have fellowship "forever." The contrast between "for a while" and "forever" is obvious (observed by many commentators; e.g., O'Brien 1982: 295). The rhetorical purpose of the divine passive is to get Philemon to understand that it is God's hand that has brought about Onesimus's departure for some divine purpose, which should quell any anger that Philemon may have harbored (Garland 1998: 333). It would have been one thing to reject Paul's admonitions, but quite another to reject the ultimate divine purpose in Onesimus's departure from Philemon (Weima 2016: 225–26). Commentators often, and rightly, mention parallels like Gen. 50:20 ("You meant evil against me, but God meant it for good in order . . . to preserve many people alive")[16] and Rom. 8:28 ("We know that God causes all things to work together for good to those who love God"). If Philemon knows either or both of these passages, he may be calling them to mind, which would further induce him to accept his runaway slave more graciously.

15. I have subsequently found that Lohse (1971: 202), Dunn (1996: 333), Barth and Blanke (2000: 402), and Harris (2010: 230), among other commentators, hold to a divine passive here.

16. See Jeal (2015: 153–56) for the most viable discussion contending that the Gen. 50 background is in Paul's mind at this point.

Paul often uses the word "forever" (αἰώνιος, *aiōnios*) to refer to the "eternal life" that believers have (nine times),[17] which begins when they believe and will endure without end in this age and the age to come. It is this "eternal life" that Onesimus has come to possess in the present through his conversion, and Philemon will be able to have fellowship in Christ with his former slave for time without end. That such "eternal" fellowship is in mind, and not temporal fellowship that lasts for the rest of Philemon's and the slave's life,[18] is pointed to by the previous reference to Onesimus's conversion to Christ (v. 10) and Paul's use of αἰώνιος always to refer to some unending redemptive-historical reality (e.g., of life, comfort, glory, God's dominion).[19] Thus one purpose of Philemon's hoped for voluntary "good" deed (v. 14) is that he would have Onesimus back forever.

Commentators speculate on the exact circumstances of Onesimus's departure. Was it to seek Paul's aid in reconciling Onesimus to his master? Was it in order to get his freedom (see D. Moo 2008: 419)? There is simply not enough information in the letter to supply the answer.

16 That Philemon would have his slave back forever is now expanded upon: he will have him "no longer as a slave, but more than a slave, a beloved brother, especially to me, [and] how much more to you, both in the flesh and in the Lord." The first clause, "no longer <u>as</u> [or <u>in the manner as</u> = ὡς, *hōs*][20] a slave," does not mean that Onesimus will lose his earthly status as a slave.[21] This is pointed to from the following wording, "more than a slave," which appears not to deny slave status but to include more than a slave status.[22] Onesimus's

17. Rom. 2:7; 5:21; 6:22, 23; Gal. 6:8; 1 Tim. 1:16; 6:12; Titus 1:2; 3:7.

18. See Harris (2010: 230) for the possibility that αἰώνιος means "permanently," i.e., Onesimus would return as a permanent slave to his master. This is sometimes argued on the basis that Exod. 21:6; Lev. 25:46; Deut. 15:17; and Job 40:28 MT, LXX (41:4 Eng.) refer to a "slave forever," using αἰώνιος and meaning a slave who remains a slave till death (in the Pentateuchal passages). See further in the additional note on verse 15.

19. See BDAG (1103–4, s.v. ὡς) for the common use of ὡς to indicate the "manner" of how something proceeds.

20. So BDAG (1103, s.v. ὡς), also suggesting the rendering "in such a way as." While BDAG cites this as a possible meaning of the particle, it classifies the use in Philem. 16 as a "marker introducing the perspective from which a pers[on], thing, or activity is viewed or understood as to character, function, or role" (BDAG 1104). However, this does not seem to contribute any more to the basic sense of "in such a way as." Therefore it is unlikely that there is much difference in meaning between including the ὡς (*hōs*) and omitting it.

21. Some observe that in verse 16 Paul's use of οὐκέτι (*ouketi*, no longer) instead of μηκέτι (*mēketi*, no longer) following the subjunctive verb at the end of verse 15 breaks the grammatical rule that μηκέτι should follow a subjunctive. Since μηκέτι would continue the subjunctive's mood of uncertainty (possibility or probability), the awkward use of οὐκέτι, as with indicative verbs, is thought to indicate "no longer as a slave" as a reality or fact (e.g., Lightfoot 1875: 343; Barth and Blanke 2000: 416–17; Jeal 2015: 114). This is overanalysis, since what is stated in verse 16 depends on Paul's tentative proposal (via "perhaps" in v. 15) about the goal of the divine passive "was parted" in verse 15.

22. Some translations render ὑπέρ (*hyper*) + the accusative as "<u>better</u> than a slave" (NJB, NIV, TNIV) or "<u>above</u> a slave" (Geneva, Webster, ASV). Douay-Rheims has "<u>instead of</u> a servant." All of these translations could suggest that Onesimus was not to be considered anymore

additional status is being a "beloved brother, especially" to Paul, since he has ministered to Paul in prison. "But how much more" (πόσῳ μᾶλλον, *posō mallon*) is he a "beloved brother" to Philemon "in the flesh" as a beloved slave ministering to his master (in line with Col. 3:22–25). The only other place in the epistle where "beloved" occurs is in verse 1, where Paul refers to Philemon as "beloved" to him. The implication is that, just as Philemon is "beloved" to Paul, so Philemon should regard his slave as "beloved" to himself, following Paul's model of loving his Christian brothers. Philemon must remember that when Onesimus was "called in the Lord while a slave," he became "the Lord's freeman" (1 Cor. 7:22a). And would Philemon not recall that he himself "who was called while free" also became "Christ's slave" (1 Cor. 7:22b)? And "how much more" is Onesimus a "beloved brother" also "in the Lord" (as a fellow Christian believer)?

But how is Onesimus a "beloved brother . . . in the flesh and in the Lord" to Philemon more than to Paul? There has been a break in the relationship between Philemon and his slave, but that break is about to be mended; the mending of this disrupted relationship will bring all the more richness to it, a reuniting richness that even Paul has not experienced in his relationship with Onesimus. This reuniting richness of fellowship "in the flesh and in the Lord" at the end of verse 16 is the main point of verses 15–16. Now, even "in the flesh" (perhaps as a continuing slave?) Onesimus is a "beloved brother,"[23] since he has begun to be "in the Lord," in the Spirit,[24] while yet being still in his preresurrection body. He was a Christian brother physically and spiritually to Philemon.[25] "While God's creation includes both the visible and the

---

as a slave. Harris (2012: 208–9) contends that in Philem. 16 the preposition is to be rendered "superior to a slave" or "better than a slave." If these renderings and their implication are preferable, then this would be the clearest place in the letter that Paul is asking Philemon to manumit his slave. Most other translations have "more than a slave" (e.g., NASB, RSV, NRSV, ESV, HCSB, NET), which suggests including him still as a slave but also something more. The use of ὑπέρ + the accusative also occurs in verse 21 as "marker of a degree beyond that of a scale of extent" (BDAG 1031, s.v. ὑπέρ): "knowing that you will also do more than what things I say." This does not exclude that Philemon will do less than "what things" Paul has asked of Philemon but that, in addition to these things he will do even more. This is likely how Paul uses the same construction in verse 16, so that "more than a slave" does not deny Onesimus's status as a slave but includes it and more. BDAG (1031, s.v. ὑπέρ) places ὑπέρ + the accusative in Philem. 16 and 21 in the same category.

23. Note that Paul can use ἐν σαρκί (*en sarki*) to refer to Christian existence in the sphere of the physical body (2 Cor. 10:3; Gal. 2:20; Col. 2:1) and to Christ's bodily incarnation (1 Tim. 3:16). Paul can also use κατὰ σάρκα (*kata sarka*) to refer to "masters according to the flesh," focusing on earthly masters to whom slaves must be obedient (Eph. 6:5; Col. 3:22; cf. Bruce 1984: 218). Since "in the flesh" focuses on the sphere of the body, "in the Lord" likely also refers to existing within the sphere of "the Lord's" spiritual existence. Paul's use of σάρξ (*sarx*) as referring to sinful human existence does not appear to be in view here.

24. Or Onesimus's renewed "spirit"; cf. the implications of verse 25.

25. So Porter (2010: 28), though he says "brother . . . in the Lord" refers to Onesimus's being a brother to the Lord (Jesus). Campbell (2012: 175) sees "in the Lord" to be periphrastic for "Christian"; thus he sees Onesimus to be a human brother and a Christian brother (so also Zerwick and Grosvenor 1981: 635).

invisible, they are integrated and held together by the one Lord."[26] Thus we have an individualized conception of the "church visible and invisible."[27] The main point of verses 15–16 is that Philemon would have his slave back forever as a beloved brother "in the Lord."[28] The slave status is not denied but is transcended by the slave becoming an eternal brother (cf. Jeal 2015: 49). Thus we do not see, as do several commentators, that "in the flesh" refers to "ordinary human" existence apart from Christ and "in the Lord" refers to the new status "in Christ" (so, e.g., Wilson 2005: 357).

There is much discussion among commentators about whether this verse means that Philemon will emancipate Onesimus. While possible, there is not enough evidence here to conclude that. More likely, as we have seen, when Paul says "but more than a slave, a beloved brother," the implication is that Onesimus is still a slave but Philemon is to view his status as being more than that of a slave. Therefore it is likely that Philemon is to love his slave in his slave status because he also exists "in the Lord." Since Paul can command masters of slaves to treat them justly (Eph. 6:9; Col. 4:1) while not emancipating them, the same applies here to Philemon's treatment of his slave (following D. Moo 2008: 424).

17 The "therefore" (οὖν, *oun*) signals that verses 15–16 are the basis for verse 17b, and the "if" clause in verse 17a adds an additional basis for verse 17b (cf. Banker 1999: 46). In particular, on the ground that Onesimus is an "eternal . . . beloved brother" to Philemon "in the flesh and in the Lord" (vv. 15–16), and on the basis that Philemon is a "partner" with Paul (v. 17a), then Philemon should "receive" the slave as he would receive Paul (v. 17b). The reasoning is as follows: (1) Onesimus also is a "beloved brother . . . in the flesh and in the Lord," and (2) so is Paul, so that (3) if Philemon has "partnership"[29] with Paul as a "beloved brother" (cf. vv. 1, 7) "in the Lord" (cf. vv. 16b, 20), (4) then he should accept his slave back, (5) since he shares equally in true Christian brotherhood and existence with Onesimus, as he does also with Paul.

We saw that this notion here was anticipated in verse 6, where κοινωνία (*koinōnia*) occurs, which overlaps in meaning with κοινωνός here. There we concluded that the idea of Philemon sharing in the common faith of all the saints in verse 6 is a partial basis in verse 17 for Paul's appeal for Philemon to receive Onesimus into brotherly Christian communion in the same manner as he would accept Paul. We noted there that since Philemon shares a common

26. Thus Wall (1993: 212), who defines the "visible" as "social relationships" and the "invisible" as "the spiritual well-being of the [church] congregation."

27. Porter (2010: 29) says that Onesimus now functions "on both earthly and heavenly planes."

28. Similarly Pao 2012: 397. Callahan's (1993) proposal that Onesimus is a slave only metaphorically but an actual "brother" (by blood) is unlikely; the phrase in verse 16 "but more than a slave" is more likely an actual and not metaphorical reference to "slave" (so Barclay 1997: 99).

29. The ranges of meaning for κοινωνός (*koinōnos*) are "one who takes part in something," i.e., as "companion, partner, sharer" (BDAG 553–54, s.v. κοινωνός).

faith with all genuine Christians,[30] including Paul and Onesimus, he should receive Onesimus on the same basis as he would accept Paul as a brother believer. A good paraphrase of verse 17a would be "if you have any fellowship with me in our common faith."[31] This is a first-class condition whereby the idea is "if [and let us assume for the sake of argument that Philemon really shares in the common faith with Paul] . . . , then" he will "accept back" Onesimus.[32] In other words, this is a statement whereby Paul is exhorting Philemon about his true Christian existence: if he really is a genuine Christian, then he will bear fruit accordingly. That is, if he is an authentic believer, he will accept his slave. This is another classic Pauline example of the indicative and the imperative. Could Paul's sending Onesimus back to Philemon be testified to in Col. 4:8–9? "I have sent him [Tychicus] . . . that he may encourage your hearts, along with Onesimus, our faithful and beloved brother, who is one of your number. They will inform you about the whole situation here."[33]

Προσλαμβάνω (*proslambanō*) is translated variously as "accept, receive, welcome," which are all synonymous. The most relevant uses are in Rom. 14–15, where Paul is urging Jewish and Gentile Christians not to divide over dietary laws or observance of various holidays. In Rom. 14 he says, "Accept the one who is weak in faith" (v. 1); "God has accepted" (v. 3) both Jewish and Gentile Christians, which is the basis for them accepting one another. Paul wants them to be reconciled into unity in Christ. The basis for this reconciliation is made more explicit in Rom. 15:7: "Accept one another, just as Christ also accepted us to the glory of God." The verb προσλαμβάνω is used similarly in Philem. 16, where Philemon is to "accept" or "welcome" his estranged slave because they share a common faith in Christ ("if you have fellowship with me"). Reconciliation and unity are the point in verse 17, and this overshadows the entire letter.[34] We will see that the goal of such reconciliation and unity is to "refresh" Paul or "set him at rest" (v. 20).

The more Philemon values his "in-Christ" shared relationship with Paul, "the more Paul's relationship with Onesimus was bound to be a factor in Philemon's attitude to Onesimus" (Dunn 1996: 336) because Paul so highly values his "in-Christ" shared relationship with Onesimus.

"But" (δέ, *de*), in contrast to what has just been said in verse 17, Paul realizes 18
that there may be an obstruction to Philemon accepting his runaway slave as
himself: "If [εἰ, *ei*] he has wronged you in any way or owes you anything . . ."

30. Note again BDAG (553–54, s.v. κοινωνός), placing Philem. 17 under the semantic category of "one who takes part in something with someone," and specifically glossing its use in the passage as "consider someone a partner."

31. I have subsequently found this paraphrase in D. Moo (2008: 426) to express my conclusion here.

32. This is a paraphrase of Wallace (1996: 690), who applies the wording to a general definition of a first-class condition.

33. Barth and Blanke (2000: 492–93) discuss this possibility, though not preferring it. Fitzmyer (2000: 121) sees that Col. 4:9 suggests this.

34. In this paragraph I am following N. Wright 2013: 11–12.

Commentators speculate about what kind of precise wrong the slave did. Onesimus may have committed some wrong against Philemon (perhaps merely in running away), or he may have stolen something from him (perhaps in his haste to get away he took some things necessary for his trip), or it may simply be that Philemon's losing the service of his slave is in itself financial loss.

To remove this possible impediment from a smooth reunion, Paul says, "Charge that to my account." Paul will repay Philemon on behalf of his slave. In another change of roles, now Paul tells Philemon to accept Paul as a debtor as he would his slave who needs to pay back. Thus Paul offers to pay the slave's debts. Paul also follows the pattern of Christ's redemption, who willingly accepted the debt of his people and paid that debt himself (cf. also Wall 1993: 215; cf. Col. 2:14: God "canceled out the certificate of debt . . . against us, which was hostile to us; and He has taken it out of the way, having nailed it to the cross" through Christ's death; cf. Phil. 2:6–8). And like Christ, Paul is a mediator between sinners (Onesimus and Philemon; Pao 2012: 413). Just as "God was in Christ reconciling the world to himself" (2 Cor. 5:19), so "God is in Paul reconciling Philemon and Onesimus."[35]

We have referred to Onesimus's debt as "possible" because of the first-class condition introduced by εἰ (*ei*). This condition expresses the idea of "if [and let us assume for the sake of argument] . . . , then." Accordingly, if, for the sake of argument, Onesimus has committed some wrong or incurred some debt, then Paul will repay it. Thus Paul may not know whether Onesimus has, indeed, committed some such wrong, or he may be putting this in a conditional way in order to hear Philemon's perspective on the matter (following D. Moo 2008: 428).

19 The apostle says, "I, Paul, [have written][36] with my own hand" to provide a sure basis for guaranteeing to Philemon that he will make up for any wrongs or debts of Onesimus. Such a reference to his signature elsewhere alludes to Paul's apostolic authority behind the letters he writes (1 Cor. 16:21; Gal. 6:11; Col. 4:18; 2 Thess. 3:17), so the churches can trust that what he says carries with it such authority, which is tantamount to divine authority (e.g., cf. 1 Cor. 7:40; 1 Thess. 2:13; 4:8). In this light, here the signature shows that he is putting his apostolic authority behind his promise to stand in for the slave's wrongs and debts. To emphasize his guarantee to do this, he repeats, "I will repay it." This is Paul's "'promissory note,' . . . a χειρόγραφον [*cheirographon*] (cf. Col. 2:14), a signed statement of indebtedness by which he formally and legally assumes all the indebtedness of Onesimus toward Philemon" (Harris 2010: 237). In addition to the legal nature of the promissory note, commentators also see a Greco-Roman background for Paul's reference to "repaying" (ἀποτίνω, *apotinō*; Wilson 2005: 358–59). These legal terms underscore Paul's commitment to stand in for any debts owed by Philemon. Some speculate about how Paul can repay anything, since he is in prison. We simply do not know the

35. N. Wright 1986: 187; followed by Thompson 2005: 224–25; so also Melick 1991: 367.
36. A classic epistolary aorist; see further on verse 21.

answer to this. Possibly he has access to funds, whether from his own tentmaking work or from other supporters. Indeed, there is some evidence that Paul may have had his own sufficient funds for such a repayment.[37] Since the focus of the signature is on Paul's commitment to pay any of the slave's debts, the epistolary aorist refers not to the whole epistle but only to what has just been said in verse 18 and again in verse 19a.[38]

Then at the end of verse 19 he abruptly shifts gears and makes Philemon realize that he owes a great debt to Paul himself: "lest I should mention that you also owe me yourself."* This is an adversative statement (with an "even though" sense) that supports the directly preceding clause and highlights Paul's offer to repay. For emphasis Paul has omitted some words (an ellipsis), so that the whole clause can be rendered as follows: "[I have thus become indebted to you][39] lest [with the sense of "even though"] I should mention that you owe me your own self as well."[40] Indeed, Philemon owes Paul much more than Onesimus owes Philemon. Likely the allusion is to Philemon's conversion to Christ through Paul's own ministry. He owes Paul his very existence as a Christian. Just as Onesimus was birthed through Paul's gospel ministry (v. 10), so was Philemon. Paul abruptly shifts from speaking of Philemon as a creditor to a debtor, who owes Paul his very life, which he cannot repay (Garland 1998: 338).

Thus the main point of verse 19 is Paul's reiterated promise to repay the slave's debt to Philemon, if any. All these points about the imprisoned and weak Paul offering to pay whatever the slave owes (the main point of v. 19) and Philemon owing Paul everything (just as did Onesimus) should further touch the master's heart and induce him amicably to take back his slave without prejudice and indeed without accepting Paul's offer of repayment. Indeed, that Philemon owes Paul should make him identify with his slave, who also owes Paul his very spiritual being, thus inducing Philemon further to willingly acquiesce to Paul's request.[41]

We have seen that the first intended result or purpose of Philemon "willingly **20**
doing good" in accepting back his slave without recrimination (v. 14) was that he would have Onesimus as a Christian brother "forever" (vv. 15–17). Now in verse 20 the second intended result is given. More precisely, the consequence

37. The governor, Felix, hoped for a bribe from Paul (Acts 24:26), and Paul was able to support himself financially for two years in Rome (28:30; see Dunn 1996: 339). Wilson (2005: 358) also mentions the Philippians' financial gift to Paul, which may have provided him with funds (Phil. 4:15–18).

38. Cf. Wallace 1996: 563; our view is contra Robertson (1934: 846), who appears to see it referring to the letter thus far written from verse 1 up through verse 18.

39. This supplied ellipsis is proposed by Harris 2010: 238.

40. Pao (2012: 409) rightly adduces 2 Cor. 9:4, the only other occurrence of ἵνα μὴ λέγω (*hina mē legō*) in the NT, to show that the phrase here is possibly an idiomatic way of introducing an abrupt and grammatically unconnected parenthetical idea.

41. I have subsequently found that Pao (2012: 409) has made a very similar point. It is not clear how Philemon became a Christian through Paul, since Epaphras rather than Paul founded the church at Colossae (Col. 1:7–8) and the Colossians (including Philemon presumably) had not personally met Paul. Nevertheless, this appears to be what Paul *is* saying.

is stated of Philemon "sharing" with Paul union "in the Lord" (vv. 16b–17a) and then "accepting" the slave as he would Paul (v. 17b). That second effect is that Paul would "benefit" from Philemon's gracious action "in the Lord." This is emphasized by the fronting of "yes" (a fronting rhetorical device of emphasis also in Phil. 4:3) with the sense of "yes, in view of my willingness to pay Onesimus's debt, now I want some return from you" (N. Wright 1986: 188). The "benefit" is immediately interpreted as Philemon "refreshing Paul's heart in Christ." Several commentators see a pun between ὀναίμην (*onaimēn*) and Ὀνήσιμον (*Onēsimon*) in verse 10. The verb can mean "to be the recipient of benefit" or "to have something for one's use" (BDAG 711, s.v. ὀνίνημι). The point of the pun would be that just as Onesimus has become useful (finally living up to the meaning of his name), so Paul exhorts Philemon to become "useful" to him in granting his request, in which case Philemon would again become identified with his slave, inducing him further to have sympathy with his slave's predicament. Or the pun "Let me have some use from you" may suggest "Let me have Onesimus from you."[42] It is hard to know if Paul intends this pun, especially since it is so far from the word of which it is supposed to be a pun (v. 10!).[43] But a pun can be pointed to by three observations: (1) Paul has already made a pun between the name Onesimus and his being "useful" in verses 10–11 (see my comments there); (2) the pun can include the notion that just as Onesimus has become useful to Paul and Philemon, so Paul is asking Philemon to put himself in the role of the slave, Onesimus, in being useful to Paul. Paul's portraying of Philemon with prior descriptions of Onesimus is also apparent in verse 20 with reference to Philemon as a "brother" and being "in the Lord" (note the prior reference to Onesimus as a "brother" and being "in the Lord"[44] in v. 16). This exchange of roles fits with the exchange of roles in verse 12, where Onesimus represents Paul's "very heart," and with verse 13, where Onesimus's usefulness to Paul is "ministering" to him in his imprisonment and representing Philemon in doing so. (3) While some argue that the word ὀναίμην is too common to be considered a pun,[45] it occurs only here in all of the NT and only once in the LXX.[46]

Since Philemon already has the reputation for "refreshing the inward parts [σπλάγχνα, *splanchna*] of the saints" (v. 7) and Paul considers Onesimus his "very inward parts [σπλάγχνα]" (v. 12), whom he is sending back to the master, then for Philemon to accept the slave back by unconditional grace will "refresh

42. This view of the pun is held by Pao 2012: 410; and Weima 2016: 229.

43. I have subsequently found that Wilson (2005: 360) posits a similar objection to the wordplay, though still seeing it as possible.

44. Though this may include Paul's existence "in the Lord."

45. Like, e.g., Lohse 1971: 205; and O'Brien 1982: 302. For a list of others rejecting a pun, see Weima 2016: 229.

46. D. Moo (2008: 432) has made this last point. Dunn (1996: 341), Barth and Blanke (2000: 486), Thompson (2005: 218), and Weima (2016: 229), among numerous other commentators, also hold to a pun on the name Onesimus here. See further Weima (2016: 229), who also lists others holding to a pun.

Paul's inward parts [σπλάγχνα]." The word "inward parts" in distinction to "heart" (καρδία, *kardia*) expresses much more emotion, so that Paul is laying bare his intense feelings about Onesimus, since Onesimus is his very "inward parts" (v. 12).[47] That Paul especially has in mind "refreshing the heart" in verse 7 is apparent since he even includes the vocative address "brother" (ἀδελφέ, *adelphe*) to Philemon, which also occurs in verse 7.[48] This fact should provide further motivation for Philemon to identify with Paul's feelings and willingly to accept back his slave without any punitive consequences.

The verb ἀναπαύω (*anapauō*) carries the notion of "give rest" or "refresh" (BDAG 69, s.v. ἀναπαύω). In this context the verb may best be translated "Comfort my heart" (Geneva), "Set my heart at rest" (NJB), or more paraphrastically, "Relieve my anxiety" (NEB and Banker 1999: 54), which probably includes a nuance of "refreshment." The rendering "Set my heart at rest" suggests "relieving anxiety" and should be preferred as the focus, since it is more consistent with the translation of the same verb in verse 7 (which the NJB renders as "set at rest") and can include a notion of setting Paul's heart at rest amid any anxiety he may have had about Onesimus's fate and whether Philemon would respond positively to Paul's appeals for Philemon to be reconciled to his slave and vice versa (see further the additional note on v. 20). Such reconciliation and unity (expressed in vv. 15–16 and v. 17) will "set Paul's heart at rest," since it will give him pleasure and delight. The refreshment of Paul's heart is "in Christ," which may indicate cause ("because of Christ"), instrumentality ("through Christ"), or close association ("under the influence of Christ"). The best view is that cause and association are preferable and inextricably linked.[49]

Some see this verse as a summary of verses 15–20, if not all of verses 8–20.[50] 21
This is only very generally true. More specifically verse 21 appears to be the basis for verses 15–20, and secondarily for verses 8–14. Accordingly, ἔγραψά σοι (*egrapsa soi*, I write to you) refers respectively to the same two preceding segments and serves well as a conclusion to those segments. There is no explicit introductory logical conjunction or particle, as in verses 15 and 17. There is no obvious marker of a paragraph break.[51] Accordingly the verse functions well

47. See on verse 7 for the difference between καρδία and σπλάγχνα, especially with respect to the latter word carrying greater emotion.

48. D. Moo (2008: 431) has made the added observation about the vocative.

49. Campbell 2012: 100. Likewise, for Philemon to "benefit" Paul "in the Lord" is to do so under the influence of and because of the Lord (Campbell 2012: 170). Harris (2012: 130) prefers the notion only of cause, "because you belong to the Lord," though his rendering seems to include also the idea of close association.

50. So, e.g., Dunn 1996: 343; Weima 2016: 230; cf. likewise D. Moo 2008: 434.

51. Thus it would be an overreach to see the absence of such an explicit logical connector to suggest a paragraph break beginning with verse 21 and thus commencing the closing section, as do Dunn (1996: 343), D. Moo (2008: 434), and Pao (2012: 418), who offer subtle but no obvious indications of a paragraph break beginning in verse 21. Dunn (1996: 343) also proposes that verse 21 begins a new paragraph because of the concluding use of ἔγραψά σοι. While I agree that it has a concluding function, I see it signaling the end of verses 8–20.

as the continuation and conclusion of the segment of verses 15–20. The word πεποιθώς (*pepoithōs*) is an adverbial participle of cause.[52] That is, Paul has been motivated to "write"[53] Philemon "because he is confident" in Philemon's "obedience" to Paul's various pleas to release his slave. The context of the epistle shows that the perfect tense indicates a settled condition of trust resulting from Paul's previous experience of knowing Philemon "as one in whom confidence could be placed" (Dunn 1996: 344; similarly Fitzmyer 2000: 12). Then in the last part of the verse, Paul escalates his confidence in Philemon's positive response, which has further inspired him "to write": "because I know [εἰδώς, *eidōs*, another adverbial participle of cause][54] that even beyond what things I say you will do."*

Here Paul combines two interesting dynamics. First, after so artfully and subtly appealing to Philemon's own personal resolve to release Onesimus in verses 8–20, in verse 21a he returns to urging Philemon by his apostolic authority "to obey" (as in vv. 8b–9a).[55] This means that Philemon's obedience is ultimately to Christ and not merely to Paul, who represents Christ's authority (cf. Garland 1998: 339–40). Then Paul turns around once more, reveals his belief that Philemon's own Christian motivation will result in his "doing even more than what" he commands, and lovingly appeals to that motivation. By concluding with this, he shows continuation of the emphasis on the letter's appeal to Philemon's own personal determination.

Of what this "even more" consists is not stated. One view is that the "even more" refers to Paul's desire to have Onesimus back to aid him in prison for a time, which would be above and beyond Paul's request that Philemon graciously receive back his slave.[56] But a problem with this view is that the theme running throughout the letter is not only the appeal to accept back the slave on good terms but also the appeal to have Philemon send the slave back to serve Paul (e.g., see v. 11 and esp. vv. 13–14). Thus in the letter Paul has *already* expressed that he not only wants Philemon to accept back the slave but also to send him back to Paul. Accordingly, the "even more" would not include sending the slave back to minister to Paul.

52. Banker (1999: 55–56) sees this as an adverbial participle of manner, which is a viable alternative: "I have written to you confidently," or it could be rendered, "I have written to you in a confident manner."

53. A classic epistolary aorist, looking at the past action of the writing from the perspective of the hearers, as if it were being done in the present, since they are hearing it for the first time in the present.

54. As with the first perfect participle in verse 21a, so here the perfect focuses on a condition resulting from Paul's previous experience with Philemon (cf. Wallace 1996: 579–80).

55. Banker (1999: 56) prefers that ὑπακοή (*hypakoē*) carries the notion of "compliance" rather than "obedience," since the verb can have that idea in the NT and LXX. However, in the ten Pauline uses outside of Philem. 21, it always means "obedience," as also in the other four uses elsewhere in the NT.

56. So Pao 2012: 420; O'Brien 1982: 305–6; and Barth and Blanke 2000: 492. Dunn (1996: 345) sees this as a viable option and also cites other commentators holding this view. Perhaps this would entail turning the slave over to Paul's custody (Patzia 1990: 115).

Another view is that the "even more" seems to include Philemon not only accepting back his slave without recrimination and allowing him to return to serve Paul but also dealing in even more generous ways with his slave when he does come back (perhaps even emancipating him[?], which some think v. 16 implies; so, e.g., D. Moo 2008: 436). What these more generous measures would be is not stated. The possibility that emancipation could be included in Paul's thinking is feasible in the light of the Greco-Roman background that eventually most slaves were set free at some point. Accordingly, Paul may have been asking Philemon to emancipate his slave sooner than he had originally intended.[57]

Additional Notes

15. Some commentators view Exod. 21:6; Lev. 25:46; and Deut. 15:17 to be in Paul's mind, since these passages refer to persons being slaves "forever," using αἰώνιος (*aiōnios*) and referring to slaves who stay as slaves for the remainder of their lives.[58] Most who acknowledge the relevance of these OT references believe Paul is referring to Onesimus being a "beloved brother" (v. 16) for the rest of his human life. While some think this includes a permanent slave status for him, others focus only on his being a brother, who will probably be emancipated. The three Pentateuchal passages may well be in mind, since they refer to human slaves within the community of Israel and identify the Israelite as "your brother" (ἀδελφός σου, *adelphos sou* in Deut. 15:12, 17; implied in Exod. 21:2, 6). In Exod. 21:6 and Deut. 15:17 the Israelite decides willingly to stay as a slave for the rest of his life.[59] If at least these two passages are in mind, as many interpreters believe,[60] then it may refer to Onesimus being "a beloved brother" (v. 16) "forever." The larger narrative context of these two Pentateuchal passages is God's setting Israel free from Egyptian slavery (see Lev. 25:42, 55; Deut. 5:15; 15:15; 16:12), which may suggest that Paul is implying that Philemon should set free Onesimus (following N. Wright 2013: 15). In fact, the basis for the instructions about setting free Hebrew slaves is based specifically on God's setting free all Hebrew slaves from Egypt (Deut. 15:15; Lev. 25:42). Even Deut. 5:15 and 16:12 provide this same basis, in part, for commanding that slaves be given rest on the Sabbath (5:14–15) and for commanding that slaves be able to celebrate the Feast of Weeks along with free people (16:9–17). The notion of slaves rejecting their freedom and deciding to stay with their masters

57. See S. S. Bartchy (*ABD* 6:70–71), who notes that in the Greco-Roman world releasing slaves at a relatively young age was frequent, and that Philem. 16, 18 expresses Paul's desire that Onesimus be released from slavery. Davids (2008b: 436) notes that a person named "Onesimus," likely the "Onesimus" of the Philemon epistle, was Bishop of Ephesus toward the end of the first century. If Davids is correct, then this may mean that Onesimus had been manumitted by Philemon.

58. Reinmuth (2006: 46) says that Paul employs the language of the three Pentateuchal texts in a transferred sense. Davids (2008b: 430) sees the Exodus and Deuteronomy passages as "only a linguistic echo," without carrying over the contextual idea of the passages. Some think Job 40:28 MT, LXX (41:4 Eng.) is in mind, but it refers to the sea creature Leviathan being a "slave forever," so that humans are not in mind there. Gnilka (1982: 50) considers the possibility that Deut. 15:17 could be in the background.

59. While Exod. 21:6 and Deut. 15:17 pertain to Hebrew slaves, Lev. 25:46 relates to slaves from other nations; however, Lev. 25:39–43 refers to a Hebrew slave as being "your brother" (ἀδελφός σου, *adelphos sou*, LXX).

60. Among others also seeing an "allusion" or "echo" to Exod. 21:6 and Deut. 15:17 is N. Wright 2013: 13–15.

"forever" (Exod. 21:6; Lev. 25:46; Deut. 15:17) apparently is a kind of equivalent to freedom in that such slaves take pleasure in pursuing such a destiny. In this respect, regardless of whether Paul implies actual manumission by alluding to these passages, the Exodus and Deuteronomy texts would be understood typologically, now focusing on Onesimus not so much as a human slave but as a true Israelite "brother," whom Philemon would have back "forever" (like the use of Exod. 20:12 and Deut. 5:16 in Eph. 6:2–3, where the promise of children "living long on the land" is taken typologically to mean "living long on the earth," focusing on the new, eternal earth). Similarly Isa. 24:2 prophesies that at the eschatological time the earth is destroyed, "slaves will be like [equal to] masters," which might support a typological view of Deut. 15:17 and Exod. 21:6.

15–16. Ip (2017: 210) asserts that verses 15–16 summarize the main request section of the letter in that it points out God's design that Onesimus have a new relationship with Philemon. In the conclusion to his book, Ip says that Paul's view about a loving relationship within the church could not coexist with relationships based on the economics of the then current slavery system, which dominated and manipulated slaves. Accordingly, Paul argues for the legitimacy of the new love relationship of believers in Christ against the prevalent oppressive economic system. Thus "Paul's purpose in the letter was to persuade Philemon to transform his relationship with Onesimus from a relationship based on economic interests to one based on loving brotherhood" (Ip 2017: 220).

20. We concluded that ἀναπαύω (*anapauō*) conveys a notion of setting Paul's heart at rest due to any anxiety he may have experienced about how Philemon will respond to his appeals and about Onesimus's fate. The verb occurs also in 2 Cor. 7:13, which says that Titus's "spirit has been refreshed by you [Corinthians]." In the context, this "refreshment"[61] is due to the Corinthians having begun to submit to Paul's appeals for reconciliation between himself and them (2 Cor. 5:11–13; 7:2–3) and especially to Paul's instructions about the immoral "offender" (2 Cor. 7:8–12; cf. Harris 2005: 548–49). Titus was in Corinth to try to bring about more reconciliation in the strained relationship between Paul and the Corinthians, and their beginning positive response "set his heart at rest" (similarly G. Guthrie 2015: 383). It is the very same situation in Philemon. Paul is appealing to Philemon to "set his heart at rest" from anxiety by responding positively to his appeal to Philemon to accept Onesimus. Paul is a mediator to reconcile the two people; if they are reconciled, his "heart will be set at rest" from anxiety. This notion of the verb to "set at rest" from anxiety occurs also in the LXX, as in Deut. 28:65; Prov. 29:17; Mic. 4:4; Hab. 3:16; likewise see the use of the noun ἀνάπαυσις (*anapausis*) in Pss. 22:2; 115:7 (Eng.: 23:2; 116:7).

For Paul to be "refreshed" may imply the refreshment of Onesimus, since the two are so identified (cf. v. 17). Philemon has already "refreshed the saints" and thus comforted Paul in so doing (v. 7), and it appears to follow from this that Paul expects that Philemon's releasing of Onesimus (cf. vv. 15–17) will "refresh" Onesimus's own heart as it will "refresh" Paul's.

61. Almost all translations here render the verb as "refreshed," but the RSV and NRSV render it "set at rest"; similarly, the NLT has "set at ease."

IV. Letter Closing: Paul Asks Philemon to Show Him Pastoral Concern, and Paul Shows His Pastoral Concern for the Church in Philemon's House (22–25)

Here is a fuller statement of the main idea of this unit: *Paul asks Philemon to show pastoral concern for him, and Paul shows his sincere pastoral concern for the church in Philemon's house by reminding the believers that not only he but also his coworkers have pastoral concern for them.*

We have observed that verses 8–14 and 15–21 appear to be distinct literary units, though closely related thematically and logically. Verses 22–25 are the last distinct literary unit of the letter, though scholars are not in agreement as to where the closing actually begins.[1] Some, like Weima, begin the closing at verse 19, others at verse 21[2] or verse 22, and still others at verse 23 (for commentators holding these various views, see D. Moo 2008: 433). Though it is difficult to be confident, verses 22–25 seem to be a segment distinct from verses 15–21, since all of verses 19–21 are integrally tied to the preceding paragraph concerning aspects of Paul's plea to Philemon: Paul's repayment of any possible debts by the slave to pave the way for his return (v. 19), Paul's benefit and refreshment to come from Philemon's positive response to the appeal (v. 20), and Paul's confidence that Philemon will do above and beyond what he is requesting (v. 21). For the first time since verses 1 and 3, furthermore, verse 22b introduces the plural "you," showing the

1. The lack of agreement is acknowledged by Weima (1994: 230; 2016: 226–28), though he says there is ample evidence that the closing begins at verse 19, so that the last segment of the epistle is verses 19–25.

2. So Dunn (1996: 343), partly on the basis that the phrase "at the same time" in verse 22a so closely links the verse temporally with verse 21 that there must not be a literary break between the two verses (see above on verse 21 for his other reasons for not positing a break between the two verses). While there is a close temporal relationship between the two verses, the abrupt change of topic to final instructions and greetings appears to signal that verse 21 begins a new paragraph, though it is certainly possible that verse 21 concludes the paragraph of vv. 15–20. But ἅμα + καί (*hama* + *kai*), while not losing the temporal force, can also mean not only "at the same time" but can be rendered "besides" (BDAG 49, s.v. ἅμα), which is followed conceptually by some English versions ("one more thing" or the like: NEB, NIV, TNIV, NRSV, NLT, NJB; similarly "moreover" [= older English "withal"]: Geneva, ASV, KJV, Douay-Rheims, all of which favor grouping verse 22 with verses 23–25; "at the same time" is preferred by RSV, NASB, ESV, NET; a mediating rendering among these is "meanwhile" [HCSB]). Thus we think ἅμα + καί conveys the thought of an additional request and is better grouped with the concluding greetings and grace.

focus on the individual "you" that dominates Philemon 4–21. Accordingly, verses 22–25 seem to form an independent series of statements, not directly and logically related to the preceding paragraph but related to Philemon's and Paul's expressions of pastoral concern.

We have also observed that the general theme of the epistle is the appeal that Philemon release Onesimus in order that he return to minister to Paul in prison (vv. 8–21). The climax of that larger segment lies with Paul's appeal to Philemon to "benefit" him by "refreshing his heart" through willingly accepting Onesimus back without recrimination. Now in verses 22–25, Paul progresses to the formal conclusion of his epistle. He first asks Philemon to extend hospitality to him when he comes to Colossae (v. 22a), and he asks Philemon to pray for his safe arrival (v. 22b). Paul gives information about his coworkers and greetings from them to the church in Philemon's house (the church at Colossae or one of the house churches there, vv. 23–24), and he commends them to the grace of Christ (v. 25). That Paul is no longer addressing only Philemon is clear from the shift to the second-person plural personal pronouns "you" in verses 22b and 25.

Similar to the letter closing of Colossians (see on Col. 4:7–18), Paul's care for the hearers is implied by observing that he begins the epistle by alluding to his imprisonment (v. 1), mentions his imprisonment three times in the body of the letter (vv. 9–10, 13), and concludes with a reference to it (v. 23). Repeatedly reminding the hearers about his circumstances of suffering reveals that, despite his suffering in imprisonment, his concern for them and especially for Philemon is ever constant. The reason for book-ending the epistle with references to his imprisonment, and punctuating the letter body three times with it, is to underscore clearly that the entire epistle indirectly expresses, in one way or another, his care for them despite his adverse situation. This concern is shown not only by wishing them "grace" and "peace" (v. 3) but also by sending greetings from people they apparently know (vv. 23–24) and again commending them to Christ's grace (v. 25). The apostle wants them to know also that his fellow workers have much concern for them in giving their greetings through Paul (vv. 23–24). This pastoral interest is to have the ultimate goal of laying a further basis for Philemon to want to listen sympathetically to Paul and thus be motivated to show pastoral love to Paul by treating his own slave with pastoral care and receiving him back as a "brother in the Lord" (v. 16), thus "refreshing" Paul himself. Likewise, Paul's pastoral consideration is directed toward the church in order to involve them as overhearing participants in helping, however they appropriately can, to encourage Philemon to do what Paul is asking. Accordingly, the epistolary conclusion functions to ingratiate Paul to the listeners and to give them confidence that he has their best interests at heart.

Exegesis and Exposition

[22]And at the same time also prepare me a lodging, for I hope that through your prayers I will be given to you. [23]Epaphras, my fellow prisoner in Christ Jesus, greets you, [24]as do Mark, Aristarchus, Demas, Luke, my fellow workers.

[25]The grace of the Lord Jesus Christ be with your spirit. ⌜ ⌝

22 In addition to asking Philemon graciously to accept back his slave and so "refresh" Paul, the apostle now asks Philemon to be gracious to him by showing him hospitality: "at the same time also prepare a lodging for me." The *reason* Paul asks this is *because* (γάρ, *gar*) "I hope that through your [pl.] prayers [of the church together with Philemon] I will be given to you [pl., the church]." "I will be given" (χαρισθήσομαι, *charisthēsomai*) is clearly a divine passive, with God as the subject (this points further to "was parted" in Philem. 15 as being a divine passive). Thus, if Paul is going to come to the Colossian church, it will be by God's doing.[3] Yet Paul realizes, at the same time, that prayer to God is the means for accomplishing God's plan of bringing Paul to Colossae (if that is the divine plan). The notion of χαρίζομαι (*charizomai*) conveys the nuance of God "graciously giving" (BDAG 1078) Paul to the church at Colossae as an answer to prayer. This may or may not imply that Paul is hoping to be released permanently from prison. Paul is hoping to come to Philemon and the church in his house, and for this reason is requesting hospitality from Philemon as a representative of the church. Could this point to Philemon being an elder in the church or in some way the authoritative head of the church?

The live possibility of Paul's coming to Colossae would have put subtle pressure on Philemon concerning Paul's requests of him, since the two would certainly meet face to face (cf. Wall 1993: 217–18) within the context of the church (note again the pl. "you"). This pressure is increased by Philemon's realization that the church will be watching to see how he responds to Paul's exhortations (Weima 2016: 233).

23 Epaphras is mentioned first as "greeting" the church. He is called "a fellow prisoner" with Paul "in Christ Jesus." Interestingly, Aristarchus is called Paul's "fellow prisoner" in Col. 4:10, and Epaphras is called "a bondslave of Jesus Christ" in Col. 4:12. In the Colossians text, Epaphras is also "one of your number," so we know he is a member of the Colossian church. Furthermore, the Colossians passage says that Epaphras "sends his greetings, always laboring earnestly for you in his prayers, that you may stand perfect and fully assured in all the will of God." Then Paul says, "I bear him witness that he has a deep concern for you and for those who are in Laodicea and Hierapolis"* (Col. 4:13; see on Col. 4:10, 12–13). This indicates here also that Epaphras's greetings likely carry with them his intense pastoral interest in the best welfare of the Colossians. As in Col. 4:10, here in Philem. 23 "fellow prisoner" (lit.,

3. I have subsequently found that Harris (2010: 242) and Pao (2012: 421) also see a divine passive here.

"fellow captive"; συναιχμάλωτος, *synaichmalōtos*) is not figurative but refers to Epaphras being a real prisoner together with Paul.[4] That actual imprisonment is in mind is apparent from observing that Paul refers to his own literal imprisonment in verses 1, 9, 10, and 13.[5] While both are physically in prison, spiritually they are simultaneously also in a different dimension, "in Christ Jesus,"[6] which changes their perspective from possible pessimism to optimism.

The greeting from Epaphras is to "you" (σε, *se*), reverting back to the singular again and addressing only Philemon, and this carries over to verse 24. The reason for the singular address is that Philemon must know Epaphras, as well as Mark, Aristarchus, Demas, and Luke (Lenski 1961: 973). Indeed, Epaphras was founder of the church in Colossae (Col. 1:7).

24 Greetings to Philemon are also sent from "Mark, Aristarchus, Demas, [and] Luke," who are Paul's "fellow workers" in the ministry of the gospel. These same four people likewise send greetings to Colossae in Col. 4:10, 14 (which see for further explanation of these four figures). "Fellow worker" refers to participation in some aspect of gospel ministry together with Paul (2 Cor. 1:24; 8:23; Phil. 2:25; 4:3; Col. 4:11) or others "working together" with God in gospel work (1 Cor. 3:9; 1 Thess. 3:2). The former category is in mind here. "Fellow worker" (συνεργός, *synergos*) occurs in verse 1 and verse 24 and thus is the only lexical repetition in the epistle that forms the outermost boundaries of Philemon. This is likely not by accident. The point of the *inclusio* is to remind Philemon that he is Paul's "fellow worker," together with Paul's other "fellow workers."[7] As such, Philemon should see that Paul's exhortations to him in the letter concern part of his own work of ministry together with Paul (following Pao 2012: 423).

25 As discussed on verses 1–3 (cf. on Col. 1:1–2; 4:18), the concluding wish-prayer, "The grace of the Lord Jesus Christ be with your spirit," replaces the typical "farewell" in contemporary Hellenistic epistles. Paul returns to addressing the whole congregation with the plural "you," thereby reminding Philemon again that what Paul has written to him throughout the letter has been heard by all in the church at Colossae, which intensifies his sense of accountability to what Paul has been telling him. The letter is bounded by Paul's opening greeting of "grace" (1:3) and the final benediction of "grace" here in verse 25. The significance of this inclusion is clear: all that Paul says in the letter and all that he exhorts and commands them, and especially Philemon, can be believed and obeyed only by God's grace (building on an observation by

4. See on Col. 4:10 for the rationale for why the term is not figurative there; contra Pao (2012: 422), who takes it figuratively. Other possible literal interpretations are that Epaphras has not actually been arrested but is nevertheless residing with Paul in prison to aid him or that Epaphras has been imprisoned elsewhere with Paul or separately from Paul (Banker 1999: 59).

5. See discussion on verse 1 and Banker 1999: 60; i.e., these are people with whom Paul is closely associated in his work of the ministry.

6. Though perhaps this expresses cause, "a fellow captive because of Christ Jesus."

7. "My" is a genitive of association (Wallace 1996: 130).

O'Brien [1982: 260] on Col. 4:18; see likewise Fitzmyer [2000: 125] on Philem. 25). While Paul alludes to "grace" at the very end of every one of his epistles,[8] the word is not a superficial polite term but seems to carry theological freight. The only way one can ever have "grace" is if one is "in Christ Jesus" (vv. 16, 20). While in verses 1–2 "grace and peace" appeared to be the broad goal of the letter, now "peace" is omitted here at the end and only "grace" is mentioned." Perhaps this highlights "grace" as the broad goal because it is the necessary means for Philemon and those in the Colossian church to respond positively to his exhortations and instructions. It is the inner "spirit" from which people act, and to act in a manner pleasing to God demands that "grace" be given to one's inner "spirit"[9] or heart.[10] Indeed, because Philemon is among those who are recipients of God's grace, he should be empowered to show grace to Onesimus (Davids 2008b: 436).

Additional Note

25. "Amen" was subsequently added in some MSS (so ℵ, C, D[1], K, L, P, Ψ, and the majority of later MSS), probably because of various congregations' responses "when the letter was read aloud as part of the church's lectionary" (Bruce 1984: 224).

8. Though in Rom. 16:20 it comes seven verses before the very end, and in 1 Cor. 16:23 it is the next-to-last verse.

9. I have subsequently found that Pao 2012 also holds this view.

10. See the additional note on verse 25 about the textual variant "Amen."

Excursus 1

The Problem of Using the Criteria of Vocabulary and Writing Style to Discern Purportedly Non-Pauline Letters

It is being increasingly acknowledged that there is not enough data from Paul's widely recognized seven authentic letters to identify Paul's typical use of vocabulary and writing style. To make a valid comparison between two writings purportedly by the same author in order to determine common authorship, it has been estimated that scholars need to have samples of around ten thousand words similar in content and length between the two documents.[1] Harold Hoehner (2006) has calculated the number of words in Paul's longest epistles[2] and concludes that "the Pauline literature available is too limited conclusively to determine distinguishing characteristics in Paul's writings." Accordingly, attempting to judge one epistle as authentic and another as inauthentic in the full corpus of the Pauline Epistles cannot be done on the basis of the available data.

More precise studies in stylometrics have been done that confirm Hoehner's analysis. For example, focusing on the Pastorals but including Ephesians and Colossians (and, in principle, 2 Thessalonians), O'Donnell (1999) conducted a thorough, if sometimes abstract, methodological study on stylistic features typically used to determine authorship and concluded that there is not enough data in the entire Pauline corpus to be able to make legitimate comparisons and thereby distinguish between authentic and supposedly inauthentic epistles. His essay points out, for the most part, the inadequacy of typical past tests

1. See Hoehner 2006: 169, appealing to Yule (1944: 2, 281) for this comparative statistic.

2. Romans has 7,114 words; 1 Corinthians has 6,842; 2 Corinthians has 4,448; and Ephesians has 2,423.

of authorship based on the use of statistics.[3] He contends that numerous past studies have committed the fallacy of "statisticulating," which is "engaging in the unprincipled and statistically unjustified use of numbers to support a particular point" (1999: 207). Though his methodological study is now a little dated,[4] I will use it as an illustrative representative of the impact of linguistic studies on past stylistic studies to determine non-Pauline authorship of certain epistles attributed to Paul.

O'Donnell has produced a helpful overview and evaluation of past studies on the subject and tries to advance these studies further with his linguistic perspectives and from a functional perspective within the Greek language system. Past studies on authorship in the NT, especially the Pauline corpus, have used the criteria of once-occurring words, common words, sentence length, and words ending sentences.[5] It is not valid with respect to stylistic statistics "to claim that dissimilarity between two samples proves dissimilarity of authorship" (1999: 221). The typical stylistic criteria used to show differences between authentic and inauthentic Pauline letters (e.g., hapax legomena, sentence length, common conjunctions, and dependent genitives) are shown by Neumann (1990) to be fallacious by the statistical approach (O'Donnell 1999: 226). "To a certain extent," an "author is limited in choice of vocabulary by the theme of the discourse" (O'Donnell 1999: 230, evaluating the view of Morton 1966). But even in this case, when writing about the weather, for example, one author may use a particular style and word choice that differ from another author who is also discussing the weather (O'Donnell 1999: 230, further evaluating Morton's view). In other words, "vocabulary use and syntax measures, like sentence-length and word position, are restricted by genre and content, and yet both reflect authorial style" (O'Donnell 1999: 231, further evaluating Morton).

An implication of Yule's 1944 book is that "a work by the same author, but in two different fields, might display marked vocabulary differences—like those found between two different authors" (O'Donnell 1999: 231, taking this implication from Yule's work). Counting hapax legomena in a letter is dubious to determine the inauthenticity of a letter (like the Pastorals). The reason for this is that, while an author may have an essential or core vocabulary as well as a predilection for particular words (or combination of words), there are many factors (e.g., further education, age, rhetorical aim, social setting, and occasion, among other factors) that expand or restrict the core set of vocabulary items (O'Donnell 1999: 232).

3. These include Harrison's study of the Pastorals (1921); Yule's study of Thomas à Kempis's *De imitatione Christi* (1944); Herdan and Grayston's study on the Pastorals (1959); Ellegård's study on the Junius Letters (1962); and Morton (1966), among other works. In contrast to these preceding works, see Kenny (1986) and Neumann (1990). O'Donnell finds various problems with the first five and evaluates the last two mainly in a positive manner.

4. O'Donnell revised the 1999 article in his work of 2005: 85–101.

5. There is a logical fallacy in the test of words ending a sentence: it can demonstrate "common authorship but *not* dissimilarity of authorship" (O'Donnell 1999: 219).

An example of the inconsistency of such studies is borne out by observing that there are 274 words in Romans (26 percent of the total amount of words in Romans) that do not appear in the other twelve epistles said to be written by Paul. Intriguingly, this is a larger percentage of once-occurring words than appears in 1 Timothy (which is 24 percent). This highlights the problem of determining authorship by word statistics alone (O'Donnell 1999: 234). In addition, past statistical evaluations of the words in the Pastorals have not taken into consideration the grammatical categories to which the hapax legomena belong (most are either adjectives or nouns, which need to be considered in any such studies; O'Donnell 1999: 235).

Sociolinguists have also formulated the concept of "idiolect," which is a recognition that each writer or speaker has a unique dialect and that dialect can change over time, depending on many factors, not the least being the stage of one's life, communicative purpose, and cultural context. This may well be applicable to the Pastorals, since, if Paul is the author, they would represent a later stage in his life, not to speak of a different situation that demanded a concomitant rhetorical aim different from his earlier epistles (O'Donnell 1999: 237). O'Donnell states that with respect to the criterion of sentence length, the earliest extant manuscripts "do not distinguish between words, let alone mark sentences," so determining what is a sentence in the NT poses the first hurdle to jump over. Furthermore, sentence length "is not a fixed value determined unequivocally by an author's habits; it is rather a tendency that can be described by probability distributions of the individual sentence lengths,"[6] and thus some have concluded that it is a weak basis on which to make determinations of authorship (O'Donnell 1999: 240). The sentence length of a Danish author in his works separated by twenty years underwent "so great alterations that no proof with any certainty [can] be established to the effect that the two samples belong to the same category" (O'Donnell 1999: 241, citing Buch 1969). Furthermore, recent linguistic studies have shown that the same author can conclude a sentence with different words, depending on how prominent the author wants the word in a clause to be, and certain words will not be used at the end of a clause to show how prominent he wants a word to be in the overall discourse unit (O'Donnell 1999: 241).

Again (in summarizing part of the significance of Ellegård's 1962 work) with respect to past studies claiming that hapax legomena in the Pastorals, for example, indicate non-Pauline authorship, one needs a much larger data set than Paul's purported seven authentic letters to compare with the Pastorals. For instance, if a word appears one time in every 10,000 words, an actual sample of 10,000 words by the same author might contain no use of the word at all or even as many as three or four occurrences. One would need a sample ten times larger (100,000 words) in order to obtain a reliable empirical reading of the relative frequency of this word (i.e., to determine that it is distinctive vocabulary of a particular author; O'Donnell 1999: 246–47). As a general principle,

6. Here O'Donnell is citing Doležel 1969: 10–11.

Ellegård suggests that to gain a clear estimate for the relative frequency of any particular word, "a text sample is required that is ten times larger than the inversion of the word's relative frequency" (O'Donnell 1999: 246). By way of illustration, if one has 100,000 words available from an author's work, then a fairly accurate estimate of that author's distinctive vocabulary can be obtained only for such words as appear at least ten times in it (O'Donnell 1999: 246). To further illustrate this, one can take the word τέλειος (*teleios*, perfect, complete), used only once in Romans (12:2). This is a relative frequency of one in 7,111 words (the total words in Romans). Using Ellegård's general rule, one would need a sample of Paul's letters that contained at least 71,110 words to determine if the use of this word was a part of Paul's distinctive vocabulary. There are 32,407 words in letters said to be by Paul, which is less than half of the 71,110 words just specified. Consequently, "only words that occur ten or more times in the 13 epistles and at least twice in Romans can be employed to determine a distinctive vocabulary measure for Romans" (O'Donnell 1999: 247). This means that there is not enough of a data base in Paul's seven-letter corpus to "focus upon hapax legomena as significant indicators of non-Pauline authorship" (O'Donnell 1999: 247). The epistolary material "is barely of the length that will allow for" a full-orbed and systematic "detailed statistical analysis and comparison" (O'Donnell 1999: 247). "The same person may use very different linguistic items to express more or less the same meaning on different occasions" (O'Donnell 1999: 251, citing Hudson 1980: 48) or when writing in different genres (O'Donnell 1999: 251–53).

In light of all this, one should be very cautious about distinguishing (on the basis of vocabulary and style) between genuinely Pauline and non-Pauline letters, all of which are attributed to Paul. This is the case with Colossians as much as with Ephesians, 2 Thessalonians, or the Pastoral Epistles. O'Donnell does not mention the possible role of secretaries in Paul's writings. Once one brings that into the picture, it makes even more improbable the conclusions of inauthenticity of epistles attributed to Paul based on the kind of methodological criteria for authorship used in past Pauline studies.

In this light, confident conclusions about the inauthenticity of Colossians, such as that by Schweizer (1982: 18–19), should be taken with a grain of salt: "So the conclusion is clear; a mass of observations that can be proved statistically and evaluated carefully produce a uniform picture, and point to an author who, although following Paul completely in vocabulary and theological concepts, differs from him altogether in his mode of argument. The letter can neither have been written nor dictated by Paul."[7]

7. This quotation is cited at the very beginning of O'Donnell's essay (1999: 206) as a prime example of overconfidence about statistics in determining authorship issues.

Excursus 2

Criteria for Discerning Old Testament Allusions and Their Use

Since recognition of a number of OT allusions is significant for the argument of this commentary, it is important to elaborate on criteria for discerning such allusions and how to determine their function. With regard to recognizing allusions, some books on the use of the OT produce elaborate criteria for validating whether something is an allusion, while others set out briefer, more basic criteria. This discussion will attempt to steer a course between these two extremes.

An "allusion" may be defined simply as a brief expression consciously intended by an author to be dependent on an OT passage. In contrast to a quotation of the OT, which is a direct reference, allusions are indirect references (i.e., the OT wording is not reproduced directly as in a quotation). Some believe that an allusion must consist of a reproduction of a unique combination of at least three words or so from the OT passage. While this may be a good rule of thumb, it remains possible that fewer than three words or even an idea may be an allusion. The telltale key to discerning an allusion is that of recognizing an incomparable or unique parallel in wording or unique combination of words or syntax, in a concept, or in a cluster of motifs in the same order or structure.[1] In addition to observing unique features (e.g., verbal coherence), when the contextual theme of the OT source text and the NT context is similar, the

This excursus is based partly on Beale 2012: 31–34. I am indebted to Chris Beetham and my research students Danillo Santos and Laura Leon for reading this section and making comments, some of which I have incorporated.

1. For this latter criterion, see Alter 1981: 47–62, giving such examples in the OT as repeated betrothal scenes that follow the same basic pattern and allude to prior betrothal scenes (Gen. 24; 29; Exod. 2:15b–21; the book of Ruth; see also further Miller 2011: 296–98). This occurs

proposed allusion takes on greater probability. Recognizing allusions is like interpretation: there are degrees of probability and possibility in any attempt to identify an allusion.[2] Recognition of allusions is not only a science but also a literary art, the latter involving an interpreter's intuition.[3]

Some commentators distinguish between "echoes" and "allusions." This distinction may not ultimately be very helpful for a number of reasons. First, some scholars use the two terms almost synonymously.[4] Second, those who make a qualitative distinction between the terms hold that an echo contains less volume or verbal coherence from the OT than an allusion does. Thus the echo is merely a reference to an OT text that does not have as clear a connection to that text as an allusion does. Another way to say this is that an echo is an allusion that has less probability of being dependent on an OT text; whereas an "allusive" reference is clearly or more probably dependent.[5] Therefore, I will not propose criteria for distinguishing between "allusions" and "echoes."[6] It is fine for interpreters to make such distinctions so that readers can know the basis for the judgments they are making,[7] but the fact that scholars differ over the specifics of these criteria has led me to combine the categories of "allusion" and "echo" and to refer merely to "allusion" and varying probabilities of allusion. Thus I posit more general and basic criteria for validating only "allusions." Ultimately, it is difficult to come up with hard-and-fast criteria that can be applied to every occurrence of an OT allusion in the NT. The study must be done case by case. The proof of the pudding is in the exegesis.

---

also in the NT, for example, between Luke and Acts (see Goulder 1964), and it can be found elsewhere in the NT (e.g., see Beale 1984b: 178–228).

2. See Gladd (2008: 3–4nn5–9) and Beetham (2008: 17–20) for discussion of the nature of allusion and perspectives on the subject by various scholars. There is much literature on the literary and philosophical nature of allusion, but the limited scope of this introduction does not allow in-depth survey and interaction with this material. Thus, while the present discussion of "allusion" here could be more nuanced, we need to rest content with our more general analysis.

3. A. Lucas 2014: 100; Hays 1989: 29; Beetham 2008: 35.

4. E.g., see Hays 1989: 18–21, 30–31, 119; see likewise the critique of Hays by Shaw 2013: 241–43; yet on the other hand, Hays sometimes clearly distinguishes between quotation, allusion, and echo, viewing them to represent OT references on a descending scale of "certain," "probable," and "possible" (1989: 20, 23–24, 29), though sometimes quotations are discussed by Hays as obvious allusions (see Shaw 2013: 241).

5. Though not everyone would distinguish allusions and echoes in this way, some affirming that the difference pertains to the function of an allusion or echo in its context and the manner in which it impacts the meaning of the NT text.

6. Echoes may also include an author's unconscious reference to the OT, though such references are more subtle and more difficult to validate, so that not much exegetical value should be placed on such references. See, e.g., Beale (2007: 319–21) and Beetham (2008: 20–36) for discussion of the possibility of distinguishing conscious from unconscious allusions and echoes, though Beetham sees a clear distinction between "allusion" and "echo." His argument for such a distinction is the best that I have seen (see further below).

7. Hays (e.g., 1989: 23–33) sees quotations and allusions as intentional and some echoes as unintentional; he makes no systematic distinction between allusion and echo, except that allusions are explicit OT references and echoes are more subtle, and, as noted above, he often appears to use "allusion" and "echo" synonymously (see the discussion by A. Lucas 2014: 95, 110).

Probably the most referenced criteria for validating allusions and echoes are those offered by Richard Hays,[8] which we believe are helpful. He discusses several criteria, which have an overall cumulative effect in pointing to the presence of an allusion or echo (though, as noted above, I collapse "echo" into the category of "allusion" and see the following criteria as applicable to the general category of "allusion").

1. The source text (the Greek or Hebrew OT) must be available to the writer. The writer would have expected his audience on initial or later readings to recognize the intended allusion.
2. There is a significant degree of verbatim repetition of words or syntactical patterns.[9]
3. There are references in the immediate NT context (or elsewhere by the same author) to the same OT context from which the purported allusion derives.
4. The alleged OT allusion is suitable and satisfying in that its meaning in the OT not only thematically fits into the NT writer's argument but also illuminates it and enhances the rhetorical punch (which admittedly involves an element of subjectivity and intuition).
5. There is plausibility that the NT writer could have intended such an allusion and that the audience could have understood it to varying degrees, especially on subsequent readings of the work. Nevertheless, it is always possible that readers may not pick up an allusion intended by an author (this part of the criteria has some overlap with the first, though the focus in the first is on recognition and here on understanding). Also, if it can be demonstrated that the NT writer's use of the OT has parallels and analogies to other contemporary Jewish uses of the same OT passages, then this points further to the validity of the allusion.
6. It is important to survey the history of the interpretation of the NT passage in order to see if others have observed the allusion. This is, however, one of the least reliable criteria in recognizing allusions. Though a study of past interpretation (by the early church and modern commentators) may reveal the possible allusions proposed by others, it can also lead to a narrowing of the possibilities, since commentators can tend to follow earlier commentators and since commentary tradition always has the possibility of distorting or misinterpreting and losing the fresh and creative approach of the NT writers' intertextual collocations.

8. Hays 1989: 29–32, on which Hays elaborates further in Hays 2005: 34–44; I have added a few of my own explanatory comments to Hays's criteria and I have revised some. See also Beetham 2008: 28–34, also following and expanding somewhat on Hays's criteria. Hays applies these criteria to allusions and to echoes (which we have seen that he does not distinguish clearly), and Beetham does the same but, as we have seen, distinguishes between allusions and echoes.

9. Hays refers to this as "volume," which includes repeated words and syntactical patterns, as well as prominence (of the source text and whether the source text occurs at a key juncture in the NT text) and rhetorical stress of the phrase (see discussion of this in A. Lucas 2014: 96).

Hays's approach is one of the best ways of discerning and discussing the nature and validity of allusions (though he likes the term "echoes"), despite the fact that some scholars have been critical of his methodology.[10] It is Hays's criteria by which we have sought to discern allusions in Colossians, though Beetham's qualification of Hays should be kept in mind. Beetham divides Hays's criteria into two tiers. The first tier is the strongest of the criteria: availability, word agreement or rare concept similarity, and essential interpretive link.[11] The second tier offers help in confirming an allusion that has met the tests of the first tier: scholarly assessment, OT and Jewish interpretive tradition, other verified references from the same OT context in the NT book (e.g., in Colossians), occurrence elsewhere in the Pauline corpus, and thematic coherence (Beetham 2008: 28–34).

Beetham and I have also set forth an approach to analyze how Paul intends for an allusion or echo to function: what is the meaning of the OT reference in its NT context? I have set forth the following sevenfold steps:[12] (1) analyze the broad NT context where the OT reference occurs; (2) analyze the broad and narrow OT context of the reference; (3) survey the exegetical tradition of the OT reference in the latter parts of the OT and in Judaism; (4) compare the ancient versions (MT, LXX, targum, etc.) and the author's use of those versions; (5) analyze the NT author's interpretive or hermeneutical use of the OT, including a comparative study of uses of the same OT reference elsewhere in the NT, NT Apocrypha, and church fathers; (6) analyze the author's theological use of the OT; (7) analyze how the author wants the OT reference to function rhetorically. Thus both Beetham and I are committed to discerning an author's original intent in using an OT allusion by analyzing the parameters set by that author (immediate and broad context of a passage in an epistle and the author's other writings).

Some do not think that the author of Colossians would have alluded much at all to the OT because "he was sensitive to the background knowledge of his readers, and presupposed a lack of knowledge of the Jewish scriptures beyond a rudimentary level" (Foster 2016: 58–60).[13] This, however, does not

10. For a sampling of scholars favorable and unfavorable to Hays's approach, see in Shaw (2013: 236–41, 243) and A. Lucas (2014), both of whom have an overall positive assessment of Hays's sevenfold criteria for discerning allusions and echoes and who well criticize those (esp. Stanley Porter) who are critical of these criteria. See likewise Beale (2012: 34–35) and Gladd (2008: 3–4nn5, 9), the latter specifically discussing those who generally follow Hays's above criteria for discerning and interpreting allusions.

11. Beetham (2008: 30) defines "essential interpretive link" as the author intending that the reader recognize the OT reference and its original OT context and connecting one or more elements of the OT context to elements of the new context. He also sees this recognition as basic to the difference between an allusion and an echo, though echoes must meet the test of the first two criteria of availability and word agreement or rare concept similarity.

12. See Beale 2012: 41–54, essentially overlapping with Beetham 2008: 36–40.

13. For Foster's other reasons for skepticism about detecting OT allusions in Colossians, see also Foster 2015: 104–7; 2016: 52–60. In both works he takes a minimalist approach. See Beale forthc. for a response to this perspective. In contrast to a minimalist approach, there are scholars

take into consideration the following factors, which suggest that the author of Colossians would have had good reason to allude to the OT more than some would allow:

1. The churches in Asia Minor were composed of a core of Jewish believers formerly from the synagogue and of Gentile godfearers, who also had association with the synagogue (cf. evidence in Acts such as 13:43–49).
2. We know from Acts and elsewhere in the NT that Jewish and Gentile believers were trained in their new faith on the basis of the OT, the Bible of the early church (e.g., Acts 17:10–12; 18:24–28; Rom. 15:4; 1 Cor. 10:6, 11; 2 Tim. 2:15; 3:16–17). Subsequent training would have enabled the Colossians to better discern the OT allusions as the letter was repeatedly read and heard.
3. In connection with the preceding point, it is plausible that the audience—upon subsequent exposure to the text of Colossians in the churches—would be able to discern more of the allusions than they would have upon a first hearing/reading. This is based on what is known to be true in the second century and was likely also true in the first century that letters were read repeatedly in the early church (implied by Col. 4:16; 1 Thess. 5:27; Rev. 1:3).
4. Since Paul repeats that Tychicus's mission was to "make known" the things about Paul (Col. 4:9 KJV; cf. 4:7), many commentators think that Tychicus was also the letter carrier, which is likely correct (if so, Onesimus should be included as carrying the letter, since 4:9 mentions Onesimus as joining Tychicus in sharing news about Paul). One function of letter carriers was clarifying parts of the letter and supplying more information that was only partially revealed in the epistle.[14] In some Jewish epistolary literature, letter carriers had the role of "reinforcing and supplementing the message of the written letter and thus facilitating the communication process envisaged by the author and sender of the letter" (Head 2009a: 219). Head also asserts that in Greek epistles (i.e., Oxyrhynchus Papyri) when a letter carrier was identified and named within a letter, "the letter carrier frequently supplements the written communication with some oral supplement" (2009b: 279). This helps us understand the role of Paul's letter carriers, including Tychicus in Col. 4:7–9 (cf. Head 2009b: 280–81 and passim). Similarly, Head affirms that among other functions, the letter-carriers of 1 Clement serve to make clear the content of the epistle, "reinforcing and even personally embodying the appeal of the letter" (2015: 492–93). Thus Tychicus (and possibly Onesimus) also plausibly functioned as an authorized interpreter of the letter to the Colossians

who agree with the general approach to identifying allusions that I take here: see Beetham 2008; Fee 2006; and Sumney 2012.

14. On this function of letter carriers in early Hellenism, Judaism, and early Christianity, see Head 2009a and 2009b; see also Richards 2004: 202.

for the audience, offering comments that would probably have included at least elaboration of some of the OT references.

These last three points indicate that Paul could well have included numerous OT allusions in the letter, even if the majority of the readers would not have recognized them at a first hearing.

Another reason why some (e.g., Foster 2016: 60) think that minimal reference to the OT in Colossians would be the case is because of the circumstances of the author of Colossians, who was unlikely to have had access to written texts of the OT in prison. If Paul, however, was the author (which we affirm), then he would have had much of the OT committed to memory and would have drawn from that memory if he had no access to a written copy of the OT. Paul was brought up as a student of the well-known Pharisee Gamaliel (Acts 22:3; cf. Acts 5:34)[15] and says in Gal. 1:14, "I was advancing in Judaism beyond many of my contemporaries among my countrymen, being more extremely zealous for my ancestral traditions" (NASB). Paul probably went to a kind of secondary school when he was between ten and thirteen years old and studied oral Torah there, reading small scrolls with Torah excerpts on them. The entire Hebrew Bible would have been the main textbook in his curriculum. Memorizing large sections of OT texts was the desired result of such education.[16]

In addition to memory, it is apparent that Paul (or other authors in his tradition) would have had access to excerpts of OT Scripture. The above-cited texts[17] show that OT Scripture was available to teachers in the church. Paul's request to Timothy that he "bring the books [τὰ βιβλία, *ta biblia*], especially the parchments" (2 Tim. 4:13) would likely have included excerpts of OT Scripture.

15. We will not enter here into debates about the historicity of this statement in Acts.

16. See Beetham (2008: 258–60) on Paul's probable educational process, where several additional sources in support of this point can also be found.

17. Acts 17:10–12; 18:24–28; Rom. 15:4; 1 Cor. 10:6, 11; 1 Tim. 4:13; 2 Tim. 2:15; 3:16–17.

Excursus 3

"Christ among the Gentiles" as Part of the Mystery

How could the idea of "Christ" as the messianic king being "among the Gentiles" (Col. 1:27) be part of the mystery in Col. 1:26–27?[1] How do the Gentiles in relation to Christ play a role in the OT mystery? Keeping in mind that Col. 1:26–27 alludes specifically to the Dan. 2 mystery, the climactic interpretation of that mystery in Dan. 2:34–35, 44–45 is the stone (representing God's end-time kingdom) that smashes the statue (representing the world's evil kingdoms). After the stone annihilates the statue, "the stone . . . became a great mountain and filled the whole earth" (Dan. 2:35). One surmises that throughout the earth will be at least a remnant of Gentiles who are not part of the evil kingdoms just destroyed, who will be restored and become part of eschatological Israel's kingdom and experience salvific restoration (to which the OT elsewhere testifies: e.g., Isa. 2:1–4; 11:1–13; 49:6, 22–23; Zech. 2:11; 8:22–23). Daniel 7:14, part of the parallel to Dan. 2, makes explicit what may be implicit in the image of the stone-mountain filling the earth: "to Him [the Son of Man] was given dominion, Glory and a kingdom, that all peoples, nations, and tongues might serve him. His dominion is an everlasting dominion."* Accordingly, if we are on the right track in understanding the implications of Dan. 2, that chapter implicitly and Dan. 7 explicitly express the idea that Israel's end-time kingdom will include Gentiles as part of this kingdom. The emphasis on Christ being "among the Gentiles" in Col. 1:27 is likely not coincidental but draws out more clearly what was implied in the stone filling the entire world in Dan. 2.[2] Colossians is a clarification of the

1. See the final additional note on Col. 1:27 about whether "among the Gentiles" further defines the "mystery" or whether the focus is on "making known . . . among the Gentiles" (Col. 1:27).

2. One of my former students, Ochang Kwon (2014), first attracted me to this view of Dan. 2 in a paper on the nature of the "mystery" in Eph. 3.

mystery that was not clear in Dan. 2, though the parallel in Dan. 7 clarifies Dan. 2 to some degree. In fact, Dan. 7:14 could be echoed in Christ's being "the hope of glory" at the end of Col. 1:27, since it is one of only two passages in the Septuagint where a messianic figure is said to have "glory" amid a kingdom composed not only of Jews but also of Gentiles.[3]

While this is a specific part of the revelation of the Dan. 2 mystery, we have seen that the idea of the Gentiles becoming part of Israel's and the Son of Man's kingdom is found elsewhere in Daniel and Isaiah. The core of the mystery, however, is to be found elsewhere. Colossians 2:16–23 is parallel with Eph. 2:14–18, the latter of which underscores that Christ's coming did away with the former ethnic markers of God's people and replaced them with Christ, which is key to understanding the mystery of Eph. 3. Colossians 2:16–23 emphasizes the same thing, where the Mosaic laws pertaining to "food or drink or Jewish festivals or new moons or Sabbath days"* are no longer binding because they must now be seen as only "a mere shadow" pointing toward Christ, who is the eschatological "substance" of these things (see comments below on Col. 2:8–23 for further elaboration). The parallel passage to Eph. 2:13–18 in Col. 2 defines the "decrees" (δόγμα, *dogma*, Col. 2:14) of Eph. 2:15 that Christ abolished as the external nationalistic expressions of the law: food, drink, festivals, new moons, or Sabbaths (see Col. 2:15–17, 20–21). Colossians 2:20–21 even refers to these "decrees" with the verbal form of δόγμα (*dogma*): "Why . . . do you submit yourself to decrees [δογματίζω, *dogmatizō*], such as, 'Do not handle, do not taste, do not touch!' (which all refer to things destined to perish with use)—in accordance with the commandments and teachings of men?"

Accordingly, believers have "died with Messiah" to these things that were so important to Israel's old world but no longer are crucial for membership in God's true end-time people and kingdom (Col. 2:20–22). While, as we have seen, Gentile salvation in the latter days was a clear prophetic expectation, it would have been assumed that they would come to the land of Israel and convert to the faith of Israel, which would include taking on the nationalistic signs (e.g., circumcision) of becoming an Israelite. Ephesians 3 and Col. 1–2 reveal that it was formerly a mystery that Gentiles could become a part of latter-day Israel without submitting to the identification marks of the old theocracy and with the Messiah as their sole identification. Thus the Colossians "mystery" indicates inaugurated fulfillment not only of the Dan. 2 kingdom prophecy but also of the general prophetic expectation about how Gentiles would become part of the saved people of God in the end time. In addition, we have seen that the mystery also includes the notion that Israel's prophesied kingdom would be so thoroughly renovated that it would find its ongoing existence only in the sphere of the latter-day, Israelite messianic king himself and, of course, subsequently all those who identify with him.

3. The only other passage is Isa. 49:3, 5, where the messianic servant is glorified by God in his task of restoration, which includes Jews and Gentiles (Isa. 49:6). In Num. 24:8 LXX and Ps. 8:5 a messianic figure is said to have "glory," but not in direct connection to Gentiles.

Excursus 4

The Old Testament Background of "the Uncircumcision of Your Flesh" in Colossians 2:13

The wording "uncircumcision [lit., foreskin] of your flesh" (τῇ ἀκροβυστίᾳ τῆς σαρκὸς ὑμῶν, *tē akrobystia tēs sarkos hymōn*) in Col. 2:13 is likely an analogical allusion to Gen. 17:10–27 LXX,[1] where "the flesh of <u>your</u> uncircumcision [foreskin]" (τὴν σάρκα τῆς ἀκροβυστίας ὑμῶν, *tēn sarka tēs akrobystias hymōn*) occurs once (17:11) and the phrase "the flesh of <u>his</u> uncircumcision" (τὴν σάρκα τῆς ἀκροβυστίας αὐτοῦ) appears three times (17:14, 24, 25).[2] There the point of the narrative is that those who are in covenantal relationship with God should express that relationship through being "circumcised in the flesh of your [or his/their] uncircumcision" (e.g., Gen. 17:11). This was a symbol expressing that a true Israelite was one whose heart had been cut apart from a condition of unbelief and sin (Deut. 10:16; Jer. 4:4b; 9:26; Ezek. 44:7, 9)[3] and was set apart to God (Jer. 4:4a; see Gen. 17 below). Similarly, Paul compares this physical circumcision to the spiritual reality of the new-covenantal relationship with Christ. When believers are identified by faith with Christ's death, which "cut him off" (= "the circumcision of Christ") from the old world and led to his resurrection, they are likewise "cut off" from the old world and subsequently raised (the point of 2:11–13). Paul's reference to being "circumcised with a circumcision made without hands, <u>in the removal of the body of the flesh</u>" in

1. Beetham (2008: 181–82) prefers to call this an "echo" (cf. further 2008: 188).

2. See the phrase also in LXX: Gen. 34:24; Lev. 12:3; and Jdt. 14:10, which may be based on Gen. 17 (cf. Beetham 2008: 186). Cf. also 1QS 5.5, "Circumcise the foreskin of this nature"; 1QpHab 11.13; 4Q434 frag. 1 1.4 (the latter two: "circumcised his [their] heart's foreskin").

3. Also cf. Josh. 5:8–9, where the circumcision of the second generation of Israel is said to symbolize "roll[ing] away the reproach of Egypt from you." Though there are various interpretations of the symbolism here, we think the best identification is that the circumcision is a reference to a contrast with the Israelite generation who came *from Egypt* and were unfaithful and disobedient in the wilderness and died there because of their unbelief (Josh. 5:4–7; on which, cf. Hess 1996: 119–22). The second generation's circumcision represented a "cutting off" from their identification with such an unbelieving condition.

verse 11 anticipates the allusion to Gen. 17 in verse 13. Also in verse 13 "flesh" is part of the description of the symbolic corruptible (and for the saint, the sinful) condition directly preceding circumcision.

But Paul seems to be making more than an analogy here. His likely acquaintance with another OT background outside of Genesis suggests that he viewed circumcision in the flesh to be pointing typologically to a coming spiritual "circumcision" to be performed by the Messiah on behalf of eschatological Israel. Paul seems to be developing the forward-looking, end-time meaning of circumcision that had been expressed already in Deut. 30:6.[4] The majority of Israel are said to be in need of "circumcising" their spiritual "heart," though they are physically circumcised (Deut. 10:16; so also cf. Jer. 4:4; 9:25–26). This command to "circumcise the heart" includes both a reference to cutting oneself off from an old condition of life (i.e., in Deut. 10:16 from a "stiff . . . neck," ultimately equivalent to spiritual death) and being separated to a new condition of life. This is expressed even more explicitly in Jer. 4:4a: "Circumcise yourselves to the Lord [for life] and remove the foreskins of your heart [the old sinful heart of death]." "Circumcise" in Jer. 4:4a means to be set apart to God and "remove the foreskins of your heart," thus set apart from a negative sinful condition, as explained in 4:4b ("the evil of your deeds").[5]

However, at the time of the "latter-day" restoration of Israel, Deuteronomy prophesies that it will not be human Israelites but God who "will circumcise your heart and the heart of your descendants, to love the Lord, . . . so that you may live" (Deut. 30:6).[6] This future circumcision appears to focus more on a setting apart to love God than a setting apart from the sinful world, though these are two sides of the same coin. In this respect, Deut. 30:6 is similar to Jer. 4:4a: the future circumcision will be a setting apart to a new sphere where one can love God and have life. Genesis 17 itself indicates that circumcision is a setting apart to a positive sphere of blessing (esp. 17:15–16), since there it "is the sign of the covenant" (17:10–11), which is "everlasting" (17:7, 13, 19). The covenant of which circumcision is a sign is a pledge that "I will multiply you exceedingly" (Gen. 17:2; likewise vv. 4–7). Thus even Gen. 17 points to an eschatological "everlasting" aspect of the sign of circumcision.

4. See Beetham (2008: 156–58), who rightly sees Deut. 30:6 as an "echo" in Col. 2:11 because of the common "unique theme of a divinely accomplished circumcision" (the LXX has "cleanse" rather than "circumcise," whereas the MT has "circumcise," followed by Symmachus, so the echo is of the MT). However, he says that "Paul did not intend his audience to recall Deut. 30:6." More likely, those few in Colossae more versed in the OT would have recognized the allusion and background, as would some others under further church instruction in the OT and repeated reading of the epistle.

5. The references to the "heart" in Deut. 10:16; 30:6; and Jer. 4:4 make explicit that circumcision represents a setting apart from a spiritual condition of deadness to that of true life, since "heart" in the OT represents the inner spiritual center of one's relationship (or nonrelationship) to God, which influenced the volitional, intellectual, and emotional aspects of a person (see further on Col. 2:2).

6. For the explicit "latter-day" time of this promise, see Deut. 4:27–31; 31:29; cf. possibly 32:29; Lev. 26:41.

Similarly, Qumran affirmed that their members were to "circumcise in the community the foreskin of the evil inclination and of the stiff neck in order to lay a foundation of truth for Israel, for the community an eternal covenant" (1QS 5.5–6 [for the most part following García Martínez 1996]; so O'Brien 1982: 115). Mishnah Pesah. 8.8F says, "He that separates himself from his uncircumcision is as one that separates himself from the grave [and needs to be sprinkled on the third and seventh days following, before he becomes clean (apparently from corpse uncleanness)]." Here circumcision symbolizes a death and resurrection, followed by water sprinkling, which is unique also to Col. 2:11–12. Philo also sees circumcision to be "a symbol of the excision of pleasures" that are sinful (*Migr.* 92) and "a symbol of the excision of the pleasures which delude the mind" (*Spec.* 1.9).

Elsewhere Paul himself also expresses the notion that circumcision represents a setting apart to a positive reality: Abraham "received the sign of circumcision, a seal of the righteousness of the faith which he had while uncircumcised" (Rom. 4:11). While this does not use the word "life," the idea that circumcision signifies "righteousness" is very close to the sphere of life, since Abraham's righteousness is linked in the context to new resurrection life (4:17–25).[7] Similarly, Paul sees that fleshly circumcision should signify positively "circumcision . . . which is of the heart, by the Spirit, not by the letter" (Rom. 2:25–29). Again, this is very close to symbolizing life, since the only other place in Paul where the language of "not of the letter" together with "not of the Spirit" occurs is in 2 Cor. 3:6,[8] where also "the letter kills, but the Spirit <u>gives life</u>."

Thus from several OT and NT passages, it is apparent that physical circumcision was not merely to be a symbol for being cut off from the sphere of cursing, corruption, and sin but was also to be an outer symbol of being set apart to a positive inner spiritual reality of life or blessing for Israelite saints. In addition, likely against the background of the positive symbolism of physical circumcision, Deut. 30:6 implies that physical circumcision (e.g., from Gen. 17) was a pointer to the eschatological time when spiritual circumcision would occur on a grander scale and would result in the life of the age to come.

So, in line with this, Paul views the circumcision of Christ and of the believer to be a setting apart not only from death and the old corruptible world (and from sin for the believer) but also to resurrection life in Col. 2:11–13. After Christ's death and resurrection, the practice of the physical rite of circumcision is no longer required, since the end-time reality to which it points has come, and its proleptic purpose has been accomplished. Part of the purpose in pointing out the dual significance of circumcision up to this point is to prepare to see circumcision as quite parallel to baptism, which also signifies separation from the old world and being set apart to life (i.e., in Christ).

7. At points in Romans Paul sees the sphere of resurrection life to be overlapping with the sphere in which saints do "righteousness" (e.g., Rom. 6:13).

8. Though the dative occurs in Rom. 2:29 and the genitive in 2 Cor. 3:6.

Both circumcision and baptism are physical sacramental rites that convey a spiritual meaning. If this is on the right track, then spiritual baptism in Col. 2:12 (and, in the background, water baptism as its corresponding sacramental sign), like spiritual circumcision, is the fulfillment of that to which physical circumcision pointed.

Excursus 5

The Master-Slave Relationship

How does the above discussion of slaves and masters in my comments on Col. 3:22–4:1 bear upon the question of slavery in general and Paul's own view of the institution of slavery? First, Paul has qualified the slave-master relationship by saying that both have a Lord in heaven who will judge them for the good and bad that they do. In addition, Paul addresses both as accountable parties who are to yield voluntary obedience to the Lord in the master-slave relationship. Especially significant is that slaves are viewed as responsible parties, who are to yield responsible and sincere obedience to masters and above all faithful obedience to the Lord, since it is the Lord whom they ultimately serve.

Second, Paul views the slave Onesimus, mentioned in Col. 4:9, to be a "faithful and beloved brother," who is a full-standing member of the church at Colossae (i.e., "who is one of your number"; so likewise Philem. 16, where Paul also calls him a "beloved brother"). Onesimus is also Paul's "child" (Philem. 10). Consequently, though Onesimus is a slave in his worldly calling, he is equal in brotherhood to his other Christian brothers and sisters. In this respect, Paul further significantly qualifies the institution of slavery by saying that within the new-covenant community distinctions of "slave" and "free" have been abolished with respect to inheriting salvation and spiritual equality in fellowship (Col. 3:11; Gal. 3:28; cf. Pao 2012: 283). The nearest that Paul gets to a notion of emancipation is 1 Cor. 7:21: after saying that a person should "remain in that condition in which he was called" (1 Cor. 7:20), he asks, "Were you called while a slave? Do not worry about it; but if you are able also to become free, rather do that." This probably is to be understood against the Roman background in which deserving slaves in urban areas were regularly offered manumission as a reward. Paul is telling slaves to take advantage of such offers (MacDonald 2000: 163).

Third, masters are to treat slaves “justly and fairly” (Col. 4:1), which is an ever-present and governing ethic for them to follow.

Fourth, although Paul acknowledges the divine endorsement of the institution of marriage (1 Cor. 7:2–5; Eph. 5:31; 1 Tim. 4:3–4), the parent-child relationship (Eph. 6:1–2; 1 Tim. 2:15), and civil rulers (Rom. 13:1–7), here and elsewhere he does not understand that slavery has been divinely instituted (see Hurley 1981: 158–61). This means that Paul is “regulating an existing condition, not endorsing the institution of slavery” (Witherington 2007: 185). It is this last issue that raises very thorny problems for Paul’s view of slavery. The consensus is that all forms of first-century slavery entailed the notion that masters owned slaves as their own property and had absolute authority over them. But this may not have been Paul’s view of what he might consider a viable form of “slavery,” since his view was likely shaped by the OT idea of slavery, which appears to have been different from Greco-Roman slavery. The former had a concept that the master owned the labor of the slave and not the slaves themselves (in line with the understanding of indentured servanthood; e.g., among others see Murray 1957: 97–204), though for criminals and conquered soldiers such labor sometimes likely would have been carried out in a kind of “prison” context. On the other hand, it is important to remember that “the old antebellum” view of slavery does not overlap well with Greco-Roman slavery,[1] since various forms of this slavery were more lenient than the old South slavery (e.g., the Roman practice of releasing slaves after they served for a certain period; see again MacDonald 2000: 163). Some forms of first-century slavery may have been hard to distinguish from the OT concept.

Fifth, and troubling to many, neither Paul nor other NT writers condemn the institution of slavery as sinful, and they do not command Christians to emancipate slaves (Murray 1957: 260). However, as we have seen, Paul comes close to doing so, encouraging slaves to become free if they can.

In the light of these above five considerations, one may detect a trajectory in Paul. It is not a trajectory that involves changes from the first century to the twenty-first, as some have contended. Indeed, Paul appears to be affirming ethics that are normative for the interim, inaugurated eschatological age, though recalling that he has radically qualified ideas of slavery for Christians, including encouragement to slaves to become free. Just as the human institution of marriage and the concomitant institution of the parent-child relationship will pass away in the consummated new creation, so will the institution of slavery. In the inaugurated form of the new creation, all Christians, including slaves and masters, are spiritually equal, though each have particular roles they must continue with in “this world [that] is passing away” (1 Cor. 7:31). In fact, as some commentators suggest, it is quite possible that a slave could become an elder, so that their Christian human masters would be under their slaves’ spiritual authority in the church community.

1. On this issue, see “The Issue of Slavery” in the introduction to Philemon.

Is it appropriate to understand the ethics governing the master-slave relationship to govern the employer-employee relationship? The answer is yes. This is not merely based on discerning principles of the master-slave relationship and applying these principles to the employer-employee relationship. Indeed, such an application to employers and employees is made by Paul himself. In Eph. 6:5–9, almost the same commands are given to masters and slaves as are found in Col. 3:22–4:1. However, the most glaring difference is that Col. 3:24 says "knowing that from the Lord you will receive the reward of the inheritance," whereas the parallel in Eph. 6:8 has "knowing that whatever good each one does, this he will receive back from the Lord, whether slave or free." Paul sees that the master-slave commands and the principles expressed in them in Eph. 6:5–9 appear implicitly to be applicable also to the "free." Thus it is entirely viable to apply the instructions for masters and slaves to employers and employees in the ancient and modern world. Paul mentions "slave and free" in Col. 3:11, which refers to both as part of the corporate "new man" in Christ, and he also teaches that both are newly created "according to the image" of God (3:10).[2]

Finally, though not stated in Colossians, it is apparent that Paul viewed his instructions to slaves to have a missionary purpose. Titus 2:9–10: "Urge bondslaves to be subject to their own masters in everything, to be well-pleasing, not argumentative, not pilfering, but showing all good faith so that they may adorn the doctrine of God our Savior in every respect" (following Garland 1998: 256; so also 1 Tim. 6:1). This is parallel elsewhere to wives who are to "be submissive to your own husbands so that . . . they may be won without a word by the behavior of their wives" (1 Pet. 3:1; likewise see Titus 2:5). Indeed, the directly following paragraph (Col. 4:2–6) likely indicates the missionary purpose of every aspect of the lives of Christians (as in 3:17, "Whatever you do in word or deed, do all in the name of the Lord Jesus"), especially as they conduct their roles within the household.

2. In my introduction to Philemon I discuss the question of slavery in general and how it might relate to Paul's own view of the institution. I also discuss further the nature of OT slavery in comparison to Greco-Roman slavery.

Works Cited

Abbott, T. K.

1897 *A Critical Commentary on the Epistles to the Ephesians and the Colossians*. International Critical Commentary. Reprinted Edinburgh: T&T Clark, 1968.

ABD *The Anchor Bible Dictionary*. Edited by D. N. Freedman et al. 6 vols. New York: Doubleday, 1992.

Aletti, J.-N.

1993 *Saint Paul Épître aux Colossiens*. Études Bibliques 20. Paris: Gabalda.

Alter, R.

1981 *The Art of Biblical Narrative*. New York: Basic Books.

ANF *The Ante-Nicene Fathers: Translations of the Writings of the Fathers down to A.D. 325*. Edited by A. Roberts and J. Donaldson. Revised by A. C. Coxe. 10 vols. New York: Christian Literature, 1885–87. Reprinted Peabody, MA: Hendrickson, 1994.

Arnold, C. E.

1995 *The Colossian Syncretism: The Interface between Christianity and Folk Belief at Colossae*. Wissenschaftliche Untersuchungen zum Neuen Testament 2/77.Tübingen: Mohr Siebeck.

2002 "Colossians." Pp. 72–105 in *Ephesians, Philippians, Colossians, Philemon*. Zondervan Illustrated Bible Backgrounds Commentary. Grand Rapids: Zondervan.

BAA *Griechisch-Deutsches Wörterbuch zu den Scriften des Neuen Testaments und der frühchristlichen Literatur*. By W. Bauer, K. Aland, and B. Aland. 6th ed. Berlin: de Gruyter, 1988.

Balch, D. L.

1988 "Household Codes." Pp. 25–50 in *Greco-Roman Literature and the New Testament*. Edited by D. E. Aune. Atlanta: Scholars Press.

Bandstra, A. J.

1964 *The Law and the Elements of the World*. Kampen, Netherlands: Kok.

Banker, J.

1999 *A Semantic and Structural Analysis of Philemon*. Dallas: Summer Institute of Linguistics.

Barclay, J. M. G.

1997 *Colossians and Philemon*. New Testament Guides. Sheffield, UK: Sheffield Academic.

Barth, M.

1974 *Ephesians*. 2 vols. Anchor Bible 34–34A, with continuous pagination. New York: Doubleday.

Barth, M., and H. Blanke

1994 *Colossians*. Anchor Bible 34B. New York: Doubleday.

2000 *The Letter to Philemon*. Grand Rapids: Eerdmans.

Bauckham, R.

2008 *Jesus and the God of Israel*. Grand Rapids: Eerdmans.

Baugh, S. M.

1985 "The Poetic Form of Col. 1:15–20." *Westminster Theological Journal* 47:227–44.

Baumgarten, J. M.

1988 "The Qumran Sabbath Shirot and Rabbinic Merkabah Traditions." *Revue de Qumrân* 3:199–213.

BCP
2012 *The Book of Common Prayer.* New York: Penguin Books.

BDAG *A Greek-English Lexicon of the New Testament and Other Early Christian Literature.* By W. Bauer, F. W. Danker, W. F. Arndt, and F. W. Gingrich. 3rd edition. Chicago: University of Chicago Press, 2000.

BDF *A Greek Grammar of the New Testament.* By F. Blass, A. Debrunner, and R. W. Funk. Chicago: University of Chicago Press, 1961.

Beale, G. K.
1984a "An Exegetical and Theological Consideration of the Hardening of Pharaoh's Heart in Exodus 4–14 and Romans 9." *Trinity Journal*, n.s., 5:129–54.
1984b *The Use of Daniel in Jewish Apocalyptic Literature and in the Revelation of St. John.* Lanham, MD: University Press of America.
1989 "The Old Testament Background of Reconciliation in 2 Corinthians 5–7 and Its Bearing on the Literary Problem of 2 Corinthians 6:14–7:1." *New Testament Studies* 35:550–81.
1991 "Isaiah 6:9–13: A Retributive Taunt against Idolatry." *Vetus Testamentum* 41:257–78.
1996 "The Old Testament Background of Rev 3.14." *New Testament Studies* 42:133–52.
1998 *John's Use of the Old Testament in Revelation.* Journal for the Study of the New Testament Supplement Series 166. Sheffield, UK: Sheffield Academic.
1999a *The Book of Revelation: A Commentary on the Greek Text.* New International Greek Testament Commentary. Grand Rapids: Eerdmans.
1999b "Questions of Authorial Intent, Epistemology, and Presuppositions and Their Bearing on the Study of the Old Testament in the New: A Rejoinder to Steve Moyise." *Irish Biblical Studies* 21:1–26.
2003 *1–2 Thessalonians.* IVP New Testament Commentary Series. Downers Grove, IL: InterVarsity.
2004 *The Temple and the Church's Mission: A Biblical Theology of the Dwelling Place of God.* New Studies in Biblical Theology 17. Leicester, UK: Apollos.
2005 "The Descent of the Eschatological Temple in the Form of the Spirit at Pentecost. Part 1: The Clearest Evidence." *Tyndale Bulletin* 56:73–102.
2007 "Colossians." Pp. 841–70 in *A Commentary on the New Testament Use of the Old Testament.* Edited by G. K. Beale and D. A. Carson. Grand Rapids: Baker Academic.
2008 *We Become What We Worship. A Biblical Theology of Idolatry.* Downers Grove, IL: InterVarsity.
2011 *A New Testament Biblical Theology: The Unfolding of the Old Testament in the New Testament.* Grand Rapids: Baker Academic.
2012 *Handbook on the New Testament Use of the Old Testament.* Grand Rapids: Baker Academic.
2014 "The Cognitive Peripheral Vision of Biblical Authors." *Westminster Theological Journal* 76:263–93.
2015 "The Background of ἐκκλησία Revisited." *Journal for the Study of the New Testament* 38:151–68.
forthc. "The Old Testament in Colossians: A Response to Paul Foster." *Journal for the Study of the New Testament.*

Beale, G. K., D. J. Brendsel, and W. A. Ross
2014 *An Interpretive Lexicon of New Testament Greek: Analysis of Prepositions, Adverbs, Particles, Relative Pronouns, and Conjunctions.* Grand Rapids: Zondervan.

Beale, G. K., and D. A. Carson (eds.)
2007 *Commentary on the New Testament Use of the Old Testament.* Grand Rapids: Baker Academic.

Beale, G. K., and B. L. Gladd
2014 *Hidden but Now Revealed: A Biblical Theology of Mystery.* Downers Grove, IL: InterVarsity.

Beale, G. K., and M. Kim
2014 *God Dwells among Us: Expanding Eden to the Ends of the Earth.* Downers Grove, IL: InterVarsity.

Beale, G. K., and S. McDonough
2007 "Revelation." Pp. 1081–1161 in *A Commentary on the New*

Testament Use of the Old Testament. Edited by G. K. Beale and D. A. Carson. Grand Rapids: Baker Academic.

Beasley-Murray, G. R.
1973 "The Second Chapter of Colossians." *Review and Expositor* 70:469–79.
1980 "Colossians 1:15–20: An Early Christian Hymn Celebrating the Lordship of Christ." Pp. 169–83 in *Pauline Studies: Essays Presented to Professor F. F. Bruce on his 70th Birthday*. Edited by D. A. Hagner and M. J. Harris. Grand Rapids: Eerdmans.

Becker, J., and U. Luz
1998 *Die Briefe an die Galater, Epheser und Kolosser*. Göttingen: Vandenhoeck & Ruprecht.

Bedale, S.
1954 "The Meaning of κεφαλή in the Pauline Epistles." *Journal of Theological Studies*, n.s., 5:211–15.

Beekman, J.
2002 *A Structural and Semantic Analysis of Colossians*. Dallas: SIL International.

Beetham, C. A.
2005 "The Scriptures of Israel in the Letter of Paul to the Colossians." PhD diss., Wheaton College Graduate School.
2008 *Echoes of Scripture in the Letter of Paul to the Colossians*. Biblical Interpretation Series 96. Leiden: Brill.

Benoit, P.
1982 "Ἅγιοι en Colossiens 1.12: Hommes ou Anges?" Pp. 83–101 in *Paul and Paulinism: Essays in Honour of C. K. Barrett*. Edited by M. D. Hooker and S. G. Wilson. London: SPCK.

Bing, C. C.
2007 "The Warning in Colossians 1:21–23." *Bibliotheca Sacra* 164:74–88.

Bird, M. F.
2009 *Colossians and Philemon: A New Covenant Commentary*. Eugene, OR: Cascade.

Birdsall, J. N.
1993 "Πρεσβευτής in Philemon 9: A Study in Conjectural Emendation." *New Testament Studies* 39:625–30.

Black, D. A. (ed.)
1992 *Linguistics and New Testament Interpretation*. Nashville: Broadman, 1992.

Blinzler, J.
1963 "Lexikalisches zu dem Terminus τὰ στοιχεῖα τοῦ κόσμου bei Paulus." Vol. 2 / pp. 429–43 in *Studiorum Paulinorum Congressus Internationalis Catholicus*. Analecta Biblica 17–18. Rome: Pontifical Biblical Institute.

Bockmuehl, M.
1988 "A Note on the Text of Colossians 4:3." *Journal of Theological Studies* 39:489–94.

Borgen, P.
1966 "Moses, Jesus, and the Roman Emperor: Observations in Philo's Writings and the Revelation of John." *Novum Testamentum* 38:145–59.

Borgen, P., P. K. Fuglseth, and R. Skarsten
2000 *The Philo Index*. Leiden: Brill.

Boring, M. E., K. Berger, and C. Colpe (eds.)
1995 *Hellenistic Commentary to the New Testament*. Nashville: Abingdon.

Bornkamm, G.
1975 "The Heresy of Colossians." Pp. 123–45 in *Conflict at Colossae*. Edited by F. O. Francis and W. A. Meeks. Society of Biblical Literature Sources for Biblical Study 4. Missoula, MT: Scholars Press.

Brenton, L. C. L. (trans. and ed.)
1851 *The Septuagint in English*. London: Samuel Bagster & Sons.

Brooks, J. A., and C. L. Winbery
1979 *Syntax of New Testament Greek*. Washington, DC: University Press of America.

Brown, R. E.
1997 *An Introduction to the New Testament*. Anchor Bible Reference Library. New York: Doubleday.

Bruce, F. F.
1984 *The Epistles to the Colossians, to Philemon, and to the Ephesians*. New International Commentary on the New Testament. Grand Rapids: Eerdmans.

Buch, K. L.
1969 "A Note on Sentence-Length as Random Variable." Pp. 76–79 in

Statistics and Style. Edited by L. Doležel and R. W. Bailey. New York: American Elsevier.

Bullinger, E. W.
1968 *Figures of Speech Used in the Bible*. Grand Rapids: Baker.

Burney, C. F.
1926 "Christ as the APXH of Creation. (Prov. viii 22, Col. i 15–18, Rev. iii 14)." *Journal of Theological Studies* 27:160–77.

Burton, E. W.
1898 *Syntax of the Moods and Tenses in New Testament Greek*. Edinburgh: T&T Clark.

Buttmann, A.
1873 *Grammar of the New Testament Greek*. Andover, MA: Warren F. Draper.

Byron, J.
2008 *Recent Research on Paul and Slavery*. Sheffield, UK: Phoenix.

Caird, G. B.
1976 *Paul's Letters from Prison*. New Clarendon Bible. Oxford: Oxford University Press.

Callahan, A. D.
1993 "Paul's Epistle to Philemon: Toward an Alternative Argumentum." *Harvard Theological Review* 86:357–76.

Callow, J.
2002 *A Semantic and Structural Analysis of Colossians*. 2nd edition. Dallas: Summer Institute of Linguistics International.

Calvin, J.
1972 *The Epistles of Paul the Apostle to the Galatians, Ephesians, Philippians and Colossians*. Grand Rapids: Eerdmans.
1984 "Commentary on the Book of Genesis." Vol. 1 in *Calvin's Commentaries*. Grand Rapids: Baker.

Campbell, C. R.
2008 *Basics of Verbal Aspect in Biblical Greek*. Grand Rapids: Zondervan.
2012 *Paul and Union with Christ*. Grand Rapids: Zondervan.
2013 *Colossians and Philemon: A Handbook on the Greek Text*. Waco: Baylor University Press.

Caragounis, C.
1977 *The Ephesian Mysterion: Meaning and Content*. Coniectanea Neotestamentica: New Testament Series 8. Lund: Gleerup.

Carr, W.
1973 "Two Notes on Colossians." *Journal of Theological Studies* 24:492–500.

Carson, D. A.
1991 *The Gospel according to John*. Pillar New Testament Commentary. Grand Rapids: Eerdmans/Leicester, UK: Inter-Varsity.
1995 *Matthew: Chapters 1–12*. Expositor's Bible Commentary. Grand Rapids: Zondervan.

Carson, D. A., and D. J. Moo
2005 *An Introduction to the New Testament*. Grand Rapids: Zondervan.

Catholic Church
1994 *Catechism of the Catholic Church*. 2nd edition. Vatican City: Libreria Editrice Vaticana; Washington, DC: United States Catholic Conference.

Chadwick, H.
1979 *Origen: Contra Celsum*. Cambridge: Cambridge University Press.

Church, F. F.
1978 "Rhetorical Structure and Design in Paul's Letter to Philemon." *Harvard Theological Review* 71:17–33.

Clark, B. T.
2015 *Completing Christ's Afflictions*. Wissenschaftliche Untersuchungen zum Neuen Testament 2/383. Tübingen: Mohr Siebeck.

Clement, P. A., and H. B. Hoffleit
1969 *Plutarch: Moralia*, vol. 8: *Table Talk, Books I–VI*. Loeb Classical Library 424. Cambridge, MA: Harvard University Press/London: Heinemann.

Cohn, L., and P. Wendland
1897 *Philonis Opera*. Philonis Alexandrini opera quae supersunt. Vol. 2. Berlin: Reimer.

Cohoon, J. W.
1932 *Dio Chrysostom*, vol. 1: *Discourses 1–11*. Loeb Classical Library 257. Cambridge, MA: Harvard University Press/London: Heinemann.

Collange, J.-F.
1987 *L'Épître de Saint Paul à Philémon*. Commentaire du Nouveau

Testament. 2nd series XIc. Geneva: Labor et Fides.

Collins, C. J.
2003 "Galatians 3:16: What Kind of Exegete Was Paul?" *Tyndale Bulletin* 54:75–86.

Collins, R. F.
1984 *Studies on the First Letter to the Thessalonians*. Bibliotheca Ephemeridum Theologicarum Lovaniensium 66. Leuven: Leuven University Press.

Colson, F. H.
1935 *Philo, with an English Translation*, vol. 6: *On Abraham; On Joseph; On Moses*. Loeb Classical Library 289. Cambridge, MA: Harvard University Press/London: Heinemann.

Connolly, A. L.
1987 "Onesimus." Pp. 179–81 in *New Documents Illustrating Early Christianity: A Review of the Greek Inscriptions and Papyri Published in 1979*. Edited by G. H. R. Horsley. New Documents Illustrating Early Christianity 4. North Ryde, Australia: Macquarie University.

Copenhaver, A.
2018 *Reconstructing the Historical Background of Paul's Rhetoric in the Letter to the Colossians*. Library of New Testament Studies 585. London: Bloomsbury.

Daly, L. W.
1961 *Aesop without Morals*. New York: Thomas Yoseloff.

Dana, H. E., and J. R. Mantey
1957 *A Manual Grammar of the Greek New Testament*. Toronto: Macmillan.

Davids, P. H.
2008a "Colossians." Pp. 227–312 in *Tyndale Cornerstone Biblical Commentary*. Edited by P. W. Comfort. Carol Stream, IL: Tyndale House.
2008b "Philemon." Pp. 417–38 in *Tyndale Cornerstone Biblical Commentary*. Edited by P. W. Comfort. Carol Stream, IL: Tyndale House.

Davila, J. R.
2000a "The Dead Sea Scrolls and Merkavah Mysticism." Pp. 249–64 in *The Dead Sea Scrolls in Their Historical Context*. Edited by T. H. Lim. Edinburgh: T&T Clark.
2000b *Liturgical Works*. Eerdmans Commentaries on the Dead Sea Scrolls. Grand Rapids: Eerdmans.

Delitzsch, F.
1970 *Biblical Commentary on the Psalms I*. Grand Rapids: Eerdmans.

DeMaris, R. E.
1994 *The Colossian Controversy: Wisdom in Dispute at Colossae*. Journal for the Study of the New Testament Supplement Series 96. Sheffield, UK: JSOT Press.

Deterding, P. E.
2003 *Colossians*. Concordia Commentary. St. Louis: Concordia.

Dibelius, M.
1917 *Die Isisweihe bei Apuleius und verwandte Initiations-Riten*. Sitzungsberichte der Heidelberger Akademie der Wissenschaften, Philosophisch-historische Klasse 8. Heidelberg: C. Winter. *See 1975 English translation below.*
1953 *An die Kolosser, Epheser, an Philemon*. Revised by D. H. Greeven. Handbuch zum neuen Testament 12. Tübingen: Mohr Siebeck.
1975 "The Isis Initiation in Apuleius and Related Initiatory Rites." Pp. 61–121 in *Conflict at Colossae: A Problem in the Interpretation of Early Christianity Illustrated by Selected Modern Studies*. Rev. edition. Edited by F. O. Francis and W. A. Meeks. Society of Biblical Literature Sources for Biblical Study 4. Missoula, MT: Scholars Press. *See 1917 German original above.*

Doležel, L.
1969 "A Framework for the Statistical Analysis of Style." In *Statistics and Style*. Edited by L. Doležel and R. W. Bailey. New York: American Elsevier.

DOTP *Dictionary of the Old Testament: Pentateuch*. Edited by T. D. Alexander and D. W. Baker. Downers Grove, IL: InterVarsity, 2003.

Doty, W. G.
1973 *Letters in Primitive Christianity*. Philadelphia: Fortress.

DPL *Dictionary of Paul and His Letters*. Edited by G. H. Hawthorne and R. P. Martin. Downers Grove, IL: InterVarsity, 1993.

Dübbers, M.
2005 *Christologie and Existenz in Colosserbrief: Exegetische und Semantische Untersuchungen zur Intenton des Kolosserbriefes*. Wissenschaftliche Untersuchungen zum Neuen Testament 2/191. Tübingen: Mohr Siebeck.

Dunn, J. D. G.
1995 "The Colossian Philosophy: A Confident Jewish Apologia." *Biblica* 76:153–81.
1996 *The Epistles to the Colossians and to Philemon*. New International Greek Testament Commentary. Grand Rapids: Eerdmans.

Dunne, J. A.
2011 "The Regal Status of Christ in the Colossian 'Christ-Hymn': A Re-evaluation of the Influence of Wisdom Traditions." *Trinity Journal*, n.s., 32:3–18.

Dupont-Sommer, A.
1962 *The Essene Writings from Qumran*. Translated by G. Vermès. Cleveland: World.

Eadie, J.
1856 *Commentary on the Epistle of Paul to the Colossians*. Reprinted Grand Rapids: Zondervan, 1957.

EDEJ *The Eerdmans Dictionary of Early Judaism*. Edited by J. J. Collins and D. C. Harlow. Grand Rapids: Eerdmans, 2010.

EDNT *Exegetical Dictionary of the New Testament*. Edited by H. Balz and G. Schneider. 3 vols. Grand Rapids: Eerdmans, 1990–93.

Eichrodt, W.
1967 *Theology of the Old Testament*, vol. 2. Philadelphia: Westminster.

Ellegård, A.
1962 *A Statistical Method for Determining Authorship: The Junius Letters, 1769–1772*. Göteborg: Elanders Boktryckeri Aktiebolag.

Ernst, J.
1974 *Die Briefe an die Philipper, an Philemon, an die Kolosser, an die Epheser*. Regensburger Neues Testament. Regensburg: Pustet.

Evans, C. A.
2009 *Old Testament Pseudepigrapha*. Assisted by D. Zacharias, M. Walsh, and S. Kohler. Portions translated by D. Christiansen. Acadia Divinity College. Wolfville, NS: Oaktree Software.

Fee, G. D.
1987 *The First Epistle to the Corinthians*. New International Commentary on the New Testament. Grand Rapids: Eerdmans.
1994 *God's Empowering Presence*. Peabody, MA: Hendrickson.
2006 "Old Testament Intertextuality in Colossians: Reflections on Pauline Christology and Gentile Inclusion in God's Story." Pp. 201–21 in *History and Exegesis: New Testament Essays in Honor of Dr. E. Earle Ellis for His 80th Birthday*. Edited by A.-W. (Aaron) Son. London: T&T Clark.
2007 *Pauline Christology*. Peabody, MA: Hendrickson.

Felder, C. H.
2000 "The Letter to Philemon." Vol. 11 / pp. 881–905 in *The New Interpreters' Bible*. Edited by L. E. Keck. Nashville: Abingdon.

Finegan, J.
1989 *Myth and Mystery*. Grand Rapids: Baker.

Fitzmyer, J. A.
2000 *The Letter to Philemon*. Anchor Bible 34C. New York: Doubleday.

Fletcher-Louis, C. H. T.
1999 "The Worship of Divine Humanity as God's Image and the Worship of Jesus." Pp. 112–28 in *The Jewish Roots of Christological Monotheism*. Edited by C. C. Newman, J. R. Davila, and G. S. Lewis. Supplements to the Journal for the Study of Judaism 63. Leiden: Brill.
2004a "God's Image, His Cosmic Temple and the High Priest: Towards an Historical and Theological Account of the Incarnation." Pp. 81–99 in *Heaven on Earth*. Edited by T. D. Alexander and S. J. Gathercole. Carlisle, UK: Paternoster.
2004b "The Image of God and the Biblical Roots of Christian Sacramentality." Pp. 73–89 in *The*

Gestures of God: Explorations in Sacramentality. Edited by G. Rowell and C. Hall. London: Continuum.

Foster, P.

2015 "Echoes without Resonance: Critiquing Certain Aspects of Recent Scholarly Trends in the Study of the Jewish Scriptures in the New Testament." *Journal for the Study of the New Testament* 38:96–111.

2016 *Colossians*. London: Bloomsbury/T&TClark.

Fowl, S. E.

1990 *The Story of Christ in the Ethics of Paul*. Journal for the Study of the New Testament Supplement Series 36. Sheffield, UK: Sheffield Academic.

Francis, F. O.

1975a "The Background of EMBATEUEIN (Col 2:18) in Legal Papyri and Oracle Inscriptions." Pp. 197–207 in *Conflict at Colossae: A Problem in the Interpretation of Early Christianity Illustrated by Selected Modern Studies*. Edited by F. O. Francis and W. A. Meeks. Rev. edition. Society for Biblical Literature Sources for Biblical Study 4. Missoula, MT: Scholars Press.

1975b "Humility and Angel Worship in Col 2:18." Pp. 163–95 in *Conflict at Colossae: A Problem in the Interpretation of Early Christianity Illustrated by Selected Modern Studies*. Edited by F. O. Francis and W. A. Meeks. Rev. edition. Society of Biblical Literature Sources for Biblical Study 4. Missoula, MT: Scholars Press.

Fuller, D. P.

1992 *The Unity of the Bible*. Grand Rapids: Zondervan.

Furter, D.

1987 *Les Épîtres de Paul aux Colossiens et à Philémon*. Commentaire Évangélique de la Bible. Vaux-sur-Seine: Edifac.

García Martínez, F.

1996 *The Dead Sea Scrolls Translated: The Qumran Texts in English*. 2nd edition. Leiden: Brill/Grand Rapids: Eerdmans.

García Martínez, F., and E. J. C. Tigchelaar (eds.)

1997–98 *The Dead Sea Scrolls: Study Edition*. 2 vols. Leiden: Brill/Grand Rapids: Eerdmans.

Garland, D. E.

1998 *Colossians/Philemon*. NIV Application Commentary. Grand Rapids: Zondervan.

Gaventa, B. R.

1998 *First and Second Thessalonians*. Interpretation: A Bible Commentary for Teaching and Preaching. Louisville: John Knox.

George, T.

1994 *Galatians*. New American Commentary. Nashville: Broadman & Holman.

Gladd, B. L.

2008 *Revealing the Mysterion: The Use of Mystery in Daniel and Second Temple Judaism with Its Bearing on First Corinthians*. Beheifte zur Zeitschrift für die alttestamentliche Wissenschaft 160. Berlin: de Gruyter.

Glasson, T. F.

1969 "Col. 1.18 and Sirach 24." *Novum Testamentum* 11:154–56.

Gnilka, J.

1980 *Der Kolosserbrief*. Herders Theologischer Kommentar zum Neuen Testament 10.1. Freiburg: Herder.

1982 *Der Philemonbrief*. Herders Theologischer Kommentar zum Neuen Testament 10.4. Freiburg: Herder.

Goppelt, L.

1982 *TYPOS: The Typological Interpretation of the Old Testament in the New*. Grand Rapids: Eerdmans.

Gorday, P. (ed.)

2000 *Colossians, 1–2 Thessalonians, 1–2 Timothy, Titus, Philemon*. Ancient Christian Commentary on Scripture 9. Downers Grove, IL: InterVarsity.

Gordley, M. E.

2007 *The Colossian Hymn in Context*. Wissenschaftliche Untersuchungen zum Neuen Testament 2/228. Tübingen: Mohr Siebeck.

Goulder, M.

1964 *Type and History in Acts*. London: SPCK.

Grant, R. M.
1947 "The Decalogue in Early Christianity." *Harvard Theological Review* 40:1–17.

Grudem, W.
1985 "Does Κεφαλή ('Head') Mean 'Source' or 'Authority Over' in Greek Literature? A Survey of 2,336 Examples." *Trinity Journal* 6:38–59.
2006 *Countering the Claims of Evangelical Feminism*. Colorado Springs: Multnomah.

Gundry, R. H.
1976 *Sōma in Biblical Theology*. Society for New Testament Studies Monograph Series 29. Cambridge: Cambridge University Press.

Gupta, N. K.
2013a *Colossians*. Macon, GA: Smyth & Helwys.
2013b "What Is in a Name? The Hermeneutics of Authorship Analysis concerning Colossians." *Currents in Biblical Research* 11:196–217.

Gustafson, H.
1963 "The Afflictions of Christ: What Is Lacking?" *Biblical Research* 8:28–42.

Guthrie, D.
1970 *New Testament Introduction*. Downers Grove, IL: InterVarsity.

Guthrie, G. H.
2015 *2 Corinthians*. Baker Exegetical Commentary on the New Testament. Grand Rapids: Baker Academic.

Hafemann, S. J.
2000 *Suffering and Ministry in the Spirit*. Carlisle, UK: Paternoster. Original edition published Grand Rapids: Eerdmans, 1990.

Hanna, R.
1983 *A Grammatical Aid to the Greek New Testament*. Grand Rapids: Baker.

Harris, M. J.
2005 *The Second Epistle to the Corinthians*. New International Greek Testament Commentary. Grand Rapids: Eerdmans.
2010 *Exegetical Guide to the Greek New Testament: Colossians and Philemon*. Nashville: B&H Academic.
2012 *Prepositions and Theology in the Greek New Testament*. Grand Rapids: Zondervan.

Harrison, P. N.
1921 *The Problem of the Pastoral Epistles*. Oxford: Oxford University Press.

Hatch, E., and H. A. Redpath
1954 *A Concordance to the Septuagint and the Other Greek Versions of the Old Testament*. 3 vols. Graz, Austria: Akademische Druck- & Verlagsanstalt.

Hay, D. M.
1973 *Glory at the Right Hand: Psalm 110 in Early Christianity*. Nashville: Abingdon.
2000 *Colossians*. Abingdon New Testament Commentaries. Nashville: Abingdon.
2004 "Philo's Anthropology and a Possible Connection with Corinth." Pp. 127–42 in *Philo und das Neue Testament*. Edited by R. Deines and K.-W. Niebuhr. Tübingen: Mohr Siebeck.

Hays, R. B.
1989 *Echoes of Scripture in the Letters of Paul*. New Haven: Yale University Press.
2005 *The Conversion of the Imagination: Paul as Interpreter of Israel's Scripture*. Grand Rapids: Eerdmans.

Hayward, C. T. R.
1999 "Sirach and Wisdom's Dwelling Place." Pp. 31–46 in *Where Shall Wisdom Be Found? Wisdom in the Bible, the Church and the Contemporary World*. Edited by S. C. Barton. Edinburgh: T&T Clark.

Head, P. M.
2009a "Letter Carriers in the Ancient Jewish Epistolary Material." Pp. 203–19 in *Jewish and Christian Scripture as an Artifact and Canon*. Edited by C. A. Evans and H. D. Zacharias. Studies in Scripture in Early Judaism and Christianity 13. Library of New Testament Studies 70. London: T&T Clark/Continuum.
2009b "Named Letter-Carriers among the Oxyrhynchus Papyri." *Journal for the Study of the New Testament* 31:279–300.

2015 "'Witnesses between You and Us.'" Pp. 477–93 in *Studies on the Text of the New Testament and Early Christianity: Essays in Honour of Michael W. Holmes on the Occasion of His 65th Birthday*. Edited by D. M. Gurtner, J. Hernández Jr., and P. Foster. New Testament Tools, Studies, and Documents 50. Leiden: Brill.

Heil, J. P.
2001 "The Chiastic Structure and Meaning of Paul's Letter to Philemon." *Biblica* 82:178–206.
2010 *Colossians: Encouragement to Walk in Wisdom as Holy Ones in Christ*. Early Christianity and Its Literature 4. Atlanta: Society of Biblical Literature.

Hendriksen, W.
1964 *Colossians and Philemon*. New Testament Commentary. Grand Rapids: Baker.
1967 *Ephesians*. New Testament Commentary. Grand Rapids: Baker.

Herdan, G., and K. Grayston
1959 "The Authorship of the Pastorals in the Light of Statistical Linguistics." *New Testament Studies* 6:1–15.

Hess, R. S.
1996 *Joshua: An Introduction and Commentary*. Tyndale Old Testament Commentaries. Leicester, UK: Inter-Varsity/Downers Grove, IL: InterVarsity.

Hock, R. F.
1995 "A Support for His Old Age: Paul's Plea on Behalf of Onesimus." Pp. 67–81 in *The Social World of the First Christians: Essays in Honor of Wayne A. Meeks*. Edited by L. M. White and O. L. Yarbrough. Minneapolis: Fortress.

Hoehner, H. W.
2006 "Did Paul Write Galatians?" Pp. 150–69 in *History and Exegesis: New Testament Essays in Honor of Dr. E. Earle Ellis for His 80th Birthday*. Edited by S.-W. (Aaron) Son. London: T&T Clark.

Hollenbach, B.
1979 "Col. II.23: Which Things Lead to the Fulfillment of the Flesh." *New Testament Studies* 25:254–61.

Horsley, G. H. R. (ed.)
1987 *New Documents Illustrating Early Christianity*. Vol. 4. North Ryde, NSW, Australia: Macquarie University.

Houlden, J. L.
1977 *Paul's Letters from Prison*. London: SCM.

Householder, F. W.
1981 *The Syntax of Apollonius Dyscolus: Translated and with Commentary*. Amsterdam Studies in the Theory and History of Linguistic Science. Series 3, Studies in the History of Linguistics 23. Amsterdam: John Benjamins.

Houston, W. J.
1993 *Purity and Monotheism: Clean and Unclean Animals in Biblical Law*. Journal for the Study of the Old Testament Supplement Series 140. Sheffield, UK: Sheffield Academic.

Hübner, H.
1997a *An Philemon, an die Kolosser, an die Epheser*. Handbuch zum Neuen Testament 12. Tübingen: Mohr Siebeck.
1997b *Vetus Testamentum in Novo*, vol. 2: *Corpus Paulinum*. Göttingen: Vandenhoeck & Ruprecht.

Hudson, R. A.
1980 *Sociolinguistics*. Cambridge: Cambridge University Press.

Hugedé, N.
1968 *Commentaire de l'Épître aux Colossiens*. Geneva: Labor et Fides.

Hugenberger, G. P.
1994 *Marriage as a Covenant*. Vetus Testamentum Supplements 52. Leiden: Brill.

Hunt, A. S., and C. C. Edgar
1932 *Select Papyri*, vol. 1: *Non-literary Papyri: Private Documents*. Loeb Classical Library 266. Cambridge, MA: Harvard University Press/London: Heinemann.

Hurley, J. B.
1981 *Man and Woman in Biblical Perspective*. Grand Rapids: Zondervan.

Ip, A. H. H.
2017 *A Socio-Rhetorical Interpretation of the Letter to Philemon in Light of the New Institutional

Economics. Wissenschaftliche Untersuchungen zum Neuen Testament 2/444. Tübingen: Mohr Siebeck.

Jacob, E.
1958 *Theology of the Old Testament*. New York: Harper & Row.

Jaekel, S.
1964 *Sententiae: Comparatio Menandri et Philistionis*. Bibliotheca scriptorum Graecorum et Romanorum Teubneriana. Leipzig: B. G. Teubner.

Jeal, R. R.
2015 *Exploring Philemon: Freedom, Brotherhood, and Partnership in the New Society*. Rhetoric of Religious Antiquity 2. Atlanta: SBL Press.

Jebb, R. C. (ed.)
1989 *The Oedipus at Colonus of Sophocles*. Cambridge: Cambridge University Press.

Johnson, L. T.
1972 "Unsolved Questions about Early Christianity in Anatolia." Pp. 181–93 in *Studies in New Testament and Early Christian Literature: Essays in Honor of Allen P. Wikgren*, edited by D. E. Aune. Novum Testamentum Supplements 33. Leiden: Brill.

Johnson, S. L., Jr.
1962a "Studies in the Epistle to the Colossians, Part 5: The Minister of the Mystery." *Bibliotheca Sacra* 119:227–37.
1962b "Studies in the Epistle to the Colossians, Part 6: Beware of Philosophy." *Bibliotheca Sacra* 119:302–11.

Keesmat, S. C.
1994 "Exodus and the Intertextual Transformation of Tradition in Romans 8.14–30." *Journal for the Study of the New Testament* 54:29–56.

Kenny, A.
1986 *Stylometric Study of the New Testament*. Oxford: Clarendon.

Kim, J. H.
2004 *The Significance of the Clothing Imagery in the Pauline Corpus*. Journal for the Study of the New Testament Supplement Series 268. London: T&T Clark.

Kim, K. S.
2017 "The Meaning of χειρόγραφον in Colossians 2:14 Revisited." *Tyndale Bulletin* 68:223–39.

Knox, J.
1959 *Philemon among the Letters of Paul*. Nashville: Abingdon.

Kohler, K.
1903 "Dietary Laws." Vol. 4 / pp. 598–600 in *The Jewish Encyclopedia*. Edited by I. Singer. 12 vols. New York: Funk & Wagnalls.

Kwon, O.
2014 "A Biblical Theology of Ephesians." Unpublished paper, Westminster Theological Seminary, January.

Lähnemann, J.
1971 *Der Kolosserbrief: Komposition, Situation, und Argumentation*. Studien zum Neuen Testament 3. Gütersloh: Gerd Mohn.

Lamarche, P.
1975 "Structure de l'épitre aux Colossiens." *Biblica* 56:453–63.

L&N *Greek-English Lexicon of the New Testament: Based on Semantic Domains*. Edited by J. P. Louw and E. A. Nida. 2nd edition. 2 vols. New York: United Bible Societies, 1988–89.

LEH *Greek-English Lexicon of the Septuagint*. Edited by J. Lust, E. Eynikel, and K. Hauspie. Rev. edition. Stuttgart: Deutsche Bibelgesellschaft, 2003.

Lenski, R. C. H.
1961 *The Interpretation of St. Paul's Epistles to the Colossians, to the Thessalonians, to Timothy, to Titus and to Philemon*. Commentary on the New Testament. Minneapolis: Augsburg. Originally published Columbus, OH: Lutheran Book Concern, 1937.

Lightfoot, J. B.
1865 *St. Paul's Epistle to the Galatians*. Reprinted Peabody, MA: Hendrickson, 1999.
1875 *St. Paul's Epistles to the Colossians and Philemon*. Reprinted Peabody, MA: Hendrickson, 1999.

Lincoln, A. T.
1981 *Paradise Now and Not Yet*. Society for New Testament Studies Monograph Series. Cambridge: Cambridge University Press.
1990 *Ephesians*. Word Biblical Commentary. Waco: Word Books.
2000 "The Letter to the Colossians." Vol. 10 / pp. 551–670 in *The New Interpreter's Bible*. Nashville: Abingdon.

Lindemann, A.
1983 *Der Kolosserbrief*. Zürcher Bibelkommentar: NT 10. Zurich: Theologischer Verlag.

Llewelyn, S. R.
1992 *New Documents Illustrating Early Christianity*, vol. 6: *A Review of the Greek Inscriptions and Papyri Published in 1980–81*. Marrickville, NSW, Australia: Macquarie University.

Lohmeyer, E.
1964 *Die Briefe an die Philipper, Kolosser und an Philemon*. Kritisch-exegetischer Kommentar über das Neue Testament (Meyer-Kommentar). Göttingen: Vandenhoeck & Ruprecht.

Lohse, E.
1971 *Colossians and Philemon*. Hermeneia. Philadelphia: Fortress.

Lona, H. E.
1984 *Die Eschatologie im Kolosser- und Epheserbrief*. Forschung zur Bibel. Würzberg: Echter Verlag.

LSJ *A Greek-English Lexicon*. Compiled by H. G. Liddell and R. Scott. Revised and enlarged by H. S. Jones with R. McKenzie. 9th ed. With rev. supplement edited by P. G. W. Glare with A. A. Thompson. Oxford: Clarendon, 1996.

Lucas, A. J.
2014 "Assessing Stanley Porter's Objections to Richard B. Hays's Notion of Metalepsis." *Catholic Biblical Quarterly* 76:93–111.

Lucas, R. C.
1980 *The Message of Colossians and Philemon*. Bible Speaks Today. Leicester, UK: Inter-Varsity.

Luz, U.
1998 "Der Brief an die Kolosser." Pp. 183–244 in *Die Briefe an die Galater, Epheser und Kolosser*. Edited by J. Becker and U. Luz. Das Neue Testament Deutsch: Band 8/1. Göttingen: Vandenhoeck & Ruprecht.

Macaskill, G.
2013 *Union with Christ in the New Testament*. Oxford: Oxford University Press.

MacDonald, M.
2000 *Colossians and Ephesians*. Sacra Pagina. Collegeville, MN: Liturgical Press.

Maher, M.
1992 *Targum Pseudo-Jonathan: Genesis*. Aramaic Bible 18. Collegeville, MN: Liturgical Press.

Marcus, R.
1953 *Philo, with an English Translation*, supplement 2: *Questions and Answers on Exodus*. Loeb Classical Library 401. Cambridge, MA: Harvard University Press/London: Heinemann.

Marshall, I. H.
1973 "New Wine in Old Wine Skins: V. The Biblical Use of the Word 'Ekklesia.'" *Expository Times* 84:359–64.
1983 *1 and 2 Thessalonians*. Century Bible Commentary. Grand Rapids: Eerdmans/London: Marshall, Morgan, & Scott.

Martin, E. D.
1993 *Colossians, Philemon*. Believers Church Bible Commentary. Scottdale, PA: Herald Press.

Martin, R. P.
1974 *Colossians and Philemon*. New Century Bible. London: Oliphants.
1991 *Ephesians, Colossians, and Philemon*. Interpretation. Atlanta: John Knox.

Masson, C.
1950 *L'Épitre de Saint Paul aux Colossiens*. Commentaire du Noveau Testament 10. Neuchâtel: Delachaux & Niestlé.

McConville, J. G.
2002 *Deuteronomy*. Apollos Old Testament Commentary 5. Downers Grove, IL: IVP Academic/Nottingham, UK: Apollos (Inter-Varsity).

Melick, R. R.
1991 *Philippians, Colossians, Philemon.* New American Commentary 32. Nashville: Broadman.

Merrill, E. H.
1994 *Deuteronomy.* New American Commentary 4. Nashville: Broadman & Holman.

Metzger, B. M.
1968 *The Text of the New Testament.* 2nd edition. Oxford: Oxford University Press.
1971 *A Textual Commentary on the Greek New Testament.* New York: United Bible Societies.
1994 *A Textual Commentary on the Greek New Testament.* 2nd edition. Stuttgart: Deutsche Bibelgesellschaft.

Meyer, H. A. W.
1885 *Critical and Exegetical Hand-Book to the Epistles to the Philippians and Colossians and to Philemon.* New York: Funk & Wagnalls.

MHT *A Grammar of New Testament Greek.* By J. H. Moulton, W. F. Howard, and N. Turner. 4 vols. Edinburgh: T&T Clark, 1908–76.

Middleton, J. R.
2005 *The Liberating Image: The* Imago Dei *in Genesis 1.* Grand Rapids: Brazos.

Milgrom, J.
1990 "The Scriptural Foundations and Deviations in the Laws of Purity of the Temple Scroll." Pp. 83–99 in *Archaeology and History in the Dead Sea Scrolls: The New York University Conference in Memory of Yigael Yadin.* Edited by L. H. Schiffman. Journal for the Study of the Pseudepigrapha Supplement Series 8. JSOT/ASOR Monographs 2. Sheffield, UK: JSOT Press.
1991 *Leviticus I–XVI.* Anchor Bible 3A. New York: Doubleday.

Miller, G. D.
2011 "Intertextuality in Old Testament Research." *Currents in Biblical Research* 9:283–309.

Mitchell, M. Y.
2000 *Colossians and Ephesians.* Sacra Pagina 17. Collegeville, MN: Liturgical Press.

MM *The Vocabulary of the Greek New Testament: Illustrated from the Papyri and Other Non-literary Sources.* By J. H. Moulton and G. Milligan. Reprinted Grand Rapids: Eerdmans, 1972.

Moo, D. J.
1996 *The Epistle to the Romans.* New International Commentary on the New Testament. Grand Rapids: Eerdmans.
2006 "Nature in the New Creation: New Testament Eschatology and the Environment." *Journal of the Evangelical Theological Society* 49:469–74.
2008 *The Letters to the Colossians and to Philemon.* Pillar New Testament Commentary. Grand Rapids: Eerdmans.
2013 *Galatians.* Baker Exegetical Commentary on the New Testament. Grand Rapids: Baker Academic.

Moo, J.
2008 "Romans 8.19–22 and Isaiah's Cosmic Covenant." *New Testament Studies* 54:74–89.

Morales, L. M.
2015 *Who Shall Ascend the Mountain of the Lord? A Biblical Theology of the Book of Leviticus.* New Studies in Biblical Theology 37. Downers Grove, IL: InterVarsity.

Morris, L.
1955 *Apostolic Preaching of the Cross.* Grand Rapids: Eerdmans.

Morton, A. Q.
1966 *Paul, the Man and the Myth: A Study in the Authorship of Greek Prose.* New York: Harper & Row.

Moule, C. F. D.
1957 *The Epistles to the Colossians and to Philemon.* Cambridge Greek Testament Commentary. Cambridge: Cambridge University Press.
1959 *An Idiom Book of New Testament Greek.* 2nd edition. Cambridge: Cambridge University Press.

Münderlein, G.
1962 "Die Erwählung durch das Pleroma." *New Testament Studies* 8:264–76.

Muraoka, T.
2009 *A Greek-English Lexicon of the Septuagint.* Louvain: Peeters.

Murray, J.
1957 *Principles of Conduct*. Grand Rapids: Eerdmans.

Neumann, K. J.
1990 *The Authenticity of the Pauline Epistles in the Light of Stylostatistical Analysis*. Society of Biblical Literature Dissertation Series. Atlanta: Scholars Press.

Neusner, J.
1988 *The Mishnah: A New Translation*. New Haven: Yale University Press.

Newsom, C.
1990 "'He Has Established for Himself Priests': Human and Angelic Priesthood in the Qumran Sabbath Shirot." Pp. 101–20 in *Archaeology and History in the Dead Sea Scrolls*. Edited by L. H. Schiffman. Journal for the Study of the Pseudepigrapha Series 8. JSOT/ASOR Monographs 2. Sheffield, UK: JSOT Press.

NIDNTT *The New International Dictionary of New Testament Theology*. Edited by L. Coenen, E. Beyreuther, and H. Bietenhard. English translation edited by C. Brown. 4 vols. Grand Rapids: Zondervan, 1975–86.

Nock, A. D.
1933 "The Vocabulary of the New Testament." *Journal of Biblical Literature* 52:131–39.

O'Brien, P. T.
1977 *Introductory Thanksgivings in the Letters of Paul*. Novum Testamentum Supplements 49. Leiden: Brill.
1982 *Colossians, Philemon*. Word Biblical Commentary. Waco: Word.
1999 *The Letter to the Ephesians*. Pelican New Testament Commentaries. Grand Rapids: Eerdmans.

O'Donnell, M. B.
1999 "Linguistic Fingerprints or Style by Numbers? The Use of Statistics in the Discussion of Authorship of New Testament Documents." Pp. 206–62 in *Linguistics and the New Testament: Critical Junctures*. Edited by S. E. Porter and D. A. Carson. Journal for the Study of the New Testament Supplement Series 168. Studies in New Testament Greek 5. Sheffield, UK: Sheffield Academic.
2005 *Corpus Linguistics and the Greek of the New Testament*. New Testament Monographs 6. Sheffield, UK: Sheffield Phoenix.

Omanson, R. L.
2006 *A Textual Guide to the Greek New Testament: An Adaptation of Bruce M. Metzger's "Textual Commentary" for the Needs of Translators*. Stuttgart: Deutsche Bibelgesellschaft.

OTP *The Old Testament Pseudepigrapha*. Edited by J. H. Charlesworth. 2 vols. Garden City, NY: Doubleday, 1983–85.

Owen, J.
1867 *The Works of John Owen*, vol. 1. Edinburgh: T&T Clark.

Page, D. L.
1941 *Select Papyri*, vol. 3: *Literary Papyri: Poetry*. Loeb Classical Library 360. Cambridge, MA: Harvard University Press/London: Heinemann.

Pao, D. W.
2000 *Acts and the Isaianic New Exodus*. Wissenschaftliche Untersuchungen zum Neuen Testament 2/130. Tübingen: Mohr Siebeck.
2002 *Acts and the Isaianic New Exodus*. Grand Rapids: Baker Academic. Originally published Tübingen: Mohr Siebeck, 2000.
2012 *Colossians and Philemon*. Zondervan Exegetical Commentary on the New Testament. Grand Rapids: Zondervan.

Parke, H. W.
1985 *The Oracles of Apollo in Asia Minor*. London: Croom Helm.

Pascuzzi, M. A.
2013 "Reconsidering the Authorship of Colossians." *Bulletin for Biblical Research* 23:223–46.

Patzia, A. G.
1984 *Colossians, Philemon, Ephesians*. Good News Commentary. San Francisco: Harper & Row.
1990 *Ephesians, Colossians, Philemon*. New International Biblical Commentary. Peabody, MA: Hendrickson.

Peake, A. S.
1970 "The Epistle to the Colossians." Vol. 3 / pp. 475–547 in *The*

Expositor's Greek Testament. Edited by W. R. Nicoll. Grand Rapids: Eerdmans.

Petersen, N. R.
1985 *Rediscovering Paul: Philemon and the Sociology of Paul's Narrative World*. Philadelphia: Fortress.

Pizzuto, V. A.
2006 *A Cosmic Leap of Faith*. Leuven: Peeters.

Pokorný, P.
1991 *Colossians*. Peabody, MA: Hendrickson.

Polanyi, M.
1966 *The Tacit Dimension*. Garden City, NY: Doubleday.

Polanyi, M., and H. Prosch
1975 *Meaning*. Chicago: University of Chicago Press.

Porter, S. E.
1989 *Verbal Aspect in the Greek of the New Testament, with Reference to Tense and Mood*. Studies in Biblical Greek 1. New York: Peter Lang.
1994 *Idioms of the Greek New Testament*. 2nd edition. Sheffield, UK: Sheffield Academic.
2010 "A Functional Letter Perspective: Towards a Grammar of Epistolary Form." Pp. 9–31 in *Paul and the Ancient Letter Form*. Edited by S. E. Porter and S. A. Adams. Pauline Studies. Leiden: Brill.

Rabinowitz, H.
1972 "Dietary Laws." Vol. 6 / pp. 26–46 in *Encyclopedia Judaica*. Edited by C. Roth and G. Wigoder. 16 vols. Jerusalem: Keter.

Rahlfs, A. (ed.)
1931 *Septuaginta. Societas Scientiarum Gottingensis*, vol. 10: *Psalmi cum Odes*. Göttingen: Vandenhoek & Ruprecht.

Ramsay, W. M.
1914 *The Teaching of Paul in Terms of the Present Day*. London: Hodder & Stoughton.

Ray, C. A.
1994 "The Identity of the 'Israel of God.'" *Theological Educator* 50:105–14.

Reinmuth, E.
2006 *Der Brief des Paulus an Philemon*. Theologischer Handkommentar zum Neuen Testament 11/II. Leipzig: Evangelische Verlagsanstalt.

Rengstorf, K. H. (ed.)
1973–83 *A Complete Concordance to Flavius Josephus*. 4 vols. Leiden: Brill.

Reumann, J.
1967 "OIKONOMIA—Terms in Paul in Comparison with Lucan Heilsgeschichte." *New Testament Studies* 13:147–67.

Reyes, L. C.
1999 "The Structure and Rhetoric of Colossians 1.15–20." *Filología Neotestamentaria* 12:139–54.

Ribbens, B. J.
2011 "Typology of Types: Typology in Dialogue." *Journal of Theological Interpretation* 512:81–96.

Richards, E. R.
2004 *Paul and First-Century Letter Writing: Secretaries, Composition and Collection*. Downers Grove, IL: InterVarsity.

Ridderbos, H.
1975 *Paul: An Outline of His Theology*. Grand Rapids: Eerdmans.

Rienecker, F.
1980 *A Linguistic Key to the Greek New Testament*, vol. 2. Grand Rapids: Zondervan.

Robertson, A. T.
1931 *Word Pictures in the New Testament*, vol. 4: *The Epistles of Paul*. Nashville: Broadman.
1934 *A Grammar of the Greek New Testament in the Light of Recent Research*. Nashville: Broadman.

Robinson, J. A. T.
1952 *The Body*. Studies in Biblical Theology. Chicago: Henry Regnery.

Rosner, B. S.
2007 *Greed as Idolatry*. Grand Rapids: Eerdmans.

Ross, A. P.
1988 *Creation and Blessing: A Guide to the Study and Exposition of the Book of Genesis*. Grand Rapids: Baker.

Roth, U.
2014 "Paul, Philemon, and Onesimus: A Christian Design for Mastery." *Zeitschrift für die neutestamentliche Wissenschaft* 105:102–30.

Rowland, C.
1983 "Apocalyptic Visions and Exaltation of Christ in the Letter to the Colossians." *Journal for the Study of the New Testament* 19:73–83.

Rusam, D.
1992 "Neue Belege zu den στοιχεῖα τοῦ κόσμου (Gal 4,3.9; Kol 2,8.20)." *Zeitschrift für die neutestamentliche Wissenschaft* 83:119–25.

Salter, M.
2010 "Does Baptism Replace Circumcision? An Examination of the Relationship between Circumcision and Baptism in Col. 2:11–12." *Themelios* 35:15–29.

Sappington, T. J.
1991 *Revelation and Redemption at Colossae*. Journal for the Study of the New Testament Supplement Series 53. Sheffield, UK: JSOT Press.

Schiffman, L. S.
1985 "Purity." Pp. 843–44 in *Harper's Bible Dictionary*. Edited by P. J. Achtemeier. San Francisco: Harper & Row.

Schreiner, T. R.
1998 *Romans*. Baker Exegetical Commentary on the New Testament. Grand Rapids: Baker Academic.

Schweizer, E.
1982 *The Letter to the Colossians*. London: SPCK.
1988 "Slaves of the Elements and Worshipers of Angels: Gal 4:3, 9 and Col 2:8, 18, 20." *Journal of Biblical Literature* 107:455–68.

Scott, E. F.
1930 *The Epistle of Paul to the Colossians, to Philemon and to the Ephesians*. Moffatt New Testament Commentary. London: Hodder.

Scott, J. M.
1992 *Adoption as Sons of God: An Exegetical Investigation into the Background of Υἱοθεσία in the Pauline Corpus*. Wissenschaftliche Untersuchungen zum Neuen Testament 2/48. Tübingen: Mohr Siebeck.

Shaw, D. A.
2013 "Converted Imaginations? The Reception of Richard Hays's Intertextual Method." *Currents in Biblical Research* 11:234–45.

Shogren, G. S.
1988 "Presently Entering the Kingdom of Christ: The Background and Purpose of Col 1:12–14." *Journal of the Evangelical Theological Society* 31:173–80.

Silva, M.
1983 *Biblical Words and Their Meaning*. Grand Rapids: Zondervan.

Simpson, E. K., and F. F. Bruce
1957 *Commentary on the Epistles to the Ephesians and the Colossians*. New International Commentary on the New Testament. Grand Rapids: Eerdmans.

Slater, T. B.
2006 "Translating Ἅγιος in Col 1,2 and Eph 1,1." *Biblica* 87:52–54.

Smalley, S. S.
2007 *1, 2, 3 John*. Word Biblical Commentary. Nashville: Nelson.

Solomon, J.
2000 *Ptolemy Harmonics: Translation and Commentary*. Mnemosyne Supplement 203. Leiden: Brill.

Sprinkle, J. M.
2000 "The Rationale of the Clean and Unclean in the Old Testament." *Journal of the Evangelical Theological Society* 43:637–57.

Sterling, G. E.
2013 "Different Traditions or Emphases? The Image of God in Philo's *De Opificio Mundi*." Pp. 41–56 in *New Approaches to the Study of Biblical Interpretation in Judaism of the Second Temple Period and in Early Christianity*. Edited by G. A. Anderson, R. A. Clements, and D. Satran. Studies on the Texts of the Desert of Judah 106. Leiden: Brill.

Stern, J.
1996 *Palephatus, Περὶ Ἀπίστων (On Unbelievable Tales): Translation, Introduction and Commentary*. Wauconda, IL: Bochazy-Carducci.

Stettler, C.
2000 *Der Kolosserhymnus*. Wissenschaftliche Untersuchungen zum Neuen Testament 2/131. Tübingen: Mohr Siebeck.

Str-B *Kommentar zum Neuen Testament aus Talmud und Midrasch*. By H. L.

Strack and P. Billerbeck. 6 vols. Munich: Beck, 1922–61.

Stuckenbruck, L. T.

1995 *Angel Veneration and Christology: A Study in Early Judaism and the Christology of the Apocalypse of John*. Wissenschaftliche Untersuchungen zum Neuen Testament 2/70. Tübingen: Mohr.

Stuhlmacher, P.

2018 *Biblical Theology of the New Testament*. Grand Rapids: Eerdmans.

Sumney, J. L.

2008 *Colossians*. New Testament Library. Louisville: Westminster John Knox.

2012 "Writing 'in the Image' of Scripture: The Form and Function of References to Scripture in Colossians." Pp. 185–229 in *Paul and Scripture: Extending the Conversation*. Edited by C. D. Stanley. SBL Early Christianity and Its Literature 9. Atlanta: Society of Biblical Literature.

Talbert, C. H.

2007 *Ephesians and Colossians*. Paideia. Grand Rapids: Baker Academic.

TDNT *Theological Dictionary of the New Testament*. Edited by G. Kittel and G. Friedrich. Translated by G. W. Bromiley. 10 Vols. Grand Rapids: Eerdmans, 1964–74.

Thielman, F.

2010 *Ephesians*. Baker Exegetical Commentary on the New Testament. Grand Rapids: Baker Academic.

Thompson, M. M.

2005 *Colossians and Philemon*. Two Horizons New Testament Commentary. Grand Rapids: Eerdmans.

Tipton, L. G.

2008 "Christology in Colossians 1:15–20 and Hebrews 1:1–4: An Exercise in Biblico-Systematic Theology." Pp. 177–202 in *Resurrection and Eschatology. Essays in Honor of Richard B. Gaffin*. Edited by L. G. Tipton and J. C. Waddington. Phillipsburg, NJ: P&R.

2016 "The Comprehensive Scope of Christology, Part II: Colossians 1:15–20." Lecture given at Westminster Theological Seminary in the course "Systematic Theology 223."

Titrud, K.

1992 "The Function of *kai* in the Greek New Testament and an Application to 2 Peter." Pp. 240–70 in *Linguistics and New Testament Interpretation: Essays on Discourse Analysis*. Edited by D. A. Black. Nashville: Broadman.

TLG *Thesaurus Linguae Graecae*. Digital corpus. University of California, Irvine, 1972–; online, 2001–.

TLNT *Theological Lexicon of the New Testament*. By C. Spicq. Translated and edited by J. D. Ernest. 3 vols. Peabody, MA: Hendrickson, 1994.

Toomer, G. J.

1998 *Ptolemy's Almagest*. Princeton: Princeton University Press.

Trebilco, P.

2011 "Why Did the Early Christians Call Themselves ἡ ἐκκλησία?" *New Testament Studies* 57:440–60.

Van Kooten, G. H.

2012 "Ἐκκλησία τοῦ θεοῦ: The 'Church of God' and the Civic Assemblies (ἐκκλησίαι) of the Greek Cities in the Roman Empire: A Response to Paul Trebilco and Richard A. Horsley." *New Testament Studies* 58:522–48.

Vassar, M.

2017 "Grant Slaves Equality: Reexamining the Translation of Colossians 4:1." *Tyndale Bulletin* 68:59–71.

Vaughn, C.

1978 "Colossians." Vol. 11 / pp. 161–226 in *The Expositor's Bible Commentary*. Edited by F. E. Gaebelein. Grand Rapids: Zondervan.

Volf, J. M. G.

1990 *Paul and Perseverance: Staying In and Falling Away*. Louisville: Westminster/John Knox.

Vos, G.

1948 *Biblical Theology: Old and New Testaments*. Grand Rapids: Eerdmans.

1956 *The Teaching of the Epistle to the Hebrews*. Grand Rapids: Eerdmans.

Wall, R. W.

1993 *Colossians and Philemon*. IVP New Testament Commentary

Series. Downers Grove, IL: InterVarsity.

Wallace, D. B.
1996 *Greek Grammar beyond the Basics*. Grand Rapids: Zondervan.

Walsh, B. J., and S. C. Keesmaat
2004 *Colossians Remixed*. Downers Grove, IL: InterVarsity.

Weima, J. A. D.
1994 *Neglected Endings*. Sheffield, UK: JSOT Press.
2016 *Paul the Ancient Letter Writer*. Grand Rapids: Baker Academic.

Weiss, H.
1972 "The Law in the Epistle to the Colossians." *Catholic Biblical Quarterly* 34:294–314.

Wheeler, D. M.
1990 "Diagram of Colossians." Unpublished paper.

Whiston, W.
1987 *The Works of Josephus*. Reprinted Peabody, MA: Hendrickson.

White, J.
2017 "Paul Completes the Servant's Sufferings (Col. 1:24)." *Journal for the Study of Paul and His Letters* 6:89–106.

White, R. J.
1975 *Artemidorus Daldianus, The Interpretation of Dreams = Oneirocritica*. Noyes Classical Studies. Park Ridge, NJ: Noyes.

Wiedemann, T.
1981 *Greek and Roman Slavery*. Baltimore: Johns Hopkins University Press.

Wilson, R. M.
2005 *Colossians and Philemon*. International Critical Commentary. London: Bloomsbury T&T Clark.

Wise, M. O., M. G. Abegg, and E. M. Cook (eds.)
2005 *The Dead Sea Scrolls: A New English Translation*. New York: HarperCollins.

Witherington, B., III
2007 *The Letters to Philemon, the Colossians, and the Ephesians: A Socio-Rhetorical Commentary on the Captivity Epistles*. Grand Rapids: Eerdmans.

Wolter, M.
1993 *Der Brief an die Kolosser; Der Brief an Philemon*. Ökumenischer Taschenbuchkommentar zum Neuen Testament 12. Gütersloh: Gütersloher Verlagshaus/Würzburg: Echter-Verlag.

Wood, G. R. H.
1952 *St. Paul's First Letter: Studies in 1 Thessalonians*. London: Walter.

Wright, C. J. H.
1996 *Deuteronomy*. Understanding the Bible Commentary Series. Grand Rapids: Baker Books.

Wright, D. P.
1987 *The Disposal of Impurity*. Society of Biblical Literature Dissertation Series 101. Atlanta: Scholars Press.

Wright, N. T.
1986 *Colossians and Philemon*. Tyndale New Testament Commentaries. Leicester, UK: Inter-Varsity.
1990 "Poetry and Theology in Colossians 1.15–20." *New Testament Studies* 36:444–68.
1992a *The Climax of the Covenant: Christ and the Law in Pauline Theology*. Minneapolis: Fortress.
1992b *The New Testament and the People of God*. Minneapolis: Fortress.
1996 *Jesus and the Victory of God*. Minneapolis: Fortress.
2013 *Paul and the Faithfulness of God*. Minneapolis: Fortress.

Yates, R.
1993 *The Epistle to the Colossians*. Epworth Commentaries. London: Epworth.

Yonge, C. D.
1993 *The Works of Philo*. Reprinted Peabody, MA: Hendrickson.

Yule, G. U.
1944 *The Statistical Study of Literary Vocabulary*. Cambridge: Cambridge University Press.

Zeilinger, F.
1974 *Der Erstgeborene der Schöpfung: Untersuchungen zur Formalstruktur und Theologie des Kolosserbriefes*. Vienna: Herder.

Zerwick, M.
1963 *Biblical Greek*. Scripta Pontifici Instituti Biblici 114. Rome: Pontifical Biblical Institute.

Zerwick, M., and M. Grosvenor
1981 *A Grammatical Analysis of the Greek New Testament*. Rome: Pontifical Institute.

Index of Subjects

Index of Authors

Index of Greek Words

Index of Scripture and Other Ancient Writings

Old Testament

Proverbs

Ecclesiastes

1 Corinthians

Philippians

Colossians

1 Thessalonians

2 Thessalonians

1 Timothy

2 Timothy

Titus

Philemon

Old Testament Apocrypha

Additions to Esther

Baruch

1 Esdras

2 Esdras (4 Ezra)

Judith

1 Maccabees

2 Maccabees

3 Maccabees

4 Maccabees

Sirach

Old Testament Pseudepigrapha

New Testament Apocrypha

Qumran / Dead Sea Scrolls

Nag Hammadi Codices

Rabbinic Writings

Targumim

Josephus

Philo

Classical Writers

Church Fathers